Best Wishes

THE WORLD OF THE
BOXER

TS-273

Overleaf: Jacquet's Holden, rendered in watercolor by Yoko, the official artist of the Japanese Kennel Club.

Title page: On the court with Ch. Jacquet's Cambridge Fortune, it's *Love-Love!* Bred by author Richard Tomita and William Dunn, she is a multiple American all-breed Best in Show winner and the 1995 American Boxer Club Bitch Winning the Most Bests in Show, Group Firsts and Bests of Breed. She lives in a loving home in Japan with her owner Ikuko Otani. Photograph by Tara Darling.

The Publisher wishes to acknowledge the following professionals for photography used in this book:
Diane Abdoo, Marcia Adams, Albert Foto, Alexander Photo, Alverson Photographers, Animal World Studio, Annelie Photo, Andrews Photo, Luiz Arruda, David and John L. Ashbey, Banks Photography, Barber Photo, Rich Bergman, D. Bezerro, Blicks Photo, Linda Bohm, K. Booth Photography, William Brown, Callea Photo, Candsas Photo, Chayo Foto, Cosillas Foto, Cott/Francis Studio, Vicky & Warren Cook, C.M. Cooke & Son, Barbara Cooper, Wayne Cott, Daigle Photo, David Dalton, Tara Darling, Kay Demski, Dean Dennis, JR Dimiceli, Downey Photography, T. Dorizas, Eduardo Studio, Henry Ellison, Fall Photo, M. Flavio, Fox & Cook, Fox Photo, Isabelle Francais, Bill Francis, Frasie Studio, Gaucho Photo, William P. Gilbert, Earl Graham Studio, Bonnie Gray, Fran Hall, Bruce Harkins, John Hartley, R. Herba, Peter B Hickey, Phil Holley, En Hong, Gary Jameson (Dog Showbiz Magazine), Janine Photo, JC Photo, Jean-Jacques, Jon Photo, Karin's Studio, K. Keith, Bernard W. and J. Kay Kernan, Barbara Killworth, Kitten Photo, Stephen Klein, Kohler Photo, Kurtis Photo, Paulo Lang, Jayne Langdon, Beverly Larson, Seigi Lehmann, Linda Lindt, Lindsay Photo, Carl Lindemaier, Ludwig Photo, Joan Mac Laren, Bill Malcolm, Marcia Photos, Marianne Photo, Matsu Photo, Bill Meyer, Mikron Photos, Ltd., Montoya Foto, Andre Nendez, Luiz Nendez, Norton of Kent, Tom Nutting, Ohtu Photo, Lloyd W. Olson Photographs, Paviel Photo, Pawprints Photos, Humberto Pazos, Diane Pearce, Perfect Image Photography, Pet Portraits, Peter Photo, Petrulis Photography, Phoebe Photo, Photo Magic, Rezewski Foto, Rinehart Photo, Ritter Photo, Jan Rose, Rothadam Photo, Eddie Rubin, Sabrina Photo, Tobe Saskor, William Scolnik, Paul Scott, Lloyd and Janet Seltzer, Evelyn M. Shafer, Sho-Photo Alex Smith, L. Sosa, Stonham Photography, Sunset Cliffs, Chuck and Sandy Tatham Taylor Photo Thurse Photo, Morry Twomey, Chuck Van de Merlen, Visual Concepts, *The Washington Post,* Louise Wetzel, Wichita Eagle, and Missy Yuhl.

TFH Publications Staff
Editor, Andrew De Prisco
Art Designer & Typographer, Patti Escabi
Editorial Assistants : Gabrielle Stravelli, Amy Gilbert, Linda Lindner, Stacy Kennedy, and Jaime Gardner.
Managing Editor: Dominique De Vito
Art Department Manager, Pat Northrup
Digital Pre-Press: Robert Onyrscuk, José Reyes.

The Editor and TFH Staff remembers our long-time friend and editor, Marcy Myerovich, whose untimely passing kept her from seeing Rick's masterpiece.

Distributed in the UNITED STATES to the Pet Trade by T.F.H. Publications, Inc., One T.F.H. Plaza, Neptune City, NJ 07753; in CANADA Rolf C. Hagen Inc., 3225 Sartelon St. Laurent-Montreal Quebec H4R 1E8; Pet Trade by H & L Pet Supplies Inc., 27 Kingston Crescent, Kitchener, Ontario N2B 2T6; in ENGLAND by T.F.H. Publications, PO Box 15, Waterlooville PO7 6BQ; in AUSTRALIA AND THE SOUTH PACIFIC by T.F.H. (Australia), Pty. Ltd., Box 149, Brookvale 2100 N.S.W., Australia; in NEW ZEALAND by Brooklands Aquarium Ltd. 5 McGiven Drive, New Plymouth, RD1 New Zealand; in SOUTH AFRICA, Rolf C. Hagen S.A. (PTY.) LTD. P. O. Box 201199, Durban North 4016, South Africa; in Japan by T.F.H. Publications, Japan—Jiro Tsuda, 10-12-3 Ohjidai, Sakura, Chiba 285, Japan. Published by T.F.H. Publications, Inc.
MANUFACTURED IN THE
UNITED STATES OF AMERICA
BY T.F.H. PUBLICATIONS, INC.

THE WORLD OF THE BOXER

RICHARD TOMITA

ACKNOWLEDGMENTS

That a single name appears under the title of *The World of the Boxer* may lead our readers to believe that one man claims the authority and responsibility for this whole volume. While I have personally been involved with every single word and photograph in this book, I must acknowledge the loyal legion of contributors that has made this magnum opus a reality!

First, I must thank Isabelle Francais, photographer and friend who connected me with my Editor and began my connection to TFH Publications nearly ten years ago.

To Dee Gannon, for her loyal editorial assistance; Seigi Lehmann, for restoring and perfecting our many photographs; my sister Christine Eicher, Marylou Hatfield, Ann Rizzo, Joseph Pastella, and Barbara Sanders, for advising, organizing, typing, etc., etc.

To our guest authors from around the globe, all of whom are Boxer lovers and experts; we are especially blest to have in print for the first time the story of the legendary Bang Away, written for us by his breeder-owner Phoebe Harris. Special thanks to Sturlene Arnold for her continued support of this project and her many hours of editing our captions and compiling our Appendix of Sires and Dams of Merit. I must acknowledge two ladies whose chapters go beyond the call of duty: thank you Karla Spitzer and Eleanor Linderholm-Wood. Thanks to my friend Marianne Legere for sharing her friend Karla with us. To author and breeder, Jo Royle, for so willing sharing her book and photographs with us.

Our contributing authors include: Greg Abood, Stephanie Abraham, James N. Arnold, Sturlene Arnold, Maureen C. S. Boyd, Agnes and Daniel Buchwald, Ilze Buldere, Vi Campos, Jeanny Candamo, Sheila Cartwright, Kris Dahl, Abhinav Dhar, Muriel Dieterich, Liane Dimitroff, Charles Fortune, Peter Foster, Jane Fournier, Franz and Ute Fuglister, Dee Gannon, Ed Goldfield, Charlotte Gotz, Phoebe Harris, Joseph Heine, Connie Jankowski, Inga Karlsen, Marilyn J. Krejci, Lucy LeComte, Eleanor Linderholm-Wood, Ruben Oscar Ledesma, Ann Lettis, Henning Lund, Joan MacLaren, Diane Mallet, Michele McArdle, Dr. Alexander Mitsopoulos, Pritha Muthana, Dr. Hideaki Nakazawa, Jimmy Ng Eng Hing, Dr. Mario Perricone, Claudine Raymo, Dr. Orlando Sacay, Nariman Shakeebai, Arkadiy Sherman, Karla Spitzer, Cecilie Stromstad, Wanda Tolliver, Lorraine H. Valleau, Rita Kiekens-Van Dorpe, Piet van Melis, Ian Weeks, Barbara Widmayer, Nancy Widmayer-Doyle, and David Wollowick.

To our translators, Carole Shea; Stellario and Katherine D'Urso, our Italian section; Kurt Kiekens, our Belgian section; Kiyoko and Brad Kibble, our Japanese section.

To Patrick and Christine Beardsell, Kapil Modi, Yoshitaka Mori, Dr. Lorenzo Roca, Dr. and Mrs. Salleo, Ruth Cavalheiro Vieira, Charles Walker, for opening doors in their respective countries.

To the faithful Jacquet Kennel family: Denise Gianninoto, kennel manager, and our many helpers over the years: Debbie Alport, Pam Alsdorf-Kohler, Sandy Anderson, John Becchina, Ronald Belli, Susan Bendziewicz, Diane Curlyhead, Gregg De Phillips, Marcie De Phillips, Donna Di Palma, Bill Dunn, Dr. Sandor Hacker, Mary and Marie Hall, Veronica Hilton, Carol and CJ Hogan, Dr. Linda Katz, Debbie Kenny, Jason Kulp, Jaimie Lally, Darren Leventhal, Javier Lliso, Michelle Neglia, Tom O'Conner, Darryl Philips, Mark Siniscalchi, Todd Stanley, Tracy Van Lenten, Whitey and Jimmy Van Valkenburg, Dr. Carol Vischer, and Barbara and Nancy Widmayer,.

To all our Jacquet handlers since the beginning: Bert Brown, Robert Forsyth, Jane Forsyth, Alvin Lee, Jr., Bob MacPherson, Linda Mastrapasqua, Don Robinder, Carmen Skinner, Gary Steele, and Marylou Wilderson-Hatfield.

To the many wonderful judges around the world who have recognized the quality of our Jacquet Boxers: Amy Acklen, Ralph Ambrosio, Nellie Anderson, Michele Billings, Mr. and Mrs. Edd Bivin, Donald Booxbaum, Gerald Broadt, Mrs. James Edward Clark, Victor and Anita Clemente, Anitra Cuneo, Liane Dimitroff, Dr. and Mrs. Anthony Di Nardo, Robert and Jane Forsyth, Charles Fortune, Peter Foster, Marcia A. Foy, Jean Fournier, Dr. Richard Greathouse, Elizabeth Gunther, Eleanor Haeberle, Clayton Haviland IV, George Heitzman, Vera Hyman, Dr. Robert A. Indeglia, Patricia Laurens, Lena Ludwig, Charlotte McGowen, Dr. Hideaki Nakazawa, Anna Katherine Nicholas, Rosina Olifent-Brace, J. Council Parker, Betty Lou Parris, Eleanor Pugliese, Cheryl Robbins, Alva Rosenberg, Virginia Salomon, Lynette and Stanley Saltzman, Francine and Bernard Schwartz, R. Stephen Shaw, William Paul Shelton, Patricia Starkweather, David Strachan, Catherine M. Thompson and so many others.

To the J-B Wholesale family, our office manager Marylou Carafello and my wonderful secretary Joyce Ochs, without whose daily assistance I could not get by.

To the memory of those Boxer enthusiasts who are no longer with us, for their support over the years: Patrick Beardsell, Dolores Caprino and Helen Willis.

To my *fearless* Editor, Andrew De Prisco, who helped orchestrate our many notes, phrases and images into a symphonic whole! What a grand opera it is!

A very young Victor Clemente, Jr. with a Brayshaw puppy.

Dedication

Edward Wiener III, for my start in Boxers,
Dr. Shelly Robin, for guidance and strength, and
William Scolnik, for his encouragement and undying support.

Bill Scolnik, holding Jacquet's Holden.

In the armchair of his owner is Jacquet's Holden, the house dog of author Rick Tomita and partner Bill Scolnik. Holden, always the gentleman, whether posing with the family cat Teckel or greeting visitors to J-B Wholesale, represents the outgoing, loving, companionable temperament of the ideal Jacquet Boxer.

CONTENTS

Circa 1860, Germany, bronze Bullenbeisser bitch, nursing puppies.

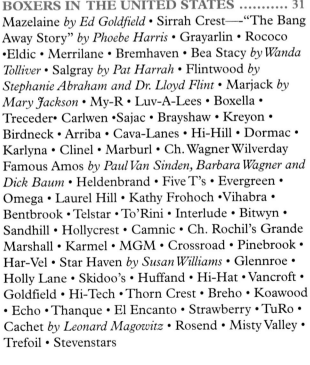

Circa mid-1800s, bronze matchholder of early Bullenbeisser type dog.

Circa 1870, France, bronze by Alphonse Arson, early Boxer with undershot jaw.

Circa 1870, oil on panel, by Frumont, flashy brindle Boxer type.

Circa 1875, France, bronze bookends on marble, Bullenbeisser.

Circa 1890, oil on canvas by Daniel V. Meinart, of white Boxer with brindle head.

Late 19th century, England, porcelain, Staffordshire Boxer, crediting theory of Boxers originating in Britain.

Circa 1930, United States, plaster by Jan Allan, early Boxer type.

Circa 1940, United States, handpainted unglazed porcelain by June Harrah, brindle Wagner Boxer.

Circa 1947, England, wire-reinforced plaster by Edward Morton, Boxer.

"The Never-ending Boxer Book" nears completion. Mr. Tomita (not pictured) began research for this book in 1990, a project that would take nearly eight years to complete. Photograph courtesy of Carl Ness.

PREFACE

In the late 1980s I was introduced to Rick Tomita of Jacquet Boxers and Shibas through my friend, TFH house photographer Isabelle Francais, with whom Rick had cooperated many times to photograph his Boxer puppies and champions for books. As an editor for TFH, I was not interested in Boxers—no, I wanted to meet his Shibas! A successful professional relationship developed into a terrific friendship: I bought two Shibas, and Rick and I were collaborating on a Shiba book and maybe even a Boxer book *"somewhere down the road."*

The contract for *The World of the Boxer* was signed on June 7, 1990 and the deadline would be extended three times in order for Rick to complete the project. Thousands of phone calls between Rick and me followed. Never before had an author so belabored over every detail of a book. His excitement as "famous" Boxer people wrote him to encourage him and send him information and irreplaceable photographs kept him going, even when many others did not respond to his countless Priority Mail requests. Knowing that TFH has wide distribution in every English-speaking country in the world, I persuaded Rick to pursue breeders in those countries as well, not just the kennels in the States. Rick became a man on a mission—to conquer the World of the Boxer. Over the years, he called me many times sounding like the impassioned warrior: "We got Canada!!"; "England's finally giving in!"; "Argentina stills says, ¡Mañana, Mañana!"

The author Richard Tomita and his editor Andrew De Prisco, spending time at the Jacquet kennels in Oakland, New Jersey.

I marveled over Rick's undeterred motivation to contact as many top breeders from around the world as possible: American, British, Canadian, Japanese, Latvian, etc., etc., as well as his persistence with those breeders who were too busy to find the time to send information and photographs. He could hardly contain his enthusiasm as the materials arrived, and the book grew and grew...and grew.

Filing cabinets later, after the acquisition of thousands and thousands of photographs from every nation but Atlantis, Rick and I sat down to discuss "the reality" of a printed book on the Boxer. Rick couldn't imagine not including all the pictures, especially the 60 champions from this kennel, the 35 offspring of this dog, and the 45 existing dogs from Latvia (It is Frau Stockmann's birthland, after all!) "We'll do a two-volume set, maybe three or four!!" The Editor, of course, needed to help Rick make selections, and approximately 1000 pictures were selected. If your dog's picture is not included in these pages, it is absolutely *not* by Rick's choice!

Finally I realized that in Rick's enthusiasm, nothing about his own kennel Jacquet had been submitted. I chided Rick, "Where's stories for Urko and Novarese?" He thought that Jacquet should only be covered minimally, if at all. I told him, No way! Jacquet Boxers were all over the world, champions in almost every country, not to mention a couple hundred in the US! After much discussion, the Editor prevailed and Rick sat down to tell the Jacquet story— his life story with Boxers—and pictures surfaced too.

I insisted that modesty had no place in this book, because our readers wanted to hear what Richard Tomita, the nation's top breeder for over a decade, had to say about Boxers and breeding Boxers, and they want to see the Jacquet dogs in photography...from Agassiz to Zephan!!

Despite the many Jacquet dogs in this book and their obvious influence on the World of Boxers, Rick has still managed to represent every important breeder and dog in the English-speaking world, and then some! Had he his way, this book would have grown to be a ten-volume set!

Putting together a book this large, with so many thousands of pictures and about 60 guest authors, has been more than the challenge I envisioned. I am proud to say that I am the Editor of the largest single volume ever published in any language on a single breed of dog (!), and Rick's even prouder to say that *that dog* is the BOXER. My hat is off to my dear friend, Rick Tomita, who never believed he could conquer *The World* and has now accomplished true greatness for his beloved breed, the Boxer. Through this man's unselfish dedication and his devotion to the breed, the international Boxer community has come together to make *The World of the Boxer* possible.

Bravissimo, Rick! The Never-ending *World of the Boxer* has finally arrived!

Andrew De Prisco

THE LEGENDARY FRAU STOCKMANN

BY KARLA SPITZER

I want to thank Rick Tomita for the opportunity to do this research and contribute this material to his wonderful book. And as a fellow lover of the breed, I want to thank him for caring enough to write it! A special thanks goes to my friend Marianne Legere, from whose extensive "Boxer Library" the information for this material comes.

Before I read the many Boxer books available to me, I wondered about the people who bred these fabulous dogs. In general, the information I'd read focused on this dog and that dog, this kennel and that kennel. But who were the people who achieved this? Through what straight or circuitous routes did my Boxers find me today? Who knew about these dogs in order to breed them? How and where did they start?

You know the old saying, "Behind every good man, there's a good woman?" Well, I wondered if the same weren't true of dogs. Somehow, it seemed logical to assume that behind every great dog, there was a person...after all, who would drive them to the shows? Fill out the show applications? Register them? More importantly, *feed* them?! Who cared enough to make these dogs champions? But there was relatively little information available about the *people* who took care of these mundane tasks.

The legendary Int. Ch. Sigurd von Dom of Barmere lived in the 1930s, just one of the many breed pillars credited to Frau Stockmann. Owner, Mrs. Hostetter Young.

While I had learned the basics about Boxers and had become acquainted with the names of some of the great Boxers of the past, I couldn't help but think, as a dog lover myself, that the people behind this fabulous breed must have been pretty remarkable themselves. And I wanted to know about *them*.

So, I jumped on the chance to satisfy my extensive curiosity by doing research on Frau Stockmann. I found that she, at least, seemed to be a pretty amazing person...just as I had suspected.

Int. Ch. Xerxes von Dom, bred by Frau Stockmann and sired by Int. Ch. Sigurd von Dom, produced Int. Ch. Dorian von Marienhof, the great brindle sire who came to Mazelaine in America, representing a half century's most selective German breeding.

The Kennel Von Dom

The dogs that Frau Stockmann bred, under the name of the von Dom Kennel, are legendary. "Von Dom" was a name that was synonymous with exceptional quality Boxers. The von Dom dogs were famous in their own time, and their fame continues today. Throughout her life as an artist, photographer and dog breeder, Frau Stockmann contributed enormously to improving the quality of the Boxer from 1911 until her death in 1973.

Outstanding dogs from the von Dom Kennel include:

Ch. Rolf von Vogelsberg

Ch. Dampf von Dom (The first dog to be sold to an American, Herbert Lehman, later Governor of the State of New York)

Ch. Urschi von Hildesberg

Ch. Rassel von Dom

Ch. Sigurd von Dom

Ch. Rolf Walhall

Ch. Zorn von Dom

Ch. Lustig von Dom

Ch. Utz von Dom.

Outstanding dogs closely related to the von Dom Kennel are:

Ch. Dorian von Marienhof

Int. Ch. Pia von Isebeck.

These are just some of the most noteworthy of the many fine dogs that were bred by the Stockmanns in the von Dom Kennel. These dogs are the ones that have placed their stamp on Boxer history.

Facing page: Frau Stockmann proved to be a consummate dog breeder, artist and photographer. "Meditation," like all of her art, brings together her love of Boxers with her aesthetic abilities. Photograph by Mrs. Friederun Miram Stockmann.

The Dog Star

The story of Friederun Miram Stockmann's life is the stuff of an old-fashioned story. Her life was not easy. It was often a very difficult, challenging life...a life of perseverance and persistence. She lived, as a German citizen, through two World Wars, and suffered hardships and obstacles that would have stopped a lesser soul.

As a child in Riga, Latvia, her playmates teased her—telling her that she was born under the Dog Star. When she questioned her father about this, he confirmed that there was a "Dog Star," Sirius, the brightest fixed star in the constellation of Canis Major (the Great Dog). Little Friederun Miram was proud of the fact that maybe she had been born under Sirius. Through her entire life, no one and no hardship could destroy her belief in the Dog Star, and that it guided and protected her.

What gives her life an almost storybook essence is her utmost, total and unwavering dedication to a breed of dog that she read about as a child. And as a child, she dreamed of one day owning such a dog. That special dog, of course, was a Boxer. It was a breed she'd never actually seen, but there was a picture of one in her brother's Christmas present—a book on dogs—and she fell totally, instantly and permanently in love.

She left home in her late teens to further her education, and everything she did after this time had something to do with Boxers. Whether through art, photography or the show ring, her knowledge and understanding of the breed were legendary even in her own time.

Frau Stockmann's knowledge of Boxers and her single dream of promoting and developing this breed led her along a challenging and interesting path in life. So enveloped was she in this childhood dream that she told her boyfriend, as she was leaving Riga for Munich to study art, not that she'd miss him, nor that she'd write. She simply told him that the first thing she intended to do was to acquire a dog!

She came onto the Boxer scene within two decades of its enthusiastic beginning. In the late 1800s there was a move all across Europe to classify and "breed to type" many of the indigenous and regional dog types.

Boxers, in the form of Bullenbeissers, had been recorded in drawings and etchings since Medieval times, but until about 1893 or 1894 the Boxer was called a Boxl or Boxel and was seen as a mutt. In 1894, a man named Friedrich Roberth took a stand in defense of Boxers. In February of 1895, the Boxer Club was formed in Munich, and the Boxer had officially arrived.

In 1896 and 1897, Herr Alt (Alt's Flora, a French dog) was bred to a dog in Germany (a Boxl) of a similar type, and one of those puppies became Herr Lechner's Box. (A sobering thought—if Herr Alt had his way, the breed might have been called Floras! A Boxer by any other name?!)

Then Tom, the Bulldog, was introduced, and the breed was off to the races, so to speak. And while many of the early dogs were white or parti-colored, we know that by 1904 solid black was a disqualification, probably due to the "unacceptable behavior" of a man referred to only as Herr Schactner. He owned the black Graf Blitz von Graudenz (dog number 178, born August 8, 1899, listed in the very first Boxer stud book) and all that Frau Stockmann or anyone else seemed to be willing to say about him was that he was totally unacceptable to members of the Munich Boxer Club.

The color white remained eligible for registration for a much longer time. It was not until 1925 or 1926 that white seemed to have been frowned upon. Collections of early pictures of Boxers show more whites in many cases than the other colors.

Various speculations are made as to why whites fell out of favor. Philip Stockmann hints that it was to distinguish them from the English Bulldog. "We have since expunged the English Bulldog from our Boxer." Another speculation is that since Boxers were beginning to become popular in use as police dogs, after a noble career as the original German war dog, the color white was too easy to see at night. Perhaps the color was a hindrance rather than an asset to the breed, given the direction it was traveling at the time.

At any rate, by 1911, when the future Frau Stockmann came onto the dog scene in Munich, the breed was well on its way to becoming popular in Germany.

Early Years: Philip Stockmann and Pluto von Dom

It was in 1911, after a childhood of art lessons, that the young Friederun Miram left her childhood home in Riga. She was 18 years old, and this was the beginning of her advanced studies in Munich. She was to become, as her mother wished, "a spinster artist." (Frau Stockmann doesn't tell us that this was her wish, only that this was when she left, and what her mother wanted. Maybe she didn't mind as long as it didn't interfere with her dream of acquiring a dog.)

At any rate, it was in Munich that Friederun Miram met Philip Stockmann, the slightly dull son (in her opinion) of a friend of her mother—someone she was expected to have dinner with at least once a month.

Needless to say, Philip's status as a dullard quickly changed when he presented her with his beloved dog, Pluto, a large brindle Boxer male. The breed of her childhood dreams! In modern times, these series of events could probably be seen as romantic, possibly even as fate! One can almost see the Dog Star twinkling. Frau Stockmann certainly believed it had led her to this outcome.

But fate is always a mixed blessing, and maybe the Dog Star was laughing—even though Frau Stockmann said that she felt she had met Pluto before long ago. Pluto, whom Frau Stockmann called "Pluto the Hellhound," sounded like he was every dog owner's worst nightmare—a dog aggressive to the extreme, totally unmanageable on a leash and with a tendency to run away and attack other animals. (Even at an advanced age, he could bring down a stag on his own.)

Such a dog does not initially strike one as a dream come true, but Frau Stockmann was not easily deterred. She loved Pluto passionately. He was a good enough Boxer "of the old type" to be entered in a stud book. He was her kennel's first entry in Stud Book Number 4, dog number 152, as "Pluto von Dom." The name "von Dom," of course, became famous among Boxer lovers in spite of Pluto.

Frau Stockmann, for her part, cheerfully admits that the name, von Dom occurred to her as a kennel name when she remembered the many dog fights Pluto had had in the vicinity of the cathedral (Dom). (Perhaps the good German Boxer lovers of the time would have frowned on "Pluto the Hellhound" or "Hellhound Kennels" as an entry in the stud book.)

Not everyone is whimsical or, perhaps, unfortunate enough to name their kennel for the vicinity of most of their dog's fights. But Frau Stockmann had, it seems, a wonderful sense of humor that enabled her to persevere when life became difficult. She had a rare belief that life, if one had one's beloved dogs, was well worth enduring.

Still, when the outrageous Pluto, despite a muzzle and all her efforts to correct him, embarrassed Frau Stockmann once too many times by fighting in front of a crowd at a butcher's shop, she returned Pluto to Philip. She refused to communicate with either of them for two weeks.

Despite the respite, she was miserable, and fate intervened again. This time, it was in the form of a letter from Philip describing Pluto's love-sick behavior—he wouldn't eat and he wouldn't play. He pined and, in general, was miserable without her.

What was a dog lover to do?! Frau Stockmann relented. All was forgiven, and both Pluto and Philip returned to her life. Never one to do things in half measures, not only did Frau Stockmann relent and take Pluto back but she quit taking expensive art classes that her parents were paying for and instead bought her first brood bitch!

Laska was a red fawn with a half-white mask, which Frau Stockmann didn't like. She only bought Laska because her mentor, Herr Albert Schmoeger from the Munich Boxer Club, recommended this particular puppy. For Pluto, however, it was love at first sight.

Being a Dog Lover Costs!

Always an innovator, Frau Stockmann may have begun what was one of the first ad agencies. Because money was tight, she and Philip (also an artist) rented a studio where she did drawings and penned slogans for advertising material in order to balance her budget. While she was no longer taking art lessons, her art was supporting her and her dogs nevertheless.

The stress of housebreaking a puppy while she was living on the fifth floor of an apartment building before the days of elevators tested her mettle. Frequently, though not surprisingly, the poor puppy couldn't make it all the way downstairs without an accident!

As the three years allotted to her by her parents to study came to an end, Frau Stockmann was faced with a dilemma. Her parents did not know that Pluto and Laska had been bought at the expense of her art education. They thought that Pluto brought fantastic stud fees and that Laska had been bought as a result of that income. And Frau Stockmann did not like living a lie. She loved her dogs, but she loved her parents, too.

She had come to the conclusion that she couldn't live in the city and keep her dogs. It was too expensive and too difficult. On the other hand, she didn't want to go to live with her uncle in the country with no access to the city either.

She discussed her problems at great length with Philip, and together, they came upon a solution. They would get married, buy a small house out of town and properly establish the von Dom Kennel so it could flourish and prosper!

Devotion to the dogs cost in very real ways. This litter of wartime von Dom puppies is eating at great expense. Few litters survived that were reared during the war.

Von Dom Kennel Is Established

In a trip to see her parents, Freiderun Miram traveled by train with her two dogs, Philip and her plans. To her great surprise and relief, her parents seemed to think that getting married, being artists, showing dogs and establishing a kennel was a perfectly reasonable thing to do.

After a rushed wedding—rushed so that Frau Stockmann could return to Munich to show her dogs—the Stockmanns rented a house in Furstenfeldbruck, near Munich, and started their lives as breeders of Boxers. It was during this time that she acquired the champion, Rolf von Vogelsberg, who became the stud for her Laska, and parted with her first love, Pluto, whom Herr Schmoeger felt was not really quite good enough to use as a stud.

Frau Stockmann decided to part with Pluto because she had the opportunity to acquire Ch. Rolf von Vogelsberg, and in those days, she could not afford to keep two male dogs. It was many years before she got over her guilt at parting with her beloved Pluto. Years later, when the wars forced her to part with many of her

woman, full of ideals, she made major personal sacrifices for her dogs. All she wanted was for them to win. And when she became miserable because of the jealousy and bickering of the dog clubs, she thought of her beautiful dogs, and that made everything worthwhile.

During the years just preceding World War I, everything continued to go well for the Stockmanns. Frau Stockmann was able to sell a couple of her carvings to Russian nobility, along with all of her best pieces of the season. So, in another innovative move, Frau Stockmann bought herself an expensive camera and became a successful and sought-after photographer of dogs. In addition to her sculptures of dogs and other projects, she was establishing herself not only as a promising breeder of Boxers but also as an artist to the dog world. In a few years, the Stockmanns parlayed their modest success into a home and small farm of their own in the parish of Emmering, near Bruck.

Always an independent spirit, Frau Stockmann was one of the few successful breeders who was able to keep her dogs unkenneled and living together as a pack. Many

Frau Stockmann feeding the von Dom pack. Few breeders were able to have their kennel dogs live together peacefully as a pack. The male on the right is Rolf von Vogelsberg.

best dogs at early ages, she looked upon these losses as punishment for having broken her pledge to Pluto, the first dog that truly belonged to her.

Pluto adapted, and the "Hellhound" spirit lived on. Pluto was seen bringing down a six-pointed stag near Starnburg, and later, he defended his owner from six attackers who were beating the young woodsman. Pluto attacked and ran them all off, and the woodsman was only slightly injured.

Despite Pluto's exit from Frau Stockmann's life, the next few years were the exciting time of a new beginning. Frau Stockmann successfully won championships, bred her dogs and learned more about Boxers with each new addition. Life had its ordinary ups and downs.

In addition to acquiring Ch. Rolf von Vogelsberg, she acquired a champion bitch, Urschi von Hildesberg. A hard lesson the young Frau Stockmann learned was that all you had to do to be hated was to own beautiful dogs. There were rumors about her being a rich Russian grandduchess. Frau Stockmann admitted that as a young

"experts" told her that she would be unable to do this, as it was impossible to keep two adult Boxers of the same sex together. Even though she did make some mistakes and had some bloody victims, Frau Stockmann believed that allowing all the animals to roam together was a better way to let them live. Her experience told her that when kenneled dogs got loose, there would be an inevitable fight. When they learn to obey their human master or mistress, and the dog in charge, all the dogs benefit from the interaction and the chance to be themselves. This is because the "turf" is clear, there is less confusion about territory and less inclination to fight.

But by 1914, with a growing and successful kennel, a baby daughter and a new farm, the rumblings of a world war were close to home. After the Archduke Franz Ferdinand and his wife were assassinated by a Serb, Austria gave an ultimatum to Serbia, which was rejected. Austria declared war and laid claim on its allies. Germany declared its solidarity with Austria, and so Germany, too, was at war.

World War I

Within weeks, Philip was drafted, leaving Frau Stockmann alone isolated from her family, who still lived in the Baltic area, to care for her new baby and pack of dogs in difficult war times.

Uncertain at first of how she would manage, Frau Stockmann was saved by her mother's ingenuity. Frau Stockmann smuggled her daughter a parcel containing an old silver compact filled with gold coins. Friends from the Artists' Union in Munich managed to send her a little monthly help, too, and so she was not forgotten. The Dog Star was still twinkling.

Eternally enterprising, Frau Stockmann turned her home and kennels into farm land, renting four acres of meadow for planting. She bought 20 chickens and 3 goats. And she had help, in the form of laborers, from a nearby hotel that had been turned into a hotel for soldiers. The soldiers—especially farmers' sons—were happy to give her a hand. She used her expensive camera to take pictures of the young soldiers to supplement her income.

Champions and ordinary dogs, including personal pets, were trained and were used by the Army. The champions, who were trained dogs, were taken first by the Army, but Frau Stockmann was instrumental in training many of the pets to be war dogs too.

Because of the way champions were chosen in those days in Germany, choosing the champions first was not as unusual as it may sound initially. In Germany, then, as now, showing a dog for a championship required that in addition to being physically of a certain type, the dog also had to demonstrate that it was able to work. The dog was required to retrieve a five-pound dummy over a six-foot wall and on flat ground, and it had to be able to perform what we now call Schutzhund work except that instead of grabbing for the arm or the sleeve, the dogs were trained to grab the back of the person's neck in order to bring him down.

Boxers, with their great speed, agility and power, were invaluable in this type of attack, and the incidence of sniper fire dropped dramatically once the soldiers started patrolling with Boxers. Later, other breeds were also

Philip Stockmann proved his utility in service to the Fatherland by working with sentry dogs, training and maintaining them for military work.

Pioneer War Dogs

Later, in 1914, the Boxer Club in Munich began a campaign to mobilize all usable Boxers to assist the German Home Guard against snipers and other enemy infiltrates who were firing on soldiers on guard duty. An officer in the area had expressed a desire for a "few keen, reliable dogs." Frau Stockmann's old friend, Herr Schmoeger, recommended Boxer breeder Philip Stockmann as the man to contact.

The Army did contact Philip Stockmann, and thus it was that Boxers were to be pioneer war dogs. Philip Stockmann was transferred from his reserve regiment to the Home Guard in order to organize the military deployment of the dogs. This was a job that he enjoyed immensely, and with Frau Stockmann's help, the Stockmanns began gathering dogs to train for the Army.

used, but in the beginning, Boxers were the principle war dog of Germany.

As much as they were valued by the German armed forces, many did not return home to their owners when the war was over. Many were killed in the line of duty, and others, who were four to six years old at the beginning of the program, served for four hard years with the armed forces and simply died of hardship and old age. Still, many soldiers who worked with the dogs made every attempt to inform the owners about the service that their dogs performed, and the reports were generally glowing.

Champion Rolf von Vogelsberg was one of the finest war dogs of the bunch. His unerring nose and instinct made it possible for him to round up and hold whole groups of smugglers and snipers by himself until human help could come and relieve him!

In spite of the war, Rolf still managed to sire a litter or two for Frau Stockmann. His most famous offspring were:

Ch. Betty von Goldrhein
Ch. Dampf von Dom
Schelm von Angertor
Ch. Rolf von Walhall
Ch. Rassel von Dom.

The glory of the war dog work and continuing the kennel lines were just one part of the war. The day-to-day reality for Frau Stockmann was that the war was just plain miserable. Food was scarce, and she had to resort to feeding her dogs vast quantities of turnips and any and all rendered meat that she could find. This included old dogs that the neighboring farmers were willing to give to her. She sold all her young dogs just to keep the old ones—too old to be war dogs—alive. She rode her bicycle 15 miles one way just to get rendered meat for her dogs.

After and during the war, many of the litters she bred fell ill. Without money and modern-day veterinary services, many of the most promising dogs died. Yet, in spite of his age, four previous championships and the long, hard war years, Rolf von Vogelsberg won a fifth championship after the war! Then Frau Stockmann retired him, undefeated.

Post-War Changes

When the war was over, Frau Stockmann and her husband were forced, once again, to re-evaluate their lives. Should they continue with her art, photography and the Boxers? Her camera was outdated, and they had no money for art. Philip tried to find work, but with little or no success.

Frau Stockmann felt she had only one way out. Once the Baltic region was re-opened, she joined forces with her mother, sold the kennels and her kiln and together, the Stockmanns and Frau Miram bought a new real farm near Alotting-Muhldorf. The Stockmanns were lucky enough to sell their house and furniture to recoup some of the losses of the war.

The price of the new house was right for the Stockmanns and Frau Miram, but the other farmers in the area thought they were nuts—they had bought what was believed to be a "haunted house." This small detail, however, did not daunt Frau Stockmann. She believed that the haunting would stop as soon as the dogs arrived.

She was wrong. Her entire kennel came down with some sort of skin disease, and many died. Then her entire herd of seven goats died. Nobody could find a reason for their deaths. Not only that, but everything in the inventory of the farm that had not been nailed down was also missing. On top of this, Frau Stockmann found that the headquarters for post-war foodstuffs was between 7 to 15 miles away! Her only transportation was her bicycle, and she was expecting her second child within five months.

The indomitable personality that she was, she eventually got plenty of food for her dogs from a local "knacker" in the form of any dead animal he could spare.

Int. Ch. Lustig von Dom, regarded by Boxer enthusiasts as the most influential of the all the von Dom dogs.

New Hope

In spite of all the hardships during and after World War I, Frau Stockmann managed to breed the sire of her new dynasty during this time. Ivein von Dom, a red fawn, while not a champion himself, sired Ch. Sigurd von Dom and Int. Ch. Pia von Isebeck. So she was back in the dog game, as she called it.

As a mate for Sigurd, Frau Stockmann chose Dudel von Pfarrhaus, and this combination produced many winning dogs. Eventually, even the post-war years sorted themselves out and Frau Stockmann was truly back in business again.

In 1933, she produced a dog that "put everything else in the shade," as she put it later—Lustig von Dom. In the early days, though, she regarded him as a "cheap pup" because of the white markings on his face! In German terms, he had a fault—pink on his nose and muzzle. How wrong she would be! (The Dog Star probably howled with laughter at just how wrong.)

To her benefit, now that the war was over, wealthy Americans were coming to Frau Stockmann for dogs. Her reputation for being a knowledgeable and impeccable breeder had reached America. The dog to have was a dog from the von Dom Kennels.

While her heart told her "no," her business head said "yes," and she sold Sigurd, at five years of age, to an American, Mrs. William Z. Breed. As much as it hurt her to do this, the money made her life easier. She was able to buy a motorcycle, and the motorcycle made running the many errands in her life much easier.

Int. Ch. Zunftig von Dom was the first von Dom Boxer to be sent to Great Britain. Zunftig sired some important dogs in England before being sent to the United States.

A Lull in the Eye of the Storm

The dog game began to flourish again to Frau Stockmann's delight, as did life in Germany in general. Lustig went on to become a champion, and it seemed that there was a continuing stream of wealthy Americans who wanted to buy the best of the German dogs. Frau Stockmann had many offers for the beautiful Lustig, but she would not sell him.

Then tragedy struck again at the "haunted farm." A valuable mare died in foal, and the cattle began dying of indeterminate diseases. The corn and potato crops rotted in the fields.

The District Veterinary Officer visited the Stockmanns' farm and said the diseases were occurring because Frau Stockmann was feeding her dogs rendered meat. By this time, the Third Reich had begun to come into power in Germany. The new Nationalist Order brought Gleichschaltung or "rationalization" to kennels and all agricultural endeavors. The upshot of this was that the Stockmanns' request for a government loan to replace their dead animals was denied because the two party members who came to examine the farm had decided that the Stockmanns were wealthy enough and didn't need the money. Frau Stockmann was furious about this, but there was nothing she could do.

Lustig Goes to America

Luck, in its own form, was always with Frau Stockmann. In the bitter winter months following this summer of disasters, a five-figure offer was made for the incomparable Lustig from an American buyer. After some hesitation on the Stockmanns' part due to genuine surprise at the size of the offer, the price went to twelve thousand marks.

The Stockmanns felt they had no other choice, so the beautiful Lustig went to America, no longer a "cheap puppy." He was one dog that Frau Stockmann could not send away. Her daughter had to take him to the railway station.

Lustig went to the Tulgey Wood Kennels owned by Erwin O. Freund. He arrived in the United States in March 1937 with a collar around his neck that read, "I am the splendid Lustig." That same month he entered the show ring and finished his championship within a week.

As painful as the sale of Lustig was for Frau Stockmann, it was extremely beneficial for US Boxers. Lustig's line eventually bred the illustrious Bang Away of Sirrah Crest. For her part, Frau Stockmann was able to trade her motorcycle for a small car, thereby making her life much easier. Once again, one of her champions was able to make life better for the Stockmanns and the rest of the von Dom Kennel.

Frau Stockmann never saw Lustig again but Philip did, when a year later, he was invited to the United States to judge at some Boxer specialties. By then, Lustig was, of course, an American champion.

Lustig left behind numerous illustrious progeny in Germany including his son, Ch. Kyrras von der Blutenau, and his sister, Liesel von der Blutenau. They were both whisked away to America after the World War II broke out. Other Lustig progeny that went to the United States were: Ajax von der Holderburg, littermate Arno von der Holderburg and Zuntfig and Volkman von Dom. Zuntfig went to England first where he left some valuable progeny but he was sold to the United States for the benefit of the Red Cross.

Of the Lustig sons that were top class, only one stayed in Germany: Danilo von Konigsee. He was a brindle, not a fawn like Lustig and Lustig's other progeny, who went to the United States.

After Lustig's departure, there were a few more years of peace and prosperity, but gradually as Germany drifted closer to its role in World War II, more and more matters were taken over and regulated by the government.

Finally, the German government created a department of "German Dog Affairs," which was governed by the Army High Command, which regulated all affairs pertaining to dogs. Large dog shows were forbidden, but for some reason, small ones were not. It was anticipated that dogs would be required again for military purposes in war time, and there was still a need for some means of assessing them. This sinister planning for the future was the reason for passing a regulation that at least one parent of a mating must have a medal for obedience to help ensure that the offspring would be trainable.

Once this policy was implemented, all the dogs were reviewed and only the obedience-trained dogs got cards for food rations. The other dogs got nothing. In the early days, it was left up to the owners to find a way to either feed them or let them starve, but dog breeders were forbidden to breed from dogs without an obedience medal.

Boxers in World War II

Possibly because of their record in World War I in Germany, Boxers were ranked second in terms of desirability (read "worthy to be fed") at this time. This ranking may have also been given because of their character and temperament. (Ranked number one was the German Shepherd Dog, which Frau Stockmann was never able to supplant. She lamented that they were dogs that anyone could train, unlike the intelligent and, sometimes, stubborn Boxer, and their coats gave them additional protection against the cold.)

With the onset of the war, Frau Stockmann was again reduced to desperate measures, in spite of her food cards, to feed her animals. Twice a week she drove to an abattoir and brought back 150 pounds of meat for her dogs. While she attended to the farm, her husband, no longer a young man, became more and more involved in local politics.

From the collection of author Richard Tomita, three von Dom Boxers carved in wood by the gifted Frau Stockmann.

There were no dog shows during the war, but Frau Stockmann continued to train her dogs with future Army training needs in mind so that when the time came, a dog could be handed over to the Army fully trained.

The training consisted of:

1) Tracking.

2) Obedience: Retrieve, recall over a jump, release of article.

3) Schutzhund: Protecting the handler, attacking the agitators, barking until help arrives.

Frau Stockmann also trained messenger dogs. These dogs had to have a special aptitude and be able to carry on in the face of all kinds of distractions. Their role, of course, was to carry messages sometimes behind and/or around enemy lines. Despite the difficulty in this, many Boxers were successful messenger dogs.

Because so many of the gallant and enterprising Boxers had a tendency to catch live hand grenades in mid-air, Frau Stockmann had to teach them to ignore anything thrown from behind them and to continue delivering their messages no matter what was happening around them. All the training had to be carried out under gunfire.

Ultimately, as the war years wore on, only the dogs who passed these tests continued to get food cards. And as the war escalated, the tests became harder and harder. Eventually, dogs had to be able to continue their retrieve over a high jump even under gunfire. Needless to say, the testing times were very tense, especially if one wasn't 100-percent certain of the dog's ability.

Firn von Dom ("Finni"), one of the Stockmanns' favorites, was extremely frightened of gunfire. The Stockmanns and their friends were afraid of what would happen to this beautiful bitch if she failed the test, and they couldn't legally feed her.

Luck held the day of the test—the Dog Star must have been watching out for her. The gun that was used as part of the test jammed just as Finni dropped the dummy after the retrieve over the jump. Finni, in her infinite Boxer wisdom, knew that the gunfire started once she was over the jump. She figured that it would not start if she weren't carrying the dummy, so she managed to avoid the noise she hated so much. What Finni didn't know was that the gun would jam, so her wonderful example of Boxer ingenuity only resulted in a substantial reduction in her score! The testers never realized that she dropped the dummy because she was afraid of the gunfire. Finni still passed her test, thus continuing to receive food cards. The Stockmanns and their friends heaved a huge sigh of relief.

Unfortunately, an order came from the Army specifically for Finni some time later. Frau Stockmann and her daughter, knowing that Finni would not be able to perform as requested, substituted Mirzl von Pfarrkirchen instead. Mirzl was a more aggressive bitch, and not as good at raising litters. Frau Stockmann reasoned that the Army would never know. She was right. The Army didn't, and their beloved Finni stayed safe with them.

As the war progressed, Frau Stockmann was reduced to dodging low-flying enemy aircraft on her trips to the abattoir to get meat to feed her dogs. Near the end, there was no shelter from the bombing even in the country. The Stockmanns speculated who would get to them first, the Americans or the Russians.

Meanwhile, near the end, the German Army, in a strange act of desperation aimed somehow at foiling the Allied Forces, began dumping all food stores. When Frau Stockmann learned of this, she managed to get 500 pounds of dried meat and flour before the remains of the German Army destroyed it. So even in this most desperate of times, she had enough food for her dogs for about two months.

Allied Forces

As it happened, the American troops arrived first. Frau Stockmann's six adult Boxers watched the tanks with great curiosity from their side of the fence as they rolled on by.

While the Allied Forces were milling around the country, still looking for pockets of German resistance, hostile Polish and Russian troops also approached the Stockmanns' farm demanding food, which the Stockmanns did not have. When the soldiers came face to face with the dogs, however, they decided to leave the Stockmanns alone. They did not plunder the Stockmanns' farm, as they did so many other, probably out of fear of the dogs.

On the other hand, the Boxers tended to win the Americans over every time! (And vice versa!) Many American soldiers stopped to admire the Boxers and told Frau Stockmann that Boxers were the most popular breed in America! The French and English troops were reserved, but the Americans' love of dogs ensured that they got on well with the

Ch. Zack von Dom commemorated on a Dog Trading Card issued by Peter Paul Candies.

Stockmanns. The dogs knew there were differences. They liked the Americans, but their attitude toward troops from the eastern countries, particularly the Russians, was quite different.

Tragedy as the War Ends

In 1945, as the war ended, at a time when the innocent country folk could have been celebrating peace, the most devastating thing possible happened to Frau Stockmann and her family. During this time, many people were taken prisoner by the Allied Forces. Philip Stockmann was taken, too. For a long time, the Stockmann family could not find out where he was imprisoned. It was not until her son was released from a prisoner-of-war camp that they found Philip. He was at an internment camp, ill with early old age and the hardships of two world wars.

At the same time, Frau Stockmann's beloved daughter was diagnosed with heart disease, probably nutritionally related due to the deprivation caused by the war. Though they could seem to do nothing to free Philip, the always resourceful Frau Stockmann sold a young Boxer. The money was enough so she could send her daughter to a health resort, the Chiemsee, for six weeks under a doctor's supervision. Her daughter's condition improved rapidly.

In September 1945, Philip was allowed to come home. He was thin and desperately ill. Despite their pleas about his health, he was home only five days when he was taken away again. This was the last time Frau Stockmann would ever see him. Nine months later, he died in a prison-camp hospital following an operation.

Three days after his death, the gun-shy Finni, a great favorite of everyone, but especially of Philip, fell ill. The next day, she died.

The 1953 Christmas edition of *Our Dogs* featured the great Frohlich von Dom on its cover, owned by Mr. Allon Dawson of the Stainburndorf kennels in England.

When Philip's belongings were returned to the Stockmanns, all that remained were a few Boxer papers and two pins, one from a political organization and the other from the Boxer Club. He had kept these small reminders of his life's work and his love of Boxers until the end.

Peace and Tranquility

Things began to settle down again, as they inevitably do. The Americans moved into Germany with all their forces, and life in rural Germany became quiet. Frau Stockmann restarted her breeding program.

She had an entirely new market. Many of the occupation soldiers (Americans) came to her for puppies. The officers brought her food and other useful items that the Stockmanns could get in no other way. And again, some homesick farm boys, this time American, helped repair Frau Stockmann's farm after the shelling.

Because of the deprivation from the war, many of these early post-war litters were not good. Years of bad or inadequate food had taken its toll on the sickly and dying puppies. Then the German currency reform came, and with it, domestic chaos. Frau Stockmann was back in a position of being uncertain of where to find the money to breed her most promising bitch, Anka von Hofbauer.

Unhesitating and always willing to gamble on her dogs, she used what little savings she had managed to hang on to from the war and what her daughter could give her. She bred Anka to Ch. Harry von der Storchenburg. It was a great sacrifice and an even bigger risk. When did that ever stop Frau Stockmann when it came to her beloved Boxers?

Luck was finally with her, and nine weeks later, Anka whelped a litter. She was the only bitch to rear her litter when all the other puppies were dying.

Coming to America

Little by little, as life returned to normal, Frau Stockmann rebuilt her kennel. Four years later, in 1949, a Mrs. Shous, the president of the Potomac Boxer Club, arrived at Frau Stockmann's farm to ask her if she would judge a series of shows in America.

As a testimony to the persistence and determination of Boxer fanciers, Frau Stockmann was given a visa to the United States when no other German civilian was allowed into the country!

ZWEI NAMENS-VETTER!

Stockmann.

Left: **"Two Name Cousins" illustrated by Frau Stockmann.**

Frau Stockmann was sent on a whirlwind tour of Boxer clubs in the United States. First she judged 140 Boxers at the Potomac show.

She gave Best in Show to a red fawn dog, Master Tutt. Best of Opposite Sex went to a brindle bitch by the name of Hot Toddy who belonged to her old friends, the Wagner family who owned the Mazelaine Kennel. This kennel was founded on Frau Stockmann's line through Ch. Sigurd, the first dog she ever sold to an American; and his grandsons, Dorian von Marienhof and Utz von Dom.

Faced with a language barrier that she had no other way to overcome, Frau Stockmann began drawing pictures in a desperate attempt to explain the flaws of some of the Boxers she saw in America, especially the dogs with heads that were too square—like "frogs." Rather than offending the Americans, the show-goers were so enchanted that the drawings were ripped out of her hands and she found her art once again bringing her some extra much-needed cash.

In Illinois, she visited Tulgey Wood, where her "cheap puppy" Lustig had lived. There she saw the memorial that Mr. Freund had built to this great dog.

In discussing the difficulties of the war, Frau Stockmann admitted that the war had taken its toll on the German dog world. At the last German show she had attended, there were no really good dogs.

Frau Stockmann had the sympathy of American Boxer lovers, and the Wagners gave her the pick of

Int. Ch. Lustig von Dom of Tulgey Wood, bred by Frau Stockmann, whelped on December 28, 1933, and owned by Edwin O. Freund. When Lustig came to Tulgey Wood Kennels in America in 1937, he won Best in Show before acquiring his AKC championship (which he did three days later, on his sixth day in the ring!).

one of their top dog's litters. Two years later, that puppy, Czardus of Mazelaine, became a German champion.

Little Lustig

It was in Los Angeles that Frau Stockmann had one of the most pleasant surprises of her wonderful journey. She judged a show that had a ten-week-old puppy belonging to Dr. and Mrs. Rafael Harris of Sirrah Crest Kennel.

She took one look at "Little Lustig," a fawn with a white mask and white paws, and he went to the head of his class. The young Bang Away of Sirrah Crest went on to become one of the greatest American champion legends of all time. He set a record for winning more than 100 Best in Show awards.

Frau Stockmann returned to Germany with three dogs from America, and new "old" blood with which to restock her kennel: Czardas of Mazelaine, Abra Dabra of Sirrah Crest and a bitch named Goody, also of Sirrah Crest. With these dogs, the von Dom bloodline returned to a depleted stock in Germany.

Later Years

In later years, Frau Stockmann had the opportunity of returning to the United States to run a kennel for a wealthy American. It would have eased

Int. Ch. Utz von Dom, grandson to Ch. Sigurd, the first von Dom dog sold to America.

Frau Stockmann judged the future great Ch. Bang Away of Sirrah Crest at the age of three months, awarding him Best in Match over an entry of 110 puppies. After the judging, Frau Stockmann asked that his handler stack him on a table and turned him at several angles for all to see. Then she said through an interpreter, "He is going to be the greatest dog in America." When she returned home to Germany, she had his photograph published in the *Boxerblatter* with the title "Little Lustig."

a lifetime of too little money and too many dogs. One condition was that she could take only three dogs of her choice with her. She could not bear to part with her four old bitches, most of whom had been born during the war. They were simply too old to abandon, although the younger dogs could be sold with little or no problem. As she had always done, Frau Stockmann put her dogs first, so her dream job in America never came to be. She couldn't and wouldn't part with her "old girls."

Inevitably, it seemed, financial problems came to the forefront again, and Frau Stockmann was forced to sell her farm. She bought a small house with four acres. In a last-ditch endeavor to keep the farm, however, she sold Czardas to a man in England, who, in turn, sold Czardas to an American officer. Thus, Czardas became the only American Boxer that had become a German champion and then returned home to America.

And so it went for Frau Stockmann. Through no fault of her own, her resolve to keep and promote her beloved dogs often out-stripped her ability to do what she really wanted for them. By her own admission, she of-

ten sold her best dogs to keep the dogs that were not the most beautiful or the best. It was her champions that saved the rest, time after time.

But she never gave up. She never stopped breeding dogs for that one perfect dog: the Sigurds, the Lustigs, the Finnis, the Ankas, the Zuntfigs, the Bang Aways, the Czardases that the rest of us can only stop to admire.

And it was this unwavering dedication of Frau Stockmann that allows the rest of us to enjoy this wonderful breed—the Boxer—with all its beauty and idiosyncrasies.

How much are we influenced by its most dedicated and enthusiastic promoter from the early days?

Perhaps like Frau Stockmann, only the true connoisseur of canine intelligence and beauty can appreciate the magic of those searching eyes, that furrowed brow, that inner sense of fun and the dedication and loyalty second to none in the dog world. It is the stuff that dreams are made of...Frau Stockmann's, and hopefully, ours. And if I'm not mistaken, the Dog Star, Sirius, twinkles on!

REMEMBRANCES OF FRIEDERUN STOCKMANN

BY LIANE DIMITROFF AND BARBARA WIDMAYER

Liane Dimitroff of Little Ferry, New Jersey, has been a member of New Jersey Boxer Club for more than 25 years and a life member of the American Boxer Club, 25 years minimum. She has been a member of the Munich Boxer Club, which she joined while in her native Germany, since the 1950s.

At that time, Frau Stockmann was living about an hour outside of Munich on a good-sized piece of property with her dogs. Liane got to know her initially through Meise Stockmann, Frau Stockmann's daughter. They were both involved in obedience where in Germany, as Liane puts it, "everyone starts." In the Fatherland, in order to become a champion, the dogs needed a Schutzhund title and had to pass another temperament exam (i.e., for shyness). Schutzhund competitions started when the dogs were between 14–16 months old. Thus, it was not until dogs were about two years old that they began conformation competitions. Most people showed their own dogs, so the only expenses were entries and travel.

Liane later met Frau Stockmann at shows. Everyone was very respectful toward Stockmann and *always* called her "Frau Stockmann," never by her first name. She was the most well-known breeder in Boxers in Germany. Even the very wealthy came to her for her opinions, although she was very cautious in giving them. If she didn't like you, she basically said "Hello" and "Goodbye." To go to her house was by invitation only...and this was an incredible opportunity to learn because she would always talk about the dogs. And when she talked, people listened because what she had to say had such meaning. Frau Stockmann knew right away what you did or didn't know by what you said. She used her drawings to help teach you what your dog had and what it was supposed to be. Never a woman to be idle, Frau Stockmann was always creating something. Her wood carvings and art work, well known around Europe, were a wonderful extension of herself.

She lived her life and did everything for the welfare of her dogs. As everyone knows, there were many hard times. With as many dogs as she had, there was always a veterinarian coming to the house. And, Liane pointed out, despite the reputation that "all of the dogs were together," there were fights from time to time. In those days of no crates it was difficult, and sometimes dogs had to be kept behind closed doors. But they really did listen to her; she was definitely in charge and had their respect at all times.

Even sitting in her living room, Frau Stockmann was always busy, either writing or carving. She was a very quiet woman by nature who never said anything or made remarks about other people. She made no criticisms or comments about dogs she saw ringside—only critiques when judging. In later years, when she realized that her health was interfering with her ability to judge, she gave it up. If someone came to her ringside, wanting to breed to a specific dog, she would be very serious and always attempt to have that person breed to the dog that she thought was the right match for the bitch. She really helped everybody.

Frau Stockmann spending time with her Boxers. Photograph courtesy of Ray Curry.

In Germany, as most people know, the statistics on breeding stock and their litters are extensive. These statistics are available to everyone through the *Boxer Blatter:* who was bred to whom; who was in the litter; how many died; how many whites; how many checks; how many cleft palates; how many harelips; how many monorchid or cryptorchid; how many breedings, etc. With this data available, it was easy to track the results of studs and bitches.

When asked to describe Frau Stockmann and her kennel, Liane recalled: "The kennels came out from the house and there were large sandy/grassy areas, maybe 50 feet by 100 feet bordered by 4–5-foot-high chain-link fencing. But the dogs never jumped the fences. As for Frau Stockmann, she had gray hair and sometimes wore glasses (plain frames). She always wore a skirt with a blouse and sweater or vest and flat sport shoes." As mentioned before, she was a very quiet person but Liane couldn't stress enough how whenever she spoke, people listened. Liane commented that she was like a god. "People listened because she was so good—so good at everything she did and such a good person. I am very glad she and her family considered me a personal friend."

Stockmann sculpture of bitch and puppies, carved from a block of wood, approximately one foot in height.

Life-size sculpture by Frau Stockmann, carved from select wood from trees fallen on her farm. This labor of love was carved in the late 1930s from wood glued together to form one large block. It took five years to complete. Collection of Mrs. R. C. Harris.

A VISIT TO FRAU STOCKMANN

BY JOAN MACLAREN

With the passing of Meise Stockmann not too long ago came the realization that the last link with the beginnings of the Boxer breed had passed into history. Meise, as she was affectionately known, was the daughter of the late Philip and Friederun Stockmann, whose Von Dom Boxers were fundamental in laying the foundations of the modern-day breed.

This sad news took me back some 20 years ago, to an occasion on which I was privileged to visit Frau Stockmann and Meise at their home.

The opportunity arose when I was invited to judge at the Olympic Show, which was run by a Munich-based German Boxer Club. It was held to celebrate Munich's hosting of the Olympic Games and the show had a truly international flavor, with judges from Italy, France, Germany and Great Britain.

During the course of the pre-show arrangements, Herr Otto Donner, the genial "host" of this group, inquired if there was anything I would like to do during my stay in Munich. As an enthusiast of the Boxer's history, and having reveled in the wonderful book *My Life With Boxers*, my special request was to meet Frau Stockmann, if this was suitable and could be arranged. During a judging career certain events are impressed in one's memory, and for myself this Olympic Show stands out. In turn it was superseded by the visit to the Von Dom Kennel.

We knew Frau Stockmann had not been in the best of health and she was more or less retired from Boxer activities. Living with a few Boxers at the time, she resided in the country, which was approximately a one and a half hour drive from Munich, sharing a cottage with Meise. Her son and his family lived in another cottage that was nearby on the same property. It was most gracious of her to agree to our visit.

As the cars drove up in front of the cottage, I noticed a rather frail old lady being awakened from her slumber by the barking of Boxers. I almost wished I had not made the request, as we were intruding on the peace and

Mounted enamal plaque by Stockmann depicts, "The Boxer fears neither death nor the devil."

Mounted enamel Boxer head, created by Frau Stockmann, from the collection of Fiona Hamilton.

tranquility of her surroundings. The originally planned visitors had included: Otto, who was a close friend of Frau Stockmann; Barbara Murray, who had assisted as interpreter at the show; Fiona Hamilton, the friend who had accompanied me on this trip; and myself. This number would not have been too much of an imposition, but somewhere along the line the French judge, plus his family and friends, had learned of the intended trip and had come along too. So it really was quite an invasion.

A grass paddock was situated to the side of the cottage and, as we watched, a large black-faced brindle jumped the wire to position himself protectively between Frau Stockmann and the cars. He did nothing spectacular but everyone with a grain of dog sense could see he meant business. He was silent, with slightly laid-back ears, an evident ruff and his tail half raised. He watched each car intently. It was most impressive and, needless to say, no one attempted to leave his car! After some conversation with Frau Stockmann from the car, Otto vacated the car and introduced himself to the Boxer. Following a short interchange between the two friends, we were told that we too could leave the cars. The "big fella" then carefully did the rounds, inspecting us all and responding to friendly advances in a reserved and dignified manner. During the visit he remained quietly alert, even when relaxed and lying at the feet of his mistress.

Meise then joined the party, the introductions were made and the chat naturally enough turned to Boxers. As neither Fiona, myself, nor some of the French party spoke German, we were reliant on the help of our German friends and our participation was limited. We learned that the brindle dog was one of Frau

Stockmann's favorites and her constant companion. We also learned that a large American offer had recently been refused for a magnificent stag red male parading in the paddock. We were told that this particular dog did not have an ideal temperament and would not be used for breeding. The other occupant of the paddock, a delightful fawn of four to five months of age complete with ears and tail, had been quite ill at the normal time for docking and cropping. As it was now too late for this, he would remain as he was, a companion. From what we could see, the only other resident Boxer then made her appearance from the house. A most typical black-faced red fawn, she rushed around greeting everyone enthusiastically in typical puppy fashion. A little small for her age, she too had suffered some setback, although she was docked and cropped. Now considered sufficiently strong enough to leave home, she was for sale. For once in my life I inwardly cursed our quarantine laws as one of the French party hastily purchased this delightful little minx for a very modest sum.

We then adjourned to the living room of the cottage. As experienced enthusiasts know, Frau Stockmann was greatly famed for her artistic ability and we did hope that some of her work would be for sale. Meise explained that there was little available—most had been sold and her mother had been unable to work recently. A number of wooden carvings and enamel artifacts were then laid on the table for our inspection and everyone was able to purchase a memento from this visit. At that point I began to feel very sad, and it must have been apparent to everyone present that these Boxer works of art would probably be the last produced by Frau Stockmann. The lady herself seemed bright and cheerful, chatting in an animated fashion to Otto and Meise about the various objects when it came to setting a price for each individual piece.

Decorating the walls of the living room were several large inscribed pewter plates which were presumably trophies won by the von Doms. Displayed also were two magnificent Boxer head plaques. Such objects were displayed with love and pride, being mementos of winners and days long gone. It was therefore somewhat embarrassing when one of the French party asked Frau Stockmann to put a price on the plaques, as these were treasured personal possessions. This awkward moment was recouped by Frau Stockmann herself who indicated that the plaques were not for sale, for they were the likenesses of her two much loved Boxers, Abra-Dabra and Goody Goody of Sirrah Crest, whom she had imported from America.

From elsewhere in the house Meise produced a large wooden carving that was not quite finished. Those fortunate enough to have a copy of Frau Stockmann's book *My Life With Boxers* would have known the twin of this model. The picture gives no indication of the actual scale but the carving shown to us was of considerable size, being at least 18 inches in height and quite splendid in appearance. It was pointed out that although the carving itself was complete, the handhold used to steady the piece while working was still attached and would need to be removed. Frau Stockmann indicated she would

Guest author Joan MacLaren visits with Frau Stockmann in Germany.

attend to this and a purchase price was set. Any Boxer enthusiast would have been privileged to own such a piece, but as soon as the information had been conveyed a rapid and noticeably increased offer was made by the Frenchman who stated he would take the carving as it was. There comes a point in some situations when it is better to walk away—noticing that Frau Stockmann had quietly dozed off, I took myself outside for some fresh air! I found it hard to put into words what most of us must have wondered on that particular morning—would Frau Stockmann in fact be able to complete her work on the carving? I also thought about some of the less than kind remarks I had heard concerning the way the lady had chosen to live—"like a peasant buried in the country."

Walking to the limits of the cottage grounds, I noticed the neatly stacked logs stored for the winter and an assortment of interesting carvings. Bird life abounded around this naturally beautiful bitch that lay at the side of the track that led to the next cottage. Since she did not object, we continued to walk. The door of the cottage stood open and the bitch stopped on the threshold

From the collection of Victor Clemente, a bronze medallion by Frau Stockmann.

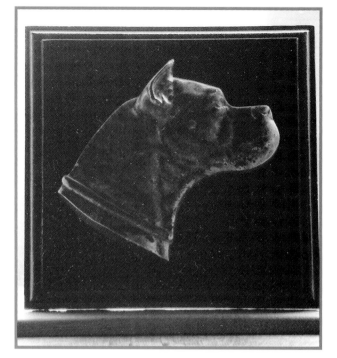

Boxer head in metal by Stockmann, from the collection of Joan MacLaren.

with a questioning expression, wondering why I didn't go inside. Having regained my composure after being charmed by the manners of this delightful Boxer lady, I retraced my steps. She stayed within the limits of her territory and I returned to the party of visitors who were by that time in the middle of a photo session.

During the course of our Munich stay, Fiona and I were royally treated, steeped in Boxer lore and given many small gifts and mementos. Among these mementos was a set of postcards produced by Frau Stockmann in her younger days. Each tells its own story. They are based on facts and the one illustration of Boxer parents

with a rather strange-looking litter apparently caused some amusement in its day. The litter was inspected and approved at an early age by the breed warden, but the puppies did not quite finish as he expected!

Through her instructive writing, Frau Stockmann left a rich legacy to the Boxer world. In this sphere, *The Boxer—His Type, Construction and Movement* stands alone in the world of pedigree dogs.

It is also an amazing fact that every Boxer alive today owes some of his beginnings to the endeavors of this most skilled of breeders. The visit to Von Dom was indeed a rare privilege.

Stockmann carving of two Boxers in play position, from the collection of Joan MacLaren.

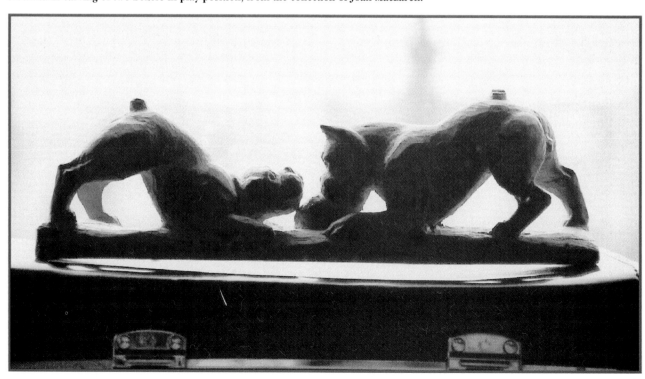

Satirical Boxer illustrations by Stockmann translate as follows (clockwise): "Born for police duty"; "Because all sins take revenge on earth"; "Rough exterior—noble cure"; "Double spawning?"; "Who is to be the chosen one?"

CH. HAPPY OURS
FORTUNE DE JACQUET

★★★★★★★★★★★★★★★★

BOXERS

IN THE
UNITED STATES

★★★★★★★★★★★★★★★★

MAZELAINE

BY ED GOLDFIELD

John and Mazie Wagner's Mazelaine Kennels was responsible for the emergence of the Boxer and its popularity, in the 1930s. More than any other Boxer kennel of the time, they promoted the breed.

Barmere Boxers imported Sigurd von Dom in 1934. He was to become the cornerstone of the Boxer in the United States. He and his three grandsons, Lustig, Dorian and Utz are considered "the four Great Pillars of the Breed." Practically every one of today's Boxers traces back to these four dogs. Ch. Dorian von Marienhof of Mazelaine and Ch. Utz von Dom of Mazelaine were both important in establishing Mazelaine as a dominant force. Dorian, however, emerged as the most important Boxer of his day.

Mazelaine Kennels was interested in Boxers as early as 1932, but it wasn't until January of 1936 that they purchased Dorian. Mrs. Mazie Wagner first saw Dorian in the fall of 1934 at the Sieger Show held in

An aerial view of the Mazelaine Kennels in the late 30s. The main dog quarters are at the right, and the Wagners' home peeps above the trees in the background.

Mazelaine existed in the heyday of the "super kennel," able to accommodate over a hundred adult dogs (plus puppies). Here are the securely fenced individual runs of the main kennel. At right center is the original kennel, and at the extreme right is the building that housed the dog food refrigeration room.

Berlin, Germany. The fame of Dorian had already reached the Boxer breeders in the U.S., even though he was still a puppy. After 18 months of negotiating, the great dog was brought to the United States. He made an immediate impact in the show ring. In less than 20 months of showing, he won 21 Bests in Show, 29 Group Ones and was undefeated in the breed, winning 34 straight Bests of Breed.

More important than his show career and the fact that he made people aware of the *new* elegance and style of the Boxer was that he stamped his get and their progeny with what we term the "Modern Boxer look." Not until his great-great-grandson, the immortal Bang Away, had one dog so changed the breed.

Mazelaine Kennels, by the 1940s, had the largest Boxer breeding program ever assembled. At times they kenneled well over 100 dogs, including stud dogs, brood bitches, show prospects and puppies.

As World War II came to a close, Mazelaine Kennels had bred the "War litter": Warbride, Warbaby and, of course, Warlord. Warlord was destined to become the first Boxer to win Best in Show at Westminster Kennel Club, the country's premier dog show. However, in the year of 1946, Warlord attained another first. He became the first Boxer to go Best American-bred in Show at Westminster (a classification that no longer exists). In the following year, 1947, Warlord went all the way to Best in Show.

Two years after Ch. Warlord's great triumphs, another Mazelaine dog came to the fore: Ch. Zazarac Brandy was the brindle son of Ch. Merry Monarch. Merry Monarch was a stunning dog with great movement and body. However, he lacked in head quality. His son,

Zazarac Brandy was most fortunate, for not only did he inherit his sire's beautiful body and movement but he had one of the best headpieces ever to adorn a Boxer. Brandy was a rather small dog, but what he lacked in size he made up in quality. Brandy was the second Boxer to go Best in Show at Westminster. The year was 1949. Zazarac Brandy, by the time he retired as a show dog, had garnered an unheard of 60 Bests in Show, a world record for a Boxer. Just as a bit of information, the immortal Bang Away was Best in Show at Westminster in 1951. Thus, Boxers enjoyed unrivaled popularity in that time period. Boxers won Best in Show at Westminster three times in a five-year span!

Furthermore, speaking of Ch. Bang Away of Sirrah Crest, he went on to amass 121 Bests in Show, more than doubling Brandy's previous record. It is a Boxer record that still stands today.

Mazelaine Boxers, between 1935 and 1950, dominated the Boxer world completely. Seventy-nine Boxers with the prefix of Mazelaine finished their championships in that period. Some of the most notable dogs were: Schoolmaster, Lucifer, Gallantry, Legend, Masterpiece, Sweepstakes, Victory Salute, Yankee Clipper, Vigilante, Pageantry and Hot Shot. Some of the important bitches were: Wild Ducas, Symphony, Serenade, Nemesis, Zenith Nocturne, Nylon, Blond Bombshell, Hot Toddy, Hells Bells, Gold Digger, Wild Fire, Zither and Yller.

After World War II and into the 1950s, due to increased costs and lack of dependable kennel help, Mazelaine Ken-

Int. Ch. Sigurd von Dom, grandsire of the three great stud influences, Lustig, Utz and Dorian. Sigurd went from Germany to Mazelaine in 1934 at the age of five.

nels, like most other large kennels, ceased to exist on the grand scale of the past. As Mazelaine started curtailing their own breeding program, they looked elsewhere for stud dogs as well as show dogs. They purchased Ch. Ursa Major, the sire of Bang Away, from the Harris's Sirrah Crest Kennels, hoping that lightning would strike twice. Unfortunately, this did not happen. They then purchased the great show prospect Ch. Warwick Kaneira, who proved to be a great Best in Show dog. However, he was only mediocre as a producer. At this same time, a Mazelaine-bred dog owned by Dr. Daniels was proving to be a top producer. He was the non-champion Mazelaine's Kapell-meister. He sired a total of 34 champions.

1955 saw the acquisition of the great bitch Ch. Baroque of Quality Hill, a litter sister to Ch. Barrage of Quality Hill, both sired by Ch. Bang Away. Baroque won 17 Bests in Show and 34 Groups in 1955. The following year, 1956, saw Mazelaine purchase a young fawn dog sired by Ch. Captain Lookout of Thorhall. This young dog, named Marjack's Golden Windjammer, won 7 Groups and 2 Bests in Shows from the classes. In 7 months of showing, he won 12 Best in Shows. Warwick's Karneira, Baroque and Windjammer accumulated some 60 Bests in Show.

By 1960, Mazelaine's stud force consisted of three dogs, none homebred. Along with Windjammer, they advertised Ch. Fielding's Freebooter, another Lookout son. The third dog at stud was a Brandy son, Ch. Rondean's Atomic Alarmist. In the following year, 1961, Mazelaine Kennels dispersed their remaining Boxers. Windjammer and Baroque were sold to Japan. The Wagners retained only one dog, Atomic Alarmist, their house dog. Thus was the end of an era.

Int. Ch. Dorian von Marienhof, born 1933, was exported from Germany to Mazelaine in 1936. The first Boxer to win the Group at Westminster, Dorian was never defeated by a Boxer in Germany or America. Ahead of his time in style and flash, this unprecedented dog could compete in the Group ring today!

Int. Ch. Utz von Dom of Mazelaine (sired by Zorn von Dom ex Esta von der Wurm) arrived in the US from Germany in April 1939. Four-time Best in Show winner and the second Boxer to win the Group at Westminster, Utz was handled by Len Brumby and became a leading sire in the US.

Commissioned by Mazelaine breeder John Wagner in 1943, "The Ideal Boxer" is a composite of 20 live Boxers and many photographs, rendered in bronze by June Harrah.

IMPORTANT BOXERS AND NUMBER OF CHAMPIONS SIRED

Ch. Bang Away of Sirrah Crest 81
Ch. Barrage of Quality Hill 45
Ch. Lustig Von Dom of Tulgey Wood 41
Ch. Dorian Von Marienhof of Mazelaine 39
Ch. Utz von Dom of Mazelaine 37
Mazelaine's Kapellmeister 34
Ch. Captain Lookout of Thorhall 31
Ch. Sigurd Von Dom of Barmere 26
Ch. Merry Monarch 24
Ch. Zazarac Brandy of Mazelaine 18
Ch. Marjack's Golden Windjammer 18
Ch. Warlord of Mazelaine 16

The Harrah bronze sculpture was also rendered in porcelain by the famous Rookwood Pottery Company, in bisque or glazed and painted.

Three Westminster Kennel Club Best in Show Boxers in the Parade of Champions at the 1952 ABC specialty: 1947 winner Ch. Warlord of Mazelaine, handled by Ernest Hamburger; 1949 winner Ch. Mazelaine's Zazarac Brandy, handled by Phil Marsh; and 1951 winner Ch. Bang Away of Sirrah Crest, handled by Nate Levine. Photograph courtesy of Charles Fortune.

SIRRAH CREST—"THE BANG AWAY STORY"

BY PHOEBE HARRIS

In the late 1930s, when America was beginning to emerge from the Great Depression, my husband and I discovered Boxers and yearned to have a puppy. Finally, we heard of a Boxer kennel near our home in southern California which was "overloaded with puppies and having a sale." When we arrived at the kennel, the owner showed us two pens of puppies. "Your choice of any puppy in this pen, $75.00, in that one, $100.00." Immediately, one of the puppies chose us. He ran toward the front of his pen, skidded into the fence, rolled over on his back and with his eyes on us, clearly said, "I love you the most! Take ME, take ME!" We were lucky. He was in the $75.00 pen and the choice had been made. So we took him home and gave him the grandest German name we could think of, Marshall v Bismark.

To us, he seemed to grow into a gorgeous Boxer and to be as good as those at the shows. So we hired a handler and, with the competition as it was at that time, he was a champion rather quickly. We wrote to the Boxer columnist of an eastern dog magazine to announce his victory and to express an interest in breeding Boxers. His reply was lengthy, kind, tactful, but the real message was that our precious champion was "the wrong type of Boxer from the wrong bloodlines." This discouraging news stunned us but, thankfully, we believed him and acted upon his suggestion to seek advice from "the fountainhead of Boxers," Mr. and Mrs. Jack Wagner of the Mazelaine Kennel in Milwaukee, Wisconsin.

Thus, Sirrah Crest, Harris spelled backwards, began in the fall of 1939 when we went to Milwaukee to meet the Wagners. Kind and gracious people, they "adopted" us and began to teach us about Boxers. We learned that the American Boxer world was dominated by four outstanding imported stud dogs: Int. Ch. Sigurd v Dom of Barmere and his three grandsons, Int. Ch. Dorian v Marienhof of Mazelaine and the two brothers, Int. Ch. Lustig v Dom of Tulgey Wood and Int. Ch. Utz v Dom of Mazelaine. Mr. Wagner said, "If you don't have Sigurd in your pedigree five times, you don't have anything." We spent two days with the Wagners seeing Boxers, reading pedigrees and listening to descriptions of the German dogs in the pedigrees. When we left, enthusiastic and inspired, we took with us the two-month-old puppy, Duke Cronian (a Dorian son ex Int. Ch. Crona v Zwergeck, a Lustig daughter) and four-month-old Quida of Mazelaine (an Utz daughter ex a Dorian daughter). The long trip home gave us plenty of time to think about our very small beginning as

Boxer breeders. Little did we realize that the two puppies in the baggage car were the first step toward a kennel of 60 dogs. Little could we imagine the years of work, trials and disappointments along with the moments of encouragement, victories and joy that would come into our lives before our ultimate achievement, the arrival of Ch. Bang Away of Sirrah Crest and his spectacular show career.

On our second visit to Mazelaine, two years later, we saw the Dorian daughter, Ch. Nocturne of Mazelaine—six years old and gorgeous! She had it all: spirit and personality along with elegance and physical beauty. We had a dream of breeding one like her! Then, Mr. Wagner showed us her daughter, Kantatrix of Mazelaine, whose four-month-old puppy looked like "a little Nocturne." We didn't even take Kantatrix out of her run; she was low on leg with a poor head and was plainly marked but both her mother and her puppy were excellent in these points. Their quality was enough to sell her to us. Kantatrix, with her brother and her nephew, each of whom were later bred to other of our bitches, places Nocturne in Bang Away's pedigree six times. We always attributed his *tremendous joie de vivre* and outstanding show spirit to Nocturne. One time after he left the ring, following an exceptional display of exuberance and showmanship, I said to Ray, "God bless Nocturne!"

Our last purchase from Mazelaine a year later was Ch. Endymion of Mazelaine, a Dorian son ex a Sigurd daughter. We were the only Boxer breeders at that time to have two Dorian sons each the exact opposite from the other. Duke Cronian was a golden brindle with an excellent head, short neck and slightly steep shoulder.

Bang Away as a pup, pictured with handler Russell Zimmerman.

Endymion was a flashy fawn with a poor head, long neck and one of the few absolutely perfect fronts and shoulders in the breed in the United States at that time.

We completed the accumulation of our foundation dogs with three breedings. Two were made when we reluctantly subjected bitches to the agony of being locked in their crates for a 60-hour train trip to Milwaukee with not only a change of trains but also a change of railroad stations in Chicago. One was bred to Utz and the other to Nocturne's son, Ch. Kavalier. The third breeding was to another Nocturne son, Whirlaway of Mazelaine, who was sold to a new owner in California.

In this discourse, I have omitted one tragic year that we have tried to forget. It was immediately after World War II when we bred six bitches to the newly imported Karlo v.d. Wolfsschlucht with the result that not one puppy from any of these litters was worth introducing into our breeding program. We sold everyone of Karlo's puppies and wrote the year off as a total loss of time, expense, labor and hopes.

As I look back it seems quite remarkable, even to me, that the purchase of four dogs plus three breedings completed our foundation stock. For the nine years we bred Boxers, no other purchase or outside breeding was made. With a population that grew to 60 Boxers, including seven champion stud dogs, we continued to concentrate the linebreeding that Mazelaine did before us and that the Germans did before them. In Bang Away's five-generation pedigree, with its 62 members, there are only 30 different individuals. His sixth generation, with its 64 additional members, gives an increase of only 13 individuals. Thus, his six-generation pedigree of 126 members contains only 43 different individuals.

Winning Best in Show at Portland, Oregon, Ch. Bang Away of Sirrah Crest is being handled by owner Mrs. R. C. Harris (one of the two times she ever handled him!)

A famous Wedgewood porcelain plate based on a 1953 drawing of Bang Away by Marguerite Kirns, from author Richard Tomita's collection, one of only two known plates in existence, the other owned by Sharlene Beckwith.

Parenthetically, let me say that linebreeding is not incest breeding. At times, we bred granddaughter to grandsire, grandson to granddam, niece to uncle and nephew to aunt, but we never did incest breeding; that is, son to dam, daughter to sire and brother to sister. Considering the stage of development in which Boxers were at this time, we felt incest breeding was harmful to the breed. Neither the Wagners nor we did it.

All of our foundation dogs had exemplary toplines with high withers, excellent hindquarters, correct bend of stifle and, most of them, good fronts and layback of shoulder. It is almost impossible to surmount the generations of breeding required to correct these major faults along with the minor ones that creep in continually. Here and there, we had plain heads, bad mouths, medium-light eyes, lowness of leg and short necks. However, also here and there, we had excellent heads, perfect mouths, very dark snappy eyes, good height of leg, long necks and perfect fronts with correct layback of shoulder.

By staying in our line, selecting and balancing the good with the bad, and never allowing the same fault to be present in two successive generations, we bred 29 champions, a number of Group winners and 2 Best in Show winners in about four generations. However, we believed we could breed a dog who would be better than any of these and kept working and waiting for the "great one." Finally, we brought our breeding program to a point where we actually expected him. This was the litter in which Bang Away's mother, Verily Verily, was born. These puppies were unusually nice and very promising for some time but, finally, none of them were quite good enough to be the answer to our hopes.

Then we bred Verily, with her exuberant spirit and vitality and her sparkling dark eyes and gorgeous head, to the tall, aloof, elegant and dignified Ursa Major, who moved like a dream. We were away from home when the puppies were born. Our first look will be always remembered. There she lay with three flashily marked fawn puppies nestled against her very dark brindle body. It was a beautiful sight! We were extremely pleased with the quality of the two males and continued to be throughout the time they were in the whelping quarters; however, we never rated our puppies until ear trimming time at seven weeks. When we stacked them on the operating table, before giving the anesthetic, each of us took a deep breath. We knew very well that no one can predict the outcome of a puppy at this age but we had reason to hope.

By the time the ears were healed I had made my choice between the two and, enthusiastically, started his show training. We had a daily workout which was mostly just having fun. We would run and jump and twist and turn and hide behind trees and play ball for a long time—ten minutes or so. Then, with me handling him very gently, talking to him kindly and gradually calming him down, he would have to stand very quiet with the lead firmly around his neck, head held high and feet planted on the ground for three seconds—just long enough to teach him that sometimes one must be subject to another's wishes. To him, though, even these 3 seconds, then 4 seconds, then 10 seconds, then on to 20 seconds soon became part of the game and he would stand perfectly quiet but very alert as he expectantly awaited my signal to break and run and jump and twist and turn and hide behind trees and play with the ball all over again. Everything was fun! Soon we graduated to the country road beside the kennel where, with me bent forward nearly double in order to hold the ball high in front of him, he learned to trot while looking up at the ball and the trees and the sky and never at the ground. Later, we went to a park where he would stand and stretch up to his full height to watch the children play at the other end of the grass. Frequently, they would come to admire and pet him. Everything was fun! Another trip was to the wide entrance in front of the movie theater when the moviegoers were leaving after the show. Some of them stopped to admire him and pet him, too. Soon, even crowds of people became fun!

When he was two-and-a-half months old, Frau Stockmann of Germany came to the United States to judge the Potomac Boxer Club Specialty in Washington, D.C. Afterwards, she visited the Wagners and, since Mr. Wagner was scheduled to judge at a show in Los Angeles, the Wagners brought Frau Stockmann with them to California. Our local Boxer club quickly organized a puppy match for her to judge. In an entry of 110 Boxer puppies, she found a little three-month-old fawn male, named V-1 of Sirrah Crest, (a temporary name,

A view of the ideal rear of puppy future Ch. Bang Away of Sirrah Crest, shown at three months old. Frau Stockmann judged him at this age and recognized his enormous potential, much to the delight of hopeful owner-breeders Dr. and Mrs. R. C. Harris.

Penelope Harris with the two Boxers that Dr. and Mrs. R. C. Harris gave to Mrs. Stockmann after World War II to help replace her dogs that suffered through the devastation of the war. On the left, Goody Goody of Sirrah Crest and on the right Abra Dabra of Sirrah Crest.

quickly chosen, the V in honor of his mother) to put Best in Match. After the judging, Frau Stockmann asked that his handler stack him on a table and turn him at several different angles for all to see. Then she said through an interpreter, "He is going to be the greatest dog in America." We were elated, of course, because she verified our hopes that he had the potential, but we didn't dare let ourselves fully believe her prophecy because he still had so much growing to do. When she returned home to Germany, she had his picture published in the *Boxer Blatter* with the title, "Little Lustig." She had bred Lustig and Utz and sold them to American breeders. It was satisfaction to us that we could show her that Boxer breeders here had appreciated these fine German imports and had used them well.

We all knew that Frau Stockmann and her daughter had suffered great hardships and had made almost impossible sacrifices during World War II to keep themselves and to preserve her Boxer breeding stock. She did not speak of it very much but one sentence was enough, "And then we ate cat."

To help her replenish her kennels, the Wagners gave her a young puppy, Mazelaine's Czardas, who became a champion. We gave her the choice of any two dogs in our kennel, except little V-1. She chose the six-month-old bitch, Goodie Goodie of Sirrah Crest, and a one-year-old male, Abra Dabra of Sirrah Crest. Abra sired her Primus v Dom who became the top winner in both show and obedience in Germany. I am accustomed to being introduced as the breeder of Bang Away, but when I was in Germany in 1985, although it had been 35 years after Abra arrived there, I was introduced as the breeder of Abra Dabra and well received because if it.

Dr. Harris poses with Bang Away and some of his winnings. Photograph courtesy of Michael Millan.

After Frau Stockmann's prophecy about V-1's future, I continued the workouts even more enthusiastically. Soon, spending the nights alone in a dog crate was added to V-1's regimen. There didn't seem to be any way in which this could be fun. Every night when I came to the stall, which he and his brother and sister occupied, I would find him sitting very stiffly on the edge of the sleeping platform, not moving a muscle and with his eyes looking straight forward. Even when the leash slipped over his head, he would stay firmly placed on the bench acting as if he didn't see me. Finally, even crating became acceptable.

Youth is a great asset when learning to be a show dog, or almost anything else.

We continued the workouts daily but, about the time V-1 was six months old, it seemed that either he was ready to graduate from training school or his teacher had reached the end of her capabilities. I was yearning for a chance to test him when a puppy match in San Diego was announced. In my mind, I had him entered and winning, but Ray and our handler were against it. They wanted to "keep him under wraps" until he was "ready for the big stuff." I continued to make plans to go to the match and, finally, Ray helped with the preparations and gave his good wishes to the kennel man and I as we drove off.

I have never known if Ray didn't go because he disapproved or because he couldn't bring himself to endure the suspense at ringside. The drive to San Diego was agonizing. I had to win!

We arrived at the match to find it well attended with a big entry. The class was easy with V-1 and V-II placing first and second. Then, we survived each elimination until the best bitch puppy and V-1 were alone in the ring for the final judging. My puppy was trying his best and was having great support from ringside. Then, just as the judge was approaching his decision, a girl at the end of the ring crossed her feet and, in the silence and suspense, the sound of little bells on her shoestrings rang out and floated across the ring. V-1 stretched up to his full height, raised his head and froze. There was no question as to who was Best in Match.

It was on that day that Bang Away began collecting his fans, who grew to be worldwide. Many times later, various San Diego Boxer enthusiasts related this match to us and bragged about witnessing one of his first victories.

His showmanship and win at the match prompted plans to launch him at the forthcoming American Boxer Club Specialty, to be held in February in New York City, where he could be shown in the 9- to 12-month puppy class. We hoped Nate Levine would handle him and in December called him. We told him that we had a puppy good enough to be entered in the puppy class at the Specialty and to go on to Best of Winners. Then we asked if he would handle him. Probably, Nate had heard many similar descriptions from many enthusiastic breeders. He hesitated but did reply that he had no conflicting commitment for the Specialty. Then, we said that we would like to send the puppy to him about five weeks before the show and added, "If you don't think he is good enough to take Best of Winners, we want you to send him back to us. We won't show at the Specialty because we think it is very important that his handler have as much confidence in him as we have." Nate agreed to this.

Now, V-1 had to have a real name. Our two best dogs had been Kobang and Yobang; so we wanted to continue with "Bang" as part of his name. One day, Ray said, "Well, now that he is going away . . ." I interrupted, "Away! That's it! That's his name! Bang Away!" His brother became Break Away.

Ch. Break Away of Sirrah Crest, litter brother to Bang Away, handled by owner Dr. Donald G. Reid in the early 1950s.

In a few weeks, Bang Away went to Nate Levine. Immediately, Nate assured us that he had "the confidence" and in February, Bang Away of Sirrah Crest took BOW at the American Boxer Club Specialty. This was the beginning of a show career that lasted five years. Nate Levine showed him north and south on the Atlantic coast and as far west as Michigan and Louisiana; Harry Sangster showed him north and south on the Pacific coast and as far east as Colorado and Texas; I showed him for a Best in Show in Portland, Oregon. He was shown in 27 of the then 48 states. He broke the record of 60 Best in Show wins before he was three years old; then, went on to be awarded Best in Show a total of 121 times. He was first in the Working Group (at that time, it contained 39 breeds), 87% of the times he won Best of Breed, and he won Best in Show 65% of the times he won Group One. We were determined that he retire when he was still in his prime. He won Best in Show eight times in the ten shows that were in his last circuit. Bang Away was never "spot shown." When he went on a circuit, he was shown at every show on the circuit. When he won Best of Breed, he was shown in the Group. He failed to win Best of Breed under four different judges at all-breed shows; later, two of these judges gave him Best in Show.

As Bang Away's popularity grew, he was featured in dog publications as well as in several national news magazines, including *Life, Sports Illustrated, Colliers, Esquire* and *Time*. Some excerpts from these are: "Despite traveling and being groomed, photographed and hounded by admirers, he remains an astounding creature of effervescent charm and personality, with the mien of an aristocrat and the 'savoir faire' of a man about town."

Another publication wrote: "Bang Away made himself immortal merely by showing up. He was 'in charge.' You talk about John Wayne or Gary Cooper walking down Main Street at high noon, when Bang Away came drifting into the ring, I mean, the town scattered. He owned the place; it was his lock, stock and barrel."

Then in *Sports Illustrated*: "A fawn and white Boxer flew to New York from California for a testimonial dinner at the Savoy-Plaza Hotel. He sat on the dias at the head table wearing a gold paper crown and was served steak in a gold bowl by the captain of waiters while 200 humans ate turkey and made elegant speeches and presentations for five hours. The occasion was the retirement from the show ring of Ch. Bang Away of Sirrah Crest, the Boxer who had won more Bests in Show than any dog in history. Bang Away's splendid record was in no small part responsible for the Boxer's becoming, in

Best in Show Westminster Kennel Club 1951 is Ch. Bang Away of Sirrah Crest, handled by Nate Levine and owned by Dr. Harris. Courtesy of Eleanor Linderholm-Wood.

the last few years, the second largest breed registered with the American Kennel Club."

In another magazine: "No wonder Boxers have grown in popularity. When people see Bang Away, they start imagining themselves walking down Fifth Avenue with one like him on the lead."

From a Canadian dog magazine: "Dog shows have a peculiar way of bringing out the worst in people, but Bang Away brought out their best. They cheered him; they didn't boo him. I remember vividly a show in Texas where he went down to defeat in the breed, and the huge crowd that had come to watch began hurling chairs and personal belongings into the ring to show their displeasure. The judge was escorted from the show by a policeman and the Boxer club members canceled the dinner that had been planned in his honor. This might befuddle the minds of today's showgoers who thrive on seeing a top dog get beaten, but it's a shining example of Bang Away's appeal."

In February 1956, as mentioned in the excerpt from *Sports Illustrated*, the American Boxer Club gave the dog, who had represented and promoted the breed so admirably, a testimonial dinner at a New York hotel. He accepted his honored position, seated on a small gold opera chair at the head table as if he always had his dinner this way. He took the roll from the bread and butter plate and gulped it down but waited patiently while I cut his steak and presented it piece by piece on a fork. Dinner was followed by gifts and tributes to the honored guest. First, a gold-colored crown was placed on

his head and he was proclaimed "The King of the Dogs." Then the president of Coro Jewelry presented him with a specially designed rhinestone-studded collar and me with a matching bracelet and earrings. Quite obviously, Bang Away sensed that he was participating in an unusual and important occasion and, like so many other events in his life, it was fun! With the crown lopped over one ear and his collar reflecting the lights here and there, he maintained his position, seated on the opera chair, while tributes and intermittent applause continued throughout the evening. Jack Wagner explained how at times in the early development of a line of animals, a "sport" appears (a "sport" being an individual who leaps forward with marked improvement in quality over those previously in the line). Then, time elapses and another "sport" appears, to make another rapid advancement in the line. He concluded, "Bang Away, like Dorian before him, is such a 'sport'." Other plaudits followed: by the judge who gave him his first win, by the judge who gave him his last win, by a professional handler whose dogs had competed with him, by the superintendent of the eastern dog shows who said that "Bang Away and his fans always bring extra excitement to any dog show" and by others who had shared important moments in his life. A "This Is Your Life" scrapbook was presented that held clippings about events in his career and pictures of his champion sons and daughters. Finally, we were given a ceramic plaque from the American Boxer Club, inscribed as follows:

Bang Away's retirement dinner held at the Savoy-Plaza Hotel in New York City, hosted by the ABC. *From left to right:* Mrs. Harris, Dr. Harris, "King of Dogs" Bang Away, Nate Levine and George Howard, President of the ABC.

"Awarded to Ch. Bang Away of Sirrah Crest and his justly proud owners and breeders, Dr. and Mrs. R. C. Harris, to whom he represents a dream come true.

"His unparalleled career spanning the past six years has carried this peerless show dog from the Northwest to the Mexican border, from the Lake States to the Gulf and from Florida to Cape Cod. While amassing the unprecedented total of 121 all-breed Best in Show wins, he has been seen at most of the major shows held in the United States. At less than seven years of age, his champion offspring already number 36. May they and others still to follow prove worthy of their illustrious sire. To all of us, Bang Away himself remains every inch a king and an inspiration to be carried forever in our hearts.

"The American Boxer Club, Inc. February 12, 1956"

When we returned to our hotel, Bang Away went into his crate, gave a big sigh and fell asleep while Ray and I relived the amazing and unbelievable evening.

When Bang Away's litters began to arrive, we saw that genetically he was blessed with the ability to transmit not only his background heredity but his own advanced quality to his offspring exceptionally well. Naturally,

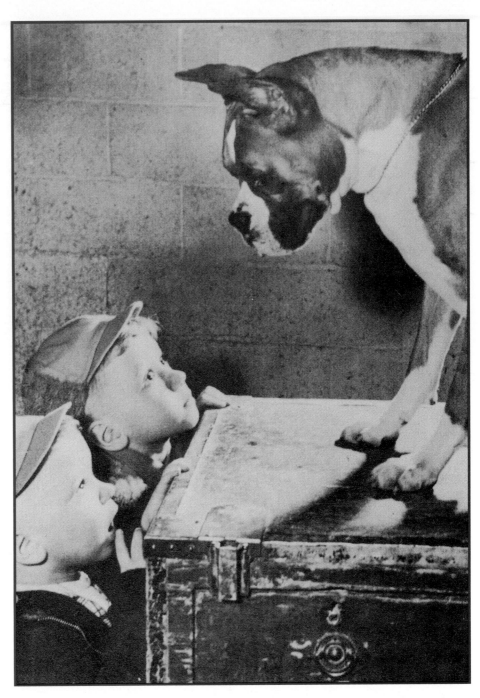

The author Richard Tomita remembers fondly what an impact this particular photograph of Bang Away and two admiring Cub Scouts had on him as a child: "I knew that I wanted a Boxer to live with just like this dog."

he was bred to many excellent bitches. However, we believed in the theory followed by agricultural animal breeders that a prepotent sire can best serve his breed by improving its overall general quality, so we bred him with bitches of lesser quality, also, and were glad to find that above-average good litters resulted. After 40 years, he still holds the record for siring the most American Boxer champions and the reputation of having contributed markedly to the improvement of the breed.

You may not know that we sold our kennel and did almost no breeding when Bang Away was about a year (or less) old and thus, never officially bred a Bang Away-sired litter. At the time of all of his breeding, we were so anxious to see a Bang Away daughter bred to Break Away or a Break Away daughter bred to Bang Away. It never

happened, but that would have been how we would have continued our breeding program. Our only regret when thinking of Bang Away's opportunities as a sire was that we never bred a litter sired by him and that he was bred to only three Sirrah Crest bitches. Unfortunately, when Bang Away was about 16 months old, a number of factors led to our selling the kennel and most of our Boxers except Bang Away and a few older dogs that we wished to keep with us for the rest of their lives. Although the three Sirrah Crest bitches to whom Bang Away was bred produced six champions, most of those who bought our other bitches outcrossed them. In this way, our close linebreeding came to an end. We were disappointed at that time, but if it contributed a small amount to the fine quality of today's American Boxers, it was worthwhile.

The final grand award was given to Bang Away in 1991, 33 years after his death, when a Dog Hall of Fame was established and he was the first show dog to be admitted. My acceptance at the award ceremony reflects the personal appeal of a Boxer who led a very rewarding and exciting life:

"If Bang Away were here, seated at a table, as he was at his retirement dinner given by the American Boxer Club here in New York City, he would be looking here and looking there, stretching and searching for some very elusive 'thing' that always seemed to be just beyond his horizon. That is what he did wherever he went and that is what he did in a show ring, greatly to his advantage, of course.

"Finally, after he was retired when visitors would come to see him (usually with a camera), I began to notice that just when he was at the peak of his stretching and looking for the 'thing' he would roll his eyes briefly toward the camera, as if to say, 'Take it now!' Bang Away's fans loved Bang Away; he loved them and we loved them, too. It was a joy for us to share the life of one so widely acclaimed by the dog fancy.

"Among the many letters that came to us (one addressed, Bang Away, Santa Ana, California) was one from a lady who lived in Ohio and who made a special trip to Washington, D.C. to see him shown. 'When he came into the ring,' she wrote, 'I sat there with tears rolling down my cheeks just as I do sometimes when I hear an especially beautiful symphony.'

"Three years ago, I was telling the judge at our national specialty show about this letter. His wife was there too, and she put up her hands and said, 'Oh, I cried every time I saw him!' Then the judge took out his wallet and from it handed me a picture of Bang Away. Had he carried it in his wallet all these years?

"Bang Away would have loved the honor you are giving him tonight and so do I.

Maybe this is the 'thing' he was always looking for just beyond his horizon!"

Ch. Bang Away of Sirrah Crest, as published in *Collier's Magazine*.

Left: Colorized photograph of Bang Away at 14 months of age.
Below: Dr. R. C. Harris poses with the Frau Stockmann wood carving that has become her lasting tribute to the breed she loved so well. This sculpture was gifted to the Harrises by Frau Stockmann after her visit to the US in 1949.

GRAYARLIN

Grayarlin began on GRAY Street in ARLINgton, Massachusetts. Jane Kamp (Forsyth) was a young girl when her mother bought an Utz von Dom daughter, a sister to the famed Ch. Mahderf's El Chico.

Starting at age 13, Jane worked for and later managed a number of prominent kennels: Elblac Dobermans, Grafmar's German Shepherds, and Renrew and Dorick Boxers. At Renrew, she showed Ch. V-E Admiral of Renrew as well as his sister, Ch. Wave of Renrew. Later, at Dorick, where Mr. and Mrs. Richard C. Kettle owned the famous Ch. Warlord of Mazelaine and Ch. Serenade of Mazelaine, she finished many of their dogs including the brothers Fiddle Faddle and Fandango.

On her own at age 19, Jane was already on her way to becoming one of the foremost handlers in the sport. Over the years, she has shown many outstanding Boxers including the great Ch. Barrage of Quality Hill, Ch. Marquam Hill's Comanche and Ch. Arriba's Prima Donna, the first Boxer bitch to win Best in Show at Westminster.

In partnership with George Pusey, from 1948 to 1959, Jane bred Boxers. Many of their dogs titled and

Am-Can. Ch. Barrage of Quality Hill won Best of Breed at the American Boxer Club Specialty in 1955 and 1957. Photograph courtesy of Eleanor Haeberle.

Am-Can. Ch. Barrage of Quality Hill, gracing the cover of *Sports Illustrated* on February 11, 1957, defeated his father Bang Away for Best American-bred dog in Show at Westminster in 1955, causing an unprecedented stir!

Sports Illustrated courtesy of Eleanor Hildebrandt.

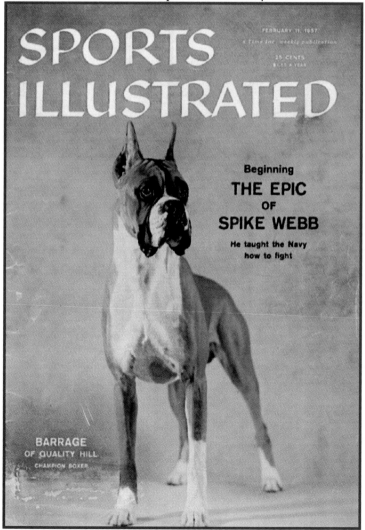

for a couple of years they were the top breeders in the country. Out of this program came Sally of Grayarlin, who was sold to Mr. and Mrs. Daniel Hamilburg. Though she had been sold as a pet, Jane talked them into letting her show the bitch on the Tar Heel circuit. Meeting in Fredericksburg, Virginia, Danny brought along his hotplate to cook for his dog, absolutely sure that she would be skin and bones. Much to his surprise, she looked great and ran right up to him at the hotel. He decided that showing dogs was great and bought two more Grayarlin dogs, Sabot and Slipper, who both finished their championships. Sabot went on to win a number of Groups and a Best in Show. Slipper, on the other hand, produced Ch. Salgray's Battle Chief, the first Salgray champion. Battle Chief won a number of Bests in Show and produced several champions. At the same time, Jane had two Marquam Hill bitches and Bob talked Dr. Burkle into buying Flamingo, who was the dam of the famous "F" litter. The entire litter titled and three became Best in Show winners. Jane had Flying High, Larry Downey had Fashion Plate and the Streichers had Flaming Ember. For many years after, they were top Boxer breeders. From pet owners to top breeders, Daniel and Phyllis Hamilburg were sincere in their love of the Boxer.

Jane also showed all of the Flintwood Boxers who, for several years, were also top breeders. Among their dogs was Ch. Flintwood's Rabble Rouser, whom she sold to Mrs. Cheever Porter, winner of many Bests in Show. Finally, until her retirement in 1981, Jane also handled for the author's Jacquet Boxers. At every show, she handled 10 to 15 Boxers, many of them the top dogs and bitches in the country.

Scott Rutherford got into Boxers in sort of a strange way. Her father played poker every Saturday night. The winnings were under her mother's pillow by Sunday morning. One Sunday—no winnings! Dad mumbled something about it being in the den. Of course, the children had discovered it. She was an eight-week-old plain brindle, a Ch. Mazelaine's Keynote daughter.

Scott had had her tenth birthday a few days before and thought it was the puppy she had wanted. It was years later that she found out that they had never intended to give her a puppy.

Impy was just the greatest. They went to obedience, then to matches. After attending several matches, she suspected she was not the world's greatest specimen. However, it was too late: Scott had been bitten by the "show bug."

In 1952, Scott saw a sign in the drug store window for the Middlesex Boxer Specialty. She entered and lost, but saw some wonderful dogs.

Scott talked her mother into driving down to the Potomac Specialty that year, a very classy event. She told her something about how educational and pleasant it would be to see Washington with her. Mother must have enjoyed it because she began to view dog showing as a reasonable activity for a teenager, though she still could not have more than one dog.

Father came home to lunch one day, not his custom. When he backed out of the driveway, he ran over Impy and killed her. He felt so badly that he allowed another puppy if it was a male.

Ch. Count Down (by Ch. On Parade of Grayarlin ex Paprika of Grayarlin), handled by Rufus Copeland and Lois Matthews. Owner, John Demetre. Judge, Nellie Anderson. Photograph courtesy of Scott Rutherford.

Ch. On Parade of Grayarlin (by Ch. Barrage of Quality Hill ex Lottery's Tortola, a Bang Away daughter), whelped November 18, 1955. Breeders, Jane Kamp and George S. Pusey. Handlers, Jane Kamp and Rufus Copeland. Owner, Scott Rutherford.

Their next-door neighbor introduced Scott to Mrs. Charles Forest Dowe. Mrs. Dowe was an active Best in Show judge and was gracious enough to take Scott along on many of her assignments. Scott is very grateful to Peggy for the wealth of information she imparted to her on those trips.

She pointed out that if the loss of Impy was too much, she should consider another breed. The family had had Scottish Terriers and maybe that was the way to go. Scott looked at several litters of Scotties and couldn't make up her mind.

Jane Kamp (Forsyth) walked by Scott at Framingham KC, while watching Scotties, with the most beautiful dog she had ever seen, Ch. Barrage of Quality Hill. The decision was made. Jane had a litter by Barrage, and On Parade of Grayarlin (Rory) came into Scott's life.

In those days, 1957, the Middlesex Specialty and Eastern Dog Club were held about a week or two before the American Boxer Specialty and Westminster. Jane entered On Parade at Middlesex and Boston because he needed the experience before the futurity at ABC. At Middlesex he won his class, handled by Anne Hone Rogers. To say the least, Scott was pleased. Saturday morning, Mother said she couldn't go to the show and that Scott would have to drive herself into Boston. She had just gotten her license. Forty minutes before the judging, she was at a traffic light on Huntington Avenue when a gravel truck's wheel locked and the brakes failed. The trucker slammed into the side of her mother's car. On Parade was thrown against the side window. By the time the police let her go, they only had five minutes before judging. On Parade had broken a canine tooth in the accident and was bleeding copiously. If she had realized that Angell Memorial was around the corner, she would have taken him there, but all she could think of

Ch. Rococo's Bright Magic (by Ch. Evo-Wen's Impressario ex Ch. Halo of Twin Willows) was handled by Rufus Copeland and owned by Scott Rutherford.

was the veterinarian at the show. Scott double parked on Huntington Avenue in front of Mechanics Hall and ran into the show. At last the dog had stopped bleeding.

Suddenly Annie appeared out of nowhere, grabbed the dog, saying, "Where have you been? He is in the ring now." As she disappeared into the crowd, Scott said, "But. . ."

Scott got to the ring just as he won the novice class. Annie handed Parade to her and said, "Don't you move." Scott bought a cold bottle of Coke because the dog's muzzle was beginning to swell. The curve of the bottle fit the muzzle perfectly. By the time Winners Dog was in the ring, the swelling had gone down and Scott knew he wasn't hurt badly.

There he was out there in Winners showing like a trooper. Maybe a slap up the side of the head was what that young dog needed. He really looked gorgeous. He won!

Then back to the cold Coke bottle compress. The Winners Bitch that day was Van's Blyth Spirit owned by Dr. Buris R. Boshell. She was a lovely bitch so when On Parade went Best of Winners, Scott was very proud to think he had beaten such a wonderful bitch.

Ch. Rococo's Major Muir (by Am-Can. Ch. Barrage of Quality Hill ex Costa's Shadow, an On Parade daughter), whelped August 12, 1959. Handled by Richard Bauer and Jane Forsyth. Owner, Scott Rutherford.

Then, in came the specials, which included Barrage. Of course, Barrage was going to win. After all, wasn't his picture on the cover of *Sports Illustrated*? He had won many BIS. He was a marvelous and magic dog.

The judge that day was Mrs. Marie Meyer. She cut quite a figure in her completely maroon outfit. The brim of her hat was so wide that if it had rained in the Mechanics Hall, Mrs. Meyer needn't have worried about getting wet. Forty-five minutes into the judging, Scott was becoming concerned about the dog being worked so hard. After all, he should be seeing the vet. The judging took forever. The ringside was now 20 deep. Scott went and got another cold Coke and lost her place at ringside. When she got back, she couldn't see but she could hear the comments. On Parade was under consideration. She ran up to the balcony and couldn't see from there either.

Ch. Rococo's Jessica (by Ch. Amity Hall's Master Key, a Barrage son, ex Opening Night of Grayarlin, a Barrage/On Parade daughter), owned by Mark and Boyd Wiltsey. Handler, Jane Forsyth.

Just as Mrs. Meyer picked On Parade for Best of Breed, the crowd parted and Scott saw it. There was such chaos that there was never a picture taken of the dog. The crowd and reporters descended on Annie with a fury that was scary. George Pusey, Jane's partner, took the dog from Annie and got him on the bench. Then Scott stood in front of the dog for hours protecting him from the public. It was not a pleasant experience.

Somebody was kind enough to call her mother. When she arrived, the crowds had somewhat abated, but she was still appalled at the rude treatment. Finally, it was time to take the dog off the bench and go home. Mother zapped her back to reality with "Dear, where did you park my car?"

On Parade went onto win many Specialties and Groups. Unfortunately, he died at four-and-a-half years of endocarditis. He sired two champions: Ch. Countdown, owned by John Demetre and handled by Lois Matthews and Rufus Copeland, and Ch. Rococo's Cricket, owned by Scott Rutherford and handled by Rufus Copeland. A sister to Cricket and Countdown was bred to Barrage and produced Ch. Rococo's Major Muir. Cricket was bred to Ch. Flintwood's Bag N'Baggage and produced Ch. Rococo's Aphrodite.

On Parade's litter sister was bred to the Barrage son, Ch. Amity Hall's Master Key and produced Ch. Rococo Jessica. Scott had reasonable success basing her breed program on Barrage. Along with the good you also get bad. Rears and feet were lacking, so Scott acquired Ch. Rococo's Bright Magic sired by Ch. Evo-Wen's Impressario ex Ch. Halo of Twin Willows. She produced three champions, two were Major Muir's and one was by Ch. Flintwood Line Backer.

When Scott decided to wind down with her Boxers, she gave a young typy bitch that she planned to show to Edgar and Florence Wilderson. This bitch was out of Ch. Brandybrook's Criteron and was named Ch. Rococo's Tangerine. In the hands of Earl Overstreet, she amassed many Bests of Breed and Group placements and became the foundation of the Wilderson's program.

Ch. Rococo's Tangerine (by Ch. Brandybrook's Criterion ex Lyric of Twin Rock), owned by Florence and Edgar Wilderson and bred by Scott Rutherford, became the foundation for the Wilderson Boxers.

Above: **Ch. Wilderson's Diana of Rococo** (by Ch. Arriba's Crescendo ex Ch. Rococo's Tangerine), handled by Marylou Wilderson and Earl Overstreet. Owners, Scott Rutherford and Marylou Wilderson. *Below:* **Ch. Wilderson's Image of Rococo,** owned by Michele Ann Sobota, bred by Scott Rutherford and Marylou Wilderson.

Eleanor Haeberle with Ch. Everready of Woodcrest.

ELDIC

As often happens, a family hobby turns into something more than a passing fancy, as it did when Eleanor Haeberle purchased a Boxer as a family pet in 1946. The male pet was with them for about six years. When faced with his loss, Eleanor attempted to purchase a top young male to exhibit in the show ring. As we all know, this task is not easy. Breeders with a top-quality male will rarely part with them; after all, they are the keystone of all good programs. Eleanor was then guided to purchase a bitch of quality to start a breeding program. The die was cast—Eldic Kennels was born.

In 1951 they purchased Everready of Woodcrest, a linebred bitch who had several points toward her championship. She was a quality bitch with a swan neck, proper topline and good movement, elegant but with very little flash.

Ch. Bang Away of Sirrah Crest was the top-winning Boxer male at the time and a sensational specimen. Believing only in linebreeding, Eleanor realized that in going out of the line to Bang Away and continuing their breeding program with the Bang Away line, they could get what was needed: flash, animation and the profit of his long linebred pedigree.

They bred Ch. Everready of Woodcrest, the foundation bitch, to Ch. Bang Away of Sirrah Crest and had three plain bitches—

very animated and sound in conformation but with very little flash.

Ch. Barrage of Quality Hill, a Bang Away son, had just won the 1954 ABC Grand Futurity. A spectacular Boxer with great flash and strong head and bone structure, he was selected for one of their Bang Away daughters, Eldic's Beaux Brite. This breeding produced Eldic's first great Boxer, Ch. Eldic's Darius. Ch. Bang Away of Sirrah Crest was the grandsire on both sides of Darius's pedigree.

Eldic continued linebreeding in the Ch. Bang Away of Sirrah Crest line, having over 70 litters in 20 years, producing both male and female champions. They bred to only about six stud dogs in this line, including grandsire breeding and double grandsire breeding whenever it was possible. In fact, in the 12th litter, a double grandsire breeding produced their second great dog, Ch. Eldic's Landlord.

Int. Ch. Eldic's Darius (May 1955–January 1964), the first champion son of Ch. Barrage of Quality Hill and double-grandson of the great Ch. Bang Away of Sirrah Crest, had a sensational record as a puppy. Quickly he proved himself an outstanding winner and sire. He was a standout showman from the start, making his debut at eight-and-a-half months of age and winning the ABC Grand Futurity. Judge Alice Groves remarked, "Once in a while, you see a dog walk into the ring who impresses you immediately as being great. Darius is one of them. He moved like a veteran show dog. I was very happy to have been able to judge such an animal."

A flashy deep red fawn, Darius went on from the 6- to 9-month puppy class to win Winners Dog and Best of Winners for a five-point major under renowned judge and breeder, Dr. R. C. Harris.

Ch. Everready of Woodcrest at 18 months of age, in whelp to Ch. Mazelaine Gallantry.

Darius was the youngest Best of Winners at any ABC Specialty and the first puppy Grand Futurity Winner to win the points. Only three times in 24 years had the final award gone to a 6- to 9-month-old puppy. He completed his championship at 11 months of age with a Best Puppy/Winners Dog/Best of Winners for another five points at Potomac Boxer Club and three more small shows within a two-month period.

At Potomac, his second show, a well-known handler remarked to Eleanor, "What are you so anxious about? If this judge doesn't put him up, he might as well fold up. You can count on your one hand the true Boxer movement at this show, and Darius is one of them."

Eleanor shares her beliefs, "Today—some 40 years later—I do believe that good true Boxer movement is not understood by many breeders. Consequently, few strive to improve it in their breeding programs. We must remember that the Boxer is a working dog."

Int. Ch. Eldic's Darius completed 32 Best of Breed wins in the 1956–1957 show season including Group wins and Group placements; he was a Sire of Merit and won many Specialty shows and the *Boxer Review* award for Best Boxer in the East. In 1957, Darius added his

Int. Ch. Eldic's Darius and litter brother Eldic's Dan Dee at seven months of age, owned and bred by Mr. and Mrs. Richard Haeberle.

Int. Ch. Eldic's Darius, handled by Jane Kamp Forsyth, owned by Mr. and Mrs. Richard Haeberle, won the ABC Specialty in 1956.

Canadian title in three consecutive shows, all in one weekend. His first competition in the Veterans class at the 1962 ABC Specialty amazed those ringside who did not realize that the lovely campaigner had reached seven years of age. He accepted the applause of his win with a proud reminiscence of his past accomplishments.

Darius was one of those dogs who was always good—great as a young puppy, as a mature dog and as a close companion to his owners, who always felt his charm and personality superseded his triumph in the ring and as a sire. Darius had much to offer, with linebreeding back to his grandsire on both sides of his pedigree. He was a clean, obedient house dog with a perfect temperament and an alert, animated, happy show dog, loving life and people without fears or problems. He was sound in conformation, perfect in balance and a great mover.

Ch. Eldic's Landlord (September 23, 1963–January 25, 1973) was a dark flashy brindle dog with deep glowing mahogany undertones and clearly defined brindle striping. He was the product of Eldic's 13 years of linebreeding on a strong pedigree of three top sires: Ch. Bang Away of Sirrah Crest, Ch. Barrage of Quality Hill and Ch. Eldic's Darius. Landlord combined all the best qualities of these three males.

As a puppy, his first win at 11 months of age was at Far Hills Kennel Club. He followed the next day with a five-point major win and Best of Winners at Westchester, a New York Boxer Specialty. His first show as an adult, at 15 months, was the 1965 Westminster show, where he won his second major for another five points. Judge Charles Hamilton took him from the Open Brindle class to Winners Dog and Best of Winners and remarked, "Excellent conformation and topline, has perfect movement." Reserve Dog at this show was a half-brother and a Darius son, helping to keep the wins in the family. Landlord completed his title at Long Island KC under Major Godsol.

In 1966, he compiled 50 Bests of Breed under 44 judges, a record at the time. He took on all the judges each weekend under whom he was exhibited and went on to win the *Boxer Review* award for Best Boxer in the East as well as an award for Sire of Merit.

Landlord was retired in triumph at three years of age, following his record-setting year by winning Best of Breed at Westminster in 1967. In 1970, Landlord won the Veterans class at the ABC Specialty, displaying the same happy animation and spirit at six-and-a-half years that captured the hearts of the fancy during his show career. Judges consistently commented about him: "Lovely flashy brindle," "Great style," "Excellent conformation, topline, tail set, strong rear and perfect movement" and "He's put together as a Boxer should be."

Like his sire Darius, Landlord was a constant joy to his owners, exhibiting a trusting nature, always eager to please and asking only to be loved in return. Obedient, yet gay and confident, his great temperament, movement and soundness were wonderful to watch. He de-

Ch. Ruda River's Best of Belle (by Int. Ch. Eldic's Darius ex Ch. Ruda Rivers Ebony Belle), handled by Jane Forsyth under judge Carl A. Wood.

Ch. Eldic's Landlord, owned and bred by Mr. and Mrs. Richard Haeberle, with his eight-week-old daughter.

ELDIC BOXERS

lighted in performing: setting himself up, moving from side to side or standing at his owner's side awaiting a command. To his last day, he was vibrant, alert, up on his toes, with not a gray hair. All who saw him maintained that his appearance would still put him in the winner's circle.

Like his predecessors—Darius, Barrage and Bang Away—Landlord was a dominant sire. He threw dark eyes and good mouths, corrected many faults in the bitches to whom he was bred. Darius's and Landlord's qualities, strengthened by sound linebreeding, were passed on to their progeny. What better legacy!

Eleanor concludes, "In the very early years of the Boxer in the U.S., our breed was thought to possess a stubborn nature. I never found this to be true. The Boxer breed is proud, loyal and a great member of the family. A very intelligent breed, my Boxers understood and respected that raising my voice slightly was a sign of my displeasure.

"I believe quality linebreeding can produce and will continue to produce. A linebred litter is a joy to behold. I advise not breeding to a top winning show dog only because of how well he represents the Boxer breed in the ring. Only breed to a good sound specimen who has a top pedigree on both sides. This philosophy has proven true to me several times during my active years of breeding Boxers.

"I offer as a point of interest and proof of good sound linebreeding the name and record of Ch. Bang Away of Sirrah Crest, a product of 26 years of linebreeding, who was Grand Futurity Winner in 1950; Ch. Barrage of Quality Hill, who was Grand Futurity Winner in 1954; Int. Ch. Eldic's Darius, who was Grand Futurity Winner in 1956. I humbly suggest that Ch. Eldic's Landlord might have won the ABC Futurity in 1965 at age 15 months had I not been judging the event and, obviously, could not enter my own dog.

"A linebred puppy should be very uniform in appearance at birth and continue the same through growth. As faults appear in a litter not so soundly linebred, be aware of these faults. They usually do not disappear. I firmly support the practice of grandsire breeding, only cautioning to do it as soon as possible as the dog might not be available by the next breeding period."

We are happy to share some more personal thoughts of Eleanor's, revealing her happiest moments in the dog sport and her truly outstanding accomplishments:

"In the approximately 20 years we bred and exhibited, we produced over 70 litters and put champion titles on both males and females. In naming our litters, we went through the alphabet twice—the first time using all 26 single letters, the second time using double letter (aa, bb) names, then using the letters of Eldic Kennels. This very happy and active period of my life took place almost four decades ago. Our participation was not only a sport but a very social activity. During this period we all had great respect for other breeder friends, congratulating them sincerely when they won and likewise when we won.

"It was also a time when we dressed up for each show season, particularly for our ABC Specialty in New York City followed by the Westminster KC show in February. I recall in early winter wearing fur hats. Later on in the spring, we wore straw hats. And in February and March, fashion called for flowered velvet hats.

"Another fond memory of mine was approaching or entering a city for a dog show early in the morning. You could safely follow the first station wagon you saw right to the show grounds.

"While exhibiting my Boxers, I devoured the dog show catalog. After becoming an AKC judge, this habit changed. I then wanted to judge each specimen as it was presented to me without knowing its background. I have been fortunate to have been able to judge all over

Ch. Eldic's Landlord (by Int. Ch. Eldic's Darius ex Eldic's Dark Dream), owned and bred by Mr. and Mrs. Richard Haeberle. Landlord amassed 50 BOBs under 44 different judges and is the celebrated sire of many champions.

the United States. I judged the ABC Futurity in 1965 and the ABC Specialty in 1977. I have also judged internationally in South America, Central America and Canada. To mention one other judging accomplishment, I was the first woman to judge at a Japanese all-breed show—Tokyo KC in 1969. In 1977, I returned to Japan to judge the Boxer Club of Tokyo Specialty.

"With all these wonderful memories and experiences, I have always felt that the best part of this outstanding period in our lives were our dear Boxers."

Your author admits more than a fondness for the great Landlord. This dog was such an inspiration to me. He was our foundation and I wanted to carry his type throughout my line. As I look at his stud card, which I studied every night before I went to bed and read about Eldic's linebreeding and breeding to grandsires and see the results in the third generation, I set my goal and my breeding program for the future. Eleanor was also an inspiration and I strove to get her type of dog to dominate my Jacquet line. Landlord also had the nicest temperament.

I will always remember my visit to Eldic Kennels in Basking Ridge, New Jersey. We took our Landlord kids for Eleanor Haeberle's approval. She then asked us to wait by the edge of a large expanse of lawn bordered by summer annuals and she brought Landlord out strutting across the grass and posing himself for Swiss cheese. He then got the okay to approach me and Bill and my young sister, immediately showering us with kisses and giving us his exuberant greeting.

Ch. Eldic's Landlord, handled by Jane Kamp Forsyth to BOB under Ted Wurmser at the 1966 Long Island show.

Int. Ch. Eldic's Darius, owned by Eleanor Heaberle, was the first champion sired by the great Ch. Barrage of Quality Hill and produced Ch. Eldic's Landlord.

Ch. Eldic's Lovely Lady Minx (by Int. Ch. Eldic's Darius ex Eldic's Dark Dream), owned by Phil and Ann Euler, is a litter sister to Ch. Eldic's Landlord, bred by Eleanor Haeberle and Mrs. Walter Amos.

Ch. Merrilane's Mad Rogue of Jofra (by Ch. Eldic's Landlord ex Merrilane's Mad Passion), bred by Eleanor Linderholm-Wood, and owned by Robert and Alma Pomeroy.

Ch. Eldic's Musetta (by Int. Ch. Eldic's Darius ex Eldic's Fairytale), at two years of age, owned by Eleanor Haeberle.

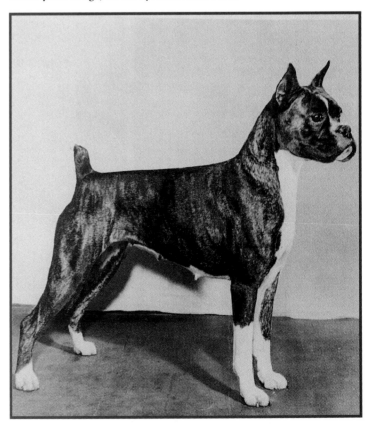

MERRILANE

Significantly important in the realm of Boxer breeding is Eleanor Linderholm-Wood, owner of Merrilane Boxers. Known to her friends as "Ellie," her devotion to the breed developed early in her teens. A friend of her mother had a Boxer bitch from Fred Hamm's Mahderf Kennel, for which he needed summer care while he traveled. This opportunity sparked Ellie's career in Boxers. During the second summer she had this bitch, she also cared for a male puppy that was later donated to The Seeing Eye in Morristown, New Jersey. He reportedly was the first Boxer and one of the earliest males trained for Seeing Eye work.

Later that fall, Ellie's parents purchased this Boxer bitch for her. Mahderf's Lucky Chance was subsequently bred and the resulting litter was cropped by Al and Mary Cousins, Rexob Boxers, then of Yonkers, New York. The friendship that developed between Ellie and the Cousins led to an invitation from Jack and Mazie Wagner to work in their Mazelaine Kennels in Milwaukee, Wisconsin, where the Cousins were the new managers. This she did for two summers while absorbing all phases of Boxer lore. It was an enviable experience in building a foundation in our breed.

It was during the school year, between these two summers, that Ellie first met Carl and Alice Wood. They solicited her help in training their newly acquired Mazelaine puppy. She showed this earliest Woodcrest Boxer for them, Robin Hood of Mazelaine. She also titled their first champion, Ysolde of Mazelaine. This led Carl and Alice Wood into developing their highly respected Woodcrest line of Boxers, which boasts some 26 homebred champions. Carl and Alice are both well known for their many years of dedication to the breed and their contributions to the dog fancy at large, especially to the American Boxer Club. Both were approved AKC judges.

It had been Ellie's ambition to become a veterinarian. She entered Cornell University's Pre-Medical College in an effort to obtain a solid background that would enhance an education in veterinary medicine. This, however, became impossible as World War II ended and the returning veterans were offered the first chances for available openings in the veterinary college. Women applicants were barely considered.

During the summer between her terms at Cornell, Ellie joined the Henry Larks, working and handling Boxers for them at their extensive Meritaire Kennels in Pennsylvania. When she left Cornell, unable to get into veterinary school, Ellie returned to Meritaire on a full-time basis. From this point on, she developed her self-

Ch. Merrilane's Knockout, SOM (by Ch. Merrilane's April Holiday ex Ch. Jacquet's Mercer), considered by owner-breeder Eleanor Linderholm-Wood to be her most important and favorite dog, has had significant influence as a sire. Breeders, Merrilane Kennels, P. and L. Small and Richard Tomita.

taught veterinary skills, as the Larks were most generous in providing equipment and supplies. Ellie worked closely with well-known professional croppers at Meritaire, adding to her abilities first learned from Jack Wagner during her stint at Mazelaine. She also learned much about the business management of a larger kennel and a great deal more about handling. Since the Larks were very seriously committed to breeding excellent Boxers, Ellie was able to put into practice what she had learned at Mazelaine about breeding principles. It was in the Larks' employ when she had the fun of showing Ch. Yller of Mazelaine to her record Best in Show awards and also others to become ABC annual award winners.

Eleanor was married in 1947 and divorced in 1954. During those years she dabbled a bit in Boxers. After having daughters, Ann (in 1948) and Gail (in 1950), she did a fair amount of handling. During much of this period, she also worked as a right-hand assistant to a

Merrilane's Mad Passion, CD (by Ch. Merrilane's Silver Dollar ex Bar Nymph's Medallion) was a top-producing bitch, the dam of ten AKC champions. Owner, Eleanor Linderholm-Wood.

Ch. Merrilane's Silver Dollar (by Ch. Space Man of Jofra ex Rococo's Enhancing) at seven years of age, owned by Eleanor Linderholm-Wood.

Silver Spring, Maryland veterinarian. Together they cropped for a number of Boxer breeders in the area and Ellie's experience in the veterinary field continued to grow.

Following her divorce, Ellie returned to Mazelaine, working at the then-Texas kennel and continuing when it was moved to the Chicago area. Later, Ellie moved to Nevada where she could concentrate principally on raising her daughters. During this time, there were, of course, Boxers with her, and she was "drafted" from her job with the State of Nevada by the City of Carson to head the newly created one-person department of dog control. This was a precarious job for some time. The residents were of mixed feelings regarding the adoption and enforcement of the new animal-control ordinance. The next seven-and-a-half years provided a many-faceted experience for Ellie and her daughters in their position in the community.

In 1966, a friend of Ellie's in Carson City bred a lovely Boxer bitch, Rococo's Enhancing, to Frances Lowman's Impressario son, Ch. Space Man of Jofra, from which litter Ellie purchased a fawn puppy. He was to become Ch. Merrilane's Silver Dollar, who completed his title at 17 months, three times along the way taking Best of Breed from the classes over Specials. He won 11 Bests of Breed, including the East Bay Specialty, before Ellie retired him from competition. She had decided to start handling again in earnest and, thus, could not keep him out against client's dogs.

Ellie married Victor Linderholm in 1968. In 1969, they moved to California where Ellie started Merrilane, the Boxer kennel for which she had so long dreamed, and began a full-time career as a professional handler. During her years of handling she finished a great many champions and gained an imposing array of top awards for her clients. In two-and-a-half years, eight homebred Merrilane champions completed titles. Silver Dollar's daughter, Merrilane's Mad Passion, CD, the kennel's foundation bitch, achieved a glowing record of ten U.S. champion get, making her the number-three producing American Boxer bitch in the breed.

Between July 1971 and July 1997, 75 homebred Merrilane champions have gained their U.S. titles and numerous other titles in foreign countries. Merrilane champions have been sold to new owners in Japan, Taiwan, Indonesia, Brazil, Spain, Norway, South Africa and Australia. Ellie is also proud that Merrilane bloodlines have strongly influenced the success of a number of kennels in this country, the most notable being the top present-day breeder, Jacquet Boxers, owned by the author Richard Tomita and William Scolnik. One example of these combined bloodlines was Ch. Merrilane's Knockout. This American Boxer Club Sire of Merit and recipient of an Award of Excellence was an ABC Top Twenty Contender in 1989 and winner of this prestigious event in 1990. This great Boxer was especially exciting to Ellie as his handler, co-breeder and owner since throughout his life he was her constant companion and dear friend.

After spouses Victor Linderholm and Alice Wood passed away in 1977 and 1980 respective, Eleanor Linderholm and Carl Wood were united in 1981. Since

Carl was an AKC-approved judge, Ellie was no longer eligible to handle dogs professionally. She "retired" to breeding and showing only her own dogs and continued to enjoy the adventures of motor-homing to dog shows all over the country with Carl and their Boxers. Their dedicated efforts for the breed are also reflected in their separate capacities with the American Boxer Club and the contributions they made in re-structuring the revised Boxer standard adopted in 1989. Carl also worked on the by-laws committee and served many years as historian to the ABC until his death in February 1990. Ellie continued with chairing the standard committee and enjoyed producing the *Illustrated Boxer Standard* approved by the American Boxer Club Board of Directors in November 1991. Her duties continue as club historian.

Photographs of the Merrilane Boxers illustrate the qualities achieved in this successful breeding program. Ellie remains alert to the trends and development in the breed and maintains a firm belief in the importance of adhering to the ideal Boxer in construction and character as described by the standard. She feels a great win record does not necessarily support or build a great breed specimen, nor will it establish a strong pattern of desirable qualities in its offspring. She also believes that it is wise to study the standard to gain the objective knowledge so necessary in individual and pedigree evaluation. This knowledge, Ellie feels, is extremely important in the development of a breeding program consistent in producing

Ch. Merrilane's Fortune de Jacquet (by Ch. Merrilane's Knockout ex Ch. Merrilane's Fortune Cookie), owned by Dorothy Mades and Richard Tomita, bred by Merrilane Kennels.

Ch. Merrilane's April Fashion, SOM (by Ch. Merrilane's Holiday Fashion ex Ch. Merrilane's April Love), owned by Coleman Cook, handled by Jane Forsyth, and bred by Merrilane Kennels, became the foundation stud for many Kennels in the Eastern United States.

prepotent qualities and diminishing undesirable characteristics.

Ellie devotes her Merrilane program to maintaining a high standard in the Boxer, keeping the Boxer a breed apart.

BREMHAVEN

Coleman Cook acquired his first Boxer in 1948, while still in the Army Air Corps. After discharge from the service, he became interested in showing and breeding. He talked to several top breeders and handlers who advised him to buy the best female that he could find. With the assistance of a top handler in Ohio, Cook purchased Canyonair's Talked About. She completed her championship in a very short period of time. Since then, he bred and/or owned 14 champions with a limited breeding program, the most well-known being Talked About (dam of champions), Ch. Bremhaven's Ringmaster, Ch. Bremhaven's Mister Roberts (BISS winner and sire of champions) and best known, Ch. Merrilane's April Fashion (multi-BISS and Group winner and the sire of 27 champions).

Cook has been a member of the American Boxer Club since 1952 and for many years in the '50s, '60s and early '70s was an AKC all-breed licensed handler.

Ch. Merrilane's Mad Madam of Jofra (by Ch. Eldic's Landlord ex Merrilane's Mad Passion, CD), owned by Neva Corboff.

Ch. Merrilane's Fashion Star (by Ch. Merrilane's Holiday Fashion ex Ch. Merrilane's Star von Heinrich) went to Yoshitaka Mori of Japan and was the sire of five AKC champions.

Ch. Merrilane's Silver 'n Gold (by Ch. Merrilane's April Holiday ex Merrilane's Silver Jewel) was the sire of five AKC champions.

Ch. Merrilane's Good As Gold (by Am-Can. Ch. Doggone Ounce of Gold ex Piccadilly's Kaleidoscope) produced three champions in her only litter.

Ch. Bremhaven's Mister Roberts (by Ch. Huffand's Nice Enough ex Ch. Keil's High Fashion), owned by Coleman Cook. This dog is the grandson of Ch. Merrilane's April Fashion, SOM.

Ch. Merrilane's Knockout, SOM, owned by Eleanor Linderholm-Wood, won an Award of Excellence at ABC and the Top Twenty in the early 1990s. Breeders, Merrilane Kennels, Rick Tomita and P. and L. Small.

Ch. Merrilane's Salute to April (by Ch. Merrilane's April Holiday ex Silver Crest Laska, a daughter of Ch. Aracrest's Jered), owned by Paul Scott of Formula Kennels in Norway, handled by Ann Keil.

Upper right: Ch. Merrilane's April Holiday, SOM (by Ch. Merrilane's Holiday Fashion ex Ch. Merrilane's April Love) was a Sire of Merit who sired two other SOMs, Ch. Merrilane's Knockout and Ch. Happy Ours Fortune de Jacquet. *Lower right:* Ch. Merrilane's Sweet Dreams (by Ch. Merrilane's Knockout, SOM ex Anton's April Memory), bred by Merrilane Kennels, and owned by Anthony and Carol Cashia.

Ch. Merrilane's Love Life of Jofra (by Ch. Eldic's Landlord ex Merrilane's Mad Passion, CD) won ABC National Specialty in 1974 and was the sire of five AKC champions, including Ch. Merrilane's April Love before his untimely death at age five.

Ch. Merrilane's April Love (by Ch. Merrilane's Love Life of Jofra ex Ch. Diamond Lil of Rio Vista) produced two SOMs in her only litter, Ch. Merrilane's April Fashion and Ch. Merrilane's April Holiday.

Ch. Merrilane's Love Song of Jofra (by Ch. Eldic's Landlord ex Merrilane's Mad Passion, CD), owned by Ronald White and Lois Matthews.

Ch. Merrilane's Holiday Fashion, SOM (by Int. Ch. Millan's Fashion Hint ex Merrilane's Mad Passion, CD), bred by Eleanor Lindholm-Wood and owned by Lois Matthews, won the ABC Futurity in 1975 and sired two SOMs out of Ch. Merrilane's April Love.

Ch. Cochise of Cherokee Oaks, SOM (by Ch. Helixview Galant Charger ex Copper Penny of Cherokee Oaks), bred by George and Beatrice Stacy, handled by Wanda Toliver, and owned by Blake and Carol Wilcox.

BEA STACY

Cherokee Oaks

At the time of Bea Stacy's death in 1981 there were 43 Cherokee Oaks champions, 13 multi-BOB winners, two BIS winners, two Sires of Merit and two Dams of Merit. To achieve Dam of Merit status was quite a feat, as Bea Stacy was very firm in her belief that each bitch should have only two litters.

Bea Stacy was the guiding hand of this kennel. She possessed a large amount of "horse sense" and an uncanny feel for the right stud for a bitch. Bea never sacrificed a loving home for any of her puppies "just so they could be shown." So 43 champions is really quite remarkable, especially for people of such strong values and limited means.

Van Nuys Branch

Bea Stacy had no children of her own and was very fond of Dolores Caprino's daughter Marianne, who loved Boxers and liked to show. Bea promised to give Marianne the most promising puppy in her kennel by Marianne's tenth birthday to show in junior handling. She gave her Cherokee Oak's Mary Rose, a Ch. Cherokee Oak's Warlord daughter, who was whelped in August 1974. Marianne put a major, plus BOW, BOS and Best Puppy on the ten-month-old puppy at the Boxer Club of Southern California Specialty. Mary Rose finished at 15 months.

As Bea Stacy's health began to fail, she asked Marianne to continue on with her kennel name. So they have continued to use the Cherokee Oaks name in her honor. They do very limited breeding but have finished one dog in each litter, all owner-handled by Marianne.

Following Bea's guidelines, they never breed a bitch more than two times and never sacrifice a loving home for a puppy for the sake of showing.

The Legend of Bea Stacy

BY WANDA TOLLIVER   (Originally printed in Boxer Review)

I first met Bea Stacy at a dog show in Southern California in 1960 and we became friends. When I had personal problems the next year, I went to live at Cherokee Oaks. From the stories Bea and George told me,

George Stacy handles Cherokee Oaks Sash of Satin and Wanda Toliver handles Ch. Flame Rose of Cherokee Oaks.

Bea Stacy handles Ch. Cherokee Oaks Cimarron Chief, winning under judge Robert Ligon. Photograph courtesy of Dolores Caprino.

Cherokee Oaks was started when they lost a Collie and George's employer, Gene Autry (yes, *the* Gene Autry), gave a puppy to the Stacys. Her name was Four D's Cherokee Miss. The name of their kennel came from that pup plus the oak trees around their home, resulting in "Cherokee Oaks."

Four D's Cherokee Miss was bred to Valley Grove's Double Trouble and produced five puppies. They kept all of them. Their first interest was in obedience: most

At eight months of age, Ch. Cherokee Oaks Blazing Jet, bred by Dolores Caprino and owned by Marianne Caprino-Amado.

of them earned their CDs and one, Cherokee Oak's Chief, attained his CDX. It was Trella White of Helixview Kennels who was responsible for their entry into the "other ring." One female, Cherokee Oaks Flame Princess, was bred to Int. Ch. Helixview Noble Knight. From that litter came their first two champions: Ch. Wichita of Cherokee Oaks and Ch. Cherokee Oaks Satin Slippers. Chuck Vroom finished Wichita, and other handlers like George Payton and even George Stacy himself put points on Satin Slippers. They all got really carried away and had such fun with these two puppies.

The beginning of their own breeding program began with a repeat breeding to Ch. Helixview Noble Knight, a breeding that produced Ch. Cherokee Silver Sandals, and they kept their little deep red fawn puppies—I think Cherokee Oaks was always known for its marvelous stag red fawns. They bred Wichita to Sable Sheen and that mating produced two more champions: Jaurez and Amber Elegance. Juarez, in turn in his first litter, sired Ch. Tequila of Cherokee Oaks. Then followed Ch. Wabash and Ch. Tangerine of Cherokee Oaks and the bitch I finished (the first points I ever put on a Boxer), Ch. Flame Rose of Cherokee Oaks. And what fun I had handling and finishing Ch. Cochise of Cherokee Oaks!

The love they had for their Boxers and for the breed is well known. While they were not "well-to-do" from a monetary perspective, they were rich in their love and understanding of the breed. Bea, it seemed, could always manage to sell a beautiful puppy to come up with entry fees. While George worked as a maintenance man on Autry's Coldwater Canyon property, Bea just stayed home, taping ears, running up and down the driveway with the puppies, spending hours and hours talking with people, telling them how to groom the puppies and just getting them interested in the Boxer as she knew it and loved it. I saw days when I was there that I didn't know where the next bag of dog food was coming from, but Bea always had the "Unity" book, which she believed in and she would read the verse for the day. She always called me "Kid" and she would say, "Kid, before the day is over, we will have entries for Santa Rosa because the judge likes Flame Rose and we will go there and we will get the points." And, as God is my witness, before the day was over, we would have sold a pup and we'd go to Santa Rosa, or whatever show it was, and we'd get the points! The Stacys had beautiful Boxers and they were influenced by people like Trella White and Phyllis King and the handlers of the day, like Ben Brown, Harry Sangster, George Payton, and Roland Mueller, all of whom did some fabulous work for them. The handlers loved to get a Cherokee Oaks dog because they could always win. Who could ever forget Amber Elegance of Cherokee Oaks? She won the Regional from the American-bred class with George Payton handling. At that time, they did not separate fawn and brindles so, if I remember correctly, there were 24 in her class and she went on to Best of Breed, beating her sire, Ch. Wichita and her grandsire, Ch. Noble Knight.

I can still hear Lena Ludwig screaming, "No, No, No!" when, in the photograph session, the tray and the cups were dropped on her head, which spooked her to no end. The next day, she took fourth in her class.

After we got back to the kennel, sitting around talking and laughing, we all agreed that "every dog has its day." She never looked like that before and she never looked like that again—but that day she was beautiful.

I remember some of the people Bea coached and started in Boxers—like Jim and Barbara Harris, who owned Ch. Tequila, sire of Ch. Bravado; the Wilcoxes, who owned Ch. Cochise, sire of 17 champions, and who later gave him back to Cherokee Oaks; and Don and Kathleen Noel, who owned Ch. Maverick of Cherokee Oaks and so many others.

I also recall all the great work Bea did with the Boxer Club of San Fernando Valley. I remember our first puppy match held on the R.C. Harris estate, probably the biggest match Southern California has seen or will ever see. Larry Downey judged. If I remember correctly, we had made 41 cents after all the expenses were deducted. The next year we held the match at Mrs. Miriam Breed's estate and that also was super.

Bea taught me everything I know and in later years when I left Cherokee Oaks to manage Talked About Kennels, which was the home of Ch. Dempsey's Copper Gentlemen and Ch. Treceder's Painted Lady (the top winning bitch in the history of the breed), Bea had molded me for this job, encouraging me to take the job with the Smiths. Once I was on the judging slate with Mrs. Phoebe Harris at the BCSFV puppy match—I was assigned the Sweeps. Bea always thought how great it was that I was in the ring with the lady who had bred the top winning male in the history of the Boxer breed and that I was the kennel manager for the kennel with the top winning bitch—she felt that we had made some sort of history.

Perhaps the most beautiful thing I know of Bea and Cherokee Oaks is what made her the way she was, her downright and forthright character and her deep love for her Boxers. The points earned on their Boxers were honest ones. They were not political; they didn't ask for favors; they just took their dogs to the shows and won a great deal. They managed to enter and finish their dogs with many handlers. Jerry Beusee is known for finishing Ch. Jaurez and all the great work he did with him. I won the Working Group with him, which was probably my greatest thrill in Boxers.

Bea was a kind lady, a simple lady, but her tremendous love always shone through as she spun story after story, telling you things the way she felt them. Others will share in the recollection of Bea, Trella and Phyllis swapping stories or comparing their differences on how to train a puppy or how to show a puppy—and it was an education for all of us to absorb this wealth of information.

Bea loved to win like all of us, but she was a true sport when she lost. Perhaps the greatest victory Bea and George ever claimed was when Roland Mueller handled Ch. Wichita to Best American-bred in Show. I remember, too, Bea's reaction when Mrs. Archibald

called from New York to tell her that she was the "Breeder of the Year" for the ABC Annual Awards. Bea told her that she must have the wrong number! Of course she went to New York to accept the award and I think possibly that was one of the finest moments in her life.

So many memories to recall! One time George and I went up north to shows, taking four Boxers and winning points with them. On the way back, we were caught in a horrible snowstorm across the Grapevine pass to Southern California. All the tire chains had been sold, all motel rooms were full, so we shared one room— George would sit in the station wagon while I slept and I took my turn out there while he slept.

The dogs, of course, stayed in the room where it was warm. We called Bea and, lo and behold, it had snowed at Cherokee Oaks and she was freezing in the unusual weather. Bea solved the problem: she burnt all the living room furniture with the exception of one chair! All the show catalogues, all the precious records we had been saving were no more! Bea laughed as she told us about it later, saying she had popped corn for the Boxers and they all had a ball! That was Bea!

Ch. Taurins Thunder of Cherokee Oaks, CGC (by Cherokee Oak's Blazing Chief ex Taurin's Double Dilemma), bred by Carolyn Mason, owned by Dolores Caprino.

When Charles Hamilton awarded the first points to Flame Rose, the first points I had ever put on a Boxer, I remember taking her to that show. We had $17.00 on us and $12.00 of that was allotted for gas. We ate 14-cent hamburgers for breakfast and skipped lunch. When we got back to Chatsworth where we lived, Bea decided we should celebrate those first points on Flame Rose by spending our last $3.00 on a pint of Four Roses Whiskey! Bea, a Cherokee Indian, was not known to handle

Ch. Cherokee Oaks Mary Rose (by Ch. Warlord of Cherokee Oaks ex Tea Rose of Cherokee Oaks), handled by Marianne Caprino at ten years of age.

these situations well and after two drinks, she was standing in the driveway giving out war whoops for my first Boxer victory as she predicted how far I was going to go. It was hilarious and I never laughed as hard in my life. George was scared stiff for he never knew what she would do next. Needless to say, she went in to sleep and didn't get up until late the next morning, not feeling quite as chipper as she did the night before.

I miss Bea a lot and I will say Boxerdom lost a fine human being for her contributions to the breed. I hope the people she encouraged and got started will carry on some of the Cherokee Oaks bloodlines. There was a lot of consideration put into the breeding program and its perpetuation is a fitting and proper testimony to Bea and her dreams.

Nell Marshall fondly relays: "I remember Bea Stacy's determination way back in 1955 when we were returning from Arizona where we both had solid-colored Boxers entered in two shows. Bea stated that one day she would breed many well-known champions and she did. The Cherokee Oaks prefix certainly gained attention from all over. We will miss Bea, especially we BCSFV members. We all loved her very much!"

Fran Hall remembers Bea saying that "without her Boxers she would have been dead. George brought her home a puppy one time as a gift. She had never seen one before and told him to take it back. Since the people were gone over the weekend and it couldn't be returned until Monday, that was just what was needed. By Monday she was a Boxer breeder! One of the greatest! She was sweet, raising her dogs, minding her own business, never giving anyone any trouble. We're at a great loss trying to replace her."

Bill Renno relays: "Bea was a well-known Boxer breeder in the southern California area about 20 years ago when we came here. The biggest impression Bea made on me was her willingness to confide in you, to

share with you her experiences, to tell you the most beautiful stories about herself and her lovely Boxers. She always had time for the novice. Bea was one of those who did not hold herself above the novice in the breed, always taking time to help them in any way she could. Her success in her breeding program speaks for itself and her kennel was named 'Kennel of the Year' for at least one year that I know of. And Bea was a teller of tales all based on her experiences, and for those who never had an opportunity to listen to Bea or share her experiences with her have missed a very great joy. Bea's passing was obviously a great loss to the breed and to those who knew and loved her."

Jim Arnold shares: "What I remember most about Bea was her happiness. I never saw Bea when she wasn't happy. She always had a funny story to tell and usually that story was about her—her dogs and her experiences. I met Bea and George first at Archie and Trella White's Helixview Kennels. We sat there by the hour listening to Bea telling different stories—how she came out here from Oklahoma and her start in dogs. I'll always remember Bea as a happy-go-lucky, jolly lady who loved her dogs dearly. Her first concern was always for her dogs. The breed is going to miss her."

Sturlene Arnold adds: "The thing I remember most about Bea was her helpfulness. When I had purchased a Cherokee Oaks puppy, I was told to call Bea, since she owned the sire of my new puppy. I called and she said to come out to see her and she'd explain about showing, caring, etc. (a favorite word of hers) for my new puppy. She was so nice and friendly, showing me all of her champions. I felt so important meeting such a big-time breeder as Bea Stacy. At that time in 1970, Cherokee Oaks was the breeding to have out here. She was such a love. She

Ch. Cherokee Oaks Amber Elegance (by Ch. Wichita of Cherokee Oaks ex Sable Sheen of Cherokee Oaks) at 14 months of age, handled by George Payton and bred and owned by George and Bea Stacy.

Above: Ch. Reward's Amber Glow (by Ch. Canzonet's John Paul Jones ex Ch. Cherokee Oaks Betsy Rose, CD). Owner, Ed Goldfield. *Below:* Ch. Cherokee Oaks Blazing Jet (by Ch. Heldenbrand's Jet Breaker ex Ch. Cherokee Oak's Belle Star Fopaw), stud dog of owner Marianne Caprino-Amado in the late 1990s.

Above: Ch. Cherokee Oaks Warrior Chief at ten months of age, owned by Dolores Caprino. *Below:* Cherokee Oaks Blazing Chief (by Ch. Cherokee Oaks Warrior Chief ex Ch. Reward's Amber Glow) was structurally superior and sired three champions.

encouraged me to go to puppy matches, which I did and got the bug! Such a helpful lady, I could write a book on her stories alone—like the one of showing her first Boxer with all its faults and whiskers. You would roar with laughter. And the story of how Cherokee Oaks achieved the deep-red color. People thought she fed strawberries to get it. The truth was she told me she started with a deep-red bitch and the color held. She was never too busy to answer all my many questions in my eagerness to learn."

Marianne Caprino shares the following: "The Stacys' entire lives were centered around animals of one type or another. They seemed to have inherited an innate sensitivity toward animals from their American Indian and Anglo heritage. Bea was especially blessed by this sensitivity, along with an uncanny ability to heal ill or injured animals.

"I personally know of several occasions when Bea saved the life of someone's dog by using an old farm or Indian technique. One experience that took place was this: Bea received a frantic call from one of her friends. The woman's dog had just jumped through a sliding glass door and was bleeding profusely from a deep laceration to his leg. Bea instructed the woman to grab a box of sugar and pack the wound as fast as possible. This formed a clot and stopped the bleeding within a few minutes and the dog was then rushed to his veterinarian. The veterinarian told the lady that without Bea's advice, the dog would have bled to death before arriving at his hospital.

"The loss of this great lady to me personally has been the deepest blow in my 18 years of life. I have known her since I was a very small child, and she had been like a beloved aunt or grandmother to me. She gave me my very own Boxer for my tenth birthday, so that I would have something nice to show. That Boxer bitch became Ch. Cherokee Oaks Mary Rose and was finished before my 12th birthday. How many people would give a child her most promising puppy?"

Below is a list of champions that Bea Stacy bred (there are others with the kennel name, but Bea was not the actual breeder):

1. Ch. Wichita, BIS winner
2. Ch. Amber Elegance, multi-BOB
3. Ch. Juarez, BIS winner
4. Ch. Satin Slipper, multi-BOB
5. Ch. Silver Sandals, multi-BOB
6. Ch. Tequila, multi-BOB
7. Ch. Wabash, multi-BOB
8. Ch. Tangerine, multi-BOB
9. Ch. Flame Rose
10. Ch. Bravado
11. Ch. Amber Lady
12. Ch. Reede Chiffon, multi-BOB
13. Ch. Maverick
14. Ch. Scarlett Dottie, multi-BOB
15. Ch. Painted Rose, multi-BOB
16. Ch. Shaunta
17. Ch. Beau Bait, multi-BOB
18. Ch. Tarus
19. Ch. Smokey Joe
20. Ch. Red Chief
21. Ch. Beau Brummel
22. Ch. Luisa
23. Ch. Gentlemen Jim
24. Ch. Drakesdown's Sabo
25. Ch. Red Moon's Joy
26. Ch. Cochise, multi-BOB; Sire of Merit
27. Ch. Ringo
28. Ch. Soldier
29. Ch. Rocky Chief
30. Ch. Dapper Dan
31. Ch. Warlord, multi-BOB
32. Ch. Autumn Rose
33. Ch. Blazin Chief
34. Ch. Red Moon's Ginell
35. Ch. Lady Rebellion, multi-BOB
36. Ch. Rosa Rita
37. Ch. Apache Lady
38. Ch. Mary Rose
39. Ch. Rose
40. Ch. Durango
41. Ch. Rosemarie, BOB winner

Ch. Cherokee Oak's Belle Star of Fopaw (by Cherokee Oak's Blazing Chief ex Ch. Casey's De Ja Vu of Fopaw), owned by Dolores Caprino, handled by Marianne Caprino-Amado.

SALGRAY

BY PAT HARAH

Owned by Mr. and Mrs. Daniel Hamilburg of Brookline, Massachusetts, Salgray Kennels, in a short span of time, has become a "tradition." Not that Salgray takes any glory from foundation bloodlines such as Mazelaine Kennels, but it gives full credit to those who have gone before and to those who advise and help them presently. One must seize an opportunity at the precise moment, however, to mold a creation, for breeding dogs is a fine art.

Salgray Kennels was founded in 1952 by the Hamilburgs. Their foundation stock, obtained from Jane Kamp (Forsyth), were Sally of Grayarlin and the litter brother and sister, Sabot and Slipper of Grayarlin. Sally, though purchased as a pet for the three Hamilburg children, finished her championship the same day as Sabot at the famous Morris/Essex Show in New Jersey. Sally returned to the children and part of her name became the kennel prefix. Sabot, on the other hand, continued his show career and was never out of the Breed and Group ribbons. Slipper, after completing her title, was bred to the great Bang Away son Ch. Barrage of Quality Hill, and produced Ch. Salgray's Battle Chief, the Hamilburgs' first homebred Best in Show, Sire of Merit and the sire of the famous "F" Litter.

When Mrs. Hamilburg saw the puppy bitch Marquam Hill's Flamingo at Jane's kennel, she had to have her. Bred by Dr. Robert Burke, "Mingo" became a multiple-BIS winner, Dam of Merit and, when bred to Chief, was the dam of the ``F'' Litter. The fabulous "F" Litter, as it became known, contained two males and four bitches. The dogs, Ch. Salgray's Fashion Plate and Ch. Salgray's Flying High, became multiple Best in Show winners, Sires of Merit and the top winning Boxers in the Midwest and the East. Fashion Plate won the Working Group at the Westminster Show (before the Work-

The sire of the great "F" Litter: Am-Can. Ch. Salgray's Battle Chief, SOM (by Am-Can. Ch. Barrage of Quality Hill ex Ch. Slipper of Grayarlin), handled by Jane Forsyth. Photograph courtesy of Joe Pastella.

ing Group was split) and the American Boxer Club Specialty two years in a row. Fashion Plate was shown by Larry Downey, and Flying High by Jane Forsyth.

Of Salgray handler Larry Downey, Mr. Hamilburg said, "Larry came to us with a wealth of knowledge and many years of experience. He had the necessary ingredients that we were lacking—great knowledge based upon experience and observation. Ours is a team effort."

At the same time as the two males were being shown, Larry and Jane interspersed Ch. Salgray's Fanfare (owned by Mr. Judson Streicher) and Ch. Salgray's Flaming Ember, who also became multiple-Best in Show winners. The other two bitches, Ch. Salgray's Flamecrest and Frolic, finished their championships and each produced champions.

Chief had been whelped in August 1956; Flamingo in April 1959; and the "F" Litter in August 1961. It was Larry Downey who recognized the value of the litter. Larry saw something beyond what the Hamilburgs saw. Although they knew they had good puppies, Larry aroused their excitement, making them sense that they had extraordinary puppies. Larry grew up in the game at the Mazelaine Kennels of John and Mazie Wagner, who undoubtedly did more for Boxers than anyone during their era. These puppies fanned the fire!

"Although named after Flamingo, it was a FUN litter," said Mrs. Hamilburg.

The "F" Litter was truly a historical litter: A litter of six puppies, all six champions; four Best in Show winners; two Sires of Merit and one Dam of Merit. This is any breeder's most aspiring dream come true.

Mingo was bred one more time to Battle Chief. From this breeding came Ch. Salgray's Memory Book. When bred to Ch. Millan's Fashion Hint (sired by Fashion

Ch. Sally of Grayarlin (by Ch. Dover of El Rose ex Lady v. Emily), handled by Jane Forsyth, became the foundation bitch for Salgray (the prefix abbreviates her name).

Plate out of a Flying High daughter), she produced Ch. Salgray's Jitterbug, a multiple-BIS winner and Dam of Merit. Jitterbug, when bred to Ch. Salgray's Ambush, produced the twins, Market Wise and Minute Man; Mutineer; VIP and Venessa. Market Wise and VIP became multiple-BIS winners, as did Minute Man, who was sent to Australia where he sired many champions for Mr. and Mrs. Miles Gunther. Market Wise also became a Sire of Merit.

The Hamilburgs relay, "We shall choose carefully and inbreed. Undoubtedly there will be criticism—'You are

Ch. Salgray's Frolic (by Am-Can. Ch. Salgray's Battle Chief ex Am-Can. Ch. Marquam Hill's Flamingo), from the great "F" litter, was herself the dam of BIS Ch. Salgray's Stuffed Shirt.

We deem it necessary to produce dominant producers. This is the way the fastest racehorses are bred, also Morgan horses, outstanding milk-producing cattle, the best sheep for wool, the best poultry. (One must remember, however, that faults, too, can be 'fixed' by inbreeding.)"

Mr. and Mrs. Hamilburg decided to take a chance and bred Flying High to Flaming Ember. This breeding produced two top winning Best in Show winners, Ch. Salgray's Ambush, also a Sire of Merit, and Ch. Salgray's Auntie Mame. Ambush finished his championship with three consecutive BIS from the classes: the first by winning the Futurity and BIS at the American Boxer Club

Ch. Salgray's Flaming Ember (by Am-Can. Ch. Salgray's Battle Chief ex Am-Can. Ch. Marquam Hill's Flamingo).

Ch. Salgray's Fashion Plate, SOM (by Am-Can. Ch. Salgray's Battle Chief ex Am-Can. Ch. Marquam Hill's Flamingo), from the great "F" Litter, a multiple Best in Show winner and an American and Canadian Sire of Merit for owner-breeders Mr. and Mrs. Daniel M. Hamilburg.

kennel blind,' 'You want to stay within your own kennel', etc. However, we are prepared that it may not work: one need not be afraid to inbreed if one has quality stock. This is what we plan. Larry has a bitch, Spring Fevor, and two other top bitches from the same litter, complete inbreeding. We shall now try to 'fix' type—to breed brother to sister, daughter to sire, etc. Naturally, we intend to move out ultimately. Our experience has shown that linebreeding is good for our stock. Inbreeding is another thing—we cannot say exactly how it will work.

"We agreed that inbreeding should be tested with excellent stock with no major faults in males or females.

Specialty, which he also won the following year, and two BIS at all-breed shows. Ambush was shown by Larry Downey in the Midwest and Jane Forsyth in the East, while Stan Flowers showed Auntie Mame. Each became a Sire or Dam of Merit.

During the years that Ambush and Auntie Mame were being shown, the Hamilburgs had another multiple-champion litter, sired by Flying High out of a Barrage daughter, Can. Ch. Salgray's Roulette, herself from a litter of multiple champions. This litter consisted of Ch. Salgray's Ovation, Sire of Merit and multiple BIS winner; Ch. Salgray's On The Town; Ch. Duc D'Orleans; and Ch. Salgray's Out of Bounds, the bitch that was bred to Ambush and produced Ch. Salgray's Good Grief, a multiple-Group winner and Sire of Merit. Ovation was owned by Mrs. Hazel Cowie and the whole litter was shown by Larry Downey.

In the 1970s, due to family illness, Salgray cut way back on its breeding program. However, with limited stock, they still managed to be well represented in the Working Group. Dogs and bitches such as Double Brothers, Double Talk, Double Play, Bojangles, Stuffed Shirt, Expresso and Show Stopper, to name a few, were multiple-BIS winners.

All in all, to date, Salgray has bred and owned 19 multiple-Best in Show winners, 13 Sires of Merit and 6 Dams of Merit.

A more recent Dam of Merit is Ch. Salgray's Call Me Madam, who achieved this honor in 1992. Their successful stud dogs are Ch. Salgray's Cavalier, an Expresso son; Ch. Salgray's Retaliation, a Cavalier son; and Ch. Salgray's Black Tie. Black Tie and his litter brother Ch. Salgray's Bow Tie finished their championships within five days of each other. Both "Tie" dogs were shown by Marylou Wilderson-Hatfield. Marylou is now the only handler of Salgray Boxers. Black Tie, though shown on a limited basis, managed to compete in the 1991 Top Twenty at the

Ch. Salgray's Fanfare (by Am-Can. Ch. Salgray's Battle Chief ex Am-Can. Ch. Marquam Hill's Flamingo) from the famous "F" Litter.

American Boxer Club Specialty. He won multiple Bests of Breed and Group placements. His first born son from his first breeding completed his title and a daughter from his second litter obtained her Canadian championship in three consecutive shows. Black Tie has the honor of being the first Boxer to have sired puppies in Australia using the frozen semen method. Miles and Liz Gunther have whelped three litters, and one of these puppies, Guntop's Black Tie and Tales, won a Best Baby Puppy at an all-breed show his first time in the ring. Cavalier, an Expresso

Ch. Salgray's Jitterbug, DOM (by Int. Ch. Millan's Fashion Hint ex Ch. Salgray's Memory Book), whelped in June 1969.

Ch. Salgray's Flame Crest (by Am-Can. Ch. Salgray's Battle Chief ex Am-Can. Ch. Marquam Hill's Flamingo) is the litter sister to Flaming Ember, Fanfare and Frolic. All four of these Salgray dogs were whelped in August 1961.

son, sired Ch. Salgray's Retaliation and other champions, including one in the Philippines.

In 1969, the all-breed and Group judges, licensed handlers and members of DogWriters of America were asked to select six breeders from the entire nation as nominees for the *Kennel Review* Outstanding Breeder Award. One of the chief requirements was "a kennel whose champions genuinely have contributed to the advancement of their breed." Most appropriately, Salgray appears prominently on this important list—significant recognition by a most knowledgeable panel of judges!

The Hamilburgs reveal, "Our dogs go through a regular schooling system. After the whelping box, they graduate to a growing room; when ears are trimmed, they are

Ch. Salgray's Ambush, SOM (by Am-Can. Ch. Salgray's Flying High ex Ch. Salgray's Flaming Ember), owned by Mr. and Mrs. Daniel M. Hamilburg, was a multiple Best in Show winner and the sire of 34 champions.

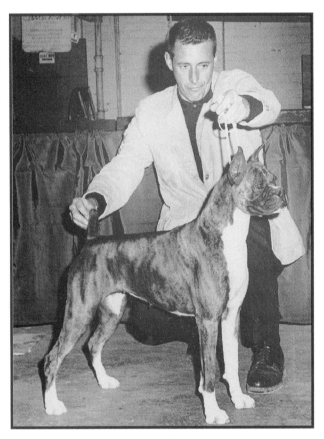

Am-Can. Ch. Marquam Hill's Flamingo (by Am-Can. Ch. Barrage of Quality Hill ex Legacy of Clover Downs), dam of the great "F" Litter, bred to Am-Can. Ch. Salgray's Battle Chief.

moved downstairs. The puppy motel is actually three rooms. When dogs mature, they go to the main kennel."

Though most people have always thought of Salgray as a large kennel, this has never been true. Mrs. Hamilburg whelped all of the pups in her sunroom, and they were raised by her with the help of her kennel man, Jim Taylor. Now that Mrs. Hamilburg is semi-retired, her daughter, Jane Hamilburg-Guy and Mrs. Pat Harrah have taken over the reins with Mrs. Hamilburg's experienced input. Together, with Marylou, Salgray hopes to continue their legacy of temperament and quality above all else.

Right: Am-Can. Ch. Salgray's Flying High, SOM (by Am-Can. Ch. Salgray's Battle Chief ex Am-Can. Ch. Marquam Hill's Flamingo), one of the "F" Litter, handled by Jane Forsyth. Owners, Mr. and Mrs. Daniel M. Hamilburg.

Ch. Salgray's Auntie Mame (by Am-Can. Ch. Salgray's Flying High ex Ch. Salgray's Flaming Ember), litter sister to Ambush, was a popular choice for Best in Show. Owners, Mr. and Mrs. Daniel M. Hamilburg.

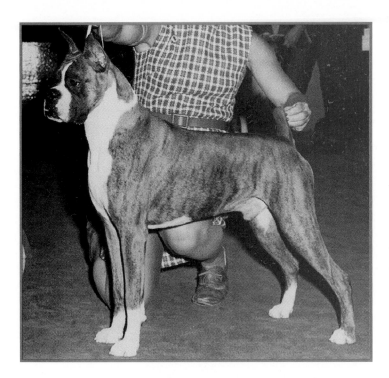

Above: **Ch. Salgray's Double Talk (by Ch. Salgray's Ambush ex Can. Ch. Bobby Pin of Blossomlea), handled by Jane Forsyth, won the ABC Best of Breed from the classes over Ch. Arriba's Prima Donna on the day before she won the Garden!**

Right: **Ch. Salgray's Market Wise, SOM (by Ch. Salgray's Ambush ex Ch. Salgray's Jitterbug), handled by Jane Forsyth. Owners, Mr. and Mrs. Daniel M. Hamilburg.**

Ch. Salgray's Ovation, SOM, owned by George Cowie, handled by Larry Downey, winning BIS under judge Maxwell Riddle on October 12, 1969.

Ch. Salgray's Retaliation (by Ch. Salgray's Cavalier ex Salgray's Serendipity), owned by Pat Harrah.

Ch. Salgray's Bow Tie (by Ch. Salgray's KO Aracrest ex Ch. Salgray's Call Me Madam), handled by Marylou Hatfield, wins under Mrs. James Edwards Clark for owner Pat Harrah.

Littermate to Bow Tie is Ch. Salgray's Black Tie, handled by Marylou Hatfield. Owners, Phyllis Hamilburg, Pat Harrah and Jane H. Guy.

Ch. Salgray's Buckaroo (by Am-Can. Ch. Salgray's Flying High ex Ch. Har-Gayle's Dubonnet) was the 1970 ABC Grand Prize Futurity winner, handled by Jane Hamilburg-Guy.

Ch. Budsobrav's Happy Days, CD (Ch. Salgray's Expresso ex Coach's Nutmeg) was a multiple BIS winner, bred by James and Joy Setzer.

Am-Can-Ber. Ch. Crescent Lane's Ramrod (by Ch. Salgray's Ambush ex Crescent's Fancy That), bred by Arlene Freer and Edward Nadella, won Best of Breed over 50 times. Handled by Arlene Freer.

Marylou Hatfield with Ch. Salgray's Bow Tie and Ch. Salgray's Black Tie. Owner, Pat Harrah.

Two future champs as pups: Ch. Tamberlaine's Polished Brass (fawn) and Ch. Tamberlaine's Fancy Me (by Ch. Salgray's Flying High ex Blazon's Bonus Bait) (brindle) with breeder Eleanor Pugliese and handler Ed Hoffman. Polished Brass went on to win multiple Best of Breeds and groups as a special. He was Best of Winners at the 1969 ABC.

Ch. Morgenshern of Kresthallo (by Ch. Steeplechase Up and Away ex Malmhus Girl About Town), a foundation bitch for Flintwood, was the litter sister of Sans Souci, owned by Dr. Lloyd D. Flint.

FLINTWOOD

BY STEPHANIE ABRAHAM AND DR. LLOYD FLINT

Dr. and Mrs. Lloyd Flint established the Flintwood Boxers in the mid-1950s, in the hey-day of Bang Away and his get. Between 1956 and 1965, in 17 carefully planned litters, they produced 26 champions. But of far more importance than mere statistics indicate, the influence of the Flintwood dogs had far-reaching implications—many of today's top winners hail back to these fine Massachusetts animals, epitomizing breed type. Indeed Ch. Arriba's Prima Donna, who was Best in Show at Westminster in 1970, was sired by Ch. Flintwood's Live Ammo, representing five generations of Flintwood breeding. The Flints won the ABC awards for "Kennel Producing the Most Champions" in 1959, 1961, 1962 and 1964. Of significant interest is the uniquely structured breeding program which emphasized the bitch lineage in the consistent production of champions.

Ch. Sans Souci of Kresthallo (by Ch. Steeplechase Up and Away ex Malmhus Girl About Town), foundation of Flintwood, owned by Dr. Lloyd D. Flint.

In the beginning, the Flints acquired the two young quality-bred litter sisters, Sans Souci and Morgenshern of Kresthallo. They were sired by Ch. Steeplechase Up and Away ex Malmhus Girl About Town. The paternal and maternal grandsires were, respectively, Ch. Bang Away of Sirrah Crest and a Bang Away son, Ch. Mazelaine's Keynote. Souci, an elegant, flashy red fawn, favored the sire's side, while Morgenshern, a plainer, darker fawn with the more typical head and a stronger topline, favored the dam's. The Flints sought a combination of the best qualities of both sisters—substance with elegance with no loss of breed type—a relatively novel concept for the time. After finishing the championships of both foundation bitches, the Flints began Phase I of their breeding program.

Ch. Flintwood's Rabble Rouser, SOM (by Ch. Brayshaw's Masquerader ex Flintwood's Banned In Boston), winning Best in Show handled by Jane Forsyth. Photograph courtesy of Charles Fortune.

To limit the variables, both sisters were first bred to Ch. Barrage of Quality Hill. Souci produced two champions, Places Please and Subtle Sequence. Morgenshern produced four: Maelstrom, After Hours, Darlin Jill and Miss Mayhem. The progeny was then bred back to their aunts, uncles or cousins, with the following results: Morgenshern to Places Please gave Bag N'Baggage and Banned in Boston. Souci to Bag N'Baggage gave three champions: Sundowner, Short Shorts and Soothsayer. Then Subtle Sequence to Baggage produced Large Charge and Tassel Dancer. Finally, After Hours to Places Please produced Flaxie Martin and Muggins Hebditch.

Phase I summarized (bitch produce only) showed Souci and her offspring had accounted for nine champions, while Morgenshern and her get had accounted for ten. Each foundation bitch tended to throw her own "type" as a whole—the majority of the offspring favored the immediate dam. So, the sought-for combination of qualities was elusive.

Phase II was the selective outcrossing of three Phase I bitches to non-Flintwood studs. Banned in Boston was

Ch. Flintwood's Bag 'N Baggage (by Ch. Flintwood's Places Please ex Ch. Morgenshern of Kresthallo) represents the fourth litter of Phase I in the Flintwood breeding program. Breeder, Dr. Lloyd D. Flint.

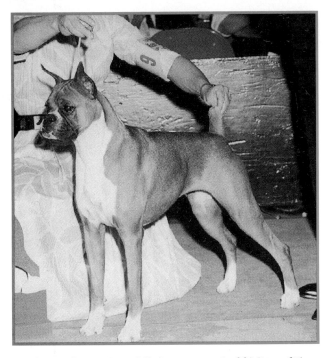

Ch. Flintwood's Muggins Hebditch represents the fifth litter of Phase I.

Ch. Flintwood's Fontessa (by Ch. Flintwood's Rabble Rouser ex Flintwood's After Hours, daughter of Morgenshern and dam of Linebacker and Live Ammo) represents Phase III in the Flintwood program.

bred to Ch. Brayshaw's Masquerader (linebred Bang Away) producing the top winning Boxer of 1962, Ch. Flintwood's Rabble Rouser and his sister. Ch. Rabble Rouser was the first Boxer to win both the ABC Futurity and Specialty at the same show. He went on to have an illustrious career under the ownership of Mrs. Cheever Porter. Banned in Boston, when acquired by the Charles Fortunes, was again bred to Masquerader, producing two more champions: Curtain Call (BOW at the 1964 ABC) and Balconyrock's Tonight Only, who went to Eileen McClintock's Holly Lane Boxers in Topeka, Kansas.

The next Phase II breeding was Rowena (Rabble Rouser's sister) to Ch. Aimebee's Apoppin', a linebred Barrage product through Ch. Eldic's Darius with an excellent Woodcrest (Carl and Alice Wood) bitch background. This produced Ch. Flintwood's Rockin' Shows. Another Phase II breeding was Flintwood's Bespoken (a Morgenshern daughter by a Souci son) to Apoppin'.

Ch. Flintwood's Sundowner (by Ch. Flintwood's Bag "N Baggage ex Ch. Sans Souci of Kresthallo) represents the sixth litter of Phase I. He won Winners Dog at ABC in 1961.

This produced three champions: Through Talkin', Tympany and Taffeta. Subtle Sequence, Souci's first daughter, had also been bred "outside the family" to Scott Rutherford's Ch. Rococo's Exhilaration, from whom she obtained Ch. Rococo's Tornado, BOW at ABC 1965. So Phase II, which was meant to be a "stepping stone," actually turned out nine champions.

Phase III brought back into the Flintwood line the more outcrossed products of Phase II. After Hours, bred to Rabble Rouser, produced Ch. Fontessa. Fontessa, when bred to Sundowner, produced two champions, Linebacker and Live Ammo, used successfully by Dr. Ted Fickes in establishing his Arriba Boxers. Curtain Call, owned by the Leopolds, bred to Sundowner, produced Ch. Blazon's Fancy Pants, ABC Grand Prize Futurity winner in 1966. Flintwood's last breeding, in 1965, used Linebacker with Morgenshern's last remaining daughter, Darlin Jill, to produce the kennel's 26th champion, Dreamsville—an appropriate name with which to end a breeding program! A tally of champion production by the Flintwood bitches only shows Sans Souci and her female offspring accounted for 10, while Morgenshern and her bitches produced 19.

Ch. Flintwood's Places Please (by Am-Can. Ch. Barrage of Quality Hill ex Ch. San Souci of Kresthallo). Photograph courtesy of Charles Fortune.

All phases of the Flintwood breeding program were an endeavor to fix type—type that the Flints envisioned as ideal for the breed. Their dogs were noted for classic heads, clean lines and exceptional toplines and tailsets, among many other outstanding qualities. Undoubtedly due to the concentration of genes through selective line-breeding, they were prepotent sires and dams and stand behind many of today's well-known show dogs, including those belonging to Holly Lane, Arriba, Huffand, Woods End and Trefoil—a testimony to the fact that the carefully constructed matriarchy that was Flintwood Boxers endures even today, over 30 years later.

Flintwood's Banned In Boston, DOM (by Ch. Flintwood's Places Please ex Ch. Morgenshern of Kresthallo), handled by Dr. Flint.

Ch. Flintwood's Subtle Sequence (by Am-Can. Ch. Barrage of Quality Hill ex Ch. San Souci of Kresthallo), a Places Please litter sister.

Ch. Flintwood's Linebacker, SOM (by Ch. Flintwood's Sundowner ex Ch. Flintwood's Fontessa), handled by Dr. Flint, represents Phase III of the Flintwood program.

Ch. Flintwood's Darlin' Jill (Am-Can. Ch. Barrage of Quality Hill ex Ch. Morgenshern of Kresthallo), with Mary Flint, represents the second litter of Phase I.

Ch. Flintwood's Rabble Rouser, SOM (by Ch. Brayshaw's Masquerader ex Flintwood's Banned In Boston), photographed by Charles Fortune, won the ABC National in 1962.

Ch. Flintwood's Bag 'N Baggage, SOM (by Ch. Flintwood's Places Please ex Ch. Morgenshern of Kresthallo), with breeder Dr. Flint.

Ch. Flintwood's Live Ammo (by Ch. Flintwood's Sundowner ex Ch. Flintwood's Fontessa) is the sire of famous Best in Show Ch. Arriba's Prima Donna and represents Phase III in the Flintwood program.

Three generations of Flintwood champions with the Souci stamp: Ch. Sans Souci of Kresthallo at eight years old, with daughter Ch. Flintwood's Short Shorts (by Ch. Flintwood's Bag 'N Baggage) at four years old, with her daughter Ch. Flintwood's Beads del Carribe (by Ch. Flintwood's Sundowner) at eight months old.

Ch. Forest Gate's Spark of Marjack (by Ch. Marjack's Golden Samurai ex Forest Gates Fair Damsel), bred and owned by Mary C. Jackson.

MARJACK

BY MARY JACKSON

In 1950, as a 12-year-old, I walked dogs for our neighbors in New Orleans. One summer our family baby-sat a Great Dane named Gorgeous Augusta (who, in retrospect, was not aptly named) for our friends, the Levys. Of course, I fell in love with Gussie and, having just lost my Welsh Corgi Laddi, *I wanted a dog!* My father, the sensible man that he is, said, "No Great Dane!!" Well, that set up a howl that could be heard throughout the nation, and the Levys' daughter Suzanne Farve came up with a Boxer puppy. My poor father realized that he couldn't win this war against three women and a Boxer puppy, and that's how I got into Boxers.

As it turned out, Suzanne had purchased an import named Enzian von Dom Alpenrose. Yes, you guessed it,

Ch. Citation's Acclaim of Marjack (by Ch. Jered's Spellbinder ex Can. Ch. Marjack Winsome v. Dorn), winning Best Puppy in Show at the Potomac Boxer Club in 1958. Owner, Mary C. Jackson.

straight out of Frau Stockmann's kennel and half-brother to Ch. Zack von Dom, their dam being Esta v.d. Wurm. The purchase of Enzian is a tale in itself that I will attempt to relay briefly.

In World War II, a group of soldiers went to the Alpenrose Castle to secure it for American forces and the grateful princess, who raised Boxers, was pleased to see them as she and her dogs were a mite hungry by this time. One of the soldiers offered to get her food in exchange for a male Boxer, so the deal was struck! Enzian von Dom Alpenrose was purchased by an American foot soldier for about $400 worth of potatoes, vegetables and canned meat (army style).

Back to camp they went and tried to hide the dog from the commanding officer—which was no easy feat— an 85-pound full-grown male Boxer really won't fit in a shoebox or a soldier's pocket. Fortunately, the CO had a Boxer at home and decided that the company needed a watchdog and a mascot. With his Schutzhund training, Enzian was in his element. Only one problem—he only understood German. So the guys learned the requisite German, and "Setzen" and "Platz," "Bleibsitzen" and "Fooey" could be heard coming from an *American* army camp!

After the war, a GI brought Enzian back home to New Orleans, but was soon transferred to an overseas assignment and couldn't take the dog. One evening this tale was being told in a local seafood pub in the French Quarter of Old New Orleans and while Enzian drank beer from a mug, Suzanne and her husband walked

Ch. Citation's Acclaim of Marjack with the Honorable Wilbur D. Brucker, Secretary of the Army, and Mrs. Janett Shouse.

through the door. "I have to have him," Suzanne exclaimed and that was that! The soldier was relieved, Suzanne was ecstatic and Enzian, slightly tipsy, was agreeably happy with his new owners.

Enzian was a tall, elegant dog of stag red color with flashy markings and was a very popular stud in New Orleans. He was bred to a Berolina bitch who was the mother of my first Boxer, Marjack's Golden Girl. The pedigree was an excellent combination of Frau Stockmann's bloodlines, and all this dropped into my lap at the tender age of 12.

So I had my dog and that should have been that, but, since my father was a naval officer, we were transferred to Norfolk, Virginia where my mother met a lad at the vet's office who showed Pekes. A lady there opened her mouth and said the fateful words, "That sure is a lovely Boxer. Have you ever shown her?" The reply was "No." "Well," the lady interjected, I know a handler." Golden Girl went to the Tidewater KC, where she won a blue ribbon and a silver cup, and my mother and I were off to the races. My father was off at sea, so he couldn't "nip this little project in the bud" this time. Such is history.

The next trip was to Seattle, and we met Ch. Salal's Sure Conceit at our first show. He was also a stag red fawn with all the attitude in the world. At 14 years of age, I had a bit of a problem scraping up $75 for a stud fee. However, one year and paper bag of coins later, Golden Girl went to Conceit and shortly thereafter Int. Ch. Marjack's Golden Mist arrived.

Misty was one of those once-in-a-lifetime dogs: she excelled in the home, the show ring and the whelping box. She won her first all-breed Best in Show from the Open class her first time shown under three different judges: Alfred LePine (Breed), Percy Roberts (Group) and Louis Muir (BIS). She was shown by Larry Ingalls, who at that time had just gotten his handler's license and was an unknown. She then produced a litter of five champions including Ch. Marjack's Golden Windjammer, who became the top-winning Boxer for three consecutive years. She was also a wonderful companion who never knew the inside of a dog crate and was insulted if walked on city streets on a leash, as she was ever-trustworthy. She was also the star in a fashion show put on by the Navy wives as a fund-raiser in the exclusive Frederick & Nelson department store.

After those two dogs, everything else has been somewhat less exciting. However, Misty's daughter produced a champion who was bred back to Windjammer and we had a litter of three males, all of whom finished with ease. We were honored with the ABC awards for Breeder of the Year, Kennel Making the Most Champions, and Dam of the Year. Each of those champions also produced champions. Ch. Marjack's Golden Samurai sired Ch. Forest Gates Spark of Marjack, who was the grandsire of Ch. Brumble Carolina Star. Carolina Star sired Ch. Wagner's Tzarina who, in turn, was the granddam of Famous Amos.

After a short handling career, I got married to a non-dog person and the dogs went the way of all things. After disposing of the jerk, I got another Boxer bitch, found one of my old studs and got Marjack's Golden Arapaho

Int. Ch. Marjack's Golden Mist (by Ch. Salal's Sure Conceit ex Marjack's Golden Girl), owned by Mary Jackson, winning Best in Show.

back after a few years of misfortune. I also purchased Ch. DT's Ibn's Legacy of Har-Vel, and he finished his championship in a month's time in top East coast competition. My next purchase was Jon-L Marjack's Three Time Gold, who finished her championship mostly owner-handled by Pam Rohr (co-owned also with Linda Dulemba) with finishing touches by Michael Shepard when Pam became ill. Three Time Gold was bred to Ch. Rochil's Grande Marshall, and then there was the flashy April Fool's Day offspring Dreamweaver's Pure Gold.

"Old dog breeders never die, and sometimes they don't even have the sense to fade away."

Ch. Marjack's Golden Sakiasan (by Ch. Marjack's Golden Windjammer ex Ch. Citation's Acclaim of Marjack). Owner, Mary Jackson.

MY-R

Lorraine Meyer's very first Boxer was purchased in 1942 and, although she proved to be an extremely poor specimen of the breed, she endeared Lorraine to Boxers as she was the epitome of what she hoped for as a friend and companion.

Beginning a show career with a Zack v Dom daughter named Clinaude's Tipped Toes, My-R's first big success was producing three champions from a magical litter out of a Marjack's Golden Windjammer daughter: Magic Maker, Magic's Geronimo, and Wizard. Bred to My-R bitches, Ch. Salgray's Fashion Plate sired some important champions, including Brag About, Wind Swept, Wind Storm, Rain Dance, Rain Maker, Marquette, and others.

Never being privileged to own a kennel, Lorraine averaged one or two litters a year, often skipping a year or two along the way. There have been 23 My-R-bred or -owned champions in the U.S. and four who finished their championships in other countries.

LUV-A-LEES

Yetta Miesel's first Boxer came over 40 years ago on the advice of a veterinarian. At that time, Dr. Gordon Boyink, who himself had been a Boxer breeder, highly recommended the breed as an excellent family dog. They purchased a plain brindle bitch with a wonderful Mazelaine pedigree and were immediately addicted. They bred her once and were rewarded with a litter of 14 puppies, raising 12 of the pups by supplementing around the clock. Suzie lived to the wonderful age of 14 years until they became involved with Irma Bircher. She introduced them to Eve Whitmore, from whom they bought Haviland's Wind Chimes, the dam of their first champion, Ch. Luv-A-Lee's Golden Nugget. They repeated that breeding to Ch. Jo-Jac's Domino and their second champion, Ch. Luv-A-Lee's Handyman, was born. When "Bucky" became a little past middle age,

My-R's Penny Ante, owned by Dr. and Mrs. F.A.C. Oehlers, was awarded all-breed Dog of the Decade in Singapore in 1971.

they decided it was time to raise another male. They were lucky enough to pick a gorgeous male pup from a litter bred by Darlene Stone. The dam was Brandi Luvs Gynger, a Bucky daughter, and the sire was Luv-A-Lee's Gristo of Shieldmont, a champion Sun N' Shadow son.

Ch. Luv-A-Lee's Pink Lady, the 1989 ABC Winners Bitch, was out of Ch. Jodiac's Fire 'N Ice bred by Jack Pickersgill and Yetta Miesel to Ch. Luv-A-Lee's Red Baron.

Ch. Luv-A-Lee's Cool Dude of Mariday ("You Be") was a stud-fee pup out of Mariday's Glory Days bred by Mary Lou Testa to Ch. Luv-A-Lee's Red Baron. "You Be's" name came from a long term of You be gone, You be quiet, You be nice, etc., etc.

Ch. Boxella's Lustig (by Ch. Wedge Hollow's Hasty Harry ex Ch. Boxella's Wand O' Magic). Owner, Joseph Heine.

Ch. My-R's Upstart of Holly Lane (by Ch. Keil's Dynasty ex Ch. Carlon's Classy Cookie), owned by Jeanette Everett, bred by Lorraine Meyer.

BOXELLA

The birth of Boxella Kennels, Reg. began in Augsburg, Germany in 1945 with Joseph Heine's acquisition of a very lovely flashy fawn female called Bella V. Steingarten (a Reichsieger Karlo vd Wolfschlucht daughter out of Siegerin Cilli vd Burg Hohenzollern). Cilli was a Reichsieger Ajax vd Holderberg daughter. Ajax and Karlo were the two best Boxers in Germany at that time. They were hidden during the war years from the Nazis who used many Boxers, Dobermans, German Shepherds and Rottweilers in concentration camps. Many of these dogs were made vicious and used to torture the prisoners. As the American forces entered these camps, these dogs were shot and destroyed. Heine wanted so much to buy Ajax as he was such a superior Boxer. However, Herr Schubert, his owner, would not let him go at any price and rightfully so, as the sincere German breeders needed him for breeding to recoup what was lost during the war years. It was interesting to note that the infamous Larry Downey was a soldier in Germany at the same time and was able to bring back not only the great Karlo but also Czech and Czech von Dom from Frau Stockmann. Karlo went to the Wagners of the famous Mazelaine Kennels and was later owned by Larry Downey. All three of these German imports produced many American champions.

Now that the war was over, Heine's major concern was to finish college and get established professionally. Along with major home responsibilities, spare time was used to study every bit of information available about the Boxer. He attended many dog shows, not as an exhibitor since there was no money to spend on such an expensive hobby, but as a spectator. He observed many judges and made up his mind that he could do a better job of judging than most whom he was observing. Heine visited many breeders and kennels including Larry Downey's Leash and Collar Kennels in Libertyville, Illinois. There he was able to see and have his hands on Karlo for the first time. What a beautiful Boxer, a head-

Zan v. Hasseler, HOF, imported to Boxella (by Jahr ATIBOX Sieger Uhtz v. Beler Ries ex Pia v. Hasseler, HOF).

Ch. Boxella's Rodger (by Ch. Dempsey's Copper Gentleman ex Rio Rita of Cross Acres), handled by Wanda Toliver and bred by Joseph Heine.

piece that exceeded anything that he'd seen in this country with an underjaw that was wide and turned up. Most Boxers in the U.S. at this time were too snipy.

He wanted to breed Bella, a.k.a. Boxi, his Karlo daughter. Since Boxi needed a bit more station, he decided to breed to Applejack of Canyonaire, a Ch. Mazelaine Endyminion son sired by the great Dorian. Although he had champion-quality puppies in this first litter, he could not afford to show them. It was a number of years and several generations later that he had the wherewithal to campaign his Boxers. Then the champions began to roll in, one after another. Boxella finished four in one year: Rodger, Ricardo, Roxella and Peg O'My Heart. All four were sired by Ch. Dempsey's Copper Gentleman and are strongly represented in the pedigrees of many present-day champions. After many years of hard work and dedication with many ups and downs, Boxella Boxers and bloodlines are well known throughout the Boxer world and have contributed much to breed improvement throughout the U.S. as well as in Finland, Sweden, Norway, England, Belgium, Iran, South Africa, Japan, Canada and Nova Scotia.

It wasn't long before Heine was invited to judge in many foreign countries. He was the first American, in fact, to judge in Finland, Sweden and Germany. It was while attending the Jahrsieger show in Bremen, Germany and seeing these beautiful-headed Boxers that he decided to breed these qualities into the Boxella line, thus the importation of Zan V. Hasseler-HOF, European Jugensieger Zethos v. Adeltrots and Aktuel v. Okler Forst. Ironically, Boxella, to the best of Heine's own knowledge, is the only American Boxer kennel that has bred American champions from German imports since the time Larry Downey brought over Karlo, Czech and Czech von Dom.

Heine relays, "Having judged this breed worldwide, it has been my observations that we have been getting away from our standard. Dogs are becoming too refined.

Ch. Boxella's Sherri (by Ch. Heldenbrand's Jet Breaker ex Boxella's Sheena, a full-sister to Ch. Boxella's Warwick sired by German import Xan v. Hasseler, HOF).

We are forgetting that the Boxer is a working breed that should be sturdy, strong, sound and of true type. This in mind, Boxella has tried for the middle of the road: to breed a Boxer that is both elegant, sound and of true type with an underjaw—one that looks like a Boxer should."

Two more champions were finished in 1992: Ch. Boxella's Black Lace II and Ch. Boxella's Sherri, making a total of 41 champions.

Top-quality females are the foundation of any kennel. No, they do not have to be champions since, for a stud fee, you can breed to the very best in the land. Rio Rita of Cross Acres, Boxella's O'Daisy Mae, Boxella's Corvetta, Ch. Boxella's Wand O'Magic, Ch. Boxella's Charo, Ch. Boxella's Nonita and Ch. Boxella's Brigitte are a few of fine females that are treasured highly at Boxella.

Ch. Boxella's Charo (by Ch. Boxella's Leonardo Da Vinchi ex Ch. Boxella's Mar-Ray's Jeanette). Breeder-owner, Joseph Heine.

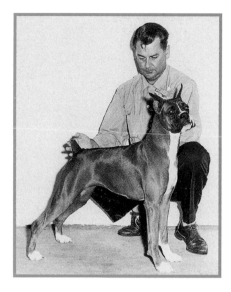

Ch. Treceder's Sequence, dam of Ch. Cajon's Calling Card, handled by Dee Anderson and owned by John and Carol Phillips.

TRECEDER

Treceder Kennels, Reg. was founded by Hollyce Stewart in Texas in 1945. Since his death in 1972, Treceder has been in the hands of Ann Harr, who has owned and bred Boxers since 1950. Her first Boxer was purchased from Lone Oak Kennels, Gina of Lone Oak, a Ch. Riot of Sirrah Crest daughter. After that, Ann's main interest was Boxers, under the prefix "Harmoney."

In 1956, Shady Lady was purchased from Hollyce Stewart. She was a Ch. Jered's Spellbinder daughter out of Ch. Treceder's High Falutin. After that, it was only Treceder for Ann. Ch. Treceder's Shady Lady was Ann's first champion. Shady Lady produced Ch. Treceder's Sequel and Ch. Treceder's Sequence, and Treceder Imprint who, though not a champion, played a part in Treceder's progress.

To name a few champions owned and/or bred by Ann: Ch. Treceder's Holy Smoke, Ch. Treceder's Candy Cane, Ch. Treceder's Sweet Stuff, Ch. Treceder's Up In Smoke, Ch. Treceder's War Paint, Ch. Treceder's Phantom of the Opera and, last but not least, Ch. Treceder's All That Jazz, the nation's top-winning Boxer in 1989 and 1990. He was also the Ken-L Ration Working Show Dog of the Year in 1989. Since 1987, Dr. Mark Harrison has been Ann's partner and co-owner of Treceder Boxers.

Ch. Cajon's Calling Card (by Ch. Barrage of Quality Hill ex Ch. Treceder's Sequence), at nine months of age, winning under legendary breeder Mazie Wagner, handled by owner John Phillips.

Left and right: Ch. Treceder's Painted Lady, known to the fancy as "Ladybug," (by Ch. Treceder's Selection ex Treceder's Discovery), with handler Joe Gregory, winning Best in Show on just two of their many occasions for owner Mary Smith.

Above left: Ladybug honored as Mayor for a day in Columbus, Ohio. Photographs courtesy of Mary Smith. *Above right:* Ladybug at home with owners Donald and Mary Smith. Bred by Don and Rita Jo Montier, she became a popular judge's choice in the early 1960s, winning 147 Bests of Breed, 98 Group firsts, and 49 Bests in Show.

Left: Ch. Treceder's Holy Smoke (by Ch. Ringmaster's Olimpian ex Treceder's Special Edition).

Right: Ch. Treceder's All That Jazz, bred by Ann Harr and owned with Mark Harrison.

Ch. Dreamweaver's Pure Gold of Marjack (by Ch. Rochil's Grande Marshall ex Ch. Jon-L's Marjack Three Time Gold).

Ch. Carlwen's Sean of Erin, SOM (by Ch. Salgray's Ovation ex Ch. Carlwen's Scotch Mischief), owned by Wendy Ness.

Ch. Carlwen's Gold Charm (by Ch. Sajac's Royal Savage ex Carlwen's Joie de Vivre).

CARLWEN

The logo Carlwen has long symbolized the dog interests of the Boxer-oriented family Ness (*Carl* and *Wen*dy). Though in dog circles Mr. Ness was not as well known as was his indomitable spouse, he was indeed a great ally and supporter in all her ambitious dog-related pursuits.

Mrs. Ness burst upon the dog show scene in the early 1950s, and from the beginning made her fame as an organizer and club person. She served many terms as president and leader of the Potomac Boxer Club, and was ever active in American Boxer Club affairs and wrote a column for *Boxer Review*.

After years of breeding and owning numerous Boxer champions, including top-producing Ch. Carlwen's Sean of Erin, Mrs. Ness retired from breeding and showing her beloved Boxers, but did continue with judging and club activities. Along the way, she was most proud of judging at the 1980 National ABC Specialty show.

Although Wendy has now left the dog scene, she in a sense lives on in the person of her ever-faithful friend and disciple, Salli Moore. Fortune smiled upon Salli as Wendy figuratively adopted her and undertook tutoring and schooling her in the intricacies of the sometimes complex Boxer world.

Today Mrs. Moore's valued presence among us serves to attest to and memorialize Wendy's legacy. Certainly Wendy has left a lasting influence on the breed that is reflected in Salli and Jack Moore's Sajac Boxers.

SAJAC

In the Boxer world, "Sajac" means *Sa*lli and *Jac*k Moore. While Colonel Jack and Salli were in the military, they met Mrs. Wendy Ness, who converted them to the "true faith" of "Boxerism." Upon retirement, the Moores settled in Florida and went about the serious business of breeding and showing Boxers. They are avid aficionados of the Boxer breed and have been successful in producing a number of fine champions.

Mrs. Moore is known to most as the active and able Chief Steward at the American Boxer Club's National Specialty, and she is also a leading force in the management of the combined all-breed shows held each January in Daytona Beach, Florida. She is noted for her efforts in canine legislation in her county, and she serves as chairman of the animal-control board.

Mrs. Moore recalls that her first encounter with Boxer folks came in the early 1970s when her husband Jack was transferred to the Washington, DC area for a tour of duty with the Joint Chiefs of Staff. Soon after their arrival, they lost their beloved dog of 16 years, "Honey Dog."

It was Honey Dog's replacement that changed the direction of Salli's life. Jack purchased, from an ad in the *Washington Post*, an "inbred Ovation daughter." Wendy Ness's stud dog was recommended. Salli called Wendy to inquire about it, and she was amazed by Wendy's knowledge of Boxers. From that instant, Wendy became Salli's dear friend and "guru." Salli recalls, "I had instant friends and complete enemies before I ever had a dog in the ring."

Ch. Sajac's Royal Savage, SOM (by Ch. Salgray's Ambush ex Carlwen's Candy Striper), owned by Salli and Jack Moore.

Ch. Sajac's Misty Morn (by Ch. Sajac's Royal Savage ex Carlwen's Joie de Vivre), owned by Salli and Jack Moore.

No breeding success came until Wendy gave Salli a plain brindle bitch, Carlwen's Candy Stuffer. She produced the last litter sired by top producer Ch. Salgray's Ambush. This union gave Salli Ch. Sajac's Royal Savage, SOM, who, according to Salli, is an "all-around good guy."

Salli says, "Someone once said that to start an insane asylum, you only need a large room and the right kind of people. Well, to have a dog show you still need that same large room and those same delightful people. I have found my niche in life."

Ch. Melfield's Witch Doctor (by Ch. Sajac's Royal Savage ex Carlwen's Joie de Vivre), owned by Melvin and Melva Hatfield.

The legendary Charlotte Brayshaw, stacking a future Brayshaw star.

Ch. Brayshaw's Victor's Rebel (by Tri Spruce's Mr. Rebel Brayshaw ex Brayshaw's Ginger Cookie), under judge Heywood Hartley at the Middlesex Boxer Club on December 17, 1965. The first show dog for Victor and Anita Clemente, Rebel won two Groups from the classes under esteemed all-rounders Alva Rosenberg and Percy Roberts.

Ch. Brayshaw's Sargeant Major (by Ch. Beaulaine's Boombo ex Brayshaw's Dandie Gem), owned by Robert Harris.

BRAYSHAW

Charlotte A. Brayshaw was a devoted breeder of Boxers as well as an advisor and true friend to many Boxer enthusiasts whom she helped get started in the breed. Charlotte got her start in Boxers in the early 1940s. She was a member of the Women's Auxiliary Army Corps as an airborne photographer. The first Boxer she met was an Army K-9 dog, and it was love at first sight. After her discharge from the WAACs, she bought a Boxer bitch named Gretchen and from then on, her life became totally devoted to the breed. She bred over 100 litters and was an active exhibitor as well. Over 50 Brayshaw Boxer have earned championship titles, and Charlotte herself was awarded every award offered by the American Boxer Club. However, regardless of all her personal achievements, her greatest joy was introducing someone new to the wonderful world of Boxers.

Charlotte had specific goals in her breeding program—temperament, soundness and beauty were the three essential qualities to strive for in breeding. She would never sacrifice temperament and soundness for beauty; that was the "icing on the cake." She felt that the Boxer should be a loyal and gentle dog with the physical capability to be a working dog. These were the principles behind her breeding program.

Charlotte passed away in 1984, but her effect on the Boxer breed and the people involved with Boxers can still be felt today, and will not be forgotten as time goes on.

Above: Ch. Brayshaw's Kissin Cousin (by Ch. Brayshaw's Morgan Boozer ex Brayshaw's Saucy Susie), winning under judge Joseph Heine, handled by Jane Kamp Forsyth. She was Winners Bitch at ABC National in 1971.

Right: One of breeder Charlotte Brayshaw's favorites, Ch. Brayshaw's Mr. Morgan Roberts (by Ch. Bang Away of Sirrah Crest ex Brayshaw's Naughty Gussie) was a multi-Group winner, handled by Nate Levine.

Left to right: Ch. Hot Shot of Bon-Ton (by Ch. Brayshaw's Masquerader ex Brayshaw's Tagalong) with handler Tom O'Neil, Ch. Brayshaw's Saucy Back Talk (by Ch. Brayshaw's Mr. Morgan Boozer ex Tremblay's Jam Session) with Victor Clemente, Ch. Brayshaw's Morgan Boozer (by Ch. Tremblay's Drummer Boy ex Brayshaw's Whistle Bait) with David Stein, Ch. Brayshaw's Saucy Freckles (by Tri-Spruce's Mr. Rebel Brayshaw ex Brayshaw's Midnite Hussy) with Anita Clemente and Ch. Tremblay's Drummer Boy (by Ch. Brayshaw's Masquerader ex Tremblay's Jam Session) with Charlotte Brayshaw.

Ch. Brayshaw's Hustler (by Ch. Brayshaw's Beau Dandy ex Howdell's Ginger Snap), Victor Clemente's most famous dog, won the ABC award for most BOBs for 1971 and became a top winner in Brazil. Handled by Anita Clemente.

Ch. Brayshaw's Calamity Ann (by Ch. Tremblay's Drummer Boy ex Brayshaw's Cynful Nightcap), handled by Jane Forsyth.

Ch. Brayshaw's Perpetual Pest (by Ch. Brayshaw's Beau Dandy ex Howdell's Ginger Snap), handled by Jane Forsyth, was the litter brother to Ch. Brayshaw's Hustler.

Ch. Brayshaw's Hustling Pest (by Ch. Brayshaw's Hustler ex Ch. Brayshaw's Perpetual Pest), handled by Robert Forsyth. Breeder-owner Anita Clemente.

Ch. Brayshaw's Saucy Freckles (by Tri-Spruce's Mr. Rebel Brayshaw ex Brayshaw's Midnite Hussy), handled by Dottie Watson in one of her famous lucky hats!

KREYON

Margaret and Walter Krey's first two Boxers were bitches, and they were "give-aways." The first, in 1955, was Lady Katrinka—uncropped, French-footed and cowhocked, with the blackest eyes you have ever seen. She was loved by the Kreys for 12 years. The second Boxer bitch was Mitzi, and, until they got into the showing game, the Kreys didn't realize what a good bitch they had been given. Mitzi passed away in 1962, and another Boxer was purchased. Their first litter was born in 1964, and the best bitch of that litter produced two champions by two different sires.

Margaret had never seen a brindle Boxer, but when she saw her first brindle she had to have one. They purchased Bartizan's Jewel, who was a double Comanche granddaughter. They hoped to finish her, but at six months of age she jumped the fence and injured her left hind leg. She was shown 13 times and always placed, but as she got tired she would favor her injured leg. She was bred to Ch. Cajon's Calling Card and produced the Best in Show bitch Ch. Kreyon's Firebrand. In 1968 she was the Grand Prize Futurity Winner and BOB at the ABC Regional.

Walter used to say that the people he met at dog shows would always say to him, "You are Margaret Krey's husband." However, after the Kreys bred Firebrand, people would say, "You own Firebrand!"

Firebrand was bred to Scher-Khoun's Shadrack and produced a quality litter. A male, Kreyon's Benchmark, earned 12 points and needed a major to finish. Another male, Kreyon's Back in Town, was used for stud in the US and his son, Rainey-Lanes Grand Slam, was sold to Mervyn Chapman of Australia. Grand Slam was the sire of 23 Australian champions. Back in Town was sold to Ivor and Marion Ward-Davies in England. "Mack," as he was called, became the sire of five English champions. Firebrand made the Kreyon name in the US, and her son made the name around the world.

Margaret joined the ABC in 1967 and remembers with great pride that her sponsors were Eleanor Haeberle and Lydia Brown. She can still recall her first ABC meeting and specialty. She has been a member of the Maryland Boxer Club since 1963, and has held the offices of president, corresponding secretary and show secretary.

Since 1966, every litter that the Kreys have bred has been futurity-nominated, and their Boxers have competed at ABC, many of them going on to finish. Walter passed away in 1982, but Margaret continues on with Boxers. She still loves to keep Boxers as house dogs, breed an occasional litter, pick a good puppy from the litter and finish his championship. Her fondest wish is to live the rest of her life with a Boxer in her home as a companion.

Ch. Kreyon's Firebrand (by Ch. Cajon's Calling Card ex Bartizan's Jewel) is Walter and Margaret Krey's most famous Boxer. Handled by Don F. Starkweather.

Ch. Becrelen's Danny Boy (by Ch. Becrelen's Shindig ex Ewo's Just Dream Girl), handled by Earl Overstreet.

BIRDNECK

Emagene and Bert Brown's beginning in Boxers was quite by accident. They got their first Boxer from a reputable breeder, and this first Boxer also became their first champion, Ch. Erica of Birdneck Point. She was of Mary Jackson's Marjack breeding.

Their second dog, Ch. Becrelen's Danny Boy, came from Cres Farrow. He was handled to his championship by Stuart Sliney. Stuart retired as a handler after the 1970 Westminster show, leaving the Browns with Danny and a barely one-year-old bitch named Becrelen's Lady Bug to show. Stuart felt that Bert should handle the dogs and Lady Bug, perhaps the most elegant bitch of her time, made a handler of him. She was by Ch. Becrelen's Charger (by Ch. Cajon's Calling Card) ex Becrelen's Plain Jane. Lady Bug defeated every male dog shown against her at one time or another. She was very popular and admirers frequently would call the Browns' home to make sure she would be shown at the next show.

Ch. Birdneck's Points Cherica (by Ch. Becrelen's Charger ex Ch. Erica of Birdneck Point) was Bert and Emagene Browns' first homebred champion.

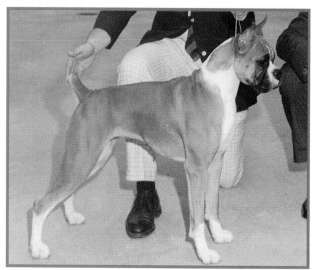

Ch. Becrelen's Lady Bug (by Ch. Becrelen's Charger ex Becrelen's Plain Jane) was one of the first Boxers that Bert Brown handled in the ring.

Lady Bug and Danny Boy were the first dogs that Bert entered, groomed and showed. At his first show he won with both: Winners Bitch with Lady Bug and Best of Breed with Danny Boy.

Ch. Birdneck's Cherica (Ch. Becrelen's Charger ex Ch. Erica of Birdneck Point) started her show career by winning the 6—9 puppy bitch class at the 1971 ABC Futurity. She completed her championship by going WB-BOB at the Eastern Boxer Club Specialty. She was from their first litter.

Ch. Birdneck's Basic Black' n Pearls, by their Ch. Ewo's Halfback and their Ch. Bar-Day's Black Velvet, began her show career with a four-point major from the puppy class. "Maggie" also won the ABC award for Bitch Making the Most Wins in the Working Group in 1977. She was beautiful and correct, and she made good Group showings because of her superior movement.

Ch. Birdneck's Basic Black 'n Pearls (by Ch. Ewo's Halfback ex Ch. Bar-Day's Black Velvet) was a top Working Group contender in the late 1970s.

Arriba's most famous Boxer, Ch. Arriba's Prima Donna (by Ch. Flintwood's Live Ammo ex Arriba's Alicia), handled by Jane Forsyth, winning under Maxwell Riddle on February 22, 1969. This bitch would go on to win Best in Show at Westminster the following year, the only Boxer bitch ever to do so. Owners, Dr. and Mrs. Pagano and Dr. Ted Fickes. Breeder, V. Baribeault.

ARRIBA

Arriba Boxers was established in 1964 by Theodore S. Fickes, DVM with a plain bitch, Nahum's Arriba ("Arriba"). She produced two flashy pups—one male and one female—who both became champions. Ch. Arriba's Amulet, Arriba's daughter sired by Ch. Mazelaine's Early Times, produced three champions by Ch. Capriana's Renegade. These dogs produced more champions, thus beginning an unbroken chain of champions who all trace back to that first Boxer, Nahum's Arriba, who was never shown.

The most notable Arriba Boxer has been Ch. Arriba's Prima Donna. She won 23 all-breed Bests in Show, including Westminster under Miss Anna Katherine Nicholas. She also was ranked as one of the Top Ten Working Dogs of All-Time, according to the *Kennel Review* system. Prima Donna's spectacular show career made the Arriba name well known in the ring.

Arriba has had many bitches who were great producers and Dams of Merit, as well as five ABC Sires of Merit. Dr. Fickes is also very proud of his success at ABC Specialties: Arriba dogs have won Best of Breed, Best of Opposite Sex, Winners Dog, Winners Bitch and other awards.

CAVA-LANES

Cava-Lanes was founded by Betty Jean Cavanaugh, BJ to those who knew her, in the early 1960s. BJ took her first Boxer, Sir Walter Biggs, a Ch. Merry Monarch son, and bred him to the bitches she had acquired through selection and found herself needing a kennel. This she acquired—in the form of the five acres where they live today—from Barney and Evelyn Owens, whose Evo-Wen Kennels is known throughout the Boxer world.

Cava-Lanes grew and prospered thanks to BJ's interest in showing and breeding together with her sincere dedication to improving the breed. The results of her efforts became apparent as she judiciously selected her breeding stock. Today Cava-Lanes is internationally respected for Boxers of soundness and elegance. The Cava-Lanes prefix can be found in the pedigrees of many Boxer kennels today.

Included in the Cava-Lanes breeding foundation stock was Forhol's Wild Irish Rose, a Ch. U-Bet's Retraction daughter, who was also a granddaughter of Ch. Marjack's Golden Windjammer. She was bred to Ch. Sorrelane's Student Prince, from which came a son, Cava-Lanes' Top Secret, who founded the Cava-Lanes dynasty.

Sorrelane's Tar Baby, a Ch. Frazer's Parademeister daughter from a Spellbinder daughter, was another early acquisition at Cava-Lanes, selected for her style. Tar

Ch. Firestar's Breakaway Express (by Ch. Heldenbrand's Heart Breaker ex Ch. Cava-Lane's Heartland Express), owned by Diane Boyle and Elizabeth J. Cavanaugh, handled by Jerry Bryant.

Ch. Cava-Lanes' New Attitude (by Ch. Salgray's KO Aracrest ex Cava-Lanes' Andromeda), owned by Elizabeth J. Cavanaugh.

Baby was bred to Top Secret, producing two outstanding foundation bitches. These were Cava-Lanes' Velvet Touch and Cava-Lanes' Flaming Star. Velvet was the ABC Brood Bitch of the Year for 1969–1970. Her litter by Ch. Treceder's Shine Boy had produced Ch. Cava-Lanes' Apollo, Ch. Cava-Lanes' Touch of Venus and Ch. Cava-Lanes' Velvet Glow, the latter a Best in Show bitch who gained the American Boxer Club's Top Winning Bitch award for 1970–1971.

Ch. Cava-Lanes' Touch of Venus's litter by Ch. Scher-Khoun's Shadrack produced Ch. Cava-Lanes' Gorgeous Babe. Ch. Cava-Lanes' Gorgeous Babe's litter by Ch. Salgray's Good Grief produced three champions that carried the Cava-Lanes prefix: Moving On, Gorgeous George and Looking Good.

In the mid 1970s, Cava-Lanes acquired a Fashion Hint daughter, Millan's Miss Palmyra, whose litter by Ch. Cava-Lanes' Moving On made her a Dam of Merit. A year later Moving On became a Sire of Merit.

After BJ's untimely death, the torch was passed to her daughter, Elizabeth. Today Elizabeth continues the Cava-Lanes tradition of breeding quality Boxers. This is demonstrated by Ch. Cava-Lanes' Heartland Express, Ch. Firestars' Breakway Express, Ch. Cava-Lanes' Thunder Storm, and Ch. Cava-Lanes' New Attitude, the latter taking Best six- to nine-month-old puppy at the American Boxer Club Futurity 1988 and finishing from the Bred-by class with four majors. The Cava-Lanes legacy continues...

In 1962, Donna Titus brought home a Boxer from the local pound for her son's first birthday and that dog turned their lives around. He lived to be 15 years old and loved and protected the family at every moment of his life.

Named for Tituses' area of town, Hiland, which was on a hill in Moline, Illinois, Hi-Hill Boxers was established in 1970. Donna acquired a Boxer bitch puppy for breeding but she never conceived. In 1973 she got a Ch. Flintwood's Rabble Rouser daughter, whom she later bred to a dog owned by John and Carol Phillips. The Phillips advised her well and taught her to be an honest breeder. Donna also met Lloyd and Mary Flint through this bitch. Due to their tutelage, she set her goal to breed as healthy a dog as possible with good temperament, movement, longevity and last, but not least, show quality. One of the best stories was that of a Linebacker daughter from the Rabble Rouser daughter. She was a plain Boxer bitch who lived for 17 years in a wonderful pet home.

Donna then bought a fawn six-month-old puppy dog from John and Carol Phillips. He was her first champion dog, Ch. Cajon's Pacemaker. He finished a couple months after her first champion, Hi-Hill's Poppin' Fresh (Duchess). She was sired by her stud dog and was bred by a 14-year-old girl. Donna then purchased Terra Oak's Souvenir, who finished but died shortly after of a brain tumor.

Ch. Hi-Hill's Rave Review, DOM (by Ch. Heldenbrand's Ks Kid by Peddler ex Hi-Hill's Summer Shadows), bred by Donna Titus.

The next to finish was Ch. Alma's Jingle Bells, a Jered daughter. Jingles produced great pups and grandpups, through whom she still lives on. Jingles gave them a dark brindle daughter, Ch. Hi-Hill Winter Classic (Holly). Holly won many Group placements and gave Jane Moog and Donna an ABC BOW, Ch. Heritage Match Point. Jingles also produced her brindle son and the littermate to Holly: Hi-Hill's Winter Fashion, a great producer who in turn produced such greats as Ch. Hi-Hill Night Lites and Ch. Hi-Hill's Night Breeze. Both finished easily.

Hi-Hill's Summer Shadows, a lovely but small bitch, was bred to Ch. Heldenbrand's Ks Kid by Peddler, which produced Ch. Hi-Hill's Rave Review, who became a Dam of Merit. Next, a lovely brindle bitch by a Winter Fashion daughter out of Ch. Shieldmont's Judge 'N Jury came on the scene: Ch. Hi-Hill's Dreaming of N Ocean Vu finished with such wins as BOW at Bucks County over 90 bitches. She placed in the Group and produced a nice litter that pointed from the Puppy class.

What joy comes in loving the town clowns of Hi-Hills whether they be champions or not. They are all special to the Titus family.

Ch. Hi-Hill's Winter Classic (by Ch. Paragon's Nite Ryder ex Ch. Alma's Jingle Bells), bred by owner-handler Donna Titus. Judge, Connie Bosold.

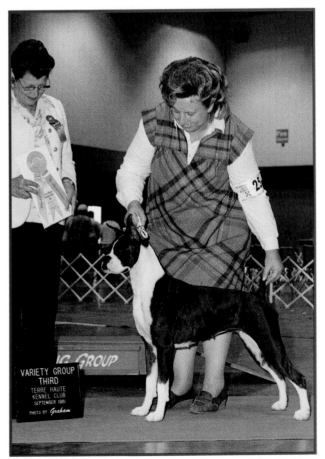

Ch. Hi-Hill's Poppin' Fresh (by Interlude's Jet Son ex Hallmark Hills April Luv) at six months old at her first show. Owner-handled by Donna Titus.

Ch. Dormac's Gunslinger, SOM (by Ch. Salgray's Ambush, SOM ex Dormac's Risque, DOM), owned by Ramon and Dorothy McNulty.

DORMAC

As all-breed professional handlers, Ramon and Dorothy McNulty bred on a very limited scale. They did produce 20 champions including a Sire of Merit, Ch. Dormac's Gunslinger, and a Dam of Merit, his dam Dormac's Risque. They also had several Group, Best in Specialty and all-breed Best in Show wins.

Some of the notable Dormac Boxers include: Ch. Dormac's Gunslinger by Ch. Salgray's Ambush ex Dormac's Risque by Ovation; Ch. Arekay N Dormac's Yu Betcha by Ch. Arekay's Photocopy of Dormac ex Ch. Dormac's On The Town; Ch. Arekay's Photocopy of Dormac by Ch. Dormac's Gunslinger ex Salgray's Promise to Dormac; Ch. Salgray's Zetta of Dormac by Ch. Salgray's Double Play ex Ch. Dormac's On The Town; and Ch. Dormac's On The Town by Ch. Dormac's Gunslinger ex Ch. Dormac's Favorite.

KARLYNA

While living abroad in the '50s, Elizabeth S. Sutton's parents bought their first Boxer. Elizabeth was a young girl at the time and fell in love with that dog. In fact, the Suttons were so impressed with the breed, they ended up with three Boxers while living in Germany.

After Elizabeth married, she and her new husband bought a wonderful male out of a Mazelaine dog. Almost 15 years later, she purchased a flashy fawn male for a pet, and was talked into going to a local show. Elizabeth thought it looked like fun, so she went through handling classes after joining the local kennel club, began reading everything about Boxers and handling available and then put five points on that flashy fawn dog. She purchased a beautiful brindle bitch from Peter Baynes, with the intent of breeding to her pet male. Though a dear, he wasn't good enough to be used for breeding, so she found a proper home for him. Elizabeth's brindle bitch, Ch. Bainridge O'Suzanna of Karlyna, became the foundation bitch and a Dam of Merit. What a beauty she was!

Elizabeth joined the Georgia Boxer Club and the American Boxer Club as well as the local kennel club, and has enjoyed showing and breeding Boxers for over a decade.

CLINEL

Clinton and Eileen Sherburne of Monte Sereno, California, purchased their first show Boxer in 1950, while Clint was still in college. The stag red fawn male was a Ch. Canyonair Hickory Dick son, acquired from Paul and Peg Davis of Canyonair fame. The Sherburnes' level of activity in showing was superseded by the establish-

Ch. Bainridge O'Suzanna of Karlyna, DOM (by Ch. Hala's Apache Rising Son ex Wesan's Sassy Sorceress), bred by Peter A. Baynes.

ment of career and raising a family, but Boxers were always a part of their household. Exhibiting and breeding became a much more active pastime in their home during the 1960s and 1970s. It was during this time that the Sherburnes established the ClinEl name, and bred and successfully campaigned their champions, ClinEl's Lil Abner and Stupifyin Jones. Clint was also approved as a Boxer judge during all this activity. In subsequent years, the Sherburnes owned several champion Boxers. The most famous was Ch. Laureate Kiss Me Kate.

There are quite a few notable dogs. Ch. ClinEl's Lil Abner, by Ch. Von Schorer's Matinee Idol ex Coburg's Second Penny, was a very smooth dog with excellent movement front and rear, very similar to his sire, Matinee Idol. Matinee Idol was a Ch. Willow Rounds Fortissimo ex Ch. Von Schorer's Miss Knock About son. Abner's dam was a very well-bred Ch. Lucky Blarney O'Downey daughter. Among Abner's get were several excellent Boxers. A breeding with Ch. Glennroe Ingenue produced the outstanding bitch, Ch. Glennroe Opensesame, DOM, who was the foundation bitch for Gene and Jennifer Tellier's Telstar Boxers. He was handled by Eleanor Wood.

Ch. ClinEl's Stupifyin' Jones, by Ch. Von Schorer's Matinee Idol ex Coburg's Second Penny, was Ch. ClinEl's Lil Abner's litter sister. Like Abner, she had a

Ch. Laureate Kiss Me Kate (by Ch. Laureate X-Cel-A-Rator ex Ch. Black Toad Penelope), bred by Margaret Benshoff and owned by Clinton and Eileen Sherburne, was a multiple BIS winner. Kate was awarded her first Best of Breed win by Jim Arnold, husband of Sturlene Arnold. She is wearing the BIS coat, a gift from the Wurmsers, owners of Terudon's Kiss Me Kate.

Ch. Karlyna's Dudley Do Right (by Ch. Karlyna's Brigadoon O'Broadway ex Ch. Karlyna's Absolutely Perfect), bred by Elizabeth S. Sutton and handled by Cheryl Robbins.

very smooth body with good front and rear angulation, she moved with great energy and she always made her presence felt in the ring.

The young adult Ch. Telstar's Tristan, by Eng. Ch. Steynmere Summer Gold ex Ch. Glennroe Opensesame, DOM, was acquired from Gene and Jennifer Tellier. He had already earned points as a puppy, and the Sherburnes campaigned him with Chery Cates handling. The combination of the great English Ch. Steynmere Summer Gold and Ch. Glennroe Opensesame was very successful. Tristan was a square dog of considerable substance whose greatest strength was his ground-covering movement. Earning his title of champion qualified his wonderful dam as an ABC Dam of Merit. As a Lil' Abner grandson, Tristan was very special to the Sherburnes.

Ch. Laureate Kiss Me Kate, by Ch. Laureate X-Cel-A-Rator ex Ch. Black Toad Penelope, was one of the truly outstanding Boxers of the 1980s. Kate was acquired by Clinton and Eileen Sherburne in May 1981, at the age of eight-and-a-half weeks, from breeder Margaret Benshoff.

She stepped out of an airline crate into their lives, exhibiting all the potential each sought in a puppy. The Sherburnes began thinking about a suitable name for this little show girl. They had always remembered Ch. Terudon's Kiss Me Kate and thought the name was ideally suited to a lovely show bitch. They watched little Katie grow over the next few weeks, and Eileen said, "This is the little girl we've been looking for, worthy of the Kiss Me Kate name."

Ch. Laureate Kiss Me Kate was owner-handled to her title, finishing at 14 months of age. As Santa Barbara KC 1982 approached, Gary Steele agreed to handle

Katie and the rest is history. Kate was shown on a limited basis during the latter part of 1982 and early 1983.

She retired from regular showing in May 1986. Her record includes 26 BIS, including 9 major all-breed shows and 17 Specialties, 150 BOBs, No. 2 Boxer 1984, No. 2 Boxer Bitch 1985, BOS ABC Specialty 1985, Award of Excellence ABC Specialty 1986, *Boxer Review* Best in the West 1984, 1985, 1986. In 1984, she was No. 15 Working and No. 68 in the top 100 all-breeds.

Mr. and Mrs. Theodore Wurmser, owners of Ch. Terudon's Kiss Me Kate, had apparently followed Katie's career. In May 1987, the Sherburnes received a surprise package in the mail. The Wurmsers sent their Kate's handmade BIS coat to Kate. "I called the Wurmsers immediately to express our heartfelt thanks," Clint said. "It was a wonderful, thoughtful thing to do. It will always be one of the highlights of our lives with Katie."

Mr. John Connolly judged the East Bay Boxer Club Specialty in March 1988, and commented: "The Veteran Bitch, Ch. Laureate Kiss Me Kate, roared into the ring and immediately captured everyone. A very good Specials class could not 'show her down' as she looked better and showed better than I've ever seen her and I've given her at least two Group firsts when she went on to Best in Show. Needless to say, she was my Best of Breed winner."

MARBURL

The Burlesons first adopted a Boxer in 1957 as a companion for Mary Frances while Rufus had to travel. Curiosity about the breed caused them to purchase their first show puppy from the Acklands in 1964 when they joined the Dallas Boxer Club. From then on everything went to the dogs!

Their first winner was a daughter of Ch. Salgray's Fashion Plate, who won her title in the states and on the CACIB circuit in Mexico City. Ch. Ackland's Fashion Belle was the granddam of the second generation of Marburl Boxers, who when bred to Al-le-lu-ia, produced Am-Can-Mex. Ch. Marburl's Joshua.

Ch. ClinEl's Lil' Abner (by Ch. Von Schorer's Matinee Idol ex Coburg's Second Penny), bred by owners Clinton and Eileen Sherburne.

John Connolly, who handled an early Marburl Boxer, helped the Burlesons acquire their first brindle puppy, a Fashion Hint daughter. Ch. Jo-Jac's Magic Moment went on to complete her title and become their first Dam of Merit.

Johnny and Joyce Johnson came on the scene and profoundly influenced the show career of Marburl Boxers. Johnny saw "Josh" at seven-and-a-half months and took him from the Burlesons and kept him until he was over three years of age. Their record was stunning:

Johnny and Josh won 27 Boxer Specialties, over 150 BOBs, two all-breed BIS and BOB at two ABC Regional Specialties, and Josh still had time to sire 23 champions.

One of the puppies Josh produced came from an outstanding brindle bitch owned and bred by the Tomhaves from Lincoln, Nebraska. Ch. Marburl's Rahab of Wesan came to the Burlesons at four-and-a-half months of age. After winning three four-point majors (including a BOB and Group placement under Larry Downey) at nine months of age, the career of a winner was die-cast. "Penny" won BOB at two ABC National Specialties (1979 and 1980); was covergirl on the *Boxer Review*, the *Gazette* and *Kennel Review;* and was a producer of the Hargreaves' DOM.

The Burlesons' Boxer career highlights include: winning 21 ABC annual awards; finishing over 35 champions; Mary Frances's judging sweeps at the Nationals in Canada, Mexico and ABC Futurity (twice); Rufus's

Ch. Marburl's Rahab of Wesan (by Ch. Marburl's Joshua ex Ch. Wesan's Dark Apache Miss), owned by Mary Frances and Rufus Burleson was a multiple Best in Show winner, having won her first all-breed BIS at the precious age of 14 months.

judging the breed across the U.S., Mexico and Australia; winning Grand Prize Futurity in 1988; and Rufus's serving as director of ABC and president of the Dallas Boxer Club.

Living in rural northern Texas about an hour north of Dallas, the Burlesons enjoy two champion ladies at the foot of the bed, a kennel of ten dogs and a separate nursery with three indoor/outdoor matron quarters. They both look forward to their next champion, their next litter and their next dog show! Their advice to the novice is to start with a well-bred bitch, breed to a proven sire and show your own (as far as you can go).

Am-Can-Mex. Ch. Marburl's Joshua, SOM (by Ch. Moreleen's Al-le-lu-ia ex Marburl's Fireball), winning the Breed at the ABC regionals.

CH. WAGNER WILVERDAY FAMOUS AMOS

BY PAUL VAN SINDEN

Once in a great while a Boxer is born whose very special qualities set him apart from the rest. Such a dog has a charisma that even the casual observer cannot forget and when this dog is shown, spectators find that they have a new standard to which they can compare to other competitors.

For those of us who had the opportunity to witness the meteoric show career of Famous Amos, the experience was unforgettable. Shown a total of 143 times as a Special, he was Best of Breed an incredible 123 times including 28 Specialty wins, 16 Group wins, 40 other Group placements and 4 all-breed Best in Show wins. Most impressive of all were his four National Specialty titles and

Ch. Wagner Wilverday Famous Amos, SOM (by Ch. Marquam Hill's Traper of TuRo ex Ch. Wagner's Vision of Wilvirday), owned by Barbara E. Wagner, won the ABC National Specialty more times than any other Boxer.

his two Regional Specialty titles—a record that will not soon, if ever, be equaled. He became the first Boxer in the history of the breed to win both the ABC National and the ABC Regional two years in succession. He is also the first dual National Specialty winner to sire a dual National Specialty winner, his son Ch. Berenas' Tribute to Fa Fa.

For those who consider Amos to be the standard of perfection for the Boxer, his success as a sire comes as no surprise. He has sired 27 known champions, 3 of which are already ABC producers of merit themselves. Two of his sons, Ch. Berenas Tribute To Fa Fa and Ch. Berenas Gemini Splashdown are National Specialty winners, and a third son, Ch. Shieldmonts Issues N' Answers was an ABC BOS winner, defeating his sire on that occasion.

As a breed enthusiast for many years, this writer has spent many hours watching Amos's show performances. As a show dog, he was always full of himself, entering the ring literally bursting with fire and enthusiasm and wearing the expression that only a Boxer can. I wish I could turn back the clock just to see Amos in the ring one more time.

Ch. Marquam Hill's Traper of TuRo, SOM (by Int. Ch. Mephisto's Vendetta ex Ch. TuRo's Whisper of Five T's), the sire of Famous Amos and the important producer for TuRo kennels. Photo courtesy of Sandy Roberts and Elizabeth Esacove.

Proud to Be a Boxer

BY BARBARA WAGNER

It has taken a long time for me to be able to talk about the wonderful memories Amos has left me. I still have times when the tears come, like now. Having such a great showman happens only once in a lifetime. Raising Amos was a joy. I think that the very first day Amos could stand on all four legs, he was *proud to be a Boxer*. God gave me a foundation to work with, and, when Amos was only five weeks old, I decided that I wanted to show the other breeders what I thought a Boxer should look like in the show ring. The day after Amos came to my home, off to work he went with me. I tried making each day a different experience. He was exposed to people and places each day. I took him to the horse track and the train station—everywhere I went, always making it fun for him. We became quite a twosome. Whenever I got ready to go anyplace, I would get his lead and say, "Let's go!" over and over so that he would get excited to go places. I was determined to make each outing an exciting one for Amos. Training him for the conformation ring was a lot of playtime, using crazy objects on and off lead, making sure that he always held his head high. I was able to do this many times during the day; my boss was very understanding! In fact, I said to him the day before I brought Amos into the office, "I'm bringing a partner to work with me tomorrow." Boy, was he surprised when the partner had four legs!

When Dick and Christine Baum first saw Amos, they both saw the same thing I saw, a *showman*. We all know that if Dick Baum likes your Boxer, no one can out-handle him in the show ring. Shortly after their first meeting, Amos entered the world of the show ring, and

the show world soon became aware of Amos and Dick. He earned his championship very quickly and began showing as a Special at a very young age. By the time he was three years old, he was at home, retired from active campaigning. Although he was perfectly content to be a good house dog, a year after his retirement I thought he looked so good that I decided the breeders should see him again, so off he went to the ABC. When I saw him in the ring sitting down with his ears back looking totally bored, I thought to myself, "Have I done the right thing?" But once his number was called and he and Dick started making their way into the ring, he went through the transformation to *showman* and again proved to everyone watching that his true joy was performing in the show ring.

The following year we repeated our visit to ABC. I will always feel that I repaid Amos for the joy he gave me by letting him return to the show world that he dearly loved. I could not have given him both worlds had he just been sent off to live with his handler like most other show dogs. He was a show dog on weekends and back home on the couch on Monday. Maybe that was the secret. But even when Amos was home, he had his fan club, because neighbors, his vet and other people treated him as if he was a famous person. Many people told me I picked the right name for him, because he was famous from the East coast to the West coast.

Amos won the National Specialty four times and the Regionals twice. Beyond that, he did his job as a producer and gave back to the breed. He not only sired

Am-Can. Ch. Wagner Wilverday Famous Amos, SOM, owned by Barbara E. Wagner, winning the Working Group at the Ravenna show in 1985.

champions, he sired producers and that's what it is all about. In May 1991, while stewarding at the National Specialty, I was able to see some of his sons, daughters and grandchildren who will carry the torch for Amos in succeeding generations.

To know Amos was to love him. Virginia Hoffman, his breeder, has since passed away, but I am sure that she was very proud to have bred him. To have owned and raised a great one was, to me, a gift from God. I will always be grateful. To this day, it is hard for me to believe he is not with me.

BY DICK BAUM

The first time I saw Amos was in April 1983. He was just six months old and shown at the Potomac Boxer Club Specialty. I remember thinking that if he ever grew into those legs he would be quite a dog. The next time I saw Amos he was 13 months old at the ABC Regional in Cincinnati. He had been Winners Dog at one of the Specialties. I recall Bobbie Wagner asking me what I thought of him. I told her, "The only thing wrong with him is that I am not showing him." She remarked that she didn't think I liked him, and I said, "What's not to like?" Shortly after that conversation, she called me and asked if I would show him.

Our first show was the Baltimore County Kennel Club under Mrs. Thelma Von Thaden. When Amos and I walked into the ring, she looked at him and looked at me and I knew she loved him. He went Best of Breed from the classes and on to a Group Two. He finished in three shows, winning five-point majors at the Christmas Classic in Cleveland under Annie Clark and Rosemary Blood.

The rest is history. In his first show as a Special, he won the Breed under Ron Herd, won the Group under John Connolly and went on to Best in Show under Ron Herd at Fort Steuben Kennel Club.

Amos was truly one of those once-in-a-lifetime dogs. He was a show dog through and through. I have many fond memories of Amos, and it is difficult to pick one particular time that was special. They were all special.

If I had to pick any particular incident though, it would be the ABC win under Joe Gregory in 1987. Amos had already won two ABC Best of Breed and had been retired when Bobbi brought him to me in April 1987 and asked if I wanted to take him back to ABC again. I told her that if he looked good, I would like for people to see him now at four-and-a-half years of age. He was not old enough for Veterans so we entered him in the Breed. I told Bobbi not to expect to win. I remember just before the Breed went in, going back to the grooming area to get him. Amos was sitting on the grooming table when I walked in. I said, "Let's go get 'em, Amos." He jumped down, shook and stood there looking at me as if to say, "What do you think? Can we do it?" He looked magnificent. I thought to myself, he can do it. One more time.

And he did.

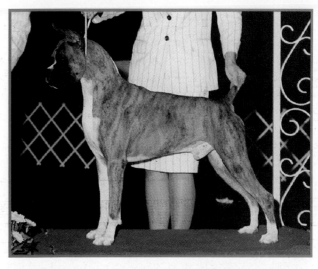

Son of Amos, this is Ch. Suncrests Seminole Chief (out of Ch. Our Delight of Shadowrock), counted among the Top Twenty Boxers in the late 1980s. Owners, Ray Culberson, Bill Weber and Olive Lee.

I think one of the finest tributes paid to Amos was by Joe Gregory, just before the final, when he pulled Amos out front, followed by his son, Ch. Shieldmont's Issues N Answers, followed by his grandson, Shieldmont's Judge N Jury, who was Winners Dog.

Amos came back to ABC once again in 1988 and won Best of Breed under judge Mrs. Olifant Brace from Australia.

Four times Best of Breed at ABC. Twice Best of Breed at ABC Regionals. A record that may never be equaled.

The last time I saw Amos was in the spring of 1989. He had been ill for some months but was getting better. Bobbie called me and said she would like to bring him over for me to see. She said, "ABC is coming up in a few months and wouldn't it be nice to take him in the Veterans Class?" When Amos walked through the door, he saw me and stopped and looked at me with that look only he had. I don't think I ever saw him look better. I got tears in my eyes and told Bobbie, "Let's go for number five!"

He died less than two weeks later.

His son, Ch. Berena's Tribute to Fa Fa was Best of Breed at the 1989 ABC under judge Patsy Connolly.

An American and Canadian Sire of Merit sired by Amos, Ch. Berena's Gemini Splashdown (out of Summerbird Leading Lady), owned by Bernie and Rena Toon, produced over 35 champions.

Ch. Heldenbrand's Jet Breaker, SOM (by Ch. Heldenbrand's Heart Breaker ex Heldenbrand's Jetta Jovina) won 21 all-breed Bests in Show and over 100 Working Groups. Breeders, Sherman and Elvinia Heldenbrand. Owners, Jeff Bennett and Judy Hunt. Handler, Gary Steele.

HELDENBRAND

The foundation sire and dam for Andy and Elvinia Heldenbrand's kennel were related quality Boxers. Their linebreeding program has produced several champions and obedience titlists including a leading Special and five Sires and Dams of Merit. Andy and Elvinia do the kennel management, show training and most of the handling, an avocation of over 25 years. Ch. Heldenbrand's Jet Breaker was the top-winning Boxer in the early 90s and a Best of Breed winner at ABC in 1990.

Ch. Heldenbrand's Heart Breaker, SOM (by Ch. Heldenbrand's Jedi Knight ex Ch. Wheatland's Gem v. Heldenbrand) is the sire of Jet Breaker. Owned by breeder Elvinia Heldenbrand.

5 T'S

5 T's Kennels was established in 1970, in Bargersville, Indiana by Jo and Don Thomson. The 5 T's Ranch, home of five Arabian horses and five Thomsons, was destined to become 5 T's Kennels.

They owned a pair of Boxers as companions for 12 years and this introduction to the breed brought about the decision to breed Boxers.

Jo and Don bred their first show litter in 1971, and from this litter the first champion, Ch. Fashion Princess of 5 T's, who was sired by Millan's Fashion Preview (a Fashion Hint littermate) and finished her title in 1972. That same year they finished a two-year-old male purchased from Canada, Am-Can. Ch. Memorylane's Sunset, a Fashion Hint son. In 1973 at Westminster, Jo finished a 15-month-old male, who was also awarded BOS from the classes over top Specials. He needs no introduction to our breed, Ch. Benjoman of 5 T's, SOM, sired by Scher Khouns Abendigo ex Tudosal's Ruffles. "Benjie" acquired 68 BOBs and 5 Group Ones, mostly owner-handled. From 1976 through 1979, he was the ABC's Top Producer, siring 38 American and 4 international champions. Many have become Sires and Dams of Merit, and more than 50 champions have completed

Ch. Kojoman of Five T's (by Ch. Benjoman of Five T's ex Bathsheba of Mud Creek), owned by Carolyn Halik, handled by Ezio Ceccarini and bred by Jo Thomson.

their title under the 5 T's banner. The last champion to finish, in 1981, was Ch. IBN Benji of 5 T's, a son from Benji's last litter. Benjoman's short life ended from cancer in 1978, just one week short of his seventh birthday.

Am-Can. Ch. Memorylane's Sunset of 5'Ts and his son Am-Can. Ch. Sunset Fonz of 5 T's both became Sires of Merit as did Ch. Kojoman of 5 T's. The 5 T's bloodlines found in present pedigrees are from the aforementioned dogs as well as: Ch. Twin Willows Mr. T. of 5 T's (ABC winner), Ch. Sunset Image of 5 T's (ABC winner), Ch. Benji's Shawn of 5 T's, Ch. Sunset Spirit of 5 T's (ABC winner), Ch.. Armant of 5 T's, Ch. Brettendale's Show Off of 5 T's, Ch. TuRo's Whisper of 5 T's, Ch. TuRo's Sugar of 5 T's, Ch. TuRo's Gabriel of 5 T's, Ch. TuRo's Ch. Risma OF 5 T's, Ch. Triple B's Baron of 5 T's, Ch. Sundance Kid of 5 T's, Ch. Benji's Citation of 5 T's, Ch. Americana's 5 T Classic and Ch. New Dawn's Farrah of 5 T's.

Last, but by no means least, do not forget all the girls who stayed home in the whelping box to make this possible.

Above: Ch. Charmant of Five T's (by Ch. Benjoman of Five T's ex Ch. Fashion Princess of Five T's), owned and handled by Jo Thomson. *Below:* Ch. IBN Benji of Five T's was Benjoman's last champion, out of Interlude's Jet Away. Handler, Chuck Steele.

Ch. Benjoman of Five T's, SOM (by Am-Can. Ch. Scher-Khouns Abendigo ex Tudosal's Ruffels) is a Sire of Merit and a multiple Group winner, much loved by Jo Thomson.

Ch. Fashion Princess of Five T's (by Millan's Fashion Preview ex Miss Brandi Mandi), owned by Jo Thomson. Handler, Bob Philips.

Ch. Evergreen's Ladyslipper (by Ch. Evergreen's Class Act ex Evergreen's Roxanne), owned by Stanley and Jane Flowers.

EVERGREEN

Evergreen Boxers of Stanley and Jane Flowers was established in 1972 with the purchase of foundation bitch Ch. Spring Willow's Suzy Q. Since 1975, over 30 Evergreen Boxers have completed their championships, including all-breed Best in Show winner Ch. Evergreen's Long Hot Summer and six Working Group winners. Ch. Evergreen's Ladyslipper was Winners Bitch at the National Specialty in 1990.

Four Evergreen Boxers: Aracrest's Stockbroker, Ch. Evergreen's Buckshot (by Ch. Salgray's KO Aracrest ex Ch. Sundancer's Autumn Flame), Ch. Evergreen's Class Act (by Ch. Salgray's KO Aracrest ex Evergreen's Image of Delight) and Ch. Evergreen's Bogart (by Ch. Salgray's KO Aracrest ex Salgray's Fame of Evergreen) with breeders Stanley and Jane Flowers.

OMEGA

In 1973, Colonel and Mrs. James Jackson purchased their first show bitch, Ch. Weber's Hustling Black Garter ("Libby," a double Fashion Hint granddaughter), who went Best of Winners at the 1974 ABC Specialty This was the beginning of Omega Boxers. In 1975, Can. Ch. Aracrest Velvet Sensation was acquired. By combining these two bitches with the lines of Ch. Scher-Khouns Shadrack, Ch. Scotlea's Billy Be Damned, Ch. Salgrays Market Wise and Tu Ro's Escappade, along with a program of linebreeding and occasional inbreeding, Omega Boxers has produced 23 champions from a limited amount of litters.

The breeding has included Ch. Aracrest's Talisman, SOM, the sire of 21 champions, 2 Sires of Merit, 1 Dam of Merit, 1 BIS winner, the 1982 ABC Specialty winner and one multi-Group winner; and Omega Windfire, DOM, the dam of 4 champions, 1 multi-BIS winner and recipient of the 1985 ABC award for dam producing the most champions.

Omega Boxers has had numerous ABC Specialty wins, including: 1974 WB, BW; 1979 RWB, Reo. Futurity winner; 1982 BOB winner; 1984 RWB; 1991 Futurity, Best Junior 12–15 months; and many class wins and placements.

Ch. Omega's Tycoon continues in the producing ways of his sire, Ch. Aracrest's Talisman, and grandsire, Ch. Omega's Rockfire. He has five champions and several very close to finishing. He is the sire of the 1992 ABC Specialty Winner, Ch. Jopa's Smolding Ember, and the multi-Group winner Ch. Omega's Desiree.

Ch. Omega's Rockfire, SOM (by Am-Ber-Can. Ch. Scher-Khoun's Shadrack ex Ch. Weber's Hustling Black Garter), owned by Jim and Lu Jackson, handled by Robert Forsyth.

Ch. Omega's Tycoon, SOM (by Ch. Aracrest's Talisman ex Ch. Omega's Maja), handled by Stan Flowers, owned by Jim and Lu Jackson.

Ch. Omega's Desiree (by Ch. Omega's Tycoon ex Ch. Omega's Manhattan), owned by Jim and Lu Jackson.

Ch. Sunset Image of Five T's (by Ch. Memorylane's Sunset ex Benj's Kandee of Five T's), bred by Jo Thomson and owned by Bruce and Jeannie Korson.

LAUREL HILL

Laurel Hill Boxers in Oyster Bay, New York, began in 1973 under the guidance of Charlotte Brayshaw. Charlotte was a wonderful breeder who shared her vast experience and knowledge with Bruce and Jeannie Korson, who showed their first dogs in 1974. Since then Laurel Hill has finished some 28 champions, over half of which were homebred. They've taken Winners Dog at the ABC twice, first with Ch. Sunset Image of Five T's and then with Ch. Sunset Spirit of Five T's. They've taken Best of Breed three times at the National Specialty and three times at an ABC Regional Specialty with Ch. Keibla's Tradition of TuRo, together with many annual awards given by the American Boxer Club. Along with breeding and showing, they have been involved in the American Boxer Club. Jeannie created the Top Twenty Event held at the National each year and has served as its Chairman. Bruce has been Secretary of ABC for five years and have served on The ABC Show Committee for some years.

Ch. Kiebla's Tradition of TurRo, affectionately called Tiggin, is bred by Kitty Barker, Sandy Roberts and Liz Esacove, owned and campaigned by the Korsons and shown by Christine Baum. Tiggin has achieved the distinction of being one of the breed's all-time winning Boxers. She has won over 50 all-breed Bests in Show, 50 Boxer Specialties (a record for the breed), 3 National Specialties and 3 Regional Specialties plus the American Boxer Club's 1991 Top Twenty Event. She was the winner of the Quaker Oats award in 1993, which made her the number one Working dog in the United States. She has won the Pedigree award for being the number-one Boxer in America for three consecutive years. Tiggin won the Working Group at the Westminster Kennel Club show in New York in 1991 under Mrs. Robert Forsyth.

Ch. Sunset Spirit of Five T's (by Ch. Sunset Fonz of Five T's ex Benj's Anji of Five T's), owned by Bruce and Jeannie Korson. Handled by Bobby Barlow.

Ch. Kieblas Tradition of TuRo, DOM (by TuRo's Escappade ex Ch. Kiebla's Mercy) is the top winning and producing bitch owned by Bruce and Jeannie Korson.

Ch. Katu's Ladawen's Sea Warlock (by Ch. Ladawen's Boston Warlock ex Kato's Hurricane Warning, CD), owned by Kathy Frohock.

KATHY FROHOCH

Kathy Frohoch's first Boxer, Pepper's Miss Suzie Q, came into her life around 1976. Ch. R. J. Token President, her first champion, was shown to his title and then Specialed by Doug Holloway.

Am-Braz. Ch. Hexastar's Royal Mark, bred by Agnes Buchwald, came to the U.S. at five years of age and finished in very short order, shown by Doug Holloway and Gerard Hughes. Royal was a very special dog and truly a "Boxer."

The first homebred champion, Ch. Katu's Ladawen's Sea Warlock, was also shown by Doug Holloway. His dam, Katu's Hurricane Warring, CD, received her obedience title at five years of age, handled by Gus Bell.

VIHABRA

Vihabra Boxers—an acronym for Virginia and Harry Bradley—have called the beautiful Pajaro Valley on California's Monterey Bay home since the late 1980s. Since first presenting their Boxers to the fancy in the late 1970s, they have produced around two dozen homebred champions. Their involvement with Boxers began in 1968 when they purchased their first pet Boxer, appropriately named "Gee Whizz" (Von Waltsiete), a male out of Ben Hame's Ch. Trigger Whizz, a noted grandson of Ch. Bang Away of Sirrah Crest.

The young Gee Whizz seemed in need of companionship and Daisy Mae, a sturdy young bitch from Ch. Canzonet's Musical Matinee, was acquired. The choice was a good one, and they soon produced a dozen brawny pups—an unusual litter of what in retrospect appeared to have been six male/female pairs of fraternal twins!

Daisy Mae was bred to the Ben Hame champion, Bold Impulse, and the Bradleys began their practice of keeping the most promising bitch—in this instance, Bold

Ch. Merrilane's Vihabra Gold 'N Key (by Ch. Merrilane's Happy to Meet You ex Merrilane's Touchdown Benroe), handled by Eleanor Linderholm-Wood at the East Bay Boxer Club in California.

Left: Am-Braz. Ch. Hexastar's Royal Mark (by Br. Ch. Pinebrook's Trademark ex Br. Ch. To'Rini's Allegria's Sequel), owned by Kathy Frohock. Judge, Anna Katherine Nicholas.

Ch. Vihabra's Stella by Starlite (by Ch. Vihabra's Gold'N Zephyr ex Ch. Vihabra's Magin's Irish Gold), owned by Peter and Magaly Cooling, bred by H.L. and Virginia J. Bradley.

Ch. Vihabra's Genesis of Jedapay (by Ch. Vihabra's Gold' N Zephyr ex B and J's Christmas Magic), bred by J. Noble, Jeanne Payne and owned by the Bradleys.

Windsong of Ben Roe (Ben Roe being the precursor to their kennel name Vihabra). "Windy" was bred to Ch. Merrilane's Holiday Fashion, and the bitch retained was Merrilane's Touchdown of Ben Roe, called "Happy." She produced their first homebred champion, Ch. Merrilane's Vihabra's Gold n Key ("Bogie") out of Ch. Merrilane's Happy to Meet You—son of Ch. Benjoman of Five T's.

A second breeding of Happy to Merrilane's Fashion Star produced Ch. Vihabra's Mister Golddust,

Ch. Vihabra's Stardust and Philippine Ch. Vihabra's Arrowhead.

The beautiful brindle bitch Ch. Vihabra's Stardust became a Dam of Merit from successive breedings to Ch. Merrilane's Salute to April, producing Ch. Vihabra's Double Take and Ch. Merrilane's Ode to Vihabra; to Ch. Merrilane's Silver & Gold, producing Chs. Merrilane's Vihabra's Gold Chip and Gold Treasure; and to Ch. Marquam Hills Trigger of TuRo, producing Ch. Vihabra's Magin's Irish Gold.

Vagabond's Lady Sunshine, winning under Phoebe Harris (breeder of the great Bang Away) at the San Fernando Valley Boxer Club on October 20, 1979. Handled by Eleanor Linderholm-Wood.

Ch. Bentbrook's Talk of the Town (by Am-Can. Ch. Jodi's Jeremiah ex Ch. Bentbrook's High Potential), bred and owned by Barb Carroll.

BENTBROOK

Bentbrook has been actively breeding and showing since 1976 when Barb Carroll acquired the outstanding foundation bitch, Ch. Huff and Highland Fling. Since then, Bentbrook has gained recognition by winning at many Boxer Specialties, as well as ABC and regional competitions. After six generations of selective linebreeding that produced nine champions, the breeding program continues.

TELSTAR

The desire to have a Boxer as a family companion stemmed from Jennifer Tellier's fond memories of a rambunctious Boxer owned by her uncle while growing up in England.

Initially, like so many fanciers, Gene and Jennifer Tellier's intention was just to find an attractive, good-natured pet. Their search for such a Boxer brought them to the home of Glenn and Zona Grupe's Glennroe Boxers, and the subsequent purchase of a very promising eight-week-old female who became Ch. Glennroe Opensesame, an ABC Dam of Merit. Gene and Jennifer, who live in San Diego, have always felt fortunate to have had such an outstanding foundation female as their very first Boxer.

In 1977, Opensesame was bred to Ch. Glennroe Eldorado, which produced an outstanding male by the name of Ch. Telstar's Court Jester. Shown from the Bred-by-Exhibitor class, this dog won a Best of Breed at the prestigious Beverly Hills Show over nine top Specials of the day.

In 1978, Opensesame was bred to Ch. Araby's Shortstop, producing Telstar's first ABC Sire of Merit, Ch. Telstar's Highflyer. A sister to Highflyer called Ch. Telstar's Pride-n-Joy, later bred to Ch. Telstar's Court Jester, produced Ch. Telstar's Front Runner, an ABC Sire of Merit.

Opensesame's third breeding was to the British import Eng. Ch. Steymere Summer Gold. This produced Ch. Telstar's Tristan.

Littermates Ch. Telstar's Stargazer and Ch. Telstar's Starmaker, SOM (by Int. Ch. Mephisto's Vendetta ex Telstar's Peppermint Pleaser), owned and bred by Gene and Jennifer Tellier, handled by Gary Steele and breeder Jennifer Tellier.

Ch. Telstar's Bravissimo, Ch. Telstar's Starmaker at 11 years old, and Ch. Telstar's Moon Pebbles, owned by Gene and Jennifer Tellier.

The 1981 breeding to Ch. Mephisto's Vendetta with a Shortstop ex Opensesame daughter produced Telstar's third ABC Sire of Merit, Ch. Telstar's Starmaker.

These earlier breedings laid the foundation for the Telstar line. The 1988 breeding to Ch. Berena's Gemini Splashdown brought their line full circle, combining the very best of some of the day's top producers. The Splashdown breeding produced a lovely bitch, Ch. Telstar's Moon Pebbles, and Ch. Telstar's Good Time Charlie. Telstar has produced over two dozen U.S. champions including three Sires of Merit.

As an avid owner-handler, Jennifer continues to reap the benefits of showing her own dogs and strives to encourage other new hopefuls to try to perfect the art of showing to experience to the fullest the thrill of being a part of a winning combination.

One of Jennifer's other endeavors is her work in bronze sculpting, in which she specializes in Boxers. Using the Boxer as her prime subject seems to come naturally, after all, breeding is an art form in itself.

TO-RINI

To-Rini Boxers of Thomas R. Squicciarini, Massapequa Park, New York, obtained its first Boxer in 1969. She was bred three years later in 1972 to produce Mex. Ch. To-Rini's Yankee (Best Puppy All-Breeds in Mexico 1974). Ch. To-Rini's Silverlining, Braz. Ch. To-Rini's Alegria's Sequel and Ch. To-Rini's Heidi's Golden Image are homebred. Ch. To-Rini's Contessa Victoria earned her championship with back-to-back five-point majors at the 1987 ABC Regional.

Tom Squicciarini is a member of the American Boxer Club and the Boxer Club of Long Island. He has served the latter as president, vice president, match show chairman, Specialty show chairman, director and delegate to the ABC. In addition he is a committee member of the ABC and serves as a steward at the annual Specialty.

Tom became licensed to judge Boxers in 1984 and was later approved to judge all Working breeds, the Working Group, Best in Show, Junior Showmanship and nine Herding breeds.

Ch. To'Rini's Heidis' Golden Image (by Ch. Kojoman of Five T's ex To'Rini's Allegria) bred by Tom Squicciarini, handled by Chic Ceccarini.

INTERLUDE

Jerry and Dot Bryant of Granger, Indiana, home of over 30 Interlude Boxer champions, obtained their first show/breeding Boxer, My-R's Interlude, from Lorraine Meyer of My-R's Boxers in 1968. With Lorraine's guidance, they bred My-R's Interlude to Ch. My-R's Marquette, and in 1970 she produced their first champion, Ch. My-R's Mohave, a Group winner. Out of this line, Ch. Interlude's Van Tug E No, who won numerous breed and Group placements, was produced.

Interlude then ventured into the Fashion Hint line and acquired Ch. Goodmanacre Jet of Interlude, who was a champion producer. Next, Abednego produced three champion littermates, Ch. Vel-Kel's Big Ben, DOM, Ch. Interlude's Current Edition and Ch. Interlude's Current Issue. Then Interlude Boxers turned to the TuRo line by purchasing a Traper son, Ch. Araby's Blackwatch, SOM. He sired 12 champions including the 1989 ABC Grand Prize Futurity winner, Ch. Thanque Joy of Interlude. Also finishing from this litter were Ch. Interlude's Punch Line, Ch. Interlude's Make My Day and Am-GR Phil. Ch. Interlude's Strike Force, top show dog all-breeds for three straight years.

Ch. Interlude's Its About Time (by Ch. Huffand's Nice Enough, SOM ex Thanque Yankee Doodle Joy, DOM) was a multiple specialty show winner for owners Jerry and Dot Bryant.

Ch. Araby's Black Watch, SOM (by Ch. Marquam Hill's Traper of TuRo ex Ch. Lilliput's Black Magic), owned by Jerry and Dot Bryant and Walter Pygman.

Ch. Thanque Joy of Interlude (by Ch. Araby's Black Watch ex Thanque Yankee Doodle Joy) was the Futurity Grand Prize winner at ABC in 1989. Owners, Jerry and Dot Bryant.

Ch. Bitwyn's Star of Kings Pt, DOM (by Ch. Vel-Kel's Big Ben ex Bitwyn's New England Summer), Ch. Bitwyn's Orion of Chal-Vic, CD (by Ch. Merrilane's April Fashion ex Ch. Bitwyn's Star of Kings Pt), Ch. Bitwyn's Star of Orion (by Ch. Bitwyn's Orion of Chal-Vic, CD ex Bitwyn's Stars and Stripes), Ch. Starfire's Flame of Bitwyn (by Ch. Bitwyn's Royal Flush ex Ch. Bitwyn's Star of Orion), and littermates Ch. Bitwyn's Dynamite v. Thorwood and Ch. Bitwyn's Debonair v. Thorwood (by Ch. Thorwood's Brigadier ex Ch. Starfire's Flame of Bitwyn), owned by Dr. and Mrs. J. Samuel Bitler.

BITWYN

Sam and Win Bitler's Bitwyn Boxers of Andover, Massachusetts, has been a family hobby since 1969, with over 30 champions to their credit. Their daughter Allison started showing in Junior Handling at age 12 and immediately went into the conformation ring, finishing over 10 Boxers as a teenager.

Although no Bitwyn champion has ever been Specialed by a professional handler, several have obtained Group placements, including a Group One by Ch. Bitwyn's Beau Brummel.

Ch. Silkwood's Coquette, Ch. Bitwyn's Flying Apache Chief and Ch. Bitwyn's Uptown Girl, owned by Jeff and Karen Ontell and Win Bitler, handled by Karen, took the Breed many times in tough Eastern competition.

Ch. Bee-Mike's Foxfire (by Ch. Shieldmont's Dimension ex Bee-Mike's Carbon Copy), bred by Bruce and Betty Mentzer and owned by Betty Aikenhead, is one of the foundations for the Sandhill breeding program.

Ch. Bitwyn's Beau Brummel (by Ch. Starfire's Brandy Alexander ex Bitwyn's Trinket of Maceire), owned by Arline Ellis and bred with Dr. and Mrs. J. Samuel Bitler and M. McNulty, and handled by Allison Bitler.

SANDHILL

Although involved for over 30 years, John and Betty Aikenhead's Sandhill Boxers has always been on a small scale (city laws limit them to three dogs). This limitation very quickly reinforced their demand for soundness of mind and body, coupled with the Boxer "type." Their ten show champions and their non-champions have all been complete family dogs. These spirited showoffs also have bed privileges!

In the early years, they were supported by the encouragement and advice of Phyllis King (Canzonet), Trella White (Helixview) and Al and Ruth Lee (True Lee), even though their dogs were not acquired from them. They strive to be worthy of these breeders.

The '80s required a new start and the Aikenheads acquired two lovely bitches, Ch. Bee-Mike's Fox Fire and Ch. Wesan's Sun Daze. They are the foundation of their current breeding and showing program. There are champion and winning youngsters on the East coast, in the South, in the Midwest and in California with Sandhill moms.

Ch. Hi Hill's Rave Review, DOM (by Ch. Heldenbrand's Ks Kid By Peddler ex Hi-Hill's Summer Shadows), bred by Donna Titus and owned by Cheryl Colby and Leon De Priest, is the foundation for the Hollycrest breeding program.

Ch. Wesan's Sun Daze, DOM (by Ch. Baldr's Sun Smoke ex Wesan's Rainy Daze) was acquired by Betty Aikenhead of Sandhill in the late 1980s and is one of the foundations of their current program.

Ch. Van Down-Kings Fire Alert, SOM (by Ch. Bropat's Red Alert of Asgard ex Ch. Vandown's Laguna Rose), owned by Fred and Carey King.

Ch. Hollycrest's Farm Hand, SOM with some of his champion progeny: Ch. Firestar's Parson, Ch. Hollycrest's Night Life, Ch. Hollycrest's Night Lite, Ch. Hollycrest's Sodbuster, and So-Am. Ch. Hollycrest's Special Export. Owner, Cheryl Colby.

HOLLYCREST

The Hollycrest Boxer of today owes much to two outstanding dogs—Ch. Hi Hill's Rave Review and Ch. Hollycrest's Farm Hand. Each of these dogs has contributed much to the breeding program and show record. Rave Review, a champion at nine months of age, finished with an impressive record in 13 shows. On to the whelping box, she achieved Dam of Merit status. Farm Hand, also a top winner, has produced 13 champions and is also a Sire of Merit. Hollycrest is a small kennel that has owned and/or bred 16 champions. They like to think that Boxer puppies are made in Heaven and God drops them off at Hollycrest!

CAMNIC

Though only "sometime" breeders and exhibitors of show Boxers, Bill and Camille Nicholson have been fortunate enough to have owned and bred a few "good ones" along the way. However, they now have only two young champion bitches with them at this time. Both are highly pedigreed and have won handily at major shows, but, as always, they must now await their hoped-for successes in the brood box.

A few years back, while at Crufts, they met Dr. Bruce Cattanach and prevailed upon him to allow them to acquire his homebred Ch. Steymere's Summer Gold. This lovely big dog then stood stud in the U.S. until his untimely death. Possibly, there may be some historical implications to this. As far as they know, he is the only English champion to have come to American shores in the last 50 years or so.

Eng. Ch. Steynmere Summer Gold (by Eng. Ch. Seefeld Goldsmith ex Eng. Ch. Steynmere Ritzi Miss), bred by Dr. Bruce Cattanach and owned by Bill and Camille Nicholson, breeder-owners of Ch. Camnic's Tom Tom, campaigned in the early 1970s.

CH. ROCHIL'S GRANDE MARSHALL

Ch. Rochil's Grande Marshall is out of Sire of Merit Ch. Har-Vel's Gold Express and Dam of Merit Ch. Rochil's Kallista of Marburl, and was bred by Perry and Sandi Combest. Affectionately called "Maxx," Grande Marshall was handled throughout his show career by Michael Shepherd.

In May 1986, Maxx completed his championship by winning Winners Dog at the American Boxer Club's Specialty at 14 months of age. Three months later, Maxx won BOB at the ABC Regional Specialty in Denver. Thus his career as a Special was born. His career record included 268 Best of Breeds; 94 Group Ones, garnered under 63 different judges; 21 all-breed Bests in Show, won under 18 different judges; and 18 Best in Show Specialty wins, under 18 different judges.

By the end of 1986, Maxx was destined to be one of the top-winning Boxers of all times. Before he was two years of age, he was awarded three all-breed Bests in Show, 24 BOBs, five Group Ones and multiple Group placements. He continued to win consistently during the next three years. In 1987 and 1988 he was the recipient of ABC awards for the dog winning most Bests of Breed, Group Ones and Bests in Show. In 1988, Maxx was recipient of the coveted Kal-Kan Pedigree Award and the *Boxer Review* named him Best in the South. Also in 1988

came the ABC's premiere Top Twenty competition and this prestigious award went to Ch. Rochil's Grande Marshall—the first Boxer to win this coveted award.

He was shown on a more limited basis in 1989, yet he still garnered an outstanding record of wins, most importantly Best of Breed at Westminster Kennel Club and second place in the Group behind the Best-in-Show-winning Doberman Pinscher. The *Boxer Review* named him Number One Boxer in the South again in 1989. Maxx was retired from the ring in the early spring of 1990, yet still received enough Best of Breed wins to be the Number One Boxer in the South once again in 1990.

Following his retirement, he was selectively shown in the Veterans class and won that class at the ABC Regional Specialties in 1991 and 1992. From the Veterans class, Ch. Rochil's Grande Marshall was BOB at the Dallas Boxer Club Specialty in 1992.

Maxx has proven to be a great producer as well. In January 1993, he was the sire of 13 champions, making him Sire of Merit. Even though Maxx is a "southern boy" and was recognized repeatedly for his wins in the South, he has shown and won from coast to coast. His progeny also can be seen from the East coast to the West coast as well in Canada, Mexico, Colombia and Thailand. In 1991, Maxx was represented in the Top Twenty competition through a champion son and daughter.

Ch. Rochil's Grande Marshall, SOM (by Ch. Har-Vel's Gold Express ex Ch. Rochil's Kallista of Marburl), handled by Michael Shepherd, ranks among the top Boxers of his day and was the first to win the ABC Top Twenty award. Owners, Perry and Sandi Combest. Judges were Anne Rogers Clark, Beverly Sachs and Gene Haupt.

KARMEL

Jacquet's Kiri Te Kanawa, DOM came to live with Karin and Melvin Wilson in the summer of 1984. While visiting with Rick Tomita, Melvin touched the koi fish in Rick's pond and made a powerful wish, and off they went with Kiri to Georgia. She became an "Army brat" and, therefore, a seasoned traveler. Tired of roaming around the world, Kiri settled down to raise a family in 1988, and the powerful wish made at the pond came true.

In three breedings to Ch. Berena's Gemini Splashdown, Kiri produced one Canadian and eight American champions. Among them was Ch. Karmel's Dream Weaver, the 1991 ABC Grand Prize Futurity winner and Reserve Winners Dog. Kiri gets placed well at the ABC Specialties, ABC Regional and Pre-ABC Specialty shows. Her daughter, Ch. Karmel's Isabelle de Aragon, an Award of Excellence Winner at the 1991 ABC Specialty, produced the 1992 ABC Grand Prize Futurity Winner Karmel's Calendar Girl.

Kiri's accomplishments include an ABC Annual Award for Brood Bitch Producing the Most Champions for 1988–1989, a Brood Bitch of Merit Award in 1991 and winner of the Brood Bitch class at the 1992 ABC Specialty.

Jacquet's Kiri Te Kanawa's excellence is continuing through future generations. She has definitely made a dramatic mark on the Boxer world.

Am-Can. Ch. Karmel's Mister Countdown (by Ch. Berena's Gemini Splashdown ex Jacquet's Kiri Te Kanawa), owned by Richard Berry of Clov-Lan Boxers.

Jacquet's Kiri Te Kanawa, DOM (by Ch. Jacquet's Gaspard ex Nutwood's Renata de Jacquet) with her winning progeny, Ch. Karmel's Dream Weaver and Ch. Karmel's Flash of Neuleben. Judge Jane Forsyth, a long-time handler of Boxers herself, and the handlers are Karin Wilson and Dick and Christine Baum.

Above: Ch. Karmel's Tess d'Urberville (by Ch. Berena's Gemini Splashdown ex Jacquet's Kiri Te Kanawa, DOM), owned by Mel and Karin Wilson. *Below:* Karmel's Calendar Girl (by Ch. Jopa's Dr. Action ex Ch. Karmel's Isabelle de Aragon).

Above: Ch. Karmel's Isabelle de Aragon (by Ch. Berena's Gemini Splashdown ex Jacquet's Kiri Te Kanawa, DOM), owned by Mel and Karin Wilson. *Below:* Ch. Karmel's Dream Weaver is a multiple BOB and Group placer, owned by Karin and Melvin Wilson.

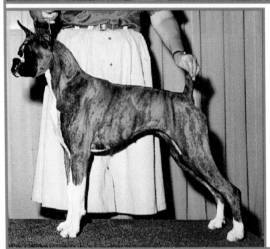

Ch. Karmel's Windsong (by Ch. King's Mojave ex Ch. Karmel's Lillie Langtree), owned by Michael, Lorin and Justin Taylor, bred by Karmel Boxers

Above: Ch. Ewo's Dream Girl (by Ch. Karmel's Dream Weaver ex Ch. Ewo's Crystal), owned by Muriel Miller. *Left:* Can. Ch. Karmel's Dante's Sassafras, DOM (by Ch. Berena's Gemini Splashdown ex Jacquet's Kiri Te Kanawa, DOM), owned by Lee and Brenda Muirhead.

Ch. Karmel's Dream Weaver, Am-Can. Ch. Karmel's Mister Countdown and Am-Can. Ch. Karmel's Flash of Neuleben, owned by Jaime Edmonson and Richard Berry. Judge, Betty Claire Frohock. Handlers, Nora McGriskin, Kim Pastella and Cindy Crawford.

In 1947, Burton Chait of Rock Tavern, New York got his first Boxer, a son of Ch. Warlord of Mazelaine. The dog was not shown at this time, as Mr. Chait was showing hunters and jumpers at horse shows, as well as breeding and racing thoroughbred horses in the United States and abroad.

After many years of successful racehorse breeding and showing, and with Burton unable to continue riding, the Chaits decided to show Boxers. It fit better into their new lifestyle of spending time on both coasts due to extensive involvement in the movie and entertainment fields.

A son of Ch. Happy Ours Fortune De Jacquet was obtained, and showing began with the now Ch. Jacquet's Sylvester, followed by Ch. Jacquet's Garbo. The first eight Boxers acquired by the Chaits were finished to their championships and some were Breed winners or Group winners.

Felice and Burt decided to develop their own Boxer line and, because of their involvement with show business, decided to use as their kennel name, "MGM Boxers Kennel of the Stars." The primary line, originating with top Jacquet Boxers, has been carefully blended with very select outside breedings. They base their breeding theory on a lesson that Mr. Chait learned while breeding racehorses with the late great thoroughbred breeder of Spendthrift Farm, Leslie Combs: "Breed the Best to the Best and hope for the Best."

They have already produced Ch. MGM's Fred Astair and Ch. MGM's Academy Award and have an extensive lineup to continue their chorus line of champions.

Ch. Jacquet's Sun Hawk (by Ch. Merrilane's April Holiday ex Ch. Jacquet's Mercer), litter brother to Ch. Merrilane's Knockout, owned by Burton and Felice Chait, bred by Rick Tomita, Paul Small and Merrilane Kennels.

Above: **Ch. Sergi 'N' BJ's Top Design of MGM (by Sergi's 'N' BJ's Junior Strut, SOM ex Sergi's 'N' BJ's Santara, CD), owned by Burton Chait, bred by Mariann Sergi and Betty Jean McVay and handled by Carmen Skinner. Judge Francine Schwartz.** *Below:* **Ch. Jacquet's Sylvester (by Ch. Happy Ours Fortune de Jacquet ex Jacquet's Bunny Bailey), owned by Burton and Felice Chait. Judge Mary Freer.**

Above: Ch. Jacquet's Garbo (by Int. Ch. Jacquet's Urko ex Jacquet's Lady Berengaria), owned by Burton and Felice Chait and bred by Richard Tomita. Judge, Dr. Donald Edwards. *Below:* Ch. Jacquet's Barrymore of MGM (by Int. Ch. Jacquet's Agassiz ex Saddleridge's Diamond Gem), bred by Richard Tomita and Loretta Lynch, owned by Burton Chait and handled by Kathy Kirk.

Above: Ch. Jacquet's Obsession (by Int. Ch. Jacquet's Urko ex Ch. Jacquet's Golay), owned by Burton and Felice Chait and bred by Richard Tomita, winning under judge Anita Clemente with handler Gerald Hughes. *Below:* MGM's Kitty Hawk, bred and owned by Burton Chait.

CROSSROAD

The mother-daughter team of Dorothy Hart and Ruth Appleby, along with their husbands, Marshall Hart and Patrick Appleby, created Crossroad Boxers in 1990. Although this is not a very long time, they have produced some very nice Boxers.

Starting off the search for a pet for the family, Ruth and Pat looked around for a Boxer. They purchased a nice fawn male that also turned out to be a pretty nice show dog. Ruth and her mother, Dorothy, decided to see just what a show Boxer should look like and went to a few local shows. From there, they were "hooked" and they started looking for a show bitch to keep their male company.

They found Vandown's Black Velvet, "Margo," and purchased her from Paul Van Sinden in April 1990. Margo was so much fun to show and was a great favorite of the ringside crowd. Margo finished her AKC championship in March 1993. She was bred three times: once to Ch. Talisman's Vigilante, producing Ch. Crossroad's Up In Smoke; second to Ch. Glennroe Rum Runner, producing Ch. Crossroad's Movin On Up; and finally to Ch. Heldenbrand's Jet Breaker, producing four very nice show puppies.

Margo was chosen Best of Breed twice, the first time she was in the Specials ring, and only four months after

Am-Can. Ch. Manor Hills My Fair Lady (by Am-Can. Ch. Siegels Sudden Empac ex Can. Ch. Manor Hills Lady Anne, CD), owned and bred by Julian and Vera Gladstone. Handler, Cindy Crawford. Judge Patsy Connolly.

Am-Can. Ch. Crossroads Movin On Up (by Ch. Glennroe's Rum Runner ex Ch. Vandowns Black Velvet), bred by Dorothy Hart and Ruth Appleby, owned by Tony and Sherti Christian and handled by Cindy Crawford under judge Stan Flowers.

her second litter was born. What a thrill that was, particularly because Paul was there to see it. He died a month later.

Margo is no longer producing puppies, but Crossroad has bred its second generation. Ch. Crossroad's Up in Smoke produced an excellent puppy, dog Jems Barcomm I'm a Lucky One. Crossroad's Night Life has already given them four very nice brindle females.

Crossroad Boxers is a young family-oriented breeding program that plans to continue breeding and showing these exceptional dogs, striving to please both judges and owners alike. Primary handler for Crossroad, Cindy Crawford of Napa, California acquired her first Boxer champion—Am-Can. Ch. Lady Katherine of the Cascades, Am-Can. UD. Cindy has been showing dogs since early 1970. She qualified for Junior Handling at Westminster four times. Boxers are always a joy for her even though she now handles other breeds too. Presently, she doesn't own a Boxer due to a potential conflict with her clients. She says that her very favorite Boxer to show has been all of them and that each one was special. Of course winning at ABC is a great thrill. Since 1989 she has won two Awards of Merit, two RWD, two Futurities and many classes.

Ch. Pinebrook's Innuendo, SOM (by Am-Can. Ch. Pinebrook's Well Tailored ex Fiero's Cassie), owned by Tom and Arlene Perret.

PINEBROOK

One cannot speak of the beloved Ch. Pinebrook's Radiation without remembering his dam, Oliver's Happy Talk, plain and brindle. "Happy" came into their home and hearts at seven weeks of age in 1966. She delivered their first two champions, Ch. Pinebrook's Radiation and Ch. Pinebrook's Radiance from her first litter. Radiation was outstanding from the beginning. At seven months of age, he was Reserve Winners Dog at the Ohio Boxer Club Specialty (his first show) under Dr. Robert Burke and repeated this feat two weeks later at Genesee Valley under Jerry Broadt. Next came the regional weekend in Texas where he acquired another Reserve and Best Puppy at the Houston Boxer Club Specialty under Dr. R. C. Harris. Two days later, at the Corpus Christi all-breed show, he gained a five-point major and Best of Breed over Specials, (one of them a Best in Show winner) under Joe Gregory, achieving a Group Three under Ray Norsworthy, all from the 9–12 Puppy class. He finished at the Ohio Boxer Club Specialty at 13 months of age under Langdon Skarda. Shown very sparingly as a Special, he was Best of Breed at the Orange Coast Boxer Specialty, Heart of America Specialty and all-breed with a Group Two. At seven years of age and still looking like a two-year-old, he won the Veterans class at ABC and was in contention with a two-year-old for Best of Breed. Radiation became a Sire of Merit, siring 13 champions. Some of his offspring have made an impact around the world, including Japan, Argentina and Brazil. Ch. Pinebrook's Trade Mark made his mark in Brazil by becoming Top Producer. He also sired Best in Show Ch. Karjean's Premonition. Ch. Pinebrook's Taste of Honey was only one of two fawns that he ever sired. One judge commented after awarding him Best of Breed that he was all dressed up in his tuxes. He was a black brindle.

Ch. Kimber-D Pinebrook Dusty Road is an outstanding young dog sired by Ch. Pinebrook's Innuendo. His first show at six months of age brought him a Reserve Winners Dog under John Connolly, starting him on his winning ways. By the time "Dusty" was seven months

old, he had eight points, one major, two Bests of Breed over Specials and a Grand Sweepstakes win. His owners are Travis and Dale Harris and Tom Perret.

Ch. Pinebrook's Replica is the son of Ch. Pinebrook's Innuendo, who finished at 13 months of age. He earned a five-point major from the 6–9 Puppy class with a Boxer entry of 140. He finished with three majors. Replica is owned by Tom and Arlene Perret.

Ch. Pinebrook's Innuendo has four champions: Ch. Pinebrook's Autumn Gold (owned by Sue Hageman and Arlene Perret), Ch. Pinebrook's Liberty Lady (owned by Holly Harris and Arlene Perret), Ch. Pinebrook's Replica and Ch. Kimber-D Pinebrook Dusty Road, who was Best of Breed at the 1995 ABC.

HAR-VEL

Harold and Velda Rounsaville of Tulsa, Oklahoma got their first Boxer in 1960. He was a Ch. Canyonair Hickory Dick, CD grandson. In 1972 they got their first bitch. She was acquired form Harold's brother, Carl, and his wife, Mary. After Harold and Velda paid the stud fee, they got the pick puppy. She was named Rounsaville's First Fancy. She was bred and produced Rounsaville's Autumn Gold. She was bred to Ich Brumble Carolina Star and gave them Har-Vel's Sweet-N'-Sassy. They quit using the Rounsaville prefix because of the length of it, which limited the use of other names with it. Sweet-N'-Sassy was the Har-Vel foundation bitch. She produced two ABC Sires of Merit: Ch. Har-Vel's Gold Express and Ch. Har-Vel's Josh's Gold, CD. The sire of these two was Int. Ch. Marburl's Joshua. Each of these Sires of Merit in turn produced a Sire of

Ch. Pinebrook's Radiation, SOM (by Candlewood's Straight Shot ex Oliver's Happy Talk) proved an outstanding show dog and producer for Tom and Arlene Perret.

Merit. Ch. Har-Vel's Gold Express produced Ch. Rochils Grande Marshall, while Ch. Har-Vel's Josh's Gold, CD produced Sire of Merit Ch. Jo-San's Future Time. He is a result of a full brother-sister breeding (Ch. Har-Vel's Josh's Gold ex Har-Vel's Gold Dust).

Harold and Velda's first champion was Ch. Har-Vel's Gold Chips, who was a litter sister to Sweet-N'-Sassy. Gold Chips produced their ABC Dam of Merit, the great producing bitch Ch. Oliver's Solid Gold, who they bought from Emmett and Mary Oliver, the owners of the famous Ch. Treceder's Sequel. Ch. Oliver's Solid Gold, fondly known as "Candy," was the ABC Dam of the Year for 1989. Can. Ch. Glencotta's Gunsmoke of Rochil, owned by the Wainwrights, a CKC Sire of Merit, is a product of Har-Vel breeding through Ch. Rochils Grande Marshall, his sire.

Velda's mentors were Virginia Latham (Valatham Boxers), Pat Childers (Childer's Boxers) and Aimee Acklen (Ackland Boxers). Velda herself is now a mentor to many new breeders who have sought her advice on breeding. Harold and Velda have always used top-quality producing sires in their breeding program.

STAR HAVEN

BY SUSAN WILLIAMS

Alaska is known as the Great Frontier: a cold and beautiful place that can be very treacherous for people, but the dangers it can hold for animals can be life-threatening.

I own five Boxers and have lived in Anchorage, Alaska for over ten years. Each winter is a new experience and offers new problems to solve.

The depth of snow we get always creates a new situation. When the snow starts getting too deep, we find ourselves shoveling a patch through the yard for the dogs so that they are able to get some exercise and relieve themselves without being literally belly-deep in snow.

I clean their feet each time they come in from outside to dry them off and get the snow that is packed in their pads. There are times when they come in with bloody paws because they have lost some of the pads

Ch. Har-Vel's Josh's Gold, CD, SOM (by Ch. Marburl's Joshua ex Har-Vel's Sweet 'N Sassy), bred by Velda I. and Harold Rounsaville, owned by Sandra Lynch.

due to the extreme cold. The temperature warming up and then freezing again creates an icy crust on top of the snow. As the dogs run around the yard, their weight causes them to break through the crust and this may also cut their feet.

However, my dogs love the snow. They chase the snowflakes and like to dig and roll around in it. They are like children and sometimes need to be reminded to come in because of the cold. Extreme cold invites the danger of frostbite. You must give special care to keep tails, ears and testicles from freezing. In extreme cases, the animal may lose a tail, etc.

I have my own "Neighborhood Watch" each time I let the dogs outside—searching for moose that roam freely in the area. A four-foot fence offers no challenge to these large animals. Needless to say, when a dog and moose meet, the situation is very dangerous. The kick from a moose hoof can cut deeply through the skin or even kill the dog.

This Alaskan beauty is warmly loved by owner Susan Williams of the Star Haven prefix.

When the snow begins to melt, called breakup, it brings the mud and standing water, which brings the mosquitoes. Although all states have mosquitoes, the Alaskan mosquitoes are so large that it has often been referred to as the state bird. On short-haired dogs, the mosquitoes have an eating frenzy, which leaves large welts on the dogs' faces and bodies. Certain types of repellents attract the mosquitoes up here, but I have found that a mixture of water and Avon® Skin-So-Soft is the safest and most effective protection for both dogs and people.

We show our Boxers in both conformation and obedience. Training has its problems too. Because our winters are so long and cold, we have to do most of our training inside. Therefore, we need a building, which isn't always available or affordable. The majority of our shows and trials are held indoors. We have to work our dogs outside in the summer to get them used to the grass, bugs and car noises that they may encounter at other shows. Boxers don't think much of going down in the wet grass for an obedience exercise. I have one dog that loves the snow, but if it's raining, forget it!

If you ever feel in an advenTuRous mood, come up to one of our shows. Enjoy the hospitality and scenery. It's an experience you will never forget.

GLENNROE

Glennroe Boxers started in 1956 with an excellent foundation bitch, Beagood Fantasy, a double Bang Away granddaughter. In 1963, bred to Ch. Cloudland Citation, she produced the first champion for Glenn and Zona Grupe, Ch. Glennroe Christina. Including "Chris," 32 Glennroe Boxers have become champions.

Glennroe has produced three Dams of Merit: Ch. Glennroe Ingenue; her daughter, Ch. Glennroe Opensesame, who became the foundation bitch for the very successful Telstar line; and Ch. Glennroe Alexandria. "Sandy" was sold as a pet and then returned to the Grupes at three years of age when her owners moved out of the country. Surprised at her show potential, they entered her in a specialty, where she went Winners Bitch and Best of Winners for her first major, and she finished shortly thereafter.

A recent Sire of Merit is Ch. Glennroe Rum Runner. "Ricky" went on the Memorial Day circuit with one point and finished that weekend. One of his champions, Am-Can. Ch. Crossroads Movin' On Up, was winner of the 1994 ABC Futurity. Several other of his get are pointed and Glenn and Zona look forward to adding them to his list of champions.

The Grupes participated in the 1992 Top 20 competition with bitch Ch. Glennroe Tequila Sunrise and in the 1993 competition with bitch Ch. Glennroe Amaretto.

Being involved in this marvelous breed has been rewarding for the Grupes. They are pleased to have people tell them that a Glennroe Boxer is recognizable in the ring, and especially pleased to have handled the majority of their dogs to their championships.

Am-Can. Ch. Glennroe's Amaretto (by Ch. Tall Oaks Desert Dazzler ex Ch. Glennroe's Tequila Gold), bred by Zona Grupe and owned with Kathy Menshew.

Ch. Glennroe Rum Runner, SOM (by Ch. Telstar's Front Runner, SOM ex Glennroe Elated Echo O'Dolor), bred by Dolores Schell and owned by Glenn and Zona Grupe.

HOLLY LANE

Dr. and Mrs. McClintock started out with a pet Boxer, a flashy fawn named Jinx, who was given to them as a gift. Jinx was a treasured companion and after she died, Dr. McClintock wanted to own another Boxer—this time a champion. They purchased an eight-week-old fawn bitch, Sarazan's Love Story, who was sired by a son of Ch. Jered's Spellbinder. Love Story was eventually bred to Ch. Flintwood's Sundowner, SOM, and produced Holly Lane Cookie. Cookie became Holly Lane's first champion and is attributed to the good start for the early breeding of champions and producers. When bred to Ch. Brayshaw's Masquerader, SOM, she produced the famous Wind litter. All four in this litter finished their championships and the male, Ch. Holly Lane's Wildwind, became a Sire of Merit as well. Litter sister Ch. Holly Lane's Windstorm produced 11 champions. One of these, Ch. Holly Lane's Inherit the Wind, became a Sire of Merit and became a Best in Show winner handled by Eileen McClintock.

Dr. McClintock passed away in 1980, but Holly Lane has continued to produce champions. Some more recent dogs include Ch. Carlon's Classy Chasis, DOM, WB and BW at ABC, co-owned by Eileen McClintock and Bob and Carol Long; Ch. Heldenbrand Holly Lane, DOM, a leading ABC dam for two years; and Ch. Holly Lane's Irish Coffee, handled by E.B. Johnson and specialed by Mr. and Mrs. J.L. Streicher, now back at Holly Lane.

Eileen McClintock loves the excitement of competition but also loves to devote time to breeding.

Ch. Holly Lane's Windstorm, DOM (by Ch. Brayshaw's Masquerader ex Ch. Holly Lane's Cookie), owned by Dr. and Mrs. E. A. McClintock produced 11 champions for Holly Lane, tying for the most producing DOM of all time.

Ch. Carlon's Classy Chasis, DOM (by Ch. My-R's Haybinder of Holly Lane ex Ch. Carlon's Sassy N' Classy), owned by Bob and Carole Long and Eileen McClintock and handled by Stan Flowers.

Ch. Holly Lane's Irish Coffee (by Ch. Shieldmont's Let's Make A Deal ex Ch. Heldenbrand Raven Holly Lane) with handler E. B. Johnson. Breeder-owner, Eileen McClintock.

SKIDOO'S

Ed Morawski got his first Boxer in 1952, long before meeting his wife Wendy. When they got married, all he talked about was his "Mazelaine-bred Boxer" and how he wanted another Boxer. In 1980, they bought Joda's Top Brass, had him neutered and entered him in obedience. He earned his Companion Dog title. Their next purchase was Enko's Brass Penny. After finishing her CD, they decided to breed her. They kept a male from the litter, Skidoo's Modest Man, and, after finishing his CD, they decided to try the breed ring. They bred Modest Man once, and the pick of the litter became their first champion, Ch. Skidoo's Instant Replay. She had one litter by Ch. Summit View's Legal Tender. In this litter were one flashy brindle bitch, who became Ch. Skidoo's Forever Amber, and one plain fawn bitch, Skidoo's No Frills Oprah. Oprah was bred to Ch. Rosend's Bo Diddley and produced some promising puppies: Ch. Skidoo's Silhouette was Best Puppy at the ABC and finished in 12 shows from the 9—12 puppy class; litter brother Ch. Skidoo's Gotcha finished at 19 months; and litter sister Skidoo's Sincerely Yours followed shortly after. Ch. Skidoo's Forever Amber, litter sister to Oprah, has had one litter by Ch. Bullock's Isaiah of TuRo.

They have only had six litters since 1980, so they only have a very limited breeding program. Three of these bitches were spayed after one litter. Oprah had her second, and last, litter—a repeat with Bo Diddley that produced two promising bitches and one male.

Ch. Skidoo's Gotcha (by Ch. Rosend's Bo Diddley ex Skidoo's No Frills, DOM), owned by Ed Morawski and handled by Cheryl Cates.

Ch. Capriana's Renegade, SOM (by Ch. Marquam Hill's Comanche ex MGM's Matched Pennies Echo) was an influential stud dog behind famous lines including Woodcrest, Eldic, Huffand, Arriba and Jacquet. Handled here by a young John Connolly.

HUFFAND

In 1970 Linda Huffman and Carole Andrews Connolly founded Huffand Boxers. They have always had small in-home kennels and bred on a very limited basis; never breeding more than one litter a year, sometimes less.

Linda had purchased Ch. Arriba's High Hopes and Carole had purchased Arriba's Ultimate, from Dr. Ted Fickes of Arriba Boxers, which was their foundation. High Hopes was a grandson and Ultimate a great-granddaughter of John Connolly's first champion, Ch. Capriana's Renegade, SOM, the producer of 19 champions.

High Hopes and Ultimate produced Ch. Huffand's Charade who was then bred back to High Hopes. The results of this breeding produced a total litter of four flashy pups, all of which became champions. From this beginning, Huffand has had the pleasure and good fortune of finishing over 30 champions. Ch. Huffand's Showtime of Arriba, co-bred with Dr. Fickes, finished in 1994, representing the sixth consecutive generation of Huffand homebred champions.

The Dams and Sires of Merit at Huffand include Arriba's Ultimate, producer of 5 champions; Ch. Huffand's Charade, 6 champions; Ch. Huffand's Irish Rebel, 7 champions; Ch. Huffand's Nice Enough, 18 champions; and Ch. Wincaster's Tyger of Huffand, 10 champions.

Above: Ch. Huffand's Nice Enough, SOM (by Ch. Merrilane's April Fashion ex Ch. Huffand's High Society), owned by Carole A. Connolly and handled by Linda Huffman. Judge, Dr. Bernard Esporite. *Below:* Ch. Huffand's Irish Rebel, SOM (by Ch. Benjoman of Five T's ex Ch. Huffand's Charade), owned by Carole A. Connolly.

Above: Am-Can. Ch. Wincasters Tyger of Huffand, SOM (by Ch. Huffand's Irish Rebel ex Can. Ch. Jocolu's Buttons and Bows), owned by Carole A. Connolly and handled by Linda Huffman. Judge, Sam Pizzino. *Below:* Ch. Arriba's Showtime of Huffand (by Ch. Moon Valley's Main Attraction ex Ch. Huffand's Obsession of Arriba), owned by Carole A. Connolly.

Ch. Hi-Hat's Moonshadow v. Jacquet (by Int. Ch. Jacquet's Novarese ex Ch. Hi-Hat's Evening Sky v. Jacquet), bred by Leni Kaplan and Richard Tomita. Handler, Jerry Kaplan. Judge, Mrs. Eve Olsen Fisher.

HI-HAT

Hi-Hat Boxers is owned by Jerry and Leni Kaplan of Hamden, Connecticut. The Kaplans started out in the early 1970s with their first champion and foundation brood bitch Am-Can. Ch. Hi-Hat's Cameo of Donessle. Cameo's second breeding was to a Fashion Hint son, Ch. Becrelen's Imports, by whom she produced two champions, Hi-Hat's Other Side of Midnite, 1979 ABC regional winner; and Ch. Hi-Hat's Summer's Prelude.

Am-Can. Ch. Hi-Hat's Evening Sky-V-Arrow, 1992 Top Twenty contender, is the daughter of Ch. Arrow's Sky High and Hi-Hat's Evening Star. Her nephew, Nebula's Adams of Hi-Hat, is a Canadian champion. These are the principal dogs from which the Kaplans have been breeding most of the splendid winners they have been putting in the rings including Ch. Hi-Hat's Gigi V. Jacquet and Hi-Hat's Moonshadow V. Jacquet, daughter of Evening Sky.

Am-Can. Ch. Hi-Hat's Evening Sky v. Arrow (by Ch. Arrow's Sky High ex Hi-Hat's Evening Star), owned by Leni Kaplan.

VANCROFT

Vancroft Boxers began in 1983 with the purchase of two brindle bitches. Beebee and Farron were entered in a few shows and received a few points, though they never finished. However, Debbie Clark and Marcia Adams were hooked on showing Boxers!

In 1985, Debbie purchased a brindle puppy bitch from Audrey Gerhardy of Gerhard Boxers: Ch. Gerhard's String Of Pearls. Pearl is a Ch. Scarborough Norman Knight daughter out of Ch. Gerhard's Harbor Lights. She was specialed for a short time and was ranked Number Five Boxer before retiring to the whelping box.

In 1986, a fawn male, Druid's Own Scarb'ro Benchmark (a Norman Knight son) was acquired and finished in May 1987 under Jane Forsyth. His specials career began almost immediately and his success garnered multiple Group placements and a place in the first Top Twenty event for the American Boxer Club in 1989. He was shown there by Alberto Berrios and was ranked number 10. At this same national specialty, Pearl and Mark's litter debuted in the futurity in the 12—15 month classes. Four competed—a fawn bitch, two brindle bitches and a brindle dog. Rudy, Vancroft's Valentino, was chosen Best Junior by Dorothy McNulty and went on to finish his championship. The fawn bitch, Ch. Vancroft's Vintage Champagne, and a brindle bitch, Ch. Vancroft's Vogue, also finished their titles.

Pearl's third litter, out of Ch. Fiero's Tally-Ho Tailo, produced her fourth champion offspring, Ch. Vancroft's Moonlighting, on April 24, 1993. Pearl is Vancroft's first Dam of Merit.

Ch. Gerhard's String of Pearls, DOM (by Ch. Scarborough Norman Knight ex Ch. Gerhard's Harbor Lights), owned by Debbie Clark and Marcia Adams and handled by Carlos Rojas.

Ch. Vancroft's Valentino (by Ch. Druid's Own Scarb'Ro Benchmark ex Ch. Gerhard's String of Pearls), owned by Debbie Clark and Marcia Adams.

Ch. Vancroft's Primetime, SOM (by Ch. Misty Valleys Curtain Call ex Ch. Vancrofts Vogue), owned by Marcia Adams and Debbie Clark, was the top winning Boxer in the mid-1990s.

From that foundation litter, two bitches have already produced champion offspring. Ch. Vancroft's Vintage Champagne produced Ch. Vancroft's Heartstrings. Piper made her father a Sire of Merit on November 1, 1992. Ch. Misty Valley's Curtain Call ex Ch. Vancroft's Vogue produced a flashy brindle litter. "O.D." finished on March 6, 1993 and, among other Bests of Breed and Group placements, won a specialty Best Of Breed from the 12—18 month class for his first Major under Stephanie Abraham. He continued a Specials career that ranks him in the top five Box-ers in the country and won Westminster in 1997.

In January 1992, Vancroft also purchased a flashy fawn bitch from Steve and Ann Anderson of Rummer Run Boxers. Corey became Ch. Rummer Run's Red Encore in March of 1993 the day after O.D. finished.

In ten short years, Vancroft has finished 11 Box-ers and one Rottweiler, produced a DOM, a Best Junior in Futurity, a homebred specials dog and several promising puppies. The future of Vancroft Boxers lies ahead with the breeding program es-tablished by Deborah Clark.

The Vancroft family of Boxers with partners Debbie Clark and Marcia Adams.

GOLDFIELD

Ed Goldfield's first champion, Jacquet's Goldfield Rubi Doux, became a Dam of Merit in 1984. Since that time, Goldfield Boxers has finished over 20 champions. However, Ed Goldfield's love of the Boxer started way before 1984. Ever since he could remember, he was taken with this breed. As a young boy growing up in Philadelphia, he always had a dog, though they were usually the "Heinz 57" variety. He saw his first Boxer when he was about 12 years old. In the early 1940s, there weren't that many Boxers around, but after his first encounter with one, it left him with a lasting impression and he knew he would have a Boxer one day. To Ed, the breed encompassed everything he thought a dog should be: noble, elegant, yet very sturdy and rugged.

Ed acquired his first Boxer in 1946. He was of dubious background and had no papers. Also, his temperament was poor. He finally gave him to a friend who had a large ranch in the Imperial Valley. The dog lived a long and happy life.

Ed's next Boxer was a brindle male, a son of Ch. Kobang of Sirrah Crest. He was his first show dog—or so he thought. He was seven years old and had a beautiful mouth, except for one thing: his teeth were worn down to a nub. He showed him anyway. Ed was a neophyte when it came to showing. Adam did reasonably well, winning several large open classes and two reserves. Finally, after about ten shows, the prominent handler Ben Brown told Ed not to waste his time, as he was too old to be competitive. So Adam was retired.

Ed's next Boxer was a Ch. Canyonair's Hickory Dick daughter. However, Bitsy, as he called her, never got enough size. His early experiences with the Boxer were

Ch. Goldfield's Eye Dazzler (by Ch. Marquam Hill's Traper of TuRo ex Ch. TuRo's Mirage), handled by Gary Steele for owner Ed Goldfield.

Goldfield's Jade de Jacquet (by Ch. Jacquet's Black Watch ex Ch. Jacquet's Barbet of Goldfield), bred by Ed and Bryan Goldfield and the author.

at best not very rewarding. It seemed that every dog Ed owned was ill-fated in one way or another.

Next, Ed was co-breeder of a litter by Ch. Break Away of Sirrah Crest, a litter brother of Ch. Bang Away. He had the pick of the litter and selected a very stylish flashy black brindle bitch. Ed called her Tango. She was very outgoing, with a curious, precocious nature. She was an excellent show candidate, very elegant, with beautiful movement and a great attitude. Ed was just getting her ready to show when she was killed, and Ed was devastated.

Goldfield's Top Brass, Ed's next dog, was a tall brindle male, a Bang Away grandson. He showed him to the extent that he had 13 points and both majors. But disaster struck again. "Pepe" had a heart attack that ended his show career. After this series of mishaps, Ed decided not to breed or show for a while. Other things took precedence and, after a hiatus of some 20 years, Ed decided to get back into Boxers. Even though he had had a lot of bad luck in his early years, it gave him a good perspective for his second time around. He studied pedigrees and the early history of the Boxer voraciously.

Ed wanted to go to a top breeder who was consistently producing good dogs. That brought him to Rick Tomita and his Jacquet Boxers. He purchased a seven-month-old brindle bitch who finished in short order. As stated earlier, she was Ch. Jacquet's Goldfield Rubi Doux (DOM) and the foundation of Goldfield Boxers.

Rubi was bred to Ch. Happy Ours Fortune de Jacquet and produced Ch. Goldfield's Idol Maker, Ch. Goldfield's Noble Pride, Ch. Goldfield's Tango and Ch. Goldfield's Dorian de Jacquet. When bred to Ch. Jacquet's Urko, she produced Ch. Jacquet's Aliage of Goldfield. Next Ed acquired a fawn bitch puppy from Jacquet. She became Ch. Jacquet's Miss Bangaway. At the same time, Ed purchased an eight-month-old brindle bitch from TuRo Boxers. She became Ch. TuRo's Mirage. Heather was her call name. Heather produced only eight puppies, three of which became champions.

Heather was bred to Ch. Traper and produced Ch. Goldfield's Eye Dazzler and Ch. Goldfield's Eagle Dancer. She was then bred to Ch. Goldfield's Noble Pride and produced Ch. Gem of the Season.

In this same period of time, Ed purchased half ownership in a Cherokee Oaks bitch, Ch. Amber's Reward. He next acquired a fawn puppy bitch, again from Jacquet. She became Ch. Jacquet's Skylark. Skylark was Winners Bitch in a huge entry at the ABC regional in Dallas, Texas in 1985.

Then there were Ch. Ghad and his litter sister Japanese Ch. Sabina, the top-winning Boxer bitch in Japan. Next came Ch. Gamet's Fire Danz V. Goldfield, co-owned with breeder Gail Metzger. All three of the above were sired by Gamet's Native Diver of TuRo. Then came Ch. Jacquet's Greggson, co-bred and owned by Jacquet Boxers. Greggson is the sire of a very promising litter out of Siren, namely Bravo, Baron and Barbet. Ch. Jacquet's Safire of Goldfield, a most recent champion, is the litter sister to Stylemeister and Siren.

Bravo finished his championship in no time and began a remarkable career as a special. Bravo is followed by Ch. Jacquet's Bravo of Goldfield, co-bred and co-owned with Bryan Goldfield and Rick Tomita.

HI-TECH

The Hi-Tech Kennel of Dr. William and Tina Truesdale was established in 1984. Since that time, they have finished and/or bred over 20 champions.

However, their first contact with show dogs dates back to 1962, when Bill and his family owned, bred and showed Boxers. For example, Ch. Coranado's Christmas Carol was shown by George Rood. She was also shown in Junior Handling by Bill. In 1968, Bill took a pick-of-litter puppy from a Caprianas Brag About daughter out of their Tampico's Cactus Jack (Ch. Canzanets Musical Matinee ex Ch. Coranado's Christmas Carol). This puppy became Ch. Tampico's Buster Brown, shown to his first points and BOB over specials by Chuck Steele under judge Joe Gregory. He was finished by George Rood, who also campaigned him to multiple Breeds,

Ch. TuRo's Mirage (by Ch. Mephisto's Warlock of TuRo ex Obie One Knobe), handled by Marianne Caprino-Amado.

Groups and Bests in Show. He went BIS at Oakland County KC under Roy Ayers, defeating the famous Ch. Chinoe's Adament James, a three-time Westminster Breed-winning English Springer Spaniel. He also won the Group under Alva Rosenberg that day. Through his career he was owned by C.C. Truesdale and Alfred Claramunt.

In the '70s, Tina and Bill continued on with the Tampico kennel name when they bred their Tampico's Kandy Kiss, a Christmas Carol great-granddaughter, to Ch. TuRo's Trumpet. Three flashy puppies came from this litter: Miles, Niles and Giles. They showed the puppies at matches and some all-breed shows but later decided they just didn't have what it took for the show ring.

Ch. Hi-Tech's Arbitrage, SOM (by Am-Can. Ch. Fiero's Tally-Ho Tailo ex Ch. Boxerton Hollyhock), bred by Jo Anne Sheffler, owned by Dr. and Mrs. William Truesdale and handled by Kimberly A. Pastella. "Biff," as he is known to the fancy, was BOB at Westminster in 1994 and 1995, taking Group first and second, respectively. In all, he won over 50 Bests in Show, the Group over 150 times and the Breed over 300 times.

Rightly resting on his ribbons, Am-Can. Ch. Fiero's Tally-Ho Tailo, SOM (by Am-Can. Ch. Fiero's Smash Hit ex Fiero's Iva-Natu), bred by Ingrid Feder and owned by Hi-Tech Boxers, was a top winning and producing Boxer.

In 1985, they met Kimberly Pastella at a show and inquired about purchasing a quality Boxer to begin a breeding program. Since that July a union has been formed that has proved to be very successful.

Kim found them two male Boxers which both finished their championships in short order. A year later, the Truesdales purchased two bitches who both also finished their championships. However, it was not until they acquired Ch. Anchic's Passion of TuRo (Hopie) that their program really took off.

At about the same time, they acquired Am-Can. Ch. Fiero's Tally-Ho Tailo, who made his mark in the show ring on the 1988 national circuit. He won Grand Sweepstakes and BOW at New Jersey Boxer Club under Ms. Scottie Rutherford and Mr. Walter Pinsker respectively, and Grand Sweeps at Bucks County under Mr. Jack Ireland. He later went on to become a multiple-specialty winner, Group winner and all-breed BIS winner. However, his biggest contribution to the breed has been his ability to produce quality Boxers. The combination of the Hi-Tech bitches bred to this dog has brought great attention to his ability to produce.

Hopie and Tailo together produced his first champion and the first homebred for Hi-Tech, Ch. Hi-Tech's

Heir Apparent. This breeding was later repeated and produced Hi-Tech's Dream Girl (reserve 9—12 futurity—Mrs. Luella Steele) and Hi-Tech's Magnetic Attraction.

The next homebred champion for Hi-Tech was Ch. Hi-Tech's Current Affair (Ch. TuRo's Paragon of Pax ex "Hopie") who, when bred to Tailo, produced Hi-Tech's Current Event and Current Edition, who both won their respective classes at the 1992 ABC National.

The next litter was Ch. TuRo's Vision of Pax bred to their Ch. TuRo's Apollo, which produced Ch. Hi-Tech's Emperor (co-owned with Mr. Javier Ramirez), WD at ABC under Mrs. Dorothy McNulty. Two other champions also came from this litter, Ch. Hi-Tech's Rhapsody and Ch. Hi-Tech's Harmony.

Through this time, various other breedings have taken place at Hi-Tech with Tailo, resulting in many champion dogs and bitches.

A smashing addition to the Hi-Tech team is the Tailo son, Ch. Hi-Tech's Arbitrage ("Biff"). He was 1991 Reserve Futurity at ABC under Mrs. Luella Steele and the 1992 Top Twenty winner his first year eligible. He has also added to his record multiple specialties, Groups and Bests in Show, including BOB at ABC in 1994.

Am-Jap-Tai. Ch. Hi-Tech's Heir Apparent (by Ch. Fiero's Tally-Ho Tailo ex Ch. Anchic's Passion of TuRo), bred by Dr. and Mrs. William Truesdale.

Handled by Kim Pastella, Ch. Hi-Tech's Aristocrat (by Ch. Hi-Tech's Arbitrage ex Ch. Woods End Chas'N Rainbows) awarded Best Junior At Potomac Boxer Club by author Richard Tomita. Owners, Hi-Tech Boxers. Aristocrat went on to become a top winning champion.

THORN CREST

Thorn Crest Boxers is owned by Alice and Robert Helm of Williamsport, Pennsylvania. In the first few years of their existence, they attained three champions in the first two litters. Their progeny have won Bests in Show, specialty Bests in Show and Grand Sweeps. Their foundation stud is Am-Can Ch. Salgray's HiJinx O' Thorn Crest.

Thorn Crest's Work of Art, who is owned by Ted Naranong in Thailand, has continued his winning streak, winning many more Bests in Show under a host of English, European and Asian judges. Ch. Thorn Crest's Masterpiece went to Malaysia and has already won two Challenge Certificates, with two reserve Bests in Show.

The 16-month-old Ch. Thorn Crest Safari, owned by Irene and Milt Troland, in just two months won ten Bests of Breed and nine Group placements, including two Group Ones. He has done well for such a young dog and he even won over the top Boxer twice.

Foundation stud for Thorn Crest is Am-Can. Ch. Salgray's HiJinx O' Thorn Crest (by Am-Can. Ch. Woods End Crown Sable ex Ch. Salgray's Call Me Madam), owned by Robert and Alice Helm.

Ch. Thorn Crest's Safari (by Am-Can. Ch. Salgray's HiJinx O' Thorn Crest ex Arkona's Amanda of Sand Hill), owned by Milt and Irene Troland.

Am-Mal. Ch. Thorn Crest Masterpiece (by Am-Can. Ch. Salgray's HiJinx O'Thorn Crest ex Thorn Crest's Misty Night), owned by Robert and Alice Helm.

Ch. Ell Bee's Just Watch Out, SOM (by Ch. Moreleen's Al-le-lu-ia, SOM ex Ell Bee's Young Kipper), owned by Leonard and Donna Blumberg, was the top Boxer in 1982 and a superior producer.

BREHO

Am-Can-SKC Ch. Ell Bee's Sonner Bee Travlin was bred by Donna and Lennie Blumberg of Dallas, Texas and is a double grandson of Ch. Ell Bee's Just Watch Out (SOM). Brenda Stuckey, owner of Breho Boxers in Jonesboro, Louisiana, is very proud of her Boxer, known at home as Buster Brown. Brenda has shown him in the States herself, winning his first five points and a four-point major from the puppy class with Best of Breed and a Group One. He has had several breed wins from the classes, was Winners Dog at the Boxer Club of Louisiana and finished with another four-point major and Best of Winners at the Dallas Boxer Club Specialty. He has also had a Group Three placement from the puppy class. He won his SKC championship in four shows, going Best of Breed at each, and winning three Group One placements and a Group Four. He has sired, in very limited breeding, one American champion and one Brazilian champion, and has several pups being shown.

Ch. Breho LoneStar Hearts Afire represents five generations of Heldenbrand owned and bred Boxers, and is by Ch. Heldenbrand's Heart Breaker(SOM) ex Ch. Heldenbrand's Breho Bonfire. "Charli" was Winners Bitch and Best of Winners from the 9—12 month class at the ABC regional specialty held in Dallas, Texas in 1992.

KOAWOOD

Gail and Clifford Lindsey of Koawood Boxers of Hawaii became serious exhibitors and breeders when, in 1985, Lois Matthews of Box M gave them the dog that would become their first champion—Ch. Box M Adonis of Seawest.

On July 4, 1989, Ch. Box M Adonis of Seawest and Ch. Box M Antoinette of Seawest (also owned by Koawood) produced Hawaii's top-winning Boxer for 1992, Ch. Koawood Star-Spangled Banner.

ECHO

Echo Boxers is owned by Terry and Caryl Agle of Davison, Michigan. It became apparent early on, with two dogs finishing their championships from one of the first litters whelped at Echo (one of which was Am-Can. Ch. Echo's Orange Ripple who was to become the foundation for Echo), that Boxers were to be an integral part of the Agles' future.

This small Michigan kennel has become successful with Terry guiding many Echo Boxers to their championships.

Ch. Echo's Believe It Or Not, SOM (by Ch. Araby's Black Watch ex Ch. Echo's Desiree), bred by Terry and Caryl Agle and owned by Vicki Bartlett, handled by Terry Agle.

Ch. Box M Adonis of Seawest (by Ch. Seawest Yuri Nuff of Box M ex Keka), owned by Clifford and Gail Lindsey.

Ch. Koawood Star-Spangled Banner (by Ch. Box M Adonis of Seawest ex Ch. Box M Antoinette of Seawest), owned by Clifford and Gail Lindsey.

THANQUE

The kennel name "Thanque" (*thank you*) has a meaning for owner Ruth Joste. First to Hollyce Stewart, the original "Mrs. Treceder," who started their kennel with a double Treceder bitch line and their first champion, Ch. Treceder's Adventure. To Leigh and David Hann, (Kachina Boxers), who made it possible for them to follow their breeding program. To all of their beautiful Boxers, (whom they loved) and the wonderful friends they made because of their Boxers.

Starting by outcrossing their double Treceder bitch, Treceder's Muchas Gracias, CDX, to Ch. Holly Lanes Winter Forecast, a bitch from that litter was bred to Ch. Merrilanes Holiday Fashion. This produced their first "Thanque" bitch, Thanque Poko, a Dam of Merit. With Leigh and David Hann, they bred Poko twice to Ch. Holly Lane's Diamond Replay. This produced Ch. Thanque Taos, Ch. Thanque Yopa Kachina and Ch. Thanque Kashi Kachina. Poko was then bred to Ch. Araby's Shortstop to produce Ch. Thanque Owag Kachina. Ch. Thanque Taos was bred to Ch. Virmar's Est and produced their second Dam of Merit, Thanque Yankee Doodle Joy. Joy was the dam of five champions sired by Ch. Araby's Black Watch. One of these, Ch. Thanque Joy of Interlude, better known as "Phoenix," was ABC Grand Futurity winner in 1989. Her breeders are Dorothy and Jerry Bryant, who handled her exclusively. Phoenix lived with their son and his wife—Craig and Donna Joste. They now carry on the Thanque name and breeding program.

Ch. Jacquet's Buster Brown (by Int. Ch. Jacquet's Novarese ex Ch. Jacquet's Maja), owned by Gerald and Katie Davis and bred by Carole Shea and Richard Tomita.

Am-Mex. Ch. Thanque Taos (Ch. Holly Lane's Diamond Replay, SOM ex Thanque Poko, DOM), bred by J. David Hann, was a Best in Show winner.

EL ENCANTO

El Encanto Boxers of Carole Shea of Saddle River, New Jersey, evolved from the purchase of a family pet as a companion to their aging Boxer. Carole knew she wanted a very dark brindle bitch with a black face who was pleasing to the eye. Jacquet's Sombra fit the bill, with the added features of excellent conformation and impressive pedigree. At the time, the Sheas were phasing out of showing and breeding horses, so it naturally followed that they became involved in showing and breeding Boxers.

Thet decided to follow a program of linebreeding, using top producing males. Sombra became the foundation bitch and spent all of her 13 years being *the boss* of the household.

Sombra produced two champions. Ch. Jacquet's Encanto, by Ch. Jacquet's Brass Idol, SOM, was a Best of Breed winner from the classes. He was campaigned on the West Coast by Alvin Lee, Jr. and finished in less than two months of showing. Sombra's second champion, Ch. Jacquet's Maja ("Raisin"), is the daughter of Int. Ch. Jacquet's Urko, SOM and was shown on both coasts also by Alvin Lee, Jr., finishing as a multi-Best of Breed and Group One winner from the classes.

Raisin has produced two US champions and one Brazilian champion by Int. Ch. Jacquet's Novarese, SOM. They are Ch. El Encanto's Chantaje Jacquet (finished at 14 months of age), handled by Carmen Skinner and Gerard Hughes; Ch. Jacquet's Buster Brown, owned by Gerald Davis and Katy Digulla; and Brazilian Ch. Jacquet's Mago El Encanto, the Number Three Boxer in Brazil for 1993 and 1994, and the Number One Male Boxer for those same years.

El Encanto has had five litters since 1983. All of their Boxers live in the house and are pets as well as homebred, home-raised champions.

Upper right: Ch. Jacquet's Encanto (by Ch. Jacquet's Brass Idol ex Jacquet's Sombra), bred and owned by Carole Shea and Richard Tomita.

Lower left: Ch. El Encanto's Chantaje Jacquet, DOM (by Int. Ch. Jacquet's Novarese ex Ch. Jacquet's Maja), owned by Carole Shea (handler) and Richard Tomita.

Lower right: Br. Ch. Jacquet's Mago El Encanto (Int. Ch. Jacquet's Novarese ex Ch. Jacquet's Maja), owned by Robert C. F. Bezerra and Nadja Gadelha Ponte and bred by Rick Tomita and Carole Shea, is a multiple Best in Show winner and number-one Boxer in Brazil.

Ch. Strawberry's Scintillation (by Am-Can. Ch. Strawberry's Caballero, SOM ex Am-Can. Ch. Strawberry's Evensong) is owned by Mr. and Mrs. Bruce Voran.

STRAWBERRY

Bruce E. and Judy Voran of Strawberry Boxers first obtained a Boxer male as a pup in 1980. Ch. Velmar's Howdy Kodo eventually finished his championship at the age of four under the guidance of Johnny Johnson. In the meantime, they purchased two bitches who actually finished before Kodo. They were Ch. Kar-Neil's Strawberry Sal and Ch. Indian Bend's Swiss Moca. "Sal" was a Ch. Marlbul's Joshua daughter and "Lucy" (Swiss Moca) was a Ch. Araby'sShortstop daughter. These two bitches formed the foundation of all of Strawberry's success. They took the name Strawberry as a kennel name from the small mountain community in Arizona where they have a home.

Sally was bred to Ch. Kar-Neil's Even Steven and the breeding produced Am-Can. Ch. Strawberry's Evensong ("Melody") who was finished and owned by the Burlesons of Marlburl fame and later returned to the Vorans as a gift to their son Michael. He did a great deal of successful handling while he was a high-school student both in the States and Canada. Lucy was bred to a Ch. Mephisto's Vendetta son, Can. Ch. Mephisto's Bandalero, which produced Am-Can. Ch. Strawberry's Caballero (SOM), known as "Cabby." Lucy was then bred to Am-Can. Ch. Mephisto's Zorro of LeBlanc,

Am-Can. Ch. Strawberry's Caballero, SOM (by Can. Ch. Mephisto's Bandelero ex Ch. Indian Bend's Swiss Moca) proved to be a popular choice in the Breed ring and sired champions in the US and abroad. Owners, Mr. and Mrs. Bruce Voran.

producing Ch. Strawberry's Son of Zorro. "James," as he was called, missed SOM status by just one champion having sired six champions.

Cabby was pointed mostly by the Vorans but was finished and campaigned by the late Chuck Steele of Tennessee. Cabby reached number ten during the period in which Ch. TuRo's Cachet, Ch. Wagner's Wilvirday Famous Amos, Ch. Laureate Kiss Me Kate and other greats were on the circuit. His specials career, including 15 BOBs, was quite impressive, and he produced 11 American champions, 2 Canadian champions and 4 Venezuelan champions.

His earliest Venezuelan champion was Ven. Ch. Richaire's Solid Gold. A litter brother of Solid Gold was Richaire's Christopher whom the Vorans finished and bred to "Tilly," as Ch. Strawberry's Scintillation, the product of a Cabby/Melody breeding, was known. The Tilly/Christopher breeding produced Ch. Strawberry's Blythe Spirit. Tilly was first bred to Ch. Arriba's CherKei Oh Boy and produced Ch. Strawberry's Glory Be. One of her champions out of Telstar's Starmaker (DOM) is Am-Ven. Ch. Strawberry's Star Gazer, owned by Oscar Rivero in Caracas, who also owns Am-Ven. Ch. Strawberry's Tango. Tango and her sister, Ch. Strawberry's Flamenco, are the rest of the last live breeding of Cabby to Blythe Spirit. Lastly, Monica Pinsker of Mephisto bred one of her bitches to Cabby to produce Can. Ch. Mephisto's Wine and Roses and Can. Ch. Mephisto's Red Baron.

Michael Voran handles Am-Can. Ch. Strawberry's Evensong (by Ch. Kar-Neil's Even Steven ex Ch. Kar-Neil's Strawberrry Sal) to Group placement. Owners, Mr. and Mrs. Bruce Voran.

TURO

After two years of research on the Boxer breed, Sandy Roberts and Pat Turner established TuRo Kennels in 1964 in Oklahoma City. Can. Ch. Hansparke's Fashion Fair and Hansparke's Dominique, purchased two years after Fashion Fair, became their foundation bitches. Both were sired by the famous Int. Ch. Millan's Fashion Hint.

After Fashion Fair ("Tootsie") finished her American championship, and after careful study of her pedigree, she was bred back to her sire, Fashion Hint. A product of this breeding, Ch. TuRo's Native Dancer, became a Sire of Merit with 18 champions. Tootsie also became a Dam of Merit and was the ABC's Top Producing Bitch in 1976.

Hansparke's Dominique produced one Canadian and three American champions for TuRo. One of these, Ch. TuRo's Truffian, became the foundation bitch for Bob and Carol Long's Carlon Kennels. Another important TuRo bitch was Ch. TuRo's Vanity Fair. She became a Dam of Merit and was the ABC's Top Producing Bitch in 1978.

Ch. Marquam Hill's Traper of TuRo, SOM (by Ch. Mephisto's Vendetta, SOM ex Ch. TuRo's Whisper of Five T's, DOM), bred by Dr. Robert Burke and owned by TuRo Kennels, is a Sire of Merit in the US and Canada.

Elizabeth Esacove joined TuRo in 1979 and brought with her Ch. TuRo's Touche (Ch. Benjoman of 5 T's ex Ch. Holly Lanes Baubles) and Ch. Mephisto's Warlock of TuRo (Int. Ch. Mephisto's Vendetta ex Can. Ch. Mephisto's Scarlet Lady). Touche became a Dam of Merit: she produced three champions when bred to Ch. TuRo's Trumpet, and another three champions when bred to Ch. Marquam Hill's Traper of TuRo. Traper dominated as the number one sire in the late 1980s, becoming the fourth top producing stud of all time. Ch. Mephisto's Warlock of TuRo produced Ch. TuRo's Mirage, a multiple Best of Breed winner owned by Ed Goldfield.

Native Dancer continued to impact TuRo's breeding program. His daughter, TuRo's Katrina of Cross Bar, produced a number of champions, the most notable being Ch. TuRo's Cachet. Cachet was purchased by Leonard and Susan Magowitz, and, after an extremely successful show career, became the foundation bitch for their Cachet Kennels. Some of her achievements are: being ranked in the Top Five Working Dogs for four years, including Number One in 1987; back-to-back Group firsts at Westminster in 1986 and 1987; and numerous BIS, BOB, Group firsts and specialty wins. Cachet was the cover dog for Anna Katherine Nicholas's lovely breed book *The Boxer* (also published by T.F.H.).

Pat Turner left TuRo in 1983, but Sandy Roberts and Elizabeth Esacove have continued to carry on the TuRo tradition of breeding quality Boxers. They put much research into their breeding program by carefully studying each Boxer's pedigree, selectively linebreeding and occasionally inbreeding. When they outcross, again, much research and planning go into each mating. Among the recent top winners are Ch. Kieblas Tradition of TuRo, a three-time ABC-winning bitch, and Ch. TuRo's Futurian of Cachet, the multiple-BIS and ABC winner.

Am-Can. Ch. Garnsey's Mad Max (by Ch. Cachet's Mad Max of TuRo ex TuRo's Fury of Cachet), bred and owned by Clayton Haviland IV. Handler, Debbie Struff.

Ch. TuRo's Chancellor of Donandru (by Ch. Marquam Hill's Traper of TuRo ex TuRo's Trinket of Philadel), bred by TuRo Kennels and owned by Ruth Pereira. Handler, Cheryl Robbins.

Ch. TuRo's Futurian of Cachet (by Ch. Cachet's High River Gambler ex TuRo's Charisma of Garnsey), bred by TuRo Kennels and Clay Haviland and owned by Jeffery and Nan Eisley Bennett. Handler, Gary Steele.

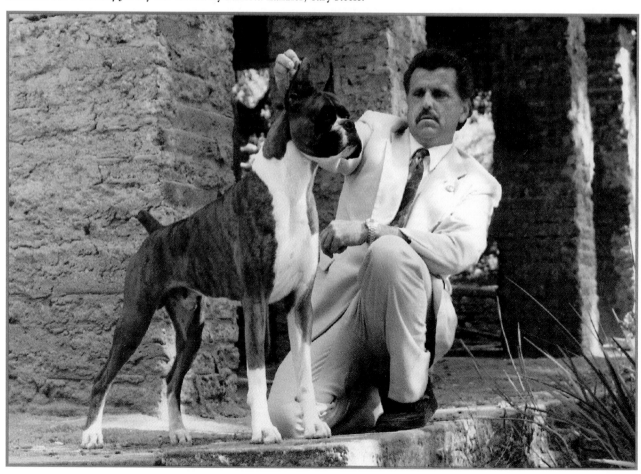

A great success was in the air for the young Cachet. Over the next four years, Cachet, handled by Chic Ceccarini, was the top Boxer in the country, all systems, and in the top five Working Dogs, including number one in 1987. When Chic took ill, his granddaughter, professional handler Kimberly Pastella, took over. Never a kennel dog, Cachet lived and slept in Chic's home. At the completion of her show career in 1987, she had compiled 33 BIS, 137 Group firsts, 40 Specialty wins and 380 BOBs. Among her prestigious wins were back-to-back Group firsts at Westminster in 1986 and 1987 and BOB at the ABC Nationals in 1986. She also went BOS at the ABC Regional in 1989 after having her second litter. Cachet was retired in 1987 to become the foundation bitch of Cachet Boxers and a beloved family companion.

Breeding Cachet was an awesome responsibility and one that we did not take lightly. There were many people with opinions on what should have been done. In the end, we went with our original plan devised with Liz and Sandy four years prior. She was bred back to her father, Ch. Marquam Hills Traper of TuRo, the fourth top-producing sire of all time. Unfortunately, none of the resulting puppies finished their titles, but two of the bitches can be found in many TuRo and Cachet pedigrees.

Cachet's second litter was by Ch. TuRo's Empire, resulting in Ch. Cachet's Mad Max of TuRo, SOM, Ch. Cachet's Casablanca of TuRo and Cachet's Minuet of TuRo. Mad Max won 14 points his second weekend out at very competitive Kentucky shows. Great plans are on the horizon for Cachet, including limited breeding and exhibiting of the Max sons.

A spectacular producer, Ch. Cachet's Mad Max of TuRo, SOM (by Ch. TuRo Empire ex Ch. TuRo's Cachet), owned by Leonard Magowitz.

Among the greatest of all Boxers is Ch. TuRo's Cachet (by Ch. Marquam Hill's Traper of TuRo ex Katrina of Cross Bar) with Chic Ceccarini.

CACHET

BY LEONARD MAGOWITZ

Cachet Boxers came into being in 1984 at a time that roughly corresponded with the acquisition of Ch. TuRo's Accolade. Accolade was a repeat breeding of Ch. TuRo's Cachet from TuRo Kennels. The Cachet prefix has been employed ever since. Cachet breeds only one or two litters per year, tightly linebred on TuRo. In the late '90s, Cachet bred a Mad Max daughter to Ch. Jacquet's Greggson after witnessing the great success Jacquet has had breeding to Mad Max.

TuRo's Cachet was acquired from TuRo Kennels in November 1982 as a birthday present for me by my wife Susan. I had actually met Sandy Roberts and Liz Esacove of TuRo Kennels at the Nationals the previous May, where I first saw a photograph of the young Cachet bitch. After much drama, she was purchased at around a year of age from Sandy and Liz—never was a puppy so carefully placed!

Left: Am-Can. Ch. TuRo's Dakota of Shar-Rea (by Ch. TuRo's Tidal Wave ex Ch. TuRo's Cherub of DJ) bred by S. Hollenshead and R. Armstrong. Owner, Willie Vicens. Owner in Japan, Dr. Nakazawa. *Right:* Ch. Cachet's Regent (by Ch. Marquam Hill's Traper of TuRo ex Ch. TuRo's Cachet), bred by Leonard Magowitz and TuRo Kennels. Owner, Leonard Magowitz.

Ch. TuRo's Accolade, SOM (by Ch. Marquam Hill's Traper of TuRo ex TuRo's Katrina of Cross Bar, DOM) is Cachet's full brother.

Left: Ch. Cachet's High River Gambler (by Ch. Cachet's Casablanca of TuRo ex Ch. Touchstone's Shara), owned by Leonard Magowitz, bred by Ken Kizzer. *Right:* Ch. Cachet's Casablanca of TuRo (by Ch. TuRo's Empire ex Ch. TuRo's Cachet), bred and owned by Leonard Magowitz and TuRo Kennels.

Ch. TuRo's Cachet, owned by Leonard and Susan Magowitz.

Ch. Rosend's Stardust (by Ch. Telstar's Starmaker, SOM ex High Crest's Desert Rose) was the first homebred champion for Jerry and Lynda Yon.

ROSEND

Rosend Boxers started in 1987 with foundation bitches from Glennroe and High Crest Boxers. Jerry and Lynda Yon finished their first champion, Glennroe Brandy N' Cream, and their first home-bred, Ch. Rosend's Stardust. Since they balance their showing and breeding activities with full-time careers and care for all of their dogs as house dogs, the number of their immediate dog family is restricted to between four and six, and their personal breeding program is limited to a litter every year-and-a-half. In 1992 they purchased Ch. Bridgewood's B.K. Kahuna, "Raider," who finished in only two weeks of competition. He went on to a very successful specials career, being the Top Boxer on the West Coast in 1993 and 1994. Through Raider's success as a sire, they have often opted for pick-of-the-litter, resulting in Top 20 contender Ch. Rosend's Bo Diddley, and other puppies who are just starting to make appearances in the ring. Ultimately, their greatest breeding achievement has been Ch. Rosend's Corporate Raider, 1994 ABC Regional RWD and Best Puppy. Their success in such a short time is a reflection of their determined dedication to excellence with a very limited breeding program.

MISTY VALLEY

Misty Valley Boxers, owned by Derek and Brenda Grice of Annapolis, Maryland, was established in 1981. They got their start in Boxers the same way so many others do—by purchasing one for a pet. They were living in England at the time, and the Boxer was a birthday present from Derek to Brenda. However, not too much time elapsed before they purchased a bitch to show—the seed had been planted. She did well in the show ring up until the birth of the Grices' first son, when showing dogs took a back seat. They moved to the US in 1970, but it wasn't until 1981 that the world of showing and breeding dogs drew them back in. This time, however, it was for good—they were hooked.

Their first American champion was a brindle bitch by Ch. Moonvalleys Sun and Shadow ex a Meshack daughter, Ch, Misty Valley's Paper Moon. She was finished by Stanley Flowers. After a trip one weekend to the Central Indiana BC, Brenda decided she would like something from the bitch Ch. TuRo's Magic Spell; however, that did not happen. When she did have the opportunity to purchase a pretty eight-week-old fawn puppy bitch, a Magic Spell granddaughter (by Ch. Gerhards Lamplighter ex Brettendale's Firecracker) bred by Carla Robinson and at that time owned by Audrey Gerhardy, Brenda was very delighted. That bitch was Ch. Gerhards RNR Encore, DOM. Bred to Ch. Fiero's Tally Ho Tailo, SOM, she produced Ch. Misty Valley's Curtain Call.

Ch. Bridgewood's B.K. Kahuna, SOM (Ch. Telstar's Goodtime Charlie, SOM ex Ginger's Gold 'N Glow) a top-winning Boxer for owners Jeff and Nan Bennett and Lynda Yon. Breeders, Jacob and Bridget Reinhold.

A very limited breeding program has produced no fewer than eight champions, the most successful and well known being Ch. Misty Valley's Curtain Call, "Jake" to his family and friends. Curtain Call finished at the age of 16 months. He was an ABC Top 20 contender for 1993/94, and in those same years he ended up Number Seven Boxer although he only specialed seven months of the year, winning numerous Bests of Breed and Group placements.

He is now carrying on the legacy of his ancestors as a producer of merit. His top-winning son is 1994's Number Four Boxer, Ch. Vancrofts Primetime. He has three American champions and one Philippine champion, with others on their way.

TREFOIL

The Trefoil Boxers of David and Stephanie Abraham in Connecticut began in 1970 with the purchase of an eight-week-old flashy fawn male puppy who grew up to be Am-Can. Ch. Gray Roy's Minstrel Boy. "Casey" sired 24 US champions and many in Canada. He left behind three ABC Sires of Merit (Ch. Trefoil's Dylan of Donessle, Ch. Trefoil's Choir Boy and Ch. Scarborough Silversmith) and one ABC Dam of Merit (Scarborough Soliloquy). Minstrel Boy's exceptional dominance is well known to the fancy. He stands behind many of today's winners and producers, including Ch. Hi-Tech's

Int. Ch. Gray Roy's Minstrel Boy, SOM (by Gray Roy's Mr. Lightning ex Gray Roy's Lollipop), handled by John Connolly for owners David and Stephanie Abraham, sired two dozen US champions including three SOMs.

Ch. Misty Valley's Curtain Call (by Ch. Fiero's Tally-Ho Tailo ex Ch. Gerhards RNR Encore), owned and bred by Brenda Grice.

Arbitrage, Ch. Woods End Crown Sable, Ch. Fiero's Tally Ho Tailo, Ch. Vancrofts Primetime, Ch. Pinepath's Night Watch, Ch. Bellcrest's Just Watch Me, Ch. Raklyn Rebellion and Ch. Holly Lane's Wild as the Wind. Other notable Trefoil Boxers include Ch. Trefoil's Scarborough Fair (ABC Regional WB and BW in 1976) and Trefoil's Esquire of Snuff Box (ABC Grand Prize Futurity Winner in 1978).

Always a small kennel whose dogs are house pets, Trefoil has won numerous ABC awards. Among them are Stud Dog Producing the Most Champions, Most Bred By Exhibitor Wins and Kennel Finishing the Most Champions. Though David and Stephanie are both licensed Boxer judges, they have been able to combine their judging with limited breeding and exhibiting. Their most recent champion, Ch. Trefoil's Lili Marlene, finished in 1994 with a breed win over specials.

In 1995 David and Stephanie had the honor of being the first husband and wife team to judge the ABC National Specialty. They look forward to another 25 years with the gentle and happy Boxers of Trefoil!

Above: Ch. Trefoil's Finesse, owned by David and Stephanie Abraham. *Below:* Ch. Trefoil's Caruso, sired by Ch. Trefoil's Choirmaster, is owned by David and Stephanie Abraham.

Ch. Gerhards R N R Encore, DOM (by Ch. Gerhard's Lamplighter ex Brettendale's Firecracker) bred by C. Robinson and owned by Brenda Grice.

Ch. Trefoil's Choir Boy, SOM (by Int. Ch. Gray Roy's Minstrel Boy ex Koseba's Show Girl), owner-handled by Stephanie Abraham.

STEVENSTARS

Marcella and Beth Ann Mushovic of Alaska have had Boxers for about 40 years, but it wasn't until "Sara" (Stevenstars Sarabeth, CDX) that they started seriously showing. When bred with Ch. Budsobrav's Happy Days, CD ("Happy"), Sara produced three very handsome boys: Am-Can. Ch. Stevenstars Summer Sunrise, Am-Can. CD ("Skeeter"); Ch. Stevenstars Summer Sunset, CDX, CGC ("Solar"); and Stevenstars Summer Solstace, Can. CD, Am. CDX ("Sabre").

Skeeter received the Award of Canine Distinction from *Dog World* magazine for never earning less than a BOB in getting his Canadian championship. Solar is owned by Susan and Dean Williams and is an active therapy dog. Sabre is working toward his Utility Dog title and is also active in agility. Both Sabre and Skeeter were active in tracking until inhibited by severe weather.

Sara and Happy were bred together again to produce a male who finished his championship and a female who has produced some very nice litters and has several pointed and near-finished get. Sara won *Dog World's* Award of Canine Distinction for having three or more champion get.

Since Sara has retired, they have added several lovely bitches to their line and have numerous dogs who have finished their championships and are working toward titles in obedience and agility. Marcella and Beth Ann enjoy conformation competition, but they also enjoy participating with their dogs in obedience, agility and other canine activities in the United States and Canada.

Ch. Budsobrav's Star of the North (by Ch. Budsobrav's Happy Days, CD ex Ch. Evergreen's Happy Luv, CD), owned by Marcella and Beth Mushovic.

Ch. Stevenstars Summer Sunset, CDX, CGC (by Ch. Budsobrav's Happy Days, CD ex Stevenstar's Sarabeth, CD), owned by Dean and Susan Williams, is an active therapy dog.

WELCOME TO JACQUET BOXERS

BY BARBARA WIDMAYER AND DEE GANNON

Rick Tomita and Bill Scolnik, long-time partners in Jacquet Boxers, are well known to the Boxer fancy throughout the world. They have produced over 150 AKC champions and at least 250 known champions worldwide. That is an average of six AKC champions and ten worldwide champions a year. Among these are many top-winning and top-producing Boxers, all bearing the Jacquet name.

It all began in 1968 when Rick and Bill wanted a Boxer as protection for their antique business, a dog that would "be a presence, friendly to our clients and their children and yet a deterrent." Thus three Boxers came into their lives. Their first dog, Jacquet Droz, was named after the 18th century French musical clockmaker, Pierre Jacquet Droz. Thus, the kennel name came to be.

Interested in showing their dogs, Rick and Bill were frustrated at their inability to obtain the quality of dog they needed, so their third Boxer, Ronel's Jacquet Satie,

Author and proprietor of Jacquet Boxers, Richard Tomita stands with Int. Ch. Jacquet's Novarese, SOM, one of the influential Boxer sires in the world.

Ch. Rocky of Shawnee Trail (by Ch. Eldic's Tecumseh ex Jo Lor's Night Song, CD) was the foundation sire for Jacquet Boxers. Rocky is seven years old in this photograph taken in May 1974.

a Ch. Eldic's Landlord daughter, was bred to Ch. Rocky of Shawnee Trail. This combination produced their first champion, Ch. Jacquet's Ronel Micah, an exciting brindle dog. He was awarded *Boxer Review's* Top Boxer in the East the same year he was killed in a tragic car accident. However, he had sired three litters. From the first litter came Ch. Jacquet's Mirah of Micah, who was to have a role in Jacquet's later success; however, the true foundation dog was Ch. Jacquet's Zephan from a repeat breeding of Satie to Rocky.

Zephan had an outstanding temperament, making him a perfect match for Ch. Barday's Chatterbox, who had been given to Rick by Tom and Barbara O'Neil. Her strong line Brayshaw breeding helped establish Jacquet's excellent heads and bites.

With a small circle of friends, including Ron and Eleanor Erickson, Richard and Mavis Thornberg, Ed and Florence Wilderson, Eleanor Haeberle, Liane Dimitroff, Gerry Broadt and Lena Ludwig, a few foundation Boxers and some sound advice from the likes of Alva Rosenberg and Victor Clemente, Jacquet began its meteoric ascent in the Boxer world.

Due to difficulties encountered at the beginning of Jacquet, Rick has taken to heart some sage advice: "Sell your best puppies and don't show against them." Thus Jacquet deliberately shares good dogs. This has brought scores of new people into Boxers, many who later entered the show ring.

The Jacquet family is a phenomenon. In addition to his dedication to the dogs, Rick has continued to make himself available to the owners of his dogs. The shared problems and successes together with sound advice and heartfelt encouragement have made this multi-faceted enterprise a legend in its own time.

While Rick has been criticized about the number of dogs that are co-owned, he has been eminently successful with the people as well the dogs without the usual problems. Anyone who has ever co-owned a Jacquet Boxer will tell you it is a pleasant experience. Rick truly feels that the dog belongs to the primary owner; his co-ownership is always secondary. What is most important is his guidance, encouragement, assistance and continued enthusiasm. Rick is truly the kindly patriarch who is justly proud of every member's success.

Of course, it helps if the dogs are of top quality. Since 1981, Jacquet has received the annual award for the Kennel Making the Most Champions 12 times and, since 1982, the award for Kennel Breeding the Most Champions 15 times. At the 1996 ABC awards dinner, after receiving the Breeder of the Year Award for the 14th time, it was noted that no other kennel in the history of the ABC has accomplished this.

Most notable among these dogs is Caleb, Ch. Happy Ours Fortune de Jacquet, who has produced over 60 champions worldwide to date. Among his get are Am-Can-Jap-Ber. Ch. Jacquet's Urko, who became the top winning dog of all time with 17 BIS in Japan; Ch. Kojak's Von San Remo, the #1 Boxer dog in 1983 with multiple BIS and BISS wins; Ch. Jacquet's Fleur de Lys, a multiple BIS and BISS winner placing consistently among the top 10 Boxers for 1986; Ch. Arrow's Sky High, a multiple BIS winner; and Jacquet's Fleur-de-Noel, WB at the 1987 ABC National Specialty over a record entry.

FCI Int.-Am.-Japanese Ch. Jacquet's Novarese, SOM and Am-Can-Jap-Ber-Int. Ch. Jacquet's Urko have strongly impacted the Jacquet breeding program.

In the tradition of many of the old German kennels and those of the golden years of the Boxer in the U.S., Jacquet has provided the foundation stock for many up and coming kennels in the United States and abroad.

Foundation bitch for Jacquet, this is Ronel's Jacquet Satie (by Ch. Eldic's Landlord ex Abruzzi's Heloise), bred by Ron and Eleanor Ericson. All the Jacquet Boxers trace back to Satie.

Am-Can-Ber-Jap-Int. Ch. Jacquet's Urko, SOM (by Ch. Happy Ours Fortune de Jacquet ex Ch. Jacquet's Candy Dancer), bred and owned by Richard Tomita. Urko was a multiple Best in Show winner and the top dog in Japan while he lived there. He came back to the U.S. to live with the author.

Ch. Jacquet's Zephan, SOM (by Ch. Rocky of Shawnee Trail ex Ronel's Jacquet Satie, an Eldic's Landlord daughter), handled by the author, winning under judge Liane Dimitroff. Zephan produced two DOMs, Ch. Jacquet's Canterbury Belle and Ch. Jacquet's Jolie. Zephan was a devoted housedog as well as foundation for the author.

JACQUET KENNELS

BY RICHARD TOMITA

In 1968, I had the good fortune to be offered the pick puppy bitch, a flashy dark brindle named Ronel's Jacquet Satie, on a breeder's agreement. This was also fortunate for me because at the time I was young with no concept about a breeding program nor any feeling about it. This puppy was an outcross sired by a stud dog with a top show record who dominated the New Jersey area, Ch. Eldic's Landlord, a strongly linebred brindle. I couldn't afford her outright so I accepted the offer, which benefited myself and the pup's breeder. They were able to carry their line on, and my cash outlay for a quality bitch was at a minimum.

When her time to breed came around during her second year, I wanted to have her bred with a top performing line further north. Eleanor and Ron Erickson would have gone along with it if I had insisted, except they pointed out to me that it was again another outcross and I would probably end up with a hodgepodge litter.

A day the author will never forget: Jacquet's first champion winning his first four-point major, Ch. Jacquet's Ronel Micah (by Ch. Rocky of Shawnee Trail ex Ronel's Jacquet Satie), under the legendary Lena Ludwig, handled by Bob McPherson.

Ch. Jacquet's Fanfare of Beaupix (by Ch. Jacquet's Brass Idol ex Jacquet's Janine), owned by Olive Beaudreau and Richard Tomita, is the foundation bitch for Beaupix. Handler, Jane Forsyth.

Ch. Happy Ours Fortune de Jacquet, SOM (by Ch. Merrilane's April Holiday, SOM ex Jacquet's Painted Lady), bred by Ann Ketchems, owned and handled by the author to finish his championship.

Author Richard Tomita with the renowned Int. Ch. Jacquet's Novarese, SOM, one of his over 250 AKC and international champions, displaying the American Boxer Club, Inc. award for Breeder of the Year/Kennel Producing the Most Champions, a distinction which he has claimed for over 15 years.

Jacquet's first Best in Show bitch—Ch. Jacquet's Fleur de Lys (By Ch. Happy Ours Fortune de Jacquet ex Ch. Jacquet's Canterbury Belle, DOM), bred by Gordon and Michele McArdle and Richard Tomita. Judge, Phillip A. Lanard III. Handler, Carmen Skinner.

The stud they had chosen was the solidly handsome Ch. Rocky of Shawnee Trail, the top winning dog sired by Ch. Eldic's Tecumseh, which would be linebreeding. Both Landlord and Tecumseh were sired by Ch. Eldic's Darius, who was a Ch. Barrage of Quality Hill son and a product of linebreeding bred by Eleanor Haeberle, who encouraged this practice to set type and consistency within a line. In two or three generations, when your dogs set foot in the ring, everyone will recognize it as your line.

This litter was whelped in 1971. I kept and campaigned Ch. Jacquet's Ronel Micah, an elegant, tall, good moving brindle male who finished at 12 months of age in one-and-a-half months of showing. "Oh how easy!" I thought, "Piece of cake!" Later, I would learn it rarely happens this way. It usually takes much longer. Micah went on to be a top ranking Boxer as a Special. He was used sparingly as a stud due to my reluctance to breed him. He was a house dog living with two other males and two bitches, and they got along so well that I didn't want to alter this peaceful balance. His first breeding was to a Rocky of Shawnee Trail champion daughter, producing Ch. Jacquet's Mirah of Micah, co-owned with Dorothy Shames. Mirah of Micah was in turn bred to Ch. Carlwen's Sean of Erin, producing Ch. Jacquet's Shana of Talisman, owned by Olive and Charles Beaudreau. She was WB and BOW at the 1979 ABC. Another bitch he bred was a Landlord daughter, producing a brindle bred to Micah's full repeat breeding brother, Ch. Jacquet's Zephan, which produced Ch. Jacquet's Candy Dancer, a wonderful moving, tall, elegant bitch who in turn was bred to Ch. Happy Ours Fortune de Jacquet, producing the Int. Ch. Jacquet's Urko, a Sire of Merit as well. He produced numerous champion

and non-champion daughters who have gone on to produce champions.

Another Micah daughter produced from Wilderson's Cheesecake, Ch. Brandybrook's Criterion linebred to Woodcrest, an outcross breeding to Ch. Tamberlaines Polished Brass, a Ch. Salgray's Flying High and Flintwood cross produced our next top winner, Ch. Jacquet's Brass Image as well as Ch. Jacquet's Chelsea, Ch. Jacquet's Branston, Ch. Jacquet's Mercer and Ch. Jacquet's Brass Idol, SOM, making their mother, Jacquet's Perigal, a Dam of Merit. Brass Image went to England to add new blood there. Chelsea was bred to Zephan and produced Ch. Jacquet's Canterbury Belle, owned by Gordon and Michele McArdle, and when she was bred twice to Ch. Happy Ours Fortune de Jacquet, she produced 1987 ABC WB, Ch. Jacquet's Noel; Ch. Jacquet's Fleur de Lys, BIS and top Boxer bitch; and three other champion sisters and brothers, making her a Dam of Merit as well. Mercer was bred to Ch. Merrilane's April Holiday and produced the famed Ch. Merrilane's Knockout, SOM. Brass Idol, producer of nine champions, produced Ch. Jacquet's Gaspard, a product of a union with a champion Markham daughter, Ch. Jacquet's Pickett. Gaspard bred to a linebred Happy Ours Fortune daughter produced ABC Dam of Merit Jacquet's Kiri Te Kanawa, dam of nine champions owned by Karen and Mel Wilson.

The full brother Zephan from a repeat breeding of Micah took over as our stud after an untimely loss of Micah. Without Ch. Jacquet's Zephan, SOM, I would

Ch. Jacquet's Gaspard (by Ch. Jacquet's Brass Idol, SOM ex Ch. Jacquet's Picket), owned by Edgar and Florence Wilderson.

Ch. Jacquet's Brass Image (by Ch. Merrilane's April Fashion ex Jacquet's Perigal), handled by Marylou Hatfield for breeders Richard Tomita and Vincent and Ginger Sbarrra, owned in the US by Edgar and Florence Wilderson.

not have been able to carry on my pursuit of Boxers. First of all, he filled that awful void left with the death of Micah at such an early age from a car accident. He was a gentle loving dog with such loyalty. He passed this quality down through his get and to our present housedog Holden, who reminds us of him so much. He is lying by my feet as I am writing this portion of the book, with his biscuit toy in his mouth, trying to entice me to play catch, keep away and hide-and-seek all at the same time. One of my favorite bitches produced by Zephan was Ch. Jacquet's Jolie, which means pretty of face, and she had a wonderful character. She was our first Dam of Merit. She became our housedog after Satie and, in turn, her daughter came into our house and then her daughter. Jolie lived to be 14 years old.

Zephan's famous daughter in Japan, Am-Jap. Ch. Jacquet's Dancing Star, was the first bitch to attain top

Am-Can. Ch. Jacquet's Mich-La-Chen (by Ch. Jacquet's Brass Idol, SOM ex Zuccini of Silver Springs), owned by Michele Cheney and Rick Tomita, was a BIS winner.

Ch. Jacquet's Jolie, DOM (by Ch. Jacquet's Zephan ex Ms. Liebschon of Rochelle), owned by Richard Tomita and William Scolnik, handled by Jane Forsyth. Jolie was Rick and Bill's house dog for many years—she lived to be 12 years old.

winning dog status there. She came out of retirement at nine years of age and won not only BOB but also Best Queen in Show (Best in Show bitch).

Zephan's first breeding was to a double Witherford Hot Chestnut granddaughter, whose dam was a Belgian import bred to another Rocky of Shawnee Trail and Ronel bitch son, and produced Charlene of Silver Spring owned by Pat Wallace. This combination produced Zuccini of Silver Springs, a big-boned European type in head and body. She was bred first to Brass Idol, producing Michele Cheney's BIS bitch Ch. Jacquet's Mich-La-Chen, who became the foundation for her line. She was then bred to Branston and produced a male, Ch. Jacquet's Sirius, and a bitch, Susannah of Silver Spring. She was a smaller version of her mother and I thought she could use some elegance, so she was bred to our stud who consistently produced elegant get, Happy Ours Fortune. This produced two champion bitches, Ch. Jacquet's Susannah and Ch. Jacquet's Fallen Monarch VSOP. Susannah was acquired by Dale and Deborah Sprivey, who owned the BIS male Ch. Smokey's Magnum Force. A result of this outcross was Ch. Shamrock's Mahogany Roxie owned by Peggy and Robert Otto of Pro Boxer, who became their foundation. Litter sister Jacquet's Shasta D'Shamrock, co-owned with John Wilkenson, was linebred with Ch. Jacquet's Grande Sonnerie owned by Walter Amos, who incidentally was co-breeder of Eldic's Landlord, producing Ch. Jacquet's Madam Butterfly Aboxa acquired by Diane and Charles Abdoo. Butterfly was bred with an Urko son, resulting in Ch. Jacquet's Bon Jovi Aboxa, now the foundation stud for co-owners Muriel Dieterich and Vi Campos. Shasta was then outcrossed with a Traper son, Ch. Goldfield's Eagle Dancer, and two champions resulted. She became a DOM with her third breeding, linebred to Novarese, resulting in Ch. Jacquet's Tribeca co-owned by Carol and Dale Brower, and Ch. Jacquet's Vacheron. Vacheron is proving to be a dominant sire with several champion get.

Zephan was bred with a third significant bitch from the Brayshaw line, Barday's Lady Tiara, a Fashion Hint granddaughter. Her dam, Ch. Barday's Chatterbox, was the youngest Boxer bitch to win a major and had finished very quickly. She possessed a strong chiseled typey head, a perfect bite and a cobby body with a sweet per-

Int. Ch. Jacquet's Novarese (by Am-Ber-Jap-Can. Ch. Jacquet's Agassiz ex Angel Angelli), bred by Richard Tomita and June Angelli, shown at the age of six months by Marylou Hatfield.

Ch. Jacquet's Susannha (by Ch. Happy Ours Fortune de Jacquet ex Susannha of Silver Spring), owned by Byron Dale and Deborah Spivey, handled by Marylou Hatfield, became the foundation of Shamrock Boxers.

sonality. She was given to us from Barbara and Tom O'Neil, kindly telling us we could use a stronger muzzle and a bit more bone and heft to our foundation. Ann Scruggs Ketchem obtained Barday's Lady Tiara to breed to Micah. Because of his early demise, she was bred instead to his brother Zephan and this union produced Jacquet's Painted Lady and Jacquet's Markham. Although none of the dogs from this litter finished, they did become our richest producers. Markham produced Angel Angelli, owned by June Angelli and bred by Richard and Mavis Thornberg (Assisi). She was bred to Ch. Jacquet's Agassiz (owned by Barbara and Ted Widmayer), himself a son of a Markham daughter, Jacquet's Hot Summer, owned by Sam Rodman, bred to Merrilane's April Fashion. His litter sister, Ch Jacquet's Goldfield Rubi Doux owned by Ed Goldfield, is a DOM with five champions. Angel produced a stag red fawn male with a short back and long arched neck, which we needed to bring back in the line, smooth strong movement and a showy personality. He won at the 1988 ABC under an international judge from Australia, Rosina Olifent-Brace. Int. Ch. Jacquet's Novarese, who is now our recent Sire of Merit, upon becoming a American champion, was invited to an international show career in Japan.

Going back a couple of generations before I get ahead of myself, Painted Lady moved to California with Ann

Scruggs Ketchem. When she was ready to be bred, I encouraged Ann to breed to Ch. Merrilane's April Holiday, the litter brother of a magnificent showy dog being campaigned in the East, Ch. Merrilane's April Fashion, who gave us beautiful heads and showmanship and enhanced what we had thus far. (When I saw the repeated high quality typey pups we were producing from him with our now strongly linebred bitches, I encouraged Ann to try the brother.) Their pedigrees connected to our bitches' pedigrees through Ch. Eldic's Landlord even though the Merrilane studs had him three generations back and, with some of our bitches through Fashion Hint, he was four generations back in our bitches. I am convinced it was our link with Landlord that clicked so well. With this union, we had a surge of wins in the show ring and finished quite a few champions in a short time.

Ann got a flashy fawn male from this breeding who would become our greatest producer. The dream prepotent stud bred to our linebred bitches produced dogs and bitches that were very similar in type. This was Ch. Happy Ours Fortune de Jacquet, Sire of Merit with 35 AKC champions and over 60 champions worldwide. Because of circumstances that prevented Ann from keeping her dogs, she sent him and his mother to my kennel. He came with a four-point major. While finding the right new owner for Fortune, we decided to prove him as a stud with one of my bitches and to show him a few times. He won another major handled by Marylou Wilderson Hatfield and at the same time his first litter was born, bred to a Merrilane's April Fash-

Ch. Jacquet's Ram (by Ch. Happy Ours Fortune de Jacquet ex Jacquet's Cinnam N Cinderella), bred by Richard Tomita and owned by Richard Miller.

ion daughter. It was a spectacular litter, so much so that I decided to keep the dog at Jacquet Kennel with Ann Ketchem's permission. Two champions finished from this first breeding. We bred other April Fashion daughters and granddaughters to him as well as Zephan daughters and got similar litters. From almost every litter one, two or three puppies went on to finish. Two of his daughters went on to Specials careers and became top ranking Boxers: Ch. Jacquet's Garnier and Ch. Jacquet's Fleur de Lys, a Best in Show winner. He also had three top-winning Best in Show sons: Ch. Kojak Von San Remo, Ch. Arrow's Sky High and Int. Ch. Jacquet's Urko, who himself became a Sire of Merit.

I bred Painted Lady once more, this time with April Fashion, and got three puppies. One of the plain black-face bitches was obtained by Bernie and Georgine Schwerdtfeger for a pet; however, the bitch was very showy and animated and had an extremely good conformation. Bernie Jr. took her to a couple of match show wins and the Schwerdtfegers were hooked. They came back for a male to keep Jacquet's Faline company. They went on to show and finish both. Faline was one of the first black-face plain bitches to finish within a 25-year memory for many Boxer fanciers. She produced two champions.

I took many of Happy Ours Fortune's tightly linebred daughters to Urko; they were his half-sisters. We bred these bitches to Novarese, who returned from a two-year stay in Tokyo after being campaigned there and ranking as Top Boxer, Top Working Dog and

Ch. Happy Ours Fortune de Jacquet is the sire of over 55 champions worldwide, bred by Ann Scruggs Ketchem, owned by Richard Tomita.

Above: The future Ch. Goldfield's Noble Pride (by Ch. Happy Ours Fortune de Jacquet ex Ch. Jacquet's Goldfield Rubi Doux, DOM), the grandsire of many champions, bred by Ed Goldfield and shown by Marianne Caprino. *Below:* As a puppy, Jacquet's Pulsar (by Jacquet's Drakkar ex Ch. Jacquet's Margetts), bred by Barbara Widmayer.

Above: At ten months of age, Jacquet's Stallone (by Ch. Jacquet's Bravo ex Jacquet's Arabella), handled by Linda Mastrapasqua, bred by Richard Tomita and Jack Majocha. *Below:* At three months, winning Best in Match, Assisi's Csillag de Jacquet (by Ch. Happy Ours Fortune de Jacquet ex Assisis Ebony Blaise), the foundation bitch for Tom and Cindy O'Conner's Assisi Boxers.

Above: Ch. Jacquet's Goldfield Rubi Doux, DOM (by Ch. Merrilane's April Fashion, SOM ex Jacquet's Hot Summer), bred by Richard Tomita and Sam Rodman, owned by Ed Goldfield and handled by Alvin Lee, Jr., is the dam of five champions. *Below:* Ch. Jacquet's Margetts (by Int. Ch. Jacquet's Novarese ex Jacquet's Ansele), bred and owned by the author.

Above: Ch. Jacquet's Garnier, at just nine and a half months, (by Ch. Happy Ours Fortune de Jacquet ex Jacquet's Brandy Wine) was the top-winning Jacquet bitch in 1983, handled by Marylou Hatfield. *Below:* Ch. Jacquet's Canterbury Belle, DOM, (by Ch. Jacquet's Zephan, SOM ex Ch. Jacquet's Chelsea), bred by Richard Tomita and owned by Gordon and Michele McArdle, is the dam of five champions.

Ch. Jacquet's Cambridge Fortune (by Jacquet's Bronson of Dieterich ex Jacquet's Murphee Noble) is a multiple Best in Show winning bitch bred by Richard Tomita and William Dunn and owned by Ikuko Otani.

a top producer. The Japanese go for a very animated, showy dog with a straight topline, high tailset, arched neckline and angulation, making a pretty picture and silhouette. They emphasize side-moving Boxers and move them very fast. Both Urko and Novarese did this well. When I saw what Novarese produced in Japan with some of the Jacquet breedings and outcross bitches, I was very anxious to have him return to Jacquet to work with his April Fashion and Zephan-Brayshaw Woodcrest pedigree to breed with my doubled and tripled Happy Ours Fortune bitches. He was bred to Urko daughters

Ch. Jacquet's Black Watch (by Ch. Cachet Mad Max of TuRo ex Jacquet's Diamond Lady), bred by Richard Tomita.

and Happy Ours Fortune daughters and this proved to be quite successful, making him a Sire of Merit by early 1995. Jacquet's Maja, the prime producer of the El Encanto Boxers, is an example. His son, Ch. Jacquet's Greggson, SOM, is producing many champions and his dual-titled daughter, Ch. Jacquet's Cebelé, CD has produced Am-Can-Ber. Ch. Jacquet's Millenium (130th champion), another dominant sire who produces strong heads; and another son, Ch. Jacquet's Attribute, who looks like he could be a dominant stud as well. Ch. Warena's Aida is a top winning bitch in Brazil and Ch. Jacquet's Mago of El Encanto is the top winning male there as well. Ch. Jacquet's Top Dream owned by Carlos and Diego Garcia is the top Boxer in Argentina. He finished on the Florida circuit with three five point majors.

Ch. Jacquet's Lord Mayor (by Ch. Jacquet's Greggson ex Ch. Jacquet's Frederica), bred by William Lyle, Dorothy Fink, and Richard Tomita. Owners, Paul and Toni Fry.

In the mid-1990s I felt it was time again to introduce another line to breed with the tightly linebred bitches half brother/half sister breedings or tripling and quadrupling back on Happy Ours Fortune breedings. Goldfield Boxers sent a linebred Ch. Marquam Hills Traper of TuRo son, Ch. Goldfield's Eagle Dancer. When he was bred to these bitches he produced several champions as well. I also tried to introduce an outside line after much research, checking into as many generations as possible for temperament problems as well as genetic defects such as heart problems, weak hindquarters, etc. We can learn much about a line through the bitches, and often we request a pick of the litter when a visiting bitch comes to be bred with one of our stud dogs. Some owners of bitches are willing to give a pick puppy in lieu of a stud fee.

I also introduced a tightly bred Ch. TuRo's Cachet granddaughter, Jacquet's Safire of Goldfield, a plainish brindle (Ch. Cachet's Mad Max of TuRo ex Ch.

Jacquet's Shasta D'Shamrock, DOM (Ch. Smokey's Magnum Force ex Ch. Jacquet's Susannha), bred by Dale and Deborah Spivey and Richard Tomita. Owner, John and Janet Wilkenson and Richard Tomita.

Goldfield's Eye Dazzler), breeding her to Greggson. A brindle male and a typey fawn bitch were produced. Both became champions. The brindle male, Ch. Jacquet's Bravo of Goldfield, finished from the puppy class with three five-point majors, two at specialties and a Group One. At this young age, he promised to be a "flyer" and went on to be in the top ten list for two years. He is bringing a "typeyness" to reinforce what we have. We liked this breeding so much that we bred Novarese daughters directly to the Cachet son, Ch. Cachet's Mad Max of TuRo, when he came back East to live with his co-breeder and owner Leonard Magowitz. We have so far produced Ch. Jacquet's Black Watch, seemingly a dominant sire; Ch. Jacquet's Flaming Brandy; a typey bitch, Ch. Jacquet's Noire; and her litter brother Jacquet's Drakkar, whose dam is Novarese daughter Ch. Jacquet's Jousseline.

The very typey brindle bitch, Ch. Jacquet's Cambridge Fortune, was campaigned to the Top Boxer Bitch of 1994. She was a result of two untitled parents, a linebred bitch combining Happy Ours Fortune, Urko and April Fashion with a sprinkling of Dieterich, Hi-Hat and California breeding thrown in.

Litter sister to Greggson, Ch. Jacquet's Jousseline (by Ch. Jacquet's Novarese ex Int. Ch. Jacquet's Aliage of Goldfield), handled by Karen Aurelius.

Jacquet's Arctic Knight (by Ch. Jacquet's Vacheron ex Jacquet's Alibert), owned by Hank and Candy Bartos.

As a seven-month-old pup, Jacquet's Pangea (by Ch. Cachet's Mad Max of TuRo ex Ch. Jacquet's Jousseline), handled by Donna DiPalma.

Ch. Jacquet's Bon Jovi Aboxa (by Aboxa's Elvis de Jacquet ex Ch. Jacquet's Madam Butterfly Aboxa), bred by Charles and Diane Abdoo and Richard Tomita, owned by Muriel Dieterich and Vi Campos.

Ch. Jacquet's Drakkar (by Ch. Cachet's Mad Max of TuRo ex Ch. Jacquet's Jousseline), bred by Richard Tomita.

Am-Jap. Ch. Jacquet's Ansonia (by Jama's Zeus ex Jacquet's Baby Luv), owned by Sadao Kikuchi and Richard Tomita.

Ch. Jacquet's Prinzee (by Ch. Jacquet's Vacheron ex Jacquet's Alibert), owned by Tom and Madeline Tomaszewski.

Jacquet's Naughty Nicole (by Int. Ch. Jacquet's Novarese ex Jacquet's Chantal), bred by Richard Tomita and owned by cobreeders Nancy and Winfield Wood.

Ch. Jacquet's Son of a Gun (by Ch. Jacquet's Vacherón ex Jacquet's Super Countess of BG), owned by John Masamillo, bred by Georgine Schwerdtfeger and Richard Tomita.

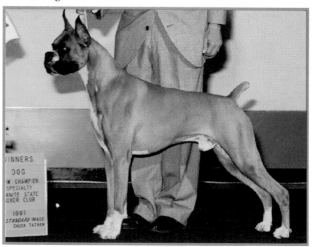

Assissi's Number One Jacquet (by Ch. Goldfield's Dorian de Jacquet ex Assissi's Muzzletuft Jacquet), bred and owned by Tom and Cindi O'Conner.

The author's good friends from the Metropolitan Opera, Michael and Kerry Hacker, visiting J-B Wholesale, posing with Holden and their dog Abercrombie.

Ch. Jacquet's Hidden Asset (by Goldfield's Saga de Jacquet ex Jacquet's Cambria Blue) was rescued at age eight months and is the beloved house pet of Bebe Ventura.

Ch. Jacquet's Destino El Encanto (by Ch. Cachet's Mad Max of TuRo ex Ch. El Encanto's Chantaje Jacquet) and Ch. Jacquet's Dinamita El Encanto (by Ch. Jacquet's Vacherón ex Ch. El Encanto's Chantaje Jacquet), owned and bred by Carole Shea and Richard Tomita.

Ch. Jacquet's Lord Wilton of Erin (by Ch. Goldfield's Dorian de Jacquet ex Erins Murphy's Law), bred by Jack O'Brien and Richard Tomita and owned by Paul and Toni Fry, became the foundation stud for Ridge Run Boxers.

Ch. Jacquet's Vacherón (by Int. Ch. Jacquet's Novarese ex Jacquet's Shasta D'Shamrock), bred by Richard Tomita. Photograph by L. D. Bohm Studios.

One of the author's favorite stud dogs, Ch. Jacquet Greggson, handled by Marylou Hatfield under Judge Anitra Cuneo.

From this journey, starting with the Eldic line, you can see I have worked with basically three lines and now a fourth, interchanging between them with grandfather to granddaughter, cousin to cousin or cousin removed, uncle to niece, half brother to half sister sometimes, but never inbreeding except for two accidental breedings that occurred in the home of the owners of the two Boxers involved. I feel I have been fortunate to be able to have plenty of room and enough Boxers with good qualities and many good friends to have these lines going so I am able to interchange within my breeding line. I am always looking for that great stud or bitch to bring into our line that has minimum faults and no genetic defects.

I am happy to see Jacquet has helped to build the foundation for many lines and kennels throughout the world, particularly in Argentina, Australia, Brazil, Canada, India, Japan, the Philippines, Taiwan and Mexico. It is a thrill to see the champions being produced by those kennels and their success. I am grateful to the devoted Boxer fanciers and breeders who have guided me with their knowledge or their strong lines that they have produced so that I was able to carry on from there to be part of furthering this wondrous world of the Boxer.

The following article written by Richard Beauchamp appeared in the July 1992 issue of *Dog Watch*:

"(Oakland, New Jersey, July 12, 1992) It's been a long time since I've had the time to do a kennel visit. Most of my time away is spent at shows, either in the ring judging or watching someone else's dog being judged, so driving through the New Jersey countryside without an airtight schedule to follow was a genuine treat.

"I had come to New Jersey to visit Rick Tomita and Bill Scolnik's highly regarded Jacquet Boxer Kennels and was met at Newark Airport.

"Off the turnpike, off the highway and off the paved road through a verdant wooded area and into a setting that most of us would consider the dream site for that 'little kennel in the country,' a lovely New England style brick home nestled up against stately pines and fronted by an expanse of beautifully trimmed, jade green lawn.

"In front of the main entrance, the first of Rick and Bill's hobbies—the Koi pond. Huge glistening multi-colored fish, some half a century old and most tame enough to eat out of your hand. The doves, the finches, the cactus greenhouses and a houseful of not only rare Boxer memorabilia but also wonderful old clocks and art, a carryover from their days as antique dealers.

"The antique business, which brought them a good many acquisitions from the late Alva Rosenberg's collection, was eventually traded in for the thriving J-B Pet Supply, which is known to and used by most of North America's dog and cat exhibitors. However, the successful business is kept well apart from the home and kennel site so as not to disturb its idyllic tranquility.

"We walked along the gravel path to the super-efficient, small kennel, immaculately maintained and arranged so that nearly every run and indoor box stall gives the dogs full view of every person that comes and goes. As every Boxer in the place, toddling puppy to seasoned stud dog, comes joyfully up to greet you, you know temperament is the bottom line in this breeding program. This is a breeding program which is currently headed by the stallion of a sire—the International, Japanese and American Ch. Jacquet's Novarese. Impressive in every sense of the word, he exudes Boxer type with that elusive and unique balance of masculinity and elegance that is a good part of the essence of this breed. His influence is observable in his many children and grandchildren in the Jacquet runs and paddocks.

"A particularly attractive dark brindle five-month-old caught our eye and, before long, we were out on the driveway getting to know each other; he already exhibiting that distinct style and movement so typical of his lineage. We learned he was a Novarese son whose name was "Tribute"—Jacquet's Tribute to Hi Hat. He would soon be on his way to Mexico to enjoy an almost certain successful show career.

"We saw them all—brindles, fawns, the boys, the girls, one more exuberant than the last. (Is there anything more jolly than a Boxer puppy?)

"Later in the evening, Angel Perez, a local lad, arrived with a litter he had bred out of his own bitch which was closely linebred to the influential sire, Ch. Happy Ours Fortune de Jacquet. She in turn had been linebred to the Novarese dog and the puppies had come for evaluation and inoculations. The consistency of the litter was obvious. They all bore the quality of their royal heritage but, even with that, one brindle bitch stood out as if under a spotlight. Both Rick Tomita and I spotted her immediately and in a flash she was up on the grooming table. Head up, tail up, everything you want and all in the right places. Ready for the shows at eight weeks!

Ch. Jacquet's Vacherón (by Int. Ch. Jacquet's Novarese ex Jacquet's Shasta D' Shamrock), bred by Richard Tomita.

Isn't it amazing how early the ones with quality recognize it in themselves?

"The litter had been raised by Angel's entire family — mother, father, brothers and sisters. The temperaments on the Boxer babies confirmed our belief that there are no puppies in the world like those raised in the family environment.

"We concluded our evening at a marvelous restaurant, gourmet Italian food, a relaxed atmosphere and stimulating conversation. We talked about many things—the world, the economy, the dog game and, of course, Boxers. But never once did I hear, 'My dog, my dog...' Interesting that those who have done the most say the least about 'My dog!'"

Ch. Jacquet's Grande Sonnerie (by Ch. Happy Ours Fortune de Jacquet ex Jacquet's Cleopatre), bred by Richard Tomita, owned by Walter Amos.

Am-Ber-Can. Ch. Jacquet's Cloud Dancer (by Ch. Happy Ours Fortune de Jacquet), owned by Karen Speck, bred by Richard Tomita.

Ch. Goldfield's Idol Maker (by Ch. Happy Ours Fortune de Jacquet ex Ch. Jacquet's Goldfield Rubi Doux, DOM), bred by Ed Goldfield.

Jacquet's Zdenka (Ch. Jacquet's Millenium ex Jacquet's Arabel), bred by Jack Majocha and the author.

Stanish's Coco de Jacquet (by Ch. Jacquet's Valentino ex Jacquet's Lucky Penny), owned by Takeshi Higuchi and bred by Chris Staniszewski and the author.

Ch. Jacquet's Corbet (by Ch. Jacquet's Gaspard ex Jacquet's Sarah Lee), owned by Lorraine Mazzei and Richard Tomita.

Ch. Jacquet's Jersey Trooper, at eight months, (by Ch. Goldfield's Eagle Dancer ex Jacquet's Shasta D'Shamrock), owned by Peter and Debra Ravettine and bred by Richard Tomita.

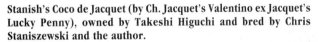

Ch. Shamrock's Kizzie de Jacquet (by Am-Can-Jap-Ber-HK. Ch. Jacquet's Agassiz), owned by Byron Dale and Deborah Spivey.

Ch. Hi Hat's Gigi v. Jacquet (by Ch. Hi Hat's Henry Higgins ex Ch. Hi Hat's Sky-V. Arrow), bred by Leni Kaplan and Richard Tomita.

Ch. Jacquet's Frederica (by Ch. Jacquet's Grande Sonnerie ex Jacquet's Bidu), bred by William Lyle, Dorothy Fink and Richard Tomita.

Ch. Jacquet's Stem Winder (Am-Br. Ch. Jacquet's Teno Fortune ex Assissis Csillag Jacquet), owned by John Purdy, was the 100th champion for Jacquet Boxers. Breeders, Tom and Cindi O'Conner.

Ch. Firesong's Jacquet My Way (by Ch. Jacquet's Windchester of B-G ex Ch. Jacquet's Firesong), owned by Dennis and Marie Snell.

Ch. Jacquet's Fleur-De-Noel (by Ch. Happy Ours Fortune de Jacquet ex Ch. Jacquet's Canterbury Belle), taking WB at the 1987 ABC under Victor Clemente, handled by Marylou Hatfield—the author and breeder looks on. Owner, Dr. H. Nakazawa. Co-breeders, Gordon and Michele McArdle.

Jacquet's Inspector, CD acquired his Companion Dog title at seven-and-a-half years of age. "Bud" is owned by Susan Bendziewicz.

Ch. Mich-La-Chen's Prince Charming (by Ch. Vindex Hirem of Bif ex Mich-La-Chen's Muguet Jacquet), owned and bred by Michele L. Cheney.

Ch. Jacquet's Jesse James (by Int. Ch. Jacquet's Urko ex Samantha Jo IV), owned by Joy Iannaconi, Dr. Tina Petillo and Richard Tomita, was a top winner in the early 1980s.

Ch. Jacquet's Bravo of Goldfield (by Ch. Jacquet's Greggson ex Jacquet's Siren of Goldfield), bred by Ed and Bryan Goldfield and Richard Tomita. Bravo is pictured at ten months of age.

Jacquet's Loveladies and her lovely litter sired by Ch. Cachet's Mad Max of TuRo.

Am-Ber-Can-Jap-Int. Ch. Urko, SOM (by Ch. Happy Ours Fortune de Jacquet, SOM ex Ch. Jacquet's Candy Dancer), bred and owned by Richard Tomita, handled by Thomas O'Conner winning under Dee Gannon at the International Molosser Show.

Ch. Jacquet's Something Special (by Am-Can. Ch. Woods Ends Crown Sable ex Jacquet's Kafir), bred by Carol Brower, Virginia DeBell and Richard Tomita.

Ch. Jacquet's Barbet of Goldfield (by Ch. Jacquet's Greggson ex Jacquet's Siren of Goldfield), bred by Richard Tomita and Ed Goldfield, handled by Gina DiNardo.

Ch. Jacquet's Lord of Thunder (by Ch. Goldfield's Eagle Dancer ex Jacquet's Honey Samantha), bred by Richard Tomita and owned by Robert and Pamela Bober. "Thor" is the foundation stud for Darkstar Boxers.

Ch. Jacquet's Renard of Wilderson (by Am-Can. Ch. Shylock ex Wilderson's Orchid de Jacquet), owned by Florence Wilderson and Richard Tomita, winning under the much-loved judge Lena Basquette.

Am-Can. Ch. Jacquet's Aliage of Goldfield (by Int. Ch. Jacquet's Urko ex Ch. Jacquet's Goldfield Rubi Doux, DOM), bred by Ed Goldfield and Richard Tomita.

Jacquet's Black Brocot (by Ch. Jacquet's Black Watch ex Little Trees Express), bred by L. Taylor, J. Lotito and author.

Ch. Jacquet's El Cid (by Ch. Happy Ours Fortune de Jacquet ex Jacquet's Jacqueline), owned by Carol Brower and Richard Tomita.

Am-Jap. Ch. Jacquet's Clinton (by Int. Ch. Jacquet's Novarese ex Jacquet's Chiqua), owned by Sadao Kikachi. Bred by George Spanos and Richard Tomita.

Ch. Jacquet's Tribeca (by Int. Ch. Jacquet's Novarese ex Jacquet's Shasta D'Shamrock), bred by Richard Tomita and owned by Carol Brewer.

Am-Can. Ch. Wilderson's Chessi of Jacquet (by Ch. Jacquet's Gaspard ex Valhal's Victorian Lady), bred by Larry and Halle Kugler and owned by Edgar and Florence Wilderson.

Ch. Jacquet's Brass Idol, BOB, handled by Marylou Hatfield, owned by Vincent and Ginger Sbarra; Ch. Jacquet's First Lady, WB, handled by breeder Rick Tomita, owned by Vera and Julian Gladstone; Ch. Jacquet's Monarch, WD, handled by Kim Pastella for owners Peter and Florence Tillotson; and Ch. Jacquet's Prince of Fortune, RWD, handled by owner Ray Shupak; Ch. Jacquet's Faline, RWB, handled by Susan Fontana for owners Bernie and Georgine Schwerdtfeger. Judge, Aimee Acklen.

Left: Ch. Jacquet's Classie Lassie (by Int. Ch. Jacquet's Urko), bred by Richard Tomita and owned by Les and Jean Hagerdorn.

Below: Am-Ber-Can. Ch. Jacquet's Millenium (by Int. Ch. Jacquet's Cloud Dancer ex Ch. Jacquet's Cebele, CD), owned by Jose Quiros and handled by Karen Speck.

The very smart and lovable Ch. Jacquet's Lalique (by Ch. Happy Ours Fortune de Jacquet ex Jacquets Cecelia), owned by Bebe T. Ventura.

Am-Ber-Jap-Can-Tai-HK-Int. Ch. Jacquet's Agassiz (by Ch. Merrilane's April Fashion ex Jacquet's Hot Summer), owned by Ted and Barbara Widmayer, Richard Tomita and Lana Tsan.

ABC 1979 Winners: Ch. Jacquet's Brass Idol, WD, (by Ch. Merrilane's April Fashion ex Jacquet's Perigal, DOM), owned by Vincent and Ginger Sbarra, and Ch. Jacquet's Shana of Talisman, WB, (by Ch. Carlwen's Sean of Erin ex Ch. Jacquet's Mirah of Micah), owned by Charles and Olive Beaudreau and bred by Richard Tomita and Dorothy Shames.

Ch. Jacquet's Attribute, CGC, TDI (by Int. Ch. Jacquet's Novarese ex Jacquet's Alexis), owned and loved by Susan Pattman.

Ch. Jacquet's Attribute, CGC, TDI

BY SUSAN PATTMAN

The story of Attribute begins like that of many Jacquet Boxers. He was very carefully bred to be a member of the Jacquet show tradition of excellence, having eight Sires of Merit in his pedigree (including Jacquet's very renowned International Champions, Novarese and Urko). Rick Tomita asked me to lead train and take young Attribute to handling classes and match shows. As with his other "kids," Rick also requested that I take him home for some socializing with my family. While Attribute lived in our home, we became very attached to him. When Rick saw how attached my 18-month-old child had become and how the puppy adored the child, he agreed to sell Attribute to us with our promise that we would show him.

"Tribber," as he is called, quickly became a member of our household and seemed to be a natural babysitter for our son. They became fast friends and nearly inseparable. I was working on finishing my undergraduate degree at the time, so the two of them kept one another entertained for many hours while I studied and attended classes.

A little over one year from the time Tribber came to live with us, our three-year-old started a fire in our kitchen while experimenting with our toaster oven. I was at school at the time and my husband was working in the office on the second floor of our 100-year-old home. Tribber raced to Michael and barked at him. Thinking the dog just wanted to go out, he ignored his barking. The young dog, 18 months old at this time, did not give up. He continued

to bark, but when Michael did not get up he had to do something else. He then grabbed Michael's arm with his mouth to pull him (he had never mouthed or bit any of us before). Sensing that something must be wrong, Michael got up and called for our son. He did not answer, so Michael went to the hallway to call again. He then saw the smoke rising from the staircase. Tribber continued to bark and pull at Michael to bring him toward the stairs. Tribber quickly moved into action. The young dog charged down the stairs into the smoke-filled first floor and found his way to the kitchen. He entered the burning room, grabbed his young master by his clothing, pulled him into the adjoining dining room and held him by the front door by lying on top of the child so that he could not get up. When Michael saw the fire, he went to the basement, got the fire extinguisher and put out the blaze. He then opened the windows and doors to clear the smoke and took the scorched toaster-oven outside. Michael then began to look for Sean and Tribber. He found them by the door and the tired dog wagged his tail and got up off the baby. Michael first hugged Sean and checked him for burns. He took them both outside for some fresh air and he then looked at our "show dog"—the one that never barks or plays rough, that sleeps a lot and that does little more than play ball with our son to make him laugh. Michael looked at him and cried tears of joy and appreciation.

Ch. Jacquet's Attribute, CGC, TDI expertly handled by Marylou Hatfield. Bred by Rick Tomita and Chris Armstrong.

Ch. Jacquet's Noire (Ch. Cachet's Mad Max of TuRo ex Ch. Jacquet's Jousseline), bred by Richard Tomita, handled by Linda Mastrapasqua, under judge Marcia Foy.

I have been told by the fire inspector and the neighbors that if it were not for the actions of my brave dog, I would have lost my home in not much more time and, quite possibly, my son and my husband as well. Needless to say, our house has smoke-detectors and is "fire proofed" to the hilt today. But the gratitude I have to Tribber, and to Rick for letting me have this fine young dog, is immeasurable.

Tribber has gone on to do other notable things. He was among the first of Rick's kids to earn a Canine Good Citizen award for his wonderful temperament and obedient nature. He has also earned a TDI certification, which permits him to do therapy work. In this capacity, Tribber has brought joy to children in the burn unit and cancer ward of a local hospital as well as many of the men at a nearby VA hospital. He also goes to nursing homes to visit senior citizens who can no longer have pets. Boxers are ideal for this type of work. They are gentle and sensitive and are an ideal size for bedside visitations. They seem to have a sixth sense about illnesses, sores and emotional states. They can be very spirited and play rough, but in these environments they

seem instinctually good. Tribber loves his therapy assignments. He will sit quietly and allow patients to stroke him, and he wiggles with joy when they speak to him — he also offers kisses when he is permitted.

Incidentally, he also has proven to be quite a showman. He became Jacquet's 120th champion, as he was bred to do. He was shown less than 50 times from puppyhood to retirement. He always placed with a ribbon as a class dog, with wins at Specialty shows and placements at the American Boxer Club Show, making us all very proud. He has multiple Best of Breed awards to look back on as well. He is a proven sire, with puppies that will no doubt leave the Jacquet mark of excellence in conformation, temperament and character.

We are honored and privileged to be owned by such a fine dog. Boxers can be very silly and stubborn at times, but they are always loyal and intelligent. When the chips are down, they come through. Tribber is a Boxer to the core: brave, noble, devoted and loyal. No other breed comes close to them. Once they have bonded to you, they are worth their weight in gold and will capture your heart forever.

Upper right: Author Richard Tomita with Karin Wilson and Ch. Karmel's Dream Weaver (by Ch. Berena's Gemini Splashdown ex Jacquet's Kiri Te Kanawa).

Upper left: Jacquet's Nebraska (by Int. Ch. Jacquet's Millennium ex Jacquet's Sugar Magnolia), handled by Kriste Kaemmlein, owned by Jose Quiros.

Lower left: The very talented and crafty Maxine owned by Siegi Lehmann. Maxine is handy with a snow shovel as well as many other household appliances—she can even paint!

Lower right: Marylou Carafello spends quality time with the six-month-old Holden. As the office manager of J-B Wholesale, Marylou has spent many, many hours with their lovable office dog Holden.

Author Richard Tomita awards the grand prize at the East Bay Boxer Club sweepstakes to Ch. Topaz' Tradewinds (by Ch. Bridgewood's B.K. Kahuna ex Topaz' Jitterbug), owned by Mark Fagan and Debbie McCarrol. Handled by Chery Cates.

Below: Rick Tomita awards Best Senior and Best Junior in Sweepstakes at the BC of Southern California to Two Dreams Mangas Blancas (by Am-Mex. Ch. Dean-Erik's Razin Kane ex Vision's Ginger and Spice), handled by Wendy Mattson-Bettis for owner Shannon Sheppard, and Ch. Sandhill's Color Me Sunshine (Ch. Baldr's Sun Smoke ex Ch. Wesan's Sun Daze), handled by James Bettis for owner Betty Aikenhead.

A memorable moment for the author as he awards Best Adult in Match to Ch. Thorwood's Red Hot Pepper (Ch. Nemrac's Ali Bey ex Ch. Faust's Remember Me v. Amerbrit), bred by James B. Goodwin and owned by Carmen N. Skinner.

AKC STANDARD FOR THE BOXER

eral appearance to which attractive color and arresting style contribute. Next is overall balance with special attention devoted to the head, after which the individual body components are examined for their correct construction, and efficiency of gait is evaluated.

Size, Proportion, Substance— **Height—**Adult males 22 1/2 to 25 inches; females 21 to 23 1/2 inches at the withers. Preferably, males should not be under the minimum nor females over the maximum; however, proper balance and quality in the individual should be of primary importance since there is no size disqualification. **Proportion—**The body in profile is of square proportion in that a horizontal line from the front of the forechest to the rear projection of the upper thigh should equal the length of a vertical line dropped from the top of the withers to the ground. **Substance—**Sturdy with balanced musculature. Males larger boned than their female counterparts.

General Appearance— The *ideal* Boxer is a medium-sized, square built dog of good substance with short back, strong limbs, and a short, tight-fitting coat. His well developed muscles are clean, hard and appear smooth under taut skin. His movements denote energy. The gait is firm, yet elastic, the stride free and ground-covering, the carriage proud. Developed to serve as guard, working and companion dog, he combines strength and agility with elegance and style. His expression is alert and temperament steadfast and tractable.

The chiseled head imparts to the Boxer a unique individual stamp. It must be in correct proportion to the body. The broad, blunt muzzle is the distinctive feature, and great value is placed upon its being of proper form and balance with the skull.

In judging the Boxer, first consideration is given to gen-

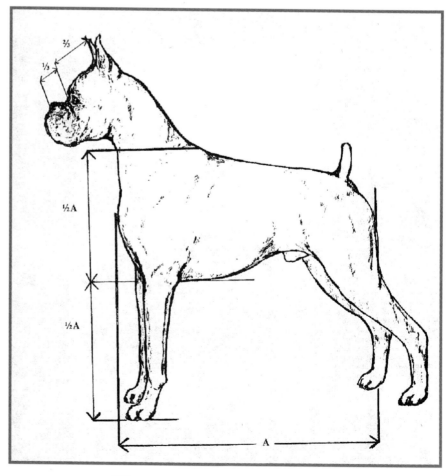

Head—The beauty of the head depends upon harmonious proportion of muzzle to skull. The blunt muzzle is one-third the length of the head from the occiput to the tip of the nose and two-thirds the width of the skull. The head should be clean, not showing deep wrinkles (wet). Wrinkles typically appear upon the forehead when ears are erect, and folds are always present from the lower edge of the stop running downward on both sides of the muzzle. **Expression**—Intelligent and alert. **Eyes**—Dark brown in color, not too small, too protruding or too deep-set. Their mood-mirroring character combined with the wrinkling of the forehead gives the Boxer head

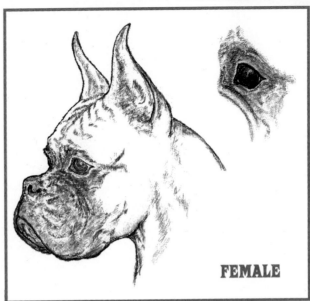

FEMALE

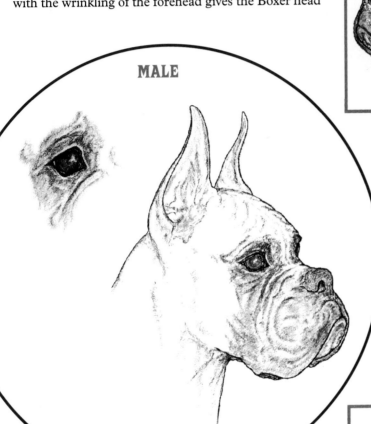

MALE

The nose should be broad and black.

The upper jaw is broad where attached to the skull and maintains this breadth except for a very slight tapering to the front. The lips, which complete the formation of the muzzle, should meet evenly in front. The upper lip is thick and padded, filling out the frontal space created by the projection of the lower jaw, and laterally is supported by the canines of the lower jaw. Therefore, these canines must stand far apart and be of good length so that the front surface of the muzzle is broad and squarish and, when viewed from the side, shows moderate layback. The chin

its unique quality of expressiveness. **Ears**—Set at the highest points of the sides of the skull are cropped, cut rather long and tapering, raised when alert. **Skull**—The top of the skull is slightly arched, not rounded, flat nor noticeably broad, with the occiput not overly pronounced. The forehead shows a slight indentation between the eyes and forms a distinct stop with the topline of the muzzle. The cheeks should be relatively flat and not bulge (cheekiness), maintaining the clean lines of the skull and should taper into the muzzle in a slight, graceful curve. **Muzzle**—The muzzle, proportionately developed in length, width and depth, has a shape influenced first through the formation of both jawbones, second through the placement of the teeth, and third through the texture of the lips. The top of the muzzle should not slant down (downfaced), nor should it be concave (dishfaced); however, the tip of the nose should lie slightly higher than the root of the muzzle.

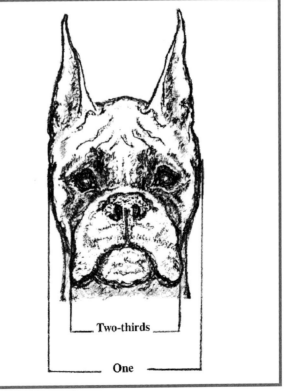

Two-thirds

One

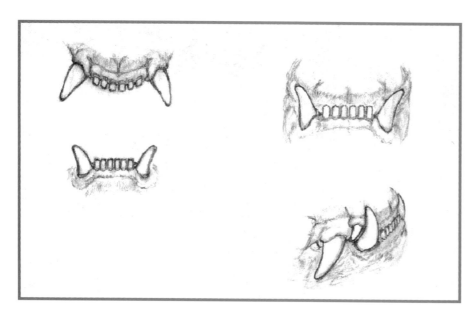

ing, but standing almost perpendicular to the ground. The dewclaws may be removed. Feet should be compact, turning neither in nor out, with well arched toes. *Faults*—Loose or loaded shoulders. Tied in or bowed out elbows.

Hindquarters—The hindquarters are strongly muscled with angulation in balance with that of the forequarters. The thighs are broad and curved, the breech musculature hard and strongly developed. Upper and lower thigh long. Leg well angulated at the stifle with a

should be perceptible from the side as well as from the front. *Bite*—The Boxer bite is undershot; the lower jaw protrudes beyond the upper and curves slightly upward. The incisor teeth of the lower jaw are in a straight line, with the canines preferably up front in the same line to give the jaw the greatest possible width. The upper line of incisors is slightly convex with the corner upper incisors fitting snugly back of the lower canine teeth on each side. *Faults*—Skull too broad. Cheekiness. Wrinkling too deep (wet) or lacking (dry). Excessive flews. Muzzle too light for skull. Too pointed a bite (snipy), too undershot, teeth or tongue showing when mouth closed. Eyes noticeably lighter than ground color of coat.

Neck, Topline, Body—*Neck*—Round, of ample length, muscular and clean without excessive, hanging skin (dewlap). The neck has a distinctly marked nape with an elegant arch blending smoothly into the withers. *Topline*—Smooth, firm and slightly sloping. *Body*—The chest is of fair width, and the forechest well defined and visible from the side. The brisket is deep, reaching down to the elbows; the depth of the body at the lowest point of the brisket equals half the height of the dog at the withers. The ribs, extending far to the rear, are well arched but not barrel shaped.

The back is short, straight and muscular and firmly connects the withers to the hindquarters.

The loins are short and muscular. The lower stomach line is slightly tucked up, blending into a graceful curve to the rear. The croup is slightly sloped, flat and broad. *Faults*—Short, heavy neck. Chest too broad, too narrow or hanging between shoulders. Lack of forechest. Hanging stomach. Slab-sided rib cage. Long or narrow loin, weak union with croup. Falling off of croup. Higher in rear than in front.

Forequarters—The shoulders are long and sloping, close-lying, and not excessively covered with muscle (loaded). The upper arm is long, approaching a right angle to the shoulder blade. The elbows should not press too closely to the chest wall nor stand off visibly from it.

The forelegs are long, straight and firmly muscled and when viewed from the front, stand parallel to each other. The pastern is strong and distinct, slightly slant-

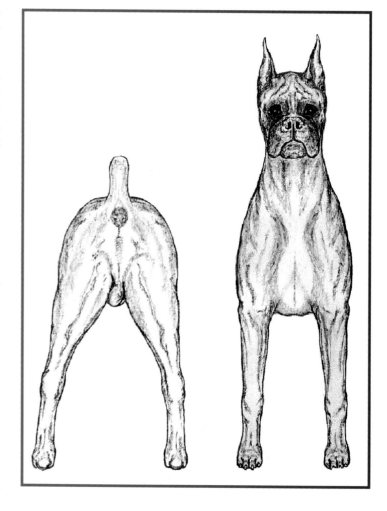

clearly defined, well "let down" hock joint. Viewed from behind, the hind legs should be straight with hock joints leaning neither in nor out. From the side, the leg below the hock (metatarsus) should be almost perpendicular to the ground, with a slight slope to the rear permissible. The metatarsus should be short, clean and strong. The Boxer has no rear dewclaws. *Faults*—Steep or over-angulated hindquarters. Light thighs or underdeveloped hams. Over-angulated (sickle) hocks. Hindquarters too far under or too far behind.

Coat—Short, shiny, lying smooth and tight to the body.

Color—The colors are fawn and brindle. Fawn shades vary from light tan to mahogany. The brindle ranges from sparse, but clearly defined black stripes on a fawn background, to such a heavy concentration of black striping that the essential fawn background color barely, although clearly, shows through (which may give the appearance of "reverse brindling").

White markings should be of such distribution as to enhance the dog's appearance, but may not exceed one-third of the entire coat. They are not desirable on the flanks or on the back of the torso proper. On the face, white may replace part of the otherwise essential black mask and may extend in an upward path between the eyes, but it must not be excessive, so as to detract from true Boxer expression. *Faults*—Unattractive or misplaced white markings. *Disqualifications*—Boxers that are any color other than fawn or brindle. Boxers with a total of white markings exceeding one-third of the entire coat.

Gait—Viewed from the side, proper front and rear angulation is manifested in a smoothly efficient, level-backed, ground covering stride with powerful drive emanating from a freely operating rear. Although the front legs do not contribute impelling power, adequate "reach" should be evident to prevent interference, overlap or "sidewinding" (crabbing). Viewed from the front, the shoulders should remain trim and the elbows not flare out. The legs are parallel until gaiting narrows the track in proportion to increasing speed, then the legs come in under the body but should never cross. The line from the shoulder down through the leg should remain straight although not necessarily perpendicular to the ground. Viewed from the rear, a Boxer's rump should not roll. The hind feet should "dig in" and track relatively true with the front. Again, as speed increases, the normally broad rear track will become narrower. *Faults*—Stilted or inefficient gait. Lack of smoothness.

Character and Temperament—These are of paramount importance in the Boxer. Instinctively a "hearing" guard dog, his hearing is alert, dignified and self-assured. In the show ring, his behavior should exhibit constrained animation. With family and friends, his temperament is fundamentally playful, yet patient and stoical with children. Deliberate and wary with strangers, he will exhibit curiosity but, most importantly, fearless courage if threatened. However, he responds promptly to friendly overtures honestly rendered. His intelligence, loyal affection and tractability to discipline make him a highly desirable companion. *Faults*—Lack of dignity and alertness. Shyness.

DISQUALIFICATIONS

Boxers that are any color other than fawn or brindle. Boxers with a total of white markings exceeding one-third of the entire coat.

Approved March 14, 1989
Effective May 1, 1989

Illustrations for this chapter drawn by Eleanor Linderholm-Wood.

REVISING THE STANDARD

The most recent revision of the Boxer standard was approved by the American Kennel Club on March 14, 1989. Many think it is more concise, clear and correct than the previous standard approved in September 1980.

The American Kennel Club required all breed standard revisions to conform with their uniform format and guidelines. This structured the American Boxer Club Standard Committee's work in organizing the order of the principal elements of the standard, condensing the description of each part and clarifying the wording. Constant attention was paid to eliminating unnecessary or repetitive wording. Only the most serious of faults were allowed to be listed. The committee consisted of Carl and Eleanor Linderholm Wood (Woodcrest and Merrilane in California), Dr. Theodore Fickes (Arriba in Massachusetts) and Lois Matthews (Box-M in Hawaii). Because of the distance between these club members, most of the work in drafting this revision was done in letters and over the telephone. Periodic review was sought with the American Kennel Club as well since the guidelines and format represented a new policy procedure at that time.

This was not a simple task, but the much clearer, more correct standard was accepted by the American Boxer Club Board and approved by the membership prior to being submitted to the American Kennel Club.

Ch. Canyonair's Talked About (Ch. Canyonair Hickory Dick, CD ex Ch. Canyonair Honey Chile), owned Coleman Cook, ranked among the top Boxers of the 1950s.

Am-Can. Ch. Barrage of Quality Hill, SOM (by Ch. Bang Away of Sirrah Crest ex Valley's Grove's Applause), winning Best in Show under the expert handling of Jane Forsyth. Owners, Mr. and Mrs. Jonette Shouse.

More recently the American Kennel Club suggested that the parent breed clubs add illustrations to enhance understanding of their individual standards. To this end, the American Boxer Club Board of Directors in November 1991 approved a series of such drawings. These were drawn by Eleanor Linderholm Wood with invaluable constructive suggestions from Dr. Theodore Fickes of the Standard Committee and Mrs. Billie McFadden, Judges' Education Chairperson. *The Illustrated Standard Booklet* was completed by Ellie and became available to the public in March 1992. Ellie used many photographs and slides to depict the particular part of the Boxer's anatomy she sketched. In addition, she had many reference books at her disposal, which she found indispensable. Of course, her main guide was the picture she carried in her "mind's eye" of how the ideal Boxer should look. This image began taking shape at Mazelaine in the early 1940s when Jack Wagner would use many Boxers

Ch. Zacksappeal (by Ch. Zack v. Dom ex Marlene v. Burcham), owned by Frances Styers Abercrombie.

Ch. Mazelaine's Zazarac Brandy, SOM (by Am-Can. Ch. Merry Monarch ex Ch. Warbaby of Mazelaine), owned by Mr. and Mrs. John P. Wagner, won the Westminster Kennel Club show in 1949 under the superb handling of Phil Marsh.

in his kennel to show as examples of particular anatomical structure. This he did routinely when visitors came to learn about Boxers, and Ellie absorbed much of his wisdom. Searching through the pictures, slides and illustrations in reference books heightened Ellie's desire to find that "perfect" visual reference she could attempt to sketch. She feels that the wish to make each drawing better, more clear and correct will always be with her.

This is the same kind of excitement a serious breeder experiences when planning his breeding program. The breeder must study of the standard, apply this knowledge and use it objectively to evaluate the pluses and minuses of individuals to be bred together as well as those in the immediate background, since they too contribute to the bank of genes and the puppies produced.

Ch. Arriba's Prima Donna (Ch. Flintwood's Live Ammo ex Arriba's Alicia) won the Westminster show in 1970, handled by Jane Forsyth and awarded Best in Show by Anna Katherine Nicholas. Owners, Dr. and Mrs. P.J. Pagano and Dr. Theodore S. Fickes. Breeder, V. Baribeault.

Ch. Barday's Chatterbox (by Ch. Hot Shot of Bon-Ton ex Ch. Brayshaw's Saucy Backtalk), bred by David Stein and Barbara O'Neil and handled by John Connolly. The breeders gave her to owners Richard Tomita and Bill Scolnik as one of their foundation Jacquet bitches.

Ch. Dempsey's Copper Gentleman, SOM (by Ch. Jered's Spellbinder ex Fontana's Crimson Mist), bred by Robert Dempsey and owned by Mary Smith. Judge, Maxwell Riddle. Handler, Joe Gregory.

Ch. Canyonair's Man on Fire, SOM (by Ch. Canyonair's Hickory Dick ex Ric-Mac's Dorable Darlin, a Bang Away daughter), owned by Ruth Wurmser and handled by Joe Gregory.

Ch. Terudon's Kiss Me Kate (by Am-Can. Ch. Barrage of Quality Hill ex Canyonair Katrinka), handled by Joe Gregory and owned by Ruth Wurmser.

Best in Show winning Ch. Capriana's Step Aside (by Ch. Capriana's Renegade ex Ch. Lesker's Ginger), bred by Charles and Isolde Stofko.

Best in Show winning Ch. Cajon's Can Can (by Am-Can. Ch. Barrage of Quality Hill ex Ch. Treceder's Sequence), handled by Ray Curry, owned by Willie Vicens.

Best in Show winning Ch. Galanjud's Blue Chip (by Ch. Salgray's Ovation ex Elharlen's Camero), handled by Jane Forsyth for owners Mr. and Mrs. Judson Streicher.

Ch. Eldic's Landlord, SOM (by Am-Can. Ch. Eldic's Darius ex Eldic's Dark Dream), owned by Eleanor Haeberle, winning BOB at WKC. Co-breeder, Mrs. Walter Amos.

Since its inception in 1936, the American Boxer Club National Specialty has attracted the greatest Boxers in the United States to come together to compete for "Boxer of the Year"—Best of Breed at the ABC. It's never as simple as "a b c" and it takes a great dog in great condition with a great handler. We salute all these "greats" in this chapter dedicated to the ABC.

Below: Seven ABC national and regional Best of Breed winners in the 1972 Parade of Champions: (*left to right*): Ch. Salgray's Ambush, SOM with Stan Flowers, Ch. Kreyon's Firebrand with owner Margaret Krey, Ch. Arriba's Prima Donna and Ch. Salgray's Double Talk with Jane Forsyth, Ch. Nadora's Black Lace with Dick Baum, Ch. Yours True Lee, SOM with Al Lee and Int. Ch. Scher-Khoun Shadrack, SOM with Shirley DeBoer.

FROM A CONVERSATION WITH MARGE ARCHIBALD

In the late '40s, the American Boxer Club was a small happy group that met monthly (or possibly bi-monthly) in a hotel in New York. Each meeting had a report of the club's finances and various members gave talks or arranged for programs about Boxers. All sorts of situations were discussed, such as taking a regional show out to the West. In those days, the Board made the decisions.

Kennels were generally bigger (and fewer). Special ones come to mind: Salgray of the Hamilburgs from Massachusetts; Dick Kettles, the owner of Warlord, from Long Island; Henry Lark from Connecticut. People generally came from Pennsylvania, New Jersey, Massachusetts and, of course, New York for the meetings, and they came on a regular basis. There was a tremendous amount of camaraderie and a sharing of mutual interests. Many good close friendships were formed in the ABC, and most of all there was good sportsmanship.

Everyone went to the local shows. There were no motor homes or vans then, so there was a lot of tailgating. Whoever had a house close to the show had a party afterward for everyone. All of the shows had good Boxer entries and, while there were many professional handlers, lots of owners showed their own dogs. This, of course, is in contrast to the membership of today (which numbers about 1000) where the primary contact is through the mail and where, needless to say, the warmth of personal contact often is lost, and the majority of members only get together once or twice a year at the national or regional Specialties.

DATE	BEST OF BREED	BEST OF OPPOSITE SEX*
1936	Ch. Corso v. Uracher Wasserfall	Bonzo v. Stolzenbergenhof ***
1937	Ch. Corso v. Uracher Wesserfall	Biene v. Elbe Bogen Sumbula ***
1938	Ch. Biene v. Elbe-Bogen se Sumbula	Eva v.d. Stuttgarter ***
1939	Ch. Biene v. Elbe-Bogen se Sumbula	Mazelaine Kelsey of Kenoosa ***
1940	Ch. Kurass v.d. Blutenau of Dorick	Mahderl's Miss Eva
1941	Ch. Serenade of Mazelaine	Ch. Adolph of Balancing Rock
1942	Ch. Overture of Mazelaine	Ch. Mahderf's El Chico
1943	Ch. Serenade of Mazelaine	Kemia Cavalier
1944	Warlord of Mazelaine	Ch. Gavotte of Mazelaine
1945	Ch. Warlord of Mazelaine	Aligau of Brielynn
1946	Wild Deuces of Mazelaine	Ch. Gentleman Jim of Rye Top
1947	Ch. Warlord of Mazelaine	Nylon of Mazelaine
1948	Ch. Apollo of San Joaquin	Ch. Victory Son of Rye Top
1949	Ch. Four Roses	Ch. Mazelaine Gallantry
1950	Ch. Yoomph of Sirrah Crest	Ch. Duchess Captain Flash
1951	Ch. Bang Away of Sirrah Crest	Ch. Tall Elms Pollyanna
1952	Ch. Barmere's Locket	Ch. Clinaude's Count v.d. Karlo
1953	Meritaire's Fancy Free	Ch. Bedazzle of Brianole
1954	Ch. Spark Plug	Ch. Jered's Sweet Stuff
1955	Barrage of Quality Hill	Bang Bang Baby
1956	Ch. Baroque of Quality Hill	Ch. Barrage of Quality Hill
1957	Ch. Barrage of Quality Hill	Ch. Galanjud's Bewitching
1958	Ch. Marjack's Golden Windjammer	Ch. Terudon's Kiss Me Kate
1959	Ch. Hollee's Top Preview	Ch. Terudon's Kiss Me Kate
1960	Ch. Mazelaine's Grand Master	Ch. Wyndyway's Headpiece
1961	Ch. Evo-Wen's Impressario	Ch. Muzzy's China Doll
1962	Ch. Flintwood's Rabble Rouser	Nagerroc's Sauci Sioux
1963	Ch. Treceder's Painted Lady	Ch. Flintwood's Rabble Rouser
1964	Ch. Treceder's Painted Lady	Ch. Flintwood's Rabble Rouser
1965	Ch. Salgray's Fashion Plate	Ch. Treceder's Sequence
1966	Ch. Salgray's Fashion Plate	Jarmac's Ginger Peachy
1967	Salgray's Ambush	Ch. Capriana's Step Aside
1968	Ch. Salgray's Ambush	Ch. Arriba's Prima Donna
1969	Ch. Arriba's Prima Donna	Ch. Rocky of Shawnee Trail
1970	Salgray's Double Talk	Ch. Arriba's Prima Donna
1971	Ch. Nadora's Black Lace	Ch. Scher-Khoun's Shadrack
1972	Ch. Scher-Khoun's Shadrack	Regency Nite Life
1973	Ch. Aracrest's Jered	Ch. Salgray's Jitterbug
1974	Ch. Merrilane's Love Life of Jofra	Ch. Regency's Nite Life
1975	Salgray's VIP	Ch. Squire Lane's Geraldine
1976	Twin-Willow's Mr. T of Five T's	Ch. Main Street Miss Liberty
1977	Ch. Galanjud's Blue Chip	Ch. Sarazak's Moon Glo
1978	Ch. Sarazak's Moon Glo	Ch. Salgray's Market Wise
1979	Ch. Marburl's Rahab of Wesan	Ch. Merrilane's April Fashion
1980	Ch. Marburl's Rahab of Wesan	Ch. Siegel's Top Contender
1981	Ch. Niklof's Empress of TuRo	Ch. Siegel's Top Contender
1982	Ch. Quebo's Miss Saturday Night	Ch. Vimar's We Believe in Magic
1983	Ch. Richaire's Domino	Ch. Kameo's Show Girl
1984	Ch. Wagner Wilverday Famous Amos	Ch. TuRo's Monogram of Sarazak
1985	Ch. Wagner Wilverday Famous Amos	Ch. Laureate Kiss Me Kate
1986	Ch. TuRo's Cachet	Ch. Shieldmont's Issues N Answers
1987	Ch. Wagner Wilverday Famous Amos	Ch. Wood's End Chas 'N Rainbows
1988	Ch. Wagner Wilverday Famous Amos	Ch. Breezewood's One Mo Time
1989	Ch. Berena's Tribute To Fa-Fa	Ch. Jodi Emmy Murphy of Heritage
1990	Ch. Heldenbrand's Jet Breaker	Ch. Kiebla's Tradition of TuRo
1991	Ch. Kiebla's Tradition of TuRo	Ch. Fiero's Tally Ho-Tailo
1992	Ch. Kiebla's Tradition of TuRo	Ch. Shieldmont's Let's Make a Deal
1993	Ch. Kiebla's Tradition of TuRo	Ch. High-Tech's Arbitrage
1994	Ch. Hi-Tech's Arbitrage	Ch. Kiebla's Tradition of TuRo
1995	Ch. Kimber-D Pinebrook Dusty Road	Carlon's Red Hot**
1996	Ch. TuRos Futurian of Cachet	Ch. Kiebla's Tradition of TuRo
1997	Ch. Hi-Tech Johnny J of Boxerton	Ch. Kiebla's Tradition of TuRo

*The official designation of Best of Opposite Sex was not introduced until 1940.
**Winners Bitch at 1995 ABC not a champion at time of win (BOS)
***1936 through 1939 represent Best of Winners not BOS

CH. CORSO V. URACHER WASSERFALL SE SUMBULA.

INT. CH. KURASS VD BLUTENAU OF DORICK.

(BY INT. SIGURD VON DOM EX GER. CH. GRETEL V. HOHENNEUFFEN)
Ch. Corso won the first and second American Boxer Club Specialties.
The 1936 show, with 56 entries, was judged by F. W. Simmons and
the 1937 show, with 44 entires, was judged by Hubert Doll. Ch. Corso,
the sire of three champions for the Sumbula kennel, was owned by
H. B. Palmedo and bred by Karl Walz of Germany.

Ch. Biene, a lovely bitch owned and bred by the same gentlemen
connected with Ch. Corso, won the ABC Specialties in 1938 and
1939, judged by Enno Meyer and F.W. Simmons, respectively. Both
shows drew an entry of 74 dogs.

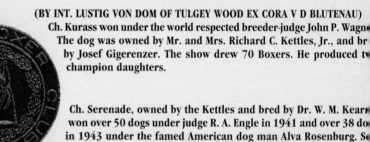

(BY INT. LUSTIG VON DOM OF TULGEY WOOD EX CORA V D BLUTENAU)
Ch. Kurass won under the world respected breeder-judge John P. Wagne
The dog was owned by Mr. and Mrs. Richard C. Kettles, Jr., and br
by Josef Gigerenzer. The show drew 70 Boxers. He produced tw
champion daughters.

Ch. Serenade, owned by the Kettles and bred by Dr. W. M. Kearr
won over 50 dogs under judge R. A. Engle in 1941 and over 38 do
in 1943 under the famed American dog man Alva Rosenburg. Se
enade was the first Best in Show dog for Mazelaine and produc
two champions.

CH. BIENE V. ELBE-BOGEN SE SUMBULA.

(BY INT. CH. DORIAN V. MARIENHOF OF MAZELAINE EX ELGA V. RAUENSTEIN)

CH. SERENADE OF MAZELAINE.

(INT. CH. DORIAN V. MARIENHOF OF MAZELAINE EX CH. CRONA V. ZWERGECK

1942

CH. OVERTURE OF MAZELAINE.

1944
1945
1947

CH. WARLORD OF MAZELAINE, SOM.

(BY INT. CH. UTZ VON DOM OF MAZELAINE EX MAZELAINE'S CHLOE) Ch. Overture, sired by the great Int. Ch. Utz von Dom, was the second Mazelaine Boxer to win the National, though the first bred by John P. Wagner. Overture won over 56 dogs under Dr. S. Potter Bartley. Overture was owned by Mrs. Lawrence A. Slesinger and produced three champion sons, including a Sire of Merit.

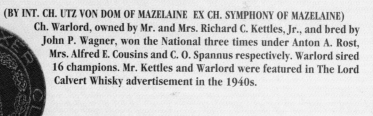

Ch. Apollo, owned and bred by Mr. and Mrs. J. Howard Davis, won over 235 Boxers under judge Hans Oberhammer. In his career, he sired eight American champions and one Canadian champion.

(BY INT. CH. UTZ VON DOM OF MAZELAINE EX CH. SYMPHONY OF MAZELAINE) Ch. Warlord, owned by Mr. and Mrs. Richard C. Kettles, Jr., and bred by John P. Wagner, won the National three times under Anton A. Rost, Mrs. Alfred E. Cousins and C. O. Spannus respectively. Warlord sired 16 champions. Mr. Kettles and Warlord were featured in The Lord Calvert Whisky advertisement in the 1940s.

Winning the 1945 Specialty over 178 Boxers entered.

1948

CH. APOLLO OF SAN JOAQUIN, SOM.

(BY WHIRLAWAY OF MAZELAINE, CD EX GAY LADY INGA OF SAN JOAQUIN)

1945

CH. WARLORD OF MAZELAINE.

CH. WILD DEUCES OF MAZELAINE.

(BY CH. ARCHDUKE OF VALCAR EX CH. VOLANTE OF MAZELAINE)
Wild Deuces, owned and bred by John P. Wagner, won under Alva Rosenberg over 175 entries. Wild Deuces won the 1946 National before she was herself a champion.

Ch. Four Roses, owned and bred by Mr. and Mrs. Henry W. Lark of Apple Hill Farm, won under Dr. R.C. Harris (the famed breeder of Ch. Bang Away) over a spectacular entry of 241 Boxers.

CH. YOOMPH OF SIRRAH CREST.

(BY CH. RIOT OF SIRRAH CREST EX ULTRA OF SIRRAH CREST)
Ch Yoomph, bred and owned by Dr. and Mrs. R. C. Harris, won under Irwin B. Hollenbach over 257 Boxers. She produced three champions in whelp to Ch. Bang Away of Sirrah Crest, SOM.

Ch. Bang Away, arguably the most famous Boxer ever to live, an American and Canadian Sire of Merit and the record holder for Best in Show victories, of which he won 121 all-breed events, handled by Nate Levine and owned and bred by Dr. and Mrs. R.C. Harris. Shown taking BOS is Ch. Tall Elm's Pollyana (by Ch. Meritaire's Pinnocchio ex Meritaire's Encore), owned by Dr. and Mrs. Milton Harkrader. The judge was Lena Ludwig. Bang Away sired 81 American champions and 12 Canadian champions, including 7 SOMs and 4 DOMs.

CH. FOUR ROSES.

(BY CH. WAR MAJOR OF CRYSTAL EX ROWDY OF ROWAYTON)

CH. BANG AWAY OF SIRRAH CREST, SOM.

(BY INT. CH. URSA MAJOR OF SIRRAH CREST EX VERILY VERILY OF SIRRAH CREST)

CH. BARMERE'S LOCKET.

(BY CH. YACHTMAN OF BARMERE EX CH. NEW DEAL OF BARMERE)
Ch. Locket, owned and bred by Barmere Kennels of Mrs. William Z. Breed, won under Alva Rosenberg over 331 Boxers. She produced three American and Canadian champion get to three different sires, Ch. Elixie of Raineylane, Ch. Bang Away of Sirrah Crest, and Mazelaine's Kapelmeister.

AM-CAN. CH. SPARK PLUG, SOM

(BY CH. ZACK VON DOM EX ROYAL LESSA V. KOENIG)
Ch. Spark Plug, owned and handled by Larry Downey and bred by Steven N. Lovett, won over 254 Boxers under judge John P. Wagner.

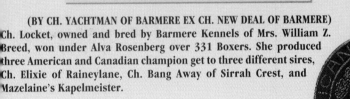

Fancy Free, handled by Jane Kamp (Forsyth), won over 256 Boxers from the classes. The judge was Dr. Lewis E. Daniels. Fancy Free, the sire of four champions, was owned and bred by Mrs. Henry W. Lark.

Ch. Baroque, litter sister to Best in Show and ABC-winning Barrage, was bred by Mr. and Mrs. M.E. Greiner, Jr. and owned by Mr. and Mrs. John P. Wagner. She mothered two Mazelaine champions.

CH. MERITAIRE'S FANCY FREE.

(BY CH. BANG AWAY OF SIRRAH CREST EX MERITAIRE'S WATER WITCH)

CH. BAROQUE OF QUALITY HILL.

(BY CH. BANG AWAY OF SIRRAH CREST EX VALLEY GROVE'S APPLAUSE)

AM-CAN. CH. BARRAGE OF QUALITY HILL, SOM

CH. HOLLEE'S TOP PREVIEW.

(BY CH. BANG AWAY OF SIRRAH CREST EX VALLEY GROVE'S APPLAUSE) Ch. Barrage, owned and bred by Mr. and Mrs. M. E. Greiner, Jr., won ABC twice, as well as BOS in 1956 to Baroque. Handled by Jane Kamp (Forsyth), Barrage is shown winning the 1957 Specialty with Ch. Galanjud's Bewitching, handled by Peter Knoop, taking BOS. The judge in 1955 was Robert Kerns and in 1957, Hugo Krave. Barrage sired a total of 47 champions in the US and Canada, including 3 SOMs and 4 DOMs.

Windjammer, bred by Mary Jackson and owned by Mr. and Mrs. John P. Wagner, won under Alfred Putnam over 186 dogs. He sired 21 American and Canadian champions.

(BY CH. SIR TOPPER OF HOLLEE EX MAROTAI'S FANCY DANCER) Ch. Top Preview, bred by J.C. Paine and owned by D. F. Starkweather and P. Mitchell, won under Carl A. Wood over 179 dogs. He sired three champions.

Grand Master, sired by 1958 ABC winner, was owned by Bernice and Bruce Dilly and bred by Mr. John P. Wagner, who judged on this prestigious occasion.

CH. MARJACK'S GOLDEN WINDJAMMER, SOM.

(BY CH. CAPTAIN LOOKOUT OF THORHALL EX INT. CH. MARJACK'S GOLDEN MIST)

CH. MAZELAINE'S GRAND MASTER.

(BY CH. MARJACK'S GOLDEN WINDJAMMER EX MAZELAINE'S HI-DE-HO)

CH. EVO-WEN'S IMPRESSARIO, SOM.

CH. TRECEDER'S PAINTED LADY.

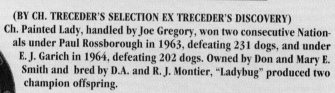

(BY CH. EVO-WEN'S BIG STORY EX EVO-WEN'S MECQUE MECQUE)
Impressario's record was nothing shy of impressive, as he won every Specialty in which he was entered. Owned by Mrs. George M. Cowie and bred by R. B. Owens, he sired over 20 champions and won 45 all-breed Best in Shows. The judge of the 1961 National was Lena L. Ludwig and there were 200 Boxers entered. He sired 27 American and Canadian champions as well as 2 DOMs.

Ch. Rabble Rouser, owned by Robert and Enid Randall and bred by L. D. Flint, won under judge R. S. Salomon over 158 dogs. In 1963 and 1964, he went BOS to Painted Lady, who proved a tough gal to beat. He sired ten American and Canadian champions with one SOM.

(BY CH. TRECEDER'S SELECTION EX TRECEDER'S DISCOVERY)
Ch. Painted Lady, handled by Joe Gregory, won two consecutive Nationals under Paul Rossborough in 1963, defeating 231 dogs, and under E. J. Garich in 1964, defeating 202 dogs. Owned by Don and Mary E. Smith and bred by D.A. and R. J. Montier, "Ladybug" produced two champion offspring.

A Sire of Merit in the US and Canada, Ch. Fashion Plate took home the trophies in both 1965 and 1966, owner-bred by Mr. and Mrs. D. M. Hamilburg. The judge in 1965 was A. Peter Knoop, who placed Fashion Plate over 235 dogs, and Bernard Brown in 1966, over 248 dogs. Fashion Plate sired 68 American and Canadian champions with 2 SOMs.

AM-CAN. CH. FLINTWOOD'S RABBLE ROUSER, SOM.

CH. SALGRAY'S FASHION PLATE, SOM.

(BY CH. BRAYSHAW'S MASQUERADER EX FLINTWOOD'S BANNED IN BOSTON)

(BY AM-CAN. CH. SALGRAY'S BATTLE CHIEF EX AM-CAN. CH. MARQUAM HILL'S FLAMINGO)

CH. SALGRAY'S AMBUSH, SOM.

CH. SALGRAY'S DOUBLE TALK.

(BY AM-CAN. CH. SALGRAY'S FLYING HIGH EX CH. SALGRAY'S FLAMING EMBER)
Salgray's Ambush, handled by Stan Flowers and owner-bred by Mr. and Mrs. D. M. Hamilburg, won the National from the classes in 1967 and as a champion in 1968. Hugo Krave judged in 1967 with an entry of 236 dogs, and James T. Culp over a record 351 entries in 1968. He sired 33 champions, 7 of which became SOMs!

Prima Donna, handled by Jane Forsyth, won the 1969 National under Joe Gregory with an entry of 245. Prima Donna was bred by Virgil J. Baribeault and owned by Dr. and Mrs. P. J. Pagano and Dr. Ted Fickes. The following year, Prima Donna would go on to win Best in Show at the Westminster Kennel Club show. In 1968 and 1970, she was BOS at the National.

(BY SALGRAY'S AMBUSH EX CH. SALGRAY'S FLAMING EMBER)
Double Talk, bred by Mr. and Mrs. Harold F. Foley and owned by Mr. and Mrs. Daniel M. Hamilburg, won the National from the classes under Phoebe Harris with the expert handling of Stan Flowers. Over 26. Boxers, Double Talk won the Breed over Prima Donna (who would go on to win BIS at Westminster within just days of the Specialty). He sired six champions for the Hamilburgs.

Black Lace, bred by Dorothy E. Allgair and owned by Josephine Waters, won under Landon Skarda, handled by Dick Baum, over 297 dogs. She produced only one champion who was Am-Can. Ch. Von Schorers Moon Shadow, SOM.

CH. ARRIBA'S PRIMA DONNA.

(BY CH. FLINTWOOD'S LIVE AMMO EX ARRIBA'S ALICIA)

CH. NADORA'S BLACK LACE.

(BY CH. VON SCHORER'S MOUNTAIN MUSIC EX SUEDEE'S NATASHA)

AM-CAN-BER. CH. SCHER-KHOUN'S SHADRACK, SOM.

CH. MERRILANE'S LOVE LIFE OF JOFRA.

(BY INT. CH. MILLAN'S FASHION HINT EX CAN CH. SCHER-KHOUN'S CAROUSEL) Shadrack, owned and bred by Ben and Shirley de Boer and handled by Shirley de Boer won the National under Larry Downey over 245 Boxers. Shadrack became a Sire of Merit in both the US and Canada, producing at least 111 champions, including 9 SOMs and 4 DOMs.

Jered, handled by Elgan (Johnny) Johnson) won the National under Paul Rossborough over 217 Boxers. Jered was owned by Al and Thelma Coffee and bred by Mr. and Mrs. J. V. McGriskin. This Sire of Merit produced 24 champions in the US and Canada, along with 2 SOMs.

(BY CH. ELDIC'S LANDLORD EX MERRILANE'S MAD PASSION, CD) Love Life, bred and handled by Eleanor Linderholm and owned by D. Crosier, won the National under Mrs. Virginia Salomon over 242 Boxers. He sired five champions.

V.I.P., owner-bred by the Hamilburgs, won the National from the classes over 268 Boxers under A. Peter Knoop. Stan Flowers handled to this important win. He sired three champion offspring.

AM-CAN. CH. ARACREST'S JERED, SOM.

CH. SALGRAY'S V.I.P.

(BY INT. CH. SCHER-KHOUN'S SHADRACK EX CAN. CH. JOCOLUS CHARMING FASHION)

(BY CH. SALGRAY'S AMBUSH EX CH. SALGRAY'S JITTERBUG)

CH. TWIN-WILLOWS MR. T. OF FIVE T'S.

CH. SARAZAK'S MOON-GLO.

(BY CH. BENJOMAN OF FIVE T'S EX TWIN WILLOW'S TEATIME)
Mr. T, handled by Leon De Priest, won the National from the Puppy classes under judge Joe Gregory over 253 Boxers, bred by Mary Thuemling and owned with his handler.

(BY AM-CAN CH. VON SCHORER'S MOON SHADOW EX CH. SARAZAK'S SCHEHEROZADE, CD)
Moon-Glo, owner-bred by Sarah Zavakos, handled by Stan Flowers won the National under Donald Starkweather over a record 38 dogs entered. She produced one champion son.

Blue Chip, handled by Jane Forsyth, was owned by Judson and Dorothy Streicher and bred by Phil and Sue Shimmin. He won the National under English breed authority and breeder Pat Heath over a record 361 dogs entered. The third son of Ch. Salgray's Ovation, SOM to win the National, Blue Chip sired only one champion.

Rahab of Wesan, bred by Wes and Ann Tomhave and owned by Mary Francis and Rufus Burleson, won the National in 1979 under Don Bradley over 334 dogs entered and in 1980 under Bea Goodman defeating 331 dogs. Handling was Johnny Johnson. She produced one champion daughter who was Ch. Marburl's Scarlet Cord, DOM.

CH. GALANJUD'S BLUE CHIP.

(BY CH. SALGRAY'S OVATION EX ELHARLEN'S CAMERO)

CH. MARBURL'S RAHAB OF WESAN.

(BY INT. CH. MARBURL'S JOSHUA EX CH. WESAN'S DARK APACHE MISS)

CH. NIKLOF'S EMPRESS TO TURO.

CH. RICHAIRE'S DOMINO.

(BY CH. TURO'S NATIVE DANCER EX CH. NIKLOFS LADY CAMILLA)
Empress, handled by Chic Ceccarini, owned by Arthur and Mary Ann Sergi, Patricia Turner, Sandra Roberts and Elizabeth Esacove, was bred by P. and S. Folkins. The judge was Theodore Wurmser, who picked Empress over 298 dogs. Although she never produced a champion, she produced a great producer in Sergi N BJ's Junior Strut.

Miss Saturday Night won the National over 375 dogs, selected by judge Eve Whitmore. She was bred by Lu Jackson and owner Martha Vidana. The handler was Chris Baum. She produced two champions.

(BY CH. TELSTAR'S HIGHFLYER EX TIFFANY OF BROOKWOOD)
Domino, handled by Richard Mysliewicz, was owner-bred by R. and C. Tolagian and won the National under Alice Downey over a record 411 dogs. He produced two champion sons.

Amos, bred by V. Hoffmann and owned by Barbara Wagner, was the only four-time winner of the ABC National. He won the National under John T. Connolly in 1984 and under Rufus C. Burleson in 1985. His handlers were Donald V. Simmons and Richard Baum. In 1987, he won under judge Joe Gregory; and in 1988 under judge Rosina Olifent-Brace. Amos sired 27 champions, including 4 SOMs and 2 DOMs.

CH. QUEBO'S MISS SATURDAY NIGHT.

(BY CH. ARACREST'S TALISMAN EX VIDANA D CAPIGUA)

AM-CAN. CH. WAGNER WILVERDAY FAMOUS AMOS, SOM.

(BY CH. MARQUAM HILL'S TRAPER OF TURO EX CH. WAGNER'S VISION OF WILVIRDAY)

CH. TURO'S CACHET.

CH. HELDENBRAND'S JET BREAKER, SOM.

(BY CH. MARQUAM HILL'S TRAPER OF TURO EX TURO'S KATRINA OF CROSS BAR) Cachet, winning under Mrs. Josephine W. Thomson, handled by Kimberly Pastella. She produced two champion sons including Ch. Cachet's Mad Max of TuRo, SOM.

(BY CH. HELDENBRAND'S HEART BREAKER EX HELDENBRAND'S JETTA JOUINA) Jet Breaker, bred by Elvina Heldenbrand and handled by Earl Overstreet won under German authority Joseph Heine. He has sired no fewer than 44 champions in the US and Canada, including 2 SOMs.

Fa-Fa, owned by Larry and Gene Neuman is the son of Famous Amos, handled by Richard and Christine Baum, winning under judge Patsy Connolly. Co-owned by breeders Bernie and Rena Toon. He was an SOM in the US and Canada. He has produced no fewer than 28 American and Canadian champions.

Tradition's tradition was winning the National. She won BOB three consecutive years and was BOS in 1990, 1994, 1996 and 1997. Owned by Jeannie and Bruce Korson, Laurel Hill Boxers, TuRo and K. Barker. She is shown winning the 1993 National under Mrs. James Edward Clark.

CH. BERENA'S TRIBUTE TO FA-FA, SOM

CH. KIEBLA'S TRADITION OF TURO, DOM

(BY AM-CAN. CH. WAGNER WILVERDAY FAMOUS AMOS, SOM EX SUMMERBIRD LEADING LADY)

(BY TURO'S ESCAPPADE EX CH. KIEBLA'S MERCY)

192

CH. HI-TECH'S ARBITRAGE, SOM.

CH. TURO'S FUTURIAN OF CACHET.

(BY AM-CAN. CH. FIERO'S TALLY-HO TAILO EX CH. BOXERTON HOLLYHOCK)
Arbitrage, known to many as "Biff," won the National in 1994, having
been BOS in 1993. Handled by Kim Pastella, Biff is owned by Dr. and
Mrs. William Truesdale and won under judge Michele Billings. He
has sired no fewer than 32 American and Canadian champions.

(BY CH. CACHET'S HIGH RIVER GAMBLER EX TURO'S CHARISMA OF GARNESY)
Futurian, handled by Gary Steele and bred Clay G. Haviland, Sandy
Roberts and Elizabeth Esacove, was owned by Jeff and Nan Bennett
with the breeders. The judge was Joseph Heine.

Dusty Road, bred by Travis Harris and owned with Arlene Perret,
won under judge Stephanie Abraham, handled by Tom Perret.

Johnny J, bred by Alison and Jefferson Crowther and owned by Dr.
and Mrs. William Truesdale, won under John T. Connolly, handled by
Kimberly Pastella.

CH. KIMBER-D PINEBROOK DUSTY ROAD.

CH. HI-TECH JOHNNY J OF BOXERTON.

(BY CH. PINEBROOK'S INNUENDO EX PINEBROOK'S SHADES OF AUTUMN)

(BY CH. HI-TECH'S ARISTOCRAT EX CH. BOXERTON CROWN IMPERIAL)

BOXERS
IN
CANADA

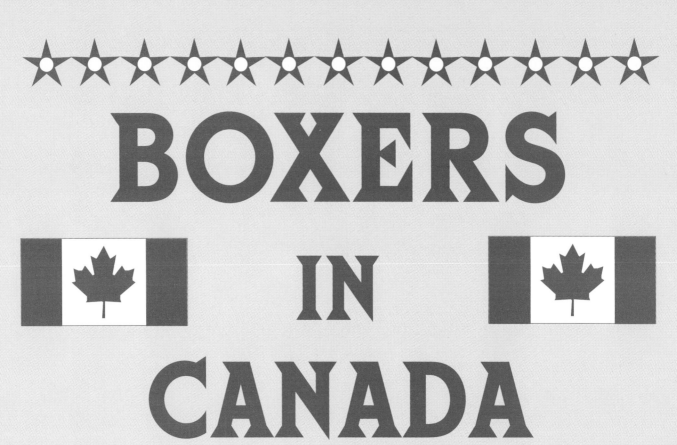

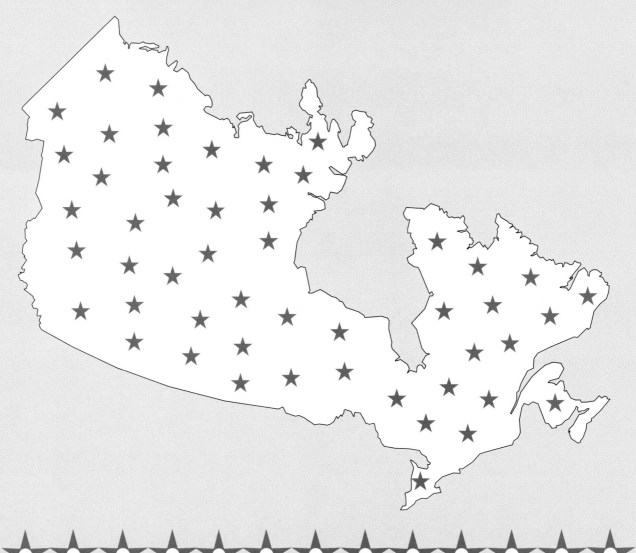

Am-Can. Ch. Bellcrest Just Watch Me, SOM (by Can. Ch. Ell Bee's Just Watch Out, SOM ex Bellcrest Encore, DOM), bred and owned by Shirley Bell, is a Sire of Merit in the U.S. and Canada, where he produced 36 Canadian champions.

By Lorraine H. Valleau, with additional material by Sturlene Arnold

The first formal recognition of the Boxer in Canada took place in 1934 with the registration of Anthony Adverse of Barmere. This dog was registered as a Boxer "Spaniel," as were all members of the breed in 1936 and 1937.

In Volume 38 of the 1935 Canadian Kennel Club stud book, he was listed as follows:

Boxer Spaniel

Anthony Adverse of Barmere 115796 by Check von Hunnenstein 115796 Anthony Adverse of Barmere 920002, Male, Boxer-Brindle, black mask, October 10, 1933, Mrs. Miriam Hostetter Young: 2nd owner, Barmere Kennels; 3rd owner, Miss Violet E. Meyers; Sir Check von Hunnenstein 819771; Casar von Deutenkofen (Moritz von Goldrainn-Liesel von Deutenkofen) Dina von Hunnenstein (Drill von Gumbertusbrunnen-Zita von Durrenberg). Dam Dodi von der Stoeckersburg 844399; Armin von der Mundsburg (Benno von der Elbe-Cuny von Flossachthal) Ulotte von der Lowernburg (Ajax von Durrenbnerg-Nanny von der Lowenburg).

Can. Ch. Greta von Wachau was the very first Boxer champion and the first bitch champion. Her entry follows:

143238 Greta Von Wachau A192553, Female, Boxer-Fawn, black mask, July 13, 1936; George H. Marcy;

owner, Mrs. A.C. Texter; sire Ch. Sigurd von Dom of Barmere 940944; Iwein von Dom (Buko von Biederstein-Zwibel von Dom) Belinde Hassia (Adi Hassia-Anita von der Schillerstadt). Dam Carla von Wachau A39866; Bimbo I von Preussenadler (Aziz Ben Satan-Murva Beth Satan) Almi von der Hohen Schrott (Nur-eddin Ben Satan-Cordelia Bath.

Next is followed by the first champion Male Am/CanCh Dago Voltenberg. Both of these Boxers were finished in 1938. His information follows:

[141551] Dago Von Valtenberg A112526, Male, Boxer-Red gold, black mask, white on breast, August 20, 1934, Willy Henneberg; imported by Ben H. Wilson; 3rd owner, Mrs. Mark E. Reed; sire Muck von der Eintracht; Hansl von Biederstein (Casar Deutenkofen-Daisy von Biederstein) Hexe von der Eintracht (Orion von der Wildburg-Adda von der Eintracht). Dam Bella von Valtenberg; Illo von Hohenneuffen (Alex von der Magdalenenquelle-Cilly von Hohenneuffen) Fricka Deutenkofen (Hermes von Diederstein-Anita von Ingersheim).

After 1937 the name "Spaniel" disappeared and subsequent dogs were known only as Boxers. Anthony Adverse of Barmere was owned by Mrs. Marion Young, who later became Mrs. Charles Breed. Barmere Kennels were highly regarded kennels in the United States that had the good fortune to purchase Sigurd von Dom of Barmere immediately after he was imported to the States by Charles Ludwig.

In 1939, the first litter of Canadian-bred Boxers was registered to Louis Fidgett of Quality Kennels in Trenton, Ontario. Of interest is the fact that the sire of this litter was Sigurd von Dom of Barmere and the dam was Melon of Mazelaine.

From the beginning, it is evident that the bloodlines of Canadian and American Boxers have much in common. The proximity of Canada to the United States and the open border that exists between the two countries have both permitted and encouraged the reciprocal breeding practices that have taken place over the years. In 1940 another Canadian kennel, Allison Kennels founded by E.A. Eaton of Pointe Fortune, Quebec, took its place beside Quality Kennels.

These were the dominant kennels in the early days of Boxer breeding in Canada. Quality Kennels began to fade from the scene by the mid-1940s while Allison Kennels were active until 1949.

In 1951 another well-known kennel, Malabar, owned by S.W. Scarpa of Pointe Fortune, Quebec, began to register Boxers. At the same time, Haviland Kennels, founded by Stan and Eve Whitmore, also became active. Haviland is one of the few Boxer kennels from this early period that continues to this day.

The number of Boxers registered in Canada was small until 1946 when, for the first time, there were over 100 dogs registered. From this time on there was a considerable increase in numbers each year until 1952 when there were 766 Boxers registered with the Canadian Kennel Club. Only five years later, in 1957, there were 1591 registrations, and the popularity of the breed escalated with kennels springing up around Ontario and Quebec. Most of the kennels at this time were located within a reasonable driving distance of Toronto or Montreal. There was, however, the occasional kennel located in the east (i.e., the Maritimes) and in the west (i.e., British Columbia and the Prairie Provinces).

Jean Grant, of Blossomlea fame, is first mentioned in the Canadian Kennel Club's stud books in 1945 as the second owner of Freeman's Ozark Jerris. This is the Lustig von Dom daughter that Jean Grant took back to England with her in 1946. At the time of importation the bitch was in whelp from a breeding to Am. Ch. Quality of Barmere. Miss Grant later returned to Canada and began to register Boxers under the Blossomlea name.

There were other kennels that were active in breeding Boxers in the 1950s. Most notable among these were Siamwill owned by Ed Williams, Unionville, Ontario; Woodhaven belonging to Mr. and Mrs. T.O. Woods of Willowdale, Ontario; and the Glen Echo Kennels of Horace King of Ancaster, Ontario. Verwood and Wildrock Kennels also began to register dogs in the mid-1950s.

The 1960s were the golden years for Boxers in Canada for the breeding programs of the early pioneers were not only strengthened but extended through the formation of newer kennels. Among these new kennels were: Aracrest, Mr. and Mrs. J. McGriskin, Pickering, Ontario; Elharlen, Mr. and Mrs. H. Foley, Nova Scotia; Gaylor, Mr. and Mrs. Len Reece, Winnipeg, Manitoba; Gaymitz, Mr. and Mrs. F.I. Northover, Weston, Ontario; Hansparke, Mr. and Mrs. G. Hanson, Oakville, Ontario; Memorylane, Vera Bartol, Thornhill, Ontario; Mephisto, Mr. and Mrs. Walter Pinsker, Surrey, British Columbia; Millan, Mike Millan, Thornhill, Ontario; Rodanna, Mr. and Mrs. R.A. Cole, Surrey, British Columbia; Scher-Khoun, Mr. and Mrs. B. deBoer, Thornhill, Ontario.

Other kennels were to follow these: Bellcrest, Mrs. Shirley Bell, Corbeil, Ontario; Donessle, Dr. and Mrs. Frank Rouse, Oakville, Ontario; Golden Haze, Mr. and Mrs. R. Burns, Alberta; Jaegerhouse, Mrs. Verena Jaeger, Thornhill, Ontario; Pinepath, Mr. and Mrs. Jack Ireland, Fingal, Ontario; Tradonalee, Mr. and Mrs. R. Verhulst, Burnaby, British Columbia.

With the passage of time, many of the kennels and their breeders have come and gone, leaving behind the mighty bloodlines of the greatest Boxers of all times. In Canada, as elsewhere, the future of the breed lies in the hands of the capable and conscientious breeders of today who respect and guard the rich heritage of the past.

The Boxer Club of Canada was formed and met for the first time on Sunday, October 26, 1947 in Hamilton, Ontario. The original list of officers reflects the close tie between the

Bred by Jean Grant, Can. Ch. Standfast of Blossomlea (by Ruda River's Happy Go Lucky ex Can-Bda. Ch. Fireside Chat of Blossomlea), whelped October 1, 1959, sired over 20 champions and was owned by Jandaire Boxers.

United States and Canada. The first officers of the club were: honorary president, J.P. Wagner, Milwaukee; honorary vice-president, C.J. Hyde, Detroit; honorary vice-president, W.D. Black Hamilton, Ontario; president, H.S. Weller, Toronto, Ontario; vice-president, Peter Smith, Hamilton, Ontario; secretary, Mrs. V. Cartledge, Guelph, Ontario; treasurer, Bruce Havitson, Hamilton, Ontario. Subsequent to the founding of the club, the first Canadian Boxer Specialty was held on May 22, 1948 in conjunction with the Hamilton Kennel Club. Mr. Charles Spannus was the judge.

The first Boxer club in Canada, the Western Boxer Club, disbanded in 1946. The second Boxer club of Canada was established in 1947. In 1948 the club held its first Specialty show in Guelph, Ontario, judged by Charles O. Spannus. Not until 1958 did a Canadian owned and bred Boxer go Best in Show at an all-breed show. In June of 1974, the Boxer Club of Canada held its first independent Specialty. Today there are seven Boxer clubs: B.C. of Canada, Alberta B.C., B.C. of Western Ontario, Dogwood B.C., Northern Ontario B.C., Prairie Region of the B.C. of Canada and the Western B.C. (again in business).

The yearly Boxer Specialty shows were held with all-breed clubs until 1974 when the show was held independently for the first time. Throughout the years, the Boxer Club of Canada has had top breed authorities judge the Specialties. Among these were John Wagner, Dr. Lewis Daniels, Joe Gregory, Donald Starkweather, Theodore Wurmser and Mrs. Pat Heath from England, to name but a few.

There has been an increase in popularity of the Boxer throughout Canada in recent years. This has led to the formation of a number of regional breed clubs. There are now three Boxer Clubs in the West: The Boxer Club of Western Canada in Burnaby, British Columbia; the Dogwood Boxer Club in Surrey, British Columbia (1991); and the Alberta Boxer Club (1988). There are two Boxer Clubs in Ontario, in addition to the parent club in Toronto: The Boxer Club of Western Ontario (1993) and the Boxer Club of Northern Ontario (1994).

In June 1964, *Dogs in Canada*, the official magazine of the Canadian Kennel Club, inaugurated its Top Dog Point System. This award system was much coveted from its beginning and has become even more prestigious through the years. Simply stated, the individual dog's breed wins, based on the records submitted by Show Secretaries to the Canadian Kennel Club and published in *Dogs in Canada*, are calculated in relation to his own breed. The total number of points the top breed dog has is then ranked with the other top breed dogs in his Group, thus his Group standing is determined. Finally, the total number of points he has and his Group ranking determine his placement in relation to all breeds.

Since this system was established, the honor of being number one of all breeds has been won five times by a

Judge Charles Spannus presiding over the first Canadian Boxer Specialty, held on May 22, 1948.

Boxer. The first to win this honor was Ch. Bonnie Lee's Sweetie Pie in 1964. In 1969 and 1970 the top position was won by Am-Can. Ch. Scher-Khoun's Shadrack, in 1976 by Am-Can-Ber. Ch. Mephisto's Soldier of Fortune and in 1979 by Ch. Haviland's Count Royal.

The history of many Canadian kennels is recorded on these pages. Some are from the past, some from the present, but all in their own way have impacted our breed in Canada. It is impossible to list all the breeders and all the kennels that have contributed to our breed.

Many thanks are due to the people who encouraged and supported me as I did the research for the data about Boxers in Canada. Special thanks to the staff of the Canadian Kennel Club who assisted me in the research, and to the members of the Boxer Club of Canada, particularly those who loaned me magazines and articles. I have written and spoken for some people who were unable to do so themselves. I am now happy to let those who can speak for themselves do so in the kennel accounts that follow.

VALSTAN

A notable small home-based kennel, Valstan Boxers began in Toronto in December 1969 with the purchase of pet bitch, the plain fawn black-masked Pandora (Haviland's Sommet). Thus began the love of Boxers shared jointly by Lorraine Valleau and Nancy Stantial. Their CKC-registered kennel name, devised from the first syllable of each of their last names, is recognized as being synonymous with quality and caring.

Two years after Pandora's arrival, Nancy and Lorraine purchased a pet companion for Pandy, a flashy brindle bitch named Angelique of Aracrest; Angie was her callname. These two bitches ruled the Valstan household for many years, providing their owners with much love and laughter, and a conviction that there would only be one breed for them in the future.

Guest author Lorraine Valleau of Valstan Boxers holds a two-week-old "Minerva."

As their interest in the breed grew, Nancy and Lorraine began a search for their "ideal" Boxer. This led them to the purchase of Josephine (Hershey's Miss Honesty) in July 1980. This beautifully marked, flashy fawn bitch was not destined, however, for the show career her owners had hoped for and so their search continued.

With the purchase of Blueline's Light of My Life, and her subsequent mating with Donessle's Spring Fever, Valstan Boxers had their first show-bound litter. The best known offspring from this breeding was Am-Can. Ch. Shylock and his litter sister Can. Ch. Frolic. Frolic retired from the ring shortly after she received her championship to allow her to mature in preparation for motherhood. Shylock enjoyed a brief retirement as a "grow-

ing boy" before he was shown as a Special late in the 1983 season. Both Shylock and Frolic were shown to their Canadian championships by Shirley de Boer.

Shylock's career as a Special really began in 1984 under the direction of Scott McNair. At the end of the 1984 season, Shylock had achieved 45 Bests of Breed and 3 Group Ones—he was ranked No. 2 Boxer in Canada that year.

In late September 1985, Shylock began his American show career. Trained, loved and cared for by Marylou Wilderson Hatfield, he completed his American championship with back-to-back majors at Cleveland in December 1985 at the Ohio Boxer Specialty. Shylock was the result of the careful linebreeding program of the Scher-Khoun, Pinepath and Donessle Kennels. His bloodlines go back to the famous Shadrack and Meshack.

Shylock will always be remembered as the spirited Boxer with the magnificent head and body to match. He was a frequent and welcome visitor at Jacquet, where he was always treated with respect and admiration.

Shylock succumbed to cancer in August of 1990 at the age of eight, leaving behind Can. Ch. Valstan Hannalora's Skywalker, "Luke" by name; Am-Can. Ch. Valstan's Dawn of Hannalora; and Am-Can. Ch. Jacquet's Renard of Wilderson. Dawn distinguished herself by obtaining her American championship in 1989 with three majors—two of these majors at Specialties. Renard also had a remarkable career, finishing his American championship at 16 months of age from the American-bred class.

The co-owners of Valstan Boxers, Nancy and Lorraine, have a simple and direct philosophy: They believe that all dogs should be pets as well as show dogs. They feel obligated to scrupulously maintain the quality of their dogs and to advance the breed in every way they can. Their program has been on a small selective scale, for all Valstan puppies are home-raised as members of the family.

Can. Ch. Karmel's Dante's Sassafras, DOM (by Ch. Berena's Gemini Splashdown ex Jacquet's Kiri Te Kanawa), owned and bred by Lee and Brenda Muirhead.

Am-Can.Ch. Valstan's Dawn of Hannalora, handled by Marylou Hatfield.

DAUNTAE

In September 1988, Dauntae Boxers was founded by Lee and Brenda Muirhead of Sooke, British Columbia. The original name "Dante" was changed in November 1992 due to a conflict with a kennel in the United States. The first Boxer owned by the Muirheads was a locally produced bitch, Ironbark's Aralias Lace. Their second Boxer, Karmel's Dante's Sassafras was sired by Ch. Berena's Gemini Splashdown ex Jacquet's Kiri Te Kanawa. She came from the east coast of the United States out of Karin and Melvin Wilson's Karmel Kennels. Sassy has become the foundation bitch for their kennel.

With her first litter, Sassy was bred to Am-Can-Mex-Int. Ch. Mephisto's Citizen Kane (CSOM). (Ch. Berena's Tribute to Fa-Fa's son). This breeding produced Can. Ch. Dauntae's Allegro of Mephisto, Can. Ch. Dauntae's Toreador, Can. Ch. Dauntae's Getting Into Mischief and Can. Ch. Dauntae's Cassandra of Mephisto. Allegro finished his Canadian championship at the Western Canada Boxer specialty, under Judge Louella Steele.

A repeat breeding to Rosenkavalier produced Can. Ch. Dauntae's Rigoleto of Mephisto. Rigoleto has joined his litter brother Allegro and both are being shown in the U.S. by Mihaly and Gisela Toth of Sunar Boxers.

In 1992 Sassy was recognized by the Boxer Club of Canada as top producing bitch in Canada. In 1993 Sassy acquired her Boxer Club of Canada's Canadian Dam of Merit award. Sassy has produced nine puppies with seven acquiring their Canadian championships.

Lee and Brenda Muirhead would like to thank Monika and Walter Pinsker, of Mephisto Boxers for their continuous advice and support. Without the Pinskers' help and encouragement they would not be enjoying the success they've achieved. Lee and Brenda would like to give special thanks to Michelle Pinsker, their show hand, for always presenting their dogs to their optimum.

Am-Can. Ch. Shylock (by Can. Ch. Donessle's Spring Fever ex Can. Ch. Blueline's Light of My Life), owned and bred by Lorraine Valleau and Nancy Stantial.

Am-Can. Ch. Trimanor's Baccus, SOM, (by Can. Ch. Donessle's Crusader ex Am-Can. Ch. Trimanor's Fair Antoinette), winning BOB at the Boxer Club of Canada specialty.

TRIMANOR

Judy Jury of Trimanor Kennels bought her first Boxer from John and Kathy Ireland, and bred her to her own Gemini dog. From this breeding came two Am-Can. champions, Ch. Trimanor's Fair Antoinette and Ch. Trimanor Pinepath's Hudson Bay (owned by the Irelands).

Antoinette was a beautiful fawn bitch, with a gorgeous head and terrific movement. She won the Boxer Club of Canada specialty when she was five years old, and produced three litters. On that same competition day, the judge gave Antionette Best Brood Bitch for producing Am-Can. Ch. Trimanor's Baccus and Can. Ch. Trimanor's Scarlet O'Hara. These littermates were Scher Khoun Meschack's grandchildren and have been the foundation dogs for many champions. They passed along soundness, terrific movement and excellent heads.

Am-Can. Ch. Trimanor's Baccus won BOW at the 1984 ABC regional in Seattle, Washington. He followed in his mother's footsteps and the following June won BOB at the Boxer Club of Canada specialty under John Forsyth.

Meanwhile, his sister Scarlet O'Hara was bred to Moon Valley's Solar Flare and produced Ch. Trimanor's Lincoln Continental, who was top Boxer in Canada in 1987. She also produced, when bred to Bellcrest's Just Watch Me, Ch. Trimanor's I Don't Give a Damn, who has proven to be an excellent stud dog.

Lincoln son of Can. Ch. Trimanor's Rolls Royce Bentley earned his Canadian championship at eight months of age and then on to his AKC championship.

Can. Ch. Trimanor's Rolls Royce Bentley (*above*) and Can. Ch. Trimanor's Scarlet O'Hara (*below*), both owned and shown by Judy Jury.

JAEGERHOUSE

Boxers have always been an important part of the Jaeger family. In 1979 Jaegerhouse Kennels was established, enabling them to participate in the dog world.

Jaegerhouse has produced more than 40 Canadian champions, several obedience titlists, one Utility Dog and countless loving companions. In 1989 their Am-Can. Ch. "Cody" went Best of Winners at the ABC as well as Best of Breed at the BCC. Three years later his daughter went RWB at both nationals. They hope to continue breeding and exhibiting for many years to come.

Am-Can. Ch. Jaegerhouse's Cody Curacao (by Can. Ch. Jaegerhouse's Victorara, SOM ex Ch. Jaegerhouse's Scotia Blue Nose, DOM), bred by Verena Jaeger.

Above: Am-Can. Ch. Trimanor's Fair Antoinette (by Can Ch. Pinepaths Gemini ex Pinepaths Fair Cleopatra), winning Best Brood Bitch with her two puppies, Can. Ch. Trimanor's Baccus and Can. Ch. Trimanor's Scarlet O'Hara.
Below: Can. OTCh. Jaegerhouse's Emily Bronte, UD at eight-and-a-half years old. Owner, Linda Roberts.

201

Michele Pinsker with Am-Can. Ch. Mephisto's Rosenkavalier, SOM (by Ch. Berena's Tribute to Fa Fa ex Am-Can. Ch. Mephisto's Black Sabbath), bred by her parents Walter and Monika Pinsker. He is a SOM in the US and Canada, having sired 10 Am. champions and 39 Canadian champions.

MEPHISTO

In 1968 Walter and Monika Pinsker of Surrey, British Colombia, Canada purchased their first Boxer, who, handled by Walter, became Ch. Haviland's Gold Rebel.

The Pinskers then decided to breed their own champions, so they purchased Ch. Scher-Khoun's Autumn Concerto, an outstanding fawn bitch who not only was their foundation bitch but ranks among the top-producing bitches in Canada. Thus, in 1969, Mephisto Kennels was founded.

Autumn Concerto produced ten champions, four of whom were: Am-Can-Bda. Ch. Mephisto's Vendetta, Am-Can-Bda-Mex. Ch. Mephisto's Stakatto; Am-Can-Nor. Ch. Mephisto's Intermezzo and Can. Ch. Mephisto's Battlecry. Together they won over 28 Best in Show awards in three different countries.

Shortly after acquiring Autumn Concerto, Walter and Monika purchased an equally outstanding brood bitch, Ch. Verwood's Lollipop. This bitch set a record producing 11 champions—one of them is noteworthy as Triple Ch. Mephisto's Soldier of Fortune, sire of over 100 champions worldwide, winner of 24 Bests in Show and top dog winner in Canada.

Their continued breeding program led to one of their most important achievements: Am-Can-Bda. Ch. Mephisto's Vendetta. They are proud that this truly outstanding dog's pedigree is reflected in two top producers in the U.S.: Ch. Marquam Hill's Traper of TuRo and Ch. Doggone Ounce of Gold. Also Ch. Doggone Ounce of Gold has passed his showmanship on to two of his kin, Ch. TuRo's Cachet and Ch. Wagner Wilverday Famous Amos, both outstanding winners in the show ring.

The Mephisto Kennel has rarely had more than five Boxers in residence, but it has produced 80 champions in seven countries, many of whom are double or triple champions. They have won over 100 BIS among them.

Monika has involved herself in the day-to-day routine of the kennels, while Walter has involved himself with exhibiting the dogs. Their daughter, Michelle, has taken over handling in recent years and is the youngest handler to win an all-breed Best in Show award with a Boxer in Canada.

Walter is licensed to judge all breeds and has officiated at shows in the United States, Mexico, Southeast Asia, Africa, Europe, Canada, Japan, Brazil and Argentina.

Am-Can-Bda. Ch. Mephisto's Vendetta, SOM (by Can-Nor. Ch. Mephisto's High Noon ex Can. Ch. Scher-Khoun's Autumn Concerto) became a top producer for Mephisto Kennels.

Int. Ch. Mephisto's Soldier of Fortune, SOM (by Int. Ch. Scher-Khoun's Shadrack ex Can. Ch. Verwood's Lollipop), owned by Donna Cole, has sired over 100 champions and is the top winning dog in Canada.

Am-Can-Jap. Ch. Mephisto's Guns and Roses, SOM (by Am-Can. Ch. Mephisto's Rosenkavalier ex Mephisto's Queen of Spades), bred by Walter and Monika Pinsker, ranked as No. 1 Boxer. All breed in 1997 in Japan, winning 15 Best in Show for owner Eiji Takahashi.

Ch. Mephisto's Citizen Kane (by Am-Mex. Ch. Dean-Erik's Razin Kane ex Am-Can. Ch. Mephisto's Black Sabbath), bred by Walter and Monika Pinsker.

DAWNWOLF

Dawnwolf Registered is located in Halifax Regional Municipality Nova Scotia and owned by Donna MacKenzie-Wheten. Although Donna Wheten has owned Boxers for over 30 years, she did not become interested in showing and breeding until 1989. Her first Canadian champion was Ch. C. and M.'s Mae West, a natural-eared bitch sired by Can. Ch. Jacquet's Maine Trooper and one of Bropat's Red Alert of Asgard's granddaughters.

Mae's show career was a true Cinderella story. Honoring a commitment to show their new champion bloodline Springer Spaniel puppy, the Whetens also decided to show their new Boxer puppy. Although Mae had been purchased as a pet, she had an excellent pedigree and looked promising. Mae was the only uncropped Boxer being shown in the Atlantic region of Canada during the 1990 and 1991 show years. The Whetens soon learned it was very uncommon to show an uncropped dog in that area of the country. Reactions from spectators, exhibitors, breeders and judges were mixed and at times extreme. It was these reactions, perhaps the negative ones more so than the positive, that kept the Whetens

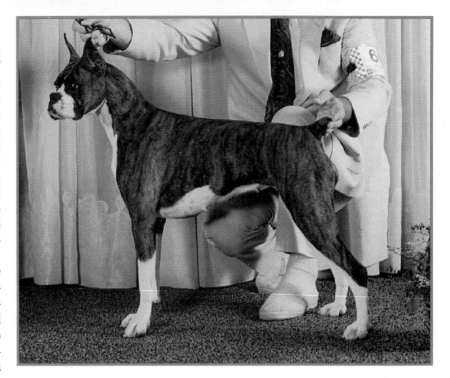

Can. Ch. Jacquet's Summer Angel (by Ch. Goldfield's Eagle Dancer, a Traper son, ex Jacquet's Honey Samantha) at 14 months of age.

and Mae going. She was awarded her Canadian championship shortly after their Springer Spaniel, being novice-owner-handler all the way! Her debut in specials then won her a Best of Breed. Mae then went on to the obedience ring where she received two qualifying scores in her first weekend out, again novice-owner-handled. Mae's story does not have a fairy-tale ending. Several weeks later she was diagnosed with cancer and died at two-and-a-half years of age.

After speaking and corresponding with a number of breeders, the Whetens acquired two Jacquet bitches—an Urko granddaughter and a Traper granddaughter, whom they co-own with Richard Tomita—to become the foundation of Dawnwolf. The Traper bitch, Ch. Jacquet's Summer Angel proved to be the primary foundation bitch. Her first litter, sired by Ch. Jacquet's Greggson, produced five puppies with one truly outstanding bitch, Jacquet's Anhthill of Dawnwolf, later sold as the foundation of another kennel. Angel's second litter, sired by Ch. Jacquet Bravo of Goldfield, was more spectacular with eight flashy brindle pups.

Dawnwolf's hope is to breed quality home-raised puppies on a limited basis under the mentorship of Mr. Tomita and to re-introduce natural-eared Boxers to the Maritimes.

For MacKenzie-Wheten, Boxers are a hobby not a business. She trains and handles her own dogs (and on occasion, other dogs) in the conformation and obedience rings. She also places particular emphasis on the degree of socialization her puppies receive, as well as the proper health clearances to ensure the longevity of her Boxers. Her dogs are all household companions, who are treasured family members who participate within the community as therapy dogs.

Dawnwolf Boxers and spaniel friend, owned by Donna Wheten.

Int. Ch. Millan's Fashion Hint, SOM (by Ch. Salgray's Fashion Plate ex Int. Ch. Gaymitz Jet Action) with breeder and owner Mike Millan.

AN ODE AND HOMAGE TO FASHION HINT

BY MICHAEL MILLAN

I have been writing this article, on request, for some time in correspondence with this task for it is my own deeply felt and personal need to pay homage to one of the greatest sires we have ever had. After his premature loss, I do this with great sadness and grief, the wounds I have suffered at his passing have barely healed.

I was his breeder and owner, but he was also my roommate. His passing not only is my personal loss but also represents a distinct loss to all breeders and lovers of our breed. Nobody can say it better than a letter from the Potomac Boxer Club, written by V. E. Kugler.

"In a very real and meaningful way, all of us in the Boxer world have experienced loss with his passing. Yet, we have so much to be thankful. Fashion Hint wrote a brilliant chapter in Boxer history, one without ending, as his indelible mark shall be present as long as there are

Boxers on this earth. He completed the mission God gave him with greater success than most of us could ever hope for. This great dog's contribution to the breed is immeasurable. We are most grateful and through you, Mike, we thank him."

As I once said, pedigree was what built Fashion Hint, or as Col. Jack Emery puts this in his own words:

"Pedigree: Fashion Hint had one of the best pedigrees that I have ever seen! Appearance, very impressive: he looked as a male Boxer is supposed to look. Show Dog: he was and could set records in the show ring. Mike Millan felt that to show and to be at stud would be too much of a drain on the dog and I agree with Mike. Stud dog: in my opinion, Fashion Hint is the greatest Boxer stud dog that ever lived."

Fashion Hint is a product of the great Salgray's "F" Litter. His dam Int. Ch. Gaymitz Jet Action came from Flying High and became the very first Canadian bitch to become an American champion. For over 20 years, no Canadian breeder produced an American champion,

Int. Ch. Millan's Fashion Hint, SOM, sire of over 100 champions and producer of the most Sires of Merit. Fashion Hint is a SOM in the US and Canada.

but Flying High produced three in the same litter! So I went back to the "F" litter—Fashion Plate and created Fashion Hint.

Dr. Lloyd Flint in 1981 wrote a very brief statement which became a formula for today's breeding. "Fashion Hint was proven to be the most prepotent sire of the past 25 years for the qualities set forth in the standard. It is still unusual for so many genes to have doubled up in one animal as to have stamped his offspring to the extent that they are unmistakable in the show ring through several generations. The latter, of course, occurred: knowing breeders wisely linebred to Fashion Hint often doubling him on both sides of the pedigree. Fashion Hint produced correct Boxer type: beautifully

Int. Ch. Verwoods Pollyana (by Int. Ch. Millan's Fashion Hint ex Verwood's Miss Muffet) is the only bitch to gain an American championship in four consecutive shows owner-handled.

balanced, compact specimens with sloping toplines, nice angulation and beautifully chiseled heads."

Fashion Hint was born in 1966; his very first champion was "Shadrack" born in 1969. Inasmuch as he was born and spent all his life in Canada, he dominated most of the 1970s in the U.S. In 1974 he equaled the "TMX Bangaway's" record for producing most of the champions of the year, but in the same year he passed away. By the end of the 1970s he shattered the 33-year-old record for producing the most Sires of Merit, then he increased that record three times and left over 100 champions. Let me give you one more quotation from the famous judge Anna Katherine Nicholas: "This is a unique accomplishment and one that has never before been achieved by a member of this breed."

What impact did Fashion Hint have on today's Boxers?

By far the most impressive male we have had for some time was the great Ch. Wagners Wilvirday Famous Amos and if you look at his pedigree you can see Fashion Hint five times.

If we are going to talk about bitches, we have to give the credit to TuRo breeding. *TuRo,* of course, comes from *Tu*rner *Ro*berts. They called me one day and I suggested two bitches by Fashion Hint from Ontario. It was a great start. They did exactly what Dr. Flint stated and the result is in front of your eyes: The greatest of them all in the tradition of TuRo.

Can. Ch. Gaymitz's Dash O'Fire, DOM (by Can. Ch. Standfast of Blossomlea ex Can-Ber. Ch. Gaymitz Spelling Bee), bred and owned by Jack Northover.

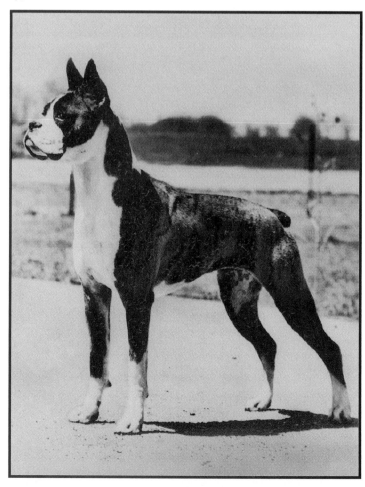

Am-Can. Ch. Millan's Queen of Fashion (by Int. Ch. Millan's Fashion Hint ex Tagwood's Spring Fashion) with Michael Millan.

HANSPARKE

While a stud dog may have many more get to his credit than a bitch ever could, the strength of the breed lies in the soundness of the dams. Pat and Gerry Hanson of Oakville, Ontario recognized this truth when they established Hansparke Kennels in 1965 with the purchase of Kerra Laine's Step Aside from Mr. and Mrs. Les Kingdon. In achieving their goal of producing quality bitches, the Hansons were able to provide two of today's prominent kennels with their foundation bitches: TuRo and Donessle. Am-Can. Ch. Hansparke's Fashion Fair, TuRo's foundation, became a Dam of Merit and, in 1976, was the ABC Top Producing Bitch. TuRo later purchased Hansparke's Dominique, sired by Int. Ch. Millan's Fashion Hint, as was Fashion Fair. Donessle Boxers in Canada established their line on the Fashion Hint daughter, Hansparke's Dynamite Dot.

The Hanson bred to Fashion Hint seven times, each time producing a successful liter. Due to the death of Pat, Hansparke did not breed from 1979 to 1987, at which time Gerry entered into partnership with Ida Baum. Back in business with Can. Ch. Hansparke's Stars 'N Stripes who debuted in Canada and won the national in 1991, acquiring his SOM in 1993.

Int. Ch. Gaymitz Jet Action (by Am-Can. Ch. Salgray's Flying Figh ex Can. Ch. Gaymitz Dash O' Fire) is the dam of the celebrated Int. Ch. Millan's Fashion Hint.

Ch. Hansparke's Fashion Fair, DOM (by Int. Ch. Millan's Fashion Hint ex Can. Ch. Hansparke's Pride of Step Aside), bred by Mr. and Mrs. Gerald Hansen, owned by Pat Turner and Sandy Roberts, is the foundation bitch for TuRo Boxers.

RINGSIDE

Peter and Linda Lariviere have lived with Boxers for over 15 years. In December 1990, a dog was purchased as a house pet called Sundance Warrior. He had won Best of Breed in Ottowa, Ontario at 11 months of age. His breeding was mostly with Holiday Kennel and Arriba. After meeting several Boxer owners at dog shows in 1991, an interest was sparked in showing. Sundance was owner-handled and won his Canadian championship the following summer. This was the beginning of Ringside Boxers.

Can. Ch. Lounsbury's Flashback to Rupik, SOM (by Am-Can. Ch. Bellcrest Just Watch Me ex Can. Ch. Lounsbury's Divinity) was Canada's top Boxer puppy in 1988.

Can. Ch. Trevtel's Sundance Warrior (by Can. Ch. Holiday's Giant, CDX ex Can. Ch. Holiday's April Blossom), bred and handled by Eric Knitel.

WARLENE

Warlene Kennels is located in the birthplace of Confederation, Canada's smallest province, Prince Edward Island. Warren and Arlene Hood, hence the prefix Warlene, have been interested in Boxers since the early 1950s, and in September 1954, Warren bought his first registered female, Miss Ginny of Shady Lane, whose parents were both from Jean Grant's Blossomlea dogs. In 1956 this female was bred to Fritz von Brinful and produced a litter of seven.

Education took priority for the next few years, and in 1967 Warren and Arlene purchased a fawn male from Stan and Eve Whitmore of Haviland Kennels. Jake, as this son of Shadrack was called, finished his Canadian championship and became Ch. Haviland's Huckleberry Finn. The Hoods were more than gratified when Jake was the first Island-owned dog ever to go BIS at an Island show. This happened in 1973 during Charlottetown's centennial celebration.

The early 1970s saw purchases from Haviland and Gaylord, plus an imported female from England, Marbelton's Black Pearl (by Marbelton's Desperate Dan). Warlene's first homebred champion was Warlene's Nifty Nabob. He was sired by Ch. Haviland's Jacks or

Better out of Haviland's Bobbin Robin. Nabob was owned by daughter Shauneen Jori Hood, who handled all the Warlene dogs.

The following years saw Warlene adding bloodlines form Donessle, Shawdondale and Ray-Shar Kennels. The Ray-Shar female from Alberta was a Traper daughter. Following came a female pup from Haviland, Haviland's Royal Magic (by Ch. Keil's Circuit Breaker).

Warren Hood has been a CKC all-breed judge for several years and has judged all across Canada, New Zealand, and some parts of the US.

Can. Ch. Bellcrest Sooner Bee Me, DOM (by Am-Can. Ch. Ell Bee's Son of BIS ex Am-Can. Ch. Bellcrest Just It From Ell Bee), dam of four champions.

Now we shall explore many of the main Boxer kennels and breeders of Canada.

Allison Boxers—E.A. Eaton has produced 13 champions with the Allison prefix. An important breeder of the late 1930s and 1940s. Breed lines through Mazelaine and Lilac Hedge.

Ainsdale—Irene Ainslee has produced 23 champions to date along with 2 CKC/DOM. Breeding behind her success is Donessle, Pinepath, Scher-Khoun & Bellcrest.

Ajay Boxers—Angela and John Smith have been successful since the '70s. So far 26 champions carry the Ajay name, and they have produced a CKC/DOM. Their breeding comes from Mephisto, Golden Haze and Berena lines.

Aracrest Boxers—Norah McGriskin from the '70s to present has had 14 champions with 5 Sires of Merit and 2 Dams of Merit. Breeding lines from Salgray, Fashion Hint, Joculu and others.

Beaucrest—Catherine Munro since 1957 has produced 15 champions and 2 CKC/DOM. Breeding stems from Blossomlea, Gaymitz, Wild Rock, Memorylane and Wo-Kan-Da, to name a few.

Bellcrest Boxers—Shirley Bell has been breeding since the '70s with 20 champions to her success along with 2 DOM and a SOM to her credit. Shirley's lines are from Tayside, Jocolu, Scher-Khoun, Vanan, Gaymitz and the English lines of Lounsbury and Rupik, etc.

Bellegray Boxers—Ray and Carol Rath have produced 18 champions. They started their success in the '80s with lines from Verwood, Haviland, Chardepado, Moss Wood, Golden Haze and others.

Berlane Boxers—Ron and Sharon Berry have produced eight champions. Sharon's previous kennel name was Rayshar, which produced 13 champions with a SOM and a DOM. Lines from Verwood, Golden Haze, TuRo, Diamondaire and Moon Valley.

Am-Can. Ch. Donessle's Northern Knight (by Am-Can. Ch. Gray Roy's Minstrel Boy ex Can. Ch. Donessle's Miss Fancy) was the first American Champion for the Donessle Kennel.

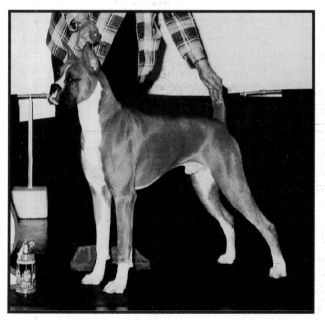

Am-Can. Ch. Bellcrest Just Watch Me, SOM (by Can. Ch. Ell Bee's Just Watch Out ex Bellcrest's Encore), bred and owned by Shirley Bell, is a Sire of Merit in the US and Canada.

Billies Boxers—Walter Brabas has five champions and a DOM to their credit. Gaylord, Golden Haze, Gaymitz and Memorylane, among others, make up their lines. Ch. Bracara's Country Classic, DOM, whom they bred, was owned by Don and Karen Harrison of Starview Boxers and produced eight champions.

Blossomlea—One of the most important early kennels was Jean Grant's Blossomlea. In almost all of our studies of pedigrees of the Sires and Dams of Merit, the breedings stemmed from Jean's breeding. We feel this gracious lady deserves great recognition for her part in the Canadian Boxer history; she deserves so much credit for her work and for getting so many kennels started on the road to success. She produced 28 champions along with several Sires and Dams of Merit.

Blueline Boxers—Elizabeth and William Stone had seven champions. They began breeding in the '70s. Their main lines were Pinepath and Scher-Khoun. They owned Scher-Khoun's Carbon Copy, DOM.

Boxella Boxers—Joe Heine of Ohio sent two champions to Canada. Back in the early '60s went Ch. Boxella's Wyatt Earp, and in the '80s went Ch. Boxella's Blackjack Wyatt Earp, who produced many Malabar champions and a DOM.

Boxjoy Boxers—Five champions for Corry Van Der Ende finished in the '80s. Main lines were Scher-Khoun, Kamursart, Mephisto and Myshadow breeding.

Am-Can. Ch. Elharlen's Illusive Dream (by Can. Ch. Elharlen's Zipcode ex Can. Ch. Salgray's Chantilly Lace), bred and owned by Eleanor and Harold Foley.

Bracara Boxers—Mr. and Mrs. L. Waddell and I. Levers have produced some 38 champions including 2 SOMs and 2 DOMs. Breed lines started with the Salgray and Gaylord lines. They have had success since the '70s and are still actively producing.

Brintan—Kevin Reid produced seven champions and a DOM from the '70s and '80s. His lines were from the English kennels of Marbelton, Rodonna and Mephisto.

Britannian Kennels—Des Lindsey-Hawkins was successful from the early '60s through the '80s. Fifteen champions were produced. Canyonair, Waagmeester and Salgray were the lines incorporated into his program.

Bullock Boxers—Greg Bullock has gained success by starting with Elharlen, Salgray, Donessle and Mephisto lines. Greg has had success both in Canada and the U.S., with six champions and a DOM to his credit.

Am-Can. Ch. Donessle's Cassino, SOM (by Can. Ch. Donessle's Crusader ex Donessle's Solitaire) was the sire of 35 Canadian champions and 11 American champions. Owners, Dr. and Mrs. Frank Rouse.

Calmar Boxers—Mr. and Mrs. Ralph Marshall produced six champions from the '70s to the '80s. Their breeding was primarily from Donessle, Honeywood and Shieldmont.

Capecod Boxers—Patsy Sayers is having success, presently with two champions so far to her credit. Her lines are Trimanor and Cinnrhee.

Carondale Boxers—Mr. and Mrs. Donald Heys were active in the '70s. Their lines were mainly Scher-Khoun and Fashion Hint.

Cedarlodge Boxers—Georgina Kvapil-Newberg had much success in the '70s and '80s. She had six champions and a DOM. Her bloodlines were Malabar, Seefeld from England and the Ch. Omega's Rockfire line.

Ceejay Boxers—C.J. Holman had eight champions and an SOM to his credit. His lines came from Donessle, Jaegerhouse, Calmar and a German line.

Am. Ch. Donessle's Night Wind (by Am-Can.Ch. Moon Valley's Sun N'Shadow ex Can. Ch. Donessle's Enchantress) was the Grand Prize Futurity Winner and Best of Winners at the ABC National in 1980.

Chabodach Boxers—Charles Proulx has done quite well in the '90s with nine so far finishing their titles. Breed lines are Donessle, Holiday, Berena, Farenny, etc. He owns Ch. Donessle's On the Double, DOM.

Chardepado's Boxers—Doug and Donna Squires have been breeding and showing since the '50s. They have to date produced 20 champions plus 2 DOMs. Their bloodline stems from Blossomlea, Terid-Don, Haviland, Pinepath, Acadia, Blueline and Keil.

Chrislen Boxers—Mr. and Mrs. L. McLellandm began in the '60s. Breeding lines were from Blossomlea and Salgray.

Cinnrhee Boxers—H. Medley Small has had nice success with the stock she has had. Fifteen champions have finished, two of which are SOM. Medley has been breeding since the '80s. Lines stem from Cedarlodge, Triamanor, Blueline, Dallenlee, Pinepath and TuRo.

210

Can. Ch. Elharlen's Opening Knight (by Can. Ch. Elharlen's Critics Choice ex Can. Ch. Elharlen's Great Expectations) at eight months of age, owned and bred by Eleanor Foley.

Conquistador Boxers—Christine Mukanik bred during the '70s and '80s. Her foundation bitch was Conquistador's E of Snuffbox, DOM from Carolyn Spencer. Two SOMs add to her collection along with a total of 11 champions carrying her kennel name. Her breeding stemmed from Gray Roy, Verwood, Scher-Khoun and Mephisto lines.

Copper Dell Boxers—Mr. and Mrs. Laurie Spears owned a kennel in the '60s that produced two champions. Lines were Haviland, Wo-Kan-Da and Blossomlea.

Crickenheim Boxers—Ingrid Sabatier has had a lot of success beginning in the late '80s. She has had eight champions with her kennel name, and her main bitch is Ch. Piccadillys Amber Magic, DOM. Lines include Billies, Starview, Norbourne and Tarabran.

Dallenlee Boxers—Gloria Bell, breeder of the late '70s and '80s, produced seven champions and two DOMs. Her bloodlines are Haviland, Cedarlodge, Malabar, Seefeld, Holiday and Verwood.

Dauntea Boxers—James and Brenda Muirhead changed the spelling from Dante and racked up six more champions. Ch. Karmel's Dante's Sassafras is still the head of the household with Mephisto, TuRo, Jacquet and Berena breeding.

Dawnwolf Boxers—Donna MacKenzie-Wheton based breeding on Jacquet in 1989.

Diamondaire Boxers—Mr. and Mrs. C. King have been producing champions since the '70s. They are still active and their champions number 26 with 4 DOMs and one SOM to their credit. Their bloodlines are Verwood, Scher-Khoun, Aracrest, Jocolu and many more.

Donaby Boxers—Mr. and Mrs. Paul Dulong have produced five champions since the late '80s. Lines include Parkdale, Donessle and Scher-Khoun mainly.

Donnell Boxers—Donna Bilodeau has so far produced 5 champions. Her success started in the late '80s. Lines are from Wyncroft, Conquistador, Mephisto, Myshadow, Miksa, Rodonna and Seefeld.

Donessle Boxers—Dr. Frank and Betty Rouse have bred 48 champions to date, with 6 DOMs and five SOMs. Breed lines contain Gray Roy, Scher-Khoun, Donfaral and Moon Valley mostly, with foundation bitch Hansparke's Dynamite Dot.

Donfaral Boxers—Mr. and Mrs. Allen Ford produced six champions from the late '60s to early '70s. Their Fashions Fancy produced the DOM Ch. Scher-Khoun's Dark Rhapsody. Their breeding stock was from Jandaire, Blossomlea, Fashion Hint and Scher-Khoun.

Dorado Boxers—Karen Know has had eight champions with the Dorado prefix. Her foundation bitch DOM Ch. McAdam's Rodonna Pride In Mind sure did her proud. Her other DOM is Tokyo Rose. Bloodlines are Golden Haze, Ajay, Verwood, Mephisto, TuRo and Berena.

Downwright Boxers—Louise Wright has produced four champions. Her lines stem from Wyncroft (English Seefeld blood), Pinepath, Scottlea, Memorylane and Mephisto.

Dreamboat Boxers—Pam and Murray Riley produced the dog Dreamboats Future Hope, who in turn produced Ch. Diamondaire's New Sensation, DOM.

Elharlen Boxers—Eleanor and Haroly Foley's foundation bitch was none other than Ch. Bobby Pin of Blossomlea, DOM, who has so far produced 65 champions. They also have two other DOMs and an SOM to their credit. Their bloodlines come mostly from Salgray and, of course, Blossomlea lines.

Esparanza Boxers—Beverley Smith bred four champions finishing in the mid '70s. Her lines were Memorylane, Golden Haze, Fashion Hint, Blossomlea, Wo-Kan-Da and Beaucrest with a little Rodonna too.

Falconhurst Boxers—Laurie Schmidt has produced five champions. Her lines are Rodonna, Rayshar, TuRo and Mephisto.

Farenny Boxers—M. and P. Ouimet have had 14 champions since the mid-'70s. Their lines are Haviland, Holiday, Scher-Khoun, Memorylane, Donessle and Cedarlodge.

Fisher Boxers—Art Fisher has produced an SOM and 25 champions. Bloodlines include Beaucrest, Haviland, Vannassau, Rodonna, Memorylane, Donessle, Shadowdale, Gayland, Wild Rock and Ellen's Alley.

Foresthill Boxers—Joe and Joan Drury (also known under prefix Jocolu) have bred seven champions that carry the Foresthill name. Lines originate from Donessle, Shadowdale, TuRo, Salgray and Bellcrest. Foresthill's The Magic Touch is their DOM.

Gayland Boxers—Audrey and Jack Peach were breeding in the '70s with seven champions finished. Their lines are Mephisto, Scher-Khoun, Verwood, Memorylane, Blossomlea, Gaylord, Jered and Treceder.

Gaylord Boxers—Len and Jean Reece have 51 champions under the Gaylord prefix, along with a whopping total of 8 DOMs and 2 SOMs. They have been breeding since the '60s. Their foundation bitch was the great Ch. Gaymitz Jet Flight, DOM, who's produced seven champions herself. Their bloodlines come from Treceder, Fashion Hint, Donessle and Tarabran, to name a few.

Gaymitz Boxers—Mr. and Mrs. F.T. Northover had 12 champions finish under the Gaymitz name along with 2 DOMs and an SOM. They began breeding in the early '60s. Lines were Eldic, Blossomlea, Jered, Markmor, Gaylord, Salgray and Ruda River mostly.

Glencotta Boxers—Thomas and Lililan Wainwright have produced 32 champions so far with 3 DOMs and an SOM. They have been successful since the early '70s. Bloodlines include Honeywood, Jodi, Vanan, Aracrest, Salgray, Scher-Khoun and Haviland.

Glen Echo—Horace King began breeding in the early '50s. There are six Glen Echo champions. Lines involved were Sirrah Crest, Raineylane, Mazelaine and Allison among others.

Golden Haze Boxers—Robert and Joanne Burns have accumulated 28 champions. Golden Haze also has a DOM and 2 SOMs. Bloodlines carry Memorylane, Verwood, Moss Wood, Moon Valley, Cher-Lane, Gaymitz, Gaylord, Treceder, Salgray, Claymar, Richmar and TuRo.

Can. Ch. Hansparke's Stars n' Stripes (by Am. Ch. Tolfan's Total Eclipse ex Am. Ch. Moon Valley's Steal A Kiss), owned by Gerald Hanson.

Greenhaven Boxers—Nancy Strange bred six champions in the '80s. Am. Ch. Greenhaven's Ebony at Pinepath is the dam of Am.Ch. Pinepaths Night Watch, SOM, owned by the Irelands.

Hansparke Boxers—Gerald and Mrs. Hanson's long-established kennel has 15 champions with 2 DOMs to its credit. The ABC-producing bitch that put TuRo on the map was Am. Ch. Hansparke's Fashion Fair. She produced producers: Ch TuRo's Native Dancer ABC/SOM and Ch TuRo's Vanity Fair ABC/DOM. Lines go to Fashion Hint, Boxella, Kerra-Laine, Markmor, Gaymitz and the great Blossomlea.

Har-Bet Boxers—Produced four champions in the '60s. Lines were Khorasan, Bang Away, Shir-Jax, Malabar and Janacee's.

Harrod Boxers—John Harrod bred in the early '70s to produce four champions. His main lines were Rodonna, Wo-Kan-Da, Beaucrest, Tradonalee and Haviland.

Haviland Boxers—Stan and Eva Whitmore began in 1948 and have had huge success, breeding well over 150 champions. Nine of these have been Best in Show winners in Canada. They have many Sires and Dams of Merit plus many other champions that don't carry the Haviland name, bred by other Boxer breeders. Lines are Blossomlea, Jered, Bang Away, Scher-Khoun, Capriana, Bonel, Diamondaire, Asgard and Keil.

Hershey Boxers—Edwin Hershey II has six champions that carry the Hershey name, but many others that do not. His breeding consists of Aracrest, Millan's, Salgray, Gaylord and Scher-Khoun lines.

Holiday Boxers—Andrew Jeannotte has bred 26 champions and an SOM and a DOM. Andrew's lines are TuRo, Karjean, Mephisto, Donessle, Eracy, Har-Vel and others.

Hollyline Boxers—Paul Murray produced two DOMs belonging to Verena Jaeger of Jaegerhouse Boxers: Irish Gold and Irish Mist. Lines include Huffand, Haviland, Five T's, Arriba, Scher-Khoun and others.

Honeycrest Boxers—Marnee Moore has bred four champions. The lines are Trimanor, Fiero, Donessle and Moon Valley, among others.

Jaegerhouse Boxers—Top kennel belonging to Verena Jaeger has finished 53 champions, 3 DOMs and an SOM. Her bloodlines include Aracrest, Donessle, Jocolu, Omega, Scher-Khoun, Donessle, Huffand, Ceejay, Calmar, Bonel, Diamondaire and many more.

Janacee's Boxers—A.H. Campbell in the early '50s saw four champions finish. Main bloodlines were Canyonair, Clinaude, Lober, Edmar, Thurzalaine and Mazelaine.

Jandaire Boxers—Suzanne Janda has 11 champions finished under the Jandaire name. Burnt Sienna was a DOM while Her Justice of Peace went to South Africa to L. and E. Van Aswegen to become an SOM of 16 champions. Bloodlines were Blossomlea, Flintwood, Barmere, Ruda River and others.

Jocolu Boxers—Joe and Joan Drury (also bred under Foresthill prefix) bred 17 champions under the Jocolu prefix with some 4 DOMs. Buttons and Bows was a good producer, and her son Am. Ch. Wincaster's

Tyger of Huffand was an SOM. The famous Charming Fashion, DOM was owned by the McGriskens and produced 2 SOMs: Ch Aracrest's Jered and Ch Aracrest's Kaylib. Bloodlines include Fashion Hint, Blossomlea, Salgray and many other important lines.

Jordannas Boxers—Evelyn Beilhartz has nine champions and a DOM (Jordannas Chantilly Lace). Her blood comes from Bellcrest, Ainsdale, Donessle, Parkdale, Ell Bee, Trimanor, Pinepath and more.

Kargotor Boxers—Irene Cauldwell had much success in the '50s with eight champions finished. Her blood came from Wo-Kan-Da, Janacee, Bob-Ell, Sirrah Crest, Allison and more.

Kalamor Boxers—Mr. and Mrs. J. Wetmore had four champions finish in the '70s. Lines from Elharlen, Haviland, Shadowdale, Scher-Khoun, Gaymitz, Malabar, Boxella, Millan and others.

Kiritowi Boxers—Helen St. Hilaire had 12 champions along with a DOM. Her blood comes from Holiday, Laroche, Gaylord, Salgray, Pinepath, Woods End, Keil, Greenhaven, Acadia, Fiero, Donessle and more.

Kpark Boxers—Donald Craig produced ten champions. He and his wife Anne were the owners of Can.Ch. Lounsbury's Sweet Miss Conduct, DOM, along with Can. Ch Hyde Park Hi Hopes of K-Park, DOM. Lines stem from Bellcrest, Hyde Park, Red Clay, Qinxaster, Gray Roy, Jocolu, Donessle, Woods End and many more.

L.A. Boxers—Laurie Schmidt finished five champions in the mid-'80s. Lines include Shadowdale, Scottlea, Peterlane, Haviland, Fisher, Terid-Don, Esparanza and Cher-Lane.

Leopold Boxers—Louise and Cec Semenoff had 11 champions. Their Leopold's Knockout Kelly was a DOM. Their breeding stock was Gaylord, Verwood, Scher-Khoun, Treceder and Mephisto.

Limehouse Boxers—Ruth Kilner has seven champions finished with her prefix. Ruth was active in the '70s. Her lines come from Marbelton in England, Scher-Khoun, Donessle, Tagwood, Millan, Glencotta, Honeywood and others.

Lounsbury Boxers—Anne Lucas has bred seven champions plus a DOM and an SOM. Lines go to Bellcrest, Donessle, Belfountain, Dunkalk, Scher-Khoun, Jocolu and more.

Am-Can. Ch. Pinepath's Night Watch, SOM (by Am-Can. Ch. Fiero's Tally-Ho Tailo ex Am-Can. Ch. Greenhaven's Ebony at Pinepath), bred and owned by Jack and Kathy Ireland is a SOM in the US and Canada.

Lynlea Boxers—Mr. and Mrs. Fred Smith had four champions in the '60s. Breeding was from Scher-Khoun, Haviland, Mazelaine and Blossomlea.

Malabar Kennels—S.W. Scarpa and L. Boileau total 38 champions and 2 DOMs. Lines are Canyonair, Boxella, Allson, Mazelaine, Clinaude, Scher-Khoun and more.

Malimi Boxers—Lisa Beaulieu and Marnie Eager-Macrae have 13 champions, along with an SOM. They have been breeding since the '80s. Lines include Golden Haze, Bellegary, Mephisto and more.

Marshall Boxers—A. Holt-Marshall bred four champions, with an SOM. Lines come from: Rodonna, Kamursart, Vimar, Warjoy, Ellen's Alley, Mephisto, Scher-Khoun and others.

Am-Can. Ch. Pinepath's Night Watch, SOM, bred and owned by Jack and Cathy Ireland.

Memorylane Boxers—Vera Bartol bred 32 champions along with 3 SOMs and a DOM. Vera's lines consisted of Millan, Gaylord, Salgray, Blossomlea, Gaymitz and many others.

Mephisto Boxers—Top breeders Walter and Monika Pinsker and their daughter Michelle purchased as their foundation bitch Can. Ch. Scher-Khoun's Autumn Concerto, DOM, who produced nine champions. Can. Ch. Verwood's Lollipop, DOM followed and produced 11 champions for them. In total there are no fewer than 65 champions with the Mephisto prefix, including 6 SOMs and 5 DOMs. There are many others owned by Pinskers not bearing their own prefix.

Merln Boxers—Mary and Ralph Lento are a fairly new kennel with two champions finishing for them so far. Their lines are Kaynine, Donessle, Arriba, Karjean, Howcurt and others.

Miksa Boxers—Mike and Sandra Todosychcuk. Another couple form the '80s have so far finished three champions. Their lines come form Mephisto, Rodonna, Verwood, Beaucrest, Scher-Khoun and more.

Millan Boxers—Mike Millan—everyone "in" Boxers knows who he is—the human dad of the great Fashion Hint, has four champions under the Millan name. He has bred the Millan's Miss Palmyra DOM, bought by the Cavanaughs. Fashion Hint produced 67 champions who were either American or American-Canadian, plus 37 others who were Canadian champions. He produced 17 Sires and Dams of Merit, being either ABC or CKC.

Minnetonka Boxers—Sharon Hodges bred nine champions. Her lines include Donessle, Leopold, Karjean, Tradonalee, Golden Haze, Berena, Carlon and more.

Myshadow Boxers—Dawn Gely has bred 17 champions. Myshadow's Sparkle is a DOM who produced five champion offspring. Lines are from Mephisto, Verwood, Millan, Scher-Khoun, Marshall's, Conquistador, Teashshur, Wedge Hollow and many more.

Nikita Boxers—Bradley and Marsha Fishleigh have finished six champions with their prefix. They also own Prina Pro Patria Cheslie, DOM. Pinepath, Trimanor, Terid-Don and Cinnrhee are the lines.

Norbourne Boxers—Mr. and Mrs. John Neff bred nine champions in the '80s. The Neffs also bred two SOMs. Their bloodlines were Mephisto, Beaucrest, Verwood, Rodonna and more.

Notgnillew Boxers—Nick Skinner finished six champions under his kennel name. His Unity bitch was a DOM. Lines include Rayshar, Verwood and Moon Valley.

Nubyu Boxers—Thea Dymott finished seven champions under Nubyu and others with different prefixes. Her lines are Fisher's, Wild Rock, Byu's, Ellen's Alley and Haviland.

Packapunch Boxers—Judy Grandmont has seven champions in just a few short years. Her blood comes from Golden Haze, Zephyr, Mephisto, TuRo and others.

Pandora Boxers—Tom and Lillian Wainwright of the Glencotta fame gave them a champion and two Canadian DOMs. Lines consisted of Honeywood, Jandaire, Millan, Blossomlea, Haviland, Scher-Khoun and more.

Pengalli Boxers—Mary and Grace Lewis have had nice success, finishing seven champions so far. The lines are Rodonna, Kayandar, Nickels, Myshadow, Candy Kisses, Marshall, Droado, Norbourne, Golden Haze, Gaylord, Teashshur, Holiday, TuRo and more.

Pinepath Boxers—Well-known breeders Jack and Cathy Ireland have produced 36 champions carrying the Pinepath prefix. They have had numerous other champions with other kennel names. They have had three DOMs under Pinepath and four SOMs, plus the Am. Ch. Acadia's Conquistador, SOM and the Am. Ch. Trimanor Pinepaths Hudson Bay, SOM. Breeding consists of Trimanor, Donessle, Blueline, Haviland, Scher-Khoun, Fiero, Greenhaven and more.

Rayshar Boxers—Sharon Wattres Berry bred 12 champions, an SOM and a DOM. Lines include TuRo, Mephisto, Verwood, Diamondaire, Golden Haze, Cher-Lane and more. Sharon also owned Can. Ch. Verwoods Sun Mist, CD, DOM.

Ringside Boxers—Peter and Linda Lariviere began with a Holiday-Arriba dog in 1990.

Rodlin Boxers—Linda and Rodney Norris have bred four champions. Their lines are Pinepath, Shadowdale, Donessle, Blueline, Keil and Salgray.

Rodonna Boxers—Robert and Donna Cole have had many champions along the way, and many breeders have their lines. There are no fewer than 45 champions with the Rodonna kennel name. They owned Am. Ch. Mephisto's Soldier of Fortune, SOM, along with three other SOMs carrying the Rodonna name. Lines were Wo-Kan-Da, Kargotor, Sirrah Crest, Verwood, Scher-Khoun and many other big name kennels.

Rowenda Boxers—Gwenda McDonnell has bred seven champions. Her line comes from Vannassau, Beaucrest, Boxwood, Mephisto, Tradonalee, Siegel and others. The bitch who helped her with her success is Ch. Gerlil's Flashy First, DOM.

Am-Can. Ch. Scher-Khoun's Syncopation (by Ch. Millan's Fashion Hint ex Ch. Scher-Khoun's Carousel) is the litter sister to Shadrack and the dam of Meshack, bred, owned and handled by Ben and Shirley de Boer.

Rramarr Boxers—Mr. and Mrs. Ron Herd bred five champions in the early '70s. They owned Ch. Scher-Khoun's Electioneer, who helped them greatly with their breeding program, and the bitch Ch. Donessle's Ecstacy. Their lines stem from Jodi, Donessle, Scher-Khoun, Sherilyn Von Schorer, Blossomlea, Woodcrest and more.

Rupik Boxers—Sheila Bowman of England exported fine Boxers to Canada, handled by Shirley Bell, Rod and Linda Norris and Evalyn Beilhartz. The lines are Bellcrest, Lounsbury, Braemerwood, Seefeld, Belfountain, and more.

Scher-Khoun Boxers—Ben and Shirley DeBoer are highly successful breeders whose dogs can be found on most pedigrees. There are no fewer than 26 champions bearing the Scher-Khoun name. They have had four DOMs with the Scher-Khoun prefix and three SOMs.

Int-Am-Bda-Can. Ch. Scher-Khoun's Shadrack (by Int. Ch. Millan's Fashion Hint ex Can. Ch. Scher-Khoun's Carousel) is the sire of over 100 American and Canadian champions. This important Canadian Boxer was bred, owned and handled by Ben and Shirley de Boer.

Scottlea Boxers—Charlotte Schwandt bred eight champions and an SOM. Her lines contain Scher-Khoun, Fan-Ton, Hargayle, Gaymitz, Millan, Trimanor, Pinepath, Omega, Aracrest and others.

Shadowdale Boxers—Mary Curl bred 27 champions plus a DOM and an SOM. Her lines include Donessle, Kaye-9, Memorylane, Scher-Khoun, Trimanor, Omega, Pinepath and others.

Shawdar Boxers—Doug and Ruth Shaw bred a total of four champions. The lines were mostly Vanan, Scher-Khoun, Gaylord and Haviland.

Shibar Boxers—Douglas Kaban's lines consisted of Conquistador, Rayshare, Notgnillew and Verwood, and he produced four champions with the Shibar prefix.

Siamwill Boxers—Ed Williams bred in the '50s, and his bloodlines were Blossomlea, Jered, Sirrah Crest, Canyonair and Raineylane.

Skanks—John and Carol Skanks bred five champions carrying the Skank prefix. Lines included Blossomlea, Siamwill, Malabar, Memorylane, Millan, Gaymitz, Gaylord, Ringmaster and more.

Sor-Lar Boxers—Mr. and Mrs. J. Sorenson were breeding back in the early '60s, and six champions carried their kennel name. The bloodlines contained Wo-Kan-Da, Bloosomlea, Barmere, Gaymitz, Kargotor and more.

Stamar Boxers—Mary Tlucko bred 11 champions in the late '70s and '80s. Her lines were from Honeywood, Glencotta, Diamondaire, Aracrest, Verwood and others.

Int-Am-Bda-Can. Ch. Scher-Khoun Meshack (by Int. Ch. Scher-Khoun's Shadrack ex Am-Can. Ch. Scher-Khoun Syncopation), the result of a brother-sister mating, bred, owned and handled by Ben and Shirley de Boer.

Starview Boxers—Don and Karen Harrison bred no fewer than 27 champions along with 2 SOMs and 1 DOM. Their lines are Norbourne, Billies, Mephisto, Rayshar, TuRo, Verwood and more. They also owned Ch. Billie's Country Classic, DOM.

Summit Boxers—Mr. and Mrs. Keneth Price bred in the early '70s. Their stock came from Harrods, Kalaber, Sor-Lar, Gayland, Gaymitz, Haviland, Beaucrest and others.

Tagwood Boxers—Long-established breeder Gertrude Stenhouse ahd two champions with the Tagwood name in the '50s. Her breed lines came from Canyonair, Thorhall, Millan, Scher-Khoun, Gaymitz and Blossomlea.

Tanoak Boxers—Dieter and Helga Leidel have been breeding many years. Eleven champions carry the Tanoak name. Their lines are German breeding along with Mephisto, Shadowdale, Memorylane, Millan and others.

Tarabran Boxers—Joyce and Gabe Bouchard have been breeding since the '70s. They have seven champions and an SOM with the Tarabran name. They also own Ch. TuRo's Kristian Dior, SOM. Their bloodlines are TuRo, Gaylord, Scher-Khoun, Donessle and more.

Tayside Boxers—Old established breeders Mr. and Mrs. Bert Laing have produced five champions with the Tayside prefix. Their lines consist of Gaymitz, Blossomlea, Salgray and Scher-Khoun lines.

Thurzalaine's Boxers—Grant Mahoot bred six champions under this kennel name. Treceder, Bladan, Mazelaine and Barmere are but a few on these pedigrees.

Tko Boxers—Martin and Carol Hlusko have finished four champions. Their lines are Holiday, TuRo, Pinepath, Greenhaven and Fiero, mainly.

Tonik Boxers—John and Janice Plank have bred eight champions. Prime lines are Pinepath, Trimanor, Fiero, Donessle, Terid-Don, Blueline, Bellcrest and others. Janice also owns Trimanor's Lady in Command, DOM.

Tradonalee Boxers—Mr. and Mrs. Robert Verhulst have bred 18 champions, 2 SOMs and 1 DOM—plus others without their prefix. Bloodlines are Holly Lane, Carlon, Breezewood, Berena, Haviland, Memorylane, Helixview and others.

Trimanor Boxers—Judy Jury has bred at least 25 champions carrying the Trimanor prefix. There are five DOMs and two SOMs with the Trimanor name. Her breeding consists of Donessle, Pinepath, Scher-Khoun and many other top kennels.

Valmax Boxers—Valorie and Andrew McMilen bred 13 champions beginning in the early '50s from English kennels. Their Aurora produced seven champions. Beaulaine, Sirrah Crest, Mazelaine and Woodcrest were the lines mostly involved.

Valstan Boxers—L. Valleau and N. Stantial bred four champions under this kennel name. Their lines are by Donessle, Blueline, Lynnrod, Pinepath, Scher-Khoun, Jojac, Rp's and Sergi. Can. Ch. Shylock owned by Valstan produced several champions.

Vanan Boxers—Mr. and Mrs. K. McCrum finished ten champions back in the '70s. Their lines include Scher-Khoun, Haviland, Capriana, Blossomlea and other top lines. Can. Ch. Vanan's Dreadnaught, SOM produced ten champions.

Vannassau's Boxers—Heather Meikle has produced four champions. Am. Ch. Vannassau's Step-In-Time produced a total of eight champions. His owner is C.D. Munro.

Veralyn Boxers—Four champions finished under this bannor in the early '70s. The breeding was Gaylord, Britannian, Salgray, Treceder and others, including Blossomlea, Gaymitz, Tudosal and Kingsway.

Verwood Boxers—Joan Valentini, one of the most recognizable names in Boxers, has bred 22 champions carrying the Verwood name—plus 6 DOMs and an SOM. Her lines are Merrilane, Salgray, Scher-Khoun, Millan, Mazelaine, Blossomlea, Haviland, Gaymitz, Moon Valley, Von Schorer and others.

Vic's Boxers—Vic Williams numbered four champions finishing in the late '50s. His lines were Sirrah Crest, Thurzalaine, Mazelaine, Barmere, Janacee and others.

Warlene Boxer's—Warren and Arlene Hood bred from Blossomlea, Marbelton, Haviland, and others.

Walmar Boxers—Five champions came under this kennel name. Blood from Lilac Hedge, Briarnold, Peablo, Millan, Golden Haze, Gaylord and Salgray were among many on the pedigree.

Wild Rock Boxers— Flora Hewitt began in the '50s showing all her own dogs. Not less than 15 champions

Am-Can. Ch. Tradonalee's Bismark, SOM (by Ch. Holly Lane's Diamond Replay ex Can. Ch. Cinderella of Tradonalee), owned by Boothe Roberts and bred by Robert and Sheila Verhulst. Handler, Alvin Lee.

Am-Can. Ch. Shylock (Can. Ch. Donessle's Spring Fever ex Can. Ch. Blueline's Light of My Life), owned by Valstan Boxers.

fly with the Wild Rock colors. In addition, she had two DOMs. Her number one stud dog was Ch Mazelaine's Witch Doctor in the '60s. Breeding was Blossomlea, Jered, Boxella, Mephisto, Pinepath, Santa Cruz, Scher-Khoun, Scottlea and others.

Wincaster Boxers—Host Winter had four champions finished in the '70s and '80s. Am. Ch. W. Tyger of Huffand owned by Carol Connolly and Linda Huffman was an ABC/SOM. Lines contained Vie T's Huffand, Arriba, Millan, Scher-Khoun, Jocolu and more. Stargazer was a producer as was Bellcrest's Encore of Shirley Bell, DOM.

Wo-Kan-Da Boxers—C.A. Nofield bred seven champions carrying the Wo-Kan-Da name. Many of the older champions had his breeding. He had a DOM and SOM to his credit. Line stemmed from Canyonair, Blossomlea, Sirrah Crest, Bob-Ell and others.

Zephyr Boxers—Sharon and Roy Simpson and Rob and Joanne Burns have finished eight champions. They also have a DOM and an SOM to their credit. Lines include Golden Haze, TuRo, Verwood, Moss Wood, Carlon, Bellcrest, Ell Bee, Wincaster, Cher-Lane and others. They also own Ch. Golden Haze April Showers, DOM and Am. Ch. Golden Haze Tuxedo, SOM, who has produced 17 Canadian champions and 20 American champions.

JEAN GRANT: A LEGEND IN HER OWN TIME

BY KRIS DAHL

Jean Grant, founder of the internationally known Blossomlea Kennels, passed away at the age of 94 in Marmora, Canada, in a rest home where she spent the last few years of her life.

When circumstances in her life led her to this unhappy position and irritation to her free spirit, the last remaining link with her beloved Boxers was cut. When the staff at the nursing home found that any association with the dog world was most upsetting to her, they requested that all dog publications be suspended, cutting yet another link.

Our friendship began in the 1970s when I received a letter from her regarding her subscription to the *Boxer Review*. Jean was not one to mince words, and she bluntly demanded her money back if she didn't receive the magazine faster! With my explanation to her, there began a steady flow of letters from her written in her own inimitable style—full of stories, advice, anecdotes, all of which revealed her unique personality.

It took two years of steady persuasion on my part to convince her that I would love to visit her after one of my trips to the East during the ABC Specialty time. I did visit her on three occasions.

I'll never forget the first time I made the trip to Toronto from New York. She had hired a driver to take her to Toronto to meet my plane. She was in her 80s then. As I came out of customs, here was this short little Scottish lady wearing a green beret, her blue eyes twinkling. As I towered over her, she looked up at me and said in that delightful brogue of hers, "My, but you're a big one, aren't you?"

The long drive back to her home in Marmora went by very quickly and we really began to know each other. I stayed with her for five days, enjoying all the stories she had to tell about Blossomlea, her life in Scotland, dog shows when she was active and the people in her life.

On my last trip I noticed a decided change in her and it was shortly after my return that I learned she had undergone a serious operation that she didn't want to tell me about. I may not have the time frame right here, but I think it was at this time that she stayed at the Pinskers'. She eventually returned to Marmora to see her home and place her one remaining Boxer, and then she entered into a nursing home.

To many, she remains a legendary figure in Canadian Boxer history. While we feel that she has never been properly recognized for her achievements, this writer will always hold her in the highest regard as a dear friend and for her loyal affection toward me.

Am-Can. Ch. Tradonalee's Touch of Class (by Ch. Holly Lane's Prairie Chief ex Am-Can-Bda. Ch. Carlon's Classy Catrina), owned by Cora Verhulst.

Right: **Am-Can. Ch. Greenhaven's Ebony at Pinepath (by Am-Can. Ch. Acadia's Conquistador ex Amber Autumn, CDX), owned by Jack and Cathy Ireland is the dam of Am-Can. Ch. Pinepath's Night Watch.**

BOXER CLUB OF CANADA SPECIALTY WINNERS

1968 Best of Breed: Ch. Scher-Khoun's Shadrack, bred and owned by B. and S. deBoer.
Best of Opposite Sex: Ch. Scher-Khoun's Syncopation, bred and owned by B. and S. deBoer.
1969 Best of Breed: Ch. Millan's Fashion Hint, bred and owned by M. Millan.
Best of Opposite Sex: Ch. Scher-Khoun's Syncopation, bred and owned by B. and S. deBoer.
1970 Best of Breed: Ch. Scher-Khoun's Meshack, bred and owned by B. and S. deBoer.
Best of Opposite Sex: Jocolu's Charming Fashion, bred by J. Drury and I. Lucas, owned by N. and J. McGriskin Jr.
1971 Best of Breed: Am-Can. Ch. Verwood's King of Spades, bred and owned by J. Balentini.
Best of Opposite Sex: Weber's Matinee Hustler, bred by Mrs. John Weber, owned by Mr. and Mrs. J. Weber.
1972 Best of Breed: Am-Ber-Can. Ch. Scher-Khoun's Electioneer, bred by B. and S. deBoer, owned by R. Herd.
Best of Opposite Sex: Ch. Scher-Khoun's Flash of Fire, bred by B. and S. deBoer, owned by Mr. and Mrs. G. Boyle.
1973 Best of Breed: Am-Can. Ch. Scher-Khoun's Shadrack, bred and owned by B. and S. deBoer.
Best of Opposite Sex: Carondale Catalyst, bred and owned by Mr. and Mrs. D. Heys.
1974 Best of Breed: Can. Am. Ch. Scher-Khoun's Shadrack, bred and owned by B. and S. deBoer.
Best of Opposite Sex: Ch. Lynlea's Charmer, bred by F. Smith, owned by B. and S. deBoer.
1975 Best of Breed: Ch. Haviland's Jacks or Better, bred and owned by S. and E. Whitmore.
Best of Opposite Sex: Dakley's Moonbeam of Murbe, bred and owned by D. Alexander and L. Fisher.
1976 Best of Breed: Am-Can. Ch. Scottlea's Billy Be Damned, bred and owned by C. Schwandt.
Best of Opposite Sex: Ch. Hunt Corner's Ebony Belle, bred by S. Schaller, owned by H. Winter.
1977 Best of Breed: Am-Can. Ch. Scottlea's Billy Be Damned, bred and owned by C. Schwandt.
Best of Opposite Sex: Ch. Donessle's Ecstacy, bred by F. and B. Rouse, owned by R. Herd.
1978 Best of Breed: Am-Can. Ch. Haviland's Count Royal, bred and owned by S. and E. Whitmore.
Best of Opposite Sex: Ch. Donessle's High Society, bred and owned by F. and B. Rouse.
1979 Best of Breed: Am-Can. Ch. Haviland's Count Royal, bred and owned by S. and E. Whitmore.
Best of Opposite Sex: Ch. Delightful Deedle Dandie, bred and owned by J. Tripp.
1980 Best of Breed: Am-Can. Ch. Haviland's Count Royal, bred and owned by S. and E. Whitmore
Best of Opposite Sex: Ch. Rramarr's Royal Promise, bred and owned by Mr. and Mrs. R. Herd.
1981 Best of Breed: Am-Can. Ch. Diamondaire Dealer's Choice, bred by C. and L. King, owned by S. and E. Whitmore.
Best of Opposite Sex: Am-Can. Ch. Trimanor Fair Antoinette, bred and owned by R. and J. Jury.
1982 Best of Breed: Am-Can. Ch. Donessle's Cassino, bred and owned by F. and B. Rouse.
Best of Opposite Sex: Ch. Verwood's April Bet, bred by J. Valentini, owned by S. and E. Whitmore.
1983 Best of Breed: -Am-Can. Ch. Trimanor's Fair Antoinette, bred and owned by R. and J. Jury.
Best of Opposite Sex: Ch. Pinepath's Union Jack, bred and owned by J. and C. Ireland.
1984 Best of Breed: Ch. Quebo's Enriquez Mingo, bred and owned by L. Jackson and V. Capiqua.
Best of Opposite Sex: Abbyroad's Added Touch, bred by D. Bassi, owned by P. Lemieux.
1985 Best of Breed: Ch. Trimanor's Baccus, bred and owned by J. Jury.
Best of Opposite Sex: Ch. Donessle's Centennial, bred and owned by F. and B. Rouse.
1986 Best of Breed: Ch. K-Park Winter Hawk, bred by Dr. D. Craig, owned by Kent Tingley.
Best of Opposite Sex: Echo's Fantasia of Twin-K's, bred and owned by D. Kowalak and C. Agle.
1987 Best of Breed: Ch. Echo's Fantasia of Twin-K's, bred and owned by D. Kowalak and C. Agle.
Best of Opposite Sex: Ch. Donessle's Brandy's Spirit, bred by F. and B. Rouse, owned by H. Gendek.
1988 Best of Breed: Ch. Benz Razmataz, CDX, bred by B. Cliff, owned by L. Cliff.
Best of Opposite Sex: Ch. Cin Rhee's Grand Slam.
1989 Best of Breed: Ch. Jaegerhouse's Cody Curacco, bred by V. Jaeger, owned by J.W. Simpson.
Best of Opposite Sex: Ch. Greenhaven's Ebony at Pinepath, bred by N. Strange, owned by Mr. and Mrs. J. Ireland.
1990 Best of Breed: Ch. Greenhaven's Ebony at Pinepath, bred by N. Strange, owned by Mr. and Mrs. J. Ireland.
Best of Opposite Sex: Hansparke's Stars 'n Stripes, bred by I. Baum and G.P. Hanson, owned by G.P. Hanson.
1991 Best of Breed: Ch. Hansparke's Stars 'n Stripes, bred by I. Baum and G.P. Hanson, owned by G.P. Hanson.
Best of Opposite Sex: Ainsdale Second Chance, bred and owned by I. Ainslie.
1992 Best of Breed: Aracrest's Chanel, bred and owned by N. McGriskin.
Best of Opposite Sex: Am-Can. Ch. Pinepath's Night Watch, bred and owned by J. and C. Ireland.
1993 Best of Breed: Am-Can. Ch. Pinepath's Night Watch, bred and owned by J. and C. Ireland.
Best of Opposite Sex: Ch. Saragus' Duchess Sierra, bred by K. and D. Smith, owned by M. and J. Rempel.
1994 Best of Breed: Am-Can. Ch. Pinepath's Night Watch, bred and owned by J. and C. Ireland.
Best of Opposite Sex: Ch. Acadia's Vindication, bred and owned by B. and J. Cross.
1995 Best of Breed: Ch. Elharlen's Your Choice, bred and owned by E. and H. Foley.
Best of Opposite Sex: Vanity Fair Little Miss Magic, bred and owned by R. and M. Perry.
1996 Best of Breed: Am-Can. Ch. Pinepath's Night Watch, bred and owned by J. and C. Ireland.
Best of Opposite Sex: Ch. Vanity Fair Little Miss Magic, bred and owned by R. and M. Perry.
1997 Best of Breed: Ch. Rodlin Abbie's Fancy Pants, bred and owned by R. and L. Norris.
Best of Opposite Sex: Am-Can. Ch. Josha's Linebacker, CD, owned by J. and P. Kilman.

TOP THREE BOXERS IN CANADA

1963
1. Am-Can. Ch. Stylesetter of Kargotor
   also #3 Working Group
2. Ch. Bonnie Lee's Sweetie Pie
3. Ch. Bonnie Lee's Dancing Doll

1964
1. Ch. Bonnie Lee's Sweetie Pie
   also #1 Working Group, #1 All Breeds
2. Am-Can. Ch.Stylesetter of Kargotor
3. Ch. Cave Canem Gunsmoke

1965
1. Ch. Haviland's Rebel Rouser
   also #6 Working Group
2. Ch. Bonnie Lee's Sweetie Pie
3. Ch. Rhadamanthus of Raman

1966
1. Am-Can. Ch. Gaymitz Jolly Roger
   also #2 Working Group, #3 All Breeds
2. Ch. Gaymitz Jet Flight
3. Ch. Bonnie Lee's Sweetie Pie

1967
1. Ch. Malabar's Anthony Earp
   also #3 Working Group, #8 All Breeds
2. Ch. Gaymitz Jet Flight
3. Am-Can. Ch. Gaymitz Jolly Roger

1968
1. Am-Can. Ch. Gaymitz Jolly Roger
   also #2 Working Group, #10 All Breeds
2. Ch. Gaymitz Jet Flight
3. Can-Ber. Ch. Gaymitz Northern Star

1969
1. Am-Can. Ch. Scher-Khoun's Shadrack
   also #1 Working Group, #1 All Breeds
2. Am-Can. Ch. Valatharn's Pow Wow
3. Ch. Golden Haze Triumph

1970
1. Am-Can. Ch. Scher-Khoun's Shadrack
   also #1 Working Group, #1 All Breeds
2. Ch. Golden Haze Triumph
3. Ch. Appianways Roguelita

1971
1. Am-Can. Ch. Verwood's King of Spades
2. Am-Can. Ch. Valathams Bow Wow
3. Ch. Gaylord's Eminent Escort

1972
1. Am-Can. Ch. Scher-Khoun's Meshack
   also #2 Working Group
2. Ch.Gaylord's Eminent Escort
3. Am-Can. Ch. Scher-Khoun's Shadrack

1973
1. Am-Can. Ch. Scher-Khoun's Meshack
   also #4 Working Group, #7 All Breeds
2. Am-Can. Ch. Scher-Khoun's Shadrack
3. Ch. Gaylord's Eminent Escort

1974
1. Am-Can. Ch. Mephisto's Soldier of Fortune
   also #3 Working Group, #6 All Breeds
2. Ch. Vanan's Dreadnaught
3. Ch. Mephisto's Battle Cry

1975
1. Am-Can-Ber. Ch. Mephisto's Soldier of Fortune
   also #3 Working Group, #6 All Breeds
2. Ch. Haviland's Jacks or Better
3. Ch. Scottlea's Billy Be Damned

1976
1. Am-Can-Ber. Ch. Mephisto's Soldier of Fortune
   also #1 Working Group, #1 All Breeds
2. Ch. Scottlea's Billy Be Damned
3. Ch. Haviland's Count Royal

1977
1. Ch. Haviland's Count Royal
   also #2 Working Group, #4 All Breeds
2. Am-Can-Ber. Ch. Mephisto's Vendetta
3. Ch. Scottlea's Billy Be Damned

1978
1. Ch. Haviland's Count Royal
   also #2 Working Group
2. Ch. Mephisto's Vendetta
3. Ch. Esperanza's Prince Charming

1979
1. Ch. Haviland's Count Royal
   also #1 Working Group, #1 All Breeds
2. Ch. Verwood's Thief in the Night
3. Ch. A. J.'s Something Special

1980
1. Ch. Diamondaire's Dealer's Choice
2. Ch. My Shadow Soldier's Masterpiece
3. Ch. Jodi's Jubilation

1981
1. Ch. Diamondaire's Dealer's Choice
   also #3 Working Group
2. Ch. My Shadow Soldier's Masterpiece
3. Ch. Tradonalee's Trade Win

1982
1. Ch. Diamondaire's Dealer's Choice
2. Ch. My Shadow Soldier's Masterpiece
3. Limehouses' Image of Vader

1983
1. Ch. Farenny's Gigolo
2. Ch. Elharen's Illusive Dream
3. Ch. Mephisto's Bandalero

1984
1. Ch. Golden Haze Snow Drift
2. Ch. Donessle's Final Option
3. Ch. Adagio's Andante Conquistador

1985
1. Am-Can. Ch. Acadia's Conquistador
2. Am-Can. Ch. Shylock
3. Ch. Golden Haze Snow Drift

1986
1. Ch. Acadia's Conquistador
   also #6 Working Group
2. Ch. Carlon's Classy Catrina
3. Ch. Mephisto's Calypso of Leblanc

1987
1. Ch. Trimanor's Lincoln Continental
2. Ch. Carlon's Classy Catrina
3. Chc Tradonalee's Touch'o Class

is very important, to unite the people not only of the District Federal but all of the Republic of Mexico. But equally important—the major breeders of various parts of the world are interested in the puppies of our club. It is also important to mention the trophies that the club confers are treasured by the winners."

And with pride he affirms: "Without a doubt, I feel that the prestige of the club is built on the foundation of the breeders of the club."

Members of the club are from Guadalajara, Queritaro, Celaya, Irapuato, Leon, Morelia, Puebla and District Federal. Founders of the club were Sr. Jose Luis Garcia, Sr. Rafael Tejero and Dr. Lorenzo Roca Ferrer.

Dr. Roca commented that the number of champions recognized by the Boxer Club of Mexico is low, but that is because the point system is very strict. He explained: "To obtain one point toward a championship, there must be 1 to 9 dogs or bitches on the floor; two points, 10—19; and three points, 20 or more. A dog is required to obtain one double- or one triple-point award to complete the seven required for the title of Champion."

And Dr. Roca emphasized: "The difficulty to obtain the maximum recognition has been precisely one of the reasons for the prestige and seriousness for which we are recognized internationally. But it is a fact that in every one of the all-breed shows held in Mexico, more than 50 percent of the principal prizes are won by breeders and owners of Boxers, which gives an idea of the high quality we have achieved."

MEXICAN KENNELS

COURTESY OF KRIS DAHL

Kauche

Like many others, Mario Quiroz's love of Boxers began when he was little, having owned a pet Boxer as a youngster. When his interests turned to having more than just a pet, he decided that if Boxers were to be his breed, he would get the best that he could. He turned to Pedro Rodriguez for that help, buying a bitch puppy. Shadrack and Meshack were on the sire's side, and the dam was by Ambush. Later he was to buy an Ambush male.

Unlucky Six

Marta Rodriguez is an American who was born in Tennessee and came to Mexico at the age of 15 with her family, her father having a business in Mexico. Soft-spoken with a faint southern accent, she is vibrant in a quiet way—a contrast to her husband, Pedro, with his rousing exuberant nature. Because of their children and grandchildren, they switched from top-winning Bulldogs to Boxers in 1971, feeling that Boxers were easier to play with and that their youngsters enjoyed them more.

Their first Boxers were a young male and a two-year-old female, Crescent Lane's Sweet Thing, who had a couple of Breed wins to her credit. As they enlarged their scope, they introduced lines from Notelrac,

Author Richard Tomita judges the Union Canofila Del Estado De Queretaro Boxer Specialty on August 17, 1985, photographed with his Winners Dog and Winners Bitch.

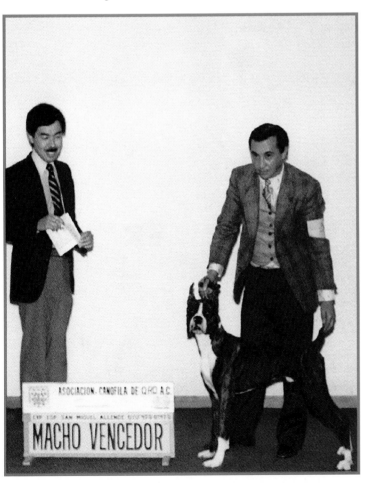

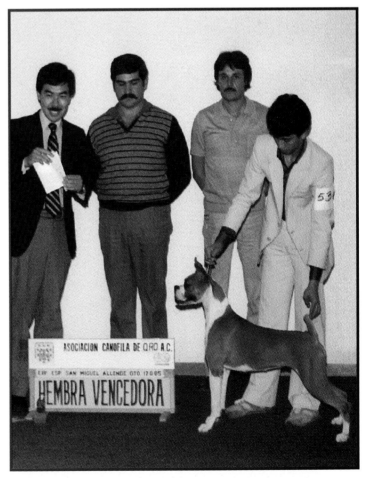

Treceder and Holly Lane, and, in 1974, the acquisition of Mephisto's Stakatto from Bob Ligon was a vital force and the cause of much of the success of the Mexican Boxer. Already an American champion when they bought him, he was sent back to Canada to earn one final point for his Canadian title, and then Arlene Freer finished his Bermudian title. He was the first Boxer ever to go Best in Show in Mexico and the first to win the International in Mexico. He is one of the few ever to have achieved four titles. He retired with ten champions to his credit, five of whom are Best in Show winners. That number could have been enhanced but, remember, there are not as many shows per year in Mexico and so many dogs are not shown. Those who have been shown have all finished.

It is to be expected that with such a top-winning stud dog that the Rodriguezes fell naturally into the role of mentors for young breeders—advising them on pedigrees and breeding, how to avoid pitfalls, etc. In fact, one person extolled their virtues in this regard most eloquently. If the intention is to buy a puppy from them, they will see that only the best in the litter is the one purchased, complete with instructions and the advice they have accumulated over the years.

To Pedro, the dog first has to be your companion, to make you feel good inside; one you can take anywhere with you, displaying courage, character and brains. Stakatto is just that to them. "That's why I get so crazy when I have Stakatto. I know he is not the perfect dog, but he's the best I've seen with the temperament, movement and everything."

Am-Can-Ber-Mex-Int. Ch. Mephisto's Stakatto (by Int. Ch. Scher-Khoun's Meshack ex Can. Ch. Scher-Khoun's Autumn Concerto), owned by Mr. and Mrs. Pedro Rodriguez of the Unlucky Six Kennels and handled in the US. by Arlene Freer.

Mex. Ch. Gorgona Medusa De Jimy's, bred, owned and handled by Ana Maria Bolio Camara.

Speaking as a breeder and a judge, Pedro sums up his observations with this: "One thing that happens to all Boxer breeders is that they are forgetting that the Boxer is not just a head. Almost everybody, even the judges, go more for the head than for the rest of the body. And I think any dog first has to move, then has to look like the standard and third, have the shoulder, angulation and topline, but they have to move."

Moon River

Miguel and Pamela Valdes were both interested in dogs at early ages. Pamela, an American whose family had lived in Indianapolis for many generations, was surrounded by many different breeds, mainly Bassets and Beagles. Miguel grew up with a St. Bernard, but early recollections recall his attraction to a brindle Boxer of his neighbors, one he played with and loved. The most important characteristic of this breed is how they get along with people, and children in particular, and they have always had the highest confidence in leaving their dogs with the children to play together.

After seeing Ch. Mephisto's Stakatto earn Best in Show, they had to have a puppy by him. They approached Pedro and Marta Rodriguez and were told they would have a litter in about two months by Stakatto and a bitch named Unlucky Six Shalimar, a Fashion Hint granddaughter. They later went to select their puppy and got a rundown on the good points of each puppy, and the Rodriguezes let them choose freely which one they liked best. As Miguel said in appreciation, "This is a very unique thing, a rare thing to find in people who breed for show. There is a natural tendency among breeders to try to keep the best puppies in each litter or to place them with people who they know will definitely show them instead of beginners who admit that this is their very first show puppy. I want to express my gratitude to Pedro and Marta for having done this with us—as they do with many other people, giving us the opportunity to get started on the right track." As it turned out, the puppy they picked was shown for the first time at about 16 months (these puppies mature slowly) and he went WD at the Boxer specialty under Ralph Willis. This a tremendous boost for these eager novices inspired them to continue showing him in Mexico City, finishing him in about five months. Since then he has won Best in Show twice at all-breed shows, won several Bests of Opposite and Best Mexican-bred champion. His name is Ch. Unlucky Six Prometeo.

Recognizing that there was no perfect dog, they wanted to get all of the qualities that were lacking in their first dog in their second dog. This time they went to Rafael Tejero, breeder of 12 champions, who sold them a bitch puppy. Tejero's Simba was a daughter of Ch. Vanan's Vega, who was imported into Mexico in 1976 or 1977. He was a Shadrack son and the dam was a Fashion Hint granddaughter.

Mex. Ch. Jacquet's Frank of Jamieson, TT (by Int. Ch. Jacquet's Novarese ex Jacquet's Brandelaine). Judge, Joseph Gregory; handler, Diego Garcia of Argentina; breeder, Richard Tomita.

Ch. Jack Jamieson Orozco was sired by Ch. Spock Jamieson and bred by Arturo Jamieson and Roberto Medrano.

Jamieson

Jamieson Boxers is owned by Arturo Jamieson and Roberto Medrano in Guadalajara, Mexico. In 1986, Arturo and Roberto acquired the Boxer that would become Mex. Ch. Spock Jamieson Orozco, son of Mex. Ch. Jacquet's El Pecos De Wilderson. Spock won 3 Best Puppy in Show, 12 Bests of Breed and 3 Group Ones. In his short life, he gave them two Mexican champions.

Since then they have acquired dogs from different lines, such as Treceder's (Treceder's Penny of Turo, full-sister of All That Jazz), TuRos (Hi Hopes to Jamieson, double-grandson of Traper), DJ's (Int-Mex. Ch. DJ's Texas Gambler, grandson of Traper and Salgray's Ambush) and our last jewel from Jacquet, Mex. Ch. Jacquet's Frank of Jamieson. Jamieson Boxers has proudly produced 15 Mexican champions.

Above: Mex. Ch. Spock Jamieson Orozco, TT (by Mex. Ch. Jacquet's El Pecos de Wilderson ex Mex. Ch. Cindy Orozco, TT), judged by Carlos Navarro. *Below:* Mex. Ch. Jamieson's Carlo Magno, TT, owned by Arturo Jamieson. Judge, Javier Ramirez.

Above: Mex. Ch. Treceder's Penny of TuRo, TT (by Ch. TuRo's Empire ex Treceder's Pride n' Joy). *Below:* Mex. Ch. Jamieson's El Tauro (by Mex. Ch. Jacquet's Frank of Jamieson ex Jamieson's Pola), bred and owned by Arturo Jamieson.

BOXER PEOPLE

Sergio Balcazar

Sergio is a person who commands center stage wherever he goes with his joyous nature, sense of humor and youthful exuberance. His dark eyes flash when he tells a story and you feel caught up in his enthusiasm. He does things with style and is the owner of the renowned Ch. Jim Pat's Assai Ben Marcotto; he was Number One Working Dog in Mexico for two years. Shown 40 times, he has 36 Bests of Breed, 29 Bests in Group and 9 Bests in Show—Sergio had Ben's retirement as a black-tie affair!

Sergio got into Boxers accidentally when his brother bred his bitch, "Real Ugly," and he got a puppy from the litter. Not knowing anything about dogs, he took him to Dr. Roca, a veterinarian and a member of the Boxer Club. Dr. Roca invited him to a meeting and little by little, Sergio started working with dogs through Dr. Roca, eventually taking them into the ring. Now wanting a show dog himself, he was promised one from Dr.

Mex. Ch. Roca's El Presidente, bred by Dr. Lorenzo Roca, won five BIS all breeds in two years, handled by Mr. Leopoldo Porras.

Roca's next litter—the best in the litter was to be his. While waiting for the puppies to arrive, he went to dog shows and began hearing from people like Pedro Rodriguez, Dr. Roca and Mr. Garcia about bringing dogs in from the US. His first import was anything but quality, a 27-inch male he bought for $600 who had a beautiful front, but his rear, shoulders and movement were anything but good. He lost as many times as he was put in the ring! It was Dorothy Hazel, on a judging assignment in Mexico, who advised Sergio not to show him anymore.

Mex. Ch. Roca's Principe Diablo (by Mex. Ch. Roca's King Devil ex Mex. Ch. Gargona Medusa de Jimyh), bred, owned and handled by Dr. Lorenzo Roca.

On a trip to Chicago, he stopped by Robert Ligon's kennels and, after Bob showed him all of his dogs, he finally brought out a beautiful brindle bitch, Holly, whom Sergio acquired. In her first show as a puppy, she won WB in the specialty, and earned WB and Best Puppy. Sergio was so happy with his first win that he persuaded his brother to co-own Rythum Master, who was also purchased from the Ligons. He is a multiple breed winner. It was after the International Show, with many Americans in attendance, that Sergio expressed his desire to acquire a champion who could compete with any champion—and that is how Ben came into his life.

Since then he's been running with the wins, often showing and campaigning seven dogs at once. He has finished four champions and another champion, Gigilo, was sold. A competitive person himself, he loves the excitement of the ring. Sometimes he will take dogs in that he knows will not win but even with that, he does his utmost to win. Case Point was a plain bitch he entered under handler Chic Ceccarini and with all of the pretty ones there, Sergio was put in front and wound up first!

Dr. Roca, who had much influence on the gradual ascent in popularity of the Boxer in Mexico, said, "To me, he is number one in Boxers in Mexico." It was Dr. Roca who brought the Fashion Hint blood to Mexico and, along with Mr. Tejero, Dr. Walker and Pedro Rodriguez, made the quality in their Boxers possible.

Mex. Ch. Routier Tejero Roca, sired by Ch. Regalaire's Whirlwind, won 18 BIS all breeds over four years (1982-86) and also was Top Dog of the Year All Breed in 1985. Judge, Eleanor Haeberle. Handled by Dr. Roca as the Tejero family join the photo session.

Dr. Lorenzo Roca

A soft-spoken man, Dr. Roca has a wealth of information about the background history of the breed in Mexico. One room of his veterinary building is devoted to a collection of books, magazines, pedigrees, etc., on the Boxer. Club members are invited to use the information freely, and Dr. Roca's willingness to help members in any way that he can speaks well of this man.

The breed in Mexico is of fairly recent origin with a handful of people such as El Marquis, Hernandez, Vega and Brown, bringing in Boxers 25 years ago. In 1971 there was some serious organization of the breed and it was in that year that Dr. Roca, Rafael Tejero, Jose Garcia and Dr. de la Vega talked about forming a club to promote the breeding of the Boxer. It was a slow process getting people interested and, in spite of this, they held their first specialty. Aimee Acklen was invited to judge this first momentous event, with an entry of 25 Boxers. The site for the show was a vacant lot next to a church. It was Aimee who expressed concern that there should be some sort of programming; a planned program for breeding was necessary. While the winner of this show, Tijuana Brass, would not be favorably compared with

today's specials, nevertheless the seeds were planted and the desire to win, to defeat, to compete and to better the Boxer breed were sown. The desire to win was further elaborated upon as Dr. Roca explained about the Latin temperament and the significance of competition. The desire to defeat the dog that had won was so strong that not even two hours had passed from the time that Aimee made her comments that several people began to investigate where they might find bloodlines that would meet this new goal. Lorenzo was among that group. At this time, the only contact they had with the Boxer world at large was through an old 1969 *Boxer Review* that Aimee had given Lorenzo at one time! They began calling people on the telephone—some of the names in the issue were Shadrack, Treceder, Fashion Hint and, after calling to Houston, California, and other kennels in North America, they finally wound up in Canada with the Vanan Kennel.

As a result of this telephone campaign, they imported dogs that we find in Mexico going back to two Fashion Hint sons, Barday's Gentleman Jim and Jim Pat's Assai Ben Marcotto; Ambush offspring, Cannon, a male and two females, Bekina and Brandy; from Shadrack, Vanan's

Dreadnaught and Vanan's Vega, who has produced many champions. From Meshack, Mephisto's Stakatto, Regalaire's Rythum Master and Regalaire's Whirlwind, all producing good stock. From Vendetta, Mephisto's Diablo and also a female, and at some point Gambling Man was brought to Mexico; there are also Diamond Replay and Benji progeny contributing to the overall quality.

Adding more information about their club, Lorenzo explained that the club is very autonomous, not just at the Mexico City level but on a national level. At their specialties, there are usually eight or nine different parts of the republic represented. The point system has been changed, making it a bit more difficult for a dog to attain a title. A major is required, based upon the number of dog and bitch entries in the categories, and this has resulted in more select champions. Selection of judges is given the greatest of importance since they welcome comments, positive and negative, from these judges who are usually breeders as well.

Dr. Roca began showing dogs in 1969 with a German Pointer, winning Breeds and Groups but always losing to a Boxer for the ultimate award. He finished ten champions, all Mexican-bred Pointers, and it was in 1972 that a Merwin Hills dog, Napoleon Solo, was to change his direction to Boxers. From 1972 to 1979, Dr. Roca obtained 28 Boxer championships—7 dogs were purchased, 21 were of his breeding. Two of them stand out in his mind: James Bond, who was a Mexican-bred specialty, Group and exhibition winner; and Sue Girl, sired by Cannon. He has produced eight champions, among them Sue Girl, who is an all-breed Best in Show winner. Vanan's Vega is another he recalls with great affection. Dr. Roca has experienced much satisfaction in his life with dogs (winning 40 BIS awards in his career—of that number, 18 have been with Boxers), but perhaps the greatest feeling has come with the fact that finally the Boxer Club of Mexico is an independent club with a real team of people who are working toward a common goal; a real team that shares his interest and enthusiasm; one that is envied by other breed clubs in Mexico.

The author awards Ch. Sherif Tejero (by Regalaires Whirlwind), and Ch. Routier Tejero Roca (by Regalaires Whirlwind), owned and bred by Rafael Tejero and Dr. Lorenzo Roca.

World-Per-Am-Mex. Ch. Roca's Red Devil III (by Mex. Ch. Roca's Principe Diablo ex Bolio Roca's B.C.), bred by Dr. Lorenzo Roca, won over 100 Bests of Breed, including at specialties.

Rafael Tejero

His involvement with dogs began with Cocker Spaniels and extended to many other breeds before he finally decided on the Boxer as the one that was the friendliest, most intelligent and most affectionate, as well as the most beautiful and elegant. His first Boxer was James Bond (a son of Shebang's Flirtation and Yours Truly), bred by Lorenzo Roca, who finished his title quickly and went on to win Best of Breed at the specialties. He was the first Mexican-bred Boxer to win a specialty in Mexico. A note of interest about this Boxer is that he actually taught their daughter Susie to walk. At the age

Mex. Ch. Routier Tejero Roca, owned by Dr. Lorenzo Roca and Jorge Pinzon. Handled by Rafael Tejero, Jr.

Ch. Hi-Tech's Emperor (by Ch. TuRo's Apollo ex Ch. TuRo's Vision of Pax), owned by Hi-Tech Boxers and Javier Ramirez, was Winners Dog at the 1992 ABC as well as the top-winning Boxer of Mexico in the early 1990s

of one-and-a-half, she still was not walking, and in spite of many visits to doctors who assured the anxious parents that nothing was physically wrong with her, she still did not walk. Her faithful companion, James Bond, loaned her his strong back and, by leaning on him, she finally gained the confidence and walked.

Their second dog was Barday's Boss Man, who proved to be a disappointment since he had no ring temperament. They later received a bitch who was to be

Bred, owned and shown by Ana Maria Bolio Camara, Mex. Ch. Tona Machetes won four BIS all breeds during 1982–1985.

Ch. Xuxa Campos, owned by Jose Luiz Campos Lopez.

their foundation bitch, Ch. Damiana, from her breeder Dr. Roca. Progeny of Barday's Gentleman Jim ex Shebang's Flirtation (both Mexican champions), she is the dam of six Mexican champions.

Recalling his greatest satisfactions, Rafael cited two things that stand out in his mind. One is winning Best of Breed with his own breeding, Tejero's Beau Geste, at a specialty, and the other is being a founding member of the Boxer Club. He has watched the growth and development of one of the most important breed clubs in Mexico; a club that has one of the highest quality levels of dogs.

For Rafael, the perfect dog would be a combination of many dogs—Fashion Hint as a producer, Shadrack for movement, Arriba's Prima Donna for topline and Benjoman for head. To produce a dog like that would require a five-time reincarnation.

He would like breeders in both Mexico and the US to know breeding is not a business; it's a hobby and a family affair. He feels the future of Boxers in Mexico is bright and with the efforts toward recognition by the AKC, many are very interested in showing their dogs in the United States. His message to the Boxer community is that every effort should be made to retain the working characteristics and quality of the dogs, to avoid what has happened in other breeds where the dog's function has been lost. The Boxer should continue to protect its home and its owners.

Speaking of dogs being a family affair, the Tejero family exemplifies this in that Rafael Jr. is a skillful handler and is the instructor in the club's handling classes. His interest in dogs began at the age of six when Dr. Roca allowed

Mex. Ch. Jacquet's El Pecos (by Am-Jap-Can-Ber. Ch. Jacquet's Urko ex Wilderson's Orchid of Jacquet), bred by Florence Wilderson and Richard Tomita and owned by Eduardo Magdaleno.

him to walk dogs at his clinic and gave him a Cocker Spaniel of his own. This dog was replaced later with Tejero's James Bond, and the young boy began training him for the ring and started winning with him. Rafael Jr. is in charge of the kennels and trains all the dogs. Susie, the youngest, is in charge of the puppies, helping to feed them and play with them. Mrs. Tejero supervises the feeding and general welfare of the dogs, and advises new owners how to care for the pups' health and welfare.

Gabriel Carrillo Rajas

Gabriel has loved dogs all of his life and has had German Shepherds, Collies and other breeds. He selected a Boxer for his grandchildren and he bought two, one for them and one for himself. They were not show dogs. Gradually, through association with club members, the bug bit him and he found himself going to dog shows and getting a new perspective on the show dog. He acquired a Fashion Hint granddaughter, Ch. Tejero's Pepper Anderson, and, to his great satisfaction, he finished her. Her credits are several Best of Breed, Best Mexican-bred and Best Opposite awards. Two more bitches were to be an integral part of his plans: Roca's Special Angel, also a Fashion Hint granddaughter; and Tejero's Farrah Fawcett. With three bitches, he decided to import more stock and his choice was to import Ch. Sylmar's Jericho of Alma.

Left: **Int. Ch. Fabela's Chic, owned and bred by Dr. Daniel and Rosalba Fabela.** *Right:* **Mex. Ch. Fabelas Fedra (by Int. Ch. Fabela's Chic), bred, owned and handled by Rafael Tejero and Rosalba Fabela, is a multiple-BIS bitch.**

BOXERS

IN THE

UNITED KINGDOM

Although the Boxer existed in Germany for about forty years before the first dog was imported to Great Britain, we must acknowledge that the English were among the first innovators to breed dogs for the specific task of baiting boars and bulls. Therefore, the Boxer, despite his German ties, is indeed quite a British breed, a "bulldog" breed, if you can bear it. Philip Stockmann, as you may know, fretted over the very word "Boxer" because it was an English word! So, the history books tell us the first imported Boxer arrived in 1933 and was registered with The Kennel Club. English or German, the Boxer and Great Britain are both better for knowing each other, as the English embraced this remarkable breed and the Boxer is one of the most popular dogs in the Kingdom! The British Boxer Club was founded in December 1936, and by 1939 it was affiliated with The Kennel Club. In that same year, a brindle male of Continental descent, Ch. Horsa of Leith Hill boasted the first English championship. He was bred by Mrs. D. Sprigg, the Club's first secretary and treasurer, and owned by Mrs. H.M. Caro, but would have no subsequent influence on the breed. Before the Second World War, the Boxer was essentially unknown in Britain, and in 1940 and 1941 only 33 and 23 Boxers were registered with The Kennel Club respectively. Credit for these early dogs is given to Mr. Allon Dawson's Stainburndorf Zulu, who was never shown but produced the stock from which the breed would descend after the war.

Gold of Uttershill, whelped in quarantine in 1939, was an early American import. Photographs courtesy of Jo Royle.

THE GREAT WAR

The Second World War, of course, was not kind to any breed of dog in any land, though the Boxer and the other working dogs fended somewhat better due to their utility to the armed forces. In war years, dogs needed to earn their keep, else they weren't kept at all! After the war, the British Armed Forces brought breed representatives back home with them, and some of these "war heroes" were utilized successfully in breeding programs.

Jo Royle, author of *Boxers Today,* shares incite and information with this author regarding Boxers and World War II: "The very old historical photos I sent you might be interesting to you as they seem to be American imports to England, the first I think, and involved some of your very early imports from Germany and Austria. There were only five shows where CCs were on offer for Boxers before the war in 1939. The Harrogate Championship Show was on September 2, 1939, the day after War was declared....all shows ceased during the war. Gold of Uttershill, an American bred, won a CC at Richmond. Unfortunately she died in whelp, or just after whelping, during the war years. I found when researching that so many bitches died in this way at that time, possibly due to lack of care or feeding difficulties or maybe lack of veterinary knowledge." Gold of Uttershill was born in quarantine in 1939 and was out on an American import So Se Sumbala to Austria. She never made her championship.

Gold of Uttershill (by Ch. Corso v. Uracher-Wasserfall ex So Se Sumbula), owned by Miss E. A. Watson.

ALLON DAWSON AND EARLY IMPORTS

Allon Dawson, the importer of Zulu, receives credit for a remarkable number of outstanding imports from Germany, Holland and the U.S. from the years 1936 to 1953. The most important of which is the fawn dog Zunftig von Dom, son of Lustig, who was in England only a short time before being sent to the U.S. Zunftig was the father of Zulu, whose influence on British Boxer pedigrees is profound. Dawson's Stainburndorf Kennel was founded on some 14 imports including Burga von Tweil (in whelp to Lustig von Dom), Florri von Dom, Bessi von Trauntal and others. In the later years of Stainburndorf in 1951 and '52, Dawson imported American Boxers including Ch. Mazelaine's Czardas and Cito von Pfarrkirchen, a fawn dog by Abra Dabra of Sirrah Crest. Also in the early '50s, Frohlich von Dom, considered to be the greatest import from Germany to the time, arrived to Dawson from Frau Stockmann. Frohlich was described as "the richest red-fawn, and a dog of grand size and wonderful substance. His body, without fear of contradiction, is about faultless, and his legs and feet could not be improved. He possesses hind-quarters so beautifully muscled in first and second thigh that he is quite outstanding. As a result his movement is just perfection. He glides over the ground with scarce a ripple, his hocks moving in perfect rhythm." (as reported in *Dog World Annual* 1954). This article continues to rave about the Stainburndorf kennels, saying that "there never was a period when a Boxer collection of such remarkable style, type and quality has been seen under the one roof in Britain." Dawson's contribution to the British gene pool cannot be overstated, though he wasn't terribly interested in competing in the shows. His lines were proven and the succession of champions utterly daunting—and when the Stainburndorf dogs did burst onto the scene—look out, for the tickets went home with Allon!

Mr. Dawson was a former Great Dane breeder, and he converted over Dane folk from the late 1930s to become Boxer enthusiasts. Among these skilled Dane converts were Mrs. Elizabeth Montgomery-Somerfield (Panfield), Mrs. E.F. Guthrie (Maspound) and Mrs. Dulcie Siggers (Cuckmere) and Major Bostock (Burstall). All four of these breeders would have some influence on the breed, though Maspound's was unfortunately short-lived, yet Mary Hambleton upon watching him win the CC at Crufts considered Ch. Mitsouko of Maspound "the greatest Boxer male I have ever seen". This noble red and white dog with a great head and body was unable to sire puppies, so he is remembered only as a show dog and not a sire.

Upper right: **Eng. Ch. Stainburndorf Vanderlion (by Stainburndorf Frohlich von Dom ex Stainburndorf Babette), one example of the unequaled quality attained by Allon Dawson and the Stainburndorf kennel.**

Middle right: **Ch. Frohlich von Dom (Ger. Ch. Heiner v. Zwergeck ex Goody Goody of Sirrah Crest), pictured with breeder Allon Dawson, was a standout even among the many great dogs produced by the Stainburndorf line.**

Lower right: **Mr. Allon Dawson judging at a championship show.**

TIRKANE

The author is delighted to have Millicent Ingram of the famed Tirkane Kennels in Ireland regale us with her story of her life with Boxers.

Half a century! It's quite a span and there is no doubt that the Boxer of 50 years ago was very different than today's elegant animal. I made my first acquaintance with the Boxer in Switzerland. He was a magnificent red male standing in bright sunshine in the centre of the path with a snow-capped mountain behind him. I had no idea what breed he was but I knew I had to find out and that this was the dog for me. Much to my father's outrage, I tracked down the owner and satisfied my curiosity. Back in Great Britain I put my mind on finding a Boxer but with little success. I went to the Crufts Jubilee Show in 1936 where the breed was classified (I think for the first time!), but there was nothing available, and even those years ago, there was considerable difference in the dog I had fallen in love with on the Continent and the one I saw at Crufts.

Puppies sired by Stainburndorf Frohlich von Dom.

Time went past, and in 1938 I saw a litter advertised in *Horse & Hound* by Mr. Allon Dawson. For the princely sum of £10 I became the proud owner of a black-faced brindle dog. Looking at his photograph and looking at today's Boxer, I must admit there is little resemblance! Even at this early date there were two distinct types: The more bulldoggy head with a heavier body, and the "Daney" type of head with a more elegant body. Both types were being shown and were winning. Much debate went on as to which was correct and I had the privilege of being taken to some of the early Boxer Club meetings by Mr. Dawson when the versions and alterations to the standard were under debate. Ironic that 50 years later the standard is again the cause of hot and strong debate.

In 1938 the Kennel Club granted the breed CCs. With the war looming it left little time to gain a title; however, the first British champion emerged, Ch. Horsa of Leith Hill. Fortunately for the survival of the breed, 1937 and 1938 saw Mr. Dawson import Burga von Twiel, in whelp to Lustig von Dom; and Zunftig von Dom, who had time to produce the dominant sire of the war years, Stainburndorf Zulu, before his departure to America.

Ch. Horsa of Leith Hill (by Ger. Ch. Hansel v. Biederstein ex Gretel von Boxerstadt), the first British champion.

On the outbreak of war, many breeders dispersed their stock. Some dogs were put down but fortunately there remained a sufficient nucleus to keep the breed going. The Boxer Club was suspended for the duration, and of course there were no Championship shows. Despite all the difficulties, many famous prefixes were to emerge during the early 1940s. Open competition was impossible. Shows were small and limited to local areas, so different dogs emerged as "kings" in their own districts. The dog papers and correspondents kept people in touch. The Boxer Club reemerged in 1946 and at the first post-war meeting in June, the American standard was authorised and sent to every member; this was the first step toward consistency of type. Imagine the excitement after all

Stainburndorf Jaguar was the son of the famous Zulu dog, the Zunftig son.

235

Breeder Millicent Ingram with early Tirkane Boxers.

all gathered, and once again a definite pattern was set for breeders to follow. I think the breed was very fortunate that two such able and positive men were picked to judge the first breed shows. Both were definite in their interpretations of the standard and both were prepared to explain their views and go into print when necessary. It is interesting that the best dog all those years ago was a Gremlin and that the record holder in the breed until recently was also a Gremlin. Sadly neither breeder nor dog are still with us, but I think that there is little doubt that the late Marion Fairbrother bred consistently to type. Thinking

the years of semi-confinement when the date of the first breed open show was announced: October 13, 1945 with Tom Scott as judge. This was undoubtedly a red-letter day when all the "kingpins" met in one spot and the results were eagerly awaited. Gremlin Gunner was best male, Mayerling Wisp was best bitch. The type and size of Wisp caused much heated discussion, but Tom Scott's decision definitely set the signpost for the direction the breed should and did follow. As I remember, Wisp would not look totally out of place in the ring today. Debate raged for weeks and the dog papers were eagerly awaited each Friday. *Dog World*, after all these years, still makes fascinating reading.

1946 saw the final guidelines for breeders to follow. The club had the foresight to invite the one and only John P. Wagner to judge the first breed Championship show on October 10, 1946. Once again we

Eng-Ir. Ch. Tirkane Toyboy (by The Jacobite of Tyegarth ex Tyegarth Sloe Gin), bred by Millicent and Ann Ingram.

Autocrat and Friston Friedl illustrate the contrasting bulldog-like head with heavy body and "Daney" head with lighter build that occurred in early English breeding.

back over the years, I can think of several dogs and bitches who could undoubtedly hold their own in today's competition. Today's breeders and exhibitors owe a lot to those early devotees of the Boxer who spent so much time, money and thought in laying the foundation of the breed in England.

Meanwhile, Ireland can lay claim to the very first Boxer imports. Dr. McMaster imported a dog and bitch after the First World War. Sadly, they never managed to produce. The next to arrive in Ireland was my Stainburndorf Autocrat, who had a marvelous personality but was very Daney in head. This was in 1938 and there were no breed classes, but he did well at open shows and gained the interest of several exhibitors of other breeds.

Eng-Ir. Ch. Tirkane's Teddyboy (by Eng-Ir. Ch. Tirkane Toyboy ex Tirkane Actress), one of the first homebred members of the Tirkane line to achieve champion status in Ireland.

The war did not affect Ireland to the same extent as England, and in October 1939 the first bitch arrived, a red daughter of Ch. Horsa of Leith Hill. She was totally different in head from Autocrat. Between them they managed to produce two bitches; one was Tirkane Vengeance, the very first Tirkane to be registered. They went to two gentlemen who became thoroughly involved in the breed for many years and who helped to form the Irish Boxer Club. Their mother went on to a Dublin girl, Miss Fitzgerald, and was the foundation for her Bisly Hill kennel, which was a force to be reckoned with for many years.

Allon Dawson continued to encourage me and gave me Stainburndorf Bombard as a 21st birthday

Ir-Eng. Ch. Tirkane Auditor (by Ir. Ch. Tirkane Toast Master ex Braxburn Vendetta), bred by Millicent Ingram.

present. He was by Florie von Dom and Bessie von Trauntal, and he proved himself very useful both at stud and in the ring. He became an Irish champion and won several Groups in Ireland, and he also won Open dog under John P. Wagner at the Championship show after the war. He was the sire of the first Irish champion bitch, Tirkane Troublemaker; and another daughter, Tirkane Telltale, a prize winner at first Open show under Tom Scott. Boxers in Ireland really were becoming popular and the quality really was improving. Tirkanes were plodding along steadily and producing quite a few Irish champions, and they were exported to many parts of the world.

My daughter Ann was also showing quite an interest in the breed. She acquired a Ch. Winking Light Juryman daughter and also a Sirocco daughter with whom she won a CC. From then on, the Tirkanes

Ir. Ch. Tirkane Toast Master (by Ir. Ch. Tyegarth Harvey Wallbanger ex Ir. Ch. Tirkane Try On) of the renowned Tirkane Kennels.

went from strength to strength. By the mid 1970s, we were able to travel more to England, and Ann campaigned Tirkane Avaunt to her English title and also to become the top-winning bitch of the year 1975. This was Tirkane's first homebred International Champion bitch and she was followed by Auditor, Chequers, Toyboy and Teddyboy, with many more Tirkanes becoming Irish champions (nearly 50 to present) and winning CCs. We have both had the privilege of judging at the championship level and Ann is now judging the breed in many different countries.

Finally, may I personally pay tribute to a wonderful breed that has given us enormous pleasure and has made us so many friends worldwide. Little did I think all those years ago what a lasting effect that early Swiss encounter was to have on my life.

PANFIELD AND ITS CONTEMPORARIES

The success of Elizabeth Montgomery-Somerfield of Panfield kennels continued to pave the way for the breed in England. The first post-war champion was bred by Panfield, and many rosette-bearing descendants followed. The Panfield champions resulted from a combination of American and German imports in the 1950s, including German import Axel von Bad Oeyn and American import Mazelaines Texas Ranger. In 1955, Mrs. Somerfield wrote the now classic volume *The Popular Boxer*, which has since enjoyed a dozen subsequent editions. In the same year, the Boxer ranked number three dog in England with 6,786 registrations, showing

Panfield dog to win an all breed Best in Show; Panfield Flash; Panfield Rhythm; and Panfield Party Piece of Greentubs, the dam of three champions.

Among Panfield's contemporaries in the '40s and '50s were George Jakeman, Mr. and Mrs. Philip Dyson, Dulcie Siggers, Mesdames Dunkels and Gample, Betty Bishonton, Winnie Sykes, Maude Payton-Smith, and Florence Cooke. The Gremlin kennel of Mrs. Marion Fairbrother yielded many post-war champions, including Gremlin Sungari, Aus. Ch. Gremlin Sundago and Ch. Gremlin Inkling, the black-masked dog who won 24 CCs. The Dysons' Knowle Crest also produced several winners. We would be remiss not to mention the Bomza Kennel of Mrs. Stephens; the Moonsfield Kennel of Mrs. E.

Five English Champions of the Panfield line (*from left to right*): Ch. Panfield Zick (by Axel von Bad Oeyn ex Panfield Flame), Ch. Panfield Ringleader (by Ch. Panfield Tango ex Panfield Serenade), Ch. Panfield Serenade (by Juniper of Bramblings ex Alma von der Frankenwarte), Ch. Panfield Rhythm (by Ch. Panfield Tango ex Ch. Panfield Serenade) and Panfield Flash (by Ch. Panfield Tango ex Panfield Comedy).

dramatic growth in popularity. Keep in mind that ten years prior in 1945, there were only 399 Boxers registered! (In 1956, the number increased a historical high of 7,570—fortunately for the breed, it subsided since then, and by the end of the century the registrations are around 5,000.)

Among the Panfield dogs that had an influence on the Boxer are Panfield Serenade, Britain's first bitch champion; Panfield Tango, a top sire who was a son of the Alma von der Frankenwarte, who was a daughter of the great Lustig; Panfield Ringleader, record-breaking sire of seven champions: Panfield Beau Jinks, the only

Harrild, Finemere Kennels of Mr. and Mrs. Michael Jellicoe, and Winkinglight Boxers of Mrs. Nan Hulluck. It was Nan Hulluck's Ch. Orburn Kekeri who was the first Boxer to win an all-breed Best in Show. She was fawn with white who is remembered as having both substance and elegance. As Mary Hambleton puts it, "...a bitch way ahead of her time....She could win in any of today's company!" She produced Ch. Winkinglight Viking and Venturer, the former of which also won a Best in Show and sired five champions. Kekeri's grandson is Winkinglight Justice, a dog of great influence on the British Boxer today.

Mrs. Elizabeth Montgomery-Somerfield shows Ch. Panfield Ringleader in 1949.

Alma von der Frankenwarte, the great Lustig daughter who had lasting influence on the breed in Britain. Owner, Mrs. Elizabeth Montgomery-Somerfield.

Eng. Ch. Panfield's Serenade (by Juniper of Bramblings ex Alma von der Frankenwarte), owned by Mrs. Elizabeth Montgomery-Somerfield.

Mazelaine's Texas Ranger (Int. Ch. Ursa Major of Sirrah Crest ex Verily Verily of Sirrah Crest), a sire of six British champions, as well as many other winners.

Mazelaine's Texas Ranger, pictured crossing from the United States to Britain, where this full brother to Bang Away had a great influence on the Boxer breed.

Eng. Ch. Panfield Texas Tycoon (by Mazelaine's Texas Ranger ex Eng. Ch. Panfield's Party Piece of Greentubs) of Panfield Kennels.

Alma von der Frankenwarte (by Int. Ch. Lustig von Dom ex Alfa van Wurzburger Blockli), owned by Elizabeth Somerfield.

The partnership of Martin Summers and Marion Fairbrother made an indelible impression on the development of the British Boxer. Summerdale Boxers were largely based on American imports, not the least of which were Raineylane Milltown and Sirocco, the latter being the true groundbreaker. Sirocco sired 13 champions and his progeny won 67 CCs and 69 RCCs. The Summerdale dogs are remembered for their lovely red and bright fawn and white coloration. Marion Fairbrother's Gremlin Kennels were carried on after Summerdale, and the most influential dog bearing this affix was Ch. Gremlin Inkling, an imposing fawn and white dog with a knockout head and expression of a true Boxer. Gremlin Mere Magic, though not a champion herself, produced the top winning Gremlin Summer Storm who thundered through 33 CCs, a record for the breed for many years, and sired seven champions, including the famous Ch. Summerdale Summer Shadow of Gremlin. The Gremlin line ended in 1983 with a not very modest 170 CC winners and 12 champions.

Eng. Ch. Panfield Ringleader (by Eng-Aust. Ch. Panfield Tango ex Eng. Ch. Panfield Serenade), sire of seven champions and numerous champion grandchildren.

FLASH!

Somerfield, Hulluck and these other breeders were among the first to strive for "flash" in Boxers, and many of the winners of this period swaggered into the ring with their white blaze and confidence. When the famous American breeder J.P. Wagner visited England to judge, he presented photographs and film footage of the great American dogs, who blazed with elegance. The English were duly impressed and began to see the breed in a whole new light and began to pursue the "correct type". Some of the Panfield dogs were "flashy", not the least of which was Panfield Flash, Panfield Rhythm and Panfield Serenade, this latter was the winning bitch under Mr. Wagner. In an article written by Mr. Wagner after the BBC show, he writes: "My greatest disappointment was in the bulkiness I found almost throughout, wide fronts, heavy shoulders going back to quite light hindquarters....In my opinion, the winning dog, Monarchist of Maspound, was far ahead of most of the competitors in general type, balance and movement, and with this he had quite a bit of elegance, whilst the head chiseling left something to be desired; he did not show the thick skull, and the muzzle was in better balance than in most of the dogs....I feel the English breeders have to some degree lost sight of the fact that the Boxer is fundamentally a working dog and such a dog must be able to jump a 6 to 8 foot fence, and must be able to travel at top speed for great distances. Such a dog cannot be found in the Mastiff and the Bulldog. He must be on the order of a powerful Terrier in the body build, with good length of leg, short, powerful back. In addition, as a companion and show dog, he should have the length of neck, head-chiseling and reasonably narrow skull that makes for great beauty in a dog."

Ch. Wardrobe's Clair de Lune (by Eng. Ch. Wardrobe's Huntersmoon ex Bartondourne Dainty Lady), owned by Wilson and Connie Wiley, was an influential bitch with over 30 CCs.

WARDROBES

The 1950s opened the door of the Wardrobes, located in Princes Risborough, Buckinghamshire, owned by Wilson and Connie Wiley. Connie handled her first champion to the ticket: Ch. Wardrobes Alma of Grenovia, a daughter of Ringleader. First attracted to Boxers "because they looked like little horses," Connie remained active in the breed, continuing to breed and show superb dogs until the mid-1970s. Wardrobes Miss Mink is remembered by British fanciers as being the most fabulous of all the Wardrobe dogs. Miss Mink was a calm, steady show dog whom many thought as close to perfection as a Boxer has ever been. Ch. Wardrobes Clair de Lune shone for the Wileys as she won 31 Challenge Certificates and was the record holder for some time. Clair de Lune was described poetically by many

Left: Eng-Aust. Ch. Panfield Tango (by Panfield Flak ex Alma von der Frankenwarte), one of the leading sires of Boxers during 1949 and 1950. *Right:* Eng. Ch. Panfield Party Piece of Greentubs (by Eng. Ch. Panfield Ringleader ex Lisa of Greentubs), dam of three champions.

Eng. Ch. Wardrobes Side-Saddle of Arnogar (by Eng. Ch. Wardrobe's Wild Mink ex Odette of Arnogar), at eight months, at an early morning training session with Mrs. Connie Wiley.

Eng. Ch. Wardrobe's Miss Mink (by Eng. Ch. Winkinglight Justice ex Wardrobe's Silver Spurs), known as the greatest of the Wardrobe line, had a profound effect on this and many other kennels, as she set a standard of excellence in temperament and beauty.

Eng. Ch. Wardrobe's Wild Mink (by Eng. Ch. Wardrobe's Swinging Kilt ex Eng. Ch. Wardrobe's Miss Mink) was a top stud dog and sire of eleven champions.

breeders as the "perfect porcelain model." Wardrobe's Miss Mink yielded Ch. Wardrobe's Wild Mink who was a top stud dog. His litter sister, Ch. Wardrobes Sapphire Mink lit up the show ring in 1960, as did Wardrobes Side Saddle of Arnogar, who was by Ch. Wild Mink out of a granddaughter of Frohlich von Dom and racked up 24 CCs. Ch. Wardrobes Miss Sable became Monica Norrington's foundation bitch of Radden and produced two litter sisters that would found Jean Heath's Starmark Kennels and Pat Heath's Seefield Kennels. Ch. Wardrobes Autumn Haze proved a stupendous sire of ten champions—he was out of Wild Mink, the son of Miss Mink. Ch. Wardrobe's Flashing Stream, sired by Haze, was a Best in Show winner in 1964. The Wardrobe dogs have had profound influence on the many kennels that utilized their stock, these include: Rytonays, Jorimour, Cloudesley, Cherryburton, Wilsiclea, Valabeau and Farfield. It is true that breeders all over the United Kingdom were keen to breed their bitches to the Wardrobe studs—nearly 50 breeders have CCs with a Wardrobe name on it. In all, the Wardrobes accumulated well over 200 CCs, and sons and daughters of the stud dogs count for over another 200 CCs. In 1973, when the "Wardrobe" door closed, they have made up a total of 31 British champions.

SEEFELD

Pat Heath of Seefeld Kennels has owned Boxers since 1954. Their first two show Boxers were Seefeld Radden Rosina and Seefeld Radden Rembrandt. Rosina was from a brother/sister mating by Ch. Wardrobes Red Sash ex Ch. Wardrobes Miss Sable, one of the breed's most influential dams. Rembrandt was by Felcign Faro ex Ch. Wardrobes Miss Sable. In due course a son of Rembrandt, Ch. Seefeld Holbein, CD, the only champion Boxer to also qualify at Working Trials, was mated to a daughter of Rosina, Ch. Seefeld Musk Rose (by the American import Wardrobes Delhart's Mack the Knife). This resulted in Int. Ch. Seefeld's Picasso, one of Britain's top winning males with 24 Challenge Certificates and 16 Bests in Show. Among the top sires of all time in the breed, Picasso sired 60 champions worldwide and is behind almost every great winning Boxer in the U.K. He is also behind Am. Ch. Berenas Gemini Splashdown, Am. Ch. Berenas Tribute to Fa-Fa, Am. Ch. Budsobravs Happy Days and others in the States. He has been dominant for type, temperament and character and his bloodlines have had a beneficial influence in many parts of the world.

Int. Ch. Seefeld Picasso (by Eng. Ch. Seefeld Holbein, CDX ex Eng. Ch. Wardrobe's Musk Rose), winner of 24 CCs with breeder Pat Heath.

Braemerwood Proclamation of Seefeld (by Ch. Salgray's Expresso ex Ch. Braemerwood Over the Rainbow), whose pedigree includes such great Boxers as Int. Ch. Millan's Fashion Hint as well as numerous other Sires and Dams of Merit.

To widen the bloodlines, Seefeld imported Norwegian Ch. Cavajes Herakles of Seefeld, which was 90% American breeding through My-R's and Boxella, together with top Finnish breeding. Next came Am. Ch. Salgray's Minute Man (by Am. Ch. Salgray's Ambush ex Am. Ch. Salgray's Jitterbug), who was with Seefeld only six months en route to Australia. These two males complimented the Seefeld breeding and laid the foundation for the next stage when Braemerwood Proclamation of Seefeld (by Am. Ch. Salgray's Expresso ex Am. Ch. Braemerwood Over the Rainbow) was imported from the States in 1983.

Proclamation blended so well with the Seefeld breeding that there are now four generations of champions down from him. His first son, Ch. Rupik Bellringer of Seefeld, was a Group and Reserve Best in Show winner. He sired Ch. Eight Bells of Seefeld, who in turn produced Ch. Ashgate Able Seaman of Seefeld, who had four Bests in Show and nine CCs before his second birthday.

With 19 British champions plus over 79 champions overseas, Seefeld has won most of the top awards in the U.K., including top sires, top dam, Best of Breed, Second Group Crufts and Champion of Champions. Aiming for good temperament, health and soundness since 1954, Seefeld Boxers are heart tested normal for aortic stenosis and all stud dogs are hip x-rayed. In the early years, all the Boxers were also first prize winners in obedience.

Mrs. Heath has judged Boxers since 1966 including Crufts, and has also judged in 13 different countries including the top specialties in America, Denmark, Holland, Britain, Australia, New Zealand, Sweden and Norway.

Top left: Int. Ch. Seefeld Picasso at 14 months, who later became a top sire of all time for the Boxer breed. *Top right:* Ch. Salgray's Minute Man (by Ch. Salgray's Ambush ex Ch. Salgray's Jitterbug). *Middle:* Eng. Ch. Mustard Seed (by Nor. Ch. Cavajes Herakles of Seefeld). *Bottom left:* Int. Ch. Seefeld Wynbok Dominic, sired by Int. Ch. Seefeld Picasso, holds titles in Norway, Sweden and Finland. *Bottom right:* Int. Ch. Seefeld Art Master (by Int. Ch. Seefeld Picasso).

Top left: Ch. Eight Bells of Seefeld (by Eng. Ch. Rupik Bellringer of Seefeld). *Top right:* Eng. Ch. Rupik Bellringer of Seefeld (by Braemerwood Proclamation) with Eng. Ch. Eight Bells of Seefeld. *Middle:* Nor. Ch. Cavajes Herakles of Seefeld (by Nor. Ch. My-R's Side Car). *Bottom right:* Eng. Ch. Seefeld Copy Cat (by Seefeld Copper Bronze ex Grandways Manhatten Woman). *Bottom left:* Eng. Ch. Ashgate Able Seaman of Seefeld (by Eng. Ch. Eight Bells of Seefeld ex Seefeld Coral Fan), at 18 months of age.

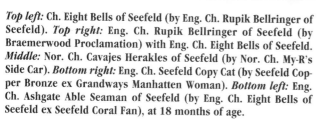

THE SIXTIES

American Boxers began to influence top breeders in 1960s, as Mazelaine's Hit Parade, Raineylane's Sirrocco and Raineylane's Milton brought success to Reg Hill, Bobbie Singleton, and Peggy Knight, directly or indirectly, as many of these top fanciers were winning with American blood in their pedigrees. Peggy Knight's Swanfield Kennels boasted champions and this can be credited to a fine selective breeding program. Other breeders of the period that thrived were Lyn Llewelyn Davies (Delapoer), Joy Malcolm (Skelder), June Grover (Ackendene), and Philip Greenaways (Rayfos).

Eng. Ch. Skelder Pot Luck (by Skelder Pot Black ex Skelder Slapstick), bred by Joy Malcolm.

Eng. Ch. Felcian Saffron Velvet of Skelder (by Felcian the Mandarin ex Viva Velvet of Skelder) with Eng. Ch. Farfield Mayfly of Skelder (by Velvet Touch of Skelder ex Farfield-Ting-A-Ling), bred by Joy Malcolm.

SKELDER

The Skelder Boxers can be traced to the great Frohlich von Dom, whom Allon Dawson had available. Portia of Skelder became the foundation bitch for Joy Malcolm. Some of the early Skelder dogs included Black Velvet, who was bred to Felcign Hot Diggotty, Red Velvet of Skelder, a Black Velvet daughter who was bred to Wardrobes Autumn Haze of Amerglo, and Velvet Touch and Viva Velvet, the offspring of that breeding. Out of Viva Velvet came Ch. Felcign Saffron Velvet of Skelder, the first champion, made up in 1967. Mrs. Malcolm says of Saffron, "I think Saffron was one of my best Boxers but she was on at the same time as Clair de Lune. I was so incensed that I couldn't make her up, and Felix (Felicia Price) seemed to be able to make up anything, so I ask her if she would go into partnership with Saffron. She said she would if she could put Felcign on her, so we stuck her prefix on her. Then half way through the partnership she found another bitch that she was determined

to make up, so she gave Saffron back to me! Fortunately I still made her up, but she was a lovely bitch and it was really tough being up against Clair de Lune with 20 or 30 tickets. That's the thing with showing dogs; so much depends on who's about at the time." Saffron was mated to Ch. Wardrobes Huntersmoon to produce Cherryburton Saffron Tartan of Skelder, and then to Ch. Cherryburton Tiger Pete to produce Ch. Tartan Tigress of Skelder. The biggest winner for the Skelders was Ch. Burnt Almond (out of Burning Bright of Skelder ex Ch. Starmark Sweet Talkin Guy), the winner of 20 CCs and 12 Reserves. In all, Joy Malcolm has finished eight champions and earned over 100 CCs, 70 percent of which have been won by the ladies!

Eng. Ch. Skallywag of Skelder (by Donovan of Skelder ex Snarestone Newscast of Skelder), bred by Joy Malcolm.

Eng. Ch. Skelder Scorching (by Eng. Ch. Starmark Sweet Talkin Guy ex Burning Bright of Skelder), bred by Joy Malcolm.

Eng. Ch. Skelder Burnt Offering (by Eng. Ch. Gremlin Summer Storm ex Skelder Burnt Amber), bred by Joy Malcolm.

Eng. Ch. Skelder Singing Sleuth (by Eng. Ch. Investigator of Abythorn ex Skelder Music Box), whose pedigree also includes fine dogs such as Eng. Ch. Faerdorn Pheasant Plucker and Eng. Ch. Starmark Sweet Talkin' Guy.

Eng. Ch. Skelder Burnt Almond (by Eng. Ch. Starmark Sweet Talkin Guy ex Burning Bright of Skelder) was the biggest winner for the Skelder Kennel with 20 CCs and 12 Reserves.

Eng. Ch. Skelder Corn Dolly (by Eng. Ch. Bailiga Rigoletto of Holwell ex Skelder Fair and Square), another example of the fine bitches of the Skelder line.

Eng. Ch. Skelder Scorching (by Eng. Ch. Starmark Sweet Talkin Guy ex Burning Bright of Skelder) with Ch. Skelder Red Rogue (by Int. Ch. Seefeld Artmaster ex Eng. Ch. Skallywag of Skelder), bred by Joy Malcolm.

Eng. Ch. Felcign Fiona (by Felcign Faro ex Eng. Ch. Felcign Cover Girl), bred by Felicia Price, won an all-breed Best in Show the same year as Eng. Ch. Wardrobe's Miss Mink.

FELCIGN

Felicia Price's Felcign Boxers, a small kennel on the outskirts of Bournemouth, owes much of its early success to Ch. Felcign Faro, a dog purchased from Jean Haggie who sired 4 champions and reaped 18 CCs. Faro, a big fawn dog, was sired by Rainey Lane Raffles, a Ch. Dion of Raineylane son. Among Faro's notably offspring is Seefeld Radden Rembrandt, the grandsire of the great Ch. Seefeld Picasso. Ch. Felcign Fiona, an outstanding bitch, quite feminine in appearance with sleek lines, was an all-breed Best in Show winner (which caused quite a stir in the Boxer world, since she did it the same year as Ch. Wardrobes Miss Mink). A very outgoing personality with a great sense of humor, a widow with a child to raise with limited resources, Felix, as her friends called her, still achieved many fine dogs with excellent toplines and tailsets. In all, Felcign claims 14 champions and about 80 CCs, truly an accomplishment for this lady among ladies who was struggling in 1950s' England against a poor economy and great odds.

Eng. Ch. Marbelton Drunken Duncan For Champions Gallery, son of the highly respected Eng. Ch. Marbelton Dressed to Kill ex Eng. Ch. Wanderobo Hurley Burley of Marbelton.

MARBELTON

The Marbelton Boxers of Mary Hambleton are credited with many champions beginning in the mid-1960s. Some of these top dogs were Ch. Marbelton Top Mark, Mosaic, Double-O Seven, Music Box and Desperate Dan. Mrs. Hambleton's autobiography entitled *I Wish I had a Champion*, published in 1991, tells the whole story of the Marbelton's success in Boxers. She credits Waylands Top Trick of Marbelton, a daughter of Ch. Winkinglight Justice, for helping them "make their mark." "Tess," as Top Trick was known, won over a hundred firsts and many Bests in Show—even though she never earned her title. Combined with Wardrobe's Wild Mink, the son of Miss Mink, Tess produced Marbelton's first big Crufts winner, Marbelton Moonraker and Marbelton Mink's Trick. Later Tess produced the flashy Marbelton Top Mark and Marbelton Top Spin, both of whom proved to be big winners, as did successors Marbelton Mosaic and Marbelton Pewter Pot. A three-

Eng. Ch. Marbelton Dressed to Kill (by Quinto Manolito v. d. Kloppeheide of Marbelton ex Marbelton Sugar Cube), winner of many prestigious awards, including RBIS at the Ladies Kennel Association.

Eng. Ch. Marbelton Pewter Pot (by Eng. Ch.. Marbelton Top Mark ex Marbelton Raindrop) won the bitch CC at the British Boxer Club at just eight months of age.

time Crufts Breed winner, Marbelton Desperate Dan broke the record at that important show in the mid-1970s. In 1982, the Hambletons claimed their first Best in Show with the one-year-old Wanderobo Hurley Burley of Marbelton, who won under breeder-judge Peggy Knight. In 1984, Mrs. Hambleton imported Dolf the Buhe Farm of Marbelton from Holland to incorporate into their breeding program. Also in the '80s came Ch. Marbelton Dressed to Kill who cleaned up some very prestigious awards, including RBIS at the Ladies Kennel Association and the Scottish KC show, as well as the British Boxer Club Golden Jubilee in 1986. "Floyd," as Dressed to Kill was called, won a total of 14 tickets, earning him the distinction of the top-winning Boxer.

Eng. Ch. Hey Good Lookin at Marbelton (by Dolf The Buhe Farm at Marbelton ex Marbelton Green Goddess), bred by Mary Hambleton.

Eng. Ch. Marbelton Dressed to Kill with Mary Hambleton, winning the 100th CC for Marbelton Kennels.

Eng. Ch. Marbelton Desperate Dan (by Eng. Ch. Marbelton Top Mark ex Marbelton Charnvyl Personality Girl), BOB at Crufts in 1971, '73 and '75, and sire of Eng. Ch. Marbelton Top Mark.

Eng. Ch. Marbelton Dressed To Kill was the top winning Boxer for Marbelton Kennels.

Eng. Ch. Marbelton Top Mark, winning his and Marbelton Kennel's first CC at the Northern Boxer Club Championship Show in 1963.

Eng. Ch. Marbelton Ooh-La-La (by Marbelton Ozone Friendly ex Ch. Look No Further at Marbelton), bred by Mary Hambleton, won her first CC at just six months of age.

Eng. Ch. Carinya Rye 'N' Dry (by Eng. Ch. Tyegarth Glenmorangie of Jenroy ex Change Key of Gremlin). Owner Debbie Theaker.

MINDENWOOD

Shirley and Arthur Butters's Mindenwood Boxers began with a serendipitous mating to Frohlich von Dom, graciously agreed to be Allon Dawson. This was one of Frohlich's last litters before he was sent to America and the Butters kept The Mindenwood Masterpiece. Dawson later sold Stainburndorf Linengown, a lovely dog but no champion producer. Masterpiece produced their first Crufts winner, the son called Mindenwood Satinsox, who produced Mindenwood Delight, who died after going Best Puppy and BOB of hepatitis. A dog named Drummage came from Audrey Stephenson of Seacrest Boxers and won 7 CCs and 6 RCCs, becoming a champion at three years of age. The Mindenwood dogs to follow helped make the mark on the Boxer world: Mindenwood Solitaire, Mindenwood Gentle Hombre, Mindenwood Jake the Fake (out of Drummage by Ch. Newlaithe Quibbler) and Mindenwood the Desert Fox (known as Dan, a Drummage daughter by Dandy Von Starenschloss of Marbelton). Mindenwood Matlow was sired by a favorite dog Fluke of Mindenwood to Dan's sister Lily Marlene, and Matlow become the foundation of Doreen Greaves's Barbarrosa Kennels. The Butters's daughter Deborah took up the reigns and began to win big with Carinya Rye 'n' Dry, a gift from Daphne North. Robbo, as he was called, produced Langbarn Lily Langtry at Mindenwood before he had to be castrated. This son has produced other dogs who have done well too. The Mindenwood dogs have been blessed with longevity and on average live to 12 years of age. Today the Butters enjoy judging Boxers and watching Deborah do her share of winning in the Mindenwood fashion.

WITHERFORD

The Witherford Kennels owned by Pat Withers in Shropshire have produced famous winners since the 1950s, including un unbroken line of four generations of UK champions. Ch. Witherford Crystal Clear, who was the father of Ch. Witherford Cool Cat, who was mother of Ch. Witherford Cool Mango, who sired four champions: Ch. French Spire of Witherford, Ch. Love Song of Witherford, Ch. In a Spin of Witherford and Ch. Mescalero Cool Breeze. The Witherford dogs go back to Collo von Dom owned by the legendary Frau Stockmann. Pat met with Frau Stockmann in the early days, one of the few priviledged English to visit her. She purchased Xanti von Dom from the brilliant breeder. Pat says of Frau Stockmann, "I hated, hated the way she was considered just a scruffy old woman by so many people—she may have been scruffy but so what? I don't suppose Rembrandt looked that good on his off days. She was a brilliant woman..." Pat bred her first champion in 1956, Ch. Witherford Crystal Clear out of Jupiter and foundation bitch Densi of Klewco (an accidental pairing). This serendipitous mating was

Int. Ch. Witherfords Hot Chestnut, (by Eng. Ch. Witherford Dawn Sky ex Bybridge Canteen Kate), bred by Pat Withers and owned by Karen Rezewski. His double grandsire is Eng. Ch. Witherfords Crystal Clear.

Eng. Ch. Marbelton Princess (by Tay Gay at Marbelton ex Ymar Modesty Blaise at Marbelton), BOB at Crufts in 1994.

repeated to yield Ch. Witherford Sweet Talk. Witherford Sun Warm, a Xanti daughter, produced Ch. Witherford Dawn Sky and Ch. Witherford Cool Cat, in subsequent litters. Cool Cat bred to Ch. Witherford Stingray yielded eleven puppies—the first eight were white, and one of the coloreds died—and then there were two, one of which became Ch. Witherford Cool Mango who took seven tickets in the late '60s and early '70s. Mango's stud work paid dividends and in total he sired seven champions who won 49 CCs and 21 RCCs. Mascalero Cool Breeze, a fourth generation champion, was a great red dog who was placed in Groups. Int. Ch. Witherfords Hot Chestnut, owned by Karen Rezewski, was exported to Germany. He lived a long and productive life of 13 years and sired 35 champions. Many of his get

and grandget were imported to the States to become foundation sires and dams for American kennels.

ACKENDENE

Dating back to the 1950s, Ackendene Kennels of June Grover has produced nice dogs over the years. Her first champion Ch. Ackendene Royal Fern, was out of Ackendene Fair Comment and Raineylane Sirocco, an American import. A granddaughter, Ch. Ackendene Precious Bane followed and won eight CCs. The Ackendene dogs have had nice successes in the ring, and Ch. Ackendene Willy Wagtail and Ch. Ackendene

Eng. Ch. Ackendene Royal Fern, (by Raineylane Sirocco ex Ackendene Fair Comment), the first champion for Ackendene Kennels.

Heritage Lucky Break (by Am-Can. Ch. Jodi Jeremiah ex New Dawns Summer Sun Heritage), the first American import to the Ackendene Kennel.

Royal Streaker of Zondora continue to rack up the CCs for Mrs. Grover, who today is a well-respected judge, regarded among the most fair and capable specialists. She says that she's aimed for "a good headed dog with sound conformation and a bit of height and showmanship." In her later years, she has looked to Germany and America for imports to improve her lines.

Ch. Wildside's Johnny 'B' Good at Ackendene (by Am. Ch. Highspire Born to Be Wildside ex Sandhill's Meet The Press) with breeder Mrs. Grover.

Kaspar of Fieldburcote served his country from 1939 to 1945. Photograph courtesy of Jo Royle.

CAMSAIL

Camsail Kennels, in Scotland, was established in 1970. Their best known dogs are Ch. Camsail Lovebird, who was top bitch in 1976, her daughter Ch. Camsail Mudlarkand and her son Camsail Bullfinch. They were followed by Ch. Camsail Firefox. Camsail Rising Lark was exported to Sweden after winning an RCC under Mary Hambleton of England. Lark went on to become Int-Sw-Norw. Ch. Korad Camsail Rising Lark. She was an excellent producer and left many Swedish champions and CC winners behind her. Other CC and RCC winners were Camsail Firefly, Camsail Heather Honey, Camsail Orange Fizz and three Swedish show dogs, Camsail Sky Diver, Camsail Dancing Fire and Camsail Foxy Fortune.

Eng. Ch. Camsail Firefox (by Eng. Ch. Braxburn Cornelius ex Camsail Tiger Moth), an outstanding dog in the Camsail line.

Onstage Diva with sister Onstage Understudy, owned by Jo Royle, at four months of age.

ONSTAGE

Jo Royle began with her Onstage Boxers back in 1952 rather as an avocation. She bred her favorite dog, Onstage Sterling Silver, in 1954 out of Mrs Cooke of the Greentubs Boxers and he proved to be worthy of his name, winning both ribbons and sterling! Since the '50s, Onstage has owned and campaigned many wonderful dogs, well over 100. Jo Royle is author of *Boxers Today* and *The Boxer* in 1976, two of the breed's most beloved and reliable books. In her dedication, Jo adds a few other Onstage winners to the list after Sterling, her "one and only": Cha Cha, Clapper, Drama, Peko, Liza, Chippy, Melba and Gracie.

Breeder Jo Royle with a litter of red Boxer pups and the parents.

WINUWUK

Marion and Ivor Ward-Davies, Jile Brown and Tim Hutchings of Gloucestershire, England founded Winuwuk Boxers on dogs imported from the U.S. and elsewhere. These dogs include Bang Away's full-brother, Mazelaine's Texas Ranger; Raineylaine's Sirocco, who sired the first champion they ever bred in 1959; and their own imports, Winuwuk Millray's Red Baron of Valvay and Kreyon's Back in Town of Winuvuk. Back in Town was owned in partnership with Mrs. M. Kray. Red Baron provided access to the great producing sires in the U.S. and Canada, including Shadrack and Fashion Hint. Back in Town and Red Baron are behind many of the top winners around the world through their producing progeny.

Eng. Ch. Roamaro Scotch Mist of Winuwuk (by Ch. Wrencliffe Flying Scotchman of Winuwuk ex Jenroy Popsicle for Belmont), bred by Marion and Ivor Ward-Davies, Julie Brown and Tim Hutchings.

Winuwuk Milray's Red Baron of Valvay (by Am-Can. Ch. Scher-Khoun's Abednego ex Milray's Flame of Candlewood) imported by Marion and Ivor Ward-Davies from the U.S.

Eng. Ch. Wrencliffe Flying Scotchman of Winuwuk (Eng. Ch. Norwatch Block Buster ex Ch. Wrencliffe's Lets Try Again), owned by Marion and Ivor Ward-Davies, Julie Brown and Tim Hutchings.

Eng. Ch. Winuwuk Heaven Forbid (by Eng. Ch. Tyegarth Glenmorangie of Jenroy ex Good Heavens of Winuwuk), owned by Marion and Ivor Ward-Davies, Julie Brown and Tim Hutchings.

RYTONWAYS

In 1956, Lorna Greathead purchased her first Boxer bitch, Tosca of Yerrom. Mated to Ch. Wardrobes Swinging Kilt, she bred the dual Crufts winner Rytonways Black Flash. She linebred into the Wardrobes strain, and this produced many top winners, including Ch. Wardrobes Rytonways Autumn Gold (top male 1964), his litter sister Ch. Rytonways Autumn Fashion and Ch. Rytonways Triple Crown. She purchased Ch. Colless Winter Gold when he was 12 weeks old and he quickly became a champion. Lorna owned Ch. Valabeau Gold Sari in partnership with the late Bill Malcolm.

Boxers being only a hobby, she's bred very few litters but has never been without a championship show winner since 1959. Wardrobes Delhart's Mack the Knife, the American import (kindly sent by Mr. and Mrs. Wilson Wiley), sired four champions. Rytonways Tamouray Dark Intrigue also sired four champions. In fact in the *British Boxer Club Records Book,* over 100 of the champions featured can be traced to this kennel.

Lorna judged her first championship show in 1968 at the Ladies Kennel Association, which was possibly a record entry including 18 champions. Since then she has judged championship shows for several breed clubs and all-breed championship shows. Lorna had the honor of judging a splendid entry at Crufts in 1990. Her husband judged his first championship show in 1979. Rytonways feels fortunate in having as a friend and partner Mrs. Lorna Baggaley, with whom she's had the pleasure of showing some excellent Boxers. Lorna expresses her thanks to Mr. and Mrs. Wilson Wiley of the world-famous Wardrobes Boxers who helped her so much in her early years in the breed.

Eng. Ch. Colless Winter Gold, (by Rytonways Tamouray Dark Intrigue ex Sukreen Hi-Life), bred by Mrs. C. Handford.

Eng. Ch. Faerdorn Flash Bang Wallop (by Eng. Ch. Faerdorn Pheasant Plucker ex Faerdorn All Things Nice), a BIS winner, owned by Carol Evans.

FAERDORN

Sue Harvey started Faerdorn in 1970 with her first champion Ch. Faerdorn Turly Scrumptious, a sensational bitch that won the Breed and Group at nine months of age. Scrumptious was mated to Ch. Seefeld Picasso to produce Ch. Faerdorn Truly Gorgeous, which she was. Among the early dogs that won nicely are Faerdorn Right on Tarket, Melting Pot, Fairy Tales, and Follow That Dream to Rayfos. In the mid-80s Ch. Faerdorn Pleasant Plucker became Sue Harvey's first all-breed Best in Show winner and the sire of eight champions (seven of these for other kennels). Ch. Faerdorn Flash Bang Wallop, also a BIS winner, won six tickets under some great breed judges including Pat Heath, Pat Dellar and Barbara Greenway. Sue bred Ch. Faerdorn With Love to Shiloh who won the Breed at Crufts under Lorna Greathead and Ch. Faerdorn Head Over Heels, who became a BIS winner for Santonoaks— two examples of the great dogs that Sue bred and sold to other prominent kennels. Few breeders have such class or claim to fame, and the Faerdorn dogs continue to do well for Sue and her contemporaries.

Eng. Ch. Faerdorn Pheasant Plucker (by Eng. Ch. Tyegarth Famous Grouse ex Faerdorn Ginger 'n' Spice), won the first all-breed BIS for Faerdorn Kennels and was the sire of eight champions.

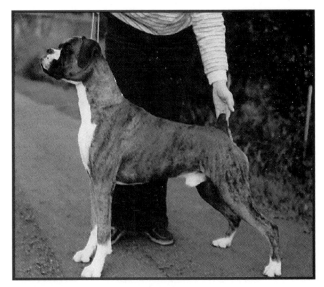

Eng. Ch. Jenroy Pop My Cork to Walkon (by Eng. Ch. Tyegarth Glenmorangie of Jenroy ex Jenroy Whoopsie Daisy), an early outstanding member of the Walkon line who by age ten had 21 CCs.

WALKON

Although a fairly recent kennel in Scotland, beginning in the early 1980s, Walkon Boxers owned by Dr. Walker G. and Yvonne Miller have an impressive list of accomplishments. They started with a Tygarth Famous Grouse son, Jenroy Pop My Cork to Walkon ("Puncher"), who by age ten had 21 CCs. The greats to follow include: Ch. Walkon Smash'd Again, a Dam of Merit, Ch. Crackers at Walkon, a Puncher daughter, and Ch. Walkon Smash 'N Grab, a Best in Show winner in Scotland. The Millers continue in their winning ways and have sold dogs to Australia, Norway and Holland.

Eng. Ch. Jenroy Pop My Cork to Walkon, winning the CC at Crufts in 1993. Handler, Yvonne Miller.

Eng. Ch. Crackers at Walkon (by Ch. Jenroy Pop My Cork to Walkon ex Ginger Lady of Marbelton), bred by Dr. Walker and Yvonne Miller.

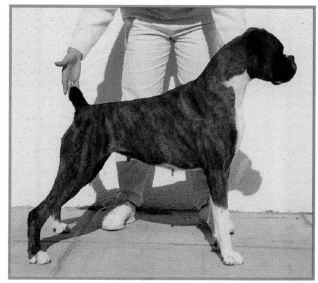

Eng. Ch. Walkon Smash'd Again (by Eng. Ch. Tyegarth Famous Grouse ex Walkon Wotta Smasha), bred by Dr. Walker and Yvonne Miller.

Walkon It's Crunchie (by Eng. Ch. Glenfall the Gladiator ex Eng. Ch. Walkon Smash'd Again), bred by Dr. Walker and Yvonne Miller.

Above and below: Eng. Ch. Blue Print Beern Skittles at Walkon (by Jenroy Pop Back to Walkon ex Aust. Ch. Walkon Skittles), at 16 months of age.

Above: Eng. Ch. Walkon Dutch Courage (by Dolf the Buhe Farm of Marbelton ex Walkon Pleasantly Pickled), winner of four CCs and ten RCCs. *Below:* Champion Walkon Smash 'N' Grab (by Eng. Ch. Tyegarth Blue Kiwi ex Eng. Ch. Walkon Smash'd Again).

WILDAX

Attempting to establish their name in the Boxer fraternity, Frank and Margaret's initial efforts were concentrated on breeding. Of course, as newlyweds in 1961, this was not restricted entirely to the rearing of Boxers! Three children and numerous litters later, the Wildman's extended the score of their activities to include the working of their dogs.

In the 1970s Frank and Margaret's involvement led them, inevitably, to the show ring. It was a move they had been contemplating for some time, but the arrival of a particularly handsome bitch by the name of Wildax Pretty By Far swung their decision to enter into the beauty stakes. Pretty By Far, or "Sophie" to her friends, proved them right by going on to do some top winning. She had the distinction of winning the post-graduate bitch class, in an entry of 40 bitches, under the eminent American breed specialist Mrs. Jane Forsyth. Sophie went on to win two CCs and two reserve CCs before, tragically, a leg injury forced her into early retirement and she never did gain that elusive third ticket which would have given her the title of champion.

Sophie proved to be the first of a long line of Wildax successes in show rings around the world. Mated to Wildax Intoxicating Company, she produced Wildax Pretty Penny, the dam of Ch. Wildax Silver Shadow and

Maltese Ch. Wildax Dimple relaxing with breeder Margaret Wildman.

Ch. Wildax Dimple, an export to Malta. Another Pretty By Far daughter, Wildax Happy Go Lucky, was just as prolific. A top show dog herself, she was once in the last three for a CC in an entry of 429 dogs under the American judge Dr. Burke. Happy Go Lucky produced yet more champions including Aus. Ch. Wildax Lucky Lad and Spanish Ch. Wildax English Rose.

Always looking to improve their bloodlines, Frank and Margaret are among the first English breeders to have imported stock from overseas. One such import in the early 1980s proved particularly productive. Quibus

Sandra Wildman with Eng. Ch. Wildax Silver Shadow, son of Wildax Pretty Penny, bred by her parents Frank and Margaret Wildman.

Dutch-Span-Germ-ATIBOX Ch. Bandolero (by Yorck v. Worikben ex Flor v. h. Slaghek), sire of Ch. Dinneke, Ch. Benno, Ch. Fedor, as well as eight other champions.

Quibus Van Rusticana of Wildax (by Lynpine Super v. Rusticus ex Nina v. Rusticana) was a Dutch import to Wildax Kennels.

Tonantron Amigo of Wildax, a grandson of Quibus Son Wildax Sheer Audacity, got off to a strong start, showing well as a puupy in large shows.

Van Rusticana, from Holland, gelled nicely with the English bitches and left his mark in no uncertain terms. He sired the Can. Ch. Wildax Gingerbread Man and the Maltese Ch. Wildax Jovita. Quibus Son, Wildax Sheer Audacity won the CC under the German specialist Herr Singlestein. Quibus, mated to Ch. Tonantron Glory Girl produced the famous brothers Ch. Tonantron True Glory and Ch. Tonantron All Glory of Wildax. The record-holding Boxer of all time, Tonantron Glory Lass, with 52 CCs and multiple Group and Best in Show wins, is in fact a Quibus granddaughter.

In the late 1980s the Dutch connection again brought dividends. Frank and Margaret had been long time admirers of a dog called Bandolero from the famous van het Slaghek Kennels owned by Leo and Truss Van Oss. An ATIBOX champion, Bandolero had also achieved champion status in Holland, Belgium, Germany, Luxembourg and Spain. As Bandolero himself was unavailable, the Wildmans bought a bitch by the name of Dinneke Vd Jamar-Hoeve from the same kennel. Dinneke, mated to Bandolero and imported in whelp, had a litter of five puppies in quarantine. Of these, three went on to become champions, including the one that Margaret and Frank kept for themselves, a beautiful bitch named Dinneke after her mother. Never before had a dog born in quarantine gone on to become a champion. Another Quibus grandson, Tonantron Arugo of Wildax won well in his first three months in the ring, including shows with entries as high as 127 pups.

The Wildmans have now bred champions in four different breeds and now show Boston Terriers and Bulldogs as well as Boxers. Boxers of course remain Margaret and Frank's first love and chief source of satisfaction and success.

Dutch Ch. Dinneke Vd Jamar-Hoeve, mated with Bandolero, produced three champions, Ch. Dinneke, Ch. Fedor and Ch. Benno.

Eng. Ch. Tyegarth Blue Kiwi (by Eng. Ch. Tyegarth Famous Grouse ex Biloran Little Claret), bred by Sheila Cartwright.

SANTONOAKS

Annabel Portlock purchased her first Boxer in 1964, though only a pet, her second dog was by Ch. Burstall Kinvike Clarion Call, whom she purchased as a show dog but was "the most God-awful specimen." Santonoaks Ziggy, the daughter of Eleanor of Bentoak, who was the foundation of the Santonoaks Boxers and by Ch. Wardrobes Huntersmoon, was the first Boxer to bear the Santonoaks affix. The first Santonoaks litter was born in 1980 by Ch. Biloran Mr. Similarity. Ziggy was bred to Marion Ward-Davies's Red Baron to produce Santonoaks Gorgeous Gussie, who is behind all the present-day Santonoaks dogs. Santonoaks Burlington Bertie, out of Gussie, did some winning, and she was followed by Ch. Tyegarth Blue Kiwi, a lovely male that Annabel managed to purchase from Sheila Cartwright. Kiwi began winning quite young and won 85 Junior Warrants as a pup. He also won the British Boxer Club's Champion of Champions trophy. The year 1986 yielded the Famous Five, a litter of flashy brindles out of Gussie (the other five were white!). The first home-bred champion came out of Miss Bourbon, one of the Famous Five, by Kiwi, and that was Ch. Slick Sammy. Other Santonoaks champions followed including: Robbie Redcoat, Kiwi Magic at Manic, a top-winning bitch, and Billy Bigshot—and it is expected that many more will follow them.

Eng. Ch. Faerdorn Head Over Hells to Santonoaks (by Eng. Ch. Santonoaks Robbie Raincoat ex Eng. Ch. Faerdorn Knobs and Knockers) poses with trophy.

From left: Eng. Ch. Tyegarth Blue Kiwi (by Eng. Ch. Tyegarth Famous Grouse ex Biloran Little Claret), Eng. Ch. Santonoaks Slick Sammy (by Eng. Ch. Tyegarth Blue Kiwi ex Santonoaks Miss Bourbon), who was the top Boxer Puppy in 1987, and Eng. Ch. Santonoaks Robbie Redcoat, winner of five CCs.

Eng. Ch. Santonoaks Robbie Redcoat (by Eng. Ch. Norwatch Glory Boy ex Santonoaks Gorgeous Gussie), bred by Mr. and Mrs. Zammit.

SUSANCAR

Susancar Boxers were started by sisters Sandra and Suzanne Carter (today married but still exhibiting under their maiden affix). They have been involved with dogs all their lives, and have worked their way through the system, and today are both qualified Championship judges. The kennels are situated midway between Manchester and Chester. Since 1980 the stock is based on a very elegant bitch puppy, daughter of Faerdorn Pheasant Plucker. With this bitch and a strong influence from the Dutch Boxer, they were very fortunate to produce Ch. Susancar Lucy Lastic, who in turn produces Susancar Al Kerholic, the very extroverted CC and multiple RCC winning dog. Alkie in turn has produced well with the classic-headed Susancar Lucinda Hedd and Ch. Gypendale Quincy Dental for Susancar. Not to be outdone, Quincy is also a consistent sire who has produced some good progeny, of which Susancar Barry Stir is just one.

Eng. Ch. Susancar Lucy Lastic (by Dolf The Buhe Farm of Marbelton ex Shy Talk of Susancar), dam of Susancar Al Kerholick, a CC-winning dog.

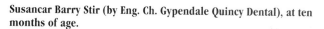

Susancar Lucinda Hedd, daughter of Eng. Ch. Susancar Al Kerholick, bred by Sandra and Suzanne Carter.

Susancar Barry Stir (by Eng. Ch. Gypendale Quincy Dental), at ten months of age.

BRAXBURN

Joan MacLaren of Glasgow, Scotland named her kennel: "Brax being the stream our Boxers splashed through en route to the Clyde to swim, and 'burn' being the Scottish term for a stream." Blazendene Gretchen, the first of Joan MacLaren's Boxers, is responsible for Braxburn's great interest in the breed—although she came before the Braxburn prefix. Gretchen was a line-bred bitch with Stainburndorf, Panfield and Bramfields in her pedigree. Gretchen, typical and sound, if not a great show dog, produced Ruthven Boomerang, a dull grey brindle but more refined than Gretchen. The MacLarens then purchased Geronimo Candy 'n' Cake from Peggy Greene. Joan shares: "Candy was a neat and shapely solid red bitch with a typey feminine head although she was a bit light in muzzle. Boomerang and

Braxburn Moonrose, bred by Joan MacLaren, at four years of age.

Braxburn Capernicum at ten years young!

Candy were bred to Winkinglight Vigilant who was sent by Mrs. Marion Fairbrother of England. He was "an impressive male, if a bit strong in skull." The girls produced 17 puppies, but the fawn puppy to make a name for herself was Braxburn Flush Royal, whose most notable win was at the 1955 British Boxer Club Championship show under Herr Leo Helbig. The MacLarens purchased Wardrobes Red Riding Hood from the Wileys—she was a repeat full sister to the legendary Miss Mink and was bred to Ch. Braxburn Flush Royal. Later in the '60s, she was bred to the import Raineylanes Sirocco, who was making a big splash in England, and that litter yielded Braxburn Minerva, the only great female out of Hoody, who seemed to produce males better until the mating to Sirocco (which was probably his last litter). Dinah was bred to Felcign Faro, a sire of considerable note owned by Felix Price, though there were many whites. A flashy puppy (with his share of white!) was Braxburn Man On Fire. These dogs and their offspring became the basis of the Braxburn Boxers. Joan reflects: "Our breeding had produced marked uniformity in litters from which a good proportion of youngsters finished well. Head type, with well rolled muzzles, was well established thanks primarily to the influence of Flush Royal."

The PA (progressive axonopathy) problem badly affected the kennel in 1982, as it did in much of Scotland. German import Uthan von Starenschloss and Ch. Braxburn Cornelius, the two sires from which all the modern Braxburn dogs derive, were affected, and retrospective clearances show that three of his six most influential sons were clear, including the solid-colored Capernicum. Joan MacLaren's enthusiasm and know-how fortunately saw her through this temporary setback and today the Braxburn line is in great shape.

Braxburn Rosabird, bred by Joan MacLaren, at 15 months of age.

Tonantron Glory Lad, son of the outstanding Eng. Ch. Tonantron Glory Lass, shown here at 12 months of age.

TONANTRON

While having owned and bred Boxers for some 23 years, it was in 1983 that this kennel first hit the headlines in the world of showing when homebred Ch. Antron Prize Guy won Best in Show at an all-breed championship show. Since then English and Norwegian champions have been made up.

The current U.K. breed recordholder, Ch. Tonantron Glory Lass, won her 40th CC with Best of Breed at Crufts 1993, to add to her British Boxer Club Champion of Champions Trophy, Top Boxer Pup 1990, Top Boxer 1991 and 1992, Best in Show all-breeds championship show winner, all achieved under the age of three-and-a-half years. Glory Lass won her first CC as a minor pup at 8 months and her champion title at 13 months. She retired with 52 CCs.

Glory Lass's sire, Ch. Tonantron True Glory (19 CC, 14 RCC), was top CC-winning male 1991 and 1992, also Best of Breed at Crufts 1992.

The Tonantron Boxers are handled by top U.K. handler Mr. Phillip Greenway, who together with his wife Barbara own the highly successful Rayfos Kennels.

Eng. Ch. Tonantron Comanchero (by Eng. Ch. Tonantron True Glory, a winner of 19 CCs and 14 RCCs, ex Tonantron Prize Doll). He followed in his father's footsteps by becoming the top CC-winning male in 1991 and 1992 and BOB at Crufts 1992.

Eng. Ch. Tonantron Glory Lass (by Eng. Ch. Tonantron True Glory ex Tonantron Bella Dora), with her British Boxer Club Champion of Champions trophy and owner Mrs. Sagra Tonkin.

Eng. Ch. Tonantron Glory Lass, the 1990s' UK breed recordholder, with an astounding 52 CCs.

Span. Ch. Janos de Loermo of Lynpine, (by Ch. Elfo v. Worikben ex Elba de Loermo) imported in 1993, was the sire of English, Spanish, French and Dutch champions.

He began considering his Boxers more seriously, and after reviewing photographs of handsome Boxers from the Continent, he decided to begin breeding more selectively to get the heads he desired.

Charles had always linebred, and these close breedings brought forth some really nice bodies and reasonable heads. Yet he reached a point where, although he was England's top Boxer breeder, he could not find a dog to breed to that would improve his existing stock. By this time he had made a number of excursions to different parts of Europe. He had seen the beautiful eyes and gorgeous mouths of Continental Boxers, although most of the German dogs had lines that were directly traced to Witherford Hot Chestnut. In the mid 1960s, he had the full litter sister of Hot Chestnut, whose name was Witherford Stolen Kiss. At an earlier time, he used Frohlich von Dom, who came to England to Allon Dawson's kennel soon after the war.

Not all of the Continental dogs are correct, in fact, many of their rear ends were terrible. If you did find the dog you really wanted to buy, they just didn't want to

Tinga von Rusticanar, Junior World Champion in 1977, pictured with owner Charles Walker.

LYNPINE

Starting back around 1948, Charles Walker of the Lynpine Kennels had his first Boxer with which he participated in some local dog shows and agricultural shows. At that time Charles was more interested in soccer. An injury to his knee stopped him from playing, but he took up refereeing and took that to the top. Soccer in England in those days was played on Saturday, the same day as the dog shows. He was very keenly interested in Boxers and got to know many of the people who were getting the breed underway after World War II. Puppies sold at an absolute premium. He got more for an eight-week-old Boxer puppy than he would earn at work for three weeks. So the random litter came in handy in the early days. He went on breeding and showing until the late 1950s and early 1960s—it was then that he began to feel too short-winded to race about a soccer field.

Eng. Ch. Cherrygate Instant Resetas at Elnathan (by Span. Ch. Janos de Loermo of Lynpine ex Lynpine Ropeke at Cherrygate).

Pedigree for Lynpine Super Rusticus, bred by Charles Walker.

Lynpine Super Rusticus (by Arko of Lynpine ex Lynpine All Gold), grandson to the great Tinga von Rusticanar of Lynpine.

sell it. The minute an Englishman was looking to buy a dog, the price doubled, tripled or worse. They felt that if an English breeder saw something in a dog, then it must be worth keeping! The ones that they really wanted to sell were the ones that Charles didn't want either.

Charles and his wife June built up a strong relationship with a young Dutchman named Issac Rusticus. Issac's father had been a breeder of Boxers from World War I, or soon after, but he was very parochial. The furthest he would go for a stud dog was 30 or 40 miles. Issac had a much wider view and went out to use German, French and Italian stock. He also was viewing some English stock, which he had seen in photographs and films. He really liked the presence of Charles's Boxers—the tighter skin and shorter coats and even their style.

Issac's big success came when his young dog, who was from his father's old bitch lines, bred to Guyus, a very good producing German dog directly from Hot Chestnut, produced Tinga von Rusticanar. Tinga won the Junior Championship in 1977 in Copenhagen at the World Show. Incidentally, the adult at that same show (was another Dutch dog named Ch. Casper Van Worikben, owned by Mr. Piet van Melis, who became one of Issac's closest friends in and out of dogs. Charles persuaded Issac to let him have Tinga on loan since Issac wouldn't sell the dog outright. Tinga, therefore, went to England and was permitted to stay for as long as Charles wished. The English show folks thought Tinga was too big, too strong and a little bit coarse, but conceded that he possessed the most gorgeous eyes and mouth. At this time teeth were badly lacking in England—and the situation hasn't improved greatly since. Although Tinga was not bred too frequently in England, those who did use him have reaped the benefits in getting stronger dogs with good bone. The English

did come to admire the bone that Tinga produced, though they still prefered a smaller dog to breed. In actuality, Tinga was only 25 inches at the withers, but he came in at a time when the English dogs were struggling to make 23 inches.

Tinga von Rusticanar of Lynpine, a well-respected dog among English Boxer breeders.

It was then that Charles returned to Holland to visit different kennels for five or six days. They were taken to see a kennel in the northeast of Holland that belonged to a Mr. Princzron. Charles couldn't even attempt to pronounce this kennel's name, for even the Dutch have problems with it. It was here that Charles happed upon a big bouncy Dutch lady who wanted to sell a dog that was growing too big for her home. Charles went to see the dog and met the nine-month-old Arko. Charles couldn't believe his luck and began to doubt that he understood the lady's broken English—Could she want to sell such a perfect Boxer? Nonetheless, he proceeded. His hands were trembling as he wrote out a check for the dog; he hoped that he was writing it correctly, that she would be able to read it and that it would be sufficient for her. He tried to ask how much she wanted, but

Ch. Tesca von Worikben of the Lynpine Kennels.

ther. They produced a top-winning bitch, Zora von Rusticana, who won at every show, including the big Dutch anniversary show. Dutch Boxer breeders admired the Walkers and held their opinion of a Boxer in high regard—so much so that they would add a naught or two to the price of any Boxer Charles looked twice at.

John Farrell from Yorkshire had gone on a holiday in Holland. Charles told him to look out for Boxers that were good specimens and let him know. He phoned Charles and said that he saw a super dog for sale that was about three or four months old. Charles instructed John to purchase him, but John decided against spending Charles's money. The following spring Charles and June went to Holland with John Farrell and saw the same

Arko of Lynpine (by Aroek von Rusticana ex Donja von Goudveugel), owned by Charles Walker was a particularly influential sire in the United Kingdom.

he couldn't understand her English. When she looked at the check and saw the amount he had written, she threw her arms around him and kissed him. The deal was complete.

Charles and wife June had found their beloved Arko, who stayed with them for 13 years. Arko was not overused in England, but it can honestly be said that many of the top winning dogs of recent times have Arko in their pedigrees. It's been some delight for Charles and June to know that they did something toward the breed that they had only dreamt of.

Considering the consternation with which Tinga was first met when he arrived to England, the Walkers certainly did prove that they were on the right track. Charles sent a bitch bred out of Tinga and some American-bred Boxers from Bruce Cattanach's kennel to Holland where the bitch was mated to Aroek von Rusticana, Arko's fa-

Miazar Juno of Lynpine, imported from Denmark in 1987, became a champion in Spain.

dog, who had grown up beautifully. He was called Tabor. After scolding John, Charles set out to buy him. The owners decided against the sale after Tabor won the junior championship at the show. Three years later, Charles tried to buy the dog again as he was scheduled to come to England but unfortunately a Dutch kennel doubled Charles's offer and he didn't come. Two years later he did come to England and he is still there with Charles today at 15 years of age. Believe it or not, in September 1994, he sired a litter of puppies when he was 14 years of age.

At the very same time as Tabor's coming to the Walkers, Piet van Melis had a very handsome plain brindle dog that was the pick of litter in Denmark. He was the progeny of Zuma von Worikben out of a Danish bitch of German descent. Charles bought him from Piet and brought him to England. Within days of Juno's having arrived in England, Charles bought Tarba, thus he had two Boxers in quarantine at the same time. Juno had terrific bone structure and the most gorgeous temperament imaginable. With Tabor coming out of quarantine at virtually the same time, Juno was overshadowed, so Piet arranged to take him back. Juno instead went on to Spain and became a Spanish champion.

On another visit to Holland, Charles met some young Spanish people who had a young dog and a bitch that had come all the way up from Valenzia through France, Belgium and Holland. They had a red dog and a brindle bitch and wanted Charles's opinions on them prior to the show. Charles said that their bitch was the better of the two, but they didn't agree. He said she will win many titles and he offered to buy the dog. They were perplexed and refused. (Charles's prediction was correct, and the bitch won the Reserve Challenge Championship that day; the dog took second). At a later date, Charles would buy Janos, that same red dog. Janos spent six months in quarantine, and was used for breeding in Charles's kennel for six months. Unfortunately the dog was stricken with cancer, never fully recovered and died six months later of leukemia.

Janos, despite his tragically premature death, sired three champions in his six months at stud. They are Ch. Shiloh Doodlebug, Ch. Newlaithe Hot Fashion and Ch. Cherrygate Instant Pesatas.

A pioneer of the Boxer in Great Britain, Charles Walker learns to accept the disappointments and to learn from them. His eye for a Boxer and unwavering devotion to the breed benefit the whole European fancy. In 1995 he imported Claudio vom Haus Roxana of Lynpine, a descendant of Tinga and World Champion Casper, and later a granddaughter of Janos, Fanfare v. Sokland Hof. The quest for better Boxers continues at Lynpine. As is the case with any true dog man, Charles awaits the day when the next great dog catches his eye and becomes his next international superstar.

Charles Walker with Claudio vom Haus Roxana of Lynpine, at stud for Lynpine in the late 1990s.

Dutch and Int. Ch. Tabor van Worikben of Lynpine is an example of Charles Walker's excellent eye for quality Boxers. At age 14, Tabor sired a litter and is still going strong!

Eng. Ch. Newlaithe Ariadne (by Eng. Ch. Hazefield Barrister ex Newlaithe Maisue Teddy Girl) at seven years set a standard for excellence by taking seven consecutive CCs beginning in 1971.

NEWLAITHE

Newlaithe Boxers was originally established with a bitch sired by Avonbard Othello, great-grandson of Axel von Bad Oeyn and the great Frohlich von Dom out of a Wardrobe-bred bitch from Ch. Justice and Wardobes Silver Spurs. Christine and Patrick Beardsell had a love for Boxers from the year they were married in 1962.

Newlaithe was extremely fortunate in producing a champion out of the third litter of the foundation bitch, however, in the early years one or two other bitches had been purchased in an endeavor to producing winning stock.

Newlaithe Ariadne was destined to set a new standard of Boxer to aim for, taking seven CCs in succession in 1971, being a Group winner and Second Best in Show, making Newlaithe Top Bitch Kennel for 1971.

Eng. Ch. Newlaithe Quibbler, bred by Christine and Patrick Beardsell, at 14 months of age.

The kennel went on to produce the lovely headed Ch. Newlaithe Quibbler. He was difficult to fault technically though he did not exhibit as well as Ariadne (as he preferred to be at home instead of in the show ring). Newlaithe Icarus failed to take top honors but was RCC at Crufts behind the famous Marbelton Desperate Dan.

Newlaithe Nestor, Christine's favorite Boxer, failed to get his third CC, probably because he was the same age as Quibbler and at that time the Beardsells were showing all three males at every show. However, Nestor did win have many Best in Show awards and 105 Junior Warrant points.

At this point, in 1980, progressive axonopathy hit Newlaithe, and Ariadne and Quibbler were totally involved as carriers and their progeny were withdrawn from the breeding program. Nestor, fortunately, was proven totally clear and he and his offspring could help continue the Newlaithe line.

A Newlaithe puppy works with an aspiring trainer!

Newlaithe went out to purchase overseas stock to help rebuild the near-decimated kennel. To that end, Ch. Jacquet Brass Image was purchased from Rick Tomita as well as a Canadian bitch from Haviland. These two imports, combined with quality dogs from Charles and June Walker of Lynpine in Holland, helped to rebuild Newlaithe kennels. Ch. Newlaithe Marietta was entirely Dutch-English bred. Ch. Newlaithe Hot Fashion is a complete composite of Dutch, American and English breeding. In the mid-80s, a son of the Canadian import bitch became a Hong Kong champion, Newlaithe Great System, the Top Boxer and Top-Winning Dog of all time in Hong Kong.

Both Christine and Patrick are international championship show judges. Christine began judging in 1979 and Patrick in 1990. Patrick serves as chairman of the Northern Boxer Club and the UK Breed Council, as well as the Judges Standard Committee. Patrick along with Margaret Kray of Kreyon Boxers in the States publishes the volume *Boxer Blarney*.

The author Rick Tomita and his selected winner from the first Supermatch in 1985, a benefit for Boxer Rescue program. Presenting the Jacquet trophy, Patrick Beardsell.

Eng. Ch. Newlaithes Quibbler winning CC at the Birmingham National in 1977.

When the author Rick Tomita went to judge the first Boxer Super Match in England, a benefit for the Boxer rescue program, I had the pleasure of staying with Patrick and Christine Beardsell in the lovely home, Newlaithe, where I had the opportunity to see their dogs. Surely the combination of American, Dutch and British lines combine here to produce some most beautiful Boxers. I remember "Nestor," Newlaithes Quibbler, who insisted on sleeping with me and kept me warm on those damp English nights. At that time, I also had the pleasure of meeting with Charles and June Walker of Lynpine Boxers, who graciously showed me their kennels where I observed the strong influence of the Dutch dogs on the British Boxers. *The World of the Boxer* is indebted to these generous folk for sharing their stories and expertise to make this section on Great Britain so very special.

Ch. Jacquet's Brass Image of Newlaithe, owned by Christine and Patrick Beardsell and Charles and June Walker.

Newlaithe Great Stuff, bred by Christine and Patrick Beardsell.

Eng. Ch. Newlaithe Great System, the top winning dog of all time in Hong Kong.

Santonoaks Jack Sprat of Newlaithe at a competition in 1989.

Breeder Christine Beardsell of Newlaithe Boxers poses with Jacquet's Young American.

Eng. Ch. Newlaithe Marietta, bred by Christine Beardsell.

Above and left:
Newlaithe Hot
Fashion, a
combination of
Dutch, American
and English
breeding, who
helped to
rebuild the
Newlaithe line
after it was
nearly destroyed
by progressive
axonapathy.

Eng. Ch. Gremlin Summer Storm (by Gremlin Famous Footsteps ex Gremlin Mere Magic), sire of Ch. Tyegarth Famous Grouse.

TYEGARTH

Sheila Cartwright began with Boxers in 1958, and Inishown Red Sand, her second Boxer by Ch. Winkinglight Justice out of a Frohlich von Dom daughter, is regarded as the foundation proper of the Tyegarth line. Sheila is a scientist and depends greatly on her understanding of genetics and gut instincts to select the proper liaisons. Tyegarth Mild and Bitter derived from a mating of Red Sand to I Red Chico (her full brother). This stocky, big dog won two CCs and two RCCs and was an important influence on the Tyegarth line. Although Tyegarth had produced a number of CC and RCC winners in its first 20 years of existence, Ch. Tyegarth Famous Grouse, born in 1978, was the first champion. Grouse won his first RCC at nine months and his

Eng. Ch. Tyegarth Famous Grouse (by Eng. Ch. Gremlin Summer Storm ex Tyegarth Old Fashioned) was the first champion for Tyegarth Kennels and an influential sire who left his mark on 17 champions.

Junior Warrant at eight-and-a-half months, a record for the breed. He went on to win 11 CCs, a Group and two Reserve Groups in his relatively short show career handled by Sheila. Ann Roslin-Williams, a *Dog World* writer, profiles Grouse by saying, "Grouse was not the big, exaggerated type that many people visualise as the ideal stallion. A medium-sized brindle, he was perfectly balanced being a natural showman who did not have to be placed into position; he adopted the correct stance. He had a good head, excellent mouth, lip placement not quite perfect, almost black eyes and black ears."

Grouse, who was by Ch. Gremlin Summer Storm out of Tyegarth Old Fashioned, proved a prepotent sire, stamping any line with which he was bred. He produced 17 champions including Ch. Glorious Twelfth of Redfyre, Ch. Tyegarth Wee Dram, Ch. Tyegarth Gin 'n' Cin and Ch. Tyegarth Double Whisky, as well as Tyegarth Boski, a top dog in Sweden and Aus. Ch. Skelder Game Chip, a proven sire "Down Under." Also a leading sire for Tyegarth is Ch. Tyegarth Glenmorangie of Jenroy, who did his share of winning as well.

Sheila Cartwright continues in her dynamic breeding program, although she's never rearing for the shows. Fortunately her many friends assist her in finishing champions and coaxing her to the shows.

Jack Daniels of Tyegarth (by Eng. Ch. Tyegarth Famous Grouse), bred by Sheila Cartwright.

Three puppies sired by Eng. Ch. Tyegarth Famous Grouse (from left): Eng. Ch. Tyegarth Wee Dram, Tyegarth Glen-Kinchie and Tyegarth AuchenToshan.

Tyegarth Boski (by Eng. Ch. Tyegarth Famous Grouse ex Eng. Ch. Tyegarth Brandiester), was the Top Sire and Top Boxer of Sweden in 1992.

Eng. Ch. Tyegarth Brain Duster, a daughter of Eng. Ch. Tyegarth Famous Grouse, bred by Sheila Cartwright.

Norwatch Mustang Wine (by Leideberge Ramsey ex Gremlin Soft Steps), receiving her DOM trophy in 1987 at eight years old.

Left: Eng. Ch. Rayfos Cock Robin (by Norwatch Glory Boy of Rayfos ex Rayfos Arf 'A' Tick), winner of 26 CCs and the United Kingdom's Top Winning Red Male. *Below left:* Eng. Ch. Sheffordian Ruby Tuesday of Norwatch, DOM (by Eng. Ch. Norwatch Brock Buster ex Sheffordian Sherry), Top Dam for 1988. *Below:* Eng. Ch. Norwatch Brock Buster (by Eng. Ch. Steynmere Night Rider ex Norwatch Mustang Wine), winner of 29 CCs, 22 RCCs and BOB at Crufts 1993.

Eng. Ch. Mitchum of Sunhawk Norwatch (by Eng. Ch. Norwatch Sunhawk Raffles ex Eng. Ch. Slightly Shocked of Sunhawk at Walkon) at home with owners Eddie and Helen Banks.

Eng. Ch. Norwatch Sunhawk Scandal (by Ch. Norwatch Sunhawk Wanneroo ex Sunhawk Norwatch Desirable), who acheived champion status in 1994, owned by Eddie and Helen Banks.

Eng. Ch. Norwatch Slightly Sozzled (by Eng. Ch. Tyegarth Famous Grouse ex Norwatch Mustang Wine), was the Top Winning Bitch of 1985 with 14 CCs.

Eng. Ch. Norwatch Sunhawk Wanneroo (by Eng. Ch. Fletcher of Sunhawk ex Eng. Ch. Sheffordian Ruby Tuesday of Norwatch), was the Top Boxer Puppy of 1991 and Top Boxer Male in 1993.

PROGRESSIVE AXONPATHY (PA)

As a result of the recent outbreak of progressive axonpathy in the United Kingdom, many breeders were forced to regenerate their stock with dogs from Holland, Belgium, Spain, Italy and Germany. Additionally, those breeders that wanted the more elegant type looked to the U.S. and Canada for stock. First defined by Dr. Ian Griffiths in 1980, this hereditary disease "apparently specific to Boxers" causes disorders in the brain and spinal cord, as well as the nerves supplying the muscles. Affected dogs display an unsteady gait, a wide-based stance and a progressive weakness that is first seen in the rear quarters. A credit to the British breeders, the problem has been dealt with forthright and is totally under control. Responsible screening to determine which dogs are affected and avoiding these dogs and their progeny have yielded positive results. Of course, such determination is not easy, as many top winners and sadly producers had to be abandoned as breeding stock. Many of the country's top kennels were forced to "start from scratch," and they have and are enduring.

Dr. Bruce Cattanach, an animal geneticist and delegate to the Boxer Breed Council, confirmed that PA is indeed a hereditary condition whose mode of inheritance was that of a recessive gene. Three well-known stud dogs were indeed carriers and therefore largely responsible for the disease's spread through the U.K. The pedigrees of the carrier dogs were distributed to breed clubs and a pamphlet prepared to educate breeders about the disease and its transmission. Removing the proven carriers from breeding programs immediately reduced the number of clinical cases. Both parents must be carriers in order for a puppy to be affected, and breeders were recommended not to breed dogs from the first or second generation. Third to fifth generation dogs should avoid having the carrier animals on both sides of the pedigree, as the degree of risk is still quite high.

Dr. Griffith, the veterinary surgeon who first defined PA, continues to research the disease, and he is able to recognize an affected puppy as young as four weeks of age (hithertofor, breeders could only recognize at three to six months). Through the continued research of excellent scientists like Dr. Griffith and his team and through the dedication and determination of British breeders, PA has been completely eradicated and the British Boxer continues to thrive as the healthy, wonderful breed it is. *(The author is indebted to Sheila Cartwright for supplying vital information about PA.)*

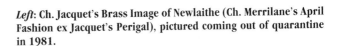

Left: Ch. Jacquet's Brass Image of Newlaithe (Ch. Merrilane's April Fashion ex Jacquet's Perigal), pictured coming out of quarantine in 1981.

Below: Stirleyhill Sullivan (by Eng. Ch. Ryecroft the Jazz Singer ex Stirleyhill Junior Miss) and Stirleyhill Flash Dancer (by Tarpen Pace Setter ex Stirleyhill Starlight). Breeder-owners, Mrs. N. Slater and Mrs. E. Waring.

Upper left: Eng. Ch. Bucksteps Charlie Brown (by Eng. Ch. Carinya Rye 'N' Dry ex Bucksteps Easy Virtue).

Lower right: Eng. Ch. Bucksteps Bittersweet (by Eng. Ch. Carinya Rye 'N' Dry ex Bucksteps Easy Virtue).

Upper right: Eng. Ch. Bucksteps Honeymoon (by Eng. Ch. Ryecroft the Jazz Singer ex Bucksteps The Bridesmaid).

Lower left: Eng. Ch. Look No Further at Marbelton has earned such prestigious honors such as the Top Boxer Puppy of 1988, the Top Boxer of 1989 and the Top Dam for 1993.

Secret Romance at Sandyne.

Eng. Ch. Maranseen Cricket Crony at Khashan (Mananseen Jiminey Cricket ex Maranseen Lollypop), whelped December 3, 1992, bred by Mrs. V. Rogers and Mr. and Mrs. G. Seeney.

Eng. Ch. Sandyne Solo Dancer.

Eng. Ch. Shiloh Doodlebug (by Span. Ch. Janus de Loermo of Lynpine ex Full Circle to Shiloh), winner of four CCs and four RCCs at two years old.

Eng. Ch. Sugarwood Didjano, owned and bred by John Cormack.

Rustar Playtime (by Rustar Play For Pleasure), bred by Paul and Tina Russell.

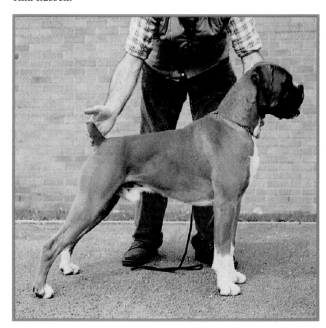

Eng. Ch. Faerdorn With Love To Shiloh (by Eng. Ch. Norwatch Sunhawk Raffles ex Faerdorn Birds 'n Bees), took BOB at Crufts 1990. Owners, S. Lockwood-Brown and A. Curtain.

Eng. Ch. Cherryside Cabarello (by Eng. Ch. Glenfall The Gladiator ex Cherryside Golden Virginia) at two years of age. Breeder/owner, David Webb.

Tyegarth Apple Pie (Tyegarth Grolsch ex Tyegarth Barn Burner).

Eng. Ch. Faerdorn With Love To Shiloh (by Eng. Ch. Norwatch Sunhawk Raffles ex Faerdorn Birds 'n Bees), winner of BOB at Crufts 1990. Owners, S. Lockwood-Brown and A. Curtain.

Limaray I'm On Fire (by Eng. Ch. Cherryside Cabarello).

Eng. Ch. Jenroy Lot Less Bother (by Eng. Ch. Norwatch Brock Buster ex Eng. Ch. Bucksteps Bit O' Bother at Jenroy).

BOXERS
on the
CONTINENT

GERMANY

BY JOSEPH HEINE

It is strange how a certain interest can draw thousands of people to one given place. In this case, the interest has been the love of Boxers from Boxer enthusiasts of many countries. They met in Bremen, Germany, on September 19, 1982, for the prestigious Jahrsieger show. Seventeen nations were represented. I was invited to represent the United States and attend their seminar the previous day. It somewhat resembled the United Nations, long tables were set up to make a "U" shape complete with microphones labeled with the names of each country. It was an excellent opportunity to speak German since most of the seminar was in German. My good friend Ute Fuglister from South Africa was able to translate for our English friends.

The seminar had to do with the problems of the Boxer and the discussion of its standard along with the understanding of the standard. In the area of the standard, it was made very clear that there is one correct type, and there can only be one correct type. In describing our breed, they described the Boxer as

Ch. Pille v. Hambacher Schloß (by Vicomte du Grand Jardin ex Ch. Bergyl de l'enfer Vert), bred and owned by J. and G. Küwens.

Europa-Klub-Jahres-ATIBOX Ch. Patrick v. Stedinger HOF, SchH. III, AD was bred by J. Trinczek and owned by Ralf Brinkmann.

a short-coupled dog that *must* have the correct layback of shoulders, depth of chest full-blown down to the elbows, straight front legs with thick cat paws, short-straight back with high tail-set and a powerful rear that is neither too over-angulated nor too straight. They went into great detail about the Boxer head, particularly the details of the mouth. The underjaw should be wide with teeth evenly spaced and an upturned chin, and the upper lip must be resting on the chin, not overlapping it. The dog should have flat cheeks, a nose with broad nostrils, dark, tight, expressive eyes and a high ear set. The proportions of the skull and muzzle developed into quite a lengthy discussion.

These discussions continued after the seminar, particularly in the areas of monorchids and the increase, in some countries, of white puppies. Where the monorchids and white puppies were concerned, the Germans have excellent records because all litters are checked and recorded by their breed wardens. I wish we could urge our Boxer breeders in the United States and Canada to keep and volunteer such information, but it is considered a mortal sin to ask the owner of any given sire whether or not his sire produces monorchids or whites. We know that they all do and that this is a world-wide problem. The Germans feel that this problem of monorchids prevails mostly in the short-nosed breeds such as the Boxers, Bulldogs, Boston Terriers, Pekingese, etc. They feel that it is genetically linked to the short-nosed breed. Whether or not this is true at this point we do not know, however, it is my understanding that the Germans are doing some research in this area. Should anyone come up with the answers to this problem, I feel that it will be the Germans.

As far as the white puppies are concerned, they feel we are going in the wrong direction simply by over-emphasizing the white markings on our breed. (I personally have been preaching this for years. It is gratifying to me that my views have been backed up by the German authorities.) It is very obvious that many breeders in the United States are coming up with litters in which half of the puppies are born white. The German standard calls for plain fawns and brindle, *some white* may be allowed. The emphasis is on *"some white."* The American Boxer has been highly criticized by the Germans particularly in the area of the steep shoulders, lack of post sternum (forechest) and the development of the breed into a very fragile dog. The standard, they say, calls for a very sturdy animal, never frail and fine boned. It is a working breed that still can be very elegant.

Ch. Helenda v. d. Burg Hilpolstein, SchH. I, AD (by Yanto v. Heideloh ex Ch. Katinga v. Wintergarten) was bred by A. Stöhler and owned by W. Winter.

Another area in which both the American and the English are highly criticized is in the show ring procedure. They feel that too much importance is placed on the handlers and how they present the Boxer when compared to the judging of the Boxer itself. They feel that we are judging personalities. They feel that our dog shows have become mostly business-oriented and that they are quite lucrative for the handlers. They say that the American and English system of judging Boxers will never prevail in Germany. I quickly learned what they were talking about when I saw their magnificent Boxers.

The 1982 Jahrsieger Show was held on a huge athletic field that was as flat as a pool table. The weather was most pleasant to say the least. Three hundred and fifty Boxers were exhibited, and judged by seven judges in seven different rings. About six thousand people attended this show. No judge is permitted to judge more than fifty dogs and he dictates a critique to a secretary of each dog. There are *no* professional handlers. If the owner is unable to handle the dog, then the ring steward will do so. The dog can not be touched by the handler. The Boxer is taught to spar with another Boxer and this is a most natural and beautiful sight to see as they pair off in the ring sparring with one another. We, in the U.S., use liver to get the dogs' attention, in Germany they use another dog. The judge will select his four best and they stand at their ring numbers in the center of the ring. He will explain the placing and reasons for them to each exhibitor, thus the faults and virtues of each Boxer. As the judge prepares to make his placing, people will swarm around that ring. Photographers rush into the ring snapping pictures. It was very difficult for me to take good pictures due to the number of people in the way, nevertheless, I did manage.

After seeing the Boxer exhibited in this manner, I realized that it is so superior to our method for several reasons. In the American system, the handler is always trying to hide a fault. Should the Boxer lack forechest, the handler will pull the head and neck back to make it appear as if his specimen is correct in this area. With the hindquarters, they will either stretch them out or bring them in to create the appearance of proper turn of stifle. Many times I have seen a Boxer handled so cleverly in the ring and looking so good; however, when the handler walked his dog back to the crate on a loose lead, all of the dog's faults "hung out." It was unbelievable that such a Boxer could be a winner with so many faults. This would never happen in the German system.

Colors are judged separately from the Judgenklasse to the Open and Korklasse. Both the fawn and brindle Korklasse were the most exciting. I have seen and judged many thousands of Boxers in time, but never have I seen such quality and perfection as I saw in these two classes. I was able to examine the mouths of about 25 Boxers. I could not believe my eyes as each had an underjaw that was wide, a turned up chin, and a row of perfectly strong, straight teeth. In all of my experience with judging Boxers in the United States, I can only think of about 10 to 12 that had such a correct foreface.

In the brindle Korklasse I spotted a male that was most outstanding with a magnificent head, neck length and body. The judge spotted him too, and Uhtz Vom Bersler Ries not only became a Jahrsieger but

The 1985 ATIBOX judging is underway. Note the handlers allow the dogs to square off while the judges look on. Photograph courtesy of Charles Fortune.

went on to become the best Boxer in the show. There are four Jahrsiegers made at this show: a brindle and fawn male, and a brindle and fawn female. The fawn was Django v Schlob Munch–hausen and the fawn female was Anka V. Insulaner, the brindle female was Titus v. Boxerkamp. Also, there is a Jahres–junsieger, who was the brindle Starky du Chemin Fleuri. There were some beautiful entries that were sired by the famous Dutch Boxer "Okko." One of his daughters won a huge Jugend brindle class and another daughter was second in a huge open fawn class. It must be remembered that for a German Boxer to become titled he must also have at least a Schutzhund title. The Jahrsieger is the most important title to be had, as this means that the

Jahres-Klub-Bundes-Europa-ATIBOX- Ger-Int. Ch. Jakoba v. Hofmannstal, SchH. III, AD (by Klub-ATIBOX Xanthos v. Bereler Ries, SchH. III, AD, FH ex Mia v. Ulisbach, SchH. I) was bred by Rosine Hofmann-Heller and owned by Dagmar Cyron.

Boxer also has the highest degree of training. It must be remembered that Germany has gone through two world wars in which their working breeds, including the Boxer, were taken for military purposes. I can personally verify this with my experiences in Germany during World War II.

The Germans have created a very compact Boxer that is most powerful and, yet, very elegant with brains as well. They reminded me of Olympic champions. Much credit must be given to the German judges for they are most disciplined and will recognize only the correct type. The judges police themselves. Should one get out of line and not judge correct type, structure and quality, he will judge no more. This discipline is carried over to the breeders because they know what is required and will make every effort to breed such a Boxer. This control has produced magnificent Boxers.

Prior to Best in Show there was a parade of Germany's Top Champions. From my vantage point I could see no major faults in any of these Boxers; they all were of the same type and structure. Again, unless one had a movie camera with a telephoto lens, it was most difficult to get good pictures due to the mass of people around each ring. They came in by the busload to see this show.

Judges on Breeding

It is the opinion of these authorities that the American Boxer is too closely bred, they call this incest breeding. There is some truth to this, should you study an 8- to 12-generation pedigrees of most American show Boxers, you will find anywhere from 15 to 50 crosses of the Bang Away-Barrage combination. A number of kennels have estab-

lished their foundation on the bloodlines of these two sires. Many fine champions were developed from these lines. It must be remembered, however, that no matter how good, too much of anything can give us reverse results. This has happened in America from the over-use and wrong use of these bloodlines. This has not happened in Germany, as they have many more sires available of superior quality yet of the same type and structure. Breeders are able to jump around and get the very best from each and they still are not so closely bred. It has been over 25 years since the United States has had such an array of quality champion-producing sires and a variety to choose from. Along with Bang Away and Barrage was Mazelaine's Kappelmeister, who was not a champion himself but produced many, such as Elixir of Raineylane, Jered's Spellbinder, his sister Sweetstuff, who in my opinion was the best Boxer ever bred in the United States, Brandy, Hickory Dick, Warwick's Karina, Captain Lookout, Zack von Dom, and Karlo. There were definitely better Boxers in the show ring in those years than we have now.

The following weekend I attended the 1982 Bundessiegerprufung, which is two days of obedience exercises that would qualify these fine Boxers for their Schutzhund titles. The most exciting phase was when the Boxers went through their man-attacking exercises on the second day. I was most impressed by the character and temperament of these fine dogs. They were very steady, sweet and gentle, yet on command they raced down a field, searched and found a man hidden behind a blockade. The man runs and on given command the Boxer makes a flying tackle, grabbing the man by the arm with terrific force and brings him to a halt, and does not let loose until commanded by the owner. These males cannot be used for breeding if they do not have a qualifying score of 80 or better. They want their Boxers to have brains as well as beauty.

When all of the judging was completed, it was then time for the awards. Platforms were set up in the middle of this beautiful field like in the Olympic Games, and trophies and awards were brought out as well as a large tub of sausages. When all of the preparations were complete, a German band came marching out onto the field playing that delightful "oom-pah-pah" music. The band was followed by the judges, who were followed by the Boxers and their handlers. A large ring was formed around the platforms. The three highest scoring Boxers' names were called and they climbed upon their respective platforms to receive their awards. Some of the awards were beautiful wood carvings of Boxers created by Katharina Gahl, the daughter of Frau Stockmann, whom I visited with later.

My good friend Otto Donner's Boxer Balduin V. D. Donnersburg (owned by Richard Kernherr) was the top winner of this event with a perfect score of 100. He was a most magnificent looking Boxer and an excellent working dog as well. As each handler received his trophy, one of the big circular sausages was placed around the neck of each Boxer. It was so comical as the Boxers were trying to eat their reward.

We went back to our hotel after the ceremonies to rest a bit and prepare for the evening's festivities. We were driven by chartered bus to a huge banquet hall the likes of which I have never seen. At least 400 people were in attendance. Tables filled with every imaginable type of food that lined the walls. We were seated in a huge hall on the second floor and entertained by the Bavarian dancers. First the children performed and then the adults, in their typical costumes of leather pants,

Hazel v. Okeler Forst, SchH. III, FH, AD (by Ch. Kim v. d. Lustigen Grille ex Agave v. Okeler Forst) was bred by Ralf Brinkmann and owned by Dr. Horst Pfeil.

danced to the tunes of a little German band. Needless to say, plenty of that good German beer and Schnapps were flowing.

September 25th was an exciting day for me as I was invited to judge Boxer movement at the Isar-Loisach show, an area a bit southeast of Munich. This club consists of about 150 members and it has its own facilities. It is on about two acres of beautiful level ground upon which the members built a modern club house with all modern equipment. Permanent outdoor kennel quarters were built so each member can house his Boxer while they are enjoying the social activities.

Conformation was judged by Herr Guy Ofcard of France and obedience was judged by Herr Gregory of Augsburg, Germany. A large ring was roped off and the Boxers that participated in movement would gait with their handlers on the outside of the ring. They must gait for 30 minutes without stopping. Should the handler get tired, he can be replaced by another but the Boxer must keep running. The Germans place great importance on movement as each must have excellent reach and drive. This exercise was right up my alley, as you will never see a Boxella Boxer campaigned that is not a good mover. Most of the Boxers moved very well for the first ten minutes or so, after which some began to crisscross or falter. The weakest were asked to drop out and I ended up with three very excellent moving Boxers. The best owned and trained by Otto Donner, was a beautiful moving female with excellent conformation and in tremendous condition. She reminded me of a champion marathon runner. I am certain that she could have continued running for another hour.

This club not only holds its shows at their location but twice a week its members go there for all phases of training. Otto Donner is quite an inspiration to the members of this club for he is knowledgeable not only about all phases of the Boxer but also about so many other areas unrelated to the dogs. For instance, Otto speaks five languages fluently. After listening to his life experiences through the war years, they could be made into a most adventurous and exciting movie. I encouraged him to write a book. Otto Donner is widely recognized for his talents and Boxer knowledge throughout Europe.

America is asking our judges to judge too many dogs too quickly at our specialty and regional shows. Judges are under pressure and simply cannot function or do a good job of judging. The dogs are crowded into a small area and put in a line-up of nose to tail that I am certain both the judge and the ringside observers get bleary-eyed looking at. The judge, having to make the decision as who will get those five points, will choose a dog "that he or she prefers" instead of selecting one that is the nearest to the Boxer standard. Wouldn't it be better to do as they do in Germany, to have more judges and more rings allowing judges to take more time in their selections? Perhaps the handlers would not like this idea should they have dogs entered in several rings, however, does everything in our country have to be based on money? The cost of putting on a show, the cost of the judges, the cost of hiring handlers…shouldn't we be thinking about our Boxers first? I say, yes.

HOLLAND

BY PIET VAN MELIS

When my very good friend Charles Walker, of the world-famous Lynpine Kennels in England, called me to ask whether it was possible for me to write an article about the Dutch influence on the Boxer for an American Boxer book, I really could not be enthusiastic.

Calls and written requests from all over the world have been coming to me asking me to tell something about the Boxer in general, and more specifically, about my breeding methods and the influence that breeding has had on the Continent. This is logical because almost 80% of the successful breeding in Holland over the last 25 years goes back to the Van Worikben lines.

I am a very busy man, breeding as well as showing dogs, and I have many jobs in the dog world. Being busy with the dogs is my priority and I want to keep it like that as long as possible. I do not spend time writing about the Boxer and breeding because I simply do not have the time to do it. However, because Charles Walker put such pressure on me to write for this American book, whose author was so impressed with the Boxers of Holland, and because I was told that this book would be one of great importance—it was not going to be "one of *those* Boxer books"—I decided to say *yes*.

Moreover, it is a challenge to tell Americans specifically about the ideas on the Boxer in that small country of Holland, where even the dogs "wear wooden shoes," and give my perception of Boxer history in Europe.

It is a fact that the Dutch Boxers have been exported and still go to all parts of the world. So, Boxer enthusiasts all over the world got, or get, involved with the successful and very typical Dutch Boxer breeding.

Esprit La Couronne du Nover, a lovely Dutch female sired by Boxella's Milo, the full-brother to Ch. Boxella's Warwick out of Dutch Ch. Aimee, owned and bred by Hans and Will Croon.

Famous Dutch Boxer breeder Piet van Melis, handling Ch. Ambrose van Worikben.

Historical Information

We are talking about the Boxer and most know that within the FCI rules, the country of origin defines the standard. In this case, it is Germany who is telling us how to breed the Boxer.

For decades the Germans ruled everything in Europe. They had the best Boxers, in beauty as well as in working quality. The winners at the most important shows on the continent of Europe were all German Boxers, and no foreigner from outside Germany even had the slightest chance to win at shows held in Germany.

The rare exhibitors who had the courage to show their Boxers in Germany were very happy to simply get the highest qualification of excellence.

I still remember being at one of the first international Boxer shows in 1971 in the city of Hanover, Germany, called the ATIBOX, with my top-winning male Eros van het Klostereind. I got Excellent four in the Open class, an unbelievably high result. We organized a huge party to celebrate that incredible rating of a Dutch Boxer.

Aside from the fact that the Germans wanted to keep the importance of the breed in their own hands, the other European countries made it easy for them to do so. Every country in Europe had its own type of Boxer. It is well known that it is much easier to have four almost equal Dobermans or German Shepherds as number one, two, three and four in the ring than to have four Boxers that resemble each other. It is almost always impos-

Europa-Klub-Jahres-ATIBOX Ch. Patrick v. Stedinger HOF, SchH. III, AD, owned by Ralf Brinkmann.

sible to have the same type of Boxer in the final, because of the fact that the Boxer is a head breed.

In England, there is far less difference between the dogs because judges and breeders are looking more for the overall quality of the dog. In the European countries, the head of the Boxer is of the highest importance, then comes the body, and movement is the last to be looked at. Most of the time, the breed is judged by a breed specialist, this especially occurs in Germany.

In every country, especially France, Italy and Holland, breeders were cooking their own soup, sometimes governed by the Boxer club in their country. The looks of the Boxers were very different in every country so they did not and could not compare their products with those of another country. It was as if there were big barriers between each country, although it was easy to cross the borders.

When there was an international Boxer show and you had the opportunity to see Boxers from several countries, you could point out which country they came from without looking in the catalogue or knowing their pedigrees.

Wardo v. Dommeldal (by Ch. Okko v. Dommeldal ex Safier v. Flowers Garden), owned by Sheila Cartwright and bred by J. Vermeulen.

The German Boxer had a big imposing body, an enormous deep chest, a very typical, (short) head with good chin and a wonderful temperament. The body was often too deep and flat and far too heavy for the bones of the legs and the feet. The head was often a little too small for this breed when compared to the rest of the body.

The German Boxer was not flashy. They preferred the plain-looking dog over the Boxer with white markings, and they still do today.

The German judges are almost all Boxer specialists and they are judging the Boxer for details in the first place; in the second place they are looking at the totality or the harmony of the whole dog. To give an example: a Boxer with overall super qualities who had small teeth, a negligible small deformation or too light eye color does not even earn an Excellent. The dog with no stardom, just a simple dog who had the descent but not the details could get the ticket. A Boxer with terrible temperament, who may have appeared high quality in beauty, did not and still does not have any chance to win.

In Germany a Boxer must pass some difficult tests based on health, type, and character (*Wesen*) to come high on the list. In a way they are right, for the standard says: "a Boxer is a guarding and defending dog."

To start with, the ZVP (*Zuchtveranlagungsprufung*), an elementary test for health, character and type, including the hip test and the AD (20 km along a bike), is done by special Boxer judges so the dog can be bred. Then the tough tests for character are administered: Schutzhund I, II and III or IPO I, II or III; and finally a very hard test for type, quality and strong character called the Selection (*Ankorung*). This last test must be repeated every two years. To pass, the amount/percentage of failures or faults the dog has brought in through breeding, like harelips, white coloration, cryptorchidism and so on, is also calculated. The Boxer Club of Germany also gives the pedigrees from which you can read many things about the dog itself and his ancestors when concerned about things for breeding.

The French and, more or less, the Italian Boxer in that period did not have that enormous strong body, it was more of a middle-sized dog and not as attractive as the German Boxer. They were missing the real high quality and temperament. The Italians always tried to copy the system used in Germany, but because an Italian Boxer does not have the character of a German Boxer they were not able to succeed.

The French interpreted the standard in their own way: they were obedient to the written standard but they did not want to be dependent on the Germans.

The Dutch Boxer, however, was a completely different story. You have to pay attention to the special character of the Dutchmen. They were, for centuries, traveling all over the world. They are extremely independent and in the years following World War II avoided contact with the Germans. The Dutch breeders originally used dogs from Germany at the turn of the century, but they did not continue using German lines. Every now and then when they got some fresh blood from another country, it came mostly from England and rarely from Germany. The most famous breeder who got his lift from a breed from England was P. Zimmermann (Of Haus Germania).

Throughout the years Holland developed a very typical Dutch Boxer, which was a heavy, strong, round dog bearing a superb but not too short expressive head proportionate to the body. It also had strong thick bones, excellent cat feet and a short coat (the Germans do not bother that much about the length of the coat) that was very important to the Dutch. The dog should be attractive with some white. They believed a plain dog did not have a future. The negative feature of the Dutch Boxer was a lack of temperament. Most Dutch breeders did not bother at all about the other point the standard is telling us: that the Boxer is a guard dog. They bred dogs for the family, for lying on the sofa and letting anyone come in and being a friend to anyone. In the show ring they did not even hold up their tails and they looked like they were standing like sheep. The Germans did not like this type of Boxer and vice-versa; the Dutchmen did not want the "aggressive" German Boxer. Breeding this type of Boxer—as a pet dog—with a lack of the high strung temperament was supported by the Boxer Club in Holland. Breeders who wanted to bring some more "gunpowder" from Germany into Holland were isolated.

Traveling Around

After being interested in the breed for some years, I started breeding in the late 1960s. My brother-in-law, Marcel van Baar (Van het Klostereind Kennels), was impressed by the German breeding and with him I traveled throughout Germany visiting kennels, seeing dogs, viewing litters, attending shows and seeing the police work with the Boxer. I saw the qualities of the Boxers in Germany, the special things France bred for and the complete opposite way of regarding the breed in England; I then noticed the missing things in our breed in Holland.

Cita v. Adeltrots (by Robin v.d. Burg-Roffhaus ex Wya v. Adeltrots), owned by H. Hetterscheidt and bred by Jan de Vries.

Sjenka v. d. Pierik (by Promisse v.d. Pierik ex Larissa v.d. Pierik), bred and owned by G.V. Leusen.

Marcel also liked the same things that I saw, but because of the policy in the Dutch Boxer Club and the overall Boxer mentality, he did not have the courage to do what his heart was telling him: breed the overall Boxer. The dog that had the strength, deepness of body and strong character of the German Boxer; the strong bones, feet and standard-head of our Dutch breed combined with the beauty, elegance and good movements of the English Boxer.

I always did everything in my life more or less "my way" and I said to him and myself: "I am going to achieve the Boxer that is in my head." I saw the German Boxers coming to our shows in Holland and winning everything, more so because of their pride and show temperament than because of their qualities. Many Dutch Boxers were better in type but they did not show off their qualities. From that very moment on I started acting against almost all the rules of the Dutch Boxer world. Very quickly I showed dogs in the ring with their tails up, showing themselves perfectly, and I started winning under foreign judges including under the Dutch judges who liked the Boxer with a kind temperament. One of the names I have to mention especially is the late judge Anton Renders, for he supported my ideas enormously. In 1974, he gave a plain dog of mine the reserve ticket for the championship in the Dutch Boxer Club which was very unusual (450 Boxers attended). The dog was only nine months old and his name was Cas van Worikben. Rather quickly I began winning many shows and ruling in the breed. Many of the breeders followed during the years thereafter.

Cas Van Worikben

I have to stop here and pay some special attention to this name. He was the basis for the success of the "modern" Dutch Boxers, who started winning all over the world. His pedigree was built up out of pure Dutch lines (Bellopark, Schapenmarkt, Heerenheide, Drie Staenen, Kleyberg, etc.) combined with some English blood brought in by Peter Zimmermann (Vom Haus Germania). His dogs had the high temperament the other Dutch kennels were missing. Cas van Worikben was a wonderful combination of type, elegance and character. He was a middle-sized, gold brindle dog with not much white, especially in the head. He had an elegant body with an excellent reach of the neck and strong bones. His strongest points were his elegant stylized head and his well-balanced strong character. Although he was basically an outcross, he put his mark on every puppy he produced and you could recognize his type in almost every progeny through him. He was so capable of giving that typical Boxer head that still will come out in a Boxer today. He was very reliable in the breed, for he did not produce major faults. Therefore, he was used hundreds of times as a stud dog.

Cas van Worikben, the famous sire of World Ch. Casper van Worikben, bred by Piet van Melis.

When he was six years old, he spent a year in Italy as a stud. They still trained him for Schutzhund and he got through with the highest points. In the 35 matings he had in Italy, he was so strong in his dominance that he produced no cryptorchid or monorchid males and no pups with "hare-lips" or any other major faults. This was a great surprise to all the breeders in Italy, because they had to deal with many faults that came with the imported German lines.

Cas was used with some very good bitches in Holland and he brought numerous super dogs into the country. His greatest success as a sire was bringing that fabulous World Champion named Casper.

Continuing the story, the biggest highlight was of course getting the World Champion title with the son of Cas van Worikben at the World Championship Show in Herning, Denmark under the famous judge Hans Lehtinen, then winning the group under Kari Jarvinen and finally being second Best in Show under Rainer Vuorinen.

I still can hear the angry remark of the Best in Show judge Vuorinen when he put me in second: "It is your fault, sir, that I can not make the best dog Best in Show, because you did not show him optimally, I am sorry." Casper was a devil in the ring, I must admit that he had a little too much temperament. At that same World Show in 1977, another Dutch Boxer got the Youth World Champion title, it was Tinga van Rusticana. The Germans were out of their minds. How was it possible that a Boxer from outside Germany could get a world title? I had to attend the *Jahressiegerzuchtschau* (Championship show) in Germany to affirm my title. I did it and I was very scared to do so. I won the complete show there under all German judges—they could not do otherwise for Casper was stealing the show with his qualities and the German temperament. The Germans were so upset that not one them came to congratulate me. Of course, all the present foreigners were very happy with this result. This was the big breakthrough and they knew that.

From that moment on, and also because I won the ATIBOX show with my Casper the year after, I finally was accepted by the Germans. I followed them completely with their breeding rules and let all my top dogs pass the other German tests to prove I was following the (German) standard completely. Champion Waldo van Worikben, another son of my famous Casper, passed all these tests including ZVP, SchH and Ankorung with the highest results. Later on came my Ch. Enkas van Motrea, who did much winning in Germany, Champion Zomar van Worikben and Champion Elfo van Worikben. The Germans liked to say to me that I was not a Dutch breeder but a German colleague—it made them feel better.

A short time later, an export of mine that went to Spain won a world title: World Champion, Italian and Spanish Champion ATIBOX-Champ. Ghia van Motrea, who was half German and half Van Worikben. Throughout the years, many breeders in other countries started following me. I was the first sheep who crossed the dike. I remember the tremendous effort of the Belgian breeder Rudy Vandersteen, the owner of the d'Amalia Kennel, who received the World Champion Title in 1989 with his Yorck d'Amalia. It was a pure inbred dog from the line of Van Worikben.

There was also the top winning dog from France, World Champion Jahressieger Perry du Chemin Fleuri. He was from my French friend Robert Genre, a guy who did more or less the same in a later stadium, some seven years later.

More and more the type of the Boxer in European countries became similar. More non-German Boxers were winning in Germany because they were of the same type and quality or even better than the Germans. The

World Ch. Casper van Worikben (by Ch. Cas von Worikben ex Olga von Zwanenbeemd), bred by Piet van Melis and owned by Di Fronzo Graziano.

Italian breeders were doing great only a few years ago. They won many important titles in Germany just like Jahressieger and Bundessieger did. I have to mention the famous Mr. Tanoni who has the Dell Coll d'Infinito Kennel. The Belgian breeders are doing a good job combining Dutch lines with German blood. I have to mention the Boksdoorn Kennels, the Hazenberg Kennels and, of course, the d'Amalia breeding.

In 1975, I bought my first Neapolitan Mastiff, and I was one of the first people owning this breed. I got in contact with them through my Italian Boxer friends. I had many contacts with Italy because I sold my World Champion Casper and also Enkas van Motrea to this country. Almost all Boxer judges in Italy also judge the Neapolitan Mastiff. I was so impressed with this breed that I got involved more and more.

Breeding this large breed was difficult, and was on a very low standard. Moreover, what more could I achieve in Boxer breeding; there were practically no titles I did not win. Aside from my Boxer breeding, I bred a litter of Mastinos every two years and in the early 1980s I

had a top winning dog in Europe. He was a multichampion, Bundessieger, European champion, etc., named Duco van Worikben. So for some years I paid all my attention and put all my energy into the Mastino breed and got focused on Boxers less intently. In the meantime I had built up a good line of bitches, and using my Italian import Dutch Ch. and Bundessieger Falcone dell'Alta Fiumara, who was one of my bitches, I got a super dog. I said to myself when this male Lumeloris was seven months old, "He is capable of winning a complete show." I was convinced of that. No one believed me, because the Mastino breed was standing on such a low level that this could not be true. So, what happened? When he was nine months old he got his first BIS. He did that another four times and did what was almost not possible: Lumerloris won the competition of Best Dog of All Breeds in 1990. This was the second dog which I brought to this title. Some years before the Boxer Bandelero, a son to Yorck van Worikben, was Best Dog of All Breeds.

Helena v. Adeltrots (by Europa-Jugend-Zethos v. Adeltrots ex Mona v. Assenstein), owned by P. V.d. Es and bred by Jan R. de Vries.

Apollohof v. Troye (by Elfo v. Worikben ex Diana v. Adeltrots) owned and bred by N. F. Koppers.

Spain: A Special Story

About 15 years ago I started having frequent contacts with some up and coming countries in the dog world. One of these countries was Spain. I exported a male Boxer, Bello, to a breeder in Madrid. This dog became the top winning dog of all breeds in Spain. A young breeder from Valencia saw the success of this Dutch dog and other top winning dogs like Fedor van het Klostereind and the World Champion bitch Ghia van Motrea, whom I exported to Spain, so he asked me for some good bitches. I liked the man and his thinking and we became very friendly. He followed my advice and very soon he had some good stock in his kennel. His seriousness brought him very far and after some years he came to the international Boxer shows and did some winning.

He became very famous because of his dogs Ch. Djerba de Loermo and Ch. Janos de Loermo, who was exported to my friend Charles Walker in England a few years ago. These two top dogs were children of Ch. Elfo van Worikben, who is the leading sire of champions in Holland in all of history.

Elfo was also a son to Yorck van Worikben. I was convinced that sooner or later my Spanish friend, Ernesto Molins-Poveda, was going to breed a super dog out of his breeding line. When his Ch. Janos had gone to England I suggested to him to use his full brother Llackson with one of his beautiful inbred bitches. A super litter was produced. I asked him to keep the best male and give him to me for some time, and he did so. This dog is World Ch. Tenor De Loermo. Tenor has done much winning all over Europe, but the highest achievement was when he became the leading dog of all breeds in Holland.

Left: Hannina v. Adeltrots (by Europa-Jugend- Zethos v. Adeltrots ex Mona v. Assenstein), owned by E. Cziesso and bred by Jan R. de Vries, was the top bitch in Holland in 1985. *Right:* Ch. Ranou v. Houdringe (by Ch. Tabor v. Worikben ex Harmke v. Houdringe), bred and owned by A. Venema, was the top bitch in Holland in 1986.

The End of My Boxer Breeding?

It is probably hard for an American to understand that there is not much harmony in ideas among the countries of Europe. We have to live with that and the reasons are rooted deep in history. You noticed the differences in ideas in the way that one bred the Boxer. These differences are sometimes very tough extremes. Ear cropping is forbidden in Germany (since 1987), Holland (since 1989), Switzerland, all the Scandinavian countries and, of course, England, but all the other European countries like France, Spain, Italy, Belgium and the Eastern European countries are still cropping ears. They can show their dogs with cropped ears in their own countries and also in countries where cropping is forbidden. The whole thing is very complex, and moreover the dog with the cropped ears has an advantage. In time, I think cropping ears will come to an end in all of Europe. I also think that almost every breeder can live with a Boxer with "natural" ears, but what is worse? In a very short period, it will also be forbidden to crop the tails. When this happens, I think that many Boxer enthusiasts are going to quit breeding. A Boxer with ears is still a Boxer, but a Boxer with a long tail is another breed to me. When and if this comes to pass, I think that I will fulfill an old wish: I will start breeding Bullmastiffs.

Right: Ming v. Adeltrots (by Quintus v. Adeltrots ex Saba v.d. Burg-Roffhausen), bred by Jan R. De Vries and owned by C. Kong-Poel.

Below: Athos v. Wilangea (by Eros v. Bessels Home ex Wende v. Dommeldal), owned by J. Vermeulen and bred by J. V. Wijck.

ITALY

BY DIANE MALLETT

In Italy, the Boxer is shown in Group Two, *Cani da Guardia, Difesa, Utilita.* He is among the bravest of the working dog class and still is the most popular family dog. Italy is about the size of New Mexico but is so spread out that they have broken each area into zones. It has seven zones, from as far south as Sicily to as far north as the Austrian Alps. There are 38 Boxer clubs in Italy, and comparing that with the United States and the ABC, it is interesting to note that the U.S. has five zones with a total of 50 Boxer clubs in the entire country.

World Ch. Nicca del Colle dell'Infinito, owned by Alessandro Tanoni.

A *Raduno* is similar to a Boxer specialty in America, given by a zone club. The classes are also similar, except they have a puppy class from 3 to 6 months and one from 12 to 18 months. The awards are given from first through fourth places with ratings of *"Excellente," "Molto Buono," "Buono"* and *"Abbastanza Buono."* The adult classes are *"Libera"* (open) and *"Lavoro"* (working), which are for dogs and bitches older than 15 months of age. The "Lavoro" class is only for dogs and bitches who have completed and been awarded the title "Cal 3" *(Certificato di Attitudine al Lavoro)* or the Schutzhund I title. It is required that each dog and bitch must pass either of these tests before becoming eligible for the title *"Champione Italiano di Bellezza"* (Italian Champion of Beauty).

The working tests are held separately from a Raduno and, while observing one of these tests, I couldn't help thinking, "What would it be like if the ABC required each Boxer to obtain at least a CD in obedience before becoming eligible for the title of champion?" Many of the other working breeds do have "temperament tests" today. I'm not trying to compare the American CD to either the Working Test or Schutzhund (we know there is no close comparison), but I'm using the CD as an example. The Cal 3 and Schutzhund I are a combination of testing for courage, gun-shyness, tracking, obedience and protection. Schutzhund II and III are much more advanced. As a dog trainer by profession, I am very impressed with all of the tests and the fine dogs who perform in them.

The classes are judged in order of age and color. I have been surprised to see some flashy dogs, as generally they are plain *"Fulvo"* (fawn) or *"Tigrato"* (brindle). The judge gives a critique of both good and bad points on each dog entered. This is done verbally to the owner and club secretary, who records it for ENCI *(Ente Nazionale della Cinofilia Italiana)*, an organization equal to the AKC. The show ring is very large, about two times the required size in America. Many of their shows are similar to bench shows, such that you must stay until a certain hour. They are very strict on health regulations and each dog is checked by a veterinarian upon entering the show grounds and cannot leave the premises until the designated hour. I find the general atmosphere very casual as one is usually seen in the appropriate attire of blue jeans—these are "working dogs," remember! There are no professional handlers, but because the Boxers are taught to "spar" in their competition with the guidance of their competent owners, these owners certainly deserve the title of "professional handlers."

The dogs are visually examined for correct structure, balance and substance. There is no baiting with food as done in America, yet they depend on the help of a friend or assistant who baits the dog with a ball or sleeve from outside the ring. This is known as double-handling and is highly discouraged in America, yet highly favored in Italy. This type of showmanship allows the dogs to set themselves up naturally, as the dogs are on leads and pull to the very end, thus showing themselves off! This is preferred to the American style of handling or stacking the Boxer.

The judge will then observe every dog individually and check its bite. I was able to observe the judging on a "selection test" (certification on a stud dog) and witnessed what I thought were the best bites anywhere! It wasn't just a few dogs, but every one of them seemed absolutely perfect! They have continued, through their breeding, such an important detail in the breed and I'd advise any American who needs to improve in that area, don't hesitate to use a European import—there are many of them in the U.S. The width of the mouth is where the American dogs are lacking, along with the size of the teeth.

Movement plays an important role here in the Boxer breed standard as he must be a "true working dog," and we all know that to work and perform properly he must be structurally sound. When judged, the dogs are moved as a group for final evaluation and will gait at their owners' sides (heel position in obedience) continuously for ten laps. As you'll agree, each owner-handler must be in good physical shape to keep up the pace. You can change handlers but this must be done without stopping or altering the dog's stride. This procedure eliminates the weaker, unconditioned or poorly constructed dogs as they tire quickly. You may see, after the third lap, crabbing, crossing over or simple pacing of a tired dog that lacks working ability. The judge will signal to those to drop out, and as the process of elimination continues it is obvious that the best dogs will remain for the final decision.

The final judging is the same as the American Best of Breed and both dogs and bitches awarded are *"Excellente."* They can be judged by one to six judges, all giving their input on the quality and faults of each dog. The dog and bitch selected are awarded a CAC (*Certificiato di Attitudine al Campionato*), which is well deserved!

It is required to obtain five CACs. One must be acquired at a Boxer Raduno and two must be acquired at an international all-breed exposition. They have added that there must be one year between each CAC—as if it isn't hard enough already.

Jacquet's Lucky Lucky (by Int. Ch. Jacquet's Urko ex Jacquet's Cappucino), owned by Verena Salleo and bred by Richard Tomita.

Tito del Colle dell'Infinito, owned by Alessandro Tanoni.

By 1992, the stud book held by the Italian Kennel Club contained a total of 4,735 Boxers. This is exceptional when you consider that German Shepherds and English Setters represent one-third of all breeds registered.

However, the Boxer is the most numerous of all defense dogs. He is popular because of his great docility and high learning capacity, the very traits that make him a nice and well appreciated family dog.

Prior to 1923, the Boxer was unknown in Italy despite the relatively proximity of Germany. The first entry in the Italian registry was in 1924 when the fawn bitch Alba v. Moss was imported and quickly became a champion. From 1925 to 1939, eight Boxers attained their Italian championships. Of these eight, seven were German bred and one was bred by Count Douglas Scotti. The Italian-bred dog Raul di Ponente came from the same bloodlines as Lustig v. Dom.

It-Int. Ch. Thomas dell Colle dell'Infinito (by Mirco v. Turmblick ex Fionda dell Colle dell'Infinito) has competed in Schutzhund and obedience. Bred by Alessandro Tanoni.

It. Ch. Friso di Valdemone was the first Italian Boxer to be registered in the Deutsche Boxer Klub Zuchtbuch.

While the German dogs had little impact on the breeding programs, Raul, who was well balanced and elegant, transmitted these qualities to the young Italian bloodlines. Then, during the war years, several sons and grandchildren of Lustig v. Dom were imported from Germany. These dogs had the capacity to imprint the Italian Boxers with the best type and temperament of this great stud dog.

Italian breeders had the best years in the 1950s with the importation of Carlo v. Fels and Eitel v. Altenau. This ten-year period could be called the Golden Years of the German Boxer. Suddenly the Boxer, in spite of being very typical and powerful, lost his original balance and elegance not only in Germany but all over Europe.

Germans who were using Abra Dabra of Sirrah Crest to lesser effect started looking to England for Boxers.

It-Int. Ch. Quiros di Valdemone, an important early Italian Boxer.

They imported the brindle Witherford Hot Chestnut, who began to dominate the German breeding, especially through Carlo uit Gutsel and Carlo v. Henninghof. However, since these dogs were always in commanding positions in the European show rings, everyone used them in their breeding programs, thus causing an uncontrolled diffusion of consanguinity whose negative results are still showing up today.

The Italians followed the German's selective line-breeding with imports Carlo uit Gutsel and Carlo v. Henninghof, but luckily the consanguinity did not occur there. Italians breed with a lot of imagination and intuition along with the German strictness. In addition, some Italian breeders looked to the Netherlands for Boxers including my own kennel, di Valdemone.

It is easy to predict that too much inbreeding will cause problems in Italy too. Breeders must look for new ways of using the European and American Boxers in their programs.

It. Ch. Orion di Valdemone, one of the early foundation dogs for the breed in Italy.

It. Ch. Vip di Tomver (by Quarzan della Gens Flaminia ex Free Fancy di Tomver), bred by Marinella Lo Bianco and owned by Giovanii Vitalesta.

Di Tomver

Marinella Lo Bianco, owner of the Boxer kennel di Tomver, chose the surname in remembrance of her first two Boxers, Tom (a fawn male) and Veronica (a brindle bitch). Marinella has been breeding Boxers for over two decades, always with the enthusiasm and the passion of the first day. Marinella, more than anything else, is a dog lover, but the Boxer, as she is sure you will also believe, is a very particular breed, and absolutely agrees with whoever said that the Boxer is a virus from which one does not recover.

Although di Tomver is an amateur kennel, Marinella desires that it remain such in order to be able to continue to provide care and love for every single Boxer. She enjoys the luxury of choosing the future owners for each of her puppies and believes that it is fundamental to the life of a Boxer to be absolutely welcome as a member of the new family. Only then will the Boxer be a happy dog and be able to express all his qualities as a companion, friend and defender of man. Many of her puppies have been chosen by parents of children who are physically or emotionally challenged. Marinella is happy to be able to say that these children have been immensely helped by the Boxer's company and its instinctive enthusiasm for little ones.

Left: It. Ch. Ninia di Tomver, bred and owned by Marinella Lo Bianco.

Upper right: Margot di Tomver (by Savas von de Pierik ex Sofia di Tomver), bred by Marinella Lo Bianco and owned by Giovanni Vichi.

Lower right: Rüde di Tomver (by Ch. Sole dei Cuordileone ex Zizzania di Tomver), bred by Marinella Lo Bianco and owned by Allessandra Pagliacci.

Ch. Marvin del Gran Mogol, owned by Giancarlo Perrotta.

A Gran Mogol male meets a youngster. Owner, Giancarlo Perrotta.

Remo del Gran Mogol relaxing at home.

Gran Mogol

Giancarlo Perrotta has been breeding Boxers for approximately 15 years, but has owned them since 1948. His achievements in the 1990s represent the culmination of his years of intense work, for he has won everything with 14 of the most important championship titles.

Researching the success of this kennel brings us to the fortuitous entrance of the great dam Olivia V. Thannhauser, mother and grandmother of his most important Boxers. Olivia descends directly from the old Bavarian German blood with excellent type and character. This line, coupled with the modern lines derived from Witherford Hot Chestnut, plus a good dose of luck and constant research, has taken Giancarlo to worldwide success.

Ch. Marilyn del Gran Mogol, SchH. I (by Ch. Hoss v. d. Goldquelle SchH. III ex Ch. Flora del Gran Mogol) is a multi-titled bitch who was among the top Boxers in Europe in the early 1990s.

Historical Overview

by Dr. Mario Perricone

The first Boxer crossed the Italian Alps in 1923—if a breed member crossed before then, it is not recorded anywhere. This Boxer was female Alba v. Moss, imported by Guido Aimone Marsan di Fossalo. In the same year, Alba won her Italian championship. In 1925, another Boxer Nathan v. Edelwanted, imported in 1923 by Mario de Croce of Turin, won his Italian championship. Nonetheless, these two first champions did not hinder the Swiss judge Fritz Leimgrube to comment after the 1928 Milan show what a pity the Italians didn't know what a great breed the Boxer was.

From 1934 to 1939, eight Boxers became champions, of which seven were imported and only one was of Italian breeding. Raoul di Ponente, sired by German Boxer Castor v. Schulzneheim and German dam Rassel v. d. Wurm, became one of the foundation dogs for Italian Boxers. Raoul's dam Rassel was by Zimmt v. Dom, the brother of the father of the famous Lustig, out of Uni v. d. Wurm, the grandmother of Lustig.

The first important Boxer, bred by the Count E. Douglas Scotti, is important in that he ignited the passion of Tomaso Bosi of the Della Val di Senio Kennels. This male was not very large but most harmonious and elegant, though his descendants were not of historical sig-

Ultra di Valdemone (by Sissi v. Bereler Ries ex Savas v. d. Pierik), owned by Ottavio and Isabella Perricone.

these years, Boxers accounted for about 12 percent of all the purebred dogs in Italy; currently they account for less than 3 percent, though their quality is higher than ever.

World Ch. Fratz del Colle dell'Infinito (by Olimpio del Colle dell'Infinito ex Playa del Colle dell'Infinito) has earned her champion titles in Italy, Austria and Holland and is a Best in Show winner in Germany.

World Ch. Nicca del Colle dell'Infinito, owned by Alessandro Tanoni, is a champion in Germany and Italy.

nificance. Bosi's kennel was founded in 1939 and today represents an important starting point for all Italian breeders.

Another vital kennel, Virmar Boxers belonging to Mario Confalonieri was established during the Second World War. Until the 1970s it contributed greatly to the Italian Boxer.

The Swiss male, Arno von Turnellen was imported by the famed dog author Piero Scanziani. Arno exhibited great working ability at the trials and became an Italian champion. The years following the war, the Boxer's numbers exploded in Italy, and the Italian Boxer Club was established on November 3, 1946. During

Aus-It. Ch. Salome Detto Zar with owner Moloshi Dimo.

Teck del Colle dell'Infinito (by Mirko v. Turmblick, SchH. III, FH, ex Fionda del Colle dell'Infinito, SchH. I), owned by Alessandro Tanoni, won the World Dog Show in Valencia, Spain.

Olimpio del Colle dell'Infinito, owned by Alessandro Tanoni, is the sire of World Ch. Fratz.

It. Ch. Tito del Colle dell'Infinito (by Bruno v.d. Morsbach ex Bellamore del Colle dell'Infinito), owned by Alessandro Tanoni.

It. Ch. Elthon del Rolanus, SchH. I (by Ch. Red del Gran Mogol ex Chela del Rolanus), owned by Pompeo Gianfranco-Torino.

It. Ch. Axel del Rolanus, SchH. II (by Ch. Oleg v. Hessen Nassau ex Hagel del Rolanus), owned by Ciervo Giovanni-Carmagnola.

Aus-It. Ch. Mel Della Carlinga (by Saiotiara Saver ex Uria di Valdemone), owned by Paolo Caloara, was the number-one Boxer in 1990.

Above: Ch. Hoeverbos (by Heros v. d. Yamarhoeue ex Linda v. d. Akkerwinde), owned by Arici Girolamo. *Below:* Bingo dell Falconara (by Enkas v. Vogelschuztpark ex Vitz di Valdemone), owned by Ottavio and Isabella Perricone.

Upper left: Dixi di San Leone (by World-Ger. Ch. Carlo v. Henningshof ex Darling v. d. Immenburg), owned and bred by Dr. Sebastino Salleo and Dr. E. Strasser.

Lower left: Biene di San Leone (by Diodoro di Zancle ex Ch. Darling v.d. Immeburg).

Upper right: Ch. Darling v.d. Immenburg (by Ger. Ch. Lerry v. Schaltz-Kastlein ex Ch. Brittaro Immenburg), owned by Dr. Sebastino Salleo.

Lower right: Diodoro di Zancle (by El Averoe ex Konni del David), bred by Dr. Sebastino and Verena Maria Salleo-Strasser.

Salome Detto Zar is a working, social and ATIBOX champion owned by Dino Mologni.

Annetta di Tomver (by Jcar del Ghiardo ex Veronica Deglietruschi), bred and owned by Di Tomver Kennels.

Bel-It-Yug-Ger-Aus-Int. Ch. Khero's v.d. Hoeverbos, owned by Arici Girolamo. Photograph courtesy of Lia Stein.

Exercise in the Italian countryside.

A wintertime gathering of the Di Tomver Boxers of Rome, Italy.

Lux. Ch. Quatro van Krato's Hof (by Ch. Otho van de Hazenberg ex Nikita van Krato's Hof) was a winning Boxer in the mid-1990s.

BELGIUM

BY RITA KIEKENS-VAN DORPE
TRANSLATED BY KURT KIEKENS

Belgium is a small country, surrounded by the big Boxer nations of Germany, France and the Netherlands. It's pretty evident that the Belgian Boxer finds its roots in those neighboring countries.

On the German side, the bloodline goes back to Eros Von Heidelogh and Carlo Von Gutsel, sons of the Witherford Hot Chestnut. Witherford was used directly by the kennel Del Trinitad, resulting in the famous male Radia Del Trinitad. On the Dutch side the most commonly used males were the champions from the kennels, Van Adeltrots, Von Worikben and Van de Klapperheide.

Through the Belgian Boxer Club's concentrated efforts and the appointment of Rene Lanoy, a noted Boxer judge, the status of the Belgian Boxer greatly improved. Mr. Lanoy is also one of the oldest Boxer breeders in Belgium. In my personal opinion, Mister Lanoy's influ-

Bel-Lux. Ch. Laike van de Hazenberg (by Ch. Jerom van de Hazenberg ex Idylle del Trinitad) was a big winner in the late 1980s and early 1990s.

ence on the evolution of the Belgian Boxer cannot be understated. Through years of consistent judging (and breeding) he succeeded, with the help of the Belgian breeders, to improve the breed considerably.

The Belgian Boxer Club had its first international exhibition in 1970. The participating dogs were described as lacking depth of muzzle and the male dogs in particular lacked substance, ruggedness, power and size in the hindquarters.

Since then, the Belgian Boxer evolved gradually. By outbreeding the German and the Dutch bloodlines, breeders created Fred Van de Hazenberg and Fantastique van de Costerhoeve—and the foundation for improvement was set.

This male brindle dog Fred Van de Hazenberg, grandson of Carlino v. Nassau-Oranien and son of Donar After Tacha, and Derby Van de Hazenberg left their permanent marks on the Belgian dog world. The current national and international champions are almost all related to these dogs.

Recently, breeders have started breeding to French champions like Athos de l'Enfer Vert, thus announcing a new generation of improved heads and temperament. The Belgian Boxer breeders have succeeded in making the stature of the Boxer square and still making its body

Plato van de Hazenberg (by Ch. Athos de l'Enfer Vert ex Bel-Int. Ch. Lady van 't Woutershof) is a BIS winner in Luxemborg as well as a Europasieger and VDH.

voluminous enough. The Belgian Boxer today has become a beautiful and very elegant dog with a very good head type and a very stable but combative character. The Belgian Boxer owners and breeders have also had good results in training their dogs. Many dogs have qualified in the CQN (Certificate de Qualification Naturelle).

By opening two training places, we succeed in obtaining good results in several I.P.O. (International Program d'Obeissance) and Schutzhund (German training program) games. There are also a lot of Belgian Boxers who have successfully participated in ATIBOX-work programs (Association Technique International de Boxer).

Quemax del Trinitad (by Int. Ch. Otho van de Hazenberg ex Nissa del Trinitad) was a World winner in 1995.

In 1988, the BCB started for the first time the selection test, acknowledged by the *Koninklijke Unie Sint Hubertus* (the coordinated organization for Belgian pedigree dogs). The selection test are very important to determine how good or bad the quality of the breed is. The results of the selection test are not to be compared with the results of exhibitions. The test contains three character tests, one behavior test (sociability) and one morphological test. Concerning the morphological test, the dog has to be very good before even being selected. The points of interest here are a square muzzle, a straight nosebridge, a moist nose, a correct mask, enough depth in the chest thorax, sufficiently developed forechest, correct topline and well-cornered hindquarters, which give the dog a correct way of running and walking.

The following dogs are not allowed to take the test: a dog whose tongue is sticking out while the mouth is closed; a dog with canine teeth shown above the top lip;

Bel. Ch. Patjero van de Hazenberg (by Ch. Jerom van de Hazenberg ex Kim van het Velpenhof).

Bel-Lux-Neth-Int. Ch. Otho van de Hazenberg (by Ch. Athos de l'Enfer Vert ex Bel. Ch. Mandi van de Hazenberg) was a top show dog and a prominent sire in Europe.

a dog who in normal position shows his incisors; a dog with one or two not pigmented eyelids or where the third eyelid has been removed; a dog whose eyes are not dark enough [the standard is set by the German as being 3b (this is a number that is given to the lightest color that is acceptable)]; a dog whose teeth are not according to the standard [good teeth have to be well formatted to vertical and broad (incorrect is when the incisors are formatted like a spoon)]; a dog whose incisors are standing before the canines, which have to be spacious enough.

The dog has to succeed the character tests before taking the morphological test. A dog can only participate twice in character tests without succeeding and is only once allowed to take the morphological tests.

The BCB also has an annual CQN test in which the dog has to prove that he has the defensive qualities that are common for his breed. The training for this test is very important and reinforces the Boxer's natural abilities, such as defending his master, protecting property, etc. Before a dog can be called a champion, he must succeed in the CQN test.

Bel. Ch. Fred van de Hazenberg, SchH. I (by Donar After Tacha ex Derby van de Hazenberg).

Sally van de Hazenberg (by Ch. Plato van de Hazenberg ex Qirra) was the World junior winner in 1995.

Bel-Lux-Int. Ch. Percival After Tacha, SchH. II, IPO III, VDH (by Neth. Ch. Ruffes van de Houtrib ex Bel. Ch. Jessica After Tacha).

Above and below: Schutzhund training being undertaken by Belgian trainers.

BY INGAR KARLSEN

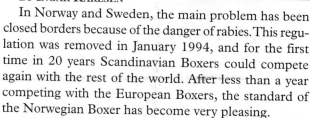

In Norway and Sweden, the main problem has been closed borders because of the danger of rabies. This regulation was removed in January 1994, and for the first time in 20 years Scandinavian Boxers could compete again with the rest of the world. After less than a year competing with the European Boxers, the standard of the Norwegian Boxer has become very pleasing.

The most successful breeder in Scandinavia in recent years is Rognerud Boxers owned by Monica Detemple and Knut Brodal, who were the Breeders of the Year in 1991 (Nor. Ch. Rogneruds Nicole), 1992 (SinJa) and 1994 (Sinia). Rognerud Boxers is a small breeder with about 10 to 15 puppies a year, but the quality is fantastic, especially with the bitches.

Knut Brodal, the man behind the Norwegian Boxer's success, is the president of the Norwegian Boxer Club, and the vice-president of ATIBOX. It took him 17 years from when he started his breeding program until he reached his greatest success, and he never faltered in his belief of what he was doing.

The two great Scandinavian Boxers must be noted, they are Rogneruds sisters: Int-Nor-Swed. Ch. Korad Rogneruds SinJa and Rogneruds Yvette. The latter was Number Two in the World Championship in Bern, Switzerland; Number Two in the ATIBOX Championship in Germany; and Number Two in the Open Finish Championship, along with being the Danish winner in 1994.

Int-Nor-Swed. Ch. Korad Rogneruds SinJa is counted among the greatest of all Scandinavian Boxers, a multiple-BIS winner and producing dam.

Nor-Swed. Ch. Korad Rogneruds Boris is regarded as the perfect combination of German and American Boxer breeding. Through a couple dozen breedings, his impact on Scandinavian Boxers has been profound.

Because of six-month quarantine after taking the rabies vaccine, SinJa did not compete outside Scandinavia. Expectations are great since SinJa has always beaten Yvette in competitions in Scandinavia. SinJa has been a star since she was born. As a puppy she was Best in Show every time except once (Number Two BIS). Even in 1993, when she had puppies, she managed to become the top-winning Boxer in Scandinavia. This first litter was born January 28, 1993 and was sired by Boris. It was a great success. The biggest Boxer show in Norway, in 1994, was won by one of the puppies—Wunderboxer Claus.

Among the top breeders of Norway, Ingar Karlsen started with Boxers 20 years ago. His first Boxer was a big dog named Wunderboxer Baron. He was wonderful with humans and bitches, but he would challenge all male dogs that he met. He was not very popular in the neighborhood. He died from cancer at ten years of age after setting a record all Boxers of the world can only dream of—350 KOs with no losses.

His next Boxer, a brindle, was Nor-Swed. Ch. Korad Rogneruds Boris. Ingar started showing him when he was close to five years old, with fantastic results. Quickly he recognized that the dog's mental condition was very strong, and he was a typical leader that never needed to fight. All dogs respected his leadership. In 1991, his mental condition was tested at the Norwegian Army's Dog School where he received 241 points, which is still the Norwegian record for a Boxer. After this test he became the most used stud Boxer in Scandinavia for three years.

At 11 years of age, Boris had been a Veteran of the Year in Norway in 1991, 1992 and 1993. In 1994 he was the only Boxer in Scandinavia, besides SinJa, that reached the "Top-Ten" in both Norway (Number Eight) and Sweden (Number Five). Boris has meant a great deal

Nor. Ch. Astovega Opuntia (by Astovega Fagus ex Astovega Rivina), owned by Cecilie Strømstad and Henning Lund and bred by Gunnar Alterskjær.

Int-Nor-Swed. Ch. Larun Your Choice (by Int. Ch. Kitwe Out of the Blue ex Nor. Ch. Larun Kalinka), owned by Solveig Sangren and bred by Unni Vestrheim.

to Scandinavian breeding with 16 combinations in Norway and 8 in Sweden. He is considered the perfect combination of American and German breeding. The American, Kreyon's Back in Town, is behind him as well as the German, Carlo V. Henninghof.

The Norwegian Boxer Club has 850 members, and the Swedish Boxer Club is approximately twice as large. Boxers are about the 20th most popular dog in Norway and Sweden. In shows for all breeds, the Boxer is always in the top five.

The difference between the Norwegian and the Swedish Boxers is that the Swedes get 95% of their Boxers imported from England. In Norway they import more Boxers from Germany, Holland and Italy, but still get many imports from England. The main reason for this big English import is due to the quarantine regulations. Before January 1994, you could import any English dog directly into your home, while you had to put all other imports in a six-month quarantine period.

Henning Lund and Cecilie Strømstad with a litter of Boxer puppies in Norway.

MORE ON SCANDINAVIA

BY HENNING LUND AND CECILIE STROMSTAD

In general, the Boxer population in Norway is not big enough to maintain a wide enough breeding base and to keep the quality up at the same time, so breeders have had to rely heavily on imported stud dogs. Norway was one of the first countries outside Germany where the Boxer was introduced and bred. By 1907 the first Boxer was registered in this country, and the breed has been bred and shown ever since. Some good Boxers were imported from Germany in these early years, among them Ch. Wotan von Dom by Rolf von Vogelsberg from the very first litter born at the von Dom kennel. It took some time, however, before a good breeding base was established, but after a somewhat slow start, some very determined enthusiasts entered the scene in the 1920s and took on an almost scientific approach to Boxer breeding to establish and maintain the required qualities. The most important of these pioneers was unquestionably Mr. L. Eyv. Dahl, who bred under the affix Kerberos. Mr. Dahl established very close connections with the German Boxer world, especially with Philip Stockmann of the von Dom kennel, and several dogs from this kennel and related breeding were imported to Norway. This breeding program enjoyed good results, and in the years preceding WWII, the quality of Boxers in Norway was among the very best in the world. To help increase the quality of Boxer breeding in Norway, the Norwegian Boxer Club was established by Dahl and his fellows in 1934.

The war meant a heavy setback of breeding of Boxers in Norway. During these years, no shows were held to monitor the breeding and the German occupational forces demanded that all dogs of working breeds were given to them for war service. However, thanks to the determination and knowledge of the enthusiasts in this country, the breed was reestab-

Int. Ch. Formula Miller (Can-Nor. Ch. Mephisto's High Noon ex Formula Merlyn), owned by Paul Scott.

Int. Ch. Formula Miller, owned by Paul Scott of Kennel Formula.

lished during the 1950s using imports from Sweden, which had not been at war, and new imports from Germany and Holland. These new foundation dogs all had a very strong von Dom background, and after some ten years of work, Norwegian Boxers had again reached world-class quality.

In the 1960s, contact was established between Norwegian breeders and the English Wardrobes Kennel, and some very influential dogs, such as Wardrobes Viking and Ch. Wardrobes Golden Tiger, came over to be used in a well-planned linebreeding program. It was Wench Paulsen (now W. Eikeseth) that imported these dogs. During this decade, also the first connections were made with American breeders, mainly through dogs that had been exported to Sweden and Finland. Ch. Treceders Mighty Dar, Boxellas Lafayette and Ch. Boxellas Yahoo were all qualitatively important stud dogs.

The 1970s were dominated mainly by dogs that were imported from North America, first Ch. My-R's Side Car, owned by Marit and Knut Andersen of Kennel Cavajes; later Int. Ch. Mephisto's High Noon, owned by Jorunn Maeland; and Int. Ch. Mephisto's Intermezzo, imported by Paul Scott of Kennel Formula who was the dominating breeder through most of this decade. These dogs did some very useful breed-

Nor. Ch. My-R's Side Car (by Ch. My-R's Marquette ex My-R's Impassioned), owned by Knut Anderson.

ing, and the dogs produced from these lines that distinguished themselves the most were Int. Ch. Formula Miller, by High Noon out of a daughter of Side Car, going back to the Wardrobes breeding on the mother's side, and Miller's son with an Intermezzo daughter, Int. Ch. Count On Barro. Barro was bred in Norway but was sold to Sweden, where he again was a useful stud dog. This father and son team consisted of the two most betitled Boxers in Scandinavia, as both had obedience championships in addition to their multiple conformation championships. There were important additions from England, mainly from Wardrobes and Seefeld breeding. Kari and Knut Sigurd Wilberg of the Kanix Kennel had great success with showing dogs of this background. Three English imports who won for them were: Int. Ch. Seefeld Wynbok Dominic, Ch. Seefeld Dark 'n Divine and Ch. Tonan Supersonic Sonmar, while the most notable winner of their own breeding was the

Can-Nor. Ch. Mephisto's High Noon, SOM, bred by Michael Millan and owned by Paul Scott, made a lasting impact on Norwegian Boxers in the 1970s. High Noon became a Canadian SOM after 20 years through the use of frozen semen.

Sonmar daughter Int. Ch. Kanix Non Stop, owned by Sjur Hall. These four Boxers all made it to "Boxer of the Year;" Dark 'n Divine took that title twice. The Wilbergs later moved to England and continued breeding there. Another winning dog from this period that deserves mention was Ch. Marikarlos Killemann, bred in Sweden by Marion Humble, but owned by Kari and Bjorn Oien of the Norwegian kennel Tirama. There were also additions from Continental Europe, the most well known of these were probably Ch. Uhu v Malefinbach and Ch. Flash von Defr Butendorfer Hohe, both descendants of the English import to Germany, Ch. Witherford Hot Chestnut.

While the American Boxers mentioned above have had an important and lasting influence in Norway, the 1980s were unquestionably dominated by dogs imported from England. Because of the quarantine, importation of dogs from the United States is costly and time consuming, and during the last decade there have been no new imports from that part of the world. Since there is no quarantine from England, it is much easier and cheaper to import dogs from there.

There have been a lot of dogs imported from England, but only a handful of them have had any big influence. Sjur Hall of Monolitten Boxers has imported several dogs, some of which have become top show winners and important studs.

Nor. Ch. Monolitten's I Believe in Sorcery (by Nor. Ch. Triglyph the Sorcerer ex Nor. Ch. Camara's Blue Monolitt), owned by Anne-Lise and Karl Holmen and bred Sjur Hall, was Boxer of the Year in Norway in 1991, 1992, and 1993.

Int. Ch. Count on Barro (by Int. Ch. Formula Miller ex Nor. Ch. Smugglers Black Velvet), owned by Paul Scott.

Int. Ch. Kitwe Out Of The Blue, by the English record-breaking dog Ch. Gremlin Summer Storm, was the first of Sjur's top winners. He was top working dog in 1983 and became the father of 17 champions. Blue's most notable get is Int. Ch. Monolitten's Future In The Blue (her mother was Ch. Kanix Non Stop, who was the first Norwegian-bred Boxer to win BIS at an international FCI all-breed show in Norway). These shows usually have an entry of 2000–4000 dogs. In 1987, Sjur went on to become the first Boxer ever to win the title of "Dog of the Year All Breeds" in Norway, which he also won in 1988. He too was an FCI BIS winner. "Sorcy" also set a record as a producer, as his get collected over 50 championships in Norway and Sweden! His most prominent sons were both bred by Sjur Hall, Ch.Monolitten's I Believe In Arco, who was top Boxer in 1989 and 1990; and Ch. Monolitten's I Believe In Sorcery, who was top Boxer no less than three years running from 1991 through 1993, and also was an FCI BIS winner. During these three years, "Billie," as he is called, had no real challenger for this title. Ch. Monolitten's I Believe In Sorcery has also taken up the legacy as a worthwhile producer of quality Boxers.

There were also other breeders that bred from a mix of English and American lines. One of these was the Tirama Kennel of Kari and Bjoern Oeien, based on English Gremlin and Cherry Burton lines with addition of American breeding that was sent to Sweden (for instance Ch. Wedge Holow's Sam's Son, a top winner in Sweden). They bred Ch. Tiramas Teddy Killemann, owned by Rolf Pedersen, who was top Boxer in 1986. Another breeder who has always gone on steadily and consistently is Gunnar Alterskjaer of Kennel Astovega, who has been breeding from stock going back to the Mephisto dogs and My-R Side Car, Boxella's Jeremiah that he imported from the USA, and Swanfield and Gremlin breeding from England.

A breeder that has gone in a slightly different direction during this period, doing her own things, is Marit Sunde of Kennel Bogerudmyra. Her breeding is heavily linebred to Treceder dogs that went to Scandinavia, and lately she has put in some Continental breeding as well.

In addition to the English and American breeding, there have been Continental dogs that have had some influence in the 1980s and early 1990s. The most notable of these as far as winning get is concerned is the German Timo von Steinmeister-Teich, who has produced ten champions. His foremost offspring is the bitch Int. Ch. Rogneruds SinJa, owned by Ingar Karlsen. SinJa has always competed among the four or so best on the Top Ten list in Norway, and she has won often in Sweden as well, where she was top Boxer in 1992 and 1994.

There is definitely a tendency for people to favor either the Continental dogs or the English/American dogs, which results in an obvious variation in type within this rather small population of Boxers. Thus, there are unending discussions on what a good Boxer is supposed to look like.

Among there top winners is our own bitch Ch. Astovega Opuntia, who in fact has done most of her winning as a veteran. In 1993, at eight years old, she was a top winning Boxer bitch in Norway and Number Three on the Top Ten list. In 1994, at age nine, she was again Number Three but was just beaten for Top Bitch by SinJa.

Am-Can-Nor. Ch. Mephisto's Intermezzo (by Int. Ch. Millan's Fashion Hint ex Can. Ch. Scher-Khoun's Autumn Concerto) greatly influenced the Larun Kennel of Unni and Lars Vestrheim, the top Norwegian kennel of the 1980s.

Ten years running, from 1981 to 1991, the honors of Top Breeder in Norway went to the Larun Kennel of Unni and Lars Vestrheim. This kennel is based mainly on the American dogs Mephisto's Intermezzo and Boxella's Jeremiah, but have used Sjur Hall's imports to some advantage during the 1980s. No less than 30 champions have been bred under the Larun prefix, quite a few of these have multiple championships. A more recent up and coming kennel belongs to Monika and Knut Brodal, the Rognerud Kennel. This kennel is mainly based upon Continental dogs that have come to Scandinavia.

Sjur Hall's English import Ch. Thatledome Perfect Partner was Top Boxer in 1994 and also won an FCI BIS. The 1990s have seen a number of quality imports enter Norway from England. While most of these imports are born in England, they come from a variety of backgrounds, some mainly from Continental breeding and others from American lines. Presently the breeding base in Norway is probably better and wider than it has been for several years. In addition to the imports, there are some good homebred Boxers as well, but of course the imports will always be most in demand at stud. There is generally a tendency for people to believe that Boxers born in another country are better than the "home made" ones! During the last years, breeders have developed very good techniques for storage and use of frozen semen, and this opens up new dimensions for dog breeding in a small country like this. Now breeders have the opportunity to use the very best dogs from other countries that would have been inaccessible earlier.

During 1988, two events negatively influenced Boxers in Norway. The Norwegian government decided to ban tail-docking. As a result, registrations went down by approximately 30% the following years. At the same

Nor. Ch. Larun Illusion (by Nor. Ch. Triglyph the Sorcerer ex Larun Waikiki), owned by Kirsten Lilleby and bred by Unni Vestrheim.

Boxer fun Norwegian style! Owner, Henning Lund.

Nor. Ch. Larun Just Fair (by Nor. Ch. Triglyph the Sorcerer ex Larun Tootsie), owned by Sverre Skalleberg, bred by Unni Vestrheim.

Int. Ch. Monolitten's Future in the Blue (by Int. Ch. Kitwe Out of the Blue ex Int. Ch. Kanux Non Stop), owned and bred by Sjur Hall.

time, it was discovered that the dreaded hereditary disease progressive axonopathy (PA), which had earlier been thought to be confined to England, had been imported to Norway through Sweden. This eradicated some of the best breeding stock in Norway, for instance, the Tirama line, and meant a disaster for breeders in some parts of Norway.

Fortunately, Boxer people are keen and don't give up that easily, and now people seem to have adjusted to the thought and sight of long-tailed Boxers. Even if some breeders were frustrated by PA, this disease was quickly brought under control thanks to the PA control scheme that had already been established in England.

Presently, approximately 250 Boxers are registered each year, and this figure has been quite constant in the last few years. The Boxer is not among the numerically most popular breeds, but as a show dog the Boxer is highly esteemed. At the bigger shows, the Boxer entry is almost always among the largest ones.

What about keeping Boxers in Norway, "the land of ice and snow"? There might be some misunderstanding about this. While the winters can be cold in Norway, the climate isn't that cold and the summers are often very hot. In fact, I get the impression that we are better off than, for instance, the northern part of Canada in the winter! Anyway, Boxers love the snow—chasing snow-

Nor. Ch. Rupik Look Back (by Can. Ch. Lounsbury's Flashback to Rupik ex Bella Dora of Rupik), owned by Cecilie Strømstad and bred by Sheila Bowman of England.

Nor. Ch. Triglyph the Sorcerer with owner Sjur Hall, the highly acclaimed Boxer who ranked number one dog in Norway and was a celebrated BIS winner of Norway's premier FCI show.

balls that disappear in the snow is a great pastime for them. If it gets too cold, you just have to put a coat on the dog when you take it out.

When you are out skiing, Boxers are great for pulling you around. With a well-exercised and eager Boxer in front of you, you don't have to work hard when going uphill, and downhill is almost dangerous! While they haven't been used much for sled dog competitions, Boxers have taken part in such activities. Nor.-Swed. Ch. Boxannas Aldebaran (Ch. Triglyph The Sorcerer ex Boxerhavens Agatha) took part in the two-day Seppala trail. We made him a sleeping bag for spending the night in a tent in the snow, and a specially designed ski suit in case the weather got too hard! This dog also competes with success in obedience trials and working competitions, and shows what a versatile all-around breed this really is, just given the chance!

In this part of the world, a Boxer is very much a member of the family. Big kennels are almost non-existent and only rarely do you find more than four or five Boxers in a household. Even the most heavily campaigned show Boxers are family pets and couch dogs, valued for their personality and company as well as for their showmanship! When it comes to dog showing, Scandinavia has nothing like the professionalism and commercialism that seems to be the rule in the USA. While many of the exhibitors in Norway find American dog shows spectacular, there is no desire to adopt that part of the "American way"!

RUSSIA

BY ARKADIY SHERMAN

At the beginning of the 20th century, Baron von Baranboyn of Russia brought the first Boxers from Germany. By 1917 he had established a sizable kennel on his estate in southern Russia. Unfortunately, during the Bolshevik Revolution, most of the dogs were destroyed or assimilated with other breeds.

Beginning in 1930, there was a renaissance in the development of the Russian Boxer. A new generation was imported from Germany and the Baltics. Moscow, Leningrad, Kharkov, Kiev and Odessa became the key breeding centers of the Boxer in Russia.

At the first dog exhibition in the USSR, only a few of these "new" Boxers were presented. However, by the end of 1930, the number of dogs began to grow and the breed gained in popularity among the nation's dog lovers. Meanwhile, the government paid more attention to German Shepherds, which, because of their longer coats, were considered more useful for working with the KGB, police department and Red Army.

The first standards for Boxers were established in 1929. There have been many changes since then. For example, the original standard for height in males was 66–68 cm, while in females it was 65–66 cm. Current standards established in 1972 for height indicate 63–68 cm for males and 58–62 cm for females. The index for bone width established in 1929 was 21–23 cm for males and 20–21 cm for females, while current standards indicate bone width of 19–21 cm for males and 18–20 cm for females. The 1984 standard indicates height for males 57–63 cm, females 53–59 cm; weight for males 30–32 kg, females 24–28 kg. Early standards did not approve of white markings on the face, neck or legs. The muzzle was supposed to be all black with no markings. The original head position was different as well: the necks were supposed to be straighter, not allowing for the "arc" configuration (arch in the neck) that is prevalent in today's Boxer.

Russia is very cold most of the year. Because Boxers are short-haired dogs, they were only useful for indoor securities so the Kennel Club for Voluntary Society for Navy, Army and Air Force (DOCAAF) made a point to develop the German Shepherd for outdoor work. The Boxer remained in the working class but lost much of its popularity. There were not many dogs in the exhibitions. Breeding became more random, resulting in many cases of inbreeding, and the price for Boxer puppies dropped. Boxer breeders definitely needed some new bloodlines.

During World War II all of the Boxers were almost lost completely, and during the post-war years purebred Boxers were once again imported from Germany. In Moscow, for example, Nikkel v.d. Dom, Scherry v. Gausenhoie, Ernst Lustig Banco v. Rick and others from Germany were used in breeding with the remaining representatives of the "old" strain, and this marked the beginning of today's dogs.

During the 1950s, two more dogs of German origin were added for breeding: Grim v. Klausdorf and Alf v. Muncbahtal. Both producers possessed excellent appearances, which they were able to reproduce in their offspring.

By the end of the 1960s, some new dogs were brought into the USSR from the German Democratic Republic and Czechoslovakia. The dark brindle color of these

Rus. Ch. Zhasta, owned by Olga Kiselev, currently lives in New York City.

A celebrated international champion Boxer photographed in the Soviet Union circa 1980.

imports initiated a new era in Boxers in Russia. The Boxer's popularity grew amazingly, and prices for puppies skyrocketed. The buying price for a puppy was comparable to the monthly salary of a Russian engineer. During this period, dogs were also imported from England, Norway and Poland.

In local, regional and national exhibitions, Boxers outnumbered most other entries. This new surge of popularity, of course, led to an increase of random overbreeding. Many cases of cryptorchidism, albinism and malformed teeth and jaws appeared. On the positive side, however, the increased popularity proved that the Boxer was a truly useful working dog. Since the rules of exhibition did not allow for the showing of untrained dogs, obedience and guard-dog training made the Boxer a more desirable dog.

Today in Russia, as was true in the 1960s, the dark red brindle Boxer is more popular than the sand-colored fawns with flashy white marks. The breed on the whole is not terribly popular, as the Russians have embraced the more exotic or the more aggressive breeds.

Nonetheless, the Boxer lovers in the country continue breeding and improving the breed, introducing new bloodlines to improve some of the skeletal problems that cropped up during the 1980s. Imports in the SNG (Union of Independent Countries), as Russia is currently called, from Israel, Germany, Italy and the United States have helped to make considerable strides in the Russian Boxers, and breeding practices are becoming more and more stable. Recent outcrossings to American Boxers have yielded dogs with the outstanding physical characteristics of the American dogs and the more trainable personality of the Russian. This is a most pleasing combination of elegance and temperament for the 21st century.

Arkadiy Sherman now lives in the United States, having left his homeland of Russia in the early 1990s. He is an all-breed conformation judge, as well as a judge in obedience and protection work. He specializes in working dogs, terriers and spaniels. He worked with military police dogs, concentrating on the training of dogs for paratroopers to look for explosives.

LATVIA

BY ILZE BULDERE

Everything started in the late 1940s when the first Boxers, as trophy dogs, were sent from Germany to the Soviet Republics including Latvia, which was a part of the USSR from 1940 to 1991. Each year the breed became more and more popular and, at the beginning of 1950, Boxers were established at the Service Dog Club. However, serious work has been done only since 1974 when Boxer breeders, together with fanciers of Great Danes and Doberman Pinchers, separated and founded their own organization, the Association of Dog Breeders.

During 1960, descendants of Onko v.d. Rennstadt Edler v. Stolzenhof and Alf. v. Hunsbacchtal improved the quality of Latvian Boxers; in the 1970s, Bil-Dzan, sired by Ben v. Barhof, produced numerous winners. At the beginning of the 1980s, Blitz-Dzoija, daughter of Blitz v. Evelynenhof, gave birth to the Blitz line. In the late 1980s there was a period of inactivity, but since the beginning of 1990, Latvian breeders have been in contact with Poland, Scandinavia and Holland. Latvian bitches have been bred to many famous dogs: Togo Szoldra, Napoleon Maxim z Grodu Merkurego, Boody Marimba CS, Dary Elismar and Sendy Im-Ka. In the 1990s there were three kennels in Latvia: Il-BI owned by Ilze Buldere, Limbic owned by Mara Bicane and Vejkalnj owned by Rolands Vindbergs.

While Latvia was a part of the USSR, fanciers abided by a Soviet breeding system. Dogs could be used only when they reached 20 months of age and bitches, 22 months of age. In addition to receiving marks of "excellent" or "very good," they also had to pass an obedience exam and guard dog test.

Guest author Ilze Buldere with Lat. Ch. Irreks Birre.

Lat. Ch. Irreks Birre (by Reks ex Saadzo-Irre) is a three-time Group winner and a multiple Breed winner, holding the VDK I, SK II, and ASD I titles

As in Germany, official club members visit the breeder shortly after whelping and verify the number of puppies (no more than eight are left) and their colors. Then at the age of two weeks, the puppies are inspected for the second time and the breeder gets instructions and advice about the next two weeks. For the third time, at the age of one month, the litter is evaluated one last time.

Under the Soviet system, there were two large all-breed shows and one specialty show held annually. The dogs were shown in three classes: youngest (10–18 months), middle (18–36 months) and senior (3–8 years). Only dogs who had passed an obedience exam could enter the senior class. The marks "excellent," "very good" and "good" and the titles "Best Junior," "Class Winner" and "Best of Breed" were given at the show.

The title "champion" was given only for breeding. There were four steps: first breeding class, elite, champion and the highest title, "Breed Champion." Dogs had to collect 72 points—a most difficult feat considering that in 18 years (1974 to 1992) there were only five "Breed Champions," four bitches and one dog, namely Balta-Gabriela, Blitc-Dzoija, Saadzo-Iterija, Irreks-Birre and Bil-Dzan.

For obedience trials, Latvia still follows the old Russian school. There are several levels and each ends with an exam and mark, the highest being step I. VDK, the first level, is the basic obedience necessary to make a good companion dog. It includes heeling off leash, sit, down, up from a distance, recall, retrieving objects and jumping over obstacles. In the second level, SK, the dog has to guard his owner's things while on a leash, find his owner's

Lotboo-Zessika Limbic owned by Mara Bicane.

things in a 200 square-meter territory, track his owner's scent and perform a scent discrimination exercise. For ASD, a dog must guard a place, defend his master from attack, hold the attacker from moving and a perform a more difficult scent discrimination test. SV dogs must perform with skiers pulling, with the commands "forward," "stop," "left" and "right."

There are several obedience competitions during the year. The highest award is the title "Master of Obedience," in which neither dog nor handler can lose even half a point during competition in two levels, VDK and ASD. It is very hard, and through the years only a few dogs have obtained this title, including two Boxers: Bujan handled by Jelena Dumbrovskaja and Blite-Dzoija handled by Ligita Zake.

Presently Latvian breeders are using stud dogs from Poland, including Napolean Maxim z Grodu Merkurego, Pol. Ch. Cyrus Eliotana, Pol. Ch. Rockefeller Nostrum, and Togo Szoldra. Given the close proximity of Poland, it's cheaper and does not require a visa, as Russia does, to make a visit for breeding purposes.

A'Nel Panna z Redy LTU, JN, LTJCH, LVJCH, as an adult, owned by Ilze Buldere.

Dimarsel-Ziskorali, bred by A. Gailis and owned by J. Dablaka, and Zersed-Udo, bred by O. Rits. Dimarsel is the most winning Boxer in Latvia in the 1990s and has done a great deal of winning in Russia, Estonia, Lithuania and Poland.

Goldrok-Gabriela (Goldsmits ex Etei-Roklenda), owned by N. Kohno.

A'Nel Panna z Redy (Rockefeller Nostrum ex Aisza Scutum), as a pup, with owner Ilze Buldere.

GREECE

BY DR. ALEXANDER MITSOPOULOS

The quality of Boxers in Greece has improved in recent times, as Greek breeders have imported prominent Boxers from the United Kingdom, Italy, Sweden and Germany in order to improve the overall quality of the breed. These imported dogs were bred by Camsail Kennels, Bailiga Boxers, J.D. Price, J. Malcolm and Mr. and Mrs. Simson. There are about 100 registered Boxers with various organizations, but the number of unregistered dogs is considerably larger. The Boxer Club of Greece was formed in 1995 under the guidance of the Greek Kennel Club, intending to promote and improve the breed. The dog sport has been on the rise in Greece, and both national and international shows have been hosted under FCI regulations and the patronage of the GKC.

Camsail Heather Honey (by Camsail Bird of Feather ex Camsail Tiger Rag), bred by L. Boyle and owned by Dr. Alexander Mitsopoulos.

Camsail Whisky Punch (by Camsail Morning Song ex Marbelton Ozone Friendly), bred by L. Boysel and owned by Dr. Alexander Mitsopoulos.

Camsail Whisky Punch and Camsail Heather Honey owned by guest author Dr. Alexander Mitsopoulos.

316

AUSTRIA

BY DR. MARIO PERRICONE

There are a few hundred Boxers registered every year in the Austrian stud books but the directors of the Boxer Club in Vienna do not complain, as they believe that the limited number makes it easier to control quality and selection. For the Austrians, the objective is to produce Boxers that have the right characteristics to make them useful to their owners. Friederich Roberth, one of the Viennese fathers of the breed, was in Munich, Germany working with military dogs for the German Colonial Army. With Roberth's background, it would be unthinkable that the Austrian breeders not take particular care in considering the working abilities of the breed.

Roberth was a true dog lover, and his interest in training military dogs led him to working with the German army, which like the Russian and French armies, was experimenting in military dogs. Roberth met Erald Conig and Rudolf Hopner, both involved in the potential employment of the Airedale Terrier. The common passion of these gentlemen gave birth to a friendship that became extremely productive in later years, as they conceived the idea of reviving the medium-sized Molossar. It was these three dog men that analyzed Flocki, considered to be the main progenitor of the modern Boxer breed. Flocki, as so many breed books tell us, was derived by Bullenbeisser on her maternal side and by the bulldog Tom on her paternal side.

Max Hohne, president of the Austrian Boxer Club, has developed a series of juvenile tests to analyze a dog's character before it is conditioned and trained. The results of these tests determine those bloodlines that are

World Ch. Otho van de Hazenberg (by Ch. Athos de l'enfer Vert ex Ch. Mandi van de Hazenberg), owned by Mevr. W. Van Dijck-Van Thielen, is a champion in Luxemburg, the Netherlands and Belgium.

Fin. Ch. Jacquet's Yankee (by Ch. Goldfield's Dorian de Jacquet ex Oota Fraulein Sparkles), bred by Richard Tomita.

best suited for work. The beliefs of the Austrian breeders are confirmed by the concrete results obtained in police services by the famous Ben Satana Boxers, utilized by Mr. and Mrs. Menzel. The Menzels were later forced to interrupt their studies due to racial persecutions and their transferring to Israel.

Austrians do not believe very much in the controlling of hip dysplasia. In Germany, breeders are obligated to use only breeding stock that is either clear of hip dysplasia or only marginally affected by it. By following these breeding practices, there is greater potential eventually to eliminate the disease. However, Austrian breeders do not follow these practices and, therefore, the Austrian Boxer Club does not require hip x-rays in order to register a dog.

BOXERS

IN

AUSTRALIA

BOXERS IN AUSTRALIA

BY PETER FOSTER

The Boxer arrived in Australia in the late 1940s. Mrs. Rena Gerardy, Mr. Fred Wheatland, Mr. Tom Hester and Mr. H. Taylor are generally recognized as the earliest importers, laying the foundation for the breed in Australia. Some of the early imports were: Tirkane Tony, T. Daybreak Jewel, T. Taffeta, Pepper Box, Anson, Klesby Blazeaway, Panfield Gambler, Panfield Jazz, Panfield Crooner, Cuckmore Kunzle, Debonair of Blossomlea, Stainburndorf Zenana and Panfield Tango, whose dam Alma Van Der Frankenwarte was a daughter of Lustig Von Dom. Mrs. Gerardy also imported that great English Champion Panfield Flash. Flash had won Best in Show in England under Frau Stockmann over 485 Boxers.

The inaugural meeting of The Boxer Club of Australia was held on December 13, 1949 at the home of Mr. and Mrs. Gerardy in Gordon, New South Wales. The meeting was chaired by Mr. Bill Spillstead, a well-known Great Dane breeder (the NSW Canine Council Showgrounds are named in his honor). Mrs. Gerardy was elected president and became the driving force behind the club for many years.

The club continued to be known as The Boxer Club of Australia despite much pressure being exerted by the controlling bodies of other states to have Australia dropped from its name. However, The Royal Agricultural Society Kennel Control insisted that the name be changed and, in November 1960, it became known as The Boxer Club of New South Wales and as such will always be recognized as the mother of all the Boxer clubs in Australia. Today there are Boxer clubs in New South Wales, Queensland, Victoria, Tasmania, South Australia and Western Australia.

Today we see a leap in the popularity of Boxers. At the all-breed dog shows, Boxers usually have the largest breed entry. With the formation of the National Breed Council and a national specialty show being held every two years, rotated to allow a different state to host it each time, enthusiasts are able to get together and exchange ideas and see the results of breeding programs from all over Australia.

As each of the various state-controlling bodies have their own rules and regulations, so each national is unique to its location, and this bi-annual event is eagerly looked forward to and attended by Boxer enthusiasts from every state in Australia and New Zealand.

Right from the beginning when the breed first arrived in Australia, knowledgeable Boxer breeders have imported stock from all over the world. Imports have come from Canada, the U.S., England, Holland and Sweden. Famous bloodlines have combined with the local stock to produce a level of quality that can more than hold its own in breed competition anywhere in the world today.

Judges come to Australia from every corner of the globe, and all are very impressed with the high standard that the breeders have attained.

Australian judges returning from overseas engagements, while praising the dogs in other countries, still feel that the local dogs would be highly placed on the world scene.

The system used to gain a dog's championship title in Australia is very different from that used in the U.S. In Australia, a dog has to gain 100 points to earn the title of champion under four different judges. The maximum points awarded at any show is 25 points, and the minimum is 6 points, depending on the number of dogs entered at the show.

The classes judged at shows are: baby puppy (3–6 months), minor puppy (6–9 months), puppy (6–12 months), junior (12–24 months), intermediate (24–36 months), Australian-bred (5 months and over, bred in Australia) and open (over 6 months).

There is no separate class for champions and the current top-winning champions are entered in their age classes, so a young Boxer has to be an extremely top-quality specimen to defeat the current winners and gain the points to earn its title.

Guest author Peter Foster with Boxhaven Hot Classic (by Aust. Ch. Westbrooks Hot Pursuit ex Aust. Ch. Boxhaven Classic Lee).

THE QUEENSLAND BOXER CLUB

BY GREG ABOOD

The history of the Boxer Club in Queensland is as colorful as the history of Australia. We appear to have had our fair share of outlaws, corrupt politicians and factional fights, and all that is normal in a club.

Our club first met in November 1958. Some of the foundation names were Blackman, Basset, Huizing, Grimwade, Underwood, Laycock, Hunter, Wheatland and Moore. There was some difficulty in obtaining affiliation with the Canine Control, with letters going to and fro, and even though the membership was quite large (about 50), affiliation was not easily attained. Despite the membership numbers, very few Boxers were being exhibited. There is no record, either with the Boxer Club or the Canine Control, of when the club was finally affiliated. Let's hope we were, as the Canine Control happily takes our affiliation dues each year!

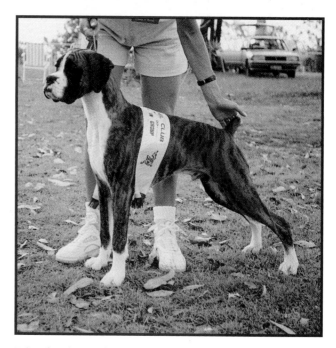

Neimad Jack Daniels (by Aust. Ch. Ascameda Justin Time ex Aust. Ch. Neimad Southern Comfort), bred by R. Pajaczkowski.

In the early days, some members appeared to stand out as contributing a lot to the club. The Underwoods were a stabilizing force in such areas as type improvement and problem resolution. There were many complaints that the Southerners were criticizing our Boxers as not being good enough. It was suggested that rather than complain, we "go south and beat the pants off them." The first Queensland Boxers to win challenge at the Sydney Royal and best puppy of breed at the Melbourne Royal were both bred by Ray and Lex Underwood. They also encouraged breeders and exhibitors not to look at the faults in their opposition but the good points, and to learn from those animals how they could improve their own breeding.

The first German import was Delf Von Alten Haust, owned by Ray and Lex Underwood. He was not shown but sired 39 champions. One of his daughters, "Bad Filly," was the first Queensland-bred Sydney Royal Challenge winner.

Aust. Ch. Betalla Shady Lady (by Aust. Ch. Betalla Charlie Boy ex Aust. Ch. Glawma Spanish Boot), whelped March 9, 1987, has won many BIS awards.

Monthly meetings in the city were very well attended. It was a close-knit community with members assisting in other areas such as providing transport to meetings and shows. Show entries were gathered by the secretary and lodged in bulk. Initial membership fees were 10 shillings, which translates to about seven dollars.

But of course, there were the more colorful moments that make history real and interesting. One member flatly refused to go in the show ring if another member was there. Others would withdraw their entries if another member entered. There were factional camps—some would sit where the "Boxer" sign was at the show, whereas others would say, "I know what a Boxer is and don't need to sit there."

Aust. Ch. Faerdorn Raise a Riot, imported from Faerdorn Kennels of the United Kingdom.

It was not easy to obtain a championship in the '60s. Three levels of challenge points were awarded, depending on the type of show. There could be two, three or five points, and it was possible to win the Group and only obtain two points for your dog.

Finances were always a problem with the club. In one of the early minutes, it is recorded that the treasurer will not need to give a report as "we are in no way financial at all!" However, unique ways of raising money were used. They had widely published gambling nights, which were strictly illegal, but good profit makers.

Despite financial problems, a regular magazine for the club began production in 1962. This provided a wealth of information for members throughout the state and assisted in pulling the members closer together. In 1962 there were 40 Boxers shown at the Brisbane Royal, compared to 113 at the Sydney Royal, and 1740 were entered at a Boxer specialty in America, but the winners that year were from the South. The comment was made that our Boxers were improving, but the Southerners were better handlers.

Aust. Ch. Betalla Charlie Boy (by Aust. Ch. Glawmar Catchme Red ex Betalla Dark Molly), whelped September 23, 1985, won many Group and BIS awards and continued to participate in veterans' shows later in his career.

Aust. Ch. Intrends Fiddlededee (by Aust. Ch. Faerdorn Raise A Riot ex Intrends Over The Moon) with owner and breeder Judy Horton.

Members of note in the '60s were the Doyles and the Midgleys. One of the more outstanding bitches was Augsburg Snowboots. The Midgleys began the Glawmar line, which dominated the Queensland scene for many years. One of their major contributions was to physically make the show trophies and donate them to the club at no charge. This was a substantial savings for the club.

During the '60s, Boxers were becoming a reasonably popular breed. A comparison of registrations shows that in 1951 only five were registered but, by 1962, 294 were registered. The preferred color seemed to change from a greater percentage of brindle in 1958 to almost 80% fawn by 1961.

In 1963 there were no overseas imports into Queensland; however, nine imports came from interstate with the significant ones coming from the Felmoor Raineylanes Raffles line. Dominant in the breeding stock were Brandenburg Brando and Von Harjo Razzle Dazzle (Underwood) and Brier-Lea Blaze Aways (Moore) from South Australia. From the mid-'60s the registrations seem to level out, but there was also a trend to go back to brindles.

In 1963, the Royal Boxer entry increased to 51 with a Queensland dog taking out the challenge and Best of Breed (Brandenburg Pinocchio). Bitch challenge went to Smestead Pink Mink from Sydney.

The club started in 1964, 2 pound 10 shillings in the red. During this time the executive members carried the finances out of their own pocket, but when it was suggested that membership fees be increased, there were complaints from members. One member stated that he drank twice as much as the membership fee at each Boxer club social activity, and he thought the fee objections were very petty.

The Underwoods and Midgleys were very supportive and complimentary to the club during this time, always encouraging good sportsmanship. There were, however, reports of a top Boxer having acid burns in its mouth as an attempt to poison or knobble it. And here's a great argument for tail docking: A top show dog had its tail broken (obviously not a Boxer), but the rivals achieved their purpose of getting it out of the ring one way or the other.

In the 1960s, membership peaked at 160. During the late '60s the show ring competition was predominantly from Brandenburg and Glawmar. The first dog of the Midgleys came from Brandenburg Kennels.

In the '70s, Midgley imported a German dog, which contributed to improvement of heads in Queensland. Some other names began appearing, such as Mack and Smitheringdale. The club became rather excitable during this time with many a heated discussion on various matters. It also appeared to be a period of consolidation, particularly as most members were open and honest with each other and matters were regularly aired at meetings, resolved and then forgotten. The club was beginning to get some

Aust. Ch. Eischied K.Z. Seven (by NZ. Ch. Tyegarth Johnny Walker ex Eischied Ever Lovin), was imported from New Zealand and went on to win the award for Queensland Boxer Club's Top Boxer in 1989, '90 and '91. He has sired 14 champions.

Ascameda Time Will Tell (by Aust. Ch. Ascameda Justin Time ex Ascameda Velvet Hammer).

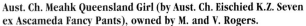

Aust. Ch. Meahk Queensland Girl (by Aust. Ch. Eischied K.Z. Seven ex Ascameda Fancy Pants), owned by M. and V. Rogers.

money together and the idea arose to have an international judge for the 21st anniversary show in 1981. Marion Ward-Davies of the United Kingdom was selected to judge and the show was a resounding success.

During the 1980s, some of the famous names were beginning to be replaced with other kennel prefixes that regularly won in the show ring. But when the lines were examined, the general trend was Brandenburg, Glawmar and Ascameda as a transition from the stock of one to the other.

This brief history is only a general overview of over 30 years of good times, bad times and proof that despite everything, people who have the common love of such a great breed as the Boxer can stay together and improve both themselves and the breed.

Above : Miscap Mischief Maker (*top*) (by Aust. Ch. Eischied K.Z. Seven ex Ascameda Miss Mischief), whelped October 5, 1990.
Right: Aust. Ch. Ascameda Summer Caper (by Aust. Ch. Betalla Prince Henry ex Ascameda Summer Mist), whelped January 2, 1987, compete in the show ring with handler Mrs. C.A. Holcombe.

Lower left: Aust. Ch. Glamorsox Moon Jewel (by Aust. Ch. Eld Moonraker ex Glamorsox Your Astar).
Lower right: Aust. Ch. Chrisharod Sun Jewel (by Aust. Ch. Glamorsox Sampson ex Aust. Ch. Glamorsox Moon Jewel), shown by breeder and owner Helen Meier.

BOXER CLUB OF AUSTRALIA (NEW SOUTH WALES)

The year 1949 was a very important one for Boxers in Australia. On the 13th of December, at the Gordon (Sydney) home of Mr. and Mrs. Gerardy (Park Royal Kennels), the first Boxer club was formed under the banner of "The Boxer Club of Australia." The following people were present: The Gerardys, Arthurs, Heaths, Spilsteads, Smalls, Gleesons, Tompson, Spiers and Swales. Bill Spilstead, now so well known by many of us, was in the chair. The constitution was adopted and office-bearers elected. These were: president, Mrs. Gerardy; vice-presidents, Miss Thompson and Mr. Symonds; secretary, Mr. Arthur; and treasurer, Mr. Heath. The head office of the Union Bank was chosen as the banker. A point-score competition was discussed and introduced using the Great Dane Club's scoring system. The point-score, besides providing a trophy for a winner and runner-up, also awarded a trophy for the most successful second prize winner. The point-score idea hasn't changed a great deal since this time, as even by the third club meeting there was discussion and some concern over the "fairness" of the point-score system.

As with most other dog clubs, the Boxer Club of Australia's major interest was in the running of shows. At early meetings, the club resolved to donate trophies for Sydney Royal Best of Breed, Best Puppy and Best Limit. At the 1951 Sydney Royal, Boxers had the second largest trophy list after Irish Setters for an entry of 32. Sydney Royal was, and still is, an important show on the Australian calendar. It may therefore be of interest to take a look at this show in the early years of Boxers.

Boxers were first exhibited at Sydney Royal in 1949. The judge was well-known British dog man Mr. Leo Wilson. There were six imported dogs shown. In 1950, under Mr. Percy Roberts of the U.S., 20 dogs were exhibited and the first Australian prefix appeared. This was Park Royal, owned by Mrs. Rena Gerardy. Mr. Mansell of Mosman also exhibited. His Cheltenham prefix was to become quite influential. Other exhibitors included Mrs. Thompson, Mrs. Gunn and Mr. and Mrs. Dove of Campsie. In 1953, more local prefixes graced the R.A.S. show rings, including Wyreema, Rexleigh and the very influential Tarakani, owned by Mrs. M. Jones. The club's long-time treasurer, Mrs. Aussell, showed for the first time. In the early '50s, Dr. and Mrs. H. Spira began a renowned era in canine affairs by showing a Cheltenham bitch. Dr. Spira became a member of the club

Skelder Pot Black, sired by the well-known Eng. Ch. Faerdorn Pheasant Plucker, was an import from the United Kingdom.

in August 1950. He was later to become a long-time patron of the club. In 1956 Mr. Wilton-Crowe, the importer of a number of English dogs, exhibited for the first time. The entry at Sydney gradually increased. By 1958 Mr. Roberts from the U.S., in a repeat judging performance, had 74 dogs. In this year, Mr. D. Taylor, a well-known all-breed judge, became a life member, and Mr. D. Glackin (Crucin) first exhibited.

Skelder Speed Trap (by Eng. Ch. Skelder Singing Sleuth ex Skelder Snakes and Ladders), imported from the United Kingdom.

Aust. Ch. Zwar In Trouble (by Skelder Speed Trap ex Boxella's Rosanna), bred and owned by J. O'Neil.

Other exhibitors who were to come to prominence in the late '50s and early '60s included Mr. and Mrs. R. Townshend (Lorac), Mr. and Mrs. J. Dobson (Wawnhill), Mr. F. Weam (Franzlaine), Mr. and Mrs. L. Williamson, Mrs. N. Evans (Innsbruck) and Mr. P. Foster (Boxhaven).

The first show of the Boxer Club of Australia was a joint effort of a three-breed committee (formed by Collie, Great Dane and German Shepherd enthusiasts). This show was held on March 6, 1950. Another show was

Zwar Interpol, a beautiful result of the breeding of British import Skelder Speed Trap with American import Boxella's Rosanna.

held in August the same year with Mr. Spilstead as show manager. The venue was at Rockdale and the judge (who kindly declined a fee) was Mr. Witton. The raffle successfully raised eight pounds! Two championship shows were approved by the RASKC for 1951. They were on the May 19 and October 6, with the judges being Mr. Spilstead and Mr. Witton. A parade was introduced in 1953. Judges at club shows in the early '50s included Mrs. Fitzgibbon, Mr. Hill and Mrs. Gerardy. In 1956, Mr. L. DeGroen judged a club championship show.

These judges had the opportunity to judge many of the early imports. The dogs were predominately from England, with an occasional American influence. English kennels that sent stock "Down Under" included Tirkane, Panfield, Cuckmere, Stainburndorf, Gremlin and Wardrobes. Dogs of note to hit NSW included the well-known English Champion Panfield Tango, Panfield Flash and the American Fireball of Ememfar imported

Aust. Ch. Vineen TuRo's Girl (by TuRo's Cross Time ex Lucentio Bessy Girl), owned by Gavin and Eileen Custance of Vineen Boxers.

by Mrs. Gerardy. Ch. Stainburndorf Rusty Pierre was imported by Mrs. J. Rees of the Casa Verdi prefix. Mr. Wilton-Crowe imported two Wardrobes dogs, Ranch Mink and Red Ribbons. Mr. D. Glackin imported Ardenoak Stirrup of Arnogar, followed by the legendary Ch. Wardrobes Morning Canter, who sired a great many winners in the late '60s. Obviously, as the '60s progressed, many other kennels in the United Kingdom sent dogs. These included Marbelton, Cherryburton and Seefield.

A major concern of the young club was fund-raising. The club began with a little over one pound, and fund-raising raffles were organized at the second club meeting. The first few raffles were a cake, a bottle of Scotch and 50 cigarettes. By the October 1950 meeting, the club had a balance of 27 pounds and 11 shillings. At regular intervals, the club had to seek new venues for meetings. In the first ten years, the club moved from Mrs. Gerardy's home, to Lovejoy's Lending Library, to the Sydney Bridge Club, to the Railway Institute and to the Glebe Town Hall.

During these years, members dealt with a number of ideas and issues that are still discussed today. At the November 1950 meeting, the establishment of a record book of pedigreed Boxer dogs owned and bred in Australia was proposed. It's a pity this record (if it began) has not been passed on over the years. The idea of an annual ball was put forth in 1954. A sub-committee was formed. Lack of support meant that it nearly didn't run, but, due to the untiring efforts of Mrs. Gerardy and Mrs. Mansell, it was a resounding success with 107 people attending.

The president Mrs. Gerardy spoke at length about indiscriminate breeding in Boxers, favoring the German system as an example of controlled breeding. Another member, Mrs. Hegger, offered to write to Germany to get full details of this breeding system. Obviously, this was never acted upon.

Throughout the first decade, there was much discussion over the club's name. Although when the club was formed there were no other Boxer clubs in Australia,

Aust. Ch. Rosemullion One Off (by Ch. Salgray's Argo of Memorylane ex Rosemullion Show Stopa), owned by Jacky Baker.

there were areas of dissent. As early as March 1950 the Victorian KC requested the RASKC to eliminate the word "Australia" from the club's name. The secretary was empowered to write a letter of defense against this action. In April of the same year, a letter was received from the RASKC recommending that "NSW: be inserted in brackets under the word 'Australia.' " However, the original name remained until 1960. In that year, the pressure from controlling state bodies and individual members saw a move to alter the club's name. In June 1960, Mr. Breety moved that the word "Australia" be deleted and replaced with "NSW." The motion was defeated by 13 votes to 9. However, in November 1960, Mr. R. Aussell again made a motion, which was carried unanimously. So was born The Boxer Club of NSW.

Jacky Baker with two Rosemullion Boxers.

Aust. Ch. Rosemullion Fast Pacer (by Swanfield Rob Roy ex Guntop Sugar N' Spice), handled by Jacky Baker.

TASMANIA

Who had the first Boxer in Tasmania is debatable. The Rev. Harold Pickup of the Canis prefix bought a bitch from England called Whirlways Sally. She was mated twice to a dog called Brackley Benneret, owned by Mrs. H. E. Patrick (Growler).

Some of the Boxer fanciers in the '60s were: Kirk, Pitchford, Heller, White, Bakker, Cruse, Jones, Strochnetter, Collicutt, Geisinger, Mamo, Summers, Ashby and Chenall. Some of these exhibitors are still actively showing and breeding Boxers today.

In early 1970, Carmel Houlmes (Bakker) was one of the driving forces in forming the Boxer Club of Tasmania. On June 19, 1980, a meeting of Boxer fanciers was held and a steering committee formed. A motion was passed that the club should be called Van Dieman Boxer Association.

On July 17, 1970, a draft constitution was presented by the steering committee and further suggestions for names for the club were called for at this meeting. The Boxer Club of Tasmania was chosen and the draft constitution was accepted as the constitution for the club.

On December 13, 1970, the first Boxer parade was held at the soccer grounds in Newstead. Nineteen classes were offered and there were 50 dogs present. Nanrae Nocturne, bred by Gwen Jones and owned by Bonnie Paul, was judged Best in Parade.

Winuwuk Look Here, imported from the United Kingdom.

Glevenshium Auntie Mame, a British import.

It was December 9, 1972 before the Boxer Club of Tasmania held its first championship show. The top award at this show went to Royal Dream Range.

Nanrae Night Sky owned by Mr. T. Collicut became the first Boxer to obtain his championship and CDX obedience title.

One other dog has achieved the title of CDX. That is Zagato Beau Debutante owned by Mr. I. Leitch. Six other Boxers have attained the title of CD.

Aust. Ch. Kingsfield Tequila (by Aust. Ch. Boystock Taksto Ttangolu ex Norwatch Sunhawk Sunset) has won numerous CCs and BOBs in all-breed shows.

BOXER CLUB OF WESTERN AUSTRALIA

The Boxer Club of Western Australia commenced in December 1984 with a few dedicated exhibitors and breeders who were willing to give up their time and make the effort to start a breed club. There had been Boxer clubs in Western Australia previously, but these had folded over the course of time and had not been recommenced.

Our first meeting records 18 members, which may seem small but to us it was a great start. Throughout the first year, our membership grew and member competitions and fun days were held. However, as we were not affiliated with the Canine Association of Western Australia, we were unable to hold any parades or championship shows. We were "on probation."

After successfully completing our probationary period, we were granted affiliation with the Canine Association of Western Australia in April 1987. Our first parade was held on April 24, 1988, followed by our first championship show on October 23, 1988.

Aust. Ch. Kimyel Crossfire (by Jacquet's Bayside of The Wind ex Phoenix Superchic), owned by Michelle Roberts.

Aust. Ch. Phoenix Ginger Rogers (by Vimar's Magic Goes On ex Phoenix The Dame).

The litter sister of Ginger Rogers, Aust. Ch. Phoenix Gloria Swanson.

Phoenix Magic Shadow (by Vimar's Magic Goes On ex Phoenix Soolaimon).

Our parades each year were judged by our trainee judges here in the West. For our championship shows, we have always strove to obtain the services of specialty judges from either interstate or overseas.

Each year our shows have been successful, with people exhibiting from our country areas and interstate. Even though our entries are small, compared with those of the Eastern States, we feel that the time and effort that our committee and members have put in has paid off.

There have been several changes in the committee over the years but those dedicated few are still among us and are still striving for bigger and better things for the Boxer Club of Western Australia. We now have some members and continue to grow in strength if not in wealth.

SOUTH AUSTRALIA

The first Boxer in South Australia was an English male imported by Tom Hester of Vimy Ridge near Bridgewater in the Adelaide Hills. He lived in England prior to and during World War II. It was there that he first saw Boxers. When he and his wife returned to SA in 1946, he arranged the importation of a male known as "Candy." This dog died tragically soon after. A most upset but undaunted Mr. Hester imported Pepperbox Anson and Klesby Blazeaway, who arrived together in 1949. These were the first representatives of the breed in South Australian show rings. Hester exhibited them to their titles. The pair was later bred with very disappointing results and, consequently, Mr. Hester lost interest in breeding and showing.

In 1950, Harry and Joan Oakes became the first breeders to show Boxers in SA. They bought their first Boxer, Baybox Royal Princess, from Victoria. She was a

Aust. Ch. Gumbrae Duet (by Vimar's Magic Goes On ex Gumbrae Looking Ahead), owned by Brian and Sue McKie of Bokson Boxers.

Aust. Ch. Phoenix Bette Midler (by Phoenix Maxwell Redman ex Phoenix Lucille Ball), owned and handled by Maxine Carter, wins a divine BIS in the third Australian National Specialty under judge Walter Pinsker.

daughter of Ch. Gremlin Sundago (Imp. UK). Their Beaconsfield was the first Boxer prefix registered in SA. Baybox Royal Princess was bred back to her father (Sandago) as there were not many stud dogs in those days, and all interstate. This mating produced their biggest winner, Ch. Beaconsfield Juneo, the 1953 CC winner at the Adelaide Royal. Tragic family circumstances ended Mrs. Oakes's breeding and showing. But these days, as Mrs. Joan Patton, she still has a keen interest in our breed and she contributed to this history.

Mrs. Wendy Newbury started her Boxendale Kennel shortly after the Beaconsfield Boxers were established. Mrs. Newbury's mother had bred Pekingese for years, so Wendy was not new to the dog scene. She remained a consistent exhibitor at dog shows for over 30 years. She purchased Inverary Lucinda from Victoria as her foundation bitch and made up her championship. Lucinda was bred to the famous champion Panfield Zest and this set Mrs. Newbury on her winning ways. She bred nine champions under the Boxendale prefix, the most noted being Boxendale Bold Beau, who also was a very famous obedience champion.

Pearl and Len Thomas began their Boxer interest in 1954 under the name of Amarina Kennels. They started with a Victorian bitch by Ch. Gremlin Sundago (Imp.

UK) whom they mated to Panfield Zest. They bred five champions. The most famous was SACA & KCC Ch. Amarina Bombshell, owned by Janet Ryrie (Egan), a very toey bitch quite apt to upholding the portion of the standard that says, "brave and determined when roused." The Thomases were regular exhibitors in Melbourne and Adelaide, holding their own with their homebred stock. Mrs. Thomas had much success with using Panfield Zest, and she sent all her bitches to him. Ch. Amarina Sparkles was Mrs. Thomas's favorite bitch. She won many Bests of Breed, but her Group attempts were always thwarted by Tom Pierce's very famous Bulldog bitch, Ch. Shiltom Jedda.

In 1956, Mr. and Mrs. Boyt-Cullis arrived from England with two of their Boxers. They left quite a team behind when they migrated. They brought their best—the stylish male Wrath of Ty-Boyt and Zilla of Ty-Boyt, his mother. These two dogs took 12 months to regain condition after the boat trip and dreadful quarantine. Wrath came out to win Best of Breed over 26 Boxers at Adelaide Royal in 1957. Zilla, a black brindle, was too plain to be shown and she was to be bred to a suitable Wrath son, but, alas, Wrath was to be a victim of our harsh bush environment.

As Boxers gained in popularity, there were soon many prominent exhibitors—Nicholson, Goodchild, Woolston, Egan, Roche and Tamblyn.

In 1958, South Australian Boxers underwent quite a revolution. Mrs. Steele (Von Harjo Boxers) came onto

Aust. Ch. Taswest Tuppany Sue, a beautiful daughter of Jacquet's Bayside Of The Wind and Phoenix The Dame, who was sired by Ch. Salgray's Minute Man.

Aust. Ch. Phoenix Jason Argonaut (by Phoenix Buck Rogers ex Phoenix Clever Coleen) was one of Australia's top show dogs, as the winner of multiple BIS awards and specialty wins and as the sire of an amazing 29 champions.

the scene. She and her husband Harry purchased a bitch from the Boyt-Cullises, Artel Fire Flash, an NSW-bred bitch sired by the Bang Away grandson imported to Sydney, Fireball of Ememfar. Flash was bred to the stylish Wrath and produced the very beautiful Ch. Von Harjo Vanity Fair and Ch. Von Harjo Vicki. These two bitches, especially Vanity, changed the face of South Australia's Boxers forever!

Von Harjo went on to win at shows all over the country. Mrs. Steele became a most proficient handler and quite a thorn in the side of the established Boxer fancy, but all to the betterment of the breed. Boxers began regularly to win Groups, and handlers became more noticed with their smart-looking Boxers. Mrs. Steele purchased a son of the imported Raffles, KCC and SACA Ch. Pampanito Peter's Pride, who produced winners for other owners in SA. Ch. Von Harjo Pattern, Mrs. Steele's greatest winner, was sired by their imported Panfield Accolade. Accolade was a son of Mazelaine's Hit Parade. Dough Jarvis imported the English Champion Wardrobes Madam Marcasite. This striking brindle bitch won many shows and, when mated to Eng-Aus. Ch. Wardrobes Joriemour Witchdoctor, produced Ch.

Ch. Phoenix Paragon (by Jacquet's Bayside Of The Wind ex Ch. Phoenix Gloria Swanson), owned by Michelle Roberts.

Robesfield Diamond Jim. Mrs. Steele purchased Diamond Jim to breed with her stock, but with the changing fortunes of health and business, the Steeles closed their kennels much to the loss of SA Boxers.

In 1959, Terry Carter (Phoenix) purchased his first Boxer as a pet from a customer of his employer. He was bitten by the show bug and went to Von Harjo for a puppy. He purchased Von Harjo Quest, out of Ch. Pampanito Peter's Pride ex Ch. Von Harjo Vicki. Quest started but never completed her title due to an injury (inexperience of the novice). Quest produced three champions, all by leading show dogs and producers of the day. This was in the early '60s. The sires were Ch. Franhope Griffo, Ch. Astex Tornado and Ch. Sno Raa Beauregard (by Tornado).

American import, Jacquet's Bayside Of The Wind (by Ch. Jacquet's Gaspard ex Ch. Jacquet's Garnier), owned by Maxine Carter.

Phoenix literally took over where Von Harjo left off and enjoyed success for quite a while, producing Boxer of the Year in 1968 and 1969. Then Phoenix went into limbo for a time and emerged again in the early 1970s with wife Maxine taking over as leading handler for the kennel. A very large kennel was established running on numerous dogs, taking out winner after winner and culminating in producing their outstanding male champion, Phoenix Jason Argonaut, who went on to represent SA at the biggest shows around Australia.

Many competitors became established and Boxers were at their strongest peak in SA history. The show scene gained impetus; entries were up at all shows. Competition was keen from kennels established during the late '60s and into the '70s—Charmore, Yookay, Boxerdom, Gumbrae and one of the most competitive of the day, Dachstein. All were breeders of champions.

Phoenix Sweet 'n' Spicy (by Am-Can. Ch. Tradonalee's Trade Win ex Titianmist Artemis), at 20 months of age.

A long established, still very active kennel and breeder of quite a few champions is Rudd's Keldaren Boxer Kennel.

A new phase in SA Boxer history began in 1981 when American Ch. Salgray's Minute Man arrived in Adelaide via NSW and the UK. His arrival inspired the establishment of a syndicate to purchase further stock from the North American continent. Am and Can. Ch. Tradonalees Trade Win arrived, closely followed by Vimars Magis Goes On. Still more came from the male Jacquet's Bayside of the Wind and the bitch Jacquet's Phoenix Playgirl, making SA the center of American Boxer blood in Australia. All of these imports have been widely used by the fancy, producing numerous winners and many champions all over Australia.

Left: Aust. Ch. Idolstyle Dancin' Queen (by Aust. Ch. Skelder Game Chip ex Ch. Capride Disco Dolly), bred and owned by Gene Frederick.

Below: Aust. Ch. Ozstock Soupa Dupa (by Aust. Ch. Ozstock Buster Douglas ex Ozstock Fancy Pants).

Owners Ruth and Terry Collicutt pose with Ch. Beawinna An Irish Acc, Ch. Sjecoin Raggedy Ann, Ch. Sjecoin Makin Whoopee and Ch. Beawinna Charlie Brown.

Aust. Ch. Idolstyle Rasputin (by Aust. Ch. Faerdorn Raise a Riot ex Ch. Idolstyle Sunny Climes) winning Res. Challenge and Best Junior in Show at the third National Boxer Specialty under judge Walter Pinsker.

Tobana Boxers, Anna, Todd, Jet and Albert at home in Woodend, Victoria, Australia.

BOXER ASSOCIATION OF VICTORIA

The first record of Boxers being shown in Victoria was in 1948 at the Royal Agricultural Show. Three were entered. The critique stated, "They have a long way to go to get the right type. My advice is to import some good bitches." Obviously, the Boxer people took notice of this and the imports started coming. Gremlin, Tirkane and Panfield provided some outstanding examples of the breed. They had improved so much that by 1952 the Best Dog at the Royal Agricultural Show was Panfield Zest. Twenty-five Boxers were shown that year.

In 1952, Boxer enthusiasts met to form the Boxer Association of Victoria. The infant association had a membership of 32. It was affiliated with the KCC in 1954. The first office bearers were: president, Dr. C. McCullagh; secretary, Mr. C. Wilson; treasurer, Mr. K. Wilson.

The first Boxer Parade was held in April and the first championship show in July 1955. Mr. A. Wheatland, who had first introduced the breed into Victoria, was the judge and he had a record entry of 63 Boxers. Karina of Juttagher was Best Exhibit and Panfield Zest was Challenge Dog.

Mr. Wheatland owned the first Boxers in Victoria (1940). Later, the Taylor Kennels became a major influence on the development of the Boxer in Victoria. The first import for them was Gremlin Sundago, who was the first Boxer to become KCC champion. In 1952, they imported a Boxer that was an outstanding example of the breed, Panfield Zest. Stella Taylor, a journalist by profession, wrote many articles about the Boxer and the history of the breed in Australia. Some of her articles were published overseas.

During the following years, Boxer enthusiasts increased in this state and more imports arrived. This excellent stock produced some very good specimens of the breed. Victoria could be considered the center of the Boxer fraternity in Australia.

With this great enthusiasm growing, the entries of Boxers grew too. Some of the biggest Boxer shows were hosted by Victoria. This developed into Victoria hosting the first Boxer National in 1988.

Thasrite

Dave Strachan of Australia began showing Boxers in 1970. However, success was not immediate. Thus, in 1978, he imported an English dog who had five Reserve CCs, quite an achievement at that time in the UK. Ch. That's Right of Panfield became a multi-BIS winner and the sire of 20 champions. In 1979, the kennel name "Kelstyle" was changed to "Thasrite" to honor this dog.

In 1979 Dave met his wife Juanita, and so began a very successful partnership. During the early 1980s, the Strachans imported two more dogs from England. They were Ch. Seefeld Sheer Delight and Ch. Steynmere Star Turn, a son of the prolific producer Eng. Ch. Steynmere Night Rider. They enjoyed great success with these dogs and with their progeny.

Aust. Ch. Thasrite Prince Charming (by Eng. Ch. Faerdorn Raise A Riot ex Aust. Ch. Kubik Amazing Grace), bred by Dave and Juanita Strachan, at four-and-a-half years old, is a multi-BIS and specialty winner.

The hugely successful sire who produced 16 champions, Ch. Faerdorn Raise A Riot, was an import from the United Kingdom. He went BIS under Mrs. Pat Heath of the UK at the second National Specialty.

Then in 1987, they imported Ch. Faerdorn Raise a Riot from Sue Harvey's famous Faerdorn Kennels in England. "Raise a Riot," an exciting, elegant, stallion type, was a dog before his time and went on to be a multi-All Breeds and Specialty BIS winner. His greatest triumph was to win BIS at the second National Boxer Specialty in Sydney in April 1990, under the world famous Boxer specialist, Mrs. Pat Heath.

"Raise a Riot" has also proven to be an exceptional sire and has clicked nicely with their "That's Right" stock. He has sired as many as four champions from one litter with three and two more in other litters. He has 16 champions, including Best in Show winners and Specialty CC winners. His most famous son is the great Ch. Thasrite Prince Charming, who at four years of age has won BIS on 18 occasions including four Specialty BIS wins.

Prince Charming ("Rudi") was Australia's Number One Boxer (ND/Friskies point score) in 1992 and led for 1993 by being Number Six All-Breeds. A culmination of a great year (1993) for Ch. Thasrite Prince Charming was winning "NSW CC Show Dog of the Year—1993," and being rated Australia's Number One Boxer, National Dog/Friskies Point Score" for the second year.

Aust. Ch. That's Right of Panfield (by Eng. Ch. Steynmere Summer Gold ex Eng. Ch. Gold Bangle of Panfield) won many BIS awards and sired an impressive 20 champions during his career.

In 1992 and 1993 the Strachans visited the U.S. and were very impressed with the style and elegance of the North American Boxer. As a consequence, they have decided to introduce more American bloodlines into their breeding program.

Dave and Juanita have owned or bred some 50 champions and these dogs have amassed nearly 50 BIS wins. They are always striving to improve their Boxers and they get immense enjoyment seeing Boxers being successful in the show ring.

Aust. Ch. Thasrite Black Night, CDX (by Aust. Ch. Boxhaven Tradition Lee ex Aust. Ch. Kubik Amazing Grace), a BIS winner of all-breed and specialty shows, bred by Dave and Juanita Strachan.

Sjecoin

Sjecoin Boxers owned by Rosina Olifent-Brace of Melbourne, Australia has, over the past twenty years, been probably the most successful Boxer kennel in Australia. Having produced 60 champions, it follows 42 bred in New Zealand under the Anisor banner and has reached an epic milestone. The hundredth international champion is promised soon and the mark of an enduring breeder is that no matter where her dogs go, her stock can mix it with the best and succeed.

It was from her grandmother that Rosina found her love of dogs and from the earliest days, she always had one as a companion. Owning her first Boxer as a teenager, she bred some puppies which, on later reflection, were quite unremarkable specimens. The turning point came when she struck up a friendship with the late Marion Fairbrother of Gremlin (UK) fame, and with

Aust. Ch. Sjecoin Winter Forecast (by Aust. Ch. Sjecoin Personality Plus ex Aust. Ch. Assissi Summer Splash), known as the best Boxer in the Sjecoin line, as well as one of the greatest Boxers in Australia, with breeder, owner and handler Rosina Olifent-Brace.

David Brace holds an armful of puppies from the first litter sired by Ch. Merrilanes Golden Gloves ex Aust. Ch. Sjecoin Showstopper.

her guidance learned about the classic Boxers of the past and their influences upon the breed. An understanding of how the breed must be seen and then bred gradually evolved in her mind. The American type Boxer became an integral part in her plan to add further elegance and charisma to the English sturdiness and sound structure that was generally evident in their stock.

Raineylanes dogs figured strongly in their pedigrees. It is a fortuitous coincidence that soon after moving to Australia, in 1973, she was able to breed her outstanding show and brood bitch Ch. Anisor Superstar to Raineylanes Grand Slam, owned by Mr. Mervyn Chapman. From this mating came the marvelous Aust-NZ. Ch. Sjecoin My T Sweet. The dam of six champions, she was without doubt the greatest influence on the later top Sjecoin Boxers.

Bitches have always figured prominently at Sjecoin. Ch. Sjecoin Fashion Parade, granddaughter of Superstar (whelped in 1979), was an illustrious winner. With nine BIS and 25 Group firsts, she was a truly elegant showgirl and produced six champions. Ch. Sjecoin Hey Look Me Over, another prolific winner, caused a sensation at her first outing when, at the age of six months, she took BOB over more than 100 Boxers at the Royal Melbourne Show (7500 total entry) under judges Irene and Edd Bivin (U.S.).

From this came the glorious bitch Ch. Sjecoin Gold Digger and later her brother Ch. Sjecoin One Mo Time. Together, these two have competed all over Australia and amassed more than 3000 challenge points between them. Gold Digger was top Boxer for Australia and New Zealand in 1991.

However, the supreme Sjecoin Boxer must surely be Ch. Sjecoin Winter Forecast, whelped in 1982 (Ch. Sjecoin Personality Plus by Ch. Assissi Summer Splash by Eng. Ch. Summer Storm). A unique Boxer in so many ways, "Simon" has stamped himself in the record books for the breed in Australia both as a sire and in exhibition by earning Best in Show 26 times and runner-up 8 times. He also won 4 BISS, 66 Group firsts, 11 Royal Challenges and 3625 Challenge points, and he has passed on his greatness by siring 30 champions. It is hard to describe the exhilaration and the honor of breeding such a dog. To repeat it is impossible and one must just be thankful. Today at ten and a half years, he is Rosina's constant companion.

There comes a time when the genes need some help. While in the U.S. in 1990, Rosina saw a young male whose pedigree and appearance fitted what she felt she needed for her Boxers. He was Merrilanes Golden Gloves, a son of Ch. Merrilanes Knockout. He was purchased and, after gaining his U.S. championship, came home to Melbourne to live and contribute to Sjecoin. A popular character with all, he has already sired champions from India, Singapore and Australia. His influence is great.

Aust. Ch. Sjecoin One Mo' Time (by Aust. Ch. Sjecoin Winter Forecast ex Aust. Ch. Sjecoin Hey Look Me Over), a very successful show dog, with his very successful owner and breeder, Rosina Olifent-Brace.

Rosina and her husband David enjoy judging the Boxer breed as well as most of the U.S. working breeds. Rosina has had Specialty assignments in several countries, the most memorable being the 1988 ABC Specialty, where she awarded BOB to Ch. Wilverdays Famous Amos.

Sjecoin Boxers have been exported to many countries. In India, Ch. Sjecoin Game Time has led for top dog All-Breeds 1992, and in Singapore, Karen Steele's Ch. Sjecoin Gold Hunter was Number One Working Dog in 1991. In the U.S., Ch. Hollycrest Ain't Misbehavin' is a granddaughter of Ch. Sjecoin Winter Forecast.

If the past is any guide, Rosina Olifent-Brace's Sjecoin Boxers will continue playing a part in keeping the breed up with the best.

Sjecoin I'm A Knockout (by American import Ch. Merrilanes Golden Gloves ex Aust. Ch. Sjecoin Showstopper), at four months of age.

Ch. Merrilanes Golden Gloves (by Ch. Merrilanes Knockout ex Vagabond's Black Onyx) has contributed to the Boxer breed all over the world, siring champions in India, Singapore and Australia.

Sjecoin Midnight Serenade, daughter of the very prominent sire Am. Ch. Merrilanes Golden Gloves out of Aust. Ch. Sjecoin Diamond Necklace, owned by Greg Abood.

Aust. Ch. Tobana August Queen (by Aust. Ch. Gremlin Sunarise ex Tobana Sea Queen), winner of over 60 Challenge Certificates and 30 plus BOB awards, was regarded by many experts as a model of perfection for the Boxer breed.

Tobana

In 1968, Wally and Robyn Robbins of Victoria, Australia purchased their first Boxer, who, handled by Wally, became dual-titled Australian Champion Tarakani Desert Haze, CD. This foundation stud dog for Tobana was placed Best Dog in Group at both the Sydney and Brisbane "Royal" Shows (Australia's equivalent of Crufts and Westminster). Desert Haze was a great-grandson of Fireball of Ememfar, the first American Boxer imported to Australia. Fireball was a grandson of Am. Ch. Bang Away of Sirrah Crest, the record holder of the most Bests in Show won by any dog of his time. Desert Haze was also used as a foundation sire for Whitechapel Kennels (Phil and Jan Lovell, Sydney).

Wanting to include the family in his great success, Wally purchased Tarakani Sea Witch, a half sister to Desert Haze, for Robyn to handle. It was obvious that dog showing was going to be a family affair when their daughter, Janelle, started in Junior Showmanship at age seven with Boxers. Janelle went on to become a Junior Handler record holder in the early 1970s and a founding member and adviser for the "PAL International JS Competition."

Tobana Kennels' first litter was the half brother/sister mating of Desert Haze to Sea Witch. This produced Tobana Sea Queen and Ch. Tobana Desert Son. Sea Queen was an outstanding producer and winner of numerous Best Head, Best Red and Best Movement at Boxer Specialty Shows. Desert Son was sold as the foundation dog of Toncris Kennels (Tony and Chris Hearne, Sydney).

Wally Robbins became a noted winning handler and was the handler of most of the imported dogs who came into Sydney at the time. One of particular importance was Ch. Gremlin Sunarise, imported from the UK. Others were Ch. Marikarlos Abra Dabra of Gremlin and Ch. Winter Frost of Gremlin.

Sunarise was mated to Sea Queen in the mid 1970s to produce a stunning red and white bitch described by American, English and German breed experts as one of the most perfect Boxers ever produced—she was Ch. Tobana August Queen. Handled by Robyn Robbins, August Queen won in excess of 60 Challenge Certificates and more than half this amount of Best of Breed wins. She was shown only until she was three years old, when she died tragically in an accident. During her three years, she was bred twice to the U.S. import Raineylanes Grand Slam. A most successful mating resulted in Tobana American Queen.

The Sunarise/Sea Queen mating was repeated after the success of the August Queen litter, and the second time around produced Ch. Tobana Academy King, who won Challenge Dog Best of Breed and Best Puppy Dog in Show at the Sydney Royal Show when only nine months old. Also, his sister Ch. Tobana Sea Charm was a prolific winner and producer who was sold to Toncris Kennels in Sydney.

Sunarise was also mated to Sea Witch and produced Ch. Tobana Allarra and Ch. Tobana Sunflower. Sunflower was sold as a foundation bitch for Luanda Boxers, owned by Harry and Sue Ward in Sydney.

Not everything went well for Tobana Boxers. In the late 1970s three of their top dogs, Ch. August Queen, Ch. Allarra and the import Ch. Gremlin Sunarise were baited with poisoned bones at a show by unidentified people. Tragically, this resulted in the death of the top sire Ch. Gremlin Sunarise.

During the early 1980s, breeding was slow at the kennel. The breeding schedule was re-planned and the kennels moved from Sydney to Woodend, Victoria, where they are now set up on some lush acreage. Breeding at this time meant crossing back into UK lines, using NZ-Aust. Ch. Gremlin Summer Spree over Tobana American Queen. This resulted in Ch. Tobana Georgia Girl, who won many Bests in Show all-breeds and BIS Boxer Specialty under UK judge Lilly Potts. In 1983, Georgia Girl was mated to the Am-Can. Ch. Tradonalee Trade Win, imported from Canada. This was a highly successful mating, resulting in three top bitches in the show ring and whelping box.

The bitch, Ch. Tobana Southern Queen, was a multiple Best in Show winner including Boxer Specialties and all-breeds. Ch. Tobana Chattahoochee was a Melbourne Royal Challenge winner and Runner-Up Best of Breed to her half brother. Another sister was Tobana Miss Albany who, although she stood in her sisters' winning shadows, excelled as a top producer. She was mated to Ch. Moljon Surprise Packet at Marbelton, an English import carrying Dutch lines, and her daughter, Tobana Rayo Sunshine, was Best Minor Puppy Bitch in Show at the first Boxer National.

Chattahoochee was mated three times to produce champions from each litter. The first litter was to her half brother, Ch. Tobana White Feather. He was given to Paul and Elaine McLaughlin and he was a multiple BIS winner and Top Boxer NSW for many years. Chattahoochee's second litter with Ch. Skelder Game Chip (imported from the UK) produced the top sire and show male at Tobana, Ch. Tobana Hard Act, handled since puppyhood by the youngest Robbins daughter, Natalie. The third litter from Chattahoochee was with Tobana Midnight Shift, a male who was never shown but is a son of Ch. Tobana Catch the Sun (Sunarise's son). A bitch from this litter, Tobana Red Velvet, has already pointed and is only one CC from her title. Shown by Janelle, Red Velvet was mated in 1993.

Tobana has been consistent in breeding and showing for 25 years. Tobana Kennels says the strength has been built by linebreeding bitches to the best bred stud dogs, all of which have been imported lines or Tobana stud dogs. Another important element is the close family unit that breeds, exhibits and cares for all the Tobana Boxers.

The family involvement goes beyond the show ring as wife and mother, Robyn and daughter Janelle, are both Committee members of the Boxer Association of Victoria. Natalie is a proven Junior Handler and has become a handler for many other breeders in various groups. Robyn loves the whelping and puppy raising duties that go with breeding Boxers and, being an excellent handler herself, she trains all the young hopeful pups at Tobana.

Wally is a licensed Boxer specialist since 1976, and has judged Boxers in many states. Janelle is a licensed Boxer specialist as well as a licensed specialist for the complete Utility and Toy groups. She is currently an apprentice judge for Terrier and Gundog groups. Janelle has judged Boxers overseas and judged the first Boxer Regional Specialty for the Boxer Club of the Philippines, Inc.

With such dedication to breeding, exhibiting and judging Boxers, Wally and Robyn are assured that their daughters will carry on the Tobana Boxer quality lines for at least another 25 years.

Aust. Ch. Walkon Skittles (by Eng. Ch. Glenfall The Gladiator ex Eng. Ch. Walkon Smash'd Again), imported from Blueprint Boxers of the United Kingdom.

BLUEPRINT

Blueprint Boxers, owned by Mark Johnston of Sydney, Australia, was established in 1976. It is based upon English bloodlines from the Gremlin Kennel, but the blood of the American-born dog Kreyons Back in Town is also valued. It is a small kennel, generally only keeping between three and five dogs, but with consistent quality always being their goal.

With this in mind, the most successful show dogs have been the Specialty and Group winning bitch, Aust. Ch. Blueprint Winter Song; her son, Ch. Blueprint Indian Summer [by Eng-Aust. Ch. Summer Shadow of Gremlin (Imp. UK)]; and her grandson, Walkon (Imp. UK), who have both won Best in Show at the Boxer Club of New South Wales Specialty. They too have been Group winners at all-breed shows.

In 1992, they imported the bitch Aust. Ch. Walkon Skittles from the United Kingdom to strengthen their bitch line. She was line bred to Eng. Ch. Gremlin Summer Storm, and is already a consistent winner.

Their hope is to continue producing quality type Boxers generation after generation.

Aust. Ch. Tobana Georgia Girl (by NZ-Aust. Ch. Gremlin Summer Spree ex Tobana American Queen), winner of several BIS awards in all-breed and specialty shows, bred by Wally and Robyn Robbins.

TASWEST

Taswest Kennels in Perth, Western Australia was founded in 1983 with the purchase of the bitch Phoenix Fancy Free. Fancy produced three Australian champions: Ch. Taswest Tifany Ikenwin (a Best in Show All-Breeds winner), Ch. Taswest Tom Sawyer (a Best in Show All-Breeds winner) by Vimars Magic Goes On (imported from the U.S.) and Ch. Taswest That's Fancy Pants by Ch. Kimyel Crossfire—a son of Jacquet's Bayside of the Wind (Imp. U.S.).

With the purchase of the bitch Phoenix the Dame, a mating to Jacquet's Bayside of the Wind (Imp. U.S.) subsequently took place. This produced the pride of Taswest—Ch. Taswest Tuppany Sue ("Becky"), who went onto become a multi-Best Exhibit in Group and Best Exhibit in Show winner (All-Breeds). Becky finished as the Number Seven Top Dog of the Year All-Breeds 1990 and was also Top Boxer of the Year 1990 (WA). She has won under judges from all over the world.

In 1988, a three-quarter brother to Becky was purchased as an eight-week-old puppy named Ch. Phoenix Paragon. Puppies at Taswest are rarely shown under 12 months, but once "Henry" made his appearance in the Junior class (12 months and over), he made quite a name for himself in Australia. He has to his credit a "hat trick"—winning Best in Show at three Boxer Club of WA Championship Shows under three world renowned specialists. In 1990, Mr. Teoh Eng Hong (Malaysia) cri-

Aust. Ch. Taswest Tifany Ikenwin (by Aust. Ch. Keldaren Kid Intrepid ex Phoenix Fancy Free) was the first champion for Taswest Kennels.

tiqued Henry with the words, "This dog would win against the top dogs in the UK and be in good company anywhere in the world." In 1991, the judge was Mr. Fred Lanting (U.S.) and in 1992, Mr. Peter Foster (Aust.). Henry was Top Boxer of the Year (WA) in 1991. Both Becky and Henry were invitees to the prestigious Contest of Winners 1991—making the Boxer breed proud.

Ch. Taswest Tom Sawyer has a story of his own that Taswest Boxers is proud to share. An ailing pup from birth, he was reared on an eye dropper for the first three weeks of his life. He finally walked unaided at five weeks, was awarded Best Baby in Show at his first outing at four months, won Best Exhibit in Show at 10 months, gained his title at 14 months and retired at the age of six years, winning Best Australian-Bred Boxer in Show at the third National Boxer Specialty Show in Queensland under the handling of Mr. Walter Pinsker (U.S.).

Taswest Kennels has bred the Top WA-Bred Boxer of the Year for at least seven consecutive years. It is a small dedicated kennel that breeds at the most one litter a year. Taswest Kennels has bred at least five Australian Champions with others well on their way for other owners. Three of these champions are Best in Show winners.

Another star for Taswest is Ch. Taswest The Lady in Red—Top WA-Bred Boxer of the Year in 1992.

Aust. Ch. Taswest Tuppany Sue (by Jacquet's Bayside Of The Wind ex Phoenix The Dame), whelped September 5, 1986, became one of the top-winning dogs for Taswest Kennels.

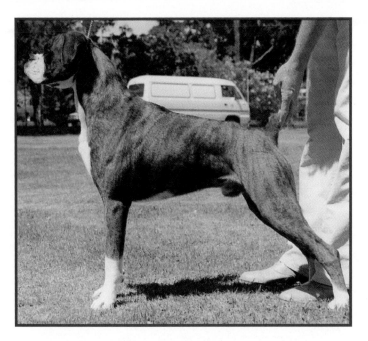

Aust. Ch. Boxhaven Mark Lee (by Aust. Ch. Boxhaven Tradition Lee ex Boxhaven Hi Mark), bred and owned by Peter and Hilda Foster, was a BIS and Puppy of the Year winner.

BOXHAVEN

The Boxhaven Boxers are owned by Hilda and Peter Foster of Leppington, New South Wales. Peter bought his first Boxer, Jawina Lord Socrates, in 1961, and entered his first show in March 1962, where "Sox" won the class, and he has been exhibiting ever since. The first litter sired by Sox [he was a Fireball of Ememfer (Imp. USA) grandson] produced two champions, both won Best Exhibit in Show.

Hilda, an experienced horsewoman, had moved to Sydney from the country. Hilda is a born animal lover,

Owner Lynn Bennett poses with Aust. Ch. Boxhaven Trivial Pursuit.

and her grandfather was a gamekeeper in England who had a kennel of Labrador Retrievers that he exhibited at the major shows in England, as well as used them for field work.

Hilda's first Boxer, Ch. Cudgewa Beau Gem, was a granddaughter of American import Hollies Po-Tan, a dog that had a profound influence on the breed in Australia, and was linebred to Ch. Elixer of Raineylanes. Their bloodlines have always been a combination of the best English and American stock. "Beauty," as she was known, won a Best in Specialty Show, Runner Up Best in Show All-Breeds and numerous Bests in Group. Not only was she a top show dog, but proved to be a top producer and is the foundation bitch of this kennel. For her first litter she was mated to Ch. Tarakani Beau Geste, the Best-in-Show-winning son of Sox. From this litter they kept the brindle bitch Boxhavens First Lady, and her bitch line has kept on producing top quality stock. All Boxhaven Boxers' bitch lines go back to Beauty and "Lady."

Aust. Ch. Taswest Tom Sawyer (by Vimars Magic Goes On ex Phoenix Fancy Free), bred and owned by Michelle Roberts.

Lady, when mated to the English import Ch. Gremlin Sunarise, produced Ch. Boxhaven Beau Jingles, who was the dam of the Puppy Point Score winner, Boxhaven Beau Jinks. Jinks is the sire of Ch. Boxhaven Ebony N Ivory, handled to her title by the Fosters' son Craig.

Jingles is also the dam of Ch. Boxhaven Quality Blend, top winning bitch of her time, Best in Specialty Show and All Breeds and winner of three Boxer Club Point Scores. Her kennel mate, the deer red Ch. Boxhaven Beau Chantre, had the honor of winning Best in Show All-Breeds on consecutive days. When retired, she was mated to Am-Can. Ch. Tradonalees Trade Win to pro-

Aust. Ch. Boxhaven Quality Blend (by Aust. Ch. Tonup Quality Street ex Aust. Ch. Boxhaven Beau Jingles) perculated many BIS wins at all-breed and specialty shows, bred and owned by Peter and Hilda Foster.

duce Ch. Boxhaven Tradition Lee and Ch. Boxhaven Robert Lee.

"Robby" won a Best in Show All-Breeds at 11 months of age, and these two dogs made up their titles within a week of each other while still in the Junior Class. Tradition Lee won numerous Groups and was Runner Up Best in Show at the prestigious Garden Island Kennel Club two years in a row. He is the sire of Ch. Boxhaven Mark Lee, Best in Specialty Show and Puppy Point Score winner. "Mark" sired Boxhaven Ash Lee, another Puppy Point Score win-

Aust. Ch. Boxhaven Hot Spice (by Aust. Ch. Westbrooks Hot Pursuit ex Aust. Ch. Boxhaven National Lee), at two years old.

ner. Trad is also the sire of Ch. Thasrite Black Knight, CDX, winner of six Bests in Show.

Robert Lee produced Ch. Boxhaven Hi Lee; Ch. Boxhaven Tem Lee, Specialty CC winner Western Australia under Lianne Dimitroff (U.S.); Ch. Boxhaven Classic Lee Specialty, CC winner; Boxhaven Rapid Lee Specialty, CC winner in Tasmania; and the beautiful deer red Ch. Boxhaven Donna Lee. She proved to be a sensation right at the start of her career when, at six and a half months of age, she won a 23 point Challenge and Minor Puppy in Group; won two more CCs and a Best in Group at nine months; and was a champion at ten and a half months. Donna won the Boxer Club Puppy Point Score and Major Point Score, Best in Futurity at the Boxer Club Specialty and Best in Show Specialty and All-Breeds. On Easter of 1989, at the prestigious Sydney Royal Show under M. VanDerWeiser (Holland), Donna won the CC and her kennel mate Ch. Boxhaven Ebony N Ivory, handled by Craig, was Reserve CC. Both were from the Junior Class. Ch. Boxhaven National Lee won the Intermediate Class, Ch. Boxhaven Hi Lee came in third in Open Bitch and the Trad son Black Knight was Reserve CC dog. It was a memorable day for Boxhaven. Donna's dam is a daughter of Am. Ch. Salgrays Minute Man and Donna was mated to the American import Ch. Westbrooks Hot Pursuit in high hopes that she would carry on the heritage of the strong bitch line at Boxhaven.

Another Robert Lee daughter, Ch. Boxhaven National Lee, when mated to Hot Pursuit produced Ch. Boxhaven Hot Gossip, an All-Breeds Best in Show winner, and with her litter brother, Boxhaven National Pursuit, won the Puppy Point Score Best Male and Best Female. Boxhaven Trivial Pursuit, a Best in Group winner; Boxhaven Silver Son; Boxhaven Hot Spice; and Boxhaven Hot Issue are all consistent winners, also.

Dogs owned/bred at Boxhaven have won Boxer Club Point Score competitions on 16 occasions and they have owned/bred 12 individual Best in Show Winners and 26 champions. Boxers from their kennel have gone to Germany and the U.S.

In the late 1980s, Hilda and Peter decided Australian Boxers were long overdue in having a specialty magazine of their own to help in promoting Australian and New Zealand Boxers. 1990 saw the first issue of *The Boxer Down Under* arrive on the scene. Its release coincided with the second Boxer National being held in Sydney, and it was met with a wonderful re-

Aust. Ch. Boxhaven Donna Lee (by Aust. Ch. Boxhaven Robert Lee ex Boxhaven Hi Mark), bred and owned by Peter and Hilda Foster.

SANDSHURI

David and Helen Weil have been involved with showing and breeding Boxers for almost 20 years. It all began with a pet Boxer who only had a short life. After he died, they decided that their next Boxer would be a really good one and that they would try showing. They bought a bitch from Ayr, North Queensland, and by luck she was a good one. She was shown successfully in North Queensland and then later in Brisbane. This bitch, Ch. Boxora Showgirl, had only one litter with Ch. Phoenix Jason Argonaut. Two puppies from this litter became champions, Ch. Sandshuri Kings Pride and Ch. Sandshuri Candy Queen.

Kings Pride had an All-Breeds Best in Show win and sired a number of notable pups. Ch. Hillcentre Morn'n Star (a bitch whose bloodlines were chiefly Phoenix Kennels) was mated to Kings Pride and in her first litter produced Ch. Sandshuri Kings Aura, a Boxer Specialty Show Best Exhibit and consistent Group winner in his short show career. He retired by the time he was two with 350 points gained in his last season of shows. A repeat of this mating produced Ch. Sandshuri Sundancer, who won many Bests in Show and Specialty Shows, and who was successful at the Brisbane Royal Show two years in a row. In 1984, Sundancer was Challenge Dog, Best of Breed and Opposite Sex in Group (his older brother Kings

Aust. Ch. Sandshuri Storm Again (by Intrends Sideshow Alley ex Thasrite Carla Zampati), whelped February 22, 1991, bred by David and Helen Weil.

ception. Now it's growing with each issue, it goes to every state in Australia and New Zealand and it has subscribers in 14 different countries. Its green and gold color and distinctive cover trade mark have made it a collectors item wherever it is sold.

Having the welfare of the breed foremost in their hearts, Hilda and Peter, working in conjunction with The University of Sydney's Veterinary Teaching Hospital, organized a Heart Murmur Clinic to be held at the Boxer Club of NSW's Easter Specialty Show. Owners of over 100 Boxers had their dogs' hearts monitored, and results of these tests were published in *The Boxer Down Under*.

Peter and Hilda were part of the syndicates that brought Am-Can. Ch. Tradonalees Trade Win and Vimars Magic Goes On to Australia. With long-time friend and Boxer enthusiast Robert Tyrrell, they have imported Eng. Ch. Mitchum of Sunhawk Norwatch from Helen and Eddie Banks, and Am. Ch. Westbrooks Hot Pursuit from Sharon Proffit. These dogs carry some of the world's top producing bloodlines and have much to offer the breed in Australia.

Peter, a well-known and respected Boxer specialist, had the honor of judging in 4 of the 6 Australian states in a period of 11 months. In the US, he has judged specialties in New York, Minnesota and New Jersey.

Aura was shown for the last time on that day, gaining Reserve Challenge). At the 1985 Royal, Sundancer again won the Dog Challenge and Best of Breed and went on to win Best Exhibit in the Group. Kings Pride also sired pups that became champions under other breeders' prefixes.

Then, for a time through the mid to late 1980s, the Weils showed less and began to work towards gaining their judging licenses. The Weils then moved away from the Brisbane area to North Queensland and have become far more disciplined in their approach to showing and breeding. They now restrict their numbers to four Boxers of the best quality they can get. Sandshuri Boxers had only two litters in the last five years. The first of these litters produced Ch. Sandshuri Storm Again, who, at two years of age, has over 500 points, 15 Best in Group wins and six Best in Show wins.

Guntop Black Label (by Ch. Salgray's Black Tie ex Guntop Fairytale) whelped April 8, 1992, belongs to the first litter of Boxers ever to be produced from frozen semen imported from another country.

Aust. Ch. Guntop Shadow Man (by Eng-Aust. Ch. Summer Shadow of Gremlin ex Aust. Ch. Guntop Up To The Minute) became a BIS winner for Guntop Kennels, owned by Liz and Miles Gunter.

GUNTOP

In 1971, Liz and Miles Gunter of Pheasant's Nest, New South Wales purchased their first Boxer, a brindle bitch named Groningen Lady Aflen, who was descended from the old Australian bloodlines tracing back to the beginnings of the breed in that country. She was not an exceptional specimen, but the Gunters entered her in a dog show and she won first prize. One might say that was the beginning of Guntop Boxers.

In 1972, the Gunters bought a flashy fawn male puppy with the unusual name of Lalaguli Woowookurung. He was from the first litter sired by Eng. Ch. Cherryburton Playboy ex Ch. Lalaguli Meekyluka. His breeder was Mrs. Chris Rangley of Sydney, who never owned a large number of Boxers but produced a succession of champions, of whom Meekyluka was the first. The Gunters also acquired "Meeky," who became their house pet until she died in 1980 at the age of 12.

Lalaguli is an Australian aboriginal word meaning "Spirit of the Billabong" (lake) or water nymph. Mrs. Rangley gave all her Boxers aboriginal names, and Woomookurung means "plentiful," as he indeed proved.

In time, "Kurung" grew into one of the top show dogs in Australia. He won 10 all-breed Best in Show awards and became a champion 20 times over. He was the Best in Show winner at the Boxer Club of New South Wales and won five Challenge Certificates at the prestigious Royal Shows. Altogether, he won 108 Challenge Certificates and 87 Bests of Breed.

Kurung sired 12 champions. Several carried the Guntop prefix, including their first champion, Ch. Guntop Scotch on the Rox, owned by Mr. Joe Gerada (Sarose Boxers) of Melbourne.

Among his other progeny were the big winners Ch. Zweckromney Zarana, Ch. Zweckromney Cavalier and Ch. Zweckromney Amber Glow, all owned by Guntop Boxers. He also produced Ch. Rosemullion Regal, a prolific winner with two Royal Challenge Certificates and ten All-Breed Best in Show wins, and Ch. Debronel Superstar and Ch. Coghurst Liza, two top-winning bitches. Kurung left many other winning get in numerous kennels, and his place as an important stud dog in the history of the Boxer in Australia seems assured. He died suddenly in 1983, at the age of 11 years.

In March 1976, the first American champion was brought to Australia. She was Am. Ch. Mazra's Miss Spitfire, by Ch. Warlord of Cherokee Oaks ex Ch. Diamond Lil of Rio Vista, bred by Colonel Carl E. Welchner in California. She accompanied her American owners, Mr. and Mrs. Raymond E. Moore, III, formerly of Hawaii, and arrived in whelp to Ch. Box M Punchline Precedent, owned by Lois Matthews. From the ensuing litter, born in quarantine in Brisbane, Mr. and Mrs. Gunter acquired their first American-bred Boxer, Kasmor's Miss America.

Later, Mr. and Mrs. Moore bred Miss Spitfire to a brindle dog they had also brought with them to Australia, a Ch. Popham's Firebrand son. Guntop Boxers acquired a bitch from this litter, who in time became Ch. Kasmor's American Maid. Two others from the same litter, Kasmor's Mr. President and Kasmor's Cincinnati Kid, also became champions.

In 1987, the well-known Am. Ch. Salgray's Minute Man arrived in Australia. He made a tremendous impact, and Guntop Boxers was among the first to use him, and continued to do so until his death in 1994. He produced the sensational littermates Ch. Guntop Rocketman and Ch. Guntop Minute Maid. Minute Man also sired a fawn male, Ch. Guntop I Like Ike and a brindle bitch, Ch. Guntop Up to the Minute. At the time of his death, Guntop had six bitches sired by Minute Man, the basis of their future breeding program.

Rocketman has been used extensively as a stud by many breeders who appreciate his type and beauty and the strength of his American bloodlines. He has produced several champions in Australia and New Zealand, where he has been used by Mrs. Maureen Boyd of the well-known Quo Vadis Boxers.

At Guntop, Rocketman produced Ch. Guntop Battle Star and the winning brindle bitch Ch. Guntop Once Upon a Time, who is from the Minute Man daughter Ch. Guntop Up to the Minute.

In 1987, Guntop Boxers imported Ch. Salgray's Argo of Memorylane, sired by Ch. Salgray's Valentino.

Ch. Salgray's Argo of Memorylane (by Ch. Salgray's Valentino ex Memorylane's Columbia) was imported from Salgray Boxers and has sired 20 champions in Australia.

His first Australian puppies made Mr. and Mrs. Gunter very confident that Argo would be very useful to the Boxer breed in Australia. Am. Ch. Salgray's Argo of Memorylane is, so far, the sire of 20 Australian champions including 5 Best in Show All-Breeds winners, and his get have been "Boxer of the Year" in New South Wales no less than 5 times (winners of the Boxer Club of NSW Major Point Score).

Sadly, Am. Ch. Salgray's Argo passed away in October of 1992 at the age of nine and a half. Guntop Boxers has recently pioneered the international use of frozen semen in Boxers, producing a litter on April 8, 1992 that was sired by Am. Ch. Salgray's Black Tie (USA), owned by Salgray's Boxers, out of Guntop Fairytale.

Ch. Guntop Bobby's Girl (by Ch. Salgray's Argo of Memorylane ex Aust. Ch. Guntop's Once Upon A Time), owned by Gary and Lynn Ryan of Blarney Boxers. Handled by Cheryl Robbins.

The Gunters believe this to be the first in the world in Boxers. Certainly, it is a first in Boxers in Australia. Guntop has retained, and is currently campaigning, two dogs and a bitch from this litter. So far, Guntop has managed to produce three litters using frozen semen from U.S. They believe this is the way to improve the breed in Australia in the future, and they are proud to have helped to pioneer this procedure. They would not have been able to do so without the help and encouragement of Mrs. Hamilburg and Mrs. Harrah of Salgray's Boxers, and they sincerely thank them.

Both Liz and Miles Gunter have been active in the Boxer Club of New South Wales. Liz was secretary for nearly ten years, and Miles was treasurer for almost as long. Both are licensed judges for Groups six (Utility) and seven (Non-Sporting) and have been enthusiastically received to judge in the US.

Aust. Ch. Guntop Minute Maid (by Ch. Salgray's Minute Man ex Kasmor's Miss America), bred and owned by Liz and Miles Gunter, was Boxer of the Year in 1983 and 1984.

Ch. Guntop Bobby's Girl (by Ch. Salgray's Argo of Memorylane ex Aust. Ch. Guntop Once Upon A Time) stands proudly as the first American Boxer champion bred in Australia.

The first Australian-bred American Boxer champion, Ch. Guntop Bobby's Girl (Kili) was bred by Liz and Miles Gunter of Guntop Boxers in New South Wales, Australia and owned by Blarney Boxers of Gary and Lynn Ryan of Hawaii. Kili is from the first Australian litter sired by Ch. Salgray's Argo of Memorylane (Bobby) ex Aust. Ch. Guntop's Once Upon A Time, a Ch. Salgray's Minute Man granddaughter.

Brought to Hawaii by the Ryans, Kili was imported to bring "new blood" to the islands. They sought out Guntop Boxers because of its outstanding international reputation and to avoid Hawaii's rigorous and restrictive 16-week rabies quarantine requirements. Hawaii, priding itself in being totally rabies-free, will only allow direct importation of animals from other rabies-free island areas such as Australia and Great Britain.

Prior to her first breeding, Kili and her owners relocated to Virginia. It was with this relocation that Kili began her show career. With intermittent breaks to whelp two litters, Kili was successfully campaigned by Cheryl Robbins. She finished her American championship with three majors and 18 championship points.

Vikenje

Registered in 1982, Vikenje has bred five champions. Their first was Ch. Vikenje Total Eclipse, by Am-Can. Ch. Tradonalees Trade Win. "Tyler" was the first Australian champion for Trade Win. Tyler was a prolific winner in both Melbourne and Adelaide, where he won two Melbourne Royal Bests of Breed and one Adelaide Royal Best of Breed, plus many Groups and Bests in Show, and was undefeated for Best of Breed until he was eight years of age, when sadly he passed away of cancer in 1991. Their breeding is based on selected American/Canadian breeding, with some English imported dogs.

From Total Eclipse there have been four Vikenje champions and three other champions for outside breeders. With many others on the way to their titles, there are at least four multiple Best in Show and Group winners.

The restrictions of moving with employment from state to state has taken its toll in regards to curbing the amount of breeding they could do and the number of dogs they have been able to keep.

Aust. Ch. Vikenje Total Eclipse (by Am-Can. Ch. Tradonalee's Trade Win ex Vikenje Top Model) on the day he gained his title in 1984.

Aust. Ch. Vikenje Total Eclipse, the first champion for Vikenje Kennels, poses majestically with breeder, owner and handler Vivienne Ashby.

OBEDIENCE

BY IAN WEEKS

My Life with Boxers, written by Frau Stockmann, is without a doubt my greatest inspiration in training and getting to know the working capabilities of the Boxer. Far too often in the obedience circles I hear "not another dumb Boxer to train" and "if you want a clown in the class just call a Boxer." This is nothing short of discrimination and narrow-mindedness. People who single out the Boxer as unmanageable and exceptionally hard to train should take time out to read *My Life With Boxers*. This is an outstanding book whose author gained great recognition not only as a breeder and exhibitor but also as a trainer, utilizing her one love "the Boxer" as a working dog in tracking, guide work, attack and message errands during World War I. On one occasion a brilliant dog named "Polly" was used as a herd dog, keeping 400 oxen in check. The book itself highlights just how obedient the Boxer really is. However, in Frau Stockmann's 50 years associated with the breed, of course there were the individual dogs who were not as eagerly inclined to work as others.

We find that with obedience, the working breeds—Border Collie, German Shepherd, Labrador Retriever, etc.—always figure predominantly in the winners circle. Naturally, this occurs because attached to the end of the lead is a dog that is most commonly sought after for obedience purposes.

Brinbox Golden Tiger (by Skelder Speed Trap ex Aust. Ch. Brinbox Gold Starfire), whelped August 19, 1991.

I'm always fascinated by the excuses used by intending obedience puppy buyers when it comes to the Boxer. The most common excuse is that the breed doesn't mature until they are at least two years old. Well, that applies to many breeds. In fact, I have trained classes where an 18-month-old Boxer was 100% more stable and reliable than its older and varied counterparts. The Boxer needs that extra variation, because repetition is great for some but it reaches a saturation point. This is where the dog that is old enough for agility should be trained as if it is a fun event and it will break the monotony. Before you can participate in an agility event the dog must be 18 months of age.

It is encouraging, however, to see more Boxers being trained and entered in Novice trials in Queensland. Obedience can be rewarding but the old adage, "you only get out of the sport what you put into it" still applies.

There are three levels of obedience to achieve. The first is Novice class and any dog six months of age or over, as long as it is trained to the prerequisites of the Novice class, may enter. Due to amendments to the rule book, however, you must first obtain 150 points in a sweepstakes before entering a Novice trial. Once you have qualified three times, with a score of 170 or over, and at least under two different judges, you may apply for your Companion Dog title (CD).

The next level is Open class and it is much more interesting, with exercises like retrieving the dumbbell, drop on recall, broad jump, etc. The total score for all exercises is 200, so to qualify you must also obtain 170 points or over. The same rules apply for the Open title,

which is called Companion Dog Excellent (CDX). You have to put a reasonable amount of training time into this class.

The third is called Utility Dog class (UD). This is where it becomes increasingly more difficult, with exercises like scent discrimination, seek back, signal exercise, directed jumping, etc. To obtain the UD title is a great achievement, and you and your dog have really worked hard and thoroughly to deserve this title.

Agility is really not looked upon as part of the obedience trial, which is why they are always run before or during the break or after the trial. Agility can be a lot of fun, and to obtain your title you must qualify three times under two different judges. Your score is taken based on the time it takes to complete the obstacle course without missing certain color jumps. Two rounds are run and if your times are placed in the first half of the first round, you run the second round. Only if you have completed a faultless round in either the first or second round will a qualifying card be obtained. Agility has its moments, but a lot of problems can be avoided if basic obedience is done first.

Once you learn to read your dog and are prepared to put in a fair amount of training, you will succeed to whatever level you desire. There are so many cases of people bringing in what is supposedly a totally unmanageable Boxer. After a couple of sessions using perseverance, patience and praise, the dog's behavior and attitude has changed for the better. There are always cases where as soon as the dogs are back with their owners they do as they please. That's the owner's fault, not the dog's.

Obedience and agility are great sports, and it is especially satisfying to have the Boxer breed recognized in it. Personally, I have reaped rewards for the hours and hours that were put into the training of my dogs.

Ranison Prince Boy, CDX, AD, whelped April 16, 1986, is an accomplished dog with many awards in obedience and agility competitions. Ali and handler Ian Weeks join in the photo.

NEW ZEALAND

BY MAUREEN C. S. BOYD

excerpted from Down Under, *courtesy of Peter Foster*

Boxers were first registered in New Zealand in 1950. The first champion was the fawn bitch, Awldogg Metz, and the first dog champion was Awldogg Kendall. NZ. Ch. Awldogg Fabian was the first Boxer to win an all-breed BIS. Bambola of Klesby mated to Eng. Ch. Panfield Ringleader whelped the first Boxer litter, and the first English champion import was Klesby Sparklet, whose influence on the breed was more than evident very soon after his first litters began appearing.

From these first two champions, the influence of the Awldoggs was obvious, being the forerunners of many of the breed to follow. It appears BIS Ch. Fabian's stamp was more than evident, especially the small ears that continued to appear in some breeding well up until the late 1960s.

Eng. Ch. Klesby Sparklet, the first English import champion, had such an impact on the breed and was behind the Leinster and Boystock Kennels, both of whom had much success in the show ring. Boystocks later leaned strongly toward the Witherford line of England, importing the brindle Witherford Tempting Touch, and then the red Witherford Weldeck Milford.

Eng. Ch. Kelfrey Merry Monarch, a beautiful headed red, was widely used at stud, and he garnered

Aust-NZ. Ch. Felmoor Astronaut (Hollee's Po-Tam ex Merriveen Midnight Mist) launched his way to BIS for breeder Jackie Barden.

Handler Ian Weeks leads his Boxer, Prince, through a fiery hoop during an obedience and agility demonstration in the Bundaberg Regional Show.

a most glamourous show career in both New Zealand and England. English imports that influenced the breed considerably in the 1960s include: NZ. Chs. Klesby Marcello, Summerdale Whipaway and Gremlin Painted Paws (all red); the English Matloe Kennel, especially Femoor Dynamic, the American Raffles imported son, along with Matloe's litter born by Eng. Ch. Summerdale Shamus.

Dynamic's progeny became the turning point in many New Zealand breeders' thinking about the Boxer, and their heads were turned forever toward the American-style dog. The acquisition of Aust. Ch. Felmoor Astronaut, a Best in Show winner for Quo Vadis Kennels and surely a before-his-time dog bred by Jackie Barden, who imported his sire Hollee's Po Tam, into Melbourne from the United States, and the English dam, Merriveen Midnight Mist, herself a double Raffles granddaughter (Jackie imported Raffles into the UK from the States when she lived there).

Then there were the Cherryburtons exported to Boxergrove Kennels, including the gorgeous reds, NZ. Chs. Cherryburton Redmead Rhythm and Cherryburton Escort and later NZ. Chs. Cherryburton Stainburndorf Sun Chariot and the beautiful English Ch. Wardrobes Cherryburton Autumn Rose.

Boxers from the Seefeld Kennels in England came in number to New Zealand's shores! NZ. Ch. Seefeld Copperplate, Seefeld Luther, Seefeld Cavallino, Seefeld Don Zachary and Seefeld Cool Blue. Vago Kennels imported the Marbelton lines, Pentagow the much used NZ. Ch. Summerdale Defiant.

By this time, Australian imports were becoming popular, considering that the English and American bloodlines were producing such good typey Boxers. The Trispias arrived from the land of OZ but regrettably for New Zealand never exhibited or bred as they had in their homeland. The Assisis came onto the scene and would be responsible for the most UK imports that would arrive for a long time, concentrating on the

Lower left: **Aust. Ch. Quo Vadis Running Wild (by Aust-NZ. Ch. Felmoor Astronaut ex Waihi Proper Pretty) at 18 months of age.**

Upper right: **NZ. Ch. Quo Vadis Impala (by Aust. Ch. Guntop Rocketman ex NZ. Ch. Quo Vadis Dolly Dazzler), bred by Maureen Boyd.**

Lower right: **NZ. Ch. Quo Vadis Ariadne (by Aust. Ch. Guntop Rocketman ex NZ. Ch. Quo Vadis Dolly Dazzler), litter sister to Quo Vadis Impala.**

Gremlin bloodlines that produced for them and many other kennels winners and producers of much merit: NZ. Chs. Gremlin Hey Pronto, Gremlin Summer Spree and Winter Frost of Gremlin, to name the dogs.

The most illustrious Assisis must surely be NZ. Chs. Assisi Hey Nice Notion and her glamorous son, Assisi Spree's Mr. Magic, whose untimely death put an end to what should have been a much more glorious stud career, one that could have continued for a good many years and added to the star-studded get he left behind.

Ten imports from the UK and Australia were owned by Quo Vadis and produced big winners consistently until the mid-1970s. The Anisor and Non Pareil kennels also had some success in the New Zealand show rings, as did the Tiaras of Australia. Curiously, the world-famous Wardrobe Kennels of England did not finish a champion in New Zealand, despite their strong influence on the breed. Currently many Boxer kennels flourish in New Zealand, some of which are based on the prominent American and English kennels of today.

Upper right: NZ. Ch. Quo Vadis Opera Phantom (by Seefeld Nijinsky ex NZ. Ch. Quo Vadis Ariadne) still looking great at seven years old.

Lower left: Quo Vadis Dark Flirt (by Quo Vadis Buds O' May ex NZ. Ch. Quo Vadis Michaela), bred by Maureen Boyd, at 11 months of age.

Middle left: NZ. Ch. Quo Vadis Michaelmas (by NZ. Ch. Quo Vadis Opera Phantom ex Quo Vadis Hot Shot), bred, owned and handled by Maureen Boyd.

Lower right: Quo Vadis Michaelmaxx, younger brother to NZ. Ch. Quo Vadis Michaelmas.

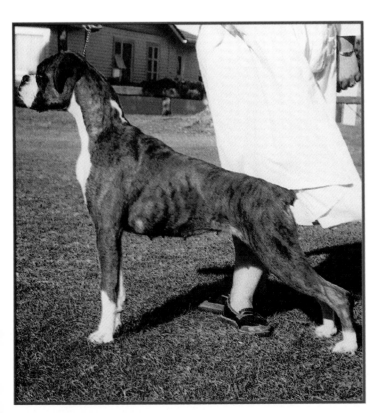

BOXERS

IN
ASIA

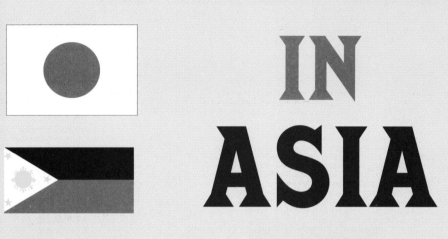

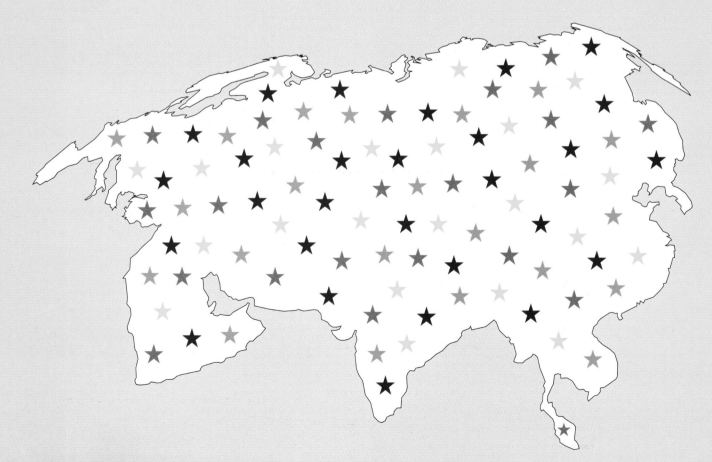

JAPAN

BY DR. HIDEAKI NAKAZAWA

The first American champion Boxer was imported into Japan around the year 1957. This first champion was Ch. Mazelaine's Captain Jinks. After this first importation, several other American champions followed and became the trendsetters of this time. Their names are as follows: Ch. Thomson's Thunderbolt, Ch. Canzonet's Minute-Minder, Ch. Canzonet's Melaine, Ch. Khorasan's Atomic, Ch. Highlight of Joffra and Ch. Von Der Hellem's Scotch 'n Soda.

In the 1960s, the Boxer world of Japan was dominated by the offspring of Ch. Canzonet's Minute-Minder. It was not a rare thing to find these offspring

roque of Quality Hill and Ch. Marjack's Golden Windjammer arrived in 1961, sold to Japan by Mazelaine.

From about 1964, it was Am. Ch. Treceder's Progression who stole the show. After the arrival of Am. Ch. Treceder's Happy Hiker, it was the Treceder's era and this continued for some time. During this time, other Boxers that arrived in Japan included: Am. Ch. Seaton's Jackpot, Am. Ch. Jubilant of Joffra and Am. Ch. Wilby's Red Commotion.

In approximately 1966, Am. Ch. Salgray's Playboy, Ch. Salgray's Marauder and Ch. Salgray's Chance Are arrived. The strong trend begun by Treceder's, however, was not yet to be broken. At around this time, Mr. Peter Delano, a handler from the Treceder's Kennel, arrived in Japan

The welcoming ceremony of the great American import Ch. Marjack's Golden Windjammer upon his arrival to Japan in 1961. Windjammer, bred by Mary Jackson and owned by Mr. and Mrs. John P. Wagner, won the 1958 ABC National.

stealing all first place awards in each category. Upon the arrival of Am. Ch. Treceder's Progression, however, this trend gradually began to change. A total of 120 entries were present at the specialty show sponsored by the Japan Kennel Club in the spring of 1961. Ch. Ba-

Ch. Salgray's Chance Play (by Ch. Salgray's Chances Are ex Kiawah Geisha), imported to Japan by owner Dr. Hideaki Nakazawa of Tokyo.

and pointed out that the Boxers in Japan were too small. Then, in 1977, Am. Ch. Salgray's Chance Play, Ch. Interlude's Jon-Jon and Ch. Salgray's Rose of Trallee arrived and changed the trend in the Boxer world of Japan.

Following Ch. Indian Bend's Red Cloud and several other champions from the Merrilane Kennel, the size of the Boxer in Japan grew larger.

After seeing the American Boxer Club show in 1981, I visited the Jacquet Kennel and received Jacquet's Urko from Mr. Richard Tomita. Having finished his championship, he was sent to Japan. Around this time, Boxers were not able to win in the Working Group. When Am. Ch. Jacquet's Urko arrived, the entire Boxer world in Japan focused its attention on this dog. Once he appeared in the ring, Boxer fanciers as well as owners and judges of other breeds marveled and commented that a "super" dog had arrived in Japan. He continuously took Best in Show awards wherever he was shown. He sired over 50 champions in Japan before returning to the United States. Following Urko's arrival, Ch. Jacquet's Agassiz, Am. Ch. Jacquet's Leon and Int. Ch. Jacquet's Novarese came to Japan. After finishing their Japanese championships, these dogs also returned to America.

In 1984, Am. Ch. Omega's Special Edition Samel arrived and in 1985 this dog became the Number One

Boxer in Japan. His offspring have received many Best of Breed awards. In 1986, Ch. Rolhi's Fancy Son of Dallas, who received the Best of Winners Award at the American Boxer Club Show, and Ch. TuRo's Emblem arrived in Japan.

Other champions and non-titled Boxers have come to Japan, but few have succeeded in leaving behind memorable names in their breed. Increased interrelations between American and Japanese Boxer fanciers is very much to be encouraged for better understanding of the current level of the breed in Japan. Fortunately, AKC and JKC (Japan Kennel Club) have direct ties and JKC dogs are recognized and registered by AKC so that Japanese-bred dogs can now be imported, shown and bred.

This daughter of Ch. Salgray's Minute Man was an historic import to Japan from the States.

American import to Japan, Ch. Interlude's Jon-Jon (by Ch. Salgray's Ambush ex Ch. Vel-Kel's Beejay), bred by Jerry and Dot Bryant and Velma Kelsey, and owned by Dr. Hideaki Nakazawa.

Ch. Cava-Lane's Steppin Out (by Cava-Lane's Born Free ex Cava-Lane's Flying Jenny), an historic import to Japan from the States.

Imported from the States to Japan by Dr. Nakazawa, Ch. Indian Bend's Red Cloud (by Ch. Holly Lane's Diamond Replay ex Indian Bend's Maria). Handled by Alvin Lee.

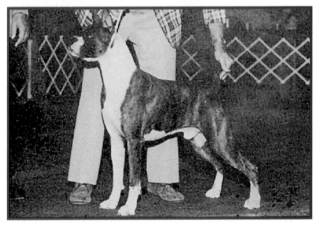

Ch. Aracrest's Ragtime (by Ch. Jim-Pat's Assai Ben Marcotto ex Ch. Aracrest's Cotton Jenny), an historic import to Japan from the States.

Excalibur of Camelot (by Ch. Salgray's Market Wise ex Ch. Catherine of Camelot), an historic import to Japan from the States, bred by Dr. H. Spey and T. Clayton.

Ch. Salgray's Rose of Tralee (by Ch. Salgray's Bojangles ex Salgray's Misbehavin), imported by Dr. Nakazawa.

Am. Ch. TuRo's Emblem (by Ch. Marquam Hill's Traper of TuRo ex TuRo's Touche), handled by Mr. Nakamura and bred by TuRo, was an important sire in Japan in the 1990s.

Am. Ch. TuRo's Emblem, the sire of many Japanese champions.

Am-Jap. Ch. Red Clay's Rockteer (by Ch. Gemini's Splashdown ex Red Clay's Rock Candy) is owned by Sadami Sato. Before being imported to Japan and gaining his championship status there, Rockteer won the Grand Prize Sweepstakes at the Potomac Boxer Club Specialty under the author, Richard Tomita. Handling on this occasion was Christine Baum.

Taking Best in Show, handled by Dr. Hideaki Nakazawa, is Am-Jap-Can-Ber. Ch. Jacquet's Urko, SOM. Bred by Richard Tomita, Urko became the most influential Boxer in all of Japan. The Shiba-inu here won Best Japanese-bred Dog in Show.

Am-Jap-Int. Ch. Jacquet's Novarese, SOM, sired by Ch. Jacquet's Agassiz, and handled by Atsuyoshi Kuroki. The judge was Masami Suzuki. Bred by Richard Tomita, Novarese became a prominent sire in the US and Japan alike.

Am-Ber-Jap-HK-Can. Ch. Jacquet's Agassiz (by Ch. Merrilane's April Fashion ex Jacquet's Hot Summer) is the sire of Int. Ch. Jacquet's Novarese and a top winner himself. Breeders, Sam Rodman and Richard Tomita. Owners, Ted and Barbara Widmayer.

Best King and Queen in Show are two Jacquet imports: Am-Jap-Can-Ber-Int. Ch. Jacquet's Urko and Am-Jap. Ch. Jacquet's Dancing Star, both bred by Richard Tomita and owned by Dr. Hideaki Nakazawa.

Left: Am-Jap. Ch. Jacquet's Dancing Star (by Ch. Jacquet's Zephan ex Susan's Lucy Midnight Star), handled by Tomokazu Mera, bred by Richard Tomita and owned by Dr. Hideaki Nakazawa.

Right: Am-Jap-Int. Ch. Tamaron's Finale de Jacquet (by Ch. Jacquet's Jessie James ex Goldfield's Onyx de Jacquet), bred by Richard Tomita and Joy Iannaconi, owned by Ryuichi Tsuruta.

Left: Am-Ber-Jap-Int. Ch. Jacquet's Razzle Dazzle (by Ch. Jacquet's Dark Donner ex Jacquet's Parlay), bred by Karen Speck and Richard Tomita, owned by Karen Speck and handled by Mr. Kuroki.

Right: Am-Ber-Jap. Ch. Jacquet's Skylark (by Ch. Jacquet's Dark Donner ex Jacquet's Parley), bred by Rick Tomita and Karen Speck, owned by Mr. Hiroaki Shijoh and handled by Mr. Nakamura.

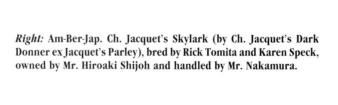

Jap. Ch. Jacquet's Sabina of Goldfield (Gamet's Native Diver of TuRo ex Lady Suzanne Jacquet), handled by Mr. Nakamura, and owned by Mr. Shijoh. The judge at this national specialty is Walter Pinsker.

Aerosmith of Stratford House (TuRo's Midnite Masquerader ex Jap. Ch. Jacquet's Sabina of Goldfield), handled by Mr. Nakamura and owned by Mr. Shijoh.

Am-Jap-Int. Ch. Jacquet's High Fashion (by Ch. Happy Ours Fortune de Jacquet ex Jacquet's Noko, an Urko daughter), owned by Sadao Kikuchi and handled by Mr. Kitagawa.

Jap-Tai. Ch. Jacquet's Todd, bred by Richard Tomita, was the top-winning Boxer in Japan in 1987 and 1988. Son of Ch. Jacquet's Urko, Todd is a Best in Show winner and is owned by Dr. Nakazawa.

Am-Jap. Ch. Jacquet's Garnet (by Am-Jap-Can-Ber-Int. Ch. Jacquet's Urko ex Roxy Keel Solomon), handled by Marylou Wilderson, bred by Richard Tomita, and owned by Tomokazu Mera. The judge at this American show was Peter Warbley of Australia.

Am-Jap. Ch. Jacquet's Trinket (by Ch. Goldfield's Dorian de Jacquet ex Ch. Jacquet's All Dolled Up), bred by Richard Tomita and Felix and Kim Cotton, owned by Sadao Kikuchi. Judge, Florence Goldenberg. Handler, Gerard Hughes.

Above: Jap. Ch. Ramancha's Big Star (by Ch. Jacquet's Razzle Dazzle ex Ch. Jacquet's Fleur de Noel), bred by Dr. Hideaki Nakazawa, owned by Mayumi Urata and handled by Mr. Kuroki.

Below: Jap. Ch. Falcon of New Trial, sired by Int. Ch. Jacquet's Novarese, bred by Mr. Imamura and handled by Mr. Kuroki, was the number-one Boxer in Japan in the early 1990s.

Ch. Ramancha's Big Star (by Ch. Jacquet's Razzle Dazzle ex Ch. Jacquet's Fleur de Noel), bred by Dr. Hideaki Nakazawa.

Jap. Ch. Mr. Rimsin of Grand Prix Road (by Can. Ch. Lounsbury's Emcee ex New Oliver's Over the Rainbow), bred and owned by Masatsugu Igaki. Judges, Mr. and Mrs. Robert Forsyth.

Beth of House Cameratt, owned by Akio Nemoto.

Ch. Suncrest's Diamond Jim (by Ch. Heldenbrand's Jet Breaker ex Ch. Beaupix Sweet Dreams), owned by Makoto Watanabe.

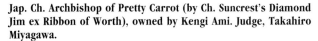

Jap. Ch. Archbishop of Pretty Carrot (by Ch. Suncrest's Diamond Jim ex Ribbon of Worth), owned by Kengi Ami. Judge, Takahiro Miyagawa.

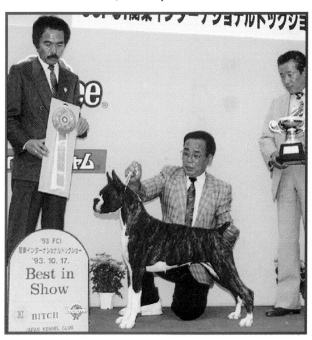

Am-Int. Ch. TuRo's Solitaire (by Ch. TuRo's Empire ex Marquam Hill's Cinder O' Philadel), owned by Hisao Sato.

Jap. Ch. Spirit Born Angel Smile (by Jap. Ch. Conbaat of Motomiya House Nakane ex Jap. Ch. Hollycrest's Flower Power), bred by Kyoko Hashimoto and owned by Junji Nonaka.

Jap. Ch. Ramancha's Beautiful Park, daughter of Int. Ch. Jacquet's Novarese, bred by Dr. Hideaki Nakazawa and owned by Hiroshi Yamamoto.

Ramancha's Red Star winning Puppy Best in Show at Gendai Boxer Specialty show, owner-breeder-handled by Dr. Hideaki Nakazawa.

Ramancha's Beautiful Me, winning Baby Best in Show from the 2—3-month puppy class. Handled by Dr. Nakazawa.

Am-Jap. Ch. Cherkei's Stampede (by Ch. Castro's Midnight Special ex Cherkei's Yarglas Shenanigan), bred by Mr. and Mrs. K. Robbins and Mr. and Mrs. G. Harrah, owner-handled by Sadao Kikuchi. The judge on this ocassion was American breeder-judge Victor Clemente.

Am-Jap. Ch. Alamo's Jameson of Aries (by Ch. Strawberry's Son of Zorro ex Aries Almost A Lady), bred by Allison Carbrey and Marilou Ruboyianes, owned by Sadao Kikuchi.

Am-Jap. Ch. Buemar's Amaretto Di Amore (by Ch. Sam-El's Maker's Mark ex Ch. Braemerwood Joy of Heritage), bred by Margaret Buechner and owned by Sadao Kikuchi.

Ramancha's Red Star, bred, owned and handled by Dr. Nakazawa, winning Baby Best in Show, handled by Dr. Nakazawa.

Am-Jap. Ch. Hala's Magnum PI (by Ch. Kricket's Jonathan ex Hala's Calico Belle), bred by Harold and Ila Young and owned by Sadao Kikuchi.

Am-Can-Jap. Ch. Red Clays Just Reward, a son of Am-Can. Ch. Bellcrest Just Watch Me out of Red Clay's Just Plain Pretty.

Jap. Ch. Morogan Flyer of Worth (by Ch. Marlindy's Beau-Jangles ex Mallow Laine's Black Jaguar), bred and owned by Kenchi Miyamoto.

Jap. Ch. Great of Mountain Angels (by Jap. Ch. TuRo's Eternal Flame ex Ch. High Justice's Sugar Candy), bred by Toyonobu Kobayashi and owned by Yoko Kobayashi.

Jap. Ch. Party Girl of Milute, daughter of Jap. Ch. Mr. Samurai of Arrox Boxers, bred by T. Nakamur and owned by Motoshi Fujita.

Jap. Ch. Puer Lady of Worth (by Jap. Ch. Morogan Flyer of Worth ex Am. Ch. Pualani of Drake Downs), bred and owned by Kenichi Miyamoto. Judge, Eleanor Linderholm.

Jap. Ch. New Oliver's Oriental Pearl (by Jap. Ch. Conbaat of Motomiya House Nakane ex New Oliver's Dadanela), bred by Akinobu Miyagawa and owned by Shoichi Yamada.

Jap. Ch. Arthur of Freedom Shuttle (by Am-Can. Ch. Aracrest's Creed ex Jap. Ch. Clara of Silkroad Day Break), bred by Kazuko Okamura and owned by Hidemichi Kobayashi.

Jap. Ch. Selection of Worth (by Ch. TuRo's Emblem ex Kathy of Worth), bred and owned by Kenichi Miyamoto.

Aerosmith of Stratford House (by TuRo's Midnite Masquerader ex Jap. Ch. Jacquet's Sabina of Goldfield), bred and owned by Hiroaki Shijo. Judge, Joseph Heine. Handler, Mr. Makamura.

Jap. Ch. TuRo's Sinsation (by TuRo's Escappade ex We-R's Class Flirt), owned by Hisao Sato, being judged by Mrs. Paula Bradley on her visit to Japan.

Ch. Moon Valley Fire Boss (by Ch. Cherkei's High Cotton ex Moon Valley Kiss of Fire), bred by Ida L. Baum and owned by Kenchi Miyamoto.

Jap. Ch. Ramancha's Black Diamond (by Int. Ch. Jacquet's Novarese ex Jap. Ch. Ramancha's Cachet), bred by Hideaki Nakazawa and owned by T. Mera.

Ch. TuRo's Solitaire, owned by Hisao Sato.

BY NARIMAN SHAKEEBAI, ABHINAV DHAR AND PRITHA MUTHANA, DAUGHTER OF LEELA RATNAM

Prior to Independence in 1947, India was a British colony, and perhaps the Boxers arrived there with the British. Most of the British, in keeping with their love for animals, carried their dogs to and from India depending on their posting and vacations. The Independence of India saw most of the British leaving the country along with their dogs. During this period, I am made to believe that the quality of dogs brought to India in general was very good. With the departure of the British, a lot of the progeny of their imported dogs was left behind. These early Boxers were very crude compared to the present-day elegant Boxers. The Boxers of that period had short necks, snipy muzzles, bulldoggy heads, and no flashy markings.

One unconfirmed source claims that the top English lines of the period, including Wardrobe, were present in India. I do not know how authentic this report is as generally the Boxers seen around India were few during the period from 1947 to 1970.

In early 1970 one of India's top breeders was Mr. S. Pathy of the kennel prefix San Craintes situated at Coimbator and owning the top winner of the time, Ind. Ch. San Craintes Pure Heart. The other top winner bred by Mr. S. Pathy and owned by Mrs. Goldsmith was Ind. Ch. San Craintes Razzle Dazzle. Later Mr. S. Pathy began breeding Dobermanns, many of which completed their American and Canadian titles. The Boxer breed's loss was the Dobermann breed's gain. Today Mr. S. Pathy is the top Dobermann breeder in India and he is an international judge.

In 1972 Mr. Askoe Mukerjee and Miss Monika Mukerjee of the Monkeberg Kennels situated at

Imported from the US, Dream Girl, granddaughter of Merrilane's April Fashion, won a Second BIS in 1990. Owner, Dr. S. W. Sawant.

Calcutta owned some of the top German imports of the time. The male dog was Ind. Ch. Artos Von Monkeberg by Griseha Von Hasseller Hof Scho Iad ex Gerch Zwiesel Von Goldhammer SchH. II, bred by Herr Peter Hoppe.

In Calcutta Dr. Nandy had imported a bitch Ch. Agita Von Recistance by Dabor-N-Worikben Youka V. Recistance, bred by Mr. J.H. Deerem Berg from Holland.

Again in Calcutta Mr. Sunitesh Chandra Mukherjee had imported a dog, Rupi K. Ring A Bell by Rupi K. Brass Tacks Seefelds Jezebella, bred by Mrs. Sheila Bowman from the UK.

In 1972 Mrs. Phyllis Bose of Calcutta owned the top-winning dogs: Ch. Perchard's Tiger by Chops ex Headline News of Skelder, bred by Mrs. Elizabeth Perchard, and her English import Ch. Chorland Seefeld of Calidad by Eng. Ch. Calidad Red Coat ex Marbelton Plum Crazy, bred by Mr. R. J. Briers. During the times these two kennels were functioning, Calcutta was considered a stronghold of Boxers in India. Quite a few of the progeny of these two kennels are still seen in and around Calcutta, but, due to the limited dogs and bitches available, the breed did not improve. In fact some of these early lines suffered from very bad bites. At the same time, the Calcutta enthusiasts should be given credit for keeping and maintaining the Boxer breed, which was becoming extinct in India.

In 1972 we had Mr. V.S. Sharma in North India with his imported dog Ch. Rolfaden Russet Gold by Eng. Ch. Boken Don Buchanan ex Rolfadan Dawn Chorus, bred by Mr. and Mrs. Wilkinson.

Ind. Ch. Aryanoush's Somersault (by Ind. Ch. Aryanoush's Birdneck's Rocky Shaizada ex Aryanoush's Sheer Delight), bred by Nariman M. Shakeebai and owned by Abhay Karkanis.

In 1974 Ms. Rangarajan, the Chairman of the Kennel Club of India and an international judge, imported a pair from UK for his Seecroft Kennels. The dog was Ind. Ch. Seefeld Poloment from the famous Mrs. Pat Heath of Seefeld, a son of the legendary Int. Ch. Seefeld Picasso ex Seefeld Turkish Delight. The bitch Ind. Ch. Gremlin Mere Vanity by Gremlin Mere Foot Steps ex NZ Ch. Gremlin Mere Braubra was from the equally famous Gremlin Kennel of Mrs. Fairbrother in the UK. Both the dog and bitch were the top Boxers to reach India's shores and created a sensation on arrival, winning all-breed BIS a number of times.

These two winners produced five champions, including Ch. Seecrofts Heretic owned by Mr. Harish Reddy at Hyderabad; Ch. Seecrofts Helonica owned by Mr. N. Adil Mirza at Hyderabad; Ch. Seecrofts Angel owned by Mr. C.V. Sundarasan. Mr. C. V. Sundarasan at Madras was also a breeder of Boxers with the kennel prefix Hack 'N Sack. Sad to say that these lines from the top UK imports were lost except for one line by Ch. Seecrofts Helonica in Hyderabad.

It is an enigma as to why the breed did not take off during the mid 1970s to the mid 1980s in spite of the arrival of top imports. During the period, the Boxer breed had nearly died off except for a few seen in dog shows. Additionally the period was plagued by an outbreak of distemper. The limited number of dogs, and therefore the small gene pool, was complicated by a breeding problem. Breeders, who could scarcely afford the costs involved with stud dogs and traveling, complained of their bitches' not conceiving, miscarriage or lack of milk. In spite of these problems, some diehard breeders especially in Calcutta kept the Boxer going in the early 1980s. These dogs, though not spectacular compared to the present-day dogs, always made their presence felt in the show rings. The 1980s saw a dramatic change. The Kennel Club of India with the infusion of new young blood started encouraging the dog game in a big way.

More shows were being held and good sponsorship of the shows encouraged better entries. New import restrictions and the increasing costs made breeders realize the value of their dogs compared to the cost of dogs offered abroad. More people took to dog breeding commercially and professionally.

In 1980 Mrs. Roswita Verma of the Roma prefix settled in Baroda imported the champion-producing German pair Ch. Argus of Roma and Ch. Elfi Vom Elchter of Roma by Bingo Vonder Wellersburg ex Dolly Von Elchter, bred by Mr. M. Falk.

In 1984 the famous international judge Mrs. Leela Ratnam at Madras of the prefix Canara Coast imported an American pair from Jacquet Boxers owned by Rick Tomita. The dog became Ind. Ch. Jacquet Canara Coast

Ind. Ch. Jacquet's Jaco Jack (by Ch. Jacquet's Agassiz ex Jacquet's Mahra), bred by Cynthia Curran, owned by Abhinav Dhar, retired undefeated as a multi-BIS winner and sire of champions.

Casey by Am. Ch. Jacquet's Dark Donner ex Jacquet's Daybreak and the bitch became Ind. Ch. Jacquet's Canara Coast Chelsea by Jacquet's Gaspard ex Jacquet's Natasha. Ind. Ch. Jacquet's Canara Coast Chelsea produced one litter by Ch. Jacquet's Canara Coast Casey.

The same year saw the arrival of another American Boxer, Ind. Ch. Aryanoush's Birdnecks Rocky Shaizada by Am. Ch. Birdneck's Touch of Class ex Birdneck's Sassy Class, bred by Mrs. E. Bert Brown and imported by Mr. Mehrioze D. Mistry. He changed hands twice before being bought by Mr. Nariman M. Shakeebai of the Aryanoush Kennels at Hyderabad. Rocky won an all-breed Best in Show at one year of age on his maiden

Ind. Ch. Jacquet's Jaco Jack with his up-and-coming puppies!

show appearance under the eminent Judge Nawab Nazir Yarjung. Ranked Top Dog in the country by many judges, Rocky was never defeated in the show ring even when showed with Mrs. Roswita Verma's German imports and Mrs. Leela Ratnam's American imports under the eminent Great Dane breeder and judge Mrs. Jean Lanning of the UK. In fact, Rocky went on to change the whole complexion of the Boxer breed in India. He has produced 21 champions to date. He is still an active stud and the All Time - All Breed Top Sire in India. Really, what Int. Ch. Seefeld Picasso did for the Boxer breed in England, and what Int. Ch. Millan's Fashion Hint did in America, Rocky has done for the breed in India.

In 1986 Mrs. Leela Ratnam imported two bitches again from Jacquet Boxers, Ind. Ch. Jacquet's Canara Coast Georgia by Am. Ch. Goldfield's Idol Maker ex Jacquet's Kiss Me Kate and Ind. Ch. Jacquet's Canara Coast Jersey. Ind. Ch. Jacquet's Canara Coast Casey has produced at least four champions, and his progeny is found in most of the top kennels in India as most of the top winners and producers carry his bloodline.

Home and Away. Photograph courtesy of S. C. Saran.

In 1987 Dr. S. V. Sawant of Bombay of the Brunswick's Kennels imported an American pair, Ind. Ch. Brunswick Classic Jewel by Mr. Herby ex Clark's Ladymebeth, bred by Mr. K.P. and Ms. A.Y. Clerk, and Ind. Ch. Brunswick's Dream Girl by Lady Boy Collins ex Jamie of the Mead, bred by Mrs. Susan Mead. Prior to this purchase, Dr. Sawant had a bitch from Mr. Roswita Verma's imported bloodline and a bitch from Mrs. Leela Ratnam. The bitch out of Casey, Brunswick's Canara Coast Carmel, could not complete her title due to her fractured leg but one litter by Ch. Birdneck's Rocky Shaizada produced three champions. Ind. Ch. Brunswick's Classic Jewel has produced four champions.

In 1987 Mr. Vijay Multani of Bombay of Vzaks Kennels acquired the English import Ind. Ch. Marbelton Look Ahead by Eng. Ch. Hey Good Looking at Marbelton ex Marbelton Little Raven, bred by Mrs. Hambleton. This dog has produced two champions.

In 1988 Mr. Nariman M. Shakeebai of Aryanoush Kennels acquired Ind. Ch. Aryanoush's Birdneck's Rocky Shaizada, the top sire all time all breeds and the producer of at least 28 champions. Aryanoush Kennels have bred no fewer than 38 champions and presently house 12 champion bitches that are all Indian bred.

Kapil Modi with his three beloved pets in India, a Boxer, St. Bernard and Afghan Hound.

In 1990 Shakeebai bought Ind. Ch. Aryanoush's Guntop Massachusetts from the Guntop Boxers of Mr. and Mrs. Miles Gunter of New South Wales, Australia. This dog produced at least seven champions and is the grand sire of seven champions. He is by Am. Ch. Salgray's Argo of Memory Lane ex Aust. Ch. Guntop Minute Maid, and his pedigree can be traced back to Int. Ch. Millan's Fashion Hint

In 1989 Mr. Avinash Dhar and Mrs. Nita Dhar of Jacko Kennels imported the dog Ind. Ch. Jacquet's Jaco Jack by Int. Ch. Jacquet's Agassis ex Am. Ch. Jacquet's Mahra from Jacquet. This dog has won all-breed Best in Show awards and has produced five champions, including a United Arab Emirates champion.

In 1990, Mr. A.D. Sharma owner of ASRA Farms imported Ch. Sjecoin Game Time by Aust. Ch. Sjecoin One Mo' Time ex Aust. Ch. Sjecoin Show Stopper from the Sjecoin Kennels of Australia and also Ch. Sjecoin Sweet Success by Am. Ch. Merrilanes Golden Grouse ex Pancho Pride Mighty Gold, bred by Mrs. J. Olifent Brace.

Also in that year, Mr. Sanjay of Dogmatix at Pune imported a number of fine dogs from Germany and Belgium. Ind. Ch. Poloma Van Boksdoon, Nigel Vande Boksdoon, who died tragically just short of his Indian title; Ind. Ch. Playful Vande Boksdoon, who was again lost but left behind some progeny. Two years later, Sanjay added Bel-Ind. Ch. Norbert Van De Boksdoon by Boreas Hufvantroys ex D. Naoin V. Eisen Bero; Ind. Ch. Marbelton Home Maid by Marbelton Home Dog ex Rowendale Too Nice for Woods; and Olympia Won De Boksdoon by Mylord Vand De Boksdoon ex Nincav. D. Boksdoon, bred by Mr. and Mrs. Jan Timmers Oyen, imported in whelp, produced Hastly of Dog Matrix and Lady of Dog Matix.

In 1991 Mr. Sanjaya Saran of Bombay of Westfeldon Kennels imported Ch. Rimarti Jean - Luc By Red Fyre Highland Flingat Rimarti ex Rimarti Belle Epoque, bred by Mr. and Mrs. M.R. Wyles from the UK.

In 1993 Messers Partha Shehar Chaterjee and Mr. Michael Hugh at Calcutta imported Ind. Ch. Cartier Diamond Trader by Aust. Ch. Thasrite Wise Guy ex Scatchard Summa Fight, bred by Mr. C. McDonald from Australia, followed by a bitch in whelp, Ind. Ch. Tarzwall Sure Thing by Aust. Ch. Panero Piping Hot ex Tarzwall Autumn Dew bred by Mrs. S.K. Smale.

The following year Mr. Jatin Sareen of Jatin Kennels imported Ind. Ch. Twice as Nice at Marbelton by Eng. Ch. Bonmeur V. Vilengea of Marbelton ex Marbelton Box of Delights, bred by Mr. M. Hambleton. Also in 1994, Mr. A.D. Sharma of Asra Farms imported Ind. Ch. Naughty But Nice of Marbelton at Towen Dale by Dolf The Buhe Farm of Marbelton ex Marbelton The Box of Delight, bred by Mrs. M. Hambleton, and Miss S. David and Ch. Vagabond's Top Gun at Asrafarm by Am. Ch. Vagabond's Son of Agun ex Vintage Dixie Peach, bred by Mrs. Harry P. Della Fields from the States.

Ind. Ch. Jacquet's Canara Coast Chelsea (by Jacquet's Gaspard ex Jacquet's Natasha), owned by Ashe and Pritha Muthanna.

Carmel was an excellent foundation bitch carrying pure Jacquet. Though she was not shown due to an injury, she did produce excellent litters of the type Brunswick aimed for. Owner, Dr. S. W. Sawant.

The arrival of the elegant American Boxers took the country by storm—the Indian show fanciers first saw the flashy markings, beautiful arch of neck, the clear cut chiseled head and the long cropped ears. These American arrivals revived and revitalized the Boxer fancy. Just about everyone wanted to own a Boxer—especially one with cropped ears, flashy markings, and an elegant neck. Fanciers were seeing the rich fawn shades of the Jacquet dogs for the first time; most Indians Boxers before the Jacquet imports were very dilute fawns or deer reds. Plus there were two Best in Show-winning Boxers: Rocky and Jacquet's Jacko Jack. The Boxer rage was full blaze!

During this upward swing, there were other imports from Germany, Belgium, Russia, England and Australia. Except for the Boxers from America and Australia, none of these Boxers produced progeny that would impact on the breed. In fact only the American Boxers have produced very well in India, and some of the progeny of American and Australian dogs have defeated the other imports in the show ring.

The biggest boost to the breed was the producing qualities of Rocky and the winning of the Australian import. Ind. Ch. Sjecoin Game Time, the Dog of the Year title in 1990—91, owned by Mr. A. D. Sharma of Delhi. Suddenly, in a short span, the Boxer took over the second position of the Working Group dog behind the German Shepherd and relegating the Dobermann to third position.

The Indian people found that, compared to the German Shepherds that had much trouble adapting to the hot Indian summer months, the Boxer with his rugged looks and build and easy-to-maintain coat was an ideally suited dog for the Indian country.

The Boxer could even adapt to a vegetarian diet, supplemented with soy bean meal and cottage cheese for protein.

All in all, the wind was favoring the Boxer breed. With the introduction of new blood, the problem of loss of milk amongst the bitches and other breeding problems were hardly heard. Boxers thrived and multiplied. Thus, the highly adaptable, sporty and elegant Boxer has found many friends in India, and, a credit to the breeders, the breed is thriving despite the earlier hardships. Today the breed is a top contender for Group and BIS wins.

There are many imported dogs from famous kennels in India but each breeder is going his own way and there is no mutual cooperation. Artificial insemination is not permitted in India, which hampers breeding programs since breeders do not take the risk to travel to different parts of the country restricting the breeder to his own limited breeding stock. Dog breeding in India is not yet accepted and dog lovers breed as a hobby keeping only four to six dogs and breeding one to two litters per year.

In the last two decades, show-quality Boxers have made their dramatic debuts in the show ring, lingered a year or two as top winners and then faded away. The chairman of the Kennel Club of India, Mr. S. Rangarajan, imported Seefeld Poloment from the famous Seefeld Kennels of the United Kingdom. Seefeld Poloment was the son of the legendary Boxer Seefeld

Ind. Ch. Jacquet's Canara Coast Casey, sired by Ch. Jacquet's Dark Donner, winning BIS at the South of India KC show, owned by Pritha and Ashe Muthanna.

Piccasso, who topped the show circuit in the 1970s. Subsequent imports faded as fast as they came.

The grand debut of the famous Jacquet family of Boxers in 1984 was and continues to be a sensation to the Boxer lovers in India. Jacquet's Canara Coast Casey and Jacquet's Canara Coast Chelsea came to India as eight- and ten-week-old puppies respectively. Both won CCs in their first appearances in the show ring. Jacquet's Canara Coast Chelsea won Best Puppy in Show under international judge Mr. Philip John. The Boxers continued the show circuit and have been big winners all along. All-breed judge Mr. Jack Flanagan (Australia) put Casey Best in Show at the prestigious South of India Kennel Club Championship Dog Show in May 1985. His comment on Casey was as follows: "Excellent dog, correct head, fine condition, moved extremely well, very alert and good temperament."

At the Canine Club of Cocbin's fourth show, Mrs. Norma Lim of the Philippines placed Casey Second Best in Show. Jim Mitchell of Australia also placed him Second Best in Show. At Madras Canine Club's 14th Championship Dog Show held in January 1986, Casey placed Third Best in Show under judge Mr. Philip John. At Poons Kennel Club's 42nd and 43rd Championship Show, with all-breed Indian

Ind. Ch. Canara Coast Alaska (by Ind. Ch. Jacquet's Canara Coast Casey ex Jacquet's Canara Coast Georgia), owned by Nita Dhar and bred by Mr. and Mrs. Ashe Muthanna. Alaska is the dam of five champions in India.

judges P.S. Chandilya from Delhi and A.K. Bose from Calcutta, Casey placed Fourth Best in Show. At Madras Canine Club's 15th & 16th Championship Dog Show, Mr. Treen (USA) placed Casey as Third Best in Show. Mr. S. Rangarajan, an international all-breed judge also placed him Third Best in Show at the same show.

Madras Canine Club is a premier club in India and has a galaxy of international judges officiating their shows. Winning at the Madras Canine Club is a big win for any dog. Both Chelsea and Casey have won Best of Breed and Best Opposite Sex with CCs at every show they have entered. The winning pair have had two litters that have been carefully placed in show homes all over India. The Jacquet Boxers have made an indelible mark in the Indian dog world. Their progeny shows promise and in good time should help to establish quality Indian Boxers as well.

Boxers have been my passport into the dog game. This story goes back 20 years and it was with this breed that I entered the show rings—ever since a lot of water has flowed down the river Hoogly. In these years, success has come as a breeder of numerous champions in various breeds, but not Boxers. Let me now justify the reason for my switching to other breeds right at the start of my dog-showing days.

Before I made this decision, I ardently carried out extensive studies in the breed's history—the greats of the breed starting with Ch. Lustig Von Dom, that great pillar of Boxer development, following with Frohlich Von Dom, a name known and talked about wherever Boxers are mentioned. Frohlich was bred by the late Frau Stockmann and imported into the

Handled by the famous Indian dog judge Mrs. Leela Ratnam, Ind. Ch. Jacquet's Canara Coast Casey, owned by Ashe and Pritha Muthanna.

Ind. Ch. Sjecoin Game Time (by Aust. Ch. Sjecoin One Mo' Time ex Aust. Ch. Sjecoin Showstopper), owned by A.D. Sharma, the son of the President of India.

UK, where he left a lasting impression on the breed's history as a sire. In the years preceding India's independence, only the rich and the royalty kept dogs, and they preferred the easy way to success at dog shows. Import and win was the order of the day. Numerous dogs of various breeds found their way to the royalties of India, but none left any lasting influence on any breed. For most of the breeds, the process had to restart and interest had to be renewed with fresh imports.

As for Boxers, I waited patiently all these years wondering why this magnificent breed did not catch the eye of the fancy. Finally, the mid-1990s will go down in the history of Boxers in India in golden letters. Imports started coming in from just about everywhere in the world—some good, others mediocre and, for the first time, Boxers in India are looking forward to a brighter future.

The focal point of such a practical development is Ch. Sjecoin Game Time, bred by Mrs. Rosina Olifent-Brace of Victoria, Australia, and imported to India by Mr. A. D. Sharma of New Delhi. "Harvey," as this dog is affectionately called, is a great credit to his breeder. He is a wonderfully constructed son of Ch. Sjecoin One Mo Time, a dog that I admired in Australia during one of my judging trips. Harvey soon compiled an enviable show record and was destined to surpass anything that any other Boxer imports might have done in India. His tremendous value as a sire has already started to be revealed in the pups that he has produced.

Brunswick's

Dr. S. W. Sawant has been a Boxer lover since 1980. In 1985 he bought a Boxer puppy Carmel from Mrs. Leela Ratnam, Madras, sired by Ch. Jacquet's Canara Coast Casey ex Ch. Jacquet's Canara Coast Chelsea. As Carmel had Jacquet's line there was not a single top-quality stud dog in India.

In the same year Mr. Mestry from Escort showed a beautiful brindle male imported from the US, Ch. Birdneck Rocky Shaizada at the Bombay show. Dr. Sawant was much impressed by this dog and hoped to use him for stud. Unfortunately this gentleman had got this dog as a gift and did not recognize his qualities and gave away the dog. After changing homes a few times, Rocky landed with Mr. Nariman Shakeebai at Hyderabad.

Finally, Mr. Nariman was kind enough to inform Dr. Sawant and Carmel had a litter of four outstanding puppies from Rocky, including two males Handsome and Sunburst and two bitches Honey and Super Trouper, who went to Mr. Nariman. All became champions except Sunburst who was not shown.

The cost of top-quality dogs from America was a bit exorbitant and to invest a large amount in a dog just for the sake of hobby was disapproved by Dr. Sawant's family members.

Ind. Ch. Status Symbol was an outstanding male, rated the best Boxer dog bred in India in the 1990s. Winning against imported dogs, he has earned 12 CCs, a Second BIS in Baroda in 1995, and became a champion before his first birthday. Owner, Dr. S. W. Sawant.

Ind. Ch. Classic Jewel became a champion in three consecutive shows, despite his incorrectly cropped ears. He is a true American-type Boxer with flashy white markings and a short bite, preferred by most Indian judges. Owner, S. W. Sawant.

In 1989 he imported a pet-quality pair, Ind. Ch. Classic Jewel and Ind. Ch. Dream Girl from the US, Dream Girl's was out of Merrilane April Fashion. She went Best in Show twice in 1990. They both became champions in three consecutive shows. They were not specialed since they were imported mainly to improve the breed quality in India.

Ch. Dream Girl produced Ch. Star Attraction sired by Ch. Handsome who went four Bests in Show in 1990. Star Attraction is with Wg. Cd. P.P. Bain at Jalandhar (Punjab) and won many CCs in the North.

Carmel had produced two litters sired by Classic Jewel: Aryanoush Honey Pot from the first litter went to Mr. Nariman Shakeebai and Ch. Oh Baby owned by Mr. Sanjaya Saran and Special Edition were from the second litter. Oh Baby won Best in Show in Baroda 1994, Poona 1994 and Bombay 1995. Super Trouper produced many champions sired by a Guntop import from Australia owned by Mr. Shakeebai. Honey produced an outstanding male Ch. Status Symbol sired by Ch. Marbelton Look Ahead imported from the UK. He won many CCs and won two Bests in Show in 1995. Today Status Symbol and Oh Baby are among the leading Boxers in India. Special Edition went to Hyderabad and her place was taken by West Feldon's Lady gifted by Mr. Sanjaya Saran. Lady is the daughter of Oh Baby sired by British import Rimarti Jean. Luc derived from the famous Tabor V. Worikben of Lynpine bloodline of Holland. Lady produced an excellent litter sired by Ch. Classic Jewel.

Ind. Ch. Hi Handsome (by Ind. Ch. Aryanoush's Birdneck's Rocky Shaizada ex Carmel) can trace 36 American champions in his pedigree. He is a multiple BIS winner and has produced outstanding pups.

Ind. Ch. Hi Honey (by Ind. Ch. Aryanoush's Birdneck's Rocky Shaizada ex Carmel) is a litter sister to Hi Handsome and is the dam of Status Symbol, sired by Marbelton Look Ahead, a UK import.

Aryanoush

Aryanoush Kennels are situated in Hyderabad, South India, owned by Mr. Nariman M. Shakeebai. The first bitch to impress Mr. Shakeebai was Ind. Ch. Seecrofts Helonica owned by his younger brother. She was out of the UK imports of Mr. S. Rangarajan, Ind. Ch. Seefeld Polomont and Ind. Ch. Gremlin Mere Vanity. Nariman acquired one male from Bangalore, and when the dog was one year old, he was stolen. After a short period, he acquired two bitches, one from Hyderabad and the other from Pune. The Hyderabad bitch became Aryanoush's First Love and carried the bloodline of Ch. Seefeld Poloment and Ch. Gremlin Mere Vanity, two of the dogs whose progeny Mr. Nariman so admired.

The top dog at Aryanoush Kennels is—and he would be top dog at any kennel anywhere!— BIS Ind. Ch. Aryanoush's Birdneck's Rocky Shaizada bred by Mrs. E. Bert Brown, imported from the States and the sire of 28 champions. Rocky is India's all-time all-breed top sire.

Ind. Ch. Aryanoush's Birdneck's Rocky Shaizada (by Ch. Birdneck's Touch of Class ex Birdneck's Sassy Class), bred by Mrs. E. Bert Brown and owned by Nariman M. Shakeebai, was the sire of 28 champions.

375

The Story of Rocky

BY MR. NARIMAN M. SHAKEEBAI

In the year 1985 I had heard that a very good brindle Boxer had arrived in Hyderabad City that went on to win an all-breed Best in Show on his maiden appearance at the age of one year. This dog changed hands and nothing was heard of him again.

Three years later in 1988 a friend called me to say that some one wanted to have a look at my bird collection and he was coming over. During our bird conversation I came to know that this particular gentleman owned an American Boxer, so I inquired if he would leave it for stud. The owner mentioned that the dog was aged four years and has never mated but he would think it over.

After a week, our common friend called to say that the gentleman wanted to give away the brindle Boxer and would I be interested to buy him. Was I interested! A week later I was the new owner of the brindle dog from America. With the arrival of Rocky, Aryanoush Kennels came into existence. Little did I realize at that time that Rocky was destined to become the country's all-time all-breed top-producing sire—plus the top sire in Asia!

The day Rocky arrived both my bitches were in season. Half an hour after Rocky's arrival I treated him to the treat of his life. Out of his very litter was born Ind. Ch. Aryanoush's Show Stopper. Later on my other bitch Aryanoush's First Love went on to produce five champions. Studying Rocky's pedigree and reading Mrs. Anna Katherine Nicholas's book *The Boxer,* I came to know that Rocky carried some of the top American bloodlines. His bloodline flowed through to Int.Ch. Scher-Khoun's Shadrack and thus to Int. Ch. Millan's Fashion Hint.

At the time of Rocky's arrival there was very few good bitches in India, and these were all out of the old lines

Ind. Ch. Aryanoush's Prima Donna (by Ind. Ch. Aryanoush's Birdneck's Rocky Shaizada ex Aryanoush's Fancy Free), bred by Nariman M. Shakeebai and owner-handled by Abhay Karkanis.

present in India. Mrs. Leela Ratnam had already imported a pair from Jacquet Kennels. Later I was to acquire some good bitches out of these lines. Hence most of Aryanoush stock is based on the inbreeding of Rocky and later the Guntop dog into the Jacquet lines. The Jacquet line was immensely helpful in straightening and strengthening my Boxer's backs, indeed Rocky himself did not have an ideal back. Rocky has sired no fewer than 28 champions; he is the grandsire of 13 champions, 4 more pointed. He has sired a Best in Show winner, two Second BIS winners, a third BIS winner, and a fourth BIS winner. Rocky's son Ch. Aryanoush's Dream Peddler was the first National Show 1993—1994 CC-BOB winner in an entry of 64 Boxers including imports. Ch. Aryanoush's Dream Peddler is the sire of three champions and owned by Mr. S. B. Krishnan and Mr. Jagannath of Bangalore.

Rocky was never defeated in the show ring.

Ind. Ch. Aryanoush's Cross My Heart winning BOB at Madras, handled by S.K. Naidu and owned by Nariman M. Shakeebai. BOS claimed by Ind. Ch. Jacko Jumping Jack, owned by Leela Ratnam. Andre Mocke of South Africa ajudicated.

His daughter Ind. Ch. Aryanoush's Miss Knock was the BOS CC winner at the Second National Show 1994—1995.

In the year 1992, due to deliberate poisoning, I lost nine litters and thus some of the best pups out of Rocky were lost, especially one out of Rocky and Aryanoush's Jacko Passion Play (a daughter of Ind. Ch. Jacquet's Jacko Jack).

The show season in India is limited to three to four months of the year. Any bitch in whelp or out of condition due to pregnancy cannot be shown. Secondly, as ours is a fledgling country as far as dog shows and showing is concerned, people want to own top show-quality dogs, but when it comes time to show, they make excuses and do not participate. All in all, the praise of Rocky is less compared to what he has done for the breed in India. It speaks volumes for a dog who, in spite of so many handicaps, could become the most influential sire in Asia. Most of the top kennels in India have the blood lines of Rocky.

Aryanoush's Firefighter (by Ind. Ch. Aryanoush's Birdneck's Rocky Shaizada ex Ind. Ch. Aryanoush's Brunswick's Honeypot, bred by Nariman M. Shakeebai and owner-handled by Azeem Farooqi.

Beyond Rocky

Shortly, the need of a second sire was felt at Aryanoush. Mentor and friend Mr. C.V. Sundarsan, an international judge, recommended some good kennels in Australia. This is how Mr. Nariman got in touch with Mr. and Mrs. Gunter of the Guntop Boxers. Guntop Massachusetts by Am. Ch. Salgray's Argo of Memorylane ex Aust. Ch. Guntop Minute Maid (a daughter of Am. Ch. Salgray's Minuteman) in no time carried the Aryanoush prefix and sported the Indian title. He has sired seven champions and is the grand sire of seven champions. His top sons are Ind. Ch. Aryanoush's Bang Bang Man and Ind. Ch. Aryanoush's Vendetta. Vendetta aged ten months on his first appearance won an all-breed Best Puppy and Second BIS in an entry of 210 dogs.

Aryanoush Boxers is the only Boxer kennel that does not have any imported bitches but has made full use of the gene pool available out of the Jacquet and other imported lines. Some of the top-producing bitches at Aryanoush are Aryanoush's First Love, dam of five champions; Ch. Aryanoush's Super Trouper, five champions; Ch. Aryanoush's Winter Forecast, three champions; Ch. Aryanoush's Sweet Heart, four champions; Ch. Aryanoush's Hint of Class, three champions; C. Aryanoush's Brunswick's Honeypot, two champions; Aryanoush's Jacko Passion Play, one champion; Asra Farm's Divine Comedy, one champion; and Aryanoush's Fancy Free, two champions.

Aryanoush Kennels has bred no fewer than 38 champions, and it is estimated that from 1989 to 1995, about 70% of Indian-bred Boxer champions were either Aryanoush-bred or carried the Aryanoush bloodlines, earning Mr. Shakeebai the distinction of being the top Boxer breeder on the Asian continent.

Ind. Ch. Aryanoush's Vendetta (by Ind. Ch. Aryanoush's Guntop Massachusetts ex Aryanoush's Jacko Passion Play), bred and handled by Nariman M. Shakeebai and owned by N. Adil Mirza, is the top boxer for 1995-1996 and top dog all-breeds in 1997.

MALAYSIA

BY JIMMY NG ENG HING

As a young boy, I got my first Boxer from an English man. I fell in love with it—and that was over 40 years ago. It was daringly difficult to own a purebred dog at that time. In 1956, I was able to acquire a good bitch, and soon I learned more about Boxers. My first beautiful bitch, Barones Suntoy Sin, purchased in 1979, propelled me to show dogs. At the first shows, under Prof. Tudie of Yugoslavia, she won Best Puppy, Junior and Reserve BPIS. Later to win CC and due to heat in a short time, I could not make her a champion. I fought for the right to show bitches in heat. After many years, we are now allowed to show them when in heat.

The only conceivable way to improve Boxers in Malaysia was through importation. So from Australia, I got a large beautiful brindle dog, Mal. Ch. Phoenix's Power Punch of Besquirel. Gradually I progressed to help import better and better dogs and bitches. The most significant was from Sjecoin Kennels; Mrs. Rosina Olifent-Brace kindly sold me Aust. Ch. Sjecoin Solid Gold. He was very strong in setting his characteristic features in our bitches and soon he gave me a very beautiful bitch, Mal. Ch. Pariville White Pearl, who went BIS at 13 months.

I give tribute to David and Rosina Olifent-Brace, Prima Donna, Aust-Mal. Ch. Sjecoin Cool William, Mal. Ch. Sjecoin That's a Knock Out, Sjecoin Cheer for Me and Lately Sjecoin Knock on Wood.

Thasrite Aristocrat (by TuRo's Cross Time ex Aust. Ch. Thasrite Hiland Lass) was imported from Australia to Malaysia.

Knock on the Wood of Besquinel (by Ch. Merrilane's Golden Gloves ex Sjecoin Tally Poppy), bred by R. Olifent-Brace and owned by guest author Mr. Jimmy Ng Eng Hing.

Thai-Phil. Ch. Tina of Phuphing Chang Puak (by Am-Mal-Phil. Ch. Thorn Crest Work of Art ex Phil. Ch. Woodcliff's Triple Threat), bred by Tanongpong Kasemboonsukri and owned by Vichien Woodtipienlert.

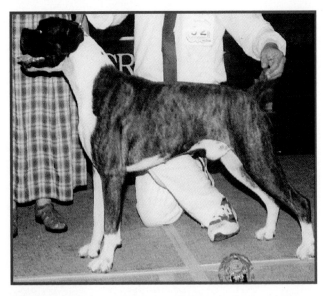

NZ. Ch. Denem Man on the Moon at Rinkenbox (by NZ. Ch. Glanmar Righton Target ex Shaylor Just a Helkat), the top dog of New Zealand imported to Malaysia, bred by C. Bradley and H. Martin and owned by Lim Koon Ngee.

NZ. Ch. Denem Man on the Moon at Rinkenbox, owned by Lim Koon Ngee.

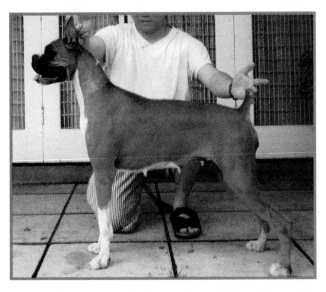

Sjecoin Silk N Sabotage (by Ch. Merrilane's Golden Glove ex Ch. Sjecoin Hot Gossip), bred by Mrs. R. Olifent-Brace and owned by Elwin Khor.

Call-T's Mister Smorking Gun (Thai Ch. Arkona Dester ex Call-T's Baby Lovely), bred and owned by Vichien Woodtipienlert.

Can-Mal. Ch. Prince Shabaka of Telstar (by Can. Ch. Tarabran's Electra Cadet, CDX ex Can. Ch. Starview's Tequilla Sunrise), owned by Yip Wai Choon.

Mal. Ch. Wescoast Autumn Storm (by Xel Shadow Boxa ex Xel Wescoast Girl), bred by L. Hoek and R. B. Bird and owned by Wong Soon Thein, imported to Malaysia from Australia.

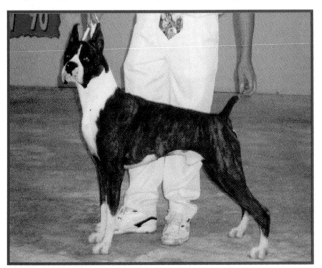

TAIWAN

BY JAMES N. ARNOLD

When you think of the Boxers of Taiwan, you must know something about the country. It is not like the U.S., with all of the open space to run and play with your Boxer. While the Boxer is the country's number-one dog, most Boxers live in apartments with their owners, where they are well cared for and pampered. When judging the Boxers in Taiwan you will not find as many bad toplines as in the U.S. The shoulders have good laybacks with good fronts. The heads as well as the mouths are good too. The movement of Boxers is adequate considering that they don't get to exercise much.

There are many different bloodlines imported into Taiwan. The breeders are always trying to improve the Boxer. They are hungry for information on how to go about doing this. It would be of great help if the people who sell dogs to Taiwan would be more considerate about the type they sell. After all, we Boxer breeders are trying to improve the breed, aren't we? This should be true not only in the U.S. but also all over the world.

When invited to judge the Boxer Club Association of Taiwan, it was an experience I will never forget. The hospitality and accommodations were of the royalty class. The show starts with the judging of the puppies (up to six months of age). Bitches are always first, then the dogs. I was told to pick as many winners as I wanted, including the Best Queen puppy and the Best King puppy. The classes then start at six months old up through the Open Class. Then there is Best Import and the Best Domestic, which means a dog bred in Taiwan.

Guest author James N. Arnold judging a Boxer specialty in Taiwan.

Lai's Echo, sired by Ch. Jacquet's Grande Sonnerie, owned by Pan-Yen Lai.

Can-HK-Tai. Ch. Mephisto's Red Baron (by Am-Can. Ch. Strawberry's Caballero, SOM ex Can. Ch. Aphrodite of Olympus), winning at the Boxer Association of Taiwan. Breeder, Monica Pinsker.

HONG KONG

The Boxer has gained significant popularity in the British colony of Hong Kong since the early 1970s. Many imported Boxers from the U.K., Australia and, in more recent years, the U.S. are seen in the show ring. There is now a tendency toward a preference for the cropped Boxers, so it seems likely that more North American dogs from the better known kennels will be imported in the future.

As a working breed, Boxers rarely win the Group in the Hong Kong show scene. This can be seen from the Kennel Club records from the 1950s. One exception in recent years was a red dog imported from the U.K. in 1975, Newlaithe Great System (sired by Norwatch Brockbuster, top Boxer in the U.K. in 1983, ex Haviland's Miss Canada, a bitch of impeccable pedigree from Canada). This impressive dog finished his championship title at three and won the Best in Show title at the Kennel Club's 50th anniversary show under Robert Curtis, from Australia. Newlaithe Great System continued on winning CCs almost undefeated until he was retired at five-and-a-half. He had a total of seven CCs, which was a Boxer record in the club's history.

In recent years there have been several North American imports from the Salgray, Evergreen, Savoye, TuRo and Elharlen bloodlines. Most of these dogs and bitches are quite elegant in stance but seem to be lacking in substance, strong bones and tight feet. Perhaps due to the lack of open space in the crowded city, the dogs are not getting sufficient exercise. Proper conditioning is so important for the this active breed to maintain its top form.

International judges who visit Hong Kong include those from the U.K., New Zealand, Australia, Japan, Singapore and the United States. These judges are primarily all-breed judges. However, Di Johnson and Andrew Brace from the U.K., who are extremely knowledgeable about the Boxer breed, and many other judges specializing in the Working Group have adjudicated on special occasions.

Upper left: Lai's Ammy, sired by Ch. Jacquet's Grande Sonnerie, owned by Pan-Yen Lai.

Lower left: Am-Jap-Tai. Ch. Jacquet's Ghad of Goldfield (by Gamet's Native Diver of TuRo ex Lady Suzanne Jacquet Bardays), bred by Ed Goldfield and Richard Tomita and owned by Dr. Hideaki Nakazawa.

PHILIPPINES

BY DR. ORLANDO SACAY

The last time a Boxer won an all-breed show, before the current "Boxer Revolution," was in 1979. In 1986, a young female fawn Boxer caught the eye of dog fanciers in the Philippines by winning the all-breed dog show of the year. This female Boxer was followed to prominence by a half-brother, who became not only top Boxer but also the Philippines's top dog. The dominance of Boxers in the show ring continues.

Phil. Gr. Ch. Rich' Lady Labyrinth (Phil. Ch. TuRo's Kodak ex Lucky's Sugar Say), bred and owned by Richard Li.

Boxer Pioneers

The history of Boxers in the Philippines is not complete without mentioning Mr. Douglas Uytengsu of Woodcliff Boxers, who established the Boxer Club of the Philippines in 1984. With a handful of Boxer lovers and total dedication, he spent time, effort and money to promote the breed. He organized a few dog shows, many of which he personally financed. His friendships with well-known breeders like Mr. Walter Pinsker of Mephisto Boxers brought some good dogs to the Philippines, who have become the foundation of the breed. Through Uytengsu's acquaintance with Ms. Patricia Forney, he was able to import what would become the first dominant Boxer sire. His contribution to the improvement of the breed was short-lived with his untimely death.

Another pioneer is Dr. Orlando Sacay of Golden Cross Boxers. Even though he was bitten by dogs four times during his younger days (which meant a total of 100 injections administered in the back), his love for dogs never waned. While looking for a Boxer puppy for his daughter, he had a chance to meet with Mr. Uytengsu. Mr. Sacay learned the details about Boxers from Mr. Uytengsu.

In search for a Boxer to bring back to the Philippines, he paid Mr. Richard Tomita of Jacquet Boxers a visit in New Jersey. There he saw a champion Jacquet bitch. Mr. Tomita introduced him to the owner of the bitch and a purchase price was agreed upon. Upon learning that the bitch would go to Manila, the owner of the bitch backed off the deal. Disappointed, he learned that some Boxer breeders in the U.S. do not like to send a dog out of the U.S.

He later called Ms. Duanna Young of Doggone Boxers, whom he learned about through a breed publication (*The Boxer Review*). He asked if he could pay her a visit. Ms. Young swore that she did not have any puppies for sale, but Dr. Sacay insisted on visiting her because he wanted to see the famous Ch. Doggone Ounce of Gold. At that time, "Troy" was the top Boxer and top producer in the U.S.

Upon arrival with his young daughter at Ms. Young's California home, he saw two beautiful puppies running around in the back yard. Intent on bringing home a Boxer, he told his daughter in their native language, "Embrace that female fawn puppy and say, within hearing distance of Ms. Young, that you want that puppy."

"What are we going to do, Duanna?" Dr. Sacay asked.

"OK, you can have her," Duanna hesitatingly said. This lovely fawn bitch would contribute to Boxer history not only in the Philippines but in the U.S as well. Their friendship led to two more Boxers exported to the Philippines. All in all, three offspring of Ch. Doggone Ounce of Gold went to the Philippines. One female be-

Vihabra's Golden Cross Lynx (by Ch. Vihabra's Gold'n Zephyr ex Vihabra's Mariah), bred by James Varano, Becky Anderson, and Virginia Bradley.

Phil. Ch. Vihabra's Arrowhead of Majent (by Ch. Merrilane's Fashion Star ex Merrilane's Touchdown Benroe), littermate to Ch. Stardust and Ch. Mister Gold Dust, bred by Eleanor Linderholm-Wood and Virginia Bradley. Owner, Menardo Jimenez.

came a Philippine Champion. Another female became a Philippine Grand Champion and Top Boxer of the Year. A male became a Grand Champion, Top Boxer and Top Dog, the first time that a Boxer ever achieved that distinction. These Boxers started the current "Boxer Revolution."

The current sponsors of the Boxer breed are Mr. Antonio Aguenza and his daughter Lian of Mainline Boxers, both of whom are totally dedicated to the further advancement of the breed. Mr. Aguenza is the president of the Boxer Club of the Philippines. They have brought in Boxers from well-known breeders such as Virginia and Harry Bradley of Vihabra Boxers and William and Tina Truesdale of Hi-Tech Boxers. He also co-owns several Boxers with Dr. Orlando Sacay.

A recently successful Boxer breeder is Ms. Barbara "Bambi" Gothong of Cebu City, an island city south of Manila. She was president of the Kennel Club of Cebu City during its initial years of existence. She was introduced to Boxers by Mr. Uytengsu. After a few false starts because of some unscrupulous Boxer breeders, yet unperturbed and intent on staying with the breed, she finally found a Boxer to her liking. Phil. Ch. Woodcliff's Gallant Charger, whom she acquired from Mr. Uytengsu, became the first dog of any breed in Cebu to become a Philippine champion. She has since imported Araby Main-Event, sired by Ch. Phil-O-Mon's Endymion out of Araby's Sweetheart on Parade, from Ms. Pat Dollar. He quickly acquired his championship by taking BIS and BISS and was the Number Seven dog of the year.

Boxers of Prominence

The Boxer to gain prominence in the early 1980s was Philippine Grand Ch. Delran's Country Gambler, sired by Ch. Marburl's Joshua out of Ch. Delran's Fancy is My Name. Bred by Ms. Patricia Forney and owned by Mr. Uytengsu, this dark brindle dog dominated the show ring for some time, winning Best of Breed several times and Working Group, the highest achievement of a Boxer at that time. This dog was also a dominant sire, having produced seven champions. This is a very large number considering that no more than 200 Boxers are born yearly and registered in the Philippines. This compares with around 20,000 Boxers in the U.S.

Philippine Grand Ch. Doggone Gold Lace was the lovely fawn puppy bitch that Dr. Sacay acquired from Ms. Duanna Young. She was sired by Ch. Doggone Ounce of Gold with Samantha of Lady's Babes. She caught the attention of dog lovers by winning the biggest all-breed dog show in 1986 under Judge Lynne Lee of Malaysia. It had been nine years since a Boxer had achieved such an honor. "Lacey," as she was fondly called, also won several Bests of Breed under noted judges such as Ms. Margaret Kilburn of the U.S. and Mr. Graham Head of Australia. She became the Top Boxer of 1986 and the Number Four Dog of the Year.

The second Boxer imported by Dr. Sacay was Philippine Grand Ch. Doggone Gold Rally, who was sired by Ch. Doggone Ounce of Gold out of Kameo's Touch of Class. This young Boxer caught the eye of the dog world. His first time out in competition, he took the breed title under well-known judge Ms. Peggy Adamson of the U.S. Since that first show, Rally did not stop winning. He was left behind to improve the Boxer breed in

Phil. Gr. Ch. Delran's Country Gambler (by Am-Int. Ch. Marburl's Joshua ex Ch. Delran's Fancy Is My Name), owner-handled by Douglas Uytengsu.

Phil. Ch. Golden Cross Sheena (by Ch. Shieldmont's Issues N Answers ex Phil. Ch. Golden Cross Stardust).

the Philippines when Dr. Sacay moved to the U.S. Mr. Jose Lim Tan and his daughter Joan, of the Supreme Boxers, continued his show career. Rally became the Top Boxer of 1988. Having won almost all of the all-breed shows in Manila, he became the Top Dog of 1989, the first ever for a Boxer. He unexpectedly died at a very young age, but left behind some outstanding offspring.

Lacey was bred to Rally and produced her only litter of three bitches. Two quickly finished their Philippine championships: Phil. Ch. Golden Cross Susie Q, whose owner was Mr. Jose Lim Tan; and Phil. Ch. Golden Cross Sunflower, whose owners were Mr. Chito Ilagan and his wife Suki. The third bitch, Golden Cross Stardust, was brought to the U.S. by Dr. Sacay when he moved to Virginia. This fawn bitch was bred to Ch. Shieldmont's Issues N Answers. Out of this breeding came Ch. Golden Cross Sheena, who was ABC Winners Bitch and Best of Winners in 1991. This is the first time that a Philippine-born bitch produced a champion Boxer in the U.S.

Am-Phil. Gr. Ch. Interlude Strike Force, bred by Jerry and Dot Bryant, was imported into the Philippines by Mr. Jose Lim Tan, who maintains a Boxer library. This brindle dog, sired by Ch. Araby's Black Watch out of Thanque Yankee Doodle Joy, was to follow in the footsteps of Rally. He became the Top Dog in 1990 and 1991.

Another outstanding dog is Phil. Gr. Ch. Golden Cross Havre de Grace. He was bred by Dr. Orlando Sacay and is owned by Mr. Eduardo Limoanco, past president of the Boxer Club of the Philippines. "Harvey" won the 1991 National Specialty under well-known Judge Alice Downey of the U.S. and the 1992 National Specialty under Judge David Strachan of Australia. Harvey was sired by Ch. Doggone Gold Bandito, a Ch. Doggone Ounce of Gold son, out of a Ch. Marquam Hills Traper and a TuRo daughter, TuRo's Charade of Golden Cross. His breeder is Dr. Orlando Sacay.

The system in the Philippines allows a dog to earn additional points after earning its championship. To earn additional points, the dog must win Best of Breed or Best of Opposite Sex. As soon as the dog earns an additional 25 points for a total of 40 points, the dog acquires a Grand Champion title. The history of Boxers in the Philippines has seen ten dogs earn their Grand Championships.

In addition to the five already mentioned, there was a 1987 Top Boxer Gr. Ch. TuRo's Kodak, sired by Ch. TuRo's Tidal Wave out of Ch. Carlon's Sassy Kate of TuRo, owned by Mr. Jaime Gosiaco. Another male is Gr. Ch. Troy of Manigo Bay, sired by Ch. Jamboree Jet of Lydk out of Tobye. Two other females also attained this coveted title; one was Gr. Ch. Rolhi's Heart Tracer, sired by Ch. Sunset Fonz of 5 T's out of Thanque Molly Brown; and the other is Gr. Ch. Rich Lady Labyrinth, sired by TuRo's Kodak out of Lucky Sugar Say. The last is Gr. Ch. Interlude's Impulse, sired by Ch. Marquam Hills Traper of Turo out of Ch. Interlude's My Chatty Doll. Of the ten Grand Champions, only two are Philippine-born, the rest are U.S. imports.

A recent import, who is taking the dog shows in the Philippines by storm, is Am-Phil. Ch. Hi-Tech Prodigy. With the assurance of Dr. Sacay that the Aguenzas would be a very good show home, William and Tina Truesdale let "Buddy" go to the Philippines. This handsome brindle dog is the son of Ch. Fiero's Tally-Ho Tailo out of Anchic's Passion of Turo. No sooner had he arrived in Manila that he started to win all the points. He acquired his Philippine championship against a very strong field of U.S. imports in five shows. He was on his way to be the next top Boxer of the Philippines.

Phil. Gr. Ch. Doggone Gold Lace (by Int. Ch. Doggone Ounce of Gold ex Samantha of Lady Babes), the top Boxer for 1986, and Phil. Gr. Doggone Gold Rally (by Int. Ch. Doggone Ounce of Gold ex Komio's Touch of Class), the top Boxer for 1988 and 1989, are credited for the Boxer revolution in the Philippines in the 1990s. Owner, Dr. Orlando J. Sacay.

Phil Ch. Clov-Lan's Hi Jack (by Ch. Fiero's Tally-Ho Tailo ex Cinnhree's Baby Doll), bred by H. M. Small and owner Richard Berry, going BIS at the KC of Cebu, Inc.

Am-Phil. Gr. Ch. Interlude's Strike Force (by Ch. Araby's Black Watch ex Thanque Yankee Doodle Joy) with owner Jose Lim Tan and daughter Joan.

Phil. Gr. Ch. Golden Cross Havre de Grace (by Ch. Doggone Gold Bandito ex TuRo's Charade of Gold 'N Cross), bred by Dr. Orlando J. Sacay, and owned by Mr. and Mrs. Eduardo Limoanco, winning the 1991 Philippine National under judge Alice Downey.

Phil. Gr. Ch. Rolhi's Heart Tracer (by Ch. Sunset Fonz of Five T's ex Thanque Molly Brown) with owner Douglas Uytengsu.

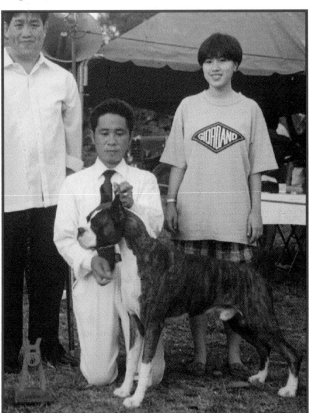

Am-Phil. Ch. Vagabond's Game Plan (by Vagabond's Big Sting ex Black Lace, daughter of Merrilane's Knockout), bred by Patricia Ventry, owned by José Quiros.

The Future of the Breed

From the days of Mr. Douglas Uytengsu to the present, more than ten years have passed. A marked improvement has been seen in the quality of Boxers in the show ring. The list of breeders of dogs entered in shows looks like a who's who of the Boxer breed in the U.S. Dog shows are still dominated by U.S. imports. Unlike before, when unfinished dogs were being imported, now U.S. champions are being brought in more often.

The gene pool of U.S. Boxers in the Philippines, especially the Vendetta line, is rapidly being enlarged. Because of this gene pool, the number of outstanding lo-

cally born Boxers is increasing. It no longer happens that an imported U.S. champion will always win his class. An outstanding local-born would now and then take the points, defeating all the imports. If the trend continues, it would not be surprising for that gene pool to one day produce Boxers of equal, if not better, quality. It may not be too long before the flow of Boxers from the U.S. to Philippines could be reversed.

More recently, four Jacquet Boxer bitches were imported, laying a firm foundation for Jose Quiros of Canlubang Sugar Estate in Laguna, Philippines. Three are Int. Ch. Jacquet's Novarese's daughters and one is a Ch. Goldfield's Noble Pride daughter. These four linebred bitches have been bred to two imports from Merrilane Kennels. The first was Main Event's Law Breaker, a progeny of Ch. Heldenbrand's Jet Breaker who was bred to Ch. Merrilane's Knockout's daughter; and the second was Ch. Vagabond's Game Plan, a Knockout son.

Several outstanding Boxers have been produced from these breedings. The Merrilane line and the Jacquet line have proved to be a successful combination in the U.S. for many years and Mr. Quiros wishes to establish this linebreeding for his kennel. Mr. Quiros is a well-known breeder of thoroughbred horses. He finished Ch. Jacquet's Millennium, Ch. Jacquet's Cloud Dancer and Ch. Jacquet's Cebel, CD.

In March 1993, Mr. Quiros imported the flashy young fawn male, Main Event's Law Breaker, from California. "Thug," as he is called, offered promising potential as a quality sire. He is a son of Ch. Heldenbrand's Jet Breaker, a noted All-Breed Best in Show winner and an American Boxer Club Sire of Merit, and Skytop's Shining Star of K O. She is a dam of three AKC champions and is sired by the Great ABC Top Twenty Winner Ch. Merrilane's Knockout, who is also a Sire of Merit. Many

Am-Phil. Ch. Hi-Tech's Prodigy (by Am-Can. Ch. Fiero's Tally-Ho Tailo ex Ch. Anchic's Passion of TuRo), owned by Antonio and Lian Aguenza and Dr. and Mrs. William Truesdale. Mr. Aguenza is the President of the Boxer Club of the Philippines.

Phil. Ch. Vagabond's Game Plan, out of Jacquet and Merrilane bloodlines, one of two imported sires to enhance Philippine quality. Owner, José Quiros.

other ABC Producers of Merit and American Kennel Club champions appear in Thug's pedigree. Due to the lack of maturity, he was not campaigned for his title in the States, but since his importation to the Philippines, he has gained his championship there.

Still anxious for an American Kennel Club champion stud, Mr. Quiros obtained the young brindle Ch. Vagabond's Game Plan in October of 1993. "Domino," as he is called, combines a strong union of Merrilane and Jacquet bloodlines, showing Ch. Merrilane's Knockout three times, as well as Ch. Jacquet's Chancellor and Jacquet's exceptional Sire of Merit, Ch. Happy Ours Fortune de Jacquet. The sire of Knockout and Happy Ours Fortune is Ch. Merrilane's April Holiday, and Chancellor's sire is the littermate, Ch. Merrilane's April Fashion. Both of these males are noted ABC Sires of Merit. The dam of Knockout is Ch. Jacquet's Mercer, a producer of three champions in this litter. Her dam and her sire are ABC Producers of Merit, Jacquet's Perigal and Ch. April Fashion.

Both Game Plan and Law Breaker will have the opportunity to mate with the quality bitches imported from Jacquet with which Mr. Quiros has further enhanced his breeding stock and program.

Phil. Ch. Main Event's Law Breaker (by Ch. Heldenbrand's Jet Breaker ex Skytop's Shining Star of KO), bred by J.J. Delmar and Reta George, and owned by Jose Quiros.

Phil. Ch. Main Event's Law Breaker, the imported fawn stud dog destined to improve bloodlines in the Philippines. Owner, José Quiros.

THAILAND

German imports have come into Thailand since the 1940s, and most of them were of pet quality. Dog shows in those days were practically unknown. American Boxers came in the late 1980s. The first American Champion import was Delmar's Bet My Boots, out of Keil's Dynasty. American imports gradually increased. Dogs and bitches came from leading kennels and breeders in the U.S., such as TuRo, Salgray, Hollylane, Moonvalley and Interludes Boxers.

Am-Thai. Ch. Thorn Crest Work of Art at Golden Sand, aka "Boomer," with Vajara Naranong, aka "Ted from Thailand."

Boomer, bred by Robert and Alice Helm of Pennsylvania, with Ted, whose interest in Boxers was sparked by author Richard Tomita.

Golden Sand

Vajara Naranong, commonly known as "Ted from Thailand," owned his first Dobe back in 1966. He was very keen in showing the dog rather than breeding in those years.

He became seriously interested in the Boxer when he met Rick Tomita of Jacquet Boxers in 1990 on a business trip to the U.S. From then on, Ted frequently visited leading kennels and breeders in the U.S. He met Edward and Lynda Woodel through an introduction from Mrs. Billie McFadden, and from them he acquired a few Boxer puppies and his foundation bitch, Chappel Legend, a fawn bitch out of Woods End Crown Sable.

Ted attended the ABC in May 1992 and acquired Ch. Thorn Crest's Work of Art from Robert and Alice Helm of Thorn Crest Boxers. Boomer is a deep red fawn dog out of Am-Can. Ch. Salgray's Hijinx O'Thorn Crest ex Thorn Crest Misty Night. Ted brought Boomer back with him to Thailand in May after the ABC. Shown at the Thailand All-Breed Championship Dog Show on October 18, 1992, he was awarded Best in Show by the U.S. judge Mrs. Barbara Jarmoluk. Boomer was shown five times with this impressive record: two all-breed Bests in Show, five Bests of Breed, three Group Ones and two Group Twos.

Benno of Lynpine, English import at four years old, owned by Song Sukampeeranont.

Lynpine

Lynpine Kennels is the name of one of the oldest dog kennels in Thailand. The founder and owner of the kennels is Mr. Song Sukampeeranont, who as a boy loved animals very much, which led him to raise dogs, the pets he best loved. Since boyhood he has been breeding dogs. However, his serious work in dog breeding started only two or three years before the Lynpine Kennels was born.

The first dog he reared was a foreign breed. The dog breed he liked best was the Boxer. Initially, he imported one Boxer puppy from England. Not long after, he ordered another stud dog from the same breeder, Mr. C.A. Walker of Lynpine Kennels in England.

From that time on, gradually Mr. Song ordered several more Boxers from England. He got two from Mrs. Marian Fairbrother of Gremlin Boxers, then a stud dog from Mrs. Hambleton of Marbelton Kennels, two from Mrs. Barbara Greenway of Rayfos Kennels and another three from Mrs. Margaret Wildman of Wildax Boxers.

Song Sukampeeranont, founder of Lynpine, with Chelsea of Lynpine, imported from England.

Lynpine Boxer taking Best in Show at an all-breed show in Thailand.

Thai. Ch. Ellen's Alley Sweet William (by Ch. Summit Views Fuzz Buster ex Shadowglen's Lady Ashley), bred by Becky Durham and owner-handled by Willie Sutan, was the first Boxer champion in Thailand.

BOXERS

IN

SOUTH AMERICA

BY AGNES BUCHWALD

The Boxer has always been one of the most popular breeds in Brazil. Their unequaled temperament and disposition, patience and playfulness with children, guardian abilities, striking appearance and easy-to-care-for coat have granted the Boxer a special place in the heart of Brazilian homes. Even though Boxers have always enjoyed much popularity in Brazil, many ups and downs have occurred along the way when it comes to breeding.

Dog breeding as a whole is deeply affected by national economical circumstances. There is a close relationship between the number and quality of pure-bred dogs and breeders and economical growth rate of the country. Therefore, there have been waves of peak splendor in the Brazilian Boxer panorama, always as a result of positive socio-economic events.

Official Kennel Club registrations date back to as early as the mid-1940s, but due to the reduced number of dogs and breeders, overall quality was quite inconsistent. Dogs were basically intended for use as guard dogs or pets with no major focus on show conformation whatsoever. Dogs related to von Dom and Mazelaine lines were brought in, and these dogs made their mark as Boxers gained growing recognition.

By the mid-1960s, the number and quality of our Boxers were increasing and some outstanding importations resulted in a fantastic time for the breed. Within a

Am-Br. Ch. Salgray's Stuffed Shirt (by Ch. Salgray's Balladeer ex Ch. Salgray's Frolic), owned by Jayme Martinelli and Evelina de Faria Toledo, had a lasting influence on Brazilian Boxers in the Southwest in the mid-1960s.

Am-Br. Ch. Brayshaw's Hustler (by Ch. Brayshaw's Beau Dandy ex Howdell's Ginger Snap), winning on this festive occasion in Brazil in the mid-1960s. Hustler, bred by R. Heller and owned by Charlotte Brayshaw and Victor and Anita Clemente, became a prominent sire and multi-BIS winner.

Br. Ch. Salgray's Miss Minx (by Ch. Salgray's Ambush ex Salgray's Diamond Lil), owned by Pent Kennels.

short period of time some remarkable specimens were imported and the strong base of the Brazilian Boxer breeding was established.

In the South, Treceder stock was used to produce compact dogs with strong square muzzles, wide bites and tight cat feet. In the North, the importation of Ch. Brayshaw's Hustler, a top winner in the USA who was bred by Charlotte Brayshaw and Victor and Anita Clemente, imprinted substance and outstanding gait to the dogs of that area. Later, he spread these features throughout the country by being a highly requested and often used stud. Hustler was a multi-BIS winner in Brazil.

In the Southwest, a heavy Salgray influence was noted with the importation of five dogs from that line. Two of them, however, deserve special mention here: Ch. Salgray's Stuffed Shirt and Ch. Barday's Country Squire (an Ambush son), both owned by Jayme and Evelina Martinelli of the Pent Kennels Boxer Fame in Sao Paulo. Besides their outstanding show records, their major influence in establishing a well-defined breeding program in Brazil is unforgettable and undeniable. These two dogs are behind the foundation stock of many of the major kennels of today. They passed on their heads, style, elegance and conformation.

Ch. Salgray's Stuffed Shirt was shown only ten times in Brazil with the amazing record of ten Bests in Show. Many of his daughters were bred to Squire with excellent results.

A most successful experience was the breeding of Squire to Ch. Ashgate Rubens, an English import daughter of the top producing Ch. Seefeld's Picasso. Ch. Manakri's Aristophanes was the most outstanding dog of this combination; a dog that could well be a top winner today. He was also the sire of many champions.

Squire sired other important dogs as well—bred to a Treceder background bitch he produced BIS Ch. Gabril De Majorca, who established the Majorca Kennel of Parana.

Another Squire daughter, Ch. Funny Girl of Pent Kennels, was the foundation bitch to Hexastar Kennels of Agnes Buchwald and sons. While Ch. Happy Girl of Pent Kennels (Squire ex a Fashion Hint daughter) was the foundation of Follow Me Boxers of the late Lilian Correa Do Carmo in Rio De Janeiro.

Continuity of such a bright start was provided by the import of other outstanding producers. Ch. Pinebrook's Trade Mark, imported by the Martinellis and owned by Hexastar, gave a new strength to the breed. Among his many champion get is Ch. Quo Vadis Augustus Caesar, the top winner and producer that gave the Quo Vadis Kennel name of Ruth Vieira, Rio De Janeiro, a great start.

Int-Br. Ch. Quo Vadis Augustus Caesar, owned by Ruth Vieira, winning under American judge Eleanor Haeberle, gave the Quo Vadis Kennel a victorious start. Sired by Ch. Pinebrook's Trademark.

Another remarkable import was Ch. Arriba's Command Performance owned by Hexastar and Domingos Aliperti Jr. He had a profound influence, both in the show ring and as a Sire of Merit in the late '70s and early '80s.

Many Brazilian breeders received imports from Merrilane, Aracrest, Tudosal, 5-T's and TuRo. By that time such imports, as well as their fine get, were already being used and highly noted by breeders from other South American countries.

Also at that time history was made as the first Brazilian-bred Boxer finished an American championship: Am-Br-Urug. Ch. Hexastar's in Legacy of Ruhlend finished with a five-point major at the Central Indiana Boxer Club. Another five Brazilian-bred Boxers finished in America, all bred by Hexastar.

A more recent influence to Brazilian breeding came via Rio de Janeiro with the importation of an outstanding producer. Ch. Jacquet Gaspard Ad Summus, the sire of many top winning champions, is also respected for being the start of the Jacquet line in Brazil. Other Jacquet winners and producers followed him; their influence is seen in the rings of today. Jacquet dogs are present in many fine present-day Brazilian kennels.

Am-Br. Ch. Jacquet's Dreams of Loriga (by Int. Jacquet's Cloud Dancer ex Jacquet's Madison), owned by Loriga Boxers and handled by Marcelo Chagas. Anitra Cuneo of the United States gives this young bitch her first all-breed BIS at the Paulist KC anniversary show in 1992.

Am-Br-Int. Ch. Arriba's Command Performance (by Ch. Arriba's Knight Revue ex Ch. Salgray's Beau Cherie), bred by Ted Fickes, became an all-breed and specialty BIS winner and one of the most influential sires in Brazil.

Ch. Ad Summus Harmony of Quo Vadis was a top winning Gaspard daughter in Rio de Janeiro while Ch. Jacquet's Mago El Encanto, bred by Richard Tomita and Carol Shea and owned by Dr. Roberto Bozerra of Ceara, is the top winning and producing Boxer in the Northwest.

Ch. Jacquet's Dreams of Loriga, owned by Beatriz and Gregorio Dotorovici and Lineu de Paula Maohado, co-owners of Loriga Boxers, was Number One Boxer in Brazil in 1992. She quickly finished her American title in 1993 after going Reserve Winners Bitch at the ABC National Specialty. Loriga Boxers are also the proud owners of the Number One Boxer in Brazil in 1993, Ch. Breezewood's Ace of Diamonds; and the Number One Boxer in Brazil in 1994, Ch. Thanque Tic Toc Time. These Loriga Boxers are all multi-BIS winners.

Brazilian breeders are thankful for the help and support of American breeders, and they look forward to a continuous exchange of information and bloodstock in order to maintain Brazil as one of the leading centers for quality Boxers in South America.

Br. Ch. Quo Vadis Julius Caesar (by Ch. Paragon's Nite Ryder ex Ch. Claudio's Sunset of Fire), owned by Henrique Magno Ferreira.

Quo Vadis Kennel began by acquiring a fawn male puppy named Gregorio. This was in 1972, and since that time the kennel has bred more than 50 litters. The basis of the breeding program was a bitch from the Treceder line. This bitch produced my Quo Vadis's top dog ,Ch. Quo Vadis Augustus Caesar, who, under Mrs. Eleanor Haeberle, became the only South American Boxer champion (South American specialty show) until recently in Brazil. He was also the sire of several champions, including the outstanding bitch Ch. Claudio's Sunset of Fire (Abednego's granddaughter) that produced our famous J litter. The star of that litter, Ch. Quo Vadis Julius Caesar, won the top Brazilian ranking in 1980 as the best Working dog and third of all breeds.

Just after that, Ruth Cavalheiro Vieira imported a very beautiful bitch, Ch. Jacquet's Harmony of Quo Vadis, who very quickly became a Brazilian champion and dam of Ch. Quo Vadis Archimedes Ad Summus and Ch. Ad Summus Helena Quo Vadis.

Quo Vadis Demostenes (by Am-Br. Ch. Breezewoods Ace of Diamonds ex Br. Ch. Quo Vadis Zuleica), owned by Ruth Vieira.

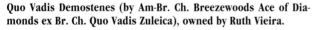

Br. Ch. Quo Vadis Archimedes (by Br. Ch. Quo Vadis Julius Caesar ex Br. Ch. Jacquet's Harmony of Quo Vadis).

Br. Ch. Claudio's Sunset of Fire, sired by Br. Ch. Augustus Caesar out of a granddaughter of Abednego with Ruth Cavalheiro Vieira.

Br. Ch. Quo Vadis Zuleika, bred by Quo Vadis Boxers who consider her "Jacquet made in Brazil," a compliment to author Richard Tomita.

Br. Ch. Jacquet's Harmony of Quo Vadis, sired by Ch. Happy Ours Fortune de Jacquet and imported from Richard Tomita, became the dam of champions in Brazil for owner Ruth Cavalheiro Vieira.

Br. Ch. Ad Summus Camila, bred by Quo Vadis Boxers.

Br. Ch. Sula of Iguassu with Magdalena Aranha, breeder of over 65 champions in her 55 years in the breed. She is pictured here at age 74.

Br. Gr. Ch. Cindy of Iguassu (by Int. Ch. Arriba's Command Performance ex Ch. Shelly of Iguassu), owned by Magdalena Aranha.

Br. Ch. Loriga's Diamonds of Fire, owned by Monica Caiado.

Am-Br. Ch. Hexastar's American Graffiti (by Int. Ch. Arriba's Command Performance ex Br. Ch. To'Rini's Allegria's Sequel), owned by Helio and Marcia Baldi, was a multiple all-breed BIS winner.

Am-Br. Ch. Jacquet's Grande Lido (by Ch. Goldfield's Eagle Dancer ex Jacquet's Honey Samantha), with Lea Palhares-Viveiros de Modena.

Ch. Jacquet's Toi of B-G, owned by Walter Steurer of Warena Boxers. (Ch. Goldfield's Dorian de Jacquet ex Ch. B-G's Lili Jacquet)

Br. Ch. Jacquet's Lion King (by Am. Ch. Jacquet's Greggson), owned by Dr. Marcezo Motta.

Ch. Warena's Aida (by Int. Ch. Jacquet's Novarese ex Ch. Jacquet's Bright Penny), top-winning BIS bitch handled by Divoney Rasera, owned and bred by Walter Steurer.

Ch. Jacquet's Bright Penny, owned by Walter Steurer of Warena Boxers.

Br. Ch. Jacquet's Harmony of Quo Vadis, sired by Ch. Happy Ours Fortune de Jacquet, owned by Ruth Vieira.

Br. Ch. Jacquet's Gaspard Ad Summus (by Ch. Jacquet's Gaspard ex Jacquet's Cinder), bred by Richard Tomita and owned by Joao Carneiro, was the top-winning Boxer in Brazil during the mid 1980's.

Br. Ch. Sunhill's Xul (by Argos del Shehuen ex Sunhill's Peppermint), bred by Dario Fogolin.

Judge Rick Tomita poses proudly with Gr. Ch. Dellie Dugran and handler Monica Bobar winning BOB from the Puppy class at the Boxer Specialty of Rio de Janiero.

Upper left: Am-Br. Ch. Breezewood's Ace of Diamonds (by Ch. Berena's Tribute to Fa-Fa ex Ch. Breezewood's One Mo' Time), winning BIS-all breed at the Brazil Kennel Club, under English judge Mrs. Pauline Gibbs. Owned by Loriga Boxers.

Lower left: Ch. Warena's Aida (by Int. Ch. Jacquet's Novarese ex Br. Ch. Jacquet's Bright Penny), owned by Walter Steurer. Top winning Boxer 93-94.

Upper right: Gioconda G. G. Di Fiore Bella (by Br. Ch. Jacquet's Gaspard Ad Summus ex Gloria dos Novos Tempos).

Lower right: Ch. Candle Light's Hexastar Kitaro (by Am-Br. Ch. Laurel Hills Mr. Fonz V. Rico ex Merrilanes Joie De Jacquet), owned by Alberto Bonfiglioli.

Br. Ch. Thanque Tic Toc Tyme, owned by Loriga Boxers of Rio De Janeiro, was the top-winning Boxer of Brazil in 1994.

Ch. Candle Light Hexastar Concot, winning Best in Sweepstakes at the Boxer Club of Estado De Sao Paulo, under judge Rick Tomita.

Am-Br. Ch. Hexastar's Royal Mark (by Br. Ch. Pinebrook's Trademark ex Br. Ch. To'Rini's Allegria's Sequel) at the New York Boxer Club Specialty.

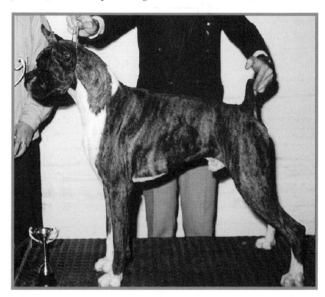

Br-Urg. Ch. Hexastar's Sundance Kid is pictured winning BOB in Uruguay.

Am-Br. Ch. Merrilane's Kiss of Fire (by Ch. Merrilane's Holiday Fashion ex Merrilane's Star Boarder), owned by Hexastar Kennels.

Br. Ch. Bee-Mike's Keepsake (by Ch. Arriba's Footloose ex Ch. Bee-Mike's Grand Illusion), bred by Betty and Bruce Mentzer.

Ch. Gold Medal's First Class, owned by Magdalena Aranha.

Ch. Bright of Talahassee (by Bach von Steinwald ex Pheonix Di Steinwald), bred by Gil Quadrado and owned by Hilton Imperatrice.

Ch. Successful With Emy Lever, bred by Carlos G. Swer of Argentina.

Br. Gr. Ch. Ronald Dos Novos Tempos, bred by Jose and Miriam da Silva and owned by Y. Pressa.

Above: Gr. Ch. Dellie Dugran (by Br. Ch. Successful With Emy Lever ex Ad Summus G. M. Tarcila) with handler Monica Borba. *Below:* Gr. Ch. Valencia do Virarvaque.

Am-Br-Int. Ch. Notelrac's Sundown (by Ch. Notelrac's Notorious ex Notelrac's Serenade), bred by São Luis, was a multiple BOB and Group winner.

Above: Am-Br. Ch. Crossroad's Up in Smoke (by Ch. Talisman's Vigilante ex Ch. Vandowns Black Velvet), handled by Marcelo Chagas, was a Group winner in the United States and a BIS winner in Brazil. *Below:* Br. Ch. Argos de Nefertite with handler Monica Borba.

Above: Br. Gr. Ch. Valencia do Virarvaque pictured going BOB at the Kennel Club Paulista Festival do Caõ in Brazil. *Below:* Ch. Bolota do Porto dos Cabritos.

Am-Br. Ch. TuRo's Gamine of Hyde Park (by Ch. Marquam Hill's Traper of TuRo ex Ch. Missy's Debutante), owned by Jayme and Evelina Martinelli, was a multiple-BIS winner.

Int. Gr. Ch. Roque Santeiro Comete da Fortaleza (by Merrilane's Comet To Arriba ex Suellyn Di Primio's), owned by Tito and Nicholas Flores, has ten BIS wins and was the first International Champion Boxer in Brazil.

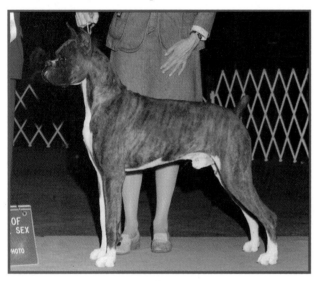

Am-Br-Int. Ch. Hexastar's in Legacy of Ruhlend (by Br. Ch. Burke of Cair Paravel ex Br. Ch. Ruhlend's Contessa of Abaro) was the first Brazilian-bred Boxer to obtain an American title.

Br. Ch. Hexastar's Legend of Xanadu (by Ch. Merrilane's Silver 'n Gold ex Am-Br-SoAm-Int. Ch. Merrilane's Kiss of Fire), finishing his Brazilian title.

Int. Gr. Ch. Dartagna Fire Fields (by Br-Int. Ch. Roque Santeiro Comete Fortaleza ex Tita da Fortaleza), owned by Luiz Nazareno dos Santos, handled by Tito Flores.

Br. Ch. Valencia do Virarvaque, winning an all-breed BIS.

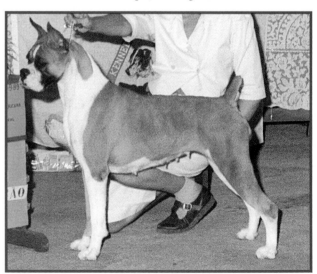

Am-Br-Int. Ch. Merrilane's Frolic of Passion (by Int. Ch. Scher-Khoun's Shadrack ex Merrilane's Mad Passion, CD), taking BOS at the Riverside Kennel Club.

Br. Ch. Merrilane's Fiesta Fortune, bred by Eleanor Linderholm-Wood, owned by Evelina Toledo and Jayme Martinelli, was a multiple BIS winner.

Am-Br-Int. Ch. Merrilane's Kiss of Fire (by Ch. Merrilane's Holiday Fashion ex Merrilane's Star Boarder), owned by Hexastar Kennels, was a multi all-breed and specialty BIS winner.

Am-Br-Int. Gr. Ch. Hexastar's Native Dancer of Ruhlend (by Int. Ch. Arriba's Command Performance ex Br. Ch. Ruhlend's Contessa of Abaro) , bred by Hexastar Kennels, was the Best Brazilian-bred Dog for 1982.

VENEZUELA

BY JEANNY CANDAMO

The Boxer in Venezuela started with the registration of dogs imported from the U.S. by Lawrence and Gene Neuman in June 1952. Neuman was active in the founding of the *Federacion Canina de Venezuela*. He and his Caribe Kennels led for a long time in our Boxer history. He imported nice dogs from the U.S. and he did win a lot with them in the few shows we had in those days. After the 1960s and the lead of the Caribe Kennels and the Venezuelan-bred Alpinas Jerry, came a small downfall of the breed.

In the '70s, some nice Boxers were seen, like Ch. Kaiser's Hombre, imported by Dr. Jaime Pinto from the U.S., who won some Breed and Group placements from 1972–1975. From 1975–1977 another U.S. import, Ch. Saxon's of Bit of Blarny of Rokays, was multi-Group placer with one Reserve BIS.

Into the decade of the '80s, Boxers started to grow once again. Some new kennels that developed in these years and are still breeding some nice dogs include: Silvia Perez's Silper Kennels, Norfay Kennels, Luis Gallegos's Kahlua's Kennels, Doris and Oscar Rivero's Ricardom and Caesar Pulido's Caesar's Palace Kennels. In addition, Dr. Jaime Pinto, always interested in the breed, bought and imported from the U.S. in a co-ownership with Richard Guevara Ch. Heritage Star Catcher, who became the first Boxer to win BIS in the decade under judge Max Magder from Canada.

Silper Kennels started with an imported bitch from the U.S., Ch. Harlock's Truda Queen, born in November 1979, winner of multiple Group placements from 1980–1984.

Norfay Kennels had a few Boxers in the limelight and they continue to breed fine dogs today.

Kahlua's Kennels, after a few national breedings, acquired an import from Arizona who has made a mark on Boxer history. A fawn bitch, Ven-PR-Col-DomRep-SoAm. Ch. Richaire's Solid Gold, has been a BIS winner and produced a multiple-BIS daughter, Ven-PR. Ch. Kahlua's Krauss of Wyoming, out of an import brought in by David Taurel, Ch. TuRo's Mandate of Will-Ves. Kahlua's import from the U.S., Ch. Triple Crown's Midnite Gambler, sired some nice puppies and continues to bring success to Kahlua's Kennels.

Caesar's Palace Kennels, after trying some imports from the States and Puerto Rico, came up with a pretty fawn bitch, Mex-Ven. Ch. Jacquet's Maxime lo Monaco, who was campaigned in Mexico with *mucho* success.

Boxers in Venezuela, as you can see, have developed a lot from the early days. I did not find any record of Boxers in obedience, but we all know they are very popular in the Venezuelan homes as guard dogs and as very good friends for the kids.

Ven-PR-Col-Dom Rep-SoAm. Ch. Richaire's Solid Gold (by Am-Can. Ch. Strawberry's Caballero ex Richaire's Christmas Love), whelped April 12, 1986, owned by Doris, Oscar and Ricardo Risero.

Caribe

Gene and Larry Neuman of Key Biscayne, Florida owned their first two Boxers in Paris in 1948. Both were the traditional "German" type—fawn with black mask, white mark on chest. When they returned to the States, the male was given to a breeder in California and an Army officer friend took the female to Guam. When Gene joined her husband in Caracas, Venezuela in June 1949, she brought with her Mazelaine's Diplomat, so named because he was going abroad. A fawn male with flashy markings, he was Best in Show at the first organized all-breed dog show in Caracas in 1950 at the Valle Arriba Golf Club. The judges were Venezuelan and American fanciers and breeders.

Ch. Linnay's Conquest came to Caracas from California in 1951. He was Working Group winner in the U.S. He competed against Ch. Bang Away of Sirrah Crest in 1950 in Chicago. The judge, John Wagner (Mazelaine) gave him Reserve to Bang Away. They subsequently met with Nate Levine and Bang Away in New York—probably after one of the shows on the Dodge Estate.

Ch. Linnay's Conquest became a champion in Cuba, Canada and Venezuela. He had a Best in Show in Mexico City in 1951 and Reserve Best in Show in Cueranavaca the following weekend. Wil Judy, owner of *Dog World*, gave "Chaunsee" (his call name) a certificate of recognition for his show wins in international competition.

Ven. Ch. Alpina's Jerry (by Am-Ven. Ch. Edymain's Sky Rocket ex Ch. Flintwood's Beads Del Caribe), bred by Maria de Peter and owned by Guillermo Gorrin Hernandez.

Ven. Ch. Triple Crown's Midnite Gambler, bred by C. Sylvester and R. Provost, at two years old.

The Neumans also imported two Venezuelan bitches to breed to Bang Away. They bred many champions there: Best in Show, Best Puppy Bred in Venezuela, Best Bred in Venezuela, etc. They bought Ch. Flintwood's Beads del Caribe as a puppy from the Flints. She had a beautiful head and sound body. There were two outstanding puppies from her first litter—Jolly Roger del Caribe and Tinker Bell del Caribe.

Ch. Berena's Tribute to FaFa, acquired by the Neumans in the late 1980's, had a great record and for a time was on the road to being Best Working Dog of the Year in 1990 when a handler's conflict of interest interfered.

The Neumans were instrumental and co-founded the Federation of Canine Clubs in Venezuela (Federacion Canina de Venezuela) in 1952, along with other breeders and exhibitors. Gene was president of the Boxer Club and editor of the *Kennel Gazette*.

Above: Three dogs bred and owned by Doris, Oscar and Ricardo Rivero, being judged by Mr. Norton Moore. *Below left:* Ven. Ch. Hardlock's Truda Queen of Silper Kennels.

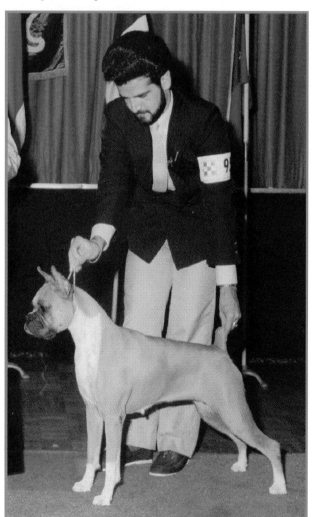

Kahlua's Kalamity Jane (by Ven. Ch. TuRo's Mandate of Will-Ves ex Ven-PR-SoAm. Ch. Richaire's Solid Gold), whelped October 19, 1991 and bred and owned by Doris, Oscar and Ricardo Rivero.

Ven-PR. Ch. Kahlua's Krauss of Wyoming (by Ven. Ch. TuRo's Mandate of Will-Ves ex Ven-PR-SoAm. Ch. Richaire's Solid Gold), whelped June 28, 1988, bred and owned by Doris, Oscar and Ricardo Rivero.

Kahlua's Kalamity Jane (by Ven-Col. Ch. TuRo's Mandate of Will-Ves ex Ven-PR-Col-Dom-SoAm. Ch. Richaire's Solid Gold), winning Best Puppy in Show under judge Norton Moore.

Finishing on the same day are Am-Ven. Ch. Strawberry's Star Gazer (by Ch. Telstar's Starmaker, SOM ex Ch. Strawberry's Scintillation) and Am-Ven. Ch. Strawberry's Tango (by Am-Can. Ch. Strawberry's Caballero ex Ch. Strawberry's Blythe Spirit), bred by Bruce Voran, both owned by Oscar Rivero and his family.

Mex-Ven. Ch. Jacquet's Maxine Lo Monaco, owned by Cesar Pulido and Richard Tomita.

Ven-Col. Ch. TuRo's Mandate of Will-Ves (by Ch. TuRo's Tidal Wave ex Ch. TuRo's Caress), bred by Roberto and Elizabeth Escove and owned by David Taurel.

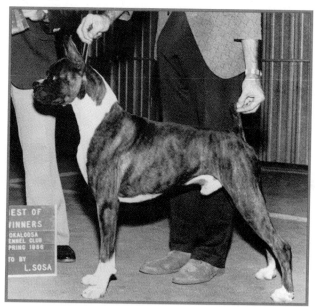

ARGENTINA

The author is greatly indebted to Ruben Oscar Ledesma and his fine book *Breviario de la Raza Boxer en la Argentina* for the information about the Boxer breed in his country.

The first Boxers competed in conformation in Argentina in 1913. All five Boxers in competition were owned by Mr. Enrique Madariaga, who is credited with being the first Boxer enthusiast in Argentina. Within two years, in 1915, one of the Boxers Mr. Madariaga bred became the first Boxer to obtain a championship. His name was simply "Box" and he was owned by Mrs. Raquel C. A. Elejalde. Box was whelped on December 8, 1913.

Don Von Grenzwall, whelped on September 4, 1936, was the first Boxer to win BIS at the Kennel Club of Argentina's 20th Anniversary Show.

In 1937, the Boxer made history in Argentina. At the 20th Anniversary Show of the Kennel Club Argentino, Don Von Grenzwall became the first Boxer to take a Best in Show award. This historical dog was owned by Mr. R. Peralta Martinez and the visiting English judge was Hamilton Adams.

The *Associacion Argentina de Criadores de Boxer* (Boxer Breeders Association) became the first Boxer club in Argentina in 1958. Its founding president was Sebastian Sanchez. The following year, on March 28–29, an entry of 65 Boxers competed in the first national specialty. Chenguiz Gipsy of Molsberg, owned by J. Aron, won the Breed under judge Ove C. Moltke.

Arg. Ch. Bosco of Keniglen, whelped August 5, 1958, was a multiple-BIS winner.

Arg. Gr. Ch. Tago Del Pozzetto (by Arg. Ch. Bosco of Keniglen ex Am-Arg. Ch. Souvenir of Cross Acres), owned by Antonio Perez, won numerous BIS awards and was the first Grand Champion Boxer in Argentina.

The golden era of the Argentine Boxer began in 1960. A revised parent club known as the Boxer Club Argentina, with Mr. Moltke as the new president, ushered in an exciting period for the growing breed in Argentina. That same year, 1960, the BCA held its first specialty. Ninety dogs participated under judge Erwin W. Rathsam of Brazil. By 1961, the BCA offered the first obedience trial for Boxers.

We acknowledge the important breeders who began producing quality Boxers to make this era truly "golden." They are Jayme Bedoya, Walter Nitsche, Ove Moltke, Martinez Reboul, Ernesto Balbian, Juan Minguillon and Osvaldo Adet, among others.

The most important Boxer in Argentina's history, Arg. Gr. Ch. Treceder's Stampede (by Ch. Treceder's Happy Hiker ex Ch. Willow Round's Protege) won an amazing 19 BIS all-breeds, 8 Reserve BIS all-breeds, 6 BIS specialties, and 5 Reserve BIS specialties.

The importation of Ch. Treceder's Ten Strike in 1968 from the United States created a major impact on Argentine Boxers. This spectacular dog, sired by Ch. Treceder's Sequel out of Treceder's Laughter, owned by J. Minguillon, became an all-breed Best in Show winner in Argentina as well as in Brazil and Uruguay. Ten Strike was the top producer all-breeds in 1968.

Arg. Gr. Ch. Memorylane's Gulliver (by Int. Ch. Millan's Fashion Hint ex Memorylane's Rosebud), a Canadian import, won numerous BIS awards, became the top dog all-breeds in 1977 and was an influential sire.

From the same kennel arrived Ch. Treceder's Stampede in the following year. Stampede is still recognized as the most important Boxer in Argentina's history. His sire was Ch. Treceder's Happy Hiker out of Willow Round's Protege. Owned by Balbiani Podesta, Stampede stampeded through 19 all-breed Bests in Show and 6 national specialties!

A clear trend toward the American Boxer was established through the influence of these two Treceder dogs. Argentine judges began praising the flashier dogs instead of the plainer ones they had favored previously. Further imports from America, or dogs sired by American champions, flooded Argentina.

Imported by Mr. and Mrs. Bruick from Canada in 1974, Ch. Memorylane's Gulliver became the top dog all-breeds in 1977, after winning 14 all-breed BIS and 35 Group Ones. Gulliver was also an influential producer.

Arg-Can. Gr. Ch. Donessle's Whistle Stop (by Am-Can. Ch. Donessle's Diplomat ex Can. Ch. Donessle's Foxfire), bred by Ted and Jean Reed, won BIS awards in Canada and Argentina.

Arg-Br-Ur-SoAm-Per. Gr. Ch. Sunhill Goliath, bred in Argentina, was the top Boxer in Argentina in 1988 and 1989 and was also a champion in Brazil, Uruguay and Peru.

Arg-SoAm-Ur. Gr. Ch. Apolo De Rumbo Kennel was an important homebred champion with numerous BIS awards.

Am-Arg. Ch. TuRo's Allure (by Ch. Marquam Hill's Traper of TuRo ex TuRo's Katrina of Cross Bar), owned by the influential breeder Monica Riccio of Buenos Aires, Argentina.

In the 1980s, the most remarkable influence on the breed came from the work of Yanquetruz-Shamrock Kennels, owned by Mrs. Graciela Baudrix and Mrs. Monica Riccio. Most notable is the Arg-Gr-Uru-Ch. of the Americas Yanquetruz Intra, Producer of Merit.

The presence of the FCI World Dog Show in Argentina in 1993 showed the world how marvelous dog shows can be in South America. The Boxer judge at this event was Mrs. Michele Billings of the USA—her choice was Blue Moon of Willsam's, owned by Gotanegra Benavides.

American imports have continued into the 1990s, as breeder-fancier Carlos Garcia purchased a champion bitch from Hi-Tech and a fawn male from Jacquet. The male became Am-Arg-Uru-Int. Ch. Jacquet's Top Dream Too, ranking Number One Boxer and Working Dog in Argentina. Later, Garcia also imported the '96 Grand Prize Futurity bitch, Ch. C-Era's Dar's Dejavu, to further his breeding program.

Other Jacquet dogs have gone to Argentina and proven exceptional. Mr. Nestor Gonzalez Sueyro imported a linebred male from Rick Tomita, Ch. Jacquet's Leo. Breeder Nelly Reggiani of Buenos Aires and well-known handler Hector Lopez turned many heads with the flashy show dog and promising dam Gr. Ch. Jacquet's Beau Monde Big Change.

Arg-Ur-Chi. Gr. Ch. Shamrock's Royal Secret won the first Argentina Boxer Club National, as well as many other BIS awards.

Arg-Ur-SoAm. Gr. Ch. Yanquetrez Indra was a Grand Champion in Argentina and also an influential sire for many years.

Arg. Gr. Ch. Jacquet's Beau Monde Big Change (by Int. Ch. Jacquet's Novarese ex Jacquet's Sweet Sensation), bred by Richard Tomita and Angel Perez, and owned by Nelly Reggiani.

Arg-Am-SoAm-Par-Int. Gr. Ch. Blue Moon's of Willsam's, a homebred champion, became an FCI World Champion in 1993.

Right: Arg-Am. Gr. Ch. Jacquet's Top Dream Too (by Int. Ch. Jacquet's Novarese ex Ch. Jacquet's Ruby Slippers), the Number One Boxer and Working Dog in Argentina, owned and handled by Diego Garcia.

Bottom left: Arg. Ch. Jacquet's Agatha, owned by Mr. Jose Hernandez and Mrs. Susana Sagula.

Bottom right: Arg. Ch. Jacquet's Thommen's (by Ch. Jacquet's Greggson ex Jacquet's Ansele), another Jacquet Boxer shown beautifully in Argentina.

Am-Arg-Int. Ch. Jacquet's Top Dream Too (by Int. Ch. Jacquet's Novarese ex Jacquet's Ruby Slipper), bred by Richard Tomita and handled by Diego Garcia, was the number-one Boxer of Argentina in 1994 and finished his American title with three five-point majors on the 1995 Florida show circuit. In 1997, Diego Garcia brought him out of retirement to reclaim his number-one status in Brazil!

Arg. Ch. Argon De Crisferjon De Wright, handled by Hector Lopez.

Arg. Ch. Merrilane's Right Time (by Ch. Merrilane's Knockout ex Merrilane's Just In Time), bred by Merrilane Kennels and Cindy Silva Hernandez and owned by Hector Lopez.

Arg-Ur. Ch. Old Pal's Babette (by Sajac's Savage Arrow ex Nicol's Gaby) was the top Boxer of Argentina in 1990 and 1991 and the Top Working Group Dog.

Arg. Ch. Agata, owned by Hector Lopez, is finishing her Argentine title at the Argentina Boxer Club National in 1994.

BOXERS
IN
SOUTH AFRICA

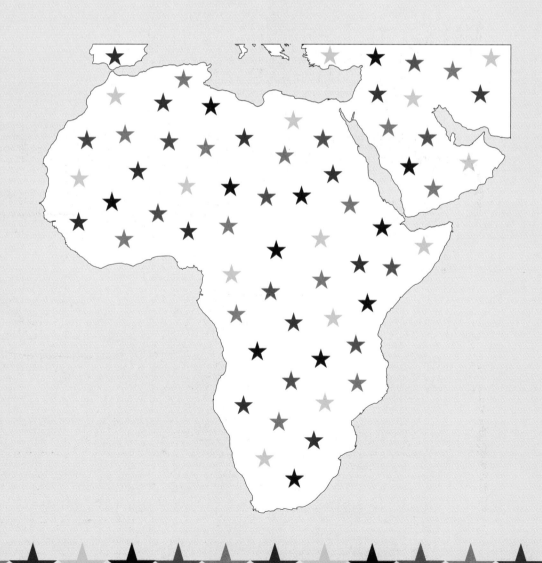

BOXERS IN SOUTH AFRICA

BY CHARLES FORTUNE, FRANZ AND
UTE FUGLISTER

The decade of the 1950s was a very exciting time for Boxers in South Africa. This was largely due to a number of stalwart people who loved the breed and were prepared to advance it in the best way they knew how. Among these were Kelvin and Yvonne Clegg, Bill Duff, Maurice Vane, Bernard Volgelnest, Peter and Daphne Harris, Alf and Louise De Young, Gordon and Ellie Wilson, Basil Allen, Mark Marincowitz, Des and Jeanette Ward Smith and Charles and Pixie Fortune.

It should be remembered that the 1950s saw the rising star of Ch. Bang Away of Sirrah Crest in the U.S. This dog's wins had a profound impact on those of us endeavoring to breed better Boxers. Even a remote place like South Africa, which was governed by a Kennel Union (which regarded itself as an extension of the Kennel Club of England), felt the impact of the sensational Bang Away and his Best in Show wins.

After the Second World War, a number of Boxers were imported, chiefly by Kelvin Clegg of N'Duna Kennels. Kelvin's role in the advent of the Boxer in South Africa is legendary. Those of us who knew him were proud of his friendship and grateful for all the advice and encouragement he gave so freely. Kelvin was a breeder at heart, whether it was Boxers or canaries, which he enjoyed until the day he died.

BOXER CLUB OF SOUTHERN AFRICA

The Boxer Club of Southern Africa began in the 1950s as an alternative to dog shows held under the auspices of the South African Kennel Union (SAKU), which was the official dog-governing body in South Africa. Many Boxer club members felt that the Boxer was seen to best advantage with cropped ears.

SA. Ch. Drum Rock's Smokin' Joe of Tortuga (by SA. Ch. Drum Rock's Diplomat ex Eldorat's Tess of Drum Rock), bred by Mark Steele and owned by Johan Keiser, is the all-time best South African Boxer with 46 BOB, 17 Group firsts, 15 Group seconds, 5 RBIS and 11 BIS!

The SAKU rules for showing forbade the exhibition of South African-bred Boxers with cropped ears, though imported dogs with cropped ears could be shown. This was an extension of the sentiment of the Kennel Club. As a result, many members of the Boxer club cropped their Boxers' ears anyway, knowing full well that they would not be able to show under the SAKU. After some years it was realized that many outstanding dogs were not being considered in serious breeding programs as they were not seen in the show ring.

The club then organized "clinics" for Boxers in which dogs with cropped ears could be shown. These clinics were staged under the auspices of the Boxer Club of Southern Africa and were in fact what we would regard as a specialty show, except no championship points were awarded. The clinics drew wonderful entries and were soon outdrawing regular shows held by the SAKU. Often overseas judges were invited, and I can recall one show in 1955 when Maxwell Riddle drew an entry of more than 100 Boxers. Riddle was very impressed with the quality of the dogs and offered the opinion that there were better quality dogs in the clinic than he had seen the previous day at an all-breed SAKU championship show.

Ch. Rojan's Columbine at five years old.

Col. Ch. Balcony Rock's Take Five (by Ch. Brayshaw's Masquerader ex Flintwood's Banned in Boston), bred by Charles and Pixie Fortune, owned by Carlos J. Echavarria, winning a puppy class under judge Ted Wurmser.

THE FEDERATION IS BORN

These clinics continued with great success without reprimand from the SAKU. The Boxer Club and the SAKU were in a state of coexistence, except the Boxer Club kept drawing greater and greater entries. In 1959, SAKU introduced a new rule whereby they would not allow the showing of imported dogs with cropped ears beginning in 1960. This new rule incurred the full wrath of the Boxer community as people felt that this would discourage the importation of good breeding stock from countries like the U.S., Germany and Holland. This rule impacted on other breeds as well. Several conferences were held to persuade the Kennel Union from passing this rule without avail. When the rule was passed, the Boxer Club of Southern Africa disassociated themselves

from the SAKU and thus the Federation of Boxer Clubs of Southern Africa was born.

The Federation of Boxer Clubs of Southern Africa was established in November 1960 to provide a controlling body, based on democratic principles, for the Boxer breed in South Africa. Until that time all Boxers were registered with the local all-breed controlling body (SAKU), which did not (and still does not) permit the registration or exhibition of cropped-eared dogs. The majority of Boxer owners and exhibitors at the time felt that owners should be allowed to decide for themselves whether to crop or not. This, combined with a need for more direct representation and better control over the destiny of the breed, finally led to the formation of an independent organization. A number of Boxer fanciers however elected to remain with the all-breed body.

Col. Ch. Sarah Olen's Luther (by Ch. Flintwood's Linebacker ex Ch. Rococo's Cinderella), bred by Gordon and Doris Laukes and owned by Carlos J. Echavarria.

At present the Federation comprises seven affiliated Boxer clubs with a total membership of approximately 650, of which some 250 are registered breeders. Control of the organization is vested in a governing body composed of elected delegates representing all the affiliated clubs. Administrative matters are the responsibility of an elected executive committee, assisted by a panel of judges, a panel of breeders and a panel of trainers.

Every year approximately twelve breed championship shows are held in various parts of the country, at each of which from 70 to 100 Boxers compete for championship points. In addition clubs stage matches and social events. To date more than 20,000 Boxers have been entered in the official stud book, of which well over 150 had achieved championship status by the mid 1990s. In order to qualify as a champion, a Boxer has to win 12 points, including one major, under various judges, in more than one province, with at least two points awarded after the age of 27 months for a dog and 21 months for a bitch. A litter must also be produced before the title is awarded.

All active accredited Boxer judges are members of an assembly of judges, responsible for the election of the panel of judges. Training courses and the theoretical and practical examination of judges and ring stewards are conducted by the panel of judges.

A breed rally, at which progeny groups as well as individual dogs are evaluated in terms of both conformation and working ability, is held every two years by the panel of breeders. They also oversee various matters related to the breeding and registration of Boxers.

Most clubs conduct regular obedience training classes and competitions under the guidance of the panel of trainers.

A third club was formed in 1995 known as the South Africa Boxer Association and it is in agreement with SAKU. While the Boxer Federation shows continue to draw twice as many dogs, SABA shows draw more American-type Boxers. The Boxer Federation attracts dogs primarily of Dutch and German breeding and seeks to affiliate itself with ATIBOX of Germany.

IMPORTS TO SOUTH AFRICA

A broad genetic base has been established for the Boxer in South Africa, through judicious importation of high-quality Boxers representing many of the best producing bloodlines in the world. Some of the imports who have made an impact on the breed in this country include:

Dog	Country of Origin	Date of Importation
Eng-SA. Ch. Stainburndorf of Dandylion	England	1956
Int. Ch. Bel Ami von Wikingblut	Germany	1958
Am-SA. Ch. Beaulaine's Parlay of Gezira	U.S.	1959
Wiking von Dom SchH. I	Germany	1961
Ch. Witherford Haralan Cavalier	England	1961
Am-SA. Ch. Flintwood's Places of Strathmere	U.S.	1961
Can-SA. Ch. Jandaire's Justice of Peace	Canada	1968
Ch. Maximum of Woodcrest	U.S.	1972
Ch. Allena's Chemain	U.S.	1973
Am-SA. Ch. Aracrest's Courier of Holly Lane	U.S.	1975
Ch. Herndon's Protege of Madleyvale	U.S.	1975
Wiking vom Schutting	Germany	1978
Ch. Arriba's Pieta of Beckleavale	U.S.	1980
Rembrandt van de Aakant	Netherlands	1981
Ch. Filou von Nassau-Oranien	Germany	1982
Ch. Juta van de Aakant	Netherlands	1982
Am-SA. Ch. Wesan's Duke of Dixieland	U.S.	1982
Am-SA. Ch. Merrilane's It Must Be Him	U.S.	1982
Ch. Zat's Purdy of Woodcrest	U.S.	1982
Ch. Aracrest's Ipso Facto	U.S.	1983
Laureate Charge of Holly Lane	U.S.	1983
Am-SA. Ch. Herndon's Belle of the Ball	U.S.	1984
Ch. Aralie vom Okeler Forst	Germany	1984
Ch. Gravin Uschiti van Adeltrots	Netherlands	1985
Salgray's Goldrush	U.S.	1989

Sieger Bel Ami von Winkingblut (by Primus Von Dom ex Herta Von Fielding Haid), a grandson of Abra Dabra of Sirrah Crest.

SIRES AND DAMS OF MERIT

The Federation awards the Sire of Merit title to stud dogs who have produced six or more Federation or International champions, while the Dam of Merit award goes to the dams of three or more champions. The following Boxers are the foundation sires and dams in South Africa and have earned this coveted award:

Am-SA. Ch. Beaulaine's Parlay of Gezira, bred by Mrs. H. Harris, whelped December 1, 1956, imported from the U.S. by Mrs. Louise de Young in 1959 (By Ch. Bang Away of Sirrah Crest ex Ch. Beaulaines' Fantasy). He is the sire of seven Federation champions including: Ch. Ridgeview's Show Girl, Ch. Silver , Ch. Strathmere's Powdered Rock von Strom, Ch. Maude's Androcles of Dengelta, and Ch. Glendan's Carbineer.

Am-SA. Ch. Flintwood's Places Please of Strathmere, bred by Dr. Lloyd Flint, whelped December 11, 1956, imported from the U.S. by Basil Allen in 1961 (By Ch. Barrage of Quality Hill ex Ch. Sans Souci of Kresthallo). He is the sire of such notable American Boxers as Ch. Flintwood's Ban 'N Baggage and Flintwood's Banned in Boston and of eight Federation champions including: Ch. Heathfield's Student Prince, Ch. Kylescue Inn's Scottish Soldier, Ch. Kylescue Inn's Golden Gentleman, Ch. Strathmere's Intimate of Round Tables, Ch. Da Cunha's Roma Arusha, Ch. Da Cunha's Spacemaster, Ch. Meristwood's Fairy Doll, and Ch. Pantabeth's Dan Patch.

SA. Ch. Denbigh Tiger, bred and owned by Bernard Vogelnest, whelped March 19, 1959 (By Int. Ch. Bel Ami von Wikingblut ex Denbigh Marcelina). He is the sire of six Federation champions including: Ch. Denbigh Bright Spot, Ch. Von Strom's Toya Tiara Ch. Glenlaw's Poppaea van Hahnenkamm, Ch. Ovambo's Ricardo of Richdale, Ch. Von Strom's Bronze Sultan, and Ch. Deprela Twinkle of Kwetu.

Can-SA. Ch. Jandaire's Justice of Peace, bred by Mrs. S. Janda, a great-grandson of Places Please, whelped on October 24, 1966, imported from Canada by Louis and Elsabe van Aswegen in 1968 (By Ch. Flintwood's Linebacker ex Can. Ch. Jandaire's Fire of Standfast). He is the sire of 16 Federation champions including: Ch. Meristwood's Show Case of Lincoln Green, Ch. Pantabeth's Make Way, Ch. Shalako of Da Cunha, Ch. Cloverview's Going Places of Strathmere, Ch. Ballyduff's Moondust of Silver Crest, Ch. Takodah's Great Topic of Alcanis, Ch. Kimberlite's Diamond Lill, Ch. Da Cunha's Last Tango, Ch. Da Cunha's Elsa of Carissa, Ch. Sanrae's Give Way, Ch. Da Cunha's Veralynn of Ballyduff, Ch. Da Cunha's Dinga Doll, Ch. Strathmere's Show Dream Ch. Ballyduff's Little Fire of Kimberlite, Ch. Carissa's Elonka of Da Cunha, and Ballyduff's Salvo of Da Cunha.

SA. Ch. Pantabeth's Make Way, bred and owned by Ian and Bill Adie, whelped on September 6, 1968 (By Can-SA. Ch. Jandaire's Justice of Peace SOM ex Strathmere's Touch and Glow DOM). He is the sire of ten Federation champions including: Ch. Pantabeth's Power Guard, Ch. Ballyduff's Melynne, Ch. Da Cunha's Fashion Glow, Ch. Strathmere's Swing High, Ch.

Am-SA. Ch. Flintwood's Places Please of Strathmere, owned by Basil Allen, taking Best Open Dog at the Rand Easter Championship Show in 1962.

Takodah's Penelope of the Barn, Ch. Kurt of Vienna, Ch. Ballyduff's Juanita, Ch. Drostdy Lane's Tailormade of Charmwood, Silver Crest's Dig My Scene, and Ch. Ballyduff's Danger Omen.

Am-SA. Ch. Aracrest's Courier of Holly Lane, bred by Mr. and Mrs. James McGriskin, Jr., whelped April 1, 1972, imported from the U.S. by Mark Steele in 1975 (By Int. Ch. Millan's Fashion Hint ex Can. Ch. Charming Fashion). He is the sire of Am. Ch. Holly Lane's Dream Pedlar and nine Federation champions including: Ch. Tisza of Hortobagy, Ch. Gezira's Clair de Lune, Ch. The Barn's Sherry Blossom of Ballyduff, Ch. Drum Rock's Senator of Thabasnduna, Ch. Florenka's Zelda of Gezira, Ch. Da Cunha's Lilla Anne of Eldoret, Ch. Da Cunha's Shane, Ch. Drum Rock's Valencia, and Ch. Drum Rock's Cascade.

SA. Ch. Drum Rock's Senator of Thabasnduna, bred by Mark Steele, whelped July 7, 1977, owned by Gerry Davison (By Am-SA. Ch. Aracrest's Courier of Holly Lane SOM ex Strathmere's Four Seasons of Drum Rock). He is the sire of seven Federation champions including: Ch. Drum Rock's Diplomate, Ch. Drum Rock's Glory Be, Ch. Drum Rock's Tiny Girl of Eldoret, Ch. Drum Rock's Magnum of Little Oaks, Ch. Drum Rock's Ike of Pentagon, Ch. Drum Rock's Touch of Class, and Ch. Drum Rock's White Lightning.

SA. Ch. Aracrest's Ipsofacto, bred by Mrs. Norah McGriskin, whelped November 28, 1982, imported

Wiking vom Schütting, SOM (by Int. Ch. Enok vom Schütting ex World Ch. Julie vom Schütting), bred by Mrs. Karin Rezewski of Germany, was the sire of 19 Federation champions.

The first South African Federation champion, Am-SA. Ch. Beaulaine's Parlay of Gezira (by Ch. Bang Away of Sirrah Crest ex Ch. Beaulaine's Fantasy), imported from the United States by Mrs. A. L. de Young from the Beaulaine Kennels. Born on February 22, 1955, he was the sire of seven Federation champions.

from the U.S. by Mark Steele in 1983 (By Ch. Salgray's Market Wise ex Ch. Aracrest's Rhinegold). He is the sire of seven Federation champions including: Ch. Drum Rock's Spike of Jalene, Ch. Drum Rock's Proud Mary, Ch. Drum Rock's JR of Borheza, Ch. Drum Rock's Fury of Borheza, Ch. Drum Rock's Princess Daisy of Borheza, Ch. Drum Rock's Bomb Squad, and Ch. Drum Rock's Sapphire of Bukhali.

Wiking Vom Schutting, bred by Karin Rezewski, whelped April 29, 1978, imported by Franz and Ute Fuglister in 1978 (by Int. Ch. Enok vom Schutting ex World Ch. Julie vom Schutting). He is the sire of 19 Federation champions including: Ch. Ballyduff's Gotterdammerung, Ch. Tambay's Ali-Baba, Ch. Tambay's Chantilly Lace, Ch. Tambay's Germania of Aurora, Ch. Jakkalsdans Fire and Ice, Ch. Tambay's Huckleberry Finn, Ch. Ballyduff's Dark Dream of Knapdaar, Ch. Ballyduff's Midnight Gambler of the Barn, Ch. Tambay's Inkosi, Ch. Tambay's Candytuft, Ch. Niconella's Buccanero, Ch. Ballyduff's Avalanche, Ch. Beckleavale's Ludovic, Ch. Tambay's Germanicus of Chief's Pride, Ch. Tambay's Julietta, Ch. Becklevale's Zack, Ch. Beckleavale's Zack, Ch. Tambay's Orinoco of Charmwood, Ch. Beckleavale's Perfect Sensation of Condor and Ch. Geolaine's Ferdinand.

SA. Ch. Jakkalsdans Fire and Ice, bred by Marlien Heystek, whelped December 10, 1981, owned by Cindy Howard (By Wiking vom Schutting SOM ex Jakkalsdans Siovain's Pride of Charmwood DOM). He is the sire of six Federation champions including: Ch. Beckleavale's Georgie Girl, Ch. Scorpio's Flame Lily of Taurus, Ch. Beckleavale's Marco Polo of Kilmurray, Ch. Beckleavale's Nippy Nina, Ch. Beckleavale's La Belle Helene, and Ch. Hendrichristie's Cindy Nannette.

SA. Ch. Filou Von Nassau-Oranien SchH. I, bred by Willibald Wendel, whelped May 19, 1979, imported from Germany in 1982 by John Clarke and Marlien Heystek. (By Ch. Valentino von Schatzkastlein ex Ratze von Heideloh). He is the sire of Int-Sp. Ch. Ballyduff's Fury and five Federation champions including: Ch. Ballyduff's Shogun, Ch. Jakkalsdans Knight Rampant, Ch. Jakkalsdans Negev of Kerberos, Ch. Jakkalsdans Malindi, and Ch. Winchester Ridge's Cezanne of Cantalibre.

Strathmere's Touch and Glow, bred by Basil Allen, whelped May 11, 1962, owned by Ian and Bill Adie (By Am-SA. Ch. Flintwood's Places Please SOM ex Strathmere's Fairlaine). She is the dam of three Federation champions including: Ch. Strathmere's Legal Love, Ch. Pantabeth's Make Way, and Ch. Sanrae's Give Way.

Strathmere's Moulin Firefly of Beckleavale and Ch. Strathmere's Honey Girl of Beckleavale.

Beckleavale's Gypsy Belinda, bred and owned by Lea Pelser, whelped February 12, 1983 (By Am-SA Ch. Wesan's Duke of Dixieland ex Ch. Strathmere's Gypsy Coquette of Beckleavale). She is the dam of four Federation champions including: Ch. Beckleavale's Perfect Sensation of Condor, Ch. Beckleavale's Foxy Josette, Ch. Beckleavale's Zack and Ch. Beckleavale's Nippy Nina.

SA. Ch. Kia Ora's Royal Velvet of Drum Rock, bred and owned by Tertius Jarrard, whelped February 28, 1978, owned by Mark Steele (By Ch. Tisza of Hortobagy ex Takodah's Tilana). She is the dam of three Federation champions including: Ch. Drum Rock's Diplomat, Ch. Drum Rock's Glory Be, and Ch. Drum Rock's Tiny Girl of Eldoret.

Drum Rock's triumvirate: SA. Ch. Aracrest's Ipsofacto, Drum Rock's Wild Card (by SA. Ch. Drum Rock's Fury of Borheza ex Ch. Drum Rock's Proud Mary) and SA. Ch. Drum Rock's Bomb Squad (by Ch. Aracrest's Ipsofacto ex SA. Ch. Drum Rock's Miss Marple), bred by Mark and Audrey Steele.

Von Strom's Grete Von Hubertus, bred by Mrs. M. G. Clarkson, whelped August 6, 1962, owned by Mrs Val Smit (By Wiking von Dom ex Olga von Hubertus). She is the dam of three Federation champions including: Ch. Von Strom's Bronze Sultan, Ch. Von Strom's Toya Tiara, and Ch. Von Strom's Tia Maria of Ward.

Bonnie Lass, bred by Mrs. Brebner, whelped February 24, 1964, owned by Mrs. R. Bennetto (By Briar Patch Zig Zag ex Cherry of Fordoun). She is the dam of three Federation champions including: Ch. Richdale's Danny Boy of Lorrin Lodge, Ch. Richdale's Bachelor Boy, and Ch. Richdale's Playboy of Telemark.

Strathmere's Amalia of Charmwood, bred by Christopher and Steven Clegg, whelped May 5, 1974, owned by Bill Allen (By Ch. Maximum of Woodcrest ex Allena's Janine). She is the dam of four Federation champions including: Ch. Strathmere's Roman, Gladiatior, Ch. Strathmere's Gypsy Coquette of Beckleavale, Ch.

SA. Ch. Drum Rock's Glory Be, bred and owned by Mark Steele, whelped September 24, 1980 (By Ch. Drum Rock's Senator of Thabasnduna SOM ex Ch. Kia Ora's Royal Velvet of Drum Rock DOM). She is the dam of four Federation champions including: Ch. Drum Rock's Magnum of Little Oaks, Ch. Drum Rock's White Lightning, Ch. Drum Rock's Ike of Pentagon, and Ch. Drum Rock's Touch of Class.

SA. Ch. Drum Rock's Touch of Class, bred and owned by Mark Steele, whelped January 26, 1982 (By Ch. Drum Rock's Senator of Thabasnduna SOM ex Ch. Drum Rock's Glory Be DOM). She is the dam of four Federation champions including: Ch. Drum Rock's Spike of Jalene, Ch. Drum Rock's Proud Mary, Ch. Drum Rock's Princess Daisy of Borheza and Ch. Drum Rock's Sapphire of Bukhali.

Eldoret's Tess of Drum Rock, bred by Emma Meades, whelped August 25, 1983, owned by Mark

Steele (By Laureate Charge of Holly Lane ex Ch. Drum Rock's Tiny Girl of Eldoret). She is the dam of three Federation champions including: Ch. Drum Rock's JR of Borheza, Ch. Drum Rock's Fury of Borheza, and Ch. Drum Rock's Miss Marple.

Wienerwald's Flying Lady of Tambay, bred by Fritz Kosa, whelped December 29, 1976, owned by Franz and Ute Fuglister (By Ch. Tisza of Hortobagy ex Wienerwald's Malvine de Nobelesse). She is the dam of four Federation champions including: Ch. Tambay's Chantilly Lace, Ch. Tambay's Ali-Baba von Wienerwald, and Tambay's Inkosi Ch. Tambay's Candy Tuft.

Jakkalsdans Siovain's Pride of Charmwood, bred by Christopher and Steven Clegg, whelped May 5, 1974, owned by Marlien Heystek (By Jakkalsdans Firebrand of Charmwood ex Ch. Allena's Siovain). She is the dam of four Federation champions including: Ch. Jakkalsdans Knight Rampant, Ch. Jakkalsdans Negev of Kerberos, Ch. Jakkalsdans Malindi, and Ch. Jakkalsdans Fire and Ice.

SA. Ch. Gravin Uschi Van Adeltrots, bred by Jan de Vries, whelped October 22, 1983, imported from the Netherlands by Hannes and Lea Pelser in 1984 (By Zethos van Adeltrots ex Glory van de Garminale). She is the dam of three Federation champions including: Ch. Beckleavale's Castizo of Jakkalsdans, Ch. Beckleavale's Prudent Lady, and Ch. Beckleavale's Saskia.

Am-SA. Ch. Balcony Rock's Tonight Only (by Ch. Brayshaw's Masquerader ex Flintwood's Banned In Boston), bred by Charles and Pixie Fortune and owned by Eileen McClintock.

MOVERS AND SHAKERS IN THE SOUTH AFRICAN BOXER WORLD

Strathmere

Established by the late Basil Allen of Johannesburg in 1960, this kennel produced a total of 13 Federation champions, many of whom were multiple Best of Breed winners and prepotent sires and dams. Strathmere bitches formed the foundation of some of the most successful kennels of today, such as Drum Rock and Beckleavale. Top producers were Am-SA. Ch. Flintwood's Places Please of Strathmere, sire of eight South African champions, and the bitch Strathmere's Amalia of Charmwood, bred by Christopher Clegg, who produced four champions. Mr. Allen was a highly respected judge of the Boxer in this country. No fewer than seven of the Federation's Dams of Merit and two Sires of Merit trace back to the remarkably prepotent bitch Strathmere's Fairlaine, bred and owned by Basil.

Da Cunha

Breeders of 12 champions, Louis and Elsabe van Aswegen registered their Da Cunha kennel in 1961. They remained active as breeders and exhibitors until forced to cut down on their activities by Elsabe's ill health. She passed away in 1985. They were the breeders and owners of a whole gallery of outstanding Boxers, probably the best known of which was their Canadian import, Can-SA. Ch. Jandaire's Justice of Peace. In addition to his highly successful show career, this beautiful fawn male sired 16 champions, making him one of the top-producing males in the Federation. Many of his progeny also produced well, such as Ch. Pantabeth's Make Way, who was the sire of ten champions.

Ballyduff

Registered in 1967 by John Clarke of De Wildt near Pretoria, the breeding program of this well-known kennel was initially based on stock linebred on Jandaire's Justice of Peace and continued with the successful introduction of other American and European bloodlines. This resulted in 16 Federation champions as well as Int-Sp. Ch. Ballyduff's Fury who won several Best in Show awards at large international all-breed shows in Europe, and is the sire of the 1988 ATIBOX Jugendsieger and other outstanding Boxers throughout Europe. Fury was sired by Ch. Filou von Nassau-Oranien SchH. I (SOM), imported from Germany in partnership with Marlien Heystek in 1962 and the sire of five Federation champions. John, who passed away in March 1992, was an accredited breed judge and for many years had been an extremely active member of the local Boxer fraternity, serving as chairman and member of numerous bodies such as the Executive, the Northern Boxer Club, the panel of judges and the panel of trainers. Fran Clarke, also an accredited judge, has served in various capacities on the committee of Northern Boxer Club, the Executive and the panel of judges.

Eldoret

The most successful Federation breeder and exhibitor of Boxers in the Cape Provence, Emma Meades of Kimberley has been registered as a breeder since 1970. Her three most successful Boxers are all bitches. Ch. Da Cunha's Lilla Anne of Eldoret, bred by Elsabe van Aswegen, was a daughter of Ch. Aracrest's Courier of Holly Lane. Ch. Drum Rock's Tiny Girl of Eldoret, bred by Mark Steele, is the dam of two champions and won the Jochen Fleming Dam of the Year Award in 1985 and the Breeders' Panel Dam of the Year Award in 1987. A daughter of Tiny Girl, Eldoret's Tess of Drum Rock, bred by Emma and owned by Mark Steele, is a Federation Dam of Merit and has also won the Jochen Fleming Dam of the Year Award. Emma is the breeder of at least five Federation champions.

Drum Rock's Bengal Tiger, owned by Mark Steele.

Flying Lady of Tambay are Dams of Merit and producers of champions. Both were sired by the imposing Best in Show-winning Courier son Ch. Tisza of Hortobagy. Mark subsequently imported several other Boxers from the United States. Of these Ch. Aracrest's Ipsofacto (SOM) proved to be a prepotent sire who has produced at least seven Federation champions. There are no fewer than 25 Federation champions that bear the Drum Rock prefix, and his American imports are still arriving.

SA. Ch. Drum Rock's Gold Squad, owned by Johan Kieser, was a son of the influential sire Ch. Aracrest Ipsofacto.

SA. Ch. Drum Rock's Bomb Squad, owned by Mark Steele, pictured at 22 months.

Drum Rock

Mark Steele of Johannesburg has been an eminently successful breeder and exhibitor since 1975, when he imported Am-SA. Ch. Aracrest's Courier of Holly Lane (SOM) from the United States. Courier is the sire of one American and nine Federation champions, including Ch. Drum Rock's Senator of Thabasnduna (SOM), who in turn sired seven champions before his premature death. Senator's two best producing offspring are Ch. Drum Rock's Glory Be (DOM), winner of the 1984 Jochen Fleming Dam of the Year Award, and Ch. Drum Rock's Tiny Girl of Eldoret, winner of the Jochen Fleming Award in 1985 and the Breeders' Panel Dam of the Year Award in 1987. Two other Courier granddaughters, Ch. Kia Ora's Royal Velvet of Drum Rock and Wienerwald's

SA. Ch. Tambay's Orinoco of Charmwood (by Wiking vom Schutting ex SA. Ch. Aralie von Okeler Forst), bred by Mr. and Mrs. Fuglister and owned by Mr. Chris Clegg.

Beckleavale

Consistent winner of the Ballyduff Breeder of the Year Award since 1986, this Johannesburg-based kennel was established in 1977 with three foundation bitches obtained from Basil Allen. These three full sisters sired by Ch. Strathmere's Riding High out of Strathmere's Amalia of Charmwood (DOM) all became champions. They provided the basis for a very successful breeding program. Although officially registered in the name of Lea Pelser, Beckleavale is very much a joint effort between Lea and her husband Hannes. The Pelsers bred the 1986 winner of the Jochen Fleming Dam of the Year Award, Beckleavale's Mon Cherie of Monalea, sired by American import Am-SA. Ch. Wesan's Duke of Dixieland, as well as a Dam of Merit, Beckleavale's Gypsy Belinda, also sired by Duke. Best known of their American imports, Ch. Arriba's Pieta of Beckleavale, acquired from Dr. Ted Fickes, enjoyed an illustrious show career with ten Bests of Breed to his credit and sired four Federation champions. A bitch imported from the Netherlands, Ch. Gravin Uschti van Adeltrots (DOM) is the dam of three Federation champions. The Pelsers have bred no fewer than 16 champions and there's a host of points winners and other youngsters waiting in the wings. A young imported male, Am-Can. Ch. Aracrest's Stand & Deliver, joined the Beckleavale ranks and started his show career with three majors and two Best in Show awards in three straight shows.

Tambay

As a breed judge, trainer, former chairman and treasurer of the Executive and member of the panels of judges, trainers and breeders, Ute Fuglister is an extremely active Boxer personality in South Africa. Husband Franz shares her enthusiasm and has been espe-

Tambay's Quandary, (by Wiking vom Schutting ex SA. Ch. Aralie von Okeler Forst) owned by Franz and Ute Fuglister, was Dam of the Year for 1990 and 1991.

cially visible at the club level, where he has been the vice-chairman and show catering manager of Northern Boxer Club for many years. Two mainstays of their Tambay kennel were Wiking vom Schutting (SOM), imported from Mrs. Karin Rezewski in Germany in 1978 and Wienerwald's Flying Lady of Tambay (DOM), both now deceased. A small hobby kennel with rarely more than five or six Boxers at any one time, the success achieved by Franz and Ute in such a short period of time is truly remarkable. Wiking, linebred to Int. Ch. Witherford Hot Chestnut, is certain to go down in the history of the Federation as one of its all-time great sires, with no fewer than 19 champion offspring to his credit. Flying Lady, bred by Fritz Kosa and a granddaughter of the great sire Ch. Aracrest's Courier of Holly Lane, is among the first six bitches in the history of the Federation to produce four champions. The Fuglisters have bred 11 breed champions and also campaigned the German import, Ch. Aralie von Okeler Forst, to her title. They also bred the 1990 and 1991 Dam of the Year, Tambay's Quandary, a daughter of Aralie and Wiking. They are situated in Midrand, halfway between Johannesburg and Pretoria.

Jakkalsdans

Marlien Heystek's involvement in Boxer affairs dates back to 1976, when she received a Boxer puppy as a gift. This little bitch eventually became a champion and the dam and granddam of several points winners and champions and started Marlien on her way toward becoming an accredited breed judge, chairman of Northern Boxer Club in 1988 and the panel of breeders in 1986, 1987 and 1992. Co-owner of German import Ch. Filou von Nassau-Oranien SchH. I (SOM), she has bred three champions from him, all out of Jakkalsdans Siovain's Pride of Charmwood (DOM). One of these, Ch. Jakkalsdans Knight Rampant, was the 1987 winner of the Hexastar Boxer of the Year award and has won Best of Breed eight times at championship shows. His half-brother, Ch. Jakkalsdans Fire and Ice, another son of Siovain's Pride by Wiking vom Schutting, has also had a successful show career and is a Sire of Merit and winner of numerous Sire of the Year awards. Rembrandt van de Aakant was imported by Marlien from the Netherlands as a puppy in 1980. Sparingly used at stud, he produced four champions, including 1991 Hexastar Boxer of the Year, Ch. Neptunus Emperor of Grunhausen. There are no fewer than nine Federation champions bearing the Jakkalsdans prefix.

Am. Ch. Firestar's Parson (by Ch. Hollycrest's Farm Hand ex Firestar's Gypsy Magic), owned by Mark Steele.

SA. Ch. Jakkalsdans Fire and Ice, SOM (by Wiking vom Schütting ex Siovain's Pride of Charmwood), bred by Ms. Marlien Heystek, was successful not only as a sire but also as a show dog.

N'Duna

Kelvin Clegg was instrumental in setting the course by breeding the first champion, Jewel of N'Duna. She was by Ch. Stainburndorf Zulu out of Bladan's Nora Belle. Stainburndorf Kennels in England were owned by Allon Dawson and the Bladan prefix was that of Dr. Dan Gordon, a noted American breeder and judge. Allon

Dawson was to play a further instrumental role in 1956 by exporting Ch. Stainburndorf Dandylion to N'Duna. Dandylion was a very handsome red fawn dog with brilliant white markings sired by the German export to England, Frohlich von Dom. Dandylion sired several champions and can be regarded as one of the cornerstones of the modern Boxer in South Africa.

The Clegg family, Kelvin, Yvonne and sons Christopher and Steven, represents four decades of intense involvement with the Boxer breed, starting with Kelvin's first encounters with Boxers in Cairo and Rome during the Second World War and continuing virtually uninterrupted to the present. Boxers carrying their various kennel prefixes (Nduna, Hedderley and Charmwood) appear in the pedigrees of numerous champions and producers in the Federation, both past and present. In addition to their many other imports, Kelvin, who presently lives in the U.S., sent Christopher and Steven a bitch in 1973 in whelp to Ch. Warlord of Cherokee Oaks. That litter produced Ch. Allena's Siovain, one of the top-winning bitches in the history of the Federation with seven Best of Breed awards won at championship shows. Chemain is also the granddam of two of the Federation's top-producing bitches, Strathmere's Amalia of Charmwood and Jakkalsdans Siovain's Pride of Charmwood, both bred by Christopher and owned by Basil Allen and Marlien Heystek respectively. Kelvin, Yvonne and Christopher are all accredited judges of the breed and have served on various committees and panels over the years.

Fortune

Charles and Pixie Fortune were bitten by the Boxer bug around 1952 but did not acquire their first Boxer until 1955. In the interim, they bred and showed Bullmastiffs. Their first Boxer was a brindle dog named Lustig Wallaby. He had no white markings and was very somber in appearance, but a wonderful companion. They yearned for a dog that looked like Ch. Bang Away and jumped at a chance to buy a young dog from the Beaulaine Kennels in the U.S. He had a lot of Bang Away and Ursa Major in his pedigree. He was imported in 1957 and shown to his championship in 1958, taking two Bests in Show. They took him back to the United States in 1960. He sired one Federation champion and was the sire of Strathmere's Fairlane out of MacDuff's Alma. Fairlane is probably the most prepotent bitch bred in U.S.

Mrs. Pixie Fortune took on the role of secretary of the Boxer Club at a critical stage of the club, particularly during the transition period when the club was de-affiliated from the Kennel Union. This involved the start-up of a breed registrar and the typing of hundreds of pedigrees of all the animals registered. Pixie handled all of this work as well as teaching school and being a mother. In addition, countless meetings were held to discuss constitutions, etc. The amount of administrative work involved in maintaining a breed is considerable and it is to the credit of the founders of the Federation that they were able to accomplish this. Pixie certainly deserved all our thanks.

Beaulaine's Ninon, owned by Donald Watson, rests with Pixie Fortune of Fortune Kennels.

Two grandchildren of Ch. Bang Away of Sirrah Crest winning BOB and BOS at the Rand Easter Show on April 21, 1962.

427

Beaulaine's Ninon (by Ch. Brayshaw's Sargeant Major ex Ch. Flintwood's Subtle Sequence), owned by Donald Watson.

MacDuff

Bill Duff, from Pretoria, imported two Boxers in 1952. The first was a son of Ch. Mazelaine's Zazarac Brandy named Birbama's Call Me Ishmael and the second was a bitch in whelp named Mazelaine's Quiver Queen, an Ursa Major daughter out of a Sieger and Ch. Karlo v.d. Wolfschlucht daughter, bred to Peg Davis' Ch. Canyonair Hickory Smoke. Quiver Queen produced a litter of seven puppies, each of which became a South African champion. Under the kennel name of MacDuff, Bill Duff showed the dog world that American Boxers were exciting to show and breed and did much to forward the cause of Boxers in the show ring. Bill Duff, who represented an American oil company, was a master at marketing and promotion. He successfully campaigned all his dogs and was probably one of the few breeders to be commercially successful. In 1958 he imported Raineylanes Bendigo from Don and Helen Starkweather of the U.S. This was a brindle grandson of Ch. Mazelaine's Kappelmeister.

Charles Fortune with SA. Ch. Beaulaine's Algisir of Balcony Rock (by SA. Ch. Beaulaine's Kentucky Bo ex Beaulaine's India), was the top winner in South Africa.

Ch. Flintwood's Places Please of Strathmere, handled by Robert Harris and imported by owner Basil Allen from breeders Dr. and Mrs. Lloyd Flint.

Maurane

Maurice Vane had established himself as a successful breeder with a number of dogs, including the first Boxer Ch. Gremlin Hiflyer (imported from Britain) to go Best in Show at an all-breed event. In 1954, he was able to obtain ownership of a dog named Joris v.d. Zaankant. Joris, imported from Holland, was a spectacular fawn dog with white markings very similar to those of Ch. Bang Away of Sirrah Crest. He won his championship in short order and under the steerage of Maurice, who showed him with great flair, he won a number of all-breed Bests in Show. He won his final all-breed Best in Show under Wil Judy from the U.S. at seven years of age. He held the record number of all-breed Bests in Show. Joris helped educate the public to the showy appearance of a flashy Boxer and let the dog world in South Africa know that the Boxer as a breed had "arrived" and was a serious contender in the show ring. Despite his magnificent record, the dog was a monorchid and did not reproduce his show quality.

In 1958, Maurice bought a dog from Frau Stockmann in Germany. This was the Seiger Ch. Bel Ami von Wikingblut SchH I, who was by Primus von Dom out of Herta von Felding Haid. Bel Ami was a double Abra Dabra of Sirrah Crest grandson (Abra Dabra was by Ch. Xebony of Sirrah Crest and the sire of Bang Away's dam.) Abra Dabra was one of the two Boxers that Dr. and Mrs. Harris of Sirrah Crest had presented to Frau Stockmann on her visit to the United States in 1948. Bel Ami was a splendid dark brindle dog with flashy white markings. He finished his championship in no time and went on to sire many champions.

MARQUE

Mark Marincowitz was not a breeder or exhibitor of dogs, but a honest-to-goodness journalist by profession, working for a large Sunday paper. This gave him a very objective approach to the problems the Boxer world was facing, particularly regarding the showing of cropped Boxers and the reaction they were causing in the Kennel Union world. His sage advice helped keep the Boxer Club on course and anchored the direction of many of us. In addition, he provided a valuable base for us in starting publication of *The Boxer Bulletin*.

The Boxer Bulletin proved invaluable to the cause of Boxers in Southern Africa, much the same way that *Boxer Briefs* did in the U.S. to sustain the breed during its early years. A publication devoted to the breed provides a unifying forum from which to promulgate ideas and generate reactions from people. The actions required to produce a publication are considerable and this is where Mark's contribution was immeasurable. During the years he was editor, the resolution of the future did not seem to be in doubt.

SA. Ch. Winchester Ridge's Cezanne of Cantalibre (by SA. Ch. Filou von Nassau Oranien ex Aurora's Miss Champagne of Winchester Ridge), owned by Winchester Ridge Boxers, was Boxer of the Year in 1990.

Am-SA. Ch. Beaulaine's Parlay (by Ch. Bang Away of Sirrah Crest ex Ch. Beaulaine's Fantasy), an import from the United States, became an extremely influential dog in South Africa.

DE YOUNG

Louise was fired by some inner spirit not only to produce the best Boxer that could be bred in South Africa but to do it as quickly as she could. Her enthusiasm was shared by her husband Alf. In 1959, I undertook to find a good Boxer for the De Youngs in the United States. I had been invited to judge the New Jersey Boxer Club Specialty that year. I spent approximately six weeks in the U.S. as a guest of Phillip and Helen Harris of Beaulaine Kennels. We attended many dog shows. In the end I persuaded the Harrises to sell Ch. Beaulaine's Parlay to the De Youngs. Parlay was sired by Ch. Bang Away out of Ch. Beaulaine's Fantasy (a Bang Away granddaughter linebred on Ursa Major). He was a striking red dog with white markings who had gone Best of Winners at Westminster Kennel Club in 1957.

Parlay, or Rocky, as he was called, was shipped to Louise and became the first Boxer to achieve championship status in the new Boxer Federation on March 11, 1961. He sired seven Federation champions and his contribution to Boxer lineage in South Africa is now legendary. It is no small tribute to these two people that, in seeking the best and following through by buying, importing, breeding and promoting an established champion from the U.S. at considerable expense, they did indeed change the future and the history of the Boxer in South Africa.

More important than the sex or color of your prospective puppy is that the puppy come from an experienced breeder with a reputation for producing not only champions but also healthy, hardy pet puppies too. Here is photographer Marcia Adams in front of the camera!

MALE OR FEMALE

Consider the following when choosing the sex of your new Boxer. A bitch is smaller than a male, if space is a factor. Do you live in a condo, an apartment, a cottage, a small house? If you are a small person, light in weight, you might find a bitch easier to manage on a leash and collar. A bitch is unlikely to roam or stray from home; however, when in season and if she has been bred before, she may run off to look for a mate.

I have found the bitch easier to housebreak than the dog. She will not likely mark in your house and other indoor areas. However, a female will mark outdoors, even raising her leg similar to a male. This is especially true if she is an alpha bitch or if she is in season. Unless you designate a spot for her in your yard or use ex-pens, your bitch could ruin a beautiful green lawn with brown burn spots. Males in turn lift their legs, usually starting at nine months, and can urinate and burn expensive ornamental shrubs or ruin furniture and rugs indoors. However, it is quite easy to teach your Boxer, male or female, to go and relieve himself in certain locations from an early age.

The cost of spaying a bitch is more costly than castrating a male dog. In dog shows, I have found the bitch competition tougher since there are more good bitches than dogs. More breeders tend to want to hang onto their best bitch or bitches to continue their line; thus, a good-quality bitch is more expensive and harder to find than a good-quality male.

Many a good breeder will tell you is that it's better to buy a bitch puppy over a male for show. If the pup does not grow into a top show dog, a male ends up being just a good pet, oftentimes not suitable for breeding. If a bitch does not turn out and has a good pedigree with no glaring faults, you can always go to a dominant top-producing champion male and perhaps produce your own future show dog. In addition, most conscientious breeders will not breed a non-titled male unless he has considerable attributes to offer.

Another factor to consider when choosing which gender is whether or not you have another dog. I find a male and a female rarely, if ever, get into fights. They may have short quarrels or spats but not the fight to the death that two bitches can get into. We are never sure what triggers this behavior, but most often the less alpha bitch decides she wants the alpha position. Unless you are in full control and an alpha figure yourself, it is a difficult problem to solve. However, I have seen and lived with two or even three bitches co-existing for their entire lives with just minor quarrels.

Take into consideration which dogs of which genders make frequent visits to your home. It is very difficult to keep a male and female apart when your female comes in season unless they are kept in different parts of the house with strong gates and closed doors. Children especially find it difficult to keep doors closed. A good solution is to use your dog crate. Without careful planning and control, it is virtually impossible to keep them apart during the heat cycle and not have them breed. Dogs are so instinctive that even males and females that have never bred will get together. Another solution is to board one of your dogs during the heat cycle with your breeder or at a good secure kennel. Also, consider the gender of your neighbor's dog, especially if their dog has access to your property.

If your home and yard are roomy enough, I do encourage the new owner never to have an "only child." Get two dogs, preferably a male and female or two females. It is usually better to take one puppy first and have that puppy trained and established in your household, then go purchase the second one. What is nice is

A new Boxer puppy is no picnic—dog ownership requires great commitment, patience, and a fair amount of expense as well. This urchin is the future Ch. Vancroft's Paper Chase.

that they have each other to play with, to occupy themselves, to exercise and to work off their abundance of energy so that they are calmer and make better house pets. I find this practice especially helpful in keeping the show Boxer in optimum condition. Boxers play a game only seen in Boxers. They romp, roll and wrestle, utilizing muscles not used in usual running or jogging. They can be lying down and playing, with their necks craning and their mouths open in mock biting, a sort of jousting while they make a cute cooing sound as if talking among themselves. I can watch these antics for hours.

Males are larger with bigger bone and many people think a big male is less manageable. However, if you properly train your male while he is young and during his maturation, he will be very responsive and you can have complete control.

Pet puppies should be typy and good-looking. Note how this pet pup bred by Pat Baxter has beautiful features and a deep black muzzle.

Sired by the Int. Ch. Jacquet's Novarese, Ch. El Encanto's Chantaje Jacquet as a puppy with breeder Carole Shea.

Boxers in America and much of Europe are preferred with cropped ears. Taping ears up to strengthen the cartilege is a simple chore, though the puppy takes time to adjust to the inconvenience. Breeders, Ottavio and Isabella Perricone.

In most breeds of dog, the bitch is considered to be more docile and affectionate to their owners and family. Also, bitches are thought to be gentler with children. I have found, and many Boxer owners will agree, that Boxer males are just as docile to their owners, gentle with children and loving to all members of their household. I have found that the males are a little more loyal and less flighty. I find their affection warmer in feeling. Until you own a male, you will not understand these subtleties. I usually have two or three Boxers living in the house, a male and two females. My entire backyard is fenced and the dogs have access to it from the kitchen door. When they want to go out, they run to the back door. I had one male that watched how I opened the door by turning the knob and then the storm door, which was a latch type. He learned to open both and let himself and the bitches out to relieve themselves. Later, he would open the doors and hold them open for the girls. Another time before I padlocked the back gate leading to the driveway, I heard barking on the back door accompanied by incessant barking. It was my male. I looked for the girls who were not in the backyard. I asked him where they had gone using their names. He ran to the open gate to show me where they had escaped, not running out himself. I, of course, gave him high praises and hugs and then ran for the girls. This made me love this dog all the more. Every male I have owned has not run off while every bitch I have lived with has taken off at one time or another.

IS THE BOXER FOR YOU?

Our line reaches maturity at around 15 to 18 months. Boxers reach maturity mentally around 12 months of age. They are housebroken often by eight to ten weeks of age because they are extremely clean.

The demand for Boxer puppies and young adults is quite tremendous for a breed that is not in the very top breeds. Families that call for them are usually couples, one of whom has grown up with a Boxer as a child. They invariably say they have never forgotten how wonderful their childhood Boxer was and now they would like a Boxer for their family.

Memories of growing up with a Boxer trigger new owners to once again share their lives with a Boxer. This charmer is Norwhite Painted Lady at Khashan, owned by Mrs. N. Sasse.

Fortunately, the Boxer is a breed that is not bred too often because of the initial expense involved, docking of the tail and cropping of ears. The temperament is so wonderfully sound with this breed that families looking at pups can concentrate on the size they prefer, the color, which should be rich, a pleasing expression on the face, the darkest eyes possible, a few wrinkles over the brow and around the muzzle and, of course, general good health and straight topline and legs. It is hard to tell movement and soundness because the bone and joints are soft and loose in youngsters.

Avoid Boxers with faults such as a pointy nose. Avoid shyness. Boxers are exuberant, outgoing and happy to meet you. Do ask to meet and see one or both parents.

Even better, meet a grandparent. I believe that the third generation is what your new puppy will reflect.

The Boxer is the ideal family dog. It is medium large with a short, easily cared for coat, ideal for indoor living with very little shedding. As the adult coat comes in during adolescence, a darker shinier coat comes with it. They are extremely clean, often licking themselves like a cat, and they have no doggy odor.

We like our Boxers to live in a home with children or children planned in the future. Boxers were bred to be baby-sitters.

Boxers are so intelligent and like human children that they make wonderful additions to households without children. They add life into any home. They give countless pleasures with their antics and their playfulness, by bringing you assortments of toys or whatever they think you would like to get your attention, by making a connection with you or just being there to greet you when you come home.

Boxers are exuberant and playful and, during their puberty, they seem to have more energy and curiosity so they might get into mischief. They are only tasting life as nature dictates. During this time, they must get more exercise. We require a fenced-in backyard. Throw balls for them. Frisbee® catching is even better. It can be fun for the owner to have this playtime and it will strengthen the bond with the Boxer. If you don't have a fenced-in area to run your dog, then jog with him or bicycle with him if you are into that.

PICKING YOUR PUPPY

Having decided on breed, gender and timing, now you begin the painstaking process of finding a breeder and selecting the puppy. In looking for and choosing a puppy, keep these criteria in mind: a great temperament, good structure and soundness; a pleasing balance of both combined with a typey head, robustness, good health and, of course, a good pedigree.

Look for advertisements or photographs in various publications such as *Boxer Review*, *Boxer Quarterly*, high-quality canine publications (*Dogs USA*, *Dog World*, *Dog Fancy*, *Dog & Kennel*, etc.) devoted

This blonde bombshell—Roxanne Westra— has her lap full with rowdy Jacquet tykes. Personalities abound... and abound...and abound in the rapidly growing litter.

to multiple breeds or monthlies dedicated to show dogs (*Breeders Digest*, *Canine Chronicle*, etc.) and of course, the AKC Gazette. These will list breeders that may be in your area. Finally you can contact the National Kennel Club to give you a list of reputable breeders closest to you. Then visit the premises where the puppies are born and reared to study their action and their parents and grandparents, if possible. I've always maintained that the puppy you choose reflects its grandparents structurally and temperamentally.

Another good resource is your veterinarian. He might have breeders as clients. Also, your vet will usually have a listing of qualified and conscientious breeders in the area in which he practices. Friends or acquaintances who own a Boxer can often refer you to the breeder they

Evaluate each puppy in the litter for its temperament, structure, soundness, balance, and health. This brindle litter comes from Vancroft Kennels.

At 25 days of age, this Boxer puppy is more than a handful! Breeder, Michele Lesca.

acquired their Boxer from—only inquire of them if their dog is a good one. Aim for highest quality possible: the healthiest, the soundest and the best personality. When you have found the right breeder, make an appointment and visit him to evaluate the puppies. See which one is active, which one is quiet, which one is more people-oriented and finally, which one connects with you. Presuming the puppy is to live with you for its lifetime, choose the temperament that is most compatible with your personality and lifestyle. Like all relationships, there needs to be compatibility or else strong bonding won't occur.

Look for very specific structure. Begin with the overall balance, then look at the head. Boxers are a "head breed." The overall impression should be pleasing to your eye. The muzzle should be broad and have depth. A bump above his nose is a good sign and a predictor of a good stop. A high occiput assures good high ear set, giving that alert look. I like to see some wrinkles, a rea-

At six weeks of age, this is the future Ch. Hi-Hill's Rave Review...adored by the critics and breeder Donna Titus alike.

sonable amount, as some of this disappears as the head grows and matures. I avoid an excess amount of wrinkling, which can give a wet look and is not desirable. Looking down on the pup, pull back the ears into the palm of your hand, the head should resemble a bunny rabbit with fat cheeks. This was pointed out to me by Gerald Broadt, a well-known handler, breeder and AKC judge. Those pups with the bunny look turn out to have the best heads when they mature with width of muzzle, clean cheeks and a narrow skull.

The topline and tail set should be good together with well-angulated hindquarters, a short back and shoulders. If you plan on showing, the deep red fawn color, well pigmented, especially down the back and head, and with the brindles, definite striations preferably in a herringbone pattern with deep red background color and markings promises to be the best. There should be white markings on the legs and chest. A white blaze is eye-catching to the judges. White, half or full, collars are a matter of taste. I prefer a solid-colored neck which, to my eyes, gives a longer look.

Consider the overall balance of the puppy as well as the specifics of structure. This well-put-together little prince was bred by English author and breeder Jo Royle.

In considering the bite, I like to see the bottom jaw line as wide as possible. This usually indicates a nice straight, wide bottom jaw when the adult teeth come in. I also like to see the jaw line as close to the top row of teeth as possible, and yet undershot. I have found that when the second set of teeth comes in, it comes forward. You must not see the tongue when the jaw is closed.

The eyes should be as dark as possible. Puppies have bluish eyes that darken as they age. I have often seen pups with light eyes that do darken with age. Dark haws, the third membranes that add to a pleasing expression, are preferred. However, I never reject a puppy having one or both haws white. That is the least worry regarding the overall quality of the pup. There are other physi-

The breeder's rapport with her puppies will tell you a lot about the breeding program. Here's Diane Bradshaw with three young Ozstock ladies sired by Jenroy Pop Back to Walkon.

I've found that what appears to be a lot of angulation does modify. Puppies seem to lose some angulation as they mature. The tail set should be straight out of the back with the tail carried high.

My advice is to seek a good, reputable breeder that has been doing this for some time—someone who knows his lines several generations back as well as other lines that he has incorporated in breeding and why he did so. Depend on him.

When you visit a breeder to see a litter of pups, take along someone who has dog sense and/or an "eye for a Boxer." Meet owners of dogs that were acquired from this breeder and question them about integrity, about their satisfaction not only for having acquired a good dog but also the breeder's help in answering their questions and about having a nice pleasant relationship with this particular breeder. I treasure the relationship and memories of the breeder and all the people who were helpful to me when I first acquired my Boxers over two decades ago. I am still on friendly terms with them. They are my teachers. They are a part of my family.

cal concerns such as poor hindquarters, roachy topline, poor feet, poor temperament, etc., which are more of a distraction. I do like to see a black muzzle, not brown. Even though there are white markings on the head, the black on the muzzle should be framed around the white. I don't like to see the black extend way over the eyes, which I believe gives a somber look.

The nose should be pigmented or nearly so by six to ten weeks of age and should be broad. A narrow nose usually indicates a narrow muzzle on maturation, giving a snipy look. I like to see a pronounced arch in the neck as well as well-angulated hindquarters. This gives the puppy a flowing line from the head to the rear hocks.

Observe the puppy's interaction with its littermates as well as how it reacts to its environment.

The best puppy will likely demand the higher price tag. As with all good things, you get what you pay for. This nicely developing youngster is the future Ven-PR. Ch. Kahlua's Krauss of Wyoming.

When you do find a puppy that has caught your eye and heart, it may be expensive, especially if it is of show quality. My motto has been "You pay for what you get." Most good reputable breeders don't spare expense for food, supplements, veterinary care, housing, proper heat in winter, proper exercise and perhaps even proper socialization by hiring good sitters and kennel help. Consider all this when purchasing a puppy.

A good breeder will want you to take over where he left off. A good breeder will have taught the puppy the first steps toward housebreaking and perhaps even leash training.

CARE OF THE PUPPY

Before bringing your new puppy home, you must purchase a crate. A crate not only will help in housebreaking but will provide the puppy with a place of its own, a place where it will feel secure. In the beginning, you might want to shred newspaper and put it in the crate. Once the puppy is housebroken, the crate will become invaluable to you, especially if you work outside the home and the puppy will be alone much of the day. Of course, the puppy will go through a chewing stage. If he is not crated, he will chew anything and everything. By crating, you will be protecting your home and your puppy from chewing something that could be dangerous, like wires, plants and indigestible small objects. Leave a couple of toys in the crate with the puppy—safe toys, such as proper sized Gumabones®. When you come home and let him out of the crate, praise him. Eventually, you will be able to leave him loose in the house while you are gone with the crate door open. Don't

Breeders monitor the individual growth of each Boxer puppy. These four littermates are looking for a hot meal and a good home. Photo by Jim Bernardo.

Well-socialized puppies (and children) are an asset to any home. Always supervise children whenever they are handling very young puppies (and keep them somewhere they can't escape!).

be surprised if you find him sleeping in the crate—it's his special place. It is important to remember that the crate should *not* be used as a punishment when the puppy does something he shouldn't have. You don't want the puppy to associate the crate with being punished. When you put him in the crate, give him a treat and praise him. As he grows, he will still use the crate because it is the place where he feels safe and secure.

BRINGING UP BABIES

When the pups all eat together in a litter, competition stimulates the appetite. When a puppy goes off with a family and is on his own, it has been known not to eat as well or, in some cases, not to eat at all. Following is the feeding instructions I give to all puppy owners:

A good basic meal would consist of dry food, about 3/4-cup of fresh hamburger cooked in about 1/2-cup water, and 1/2-cup to 3/4-cup cottage cheese. Vitamin C is the most important supplement and should be added once a day. Additional items that can be added are: boiled rice and barley, cooked egg yolks for puppies (no raw whites), cooked whole eggs for adults, wheat germ, beef stew with vegetables, chicken stew with vegetables, most cooked vegetables (carrots, tomatoes, celery, etc.). For liquid you can use meat juices, broth or soup. Canned dog food can be added to the dry food to encourage a fussy eater.

Bringing up babies is never easy work. Jeffrey Gallagher at eight months with five week old puppies bred by Pat & Donald Fink.

With his ears taped and secured, the future Ch. Donley's Torrance of Omaha takes a "time-out." Owners, Bill Brown and Bob Donley.

During this phase, supplement the pup with a high-calorie appetite stimulator that will keep him nourished and prevent too much weight loss. Don't fuss too much and the puppy will eat when it gets hungry enough. I have difficulty with this since some pups do become depressed when taken away from littermates—separation anxiety. I think coaxing is a part of the bonding process between you and your new pup. Once you have the puppy eating, then less fussing can be used. Only in a few isolated cases have we produced a fussy eater in later life, and this can be a nightmare. Eat! Eat! Please eat!

Some Boxers will increase their appetites, others may need coaxing with some added meat, preferably fresh cooked or from a can. I usually feed them two meals at this time and, as long as they are not getting obese, I feed them as much as they want. They are still growing and their bodies are developing.

Vitamins could be added. An all-natural vitamin with fatty acids is an excellent choice that can be added to a meal. Other useful vitamins are vitamin E and vitamin C, wheat germ oil, a combination of oils and elemental sulfur (helpful for fleas), brewer's yeast and garlic (this seems helpful with fleas as well as being beneficial and appetizing).

If a puppy or adult won't eat, entice him with canned cat food. Dogs love the smell and the taste. (Incidentally, they also love to eat cat droppings, so use cat litter pans that have covers or put the box in an area where your Boxer cannot access it.)

Some puppies are known to eat their own stools. I laughingly refer to this as recycling. However, it is not pleasant to have the puppy give you a lick after he has eaten his own stool. There are remedies that have been successful. Monosodium glutamate sprinkled on the puppy's food, powdered seaweed such as sea meal, or kelp in pellets or tablets has worked. Try an enzymatic-acting supplement. When these are digested, they break down the appeal of the stool, making it unappetizing for the pups. Better yet, pick up the stool immediately after each bowel movement and dispose.

During the first week away from the littermates, the puppy will be lonely. They are used to having companions. At night I suggest placing the pup in a dog crate with an artificial lambskin for warmth. The wool will feel like a littermate. You can also set the crate up in your bedroom or in a child's bedroom near the bed so the puppy can feel human presence. There are durable woolly toys with squeakers in them for the pups to play with and snuggle up to. If the pup cries in the night, reassure him by softy talking to him while putting your hand or finger into the crate. This will reassure him that he is not alone. This might go on for a few nights. Be patient and understanding. Don't rattle the crate or

"Hey, who's watching who here?" All babies need supervision.

frighten him. You want him to feel comfortable and happy in his crate, which is his bedroom, his space, his den and just a secure place. The collapsible crates are ideal for moving in and out of the bedroom.

When you awaken in the morning, take the puppy out immediately. Wait until the pup makes its bowel movement before bringing him in. They invariably seem to have to do this. If you don't, the pup will make the second load, so to speak, in the house. During the day, take the puppy out after every nap and, of course, after every meal. In the winter, many breeders will have paper trained their pups, although Boxer pups seem to train themselves on paper. Put the newspaper in front of the door that you will be using to take the pup out. I strongly recommend a fenced yard or a fenced run area or exercise pen. You know then that the puppy is in a safe area and cannot wander off and get lost, stolen or hit by a car. If you do not have a fenced yard, always walk the

Praise puppies with a happy voice with gusto, but don't overdo the cookies. Little Stephanie Grossman and her pups.

Boxer babies snuggling together. Breeders, Barry and Hope Blazer.

puppy on a leash. Never allow your puppy to walk over the threshold of your house without a leash and collar. If you get in the habit of doing this each and every time, the puppy, as it grows, will not have the tendency to dash out the door ahead of you. Many dear pets have been killed or maimed by running into the path of an oncoming vehicle.

I've also found that when Boxers, being loyal companions, are not allowed to wander off the property on or off leash until at least a year of age, there is not a tendency for the adult to leave the property. If your puppy does run away, don't chase him. He will think it is a game and he will usually continue to run away from you. Try running in the opposite direction, away from danger or toward your home, calling him vigorously and enthusiastically. If this doesn't work, drop to the ground

on your knees or completely down and pretend to cry. If you have created a bond, the puppy will usually come to see that you are all right as long as he is not distracted or chasing something.

I teach my puppies through the alpha concept, by becoming the mother or father of the puppy, praising with enthusiasm and gusto in a happy voice. If you have to discipline your puppy, use a voice that is grave, with the sound of a growl. The puppy will remember this from the time he lived with his dam. Never strike your puppy with your hand, a rolled up newspaper, etc. If you must get physical, grab the scruff of the neck gently or use a collar and leash and give a correction as in obedience. Always follow with praise to give immediate reassurance that you still love him. For people who are or have been a parent, treat them kindly as you would a

Roxanne Westra easily establishes herself as the alpha of these Jacquet pups. All dogs need someone reliable to follow.

Anais de Tomver, bred by Marinella Lo Bianco and owned by Dr. Alessandro Mutolo.

child. Boxers are so human-like in character, personality and intelligence that they will respond to you because they love to please.

I do urge going to obedience classes. Start with puppy kindergarten classes where there is less demand on the puppy. Check with local trainers. Boxers, being as bright as they are, can easily get bored with repetition and too many demands at a young age. If you own a show puppy and plan to finish his championship title, I don't recommend going through an obedience class. I do, however, recommend show-handling classes, usually run by a local kennel club or privately by a well-known professional handler. Consult your breeder. It is too big of a demand and the puppy can lose some of its spark—that ineffable characteristic of a great "show" dog. I have seen many beautiful show prospects with no spark who never attain the championships that they should have easily won.

The dam of this litter has little concern about the socialization of her four pups. These young boys are each giving ample attention.

Michael Harms and Am-Can. Ch. Sig's Star Sapphire enjoy playing with a Frisbee and a granddaughter. Owners, Paul and Cynthia Starr.

A wagonful of handsome pups bred by John Purdy, out of Ch. Jacquet's Stem Winder.

HOUSETRAINING BOXERS

BY CONNIE JANKOWSKI

Housetraining a healthy Boxer is easy—once you know the secret to success. Perhaps you've just purchased a new puppy. Maybe your companion-of-choice is a mature dog. Whether your Boxer is new in your home, or whether you've been unsuccessful in previous attempts to curb your dog's desire to eliminate in your house, take a positive attitude before beginning your quest to teach your pet the rules of the house.

Veterinary Examination

Before attempting housetraining, have your dog examined by your veterinarian. New pets should be examined before they come to your home. Dogs that have resisted housetraining should be examined to rule out underlying physical conditions that contribute to house-soiling problems.

Although most causes of house-soiling are behavioral, not physical, diabetes, bladder infections, kidney ailments and coronary conditions can cause dogs to eliminate irregularly.

Male dogs should be neutered by six months of age, unless your dog is a show-quality specimen and you plan to exhibit the dog (which requires both time and expense).

Below: **Housetraining is a cinch, given the proper encouragement and devotion to the task at foot. Jessica Starr and Michael Harms sit with puppies in the yard.**

Praise your puppy upon each piddle. Here's Diamond, owned by John Rogers.

The Secret to SUCCESS

Until your Boxer is reliably housetrained, don't let it run unsupervised through your house. Sound like common sense? It is. However, most people who have been unsuccessful in teaching their dogs where to eliminate have broken that cardinal rule.

Where do they go wrong? Unsupervised refers to your state of mind as well as your physical presence. You cannot focus your attention on your dog when you are talking on the phone, preparing dinner or doing paperwork. At these times your Boxer should be confined (put in the yard, put in its crate or restrained on a leash).

Getting on Track

Devote three days to housetraining your dog. Follow these rules and enjoy your rewards!

1. Watch your dog. It will tell you when it needs to eliminate. Dogs usually seek out corners or boundaries (such as the area next to a wall) to "make deposits." When your Boxer heads to such a spot, observe its behavior. Sniffing, walking in a circle and squatting signal that it's time to get the dog outside!

2. Select an appropriate area and deliver the dog to that spot every time it needs to eliminate. While the dog sniffs and investigates the area, resist the temptation to distract him. Don't talk to him, don't even look at him.

3. Reward your Boxer for appropriate behavior. Verbal praise or, better yet, a food reward should be offered immediately following elimination. Dogs associate rewards and punishments with whatever they are doing at the time of the reward or punishment.

4. Never ever punish after the fact. If you find an "accident," just clean it up and ignore it. The dog won't associate punishment delivered with the act of squatting or pointing and delivering. Boxers are very sensitive, and your dog may "look guilty" when feces or urine are left on a carpet, but the dog is responding to association of the presence of the excrement and your annoyance. The dog neglects to realize that its actions (squatting or pointing) are the cause of your displeasure.

Encourage your puppy to use the same place in the yard each time that you wish for him to eliminate. Owner, Brinbox Kennels.

Puppies acquired from competent breeders usually are practically housebroken before arriving to their new homes. Here's Rosina Olifent-Brace with two Sjecoin dolls.

"Doubting Thomases" should take this simple test. If you've been punishing after the fact and your dog is still eliminating in the house, it's not getting the message. Clean and disinfect soiled areas. (Use a pet-odor eliminator from a pet shop.) Dogs often return to spots that bear their scents.

5. Enroll in a dog training class. Occasionally, house-soiling is caused by a dog's over-inflated image. Dominant dogs may use elimination to mark territory. Often an obedience class will help redefine pack order and will affect a dog's elimination patterns. Many of these dogs are in desperate need of reconditioning, and enrolling in a class may prevent more serious problems (such as aggression) from developing.

Behavior problems are the biggest cause for dog/owner relationships to fail. Start off on the road to success by teaching your dog the most basic of canine good manners. If you have difficulty, contact an animal behaviorist for assistance. You *can* housetrain your dog. Don't make excuses, don't delay.

TO BREED OR NOT TO BREED

WHY BREED?

To me, there is nothing more wonderful and cute than a litter of Boxer puppies. It is extremely tempting to breed the Boxer bitch you now own to produce puppies like her. Think hard about whether you want the responsibility of bringing more puppies into an already overpopulated world. Visit your local pound or humane society and see all the sad, un-

with us and not pushed off on total strangers or, worse, out into the streets.

I agonize over every breeding: who to breed to and why. It gets more agonizing each time I breed. I give it a lot of thought before deciding. If you do breed for a specific purpose, such as to produce show-quality puppies and future champions, to improve upon the bitch you own and/or to carry on your line of

The responsibility of bringing puppies into the world should never be underestimated. Raising a litter requires an enormous commitment of time, resources and money. Don't expect to even break even—breeding dogs properly is never profitable! Breeder, Andy Casale. Photo by Sutton Studios.

wanted puppies and dogs needing homes, begging you to take them home with you, their sad eyes and eager whimpers and barks calling to you. Call your local Boxer Rescue service, a nonprofit organization staffed by dedicated, hardworking Boxer lovers trying to save all Boxers from the pounds. Ask how many Boxers they have rescued and how many still need to be rescued. You would be appalled at the number.

If you decide to breed and raise a litter, are you prepared to take back one of your pups if it doesn't work out with the new owner even if the dog you sold is now a few years old? It has happened with us many more times than I like to think about. One recently was returned at eight years of age. How sad. After living with her owners for all that time and then to be rejected and relocated into a new home. Fortunately, most Boxers are resilient, have a zest for living and can adapt to new surroundings. We tell every prospective new owner that if, for some reason, it does not work out, even years from the time the pup is sold, we will take the dog back or try to arrange for a new home. Many times we have made cash reimbursements because that is what was requested and we wanted our "kids" back

Boxers to share with other enthusiasts, then I would say go for it. Another factor for when I breed is to have a waiting list of prospective good homes. However, prepare yourself for a commitment. It is hard work, a true labor of love. It is a big responsibility and it can be expensive. Responsibility is not only to yourself and your family but to the bitch. Do you want her to go through the strenuous labor or are you willing to possibly encounter the occasional C-section, which is major surgery for the bitch and a major expense for you?

Always check with your veterinarian as to the condition of your bitch. Is she fit? Find out if your vet will be there for you during the pregnancy and, most importantly, during the whelping process. Not all vets like delivering puppies. Ask a breeder friend to help you find a vet who likes newborn puppies and who is also familiar and sympathetic with reproduction. An ideal vet is one who likes Boxers and is familiar with their characteristics and needs such as the right length of tail, the right amount of anesthesia, if needed, or any of the known problems with the breed such as tumors and cancer, hypothyroidism and Boxer cardiomyopathy, a degeneration of the heart muscle that appears later in life.

PREPARING TO BREED

Mature bitches of sound health, good temperment and proper type adhering to the allowed colors are, by a conscientious breeder's choice, the only ones to be bred. The chosen mate should represent equal or greater quality so as to enhance the quality of the offspring of which the breeder can be proud. Other important factors to consider are timing and convenience. It takes a considerable amount of time to help the bitch raise her litter well. It is a great asset for each pup to feel secure with people. This grows with consistent gentle care and handling. Essential too is a private comfortable area for the bitch to whelp that is convenient to all necessary help and care.

Preparations for breeding your bitch begin at the moment you pick out the bitch as a puppy. You want one that is of superior conformation, sound temperament, good health and the best type possible for the breed. You must raise her with top-grade nutrition and plenty of daily exercise. Proper nutrition and exercise determine fertility and the uterine tone necessary for bearing and whelping a litter. The bitch must be in good weight, hip bones and ribs covered in flesh, with the coat healthy and shiny. However, she must not be obese. I find obese bitches do not conceive as well as thinner bitches. I also found my stud dogs were not as attracted to them. One of my very choosy males absolutely refused to breed overweight bitches as well as bitches that resisted being bred by growling at him or jumping around. I encourage a crash diet for obese bitches even at the time of breeding and into the first two to three weeks of pregnancy by feeding the diet or "light" dog foods supplemented with lowfat cottage cheese and cooked vegetables like carrots, celery, green beans, etc., along with a good vitamin supplement.

For a bitch in good weight, continue feeding a high-grade adult food through the fourth and fifth week of pregnancy since the bitch cannot fit larger meals in her system with the puppies inside her. Increase her food intake by feeding at least two, three or four meals daily. Then increase the supplements with a high-grade natural ingredient and/or multiple-vitamin supplement as well as a slight increase in vitamin C and raspberry leaf tea. I find this does wonders for toning the uterus for the hard labor that will ensue. Many veterinarians recommend feeding puppy food the last week or two of pregnancy since it provides a high calcium and protein source.

I find many Boxer bitches go through morning sickness just like women when they are pregnant. In the fifth to sixth week, a thick milky discharge is seen dripping from the vulva, confirming that she is pregnant.

Continue exercising your bitch right up to her due date. Later, she will slow down and may lay around lazily, resulting in a looser muscle tone and less pushing power when she needs it to get the puppies out. Many pet owners think that she is in a "delicate" way, so she must be treated gingerly. I tell the owners that if she were in the wild, she would be hunting and running miles to procure food to feed herself and nourish the growing pups inside her, so we can take this hint from nature and apply it at home through exercise and play. When playing with the pregnant bitch, do not throw a ball into the air. This will encourage jumping, which could be detrimental to her puppies. Long brisk walks are also good exercise. Remember that Boxer bitches are known to have lazy muscle tone in their uteri. A bitch in good muscle tone and condition can overcome this by having strong abdominal muscles to help push the puppies out. I cannot emphasize enough the benefits of exercise.

With good pushing power, the bitch can overcome dystocia, which I understand was more common in the earlier history of Boxers when they had bigger heads, larger, wider skulls and perhaps narrower hips. Dystocia is common among Bulldogs and Pekingese, who have big heads and narrow hips that make for difficult deliveries. Today's Boxers are more elegant with narrow occiputs and cleaner muzzles and heads in general.

WHELPING PREPARATION AND THE BIRTHING PROCESS

As the whelping date approaches, prepare the whelping box and area of the room that the bitch will occupy. Always provide a private area away from the hustle and bustle of your house and/or kennel. In the wild, a

A Dam of Merit who has contributed many champions to the Karmel breeding program, this is Jacquet's Kiri Te Kanawa, named by the author for the creamy lyric soprano from New Zealand.

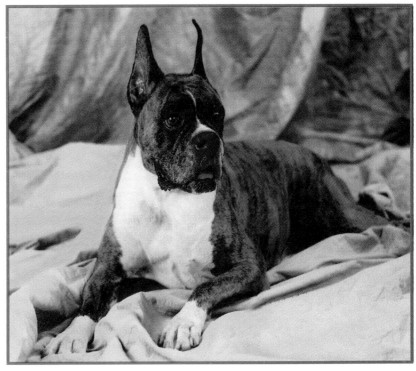

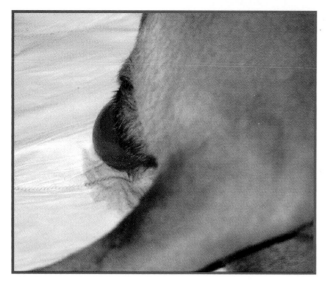

The puppy is beginning to emerge from the dam with the amniotic sac still intact. It appears as a small bubble from the pressure of the labor contractions. Sometimes this could be the water bag which could come and go until it is broken by the bitch by licking or breaks on its own from pressure of contractions. Another hour or two could pass before the first pup appears.

bitch seeks out a den away from enemies as well as her own kind. The area should be warm and dry. I use whelping boxes with guardrails that can be removed a week or two after birth. Some bitches can be clumsy, or if the whelping is a long process, they can become tired and inadvertently crush a pup against the walls of the box or a puppy can get caught in the corner and become chilled. Even if you sleep next to the box, you can rest more easily. There are boxes that can be purchased through mail order catalogs and easily put together. They are made of wood or plastic. One manufacturer has a whelping ex-pen complete with removable guardrails large enough for a Boxer and her litter. Even though wood is expensive, I prefer the whelping boxes made from wood. Some breeders use portable children's swimming pools made of plastic. I use an old blanket for the bottom in

The dam is cleaning one puppy while a second one is being pushed out, as the breeder anxiously catches it.

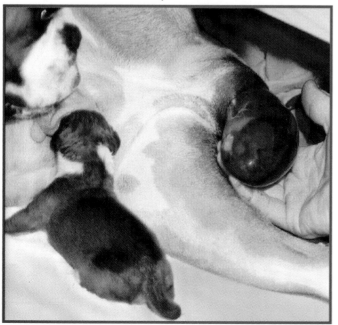

the beginning so the bitch can tear and pull and dig at it to relieve the tension created by the labor and the puppies' movements down the canal. When the pups are actually being born, you can put newspapers on the bottom with towels to soak up fluids. I then use the artificial lambskin pads, which allow the puppies to be on a warm surface that they can grip with their tiny paws. They cannot easily be torn so the puppies can't get tangled in them and they also allow any fluids to pass through, keeping the surface relatively dry.

Gestation is usually 63 days from conception. During the final days in whelp, the bitch will have a slight thick discharge, appearing creamy (like milk in color) or clear. I consider this lubrication for the vaginal canal. This is a good color. During her labor, this mucus can be tinged with a pinkish color and it is still alright. At the beginning of the final week of pregnancy and at least twice daily, two or three days prior to her due date, start to take her temperature using an anal thermometer. Use

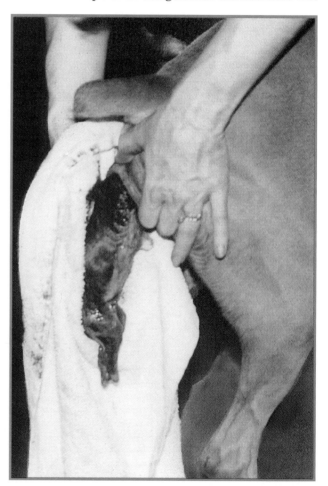

The breeder eases the whelp being born without a sac with a towel.

any water-soluble lubricant for insertion. I find this to be most accurate. Normal temperature for canines is approximately 101.5°F. As the due date approaches, the temperature runs from 101° to 99°. When her temperature drops to 98.5° or 98°, then whelping is about 12 hours away. Then I find the temperature starts to climb to 99°. There is no need to be alarmed if intermittent panting starts a day or two before the actual hard labor begins as long as the temperature has not dropped as described above.

I usually check the color of discharge, if there is any at this time. On occasion, a dark green tar-like discharge is present; this alarmed me the first couple of times, but I learned this discharge comes when the placenta breaks away from the wall of the uterus. However, if the bitch is in hard labor and discharges a watery emerald green discharge, like the color of algae, then the bitch could be in trouble. Usually, this is a sign that a puppy is stuck somewhere in her uterus and/or the vaginal canal. Call your vet! Often this occurs when a puppy from one horn collides with a puppy from the other horn as they descend down the birth canal. The hard labor, or the final phase of labor, is easily detected as the bitch will bear down with noticeable abdominal contractions accompanied by grunts. Some bitches, however, can push puppies out with minimum contractions. One or two pushes

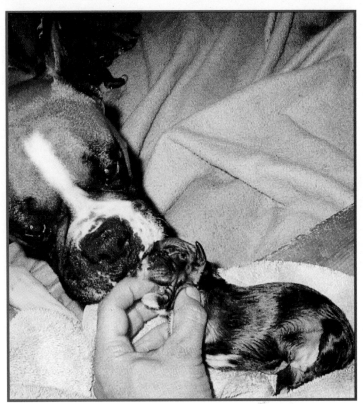

The breeder assists the newborn in breathing by inserting a finger in the mouth above the tongue and checks for any deformity in the palate at the same time.

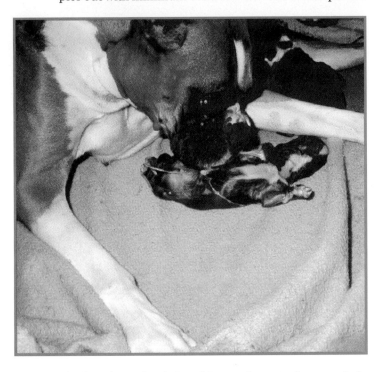

The dam cleans the whelp and ingests the protective sac and placenta, which is rich in blood and probably stimulates whelping and lets down milk.

and the puppy emerges. Puppies usually emerge anywhere from every 15 minutes to every two to three hours. If the time between puppies goes beyond three to four hours and if the bitch is bearing down hard, it might be a good time to do a vaginal examination to see if there might be an abnormality, such as malpresentation. Abnormal birth presentations are the head with one foot or neither, or the tail only with both rear legs tucked under. This is a true breech. With Boxers, we find that half the puppies come rear first. Often, if you put your mind to it, these can be straightened out by pushing the puppy back in. If after one or two attempts nothing happens, call the vet.

In those cases where a C-section is required, some vets will give the placenta to the mother, and rub it on the pups and in the bitch's mouth. This is done so that when she wakes up from the anesthesia, she will have the natural smell and taste of her puppies and not the smell of anesthesia, which could confuse her.

If inertia occurs, you can insert two fingers into the vulva and follow the canal upward toward the backbone. It will straighten out horizontally just below the anus and toward the head. During the actual labor, this is the canal that is dilated. Gently push against the ceiling of this canal toward the spine. If nothing occurs, then gently feather (massage) the top part of the canal. This usually will trigger strong contractions. Usually, after doing this a few times, a puppy will descend into this area and be in position to be born. By entering with your fingers, you can also tell that a puppy is already presented and in what position. This is always an aid to your vet when you have to report how the labor is progressing.

This is the stage when your vet may want to use oxytocin to produce heavier contractions to push the pup out. If you know how to inoculate, he may have given you an injection or two to give to her at this time. I never give oxytocin until I have consulted with my vet. If nothing is produced after 30 minutes to one hour, you *must* see your vet. If the cervix is closed or the puppy is stuck, heavy contractions stimulated by oxytocin could rupture the uterus.

During labor I suggest a brisk walk outside, weather permitting, and always on a lead. I have had bitches take off and hide on me, even in my fenced yard. The bitch may dig into a burrow and insist on having a puppy there, so take along a towel and, if at night, a flashlight in case she passes her puppy outside. I have had bitches that have been taken for a short, brisk walk, squat as if they were urinating and drop a puppy.

Sometimes a puppy will come out part-way and seem to be stuck. Take a towel and grasp the puppy, then gently but firmly pull outward in a downward movement. Puppies must be delivered as quickly as possible so that a puppy, still inside, can be born without delay. I've found that the first puppy to emerge, especially in the maiden bitch, is difficult to pass and causes some pain as it begins through the cervix and the vulva, making the bitch cry out. Application of water-soluble, sterile lubricant in the vaginal canal will help this process sometimes.

As you can gather with all that is involved in the birthing process, the bitch must not be left unattended. If you are nervous or unsure about this, ask an experienced friend to be with you. However, do not have an audience as this will make the mother nervous and she may retain the puppies. Above all, don't let your bitch sense your anxiety. Reassure her, make her feel secure and safe so that she can do what nature has instinctively instilled in her. Our Boxers are so close to us and so tuned into our emotions that a bitch in labor will sense if we are in dither or emotionally distraught, causing her to hold back or even halt the process, delaying valuable time. She may even hold back all of her puppies which, as you know, must come out as quickly as possible. The longer they stay inside her, the weaker they and their mother become.

When the puppy emerges, quickly locate the head and the nose; break the sac using your two thumbs while peeling it away to expose the head. I advise novices to put an orange or an apple in a plastic food storage bag, which has the feel of the sac, and with the thumbs, break the bag for practice before the whelping. I insert my pinky finger into the puppy's mouth on the tongue, which

Hold the end of the broken umbilical cord and with the other fingers push the blood within the cord back into the pup, before tying it off with silk thread or dental floss.

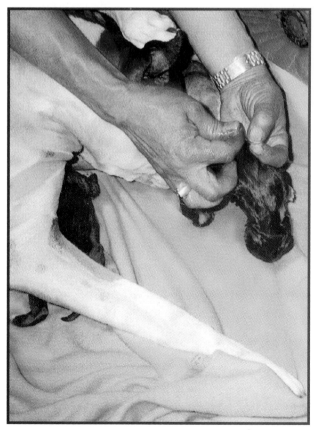

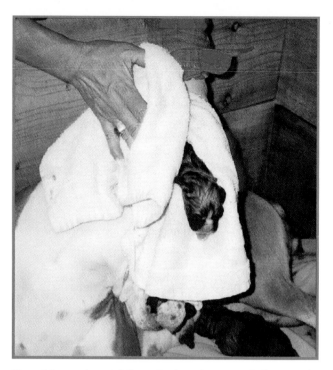

Since this pup is not fully revived, a vigorous rub down on its sides and back with a good terrycloth towel will help drain the fluids and stimulate the lungs as a mother's tongue would do. (Note the head and nose in downward position.)

will cause the puppy to suck the finger; then, in turn, the puppy pushes the fluid in the nostrils out. I then peel the sac completely away, if the bitch has not done so already. Cut the umbilical cord with blunt scissors or lacerate it in a jagged cut measuring about 3–5 inches from the navel. Try to push the blood in the cord back into the puppy before cutting. Dab povidine or tincture of iodine on the cut edge to prevent possible bacteria from entering the puppy's system. If the cord is cut too short or is bleeding, tie it off close to the body of the puppy with thread or dental floss. Shaking a pup immediately after birth is not always necessary. Rub them vigorously with a terry cloth towel, which resembles the mother's tongue and helps to get them breathing. Gently suck out the excess mucous from the mouth. With the head in a down position, rub the pup with a terry cloth towel on the sides and up and down the back. Again, open the mouth with a finger to allow the excess mucous to drip out. Scrubbing simulates the mother's tongue, which stimulates the pup until you hear it whimper or cry out.

If it doesn't get to this stage, I clasp the pup firmly between my two hands and, using my first two fingers, grasp the head securely so as not to snap the head and harm the pup. I swing it at arm's length in an arc between my parted legs. This will remove most of the mucous in the lungs and nasal cavities, which is preventing the pup from breathing, by using centrifugal force. Then towel scrub again briskly and give the pup to its mother, who will continue the scrubbing with her tongue. She will go for the umbilical cord, chomping and pulling at it. Since Boxers have an undershot bite, as opposed to scissors bites in most other breeds, cutting the cord is more difficult. Try to discourage the pulling by distracting her. By measuring off 3–5 inches,

I hold the cord with my fingers, allowing the bitch to bite and pull the end so that the pup's abdomen is not affected by the pulling pressure while the mother gets the satisfaction of having done her duty. I have seen instances where the bitch biting the cord has caused umbilical hernias, which may need to be corrected surgically a little later in the pup's life.

If a pup still has not revived after all of this, try mouth-to-mouth resuscitation by first gently sucking out the mucous from the nose and mouth before gently blowing over and into the mouth. There is a theory that carbon dioxide from breath stimulates the pup's breathing action.

Don't allow non-members of your family to visit at this point. Of course, there are some bitches that would welcome anyone to see her brood. Each bitch reacts differently. Be sympathetic to your bitch's needs.

I often have to explain to first-time owners of a new mother that the bitch goes into a protective mother mode upon whelping. It is similar to a high that a new mother experiences with her child. She becomes less aware of her human family and thinks only of her babies. She may not even recognize you. She may look at you with a worried expression. She may even try to hide her pups from your gaze by tucking them under her. Always reassure her that you are proud of her efforts. Ultimately, you may have to just leave her alone without too much fuss. Canines have had to do this in the wild in order for the pups, who are completely blind and helpless, to have the total protection and care of their mother.

You will find that the bitch will not leave the nest, whelping box, etc., unless you leash her and drag her out to do her toilet duties. She may even disregard her food. Put the food bowl in her box. If she does not find it particularly appetizing, offer her white bread with broth made from cut up chicken parts or marrow bones or chopped beef and entice her with this. I feed white bread soaked in the broth as the first meal right after whelping. I don't feed her until I make sure that the last pup is born so that she doesn't get sleepy on a full stomach. She must get those pups out. Should there be a large litter (ten or more) and the bitch has consumed numerous placentas and refuses to eat, anything goes—pizza works wonders!

Some bitches may get overprotective of their pups. This usually happens after her last puppy is born. She may be growling and ferocious looking, sometimes snapping and biting. This is what Mother Nature is telling her. It is left over from the wild state. Forgive her. She can even be this way to the owners that she normally loves and adores. I have encountered this on occasions and if I have to attend to the pups, I throw a large towel over her head so she cannot see me touching her pups. Leave a collar on her so that you can put a leash on her and take her out. Generally, these bitches, when taken out of the whelping box or out of the room where she has had her puppies (her den), revert back to themselves.

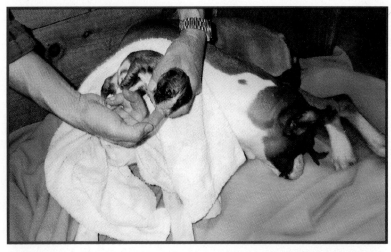

Inserting your finger into the mouth of the newborn starts the sucking motion and makes the pup able to breathe through the nostrils forcing out fluids that may still lie in the nasal passages. When you feel a good suction from the pup, place it on a the dam's nipple.

I use a heating mat, which is available with a thermostat, to control heat on the floor of the whelping box so that the pups can lay on this and be warmed by radiant heat. I also use a heat lamp during the first three days. I hang the lamp securely, 3–4 feet above the box, to quickly dry the pups' backs, especially after birth and after mother has been licking them. You will notice many mothers constantly licking them at the beginning, especially if you have touched them. This will prevent respiratory problems in a puppy. I have found that if the body temperature is maintained, the puppies are more vigorous and nurse more strongly.

Some bitches refuse to lay with their pups and will not allow them to feed from her. Comfort her and make her lie down and urge the pups to nurse from her. The sucking of the pups stimulates her milk and her maternal instinct. Try not to feed them too much. Avoid tube feeding if at all possible.

With one of the first pups born, the breeder helps by quickly breaking the bag and feeding the bitch the placenta and allowing her to chew the umbilical cord by holding it up to her.

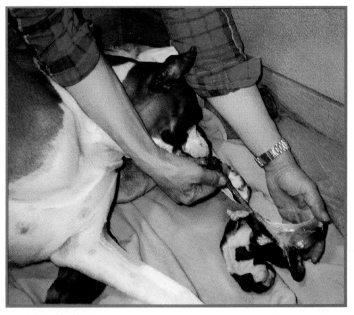

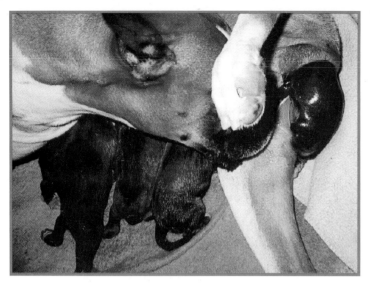

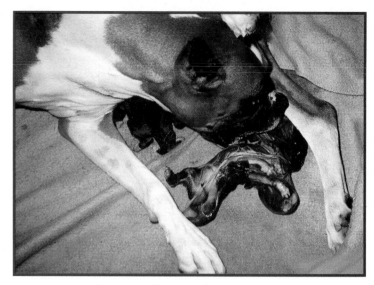

After several pups have been born the bitch is more aware of what is happening and is eagerly awaiting this next pup to break the bag on her own.

...and eagerly grabs the placenta to ingest it before it can be taken away from her. Removing it and disposing of it are advisable if she has ingested a few by this time.

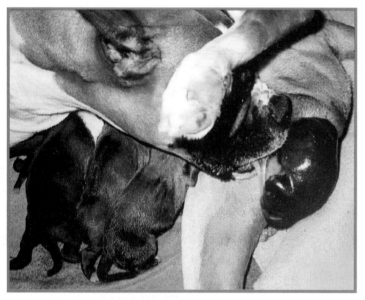

The bitch has already started breaking the bag as more of the puppy appears...

She has licked away the bag covering the pup as she awaits the placenta to emerge with another short contraction. Notice the pup has been revived still attached to the placenta.

She is biting and yanking the umbilical cord, which helps stimulate the pup but may unfortunately cause an umbilical hernia. Help by cutting the cord two to three inches away from the puppy with blunt scissors.

After the bag and the placenta are disposed of, the mother vigorously licks the puppy to stimulate and dry it.

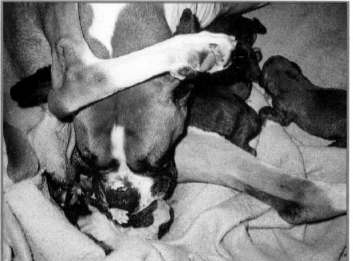

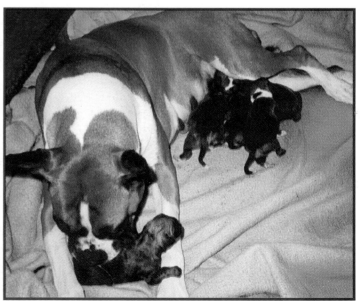

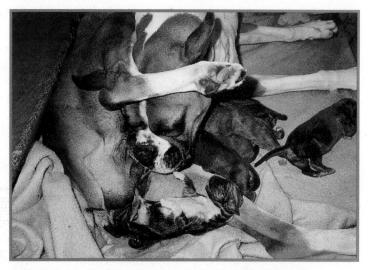

Not finished! Notice that her body is curled and she is not relaxed. There is still a slight bulge in her abdominal area. Her head rests over the pups to protect them.

She is licking and pulling the placenta which is still in her canal after she has broken the bag covering the pup with the breeder's help.

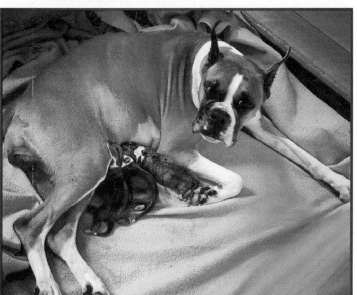

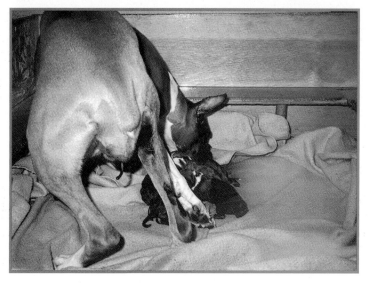

Restarting her labor...another puppy on the way. Notice the swelling of the vulva and the strained look in her eyes as contractions begin again.

Although it looks like a puppy tail, the membrane hanging out of the vulva is part of an umbilical cord attached to the retained placenta. If you can, you can grasp it gently pulling out the placenta as she contracts.

Here she is giving a real good push as the tail of the puppy emerges from the vaginal canal.

Finally the bitch is allowing herself to relax. She has completed whelping, though she may still have a placenta retained. Have her checked by your veterinarian.

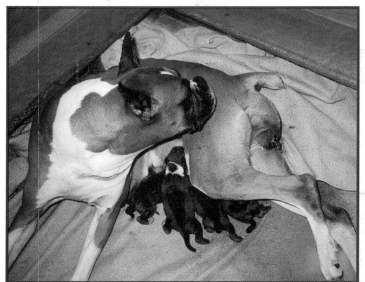

RESPONSIBLE STUD DOG OWNER

If you own a stud dog and your dog gets requests for breeding bitches to him, be very selective; allow him to breed only the best bitches. It takes two to tango, and the bitch contributes equally to the puppies that are produced. If the bitch is not of good quality and has glaring faults that your stud dog cannot correct, turn her down. Perhaps you can recommend her to another stud dog that can correct the fault or faults in the next generation. If faulty puppies come from this union, you know the stud will almost always be blamed. Ideally, the owner of the stud dog should be an experienced breeder with knowledge of three or four generations of Boxers he has bred and who knows all the shortcomings of his line. Try to be truthful with the fact that breeding the bitch will not do the Boxer breed any good. Be frank if you feel your male cannot correct the problems the bitch and her background may have that could produce mediocrity.

"Not tonight, Honey." **Photograph compliments of Verena Jaeger.**

Also, discourage the owners of the bitch from breeding if the situation is not ideal. They may have a tiny apartment or a small house where the bitch will not have her privacy. It is so important not to have distractions the first three weeks following the birth of the litter. Perhaps there are young children who would have unsupervised access to the whelping area, causing the bitch to become nervous and not do her job properly. She may also become overprotective and tuck them under her chest, smothering them, or she may lick them constantly, resulting in a loss of body heat, which can lead to fading puppies. Can the owner afford a litter? It is expensive having a litter when you are using the highest quality food and all the good supplements, purchasing all the necessary equipment and supplies to ensure a good, healthy and safe whelping. A well-made whelping box and veterinary fees for inoculations, tail docking, dewclaw removal and possibly ear cropping are all expensive.

Whelping a litter of puppies at home can have an effect on children at an impressionable age, those old enough to understand nature's way of reproduction. I was about 12 when my first Boxer bitch, who was quite well bred, had her litter. Not only was I in attendance, I helped whelp the puppies, cutting the umbilical cord and stimulating them, all the time being coached by my mother. Until this time I was told babies came via the stork. What a revelation—watching her pups being born, coming from her uterus via the vulva, watching the contractions and pushing. This was a moment I will never forget.

The stud dog owner must also be aware of communicable diseases that can be transmitted through breeding. Require tests showing that the bitch is clear of brucellosis and bacteria in the vaginal area that may cause serious problems for the stud dog. Have your stud dog checked for this yearly as well. Make sure both dogs have been checked for genetic defects such as hip dysplasia, congenital heart disease and other disabilities before you breed. If a problem shows up, don't use him no matter how beautiful he is, no matter how well bred. There are enough problems out there already. We breed to better the Boxer and to share healthy defect-free puppies with all who fancy our wonderful breed.

CARE OF THE STUD DOG

Before deciding to own and breed your stud dog, determine if your dog has the basic good conformation that the Boxer standard calls for, as well as an excellent temperament. Does he have the pedigree backed by known producers of merit? Are there many generations of known champions of quality? Are there untitled dogs in the pedigree with obvious pet names that could be the result(s) of backyard breedings? I am a firm believer in finishing a stud dog's title. Let qualified judges evaluate his merits. Of course, there are always some champions that are not of sufficient good quality and that should not have finished, but did anyway. At the same time, there are many non-champion males who are of high quality and represent good breed type.

The stud dog should be kept in the best physical condition possible. Feed him the highest grade protein-rich food. I supplement with a good vitamin based in natural ingredients fortified with natural vitamin E or wheat germ, which I believe keeps their fertility at optimum. Make sure the stud is neither too fat nor too thin. Heavy stud dogs huff and puff through a breeding, putting heavy stress on their vital organs, especially their hearts. A thin stud dog, without proper nutrition and in poor condition, could have problems with low sperm count and may lack stamina. The act of breeding is quite taxing to the male, therefore he should be in tiptop physical condition. He should have regular exercise in large paddock areas, long runs or a fenced yard. If none of this is available, a good jog in the park with you for two or three miles is a good alternative, as is fetching balls or Frisbees®. You can feel muscle tone. If the muscles are firm to the touch and in good tone to the eye, you know he is getting enough exercise and is in good condition. This is the same as when he was in great show condition. Keep up with his inoculations and check regularly for parasites.

As a responsible stud owner, you should always be available to answer questions and unselfish in guiding the owner of the bitch through the care required during pregnancy and whelping as well as the rearing of your stud dog's progeny. The knowledge of the stud dog's owner can eliminate problems and/or fears, making for a better experience and healthier puppies.

FEEDING NEWBORN PUPPIES

Good nutrition starts with mother's milk. The first protein is derived from the colostrum, followed by nu-

Bottle-feeding an extra baby, a runt or an orphan is necessary for the breeder, using a formula especially for canines.

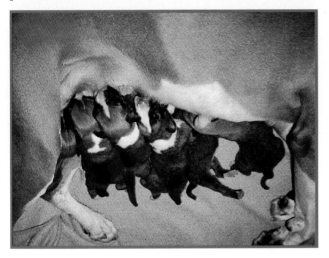

The pups are eagerly nursing, while the bitch's body is stretched and relaxed to faciliate nursing.

tritious milk. The necessary antibodies and hormones are present, especially in colostrum, as well as in the milk that follows. The mother protects her pups.

Commercial milk replacers provide needed calories and nutrients but lack growth-promoting peptides, hormones and antibodies. The usual ingredients may include dried skimmed cow's milk, vegetable oils, egg or lecithin. I find that replacers are safer than home brews, which may contain bacteria and molds and, if egg yolks are used, possibly the deadly salmonella. Unless you supplement with vitamins, replacers will not contain sufficient vitamins for the pup.

The pre-mixed milk supplement might contain more water than mixing with a dry concentrate. Several years ago, development of cataracts in wolf pups and certain purebred dogs were linked to commercial milk replacers. On researching this, I didn't get definite answers. It seems that in these cases pups were fed with replacers during the first three days of their life. I myself have not encountered this with our Boxers after many years of using top-quality commercial milk replacers. Some manufacturers stress on their label that their products will not cause cataracts. I feel that to keep the risk of cataracts low, feed the supplement in conjunction with mother's milk or, as an alternative, you can use goat's milk.

BRINGING UP BABIES

After birth, I constantly watch, check up on and monitor the newborns. I place the smaller and weaker pups on the rear nipples, the ones that are in the abdominal area. They are usually smaller in size and are more supple

so that the pups can hold onto them and get more milk to flow into their throats and tummies. I pull off the stronger and larger ones and put them on the larger nipples over the chest area. In nature, the pups all choose their favorite teat; the stronger ones choosing the easiest flowing teat. They will push off any pup that goes on their chosen nipple as they grow stronger and bigger. In a controlled atmosphere, we can help balance the litter by giving the smaller, weaker ones the advantage. Keep all the nipples flowing because they will be needed even more later as the pups grow and the demand for milk increases. I massage the breast and nipples at least twice daily to check for the beginning of mastitis and to watch the quality of the milk. The quality of the milk should not be thick after the first or second day when the colostrum is available and necessary for building up an immune system of the pups.

To stimulate milk productionof the bitch, the following recipe passed down by a succession of breeders works wonders:

> 2 servings dried oats
> 2 tbls. honey
> 1 fresh banana, mashed
> large can of evaporated milk
> 1 slice raw liver, chopped up

Feed the bitch every other day until her milk comes in. Another product I use to bring down milk is high in nutrition and calories, Pediatric Stat can be given to weak pups, as well.

If after two or three days you do not see weight gain and/or fast growth, you may have to supplement once or twice a day especially if the pelvic bones start to show.

This puppy is being hydrated using a sterile ringers solution for dehydration to prevent the pup from "fading." Courtesy, Dr. Gary Duhr.

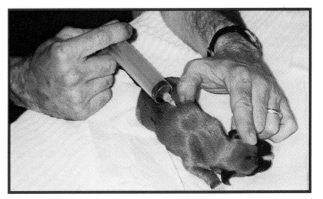

Competition among littermates entices the pups' appetites. The puppies are eating for themselves from a puppy pan especially designed by the author. Rick's Puppy Pan is the choice weaning tray for many breeders.

Use a human baby nurser that is made of soft plastic that gives as the pups nurse, so that the supplement will flow out almost like a bitch letting her milk down. The larger pet nursers are all right. Don't use the small ones that are a better size for kittens, bunnies, etc. The Boxer pups will try to suck on this and take in more air than formula. Because there will be an intake of air through bottle feeding, it is essential to burp the puppy by holding the puppy upright against your body and stroking his back gently. If you don't burp the puppy, when you put him in the whelping box he might burp up the supplement and could aspirate into his lungs, causing pneumonia or instant death.

If you have weak puppies that cannot suck from the bottle, you might have to tube feed, a very tricky procedure. Seek help from your vet or an experienced breeder. Most veterinarians can provide you with a tube-feeding kit. I use a thick catheter attached to a mouth syringe. Measure the catheter carefully from the abdomen to the tip of the nose. This is how long the tube should be inserted into the pup through the mouth. If the puppy coughs, it is going down the trachea. Pull it out immediately and re-insert until you reach the measured spot on the catheter. Mark it off with surgical tape. Put the open end into a glass of water to see that you are not getting air bubbles. If you are, the tube is down the trachea. Re-insert the tube, then attach this end to the mouth syringe and pour the warm supplement into the syringe with the plunger removed and allow the formula to funnel slowly into the puppy's stomach.

For weak puppies, select an easily assimilated formula with electrolytes. Use only a drop on the tongue. If you give too much of this type supplement, because it is so rich, it can cause colic.

If the puppy feels cold to the touch and is getting weak or is being pushed aside from the dam and is not nursing, warm the pup on a heating pad. The best method of bringing the pup's warmth to its normal level is taking it under your shirt, blouse or undershirt, against your skin, then putting on a sweater or sweatshirt and carrying the puppy around with you. The moisture from your body combined with your body heat and hearing your heartbeat can stimulate the puppy into a more vigorous state. I find, when the pup's body temperature rises, it is stimulated to nurse a bit stronger and I have also found that the bitch has a tendency not to push the pup aside.

For colicky pups, the above method is also helpful. Tucking the pup into your shirt and rocking or moving around brings the gas out of its digestive system. If you have a rocking chair sit and rock. A few drops of chamomile extract on the tongue can also be helpful. This can be purchased in health food stores. Bentil syrup from your veterinarian is also a lifesaver in extreme cases.

If you or a member of the family are suffering from strep throat, don't go near the puppies. This is the only illness that Boxer puppies can contract from a human I am told. This condition is known in canines as puppy strangles. The lymph glands in the neck near the throat get swollen, preventing the puppy from swallowing and making breathing difficult. If not treated with antibiotics, it can be fatal to your puppies. Feel the glands to check. Sometimes, if you lift the ears up, you will see blisters on the inside of the ears. Consult your vet immediately.

Do be careful not to overdo it and fill their bellies so much that they don't drink sufficiently from their mother and stimulate her milk production. The constant feeding and pulling stimulate milk to come down. I like to get the pups robust before having the tails docked and dewclaws removed so that they can withstand this first trauma in their life. A dietary supplement designed for stress relief containing *lactobacillicus* such a Bene Bac® is most helpful before and after the tail-docking trauma. I like to have the tail and dewclaws done between the fifth and seventh

Two Jacquet infants still with their eyes closed. The pups' eyes usually open by the tenth day.

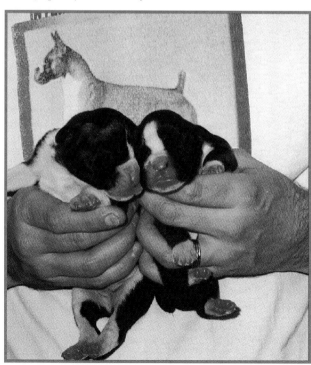

day. I find that the blood does not clot so easily when docking is performed on the first or second day. In Boxers, the ideal length (at the fifth to seventh day) is 3/4 of an inch. At that point, you will find the tail, from the base of the spine out, becomes thinner and the color of the hair turns from light to dark. There is a joint perfect for cutting at this spot. I found it is better to cut a little longer than shorter since you can never add on; but, if it is too long, you can always re-dock at a later age.

At a day old, I also like to provide a *lactobacillus* product in an easily absorbed paste form and mildly fortified with vitamins to supplement pups through this critical period, the first 10 to 14 days of life. Such a supplement helps prevent diarrhea, which can seriously dehydrate puppies.

Be sure to keep the sharp nails on the pups trimmed using a human fingernail trimmer, the snapping kind, or a cat claw trimmer. If you notice, healthy hungry pups will push with their paws on the breast in a kneading action to stimulate milk flow. Provide a sheepskin-like pad, towel or clean throw rug for traction on which the pups can grip with their hind feet and be able to push with their front paws. If everything goes well and mother's milk production is adequate, it usually takes three to seven days for the production and richness of bitch's milk to become adequate for the pups, you will not have to worry until the end of two-and-a-half weeks or the beginning of the third week to start the weaning process. I use a prepared milk-replacer formulas warmed and mixed with baby rice cereal, which gives extra nourishment and aids in the formula not running through the pup's digestive system (since rice is a binder). Jars of baby meats can be added to the rice cereal mix to make it really appetizing. The pups dive into the feeding pan. Many breeders prepare their own formula through elaborate mixtures of different ingredients. Some use goat's milk and others give lean chopped round steak. This is done by holding a portion the size of a marble between your fingers and having the pup work for it. This makes the puppy salivate and aids digestion. A prepared canned weaning formula is available and is very nutritious and fortified with the proper vitamins. The puppies love it and it makes weaning less of a chore. There is a puppy feeding dish that is just ideal for weaning a litter of puppies. It has the center of the dish raised so that the pups cannot get in the middle of the dish, messing themselves and also messing in the food. The pan is sloped, keeping the food around the outside where all the pups can get to it. It makes feeding so easy—I know since my partner and I developed it.

Play classical music throughout this period. I leave the classical music station on 24 hours a day. Our pups, when their ears pop open, which seems to happen overnight (around the second week), hear the soothing sound of rich music interrupted with the usually soothingly quiet

Much of what a puppy needs to learn begins with the dam. An experienced or instinctive dam is the mother who knows best. Owner, Pat Baxter. Photo by Lidda Brombern.

voices of the announcers. I've found this, together with a lot of gentle handling, creates a calmer, more self-confident puppy. I have been doing this for years and have gotten many positive comments on how calm and content the pups are when they go to their new homes. Much study on classical music has been done on growing plants as well as its effect on humans. It has been found to produce healthy and robust plants and calm, healthy and smart babies.

After a week of the milk-replacer and rice cereal or canned weaning food, I gradually add well-soaked dry puppy food of the highest grade possible (i.e., a pet-shop brand puppy lamb and rice formula).

After most of the puppy's teeth have come in, poor mother will not feel comfortable staying in the same whelping box as long and will begin to stop feeding. This is when some mothers will regurgitate her partially digested food for the pups. I let them eat this since I feed the bitch puppy food. The pups will find this most appetizing and devour this food with relish. In the wild, mother goes off hunting, sometimes traveling very far for game, and then carries the food conveniently in her stomach partially digested along the way and then regurgitates it for the pups, who bolt this food down. By the fifth week, puppies can be almost entirely on solid foods, fed at least three to four times daily.

If during the second or third week puppies develop diarrhea caused by mother's milk or other circumstances, feed them a mixture of formula and rice cereal in a human baby bottle with a crosscut nipple. You may want to enlarge the crosscut to make a larger opening to allow the slightly thick gruel mixture to be sucked. The rice cereal will help stop the diarrhea and stay in the pup's system for more nourishment. Do not allow them to overeat this formula, as it can cause colic.

When the pups all eat together as a litter, there is stimulation from the age-old chow-time competition, similar to the pups' fending for a nipple at the milkbar.

FADING PUPPY SYNDROME

Puppies that seem healthy at birth but fail to thrive will pass away within their first three weeks. During the first 24 hours, the puppy is vigorous and seems to nurse well. After that he usually does not gain weight and his pelvic bones show. He may develop diarrhea and cry continuously, escalating toward a high-pitched squealing sound. Such puppies are restless. Unfortunately, this upsets the bitch and she begins to neglect the rest of the litter because of her concern for the fading pup. These symptoms can be caused by bacteria in the systems such as *streptococci* and *escherichia coli*. Also various viruses, including herpes, can sometimes be combated with high heat. Bacteria can be often cured with puppy antibiotics from your vet. If the puppy becomes dehydrated, you can tell this by softly lifting and pinching the skin and if it does not lay back down in a couple of seconds, ask your veterinarian to hydrate the pup with fluids subcutaneously giving them the strength to start their nursing. Our veterinarians have saved many fading pups this way. Parasites, particularly hookworms, could also be a cause. Check the stools. Is the puppy chilled (low temperature)? Is the bitch's milk not rich or nutritious enough? To prevent this, you may choose not to breed a bitch that produced fading pups. However, oftentimes in the next litter this may not occur. Consult your vet on possibly putting the bitch on an antibiotic regimen that will not affect the fetuses during the breeding and pregnancy.

Puppies that have been given antibiotics and puppies that are born to and nurse from bitches that have been given antibiotics may have their digestive bacteria cultures destroyed. Give these puppies a dietary supplement paste (containing *Lactobacillus*) to rebuild the cultures in the lower bowels so that they will not develop diarrhea or not be able to assimilate nourishment.

It has also been found recently that another possible cause for fading puppies is attributed to collapsed lungs at birth or if the circulation of the blood, which was altered at birth, does not modify itself to the normal level through the heart and liver. The puppies will remain cold and weak and will fade away. Puppies are born with a lower body temperature than adult dogs, so it is necessary to have them absorb warmth from mother's mammary glands from her body temperature. I almost always augment heat with a heated whelping pad under the whelping box. There are pads that are moisture resistant with the cord protected against chewing that can be placed right in the whelping box. Puppies seem to absorb heat better this way than through raising the room temperature, which in many ways is a waste of energy. A second way of heating the whelping box is with an infrared heat lamp. Don't put it too close to cause burning or dehydration and, of course, don't aim it on the bitch. It could overheat her and she will start panting and sometimes try to move away from her pups. It also could scatter the puppies, causing the bitch to step or lie on a puppy. By having the heat in one spot, the puppies will gather and when they are warm, will move away, moving back when they feel the need for heat. After five to seven days, if the whelping room is a comfortable temperature, they will not need so much of the extra heat such as the heat lamp or the portable radiators, which can be placed right near the box. Kerosene heaters are dangerous and a fire hazard. Electric heaters are dangerous and can cause the pups to dry out. I also don't use human heating pads in the box because you don't want it to get wet from puppy urine or have the bitch move it with her paws or dig as many new mothers do.

This flashy litter of seven appears ready for meeting their new owners. Breeder, Ed Goldfield.

KEEPING PUPPIES HEALTHY

Healthy newborn pups do not lie still for long periods. Their sleep is interrupted by twitching and small jerky movements. This is called activated sleep and the purpose is to develop and exercise the nerve and muscle systems. Healthy pups are warm and feel plump. A pup will make a murmuring sound with a light yip if mother moves it or a littermate pushes it off a teat. If the puppy is lying very still, then you worry about it. Something is usually wrong. A puppy that cries constantly—especially if the crying becomes a high-pitched sound like a seagull—indicates trouble. The bitch will usually ignore or reject a pup that is abnormal or has a birth defect that we may not see. She may smell or hear something or the pup does not react to her licking.

Line the whelping box with an artificial lambskin pad with newspaper underneath or, even better, throwaway whelping pads made from super-absorbent paper like the material used in throwaway diapers. The lambskin pads provide warmth as well as a surface to dig in their back paws, so they are able to latch onto mother's teats and nurse more efficiently without expending wasted energy sliding about. This pad also keeps them cleaner and prevents bacterial growth. Bacteria can cause pustules usually found on the stomach and abdominal areas. If the bitch is not prudent in cleaning her pups, it can spread into the furry area on the back and rump, which can cause the fur to come off. Wash these areas with a warm aqueous solution containing povidone-iodine and rub a good antiseptic cream on them. In bad cases, they may have to go on puppy antibiotics. Consult your vet.

Sometimes even the unopened eye can get affected. You will either see discharge or, worse, pus coming from the corner of the eye, or the unopened eye will swell. Get an antibotic eye ointment from your vet and administer it under the lid. Get the eye opened as soon as you begin this treatment. This problem can also be caused by conjunctivitis.

Umbilical hernias are quite common in Boxers and other blunt-nosed dogs with undershot jaws. Unlike the scissors bite in other canines, they cannot cleanly cut the cord. There is a lot of pulling and biting by the mother. I usually try to help bitches by measuring off about 3 to 6 inches of the cord from the abdomen of the pup. Push the blood contained in the entire cord into the pup. I pinch this section with two fingers, and using a pair of blunt scissors, I lacerate the cord. I dab the cut end with a solution containing povidine-iodine or tincture of iodine for prevention of bacteria to enter the pup. This laceration action will stop the bleeding from the end. Never make a sharp cut because it will cause some bleeding. If there is bleeding, tie off with a silk thread or dental floss close to the navel.

I find that, as the puppy grows and exercises and builds up his abdominal muscle, the umbilical hernia usually disappears.

Every once in a while a pup is born with a cleft palate, a condition in which the two halves of the hard palate in the roof of the mouth are not fused together at birth. It seems to be more prevalent in short-nosed

This dam is imparting some last minute wisdom before the puppy takes on the world on his own. Breeders, Ottavio and Isabella Perricone.

breeds. If you are not certain of this condition, you may see milk coming down the nose as the pup tries to nurse. The mouth cannot create a suction power because of this opening in the roof of the mouth, and these pups have no weight gain and instead begin to lose weight and become increasingly weaker. Unfortunately, these pups must be put down. If not, the constant crying because it gets no nourishment will upset the mother and take her concentration away from the good healthy pups.

Sometimes a puppy will be born with an opening of the middle of the occiput, sometimes referred to as an open fontanelle. Usually the pup is smaller, looking like the runt of the litter. This could be a later conceived puppy being slightly premature, thus, the bony plates of the skull could not fuse together before birth. This sometimes takes a long time to close, closing way after weaning. When it does, the puppy usually makes great strides in its growth and catches up to its littermates.

BREEDING AGE

In Boxers, I have found that puppyhood lasts for a long time and the first estrous may not occur until they are 18 months to 24 months of age. Don't be alarmed. I have frequently gotten calls from owners of our bitches, seemingly worried that their bitch is close to 18 months of age and has not been in season. This is quite normal with our Boxer bitches and I have found that this also tells us that she will come into season every 8 to 12 months, which is a blessing for a bitch that is a housepet.

Denise Gianninoto, kennel manager for Jacquet Boxers, and author Richard Tomita proudly poses with a litter of future champions. Denise has been managing the Jacquet kennel for over 15 years, while Rick has been named "Kennel Breeding the Most Champions" by the American Boxer Club for about the same amount of time.

HOUSEBREAKING

Mother ingests the puppy waste during the first three weeks. As soon as you introduce solid foods to the puppies, mother usually stops. Some mothers will go on. At this point, you must take over by using newspapers, shredded is more practical. Newspapers have grains. By going with the grain and stripping as thin as possible, they fluff up better thus absorbing urine and wrapping around feces so that the pups are not rolling in it. Pick the soiled clumps out and discard. This is especially helpful when the weather is bad and you cannot take them out. We take them out if the weather is good after every naptime and after every meal. Using a run or an ex-pen, they will get to a point of not soiling in the whelping box. I have seen breeders using two boxes, one with paper and the other with a blanket, and the pups go to the one with newspapers to relieve themselves. We even-

tually have them use the doggy doors, the swinging type, and have mother teach them housebreaking. Puppies are wonderful mimickers and after seeing mommy going in and out the door, they do the same. Of course they see mother relieving herself outside and follow suit. They do what they see. In no time, they will keep their living quarters clean.

One winter, I visited some Boxer breeders when their puppies were nearly weaned and they slept in boxes inside two ex-pens put together with layers of newspapers on the floor. Fortunately for the puppies, the breeders were retired and they spent all of their waking hours picking up with pooper scoopers or moving the ex-pen and picking up the newspapers. The puppies were immaculate except for some newsprint on the white parts. All this was set up in their sunroom right off the kitchen. I was green with envy that I could not spend all of my waking hours with the puppies. I shared this experience with a friend of mine who also breeds on occasion. She exclaimed, "Why that's exactly what I do when I have a litter!" A total commitment.

What I do now is have assistant puppy sitters to constantly keep the whelping box and the pen picked up. I have found that our pups rarely messed in the crates when they entered their new homes and were just about housebroken. I tell the new owners they just have to be on their daily schedule. Many are skeptical but they call me later and say, "You were right, they are just about housebroken."

In fact, as they grow, keep all feces picked up and neutralize urine and fecal odors with enzymatic odor cleaners. Your Boxer will appreciate this. Remember most Boxers are huggers by nature so you'll be glad that your Boxer won't smear his duty on you whenever he wraps his arms around you.

"Jake" grew up to be Aust. Ch. Boxhaven Trivial Pursuit, bred by Peter Foster and owned by Andrew and Lyn Bennett.

BREEDER BONDING

Boxers love to have their croup above the tail scratched. This is a spot they usually cannot reach to scratch themselves. I scratch this area with one hand and scratch their chest at the same time. You will have them love you forever. I also rub a bitch on her stomach area just in front of the vulva, the male just in front of the penis, the abdominal area. This has a very soothing, almost hypnotic, effect and you are letting them know you are alpha. I also bite the side of the muzzle, not hard, but with affection. This is also letting your Boxer know you are alpha. Boxers have the nicest smell in this area, I think—not doggy, just Boxer. I found this show of affection imprints you onto the puppy and they will always remember you after they have left, even years later.

The cropped ears should be standing if you've been prudent in taping them upward. If there is a bit of weakness, use props with tape to help them upward.

Boxers in the United States do not drool. The Boxers have been carefully bred to eliminate excess flews (jowls) and padding around the muzzle. The modern-day Boxers are more elegant in stature and in head, softening the "mean" look that frightens people. Yet, they can still be an effective deterrent for burglars who gladly do not realize how super-friendly Boxers are.

The Boxer is everything I wanted in a dog: smart, clean, playful and very protective with children.

I grew up with a Boxer when I was a child and my love for them has never strayed to another breed of dog (except for the Shiba Inu). I am in contact with many breeds and have observed them for years; however, the sculpted beauty of the Boxer in physical stature, their wonderful sense of humor, their playfulness, their sense of loyalty make them the perfect dog in my view. The very nature of their personality I find uplifting and invariably puts me in a good mood.

The future Can. Ch. Jaegerhouse's Abracadabra, learning a little magic from his cookie-eating toddler friend.

"Everything I ever wanted in a dog," the Boxer is compelling and endearing, strong and protective with a big heart and an uplifting spirit. This charmer is the author's house dog, Jacquet's Holden.

EAR CROPPING

BY CONNIE JANKOWSKI

While many countries, especially in Europe, have banned ear cropping, it is still legal and routinely done in the United States. In fact, most breeders have their entire litters cropped between the ages of seven to nine weeks. This is especially true in the case of the longer, stylized crop required on the Boxer. Ears that are cropped later may not stand up as well as those done at younger ages. If you decide you want an uncropped Boxer, you should discuss this with your breeder early. Don't expect to find older puppies that are uncropped.

Should you have your dog's ears cropped? This elective surgery is traditionally performed on Boxers because removal of ear flaps once served a practical purpose, enabling dogs to perform their jobs more efficiently. Although few dogs today work for a living, many pet owners prefer the look of a dog with cropped ears and choose to follow the tradition established by early breeders.

Other Boxer owners prefer to keep the natural look of the Boxer and they disregard this elective surgery. Any surgery can cause stress, and some dogs have difficulty accepting the post-surgical care regimen. If you are debating the ear-crop issue, discuss the procedure with your dog's breeder and your veterinarian.

WHY CROP?

In addition to creating an image, cropping ears has practical benefits for dogs. Dogs with erect ears suffer fewer infections and health problems related to the ears. Therefore, by "creating" erect ears from pendulous ones, a Boxer owner can help his dog avoid the tendency to suffer from ear infections. When a dog's ears hang low, the ear flaps cover the entrances to the ear canals. Therefore, air circulation is limited and the warm, isolated canal can become a host for bacteria, which may result in painful infections. Cropping the ears changes the conformation of the ear, and the dogs enjoy the same benefits as dogs with naturally erect ears, such as Siberian Huskies and German Shepherd Dogs.

Breed type dictates the surgical preferences for dealing with ear problems, but pet owners faced with chronic ear infections in their dogs should consider surgical options to improve their dogs' health and comfort.

"COSMETIC" SURGERY

This term is often misleading and can cause pet owners to make dangerous decisions about their dogs. Cropping ears is not a grooming procedure. Cropping ears should not be performed by a breeder, dog handler or pet store manager. Ear cropping is a surgical procedure that should only be performed by a licensed veterinarian in a hospital setting. It is illegal for a layperson to perform surgery on animals, however, many ignore the law, and many problems result from these "back-alley butchers."

Laypeople lack the knowledge, skill, proper medications, equipment and sterile environment that is necessary for the practice of medicine.

What are the proper conditions for cropping ears? When performed by a competent surgeon, in the ap-

While the question of ear cropping is a legal one in some countries, in the United States and Canada, it is purely a question of style, elegance and grace. America has truly become the Boxer's nation, where the stylish gentleman can shine and compete with the showiest breeds. Breeders, Avis Breck and Merrilane kennels.

propriate environment, the procedure is safe and is usually free of complications. Ear cropping is not a simple surgical procedure, but a major one that involves putting the dog under general anesthesia for approximately one and a half hours. When choosing a surgeon to perform this procedure, the pet owner should look for a doctor with experience cropping that breed.

The surgery is most successful when performed at the proper age for the dog (7 to 9 weeks is recommended for Boxers) and when followed by a post-operative care period of 2 to 24 weeks. Ears can be cropped when the dog is older than the ages listed, however, there is greater chance that the aftercare will be extended.

SUCCESS?

Can a veterinarian guarantee that a dog's ears will stand following surgery? Ear cropping surgery is determined by the shape of the ear. Whether or not the ear stands correctly depends upon other factors, such as ear cartilage, muscle control, breeding, genetics, nutrition and surgical aftercare. Most of these factors are controllable when the owner participates in the recovery process.

After surgery there is a period in which the hospital staff and the pet owner work together to complete the process of creating erect ears. Choosing to have a dog's ears cropped should be a major commitment on the part of the dog owner. Without the owner's commitment, the procedure is useless.

POST-SURGERY

If surgery is performed during morning hours, your puppy should be able to go home between 4:00 and 6:00 p.m. on the same day. Boarding is strongly recommended for puppies having surgery who are older than the optimum ages, or for puppies that may have to be left alone. The first 24 to 48 hours are an important adjustment time. Should you anticipate any problems in properly taking care of your puppy following surgery, board it in the hospital.

When you arrive to take your puppy home, you will observe that the incisions on the puppy's ears are exposed to the air and are not covered with a dressing. This procedure facilitates healing and allows you to clean the incision sites.

Your puppy may be slightly ataxic during your drive home, so transport it in a kennel or bring someone to hold your puppy during the drive. When you arrive home after the surgery your puppy will be glad to be home, thirsty and hungry. Do not give food or water for the first half hour, then, give only small amounts during the next six hours. Giving too much food and water at one time may result in nausea and vomiting. Once fed and quenched, and the initial excitement of being home is over, your puppy may quickly go to sleep.

Properly taped ears do not interfere with the puppy's socialization period. Puppies quickly adjust to the inconvenience of having their ears taped.

THE ADJUSTMENT PERIOD

Often, the pet owner's attitude affects the puppy's recovery. Owners who maintain a calm attitude will aid in their dogs' recovery. Owners who overreact will stress their dogs and inhibit healing. The most difficult time for the puppy and its owner will be the first week after surgery. This is when the puppy must adjust to the incision and tape on its ears. Most puppies quickly learn not to rub or scratch the ears because scratching is uncomfortable.

Following surgery, the puppy's ears must be taped upright or supported by a plastic or metal ear rack, which is typically worn for two weeks. The pet owner must clean the ears twice each day, using cotton balls or gauze pads moistened with 3% hydrogen peroxide. Following each cleaning, antibiotic ointment should be applied to avoid infection. The puppy should be examined by the veterinarian seven to ten days after surgery. After two weeks, the veterinarian will remove the rack and sutures. Additional support tape will be required to keep the ears standing at this time. Your puppy should be seen every two weeks for the next few months for rechecks and tapings.

Of course, all puppies should receive vaccinations and examinations to ensure general good health. When shopping for veterinary services, including surgeries, remember that the lowest price isn't always the best price. With a low price tag often comes minimal care. Be sure that safety and comfort measures are taken, such as pre-operative blood panels and post-operative pain medication for your puppy.

A future star, Ch. Jacquet's Attribute at five months needed a little extra encouragement with his right ear. Sean Pattman poses with Attribute for this photo.

CARING FOR CROPPED EARS

BY RICHARD TOMITA

If you choose to have your Boxer puppy's ears cropped you will have to learn how to provide the after-care. The taping and care will continue for a period of several months due to the long, stylized cut that is used in the breed. Over the many years that I have bred Boxers, I have collected some wonderful methods for making the ears stand properly.

Initially, when the ears are still stitched and healing, apply medicated powder. This product can be found in most drug stores. It should be used twice a day for at least four or five days on the cut edge. It will promote healing and relieve the itchiness so that the puppy will not scratch and possibly tear out the stitches.

Once the edge has scabbed over, begin using aloe vera cream with natural vitamin E. After the stitches have been removed, start massaging the ears upward into the position you want them to stand. You can also use warm olive oil, ointment with vitamin E or nothing at all while massaging. This process keeps the cut edge stretched during the healing process. It will also make the ear stand more quickly.

Since most Boxer ears do not stand on their own, they will have to be taped. Some owners and breeders use mole foam and skin bond for a tapeless bracing of the ears in an upright position. This method keeps the ears stretched and up so that you can eliminate the massaging and stretching process. However, you must be on top of this technique by changing the mole foam every four or five days.

Most owners and breeders still use the standard taping method to make the ears stand. Porous cotton tape is preferred since it will let the ear "breathe" and not cut into the ear itself. Ears should not be taped until all the scabs have healed.

Ch. Hi-Hat's Moonshadow v. Jacquet began practice for show career with her ears taped. Breeders, Leni Kaplan and Richard Tomita. Owner, Nancy Wainwright.

Veterinarian Dr. Gary Duhr of Ramapo Valley, New Jersey, listens intently for a clear bill of health for this plump Jacquet puppy bred by Joe and Laura Monello.

If the ear flops outward, away from the occiput, follow the natural fold of the skin found at the base of the ear. Pull the ear upward, really stretching it, and wrap the tape in a spiral upward like a barber pole. Taping always begins at the very base of the ear. Keep the tape rather loose. If the tape is too tight it will cut off the circulation and be more difficult to remove. Leave the very tip of the ear exposed as a guide for when you cut the tape upwards using bandage scissors.

If the ears flop inward or pull toward the top of the head, taping can correct this problem. However, this is a little trickier. First, massage the ear to soften. Then wipe dry with alcohol preps. This will remove the oils and help the tape to stick better. Start taping from the base of the ear, but this time you unfold the natural fold of the ear and tape the opposite way from the method described above. This flips the muscle at the base so that the ears straighten upward. Leave the tape on for five to seven days. If left on longer than this, the muscle may break down. When you remove the tape, let the ear rest for at least a day before retaping. I usually wait until the ear flops again before I retape.

I do not use calcium supplements but do recommend vitamin C, which seems to form good connective tissue.

METHODS OF "POSTING"

BY MURIEL DIETERICH AND VI CAMPOS

When all scabs or rough edges have disappeared, it is necessary to begin the process called "posting" to train the ears to stand on their own. The word "posting" tends to overwhelm the new owner, but there are several methods that are easy to do that are non-invasive and not traumatic to the new pup. Remember...you will be posting for several months, especially if your puppy is of show quality. Ears do not just pop up!

Mole Foam

One of the easiest methods of posting is to use Dr. Scholl's Mole Foam. It keeps the ears stretched, it is light, and it is quick to do.

Supplies needed:
Mole foam (Diagram A)
Skin bond (surgical glue)
Scissors
1-inch cloth adhesive tape

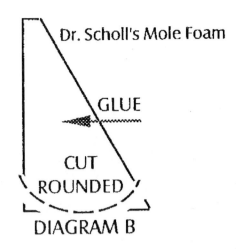

DIAGRAM B

press the glued side of the mole foam against the glued inside of the ear.

7. Take a 6-inch piece of cloth adhesive tape and secure by wrapping it around the bottom of the ear. *Do not tape tightly!*

This posting should last five to seven days and is easy to remove as it peels off.

DIAGRAM A

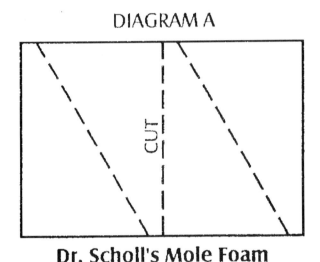

Dr. Scholl's Mole Foam

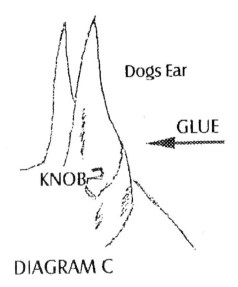

DIAGRAM C

1. Use one square of mole foam (not mole skin) per posting. Mark the square as indicated in Diagram A.

2. Leave the protective backing on the mole foam when cutting. Cut along dotted line as indicated in Diagram A. Cut bottom in a rounded arc as in Diagram B.

3. Clean the pup's ears well.

4. Remove the backing to the mole foam.

5. Apply the surgical glue (skin bond) to the inside of the pup's ears as in Diagram C and to the back of the mole foam as in Diagram B. Apply glue on the entire ear up to the knob (Diagram C) at the bottom of the ear. Let the glue become tacky before applying.

6. Make sure you pull the ear upward tautly as you

Taping with a Plug

Sometimes ears need stronger reinforcement. This happens if the ears are exceptionally long or soft in texture. Taping with a plug is a more tedious task, but it is a sure-fire taping method.

Supplies needed:
1-inch cloth adhesive tape
Tampon (slender/slim-line)
Scissors

Take a slender or slim-line tampon (the cardboard applicator style, not plastic) and measure the size of the pup's ears. The tampon can be adjusted to the length of the ear by pulling in or out. Once it is the size you need, secure the tampon with a piece of adhesive tape so that the applicator doesn't shift. Always make the plug longer

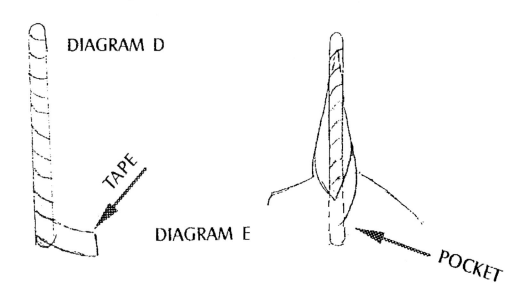

DIAGRAM D

DIAGRAM E

TAPE

POCKET

than the ear, as this prevents injury to the tip. Taking the cloth tape, wrap the entire tampon with the tape (sticky side out). You now have the plug (Diagram D).

1. Hold the ear up as high as it will go.

2. Insert the plug low in the ear pocket.

3. Lay the ear against the sticky plug.

4. Take several 6-inch pieces of cloth tape and secure the plug to the ear. (Diagram E)

5. *Do not tape tight.*

There is also a variation on this procedure that uses three pieces of tape instead of a plug. The accompanying diagrams illustrate this alternate method.

Correcting a common problem: On occasion a puppy will have an ear that tends to pitch inward (Diagram F). This pitching is caused by the muscle at the bottom of the ear. This muscle, near the knob, must be trained to go in the opposite direction. The simplest method is to take one or two cotton balls and attach them to the plug (located by the knob). This pushes in the muscle and rectifies the problem (Diagram G).

Below right: **Alternative method not using a plug.**

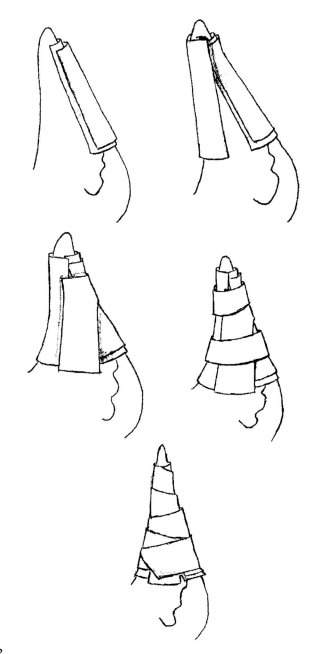

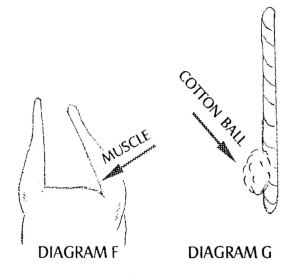

MUSCLE

COTTON BALL

DIAGRAM F   DIAGRAM G

462

The beautiful and very stylish American Boxer, Ch. Jacquet's Cambridge Fortune, the definitive argument for cropped ears. Photo by Isabelle Francais.

SHOWING YOUR BOXER

BY ELEANOR LINDERHOLM-WOOD

Naturally, a show dog must be in good condition, which includes the emotional development sufficient to be receptive to training, as well as good physical condition. General appearance is definitely enhanced if your Boxer is in proper weight with good muscle tone and a clean well-groomed coat, nails and teeth. These things, together with a willing, happy attitude and good behavior, will greatly improve your dog's chances to place well in conformation competition.

TRAINING FOR THE SHOW RING

As few dogs are reincarnated Best in Show winners, obedience training will make show training easier. Heeling on your left side (without pulling on the lead, lagging behind you or sniffing the ground) and being responsive to simple commands like come and stay are the first steps to take in order to enter this "canine college." Positive adjustment to the crate and exercise pen

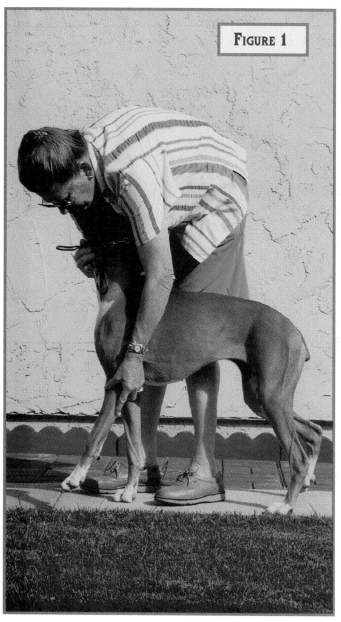

FIGURE 1

and the willingness to do potty relief exercises while on a lead are also important talents to develop. Your life with your show dog will be so much more enjoyable when these details are mastered.

The initial sessions of ring training should be short, businesslike and rewarding. Always try to begin these when your Boxer is rested and comfortable, neither full just after a meal nor just awakened from a nap. Try hard

FIGURE 1-A

to finish each session on a positive note of praise, even for a small degree of success. This way you will both look forward to the next workout.

Be careful about trying to train your dog beyond his ability, either physically or mentally. Time and good healthy encouragement will increase both. Be patient! This is vitally important. Therefore, do not attempt to start or further a session if you do not feel good about working with your dog. Since your Boxer is intelligent and perceptive, he can feel your negativity. This is likely to mar his ability to understand just what you expect. If you force a training period under adverse conditions, including uncomfortable weather, poor surface area or distracting loud noises, it can affect your chances of communicating clearly. You may then destroy the progress in training that you have previously achieved.

FIGURE 2

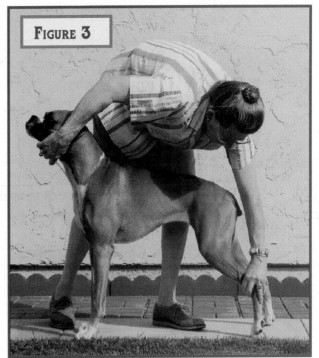

FIGURE 3

Become well informed as to the usual ring procedures and what will be expected when you and your dog perform in front of a judge. This knowledge will make your training more efficient.

As you meet with success a little at a time, you and your dog will have fun. This is what showing is about, to learn and enjoy.

FIGURE 2-A

PRESENTING YOUR BOXER

The illustrations depict basic steps in stacking your Boxer for the judge's evaluation while competing in the ring. These are suggestions you might follow in training your dog. Handlers develop their own styles in setting up their dogs, and you may have to be ready to change your technique as the individual dog or circumstances require. Be alert in the ring, attentive to the judge's instructions and aware of your dog's presence at all times. Your judge of the day will probably choose one of the individual movement patterns as diagrammed for each competitor to follow. Acquaint yourself with these so that you will be able to understand the judge's brief or possibly even mute directions. It is helpful to watch preceding classes. You will learn where to stack your dog after entering the ring and the general order of examination, including the movement pattern used that particular day. If you are nervous, you are human. This is a blessing. Turn these feelings into contained excitement and work smoothly with your dog. No doubt, your Boxer feels the same way. You must be in control or at least make it seem that way. Then your dog will be more assured and respond more readily to you. Remember, every great handler started where you are now.

Since the dog's left side will be the one the judge will view first, you should set the left front leg first (fig. 1), using a light firm grip of your left hand at the dog's elbow (fig. 1-A). I like to hold the dog's neck or jaw with my right hand so that the head points directly forward and cannot twist from side to side. I feel head movement changes the dog's balance and body line. Figures 2 and 2-A show that I have quickly and smoothly changed hands. The left hand is holding the dog's head and the right hand is setting the dog's right foreleg, again using the more effective method of gripping the elbow. Then I shift to the rear after I switch the neck- or head-controlling hand from left to right. I set the dog's left hind leg first (fig. 3 and 3-A) because this is the side the

FIGURE 3-A

FIGURE 4-A

judge is looking at first, and then the right hind leg is moved into place. (fig. 4 and 4-A). In most cases, I will set the dog's rear legs from the top, keeping my hand gently but firmly over the hock with my thumb positioned on the inside to get the best leverage to set the hocks quickly. Do not lift the legs higher than necessary or you will disturb the dog's balance and make him move. As my hand leaves the hock, it may lightly stroke the inside of the thigh to help relax the dog as it proceeds to the underside of the tail, lifting and stroking it upward to enhance the dog's topline (fig. 5 and 5-A). With some

training, hopefully, the tail will stay up. At this point, you smoothly and quickly position the dog's collar high on the neck, careful to maintain a clean underjaw skin line. Hold the collar in your left hand after lifting the neck enough to show an attractive arch with the right (fig. 6). Use your right hand to bait or attract the dog's attention forward with the muzzle level or pointing slightly downward (fig. 6-A and 6-B). Softly uttered firm tones of command, sparingly used, may be helpful during this whole exercise. Also, a hungry dog, not starving, is a more willing and alert worker.

FIGURE 4

FIGURE 5

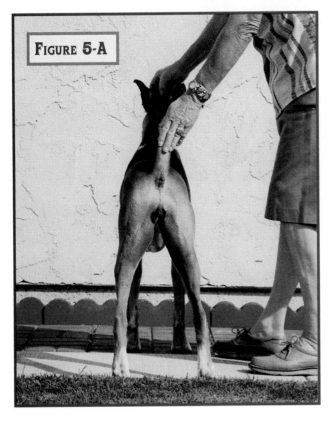

FIGURE 5-A

FIGURE 6-A

If you feel uncertain about how you are stacking your dog and how the positioning of his legs, topline and body would appear to the judge, it would be helpful for you to view these things. A large mirror conveniently placed will allow you to practice with your dog. When you feel reasonably confident, have someone take a video of you working with your Boxer. You can really learn a lot from this if you understand what you are trying to accomplish.

FIGURE 6

FIGURE 6-B

FIGURE G-1

The following is a list of some things you should guard against:

1. Permitting your dog to twist around while stacking. The balance is apt to shift and the tendency to move legs is far greater.

2. Pulling the tail to raise it. The dog will pull back and probably duck his rear under. Train the dog in advance by lifting it gently from the underside while stroking it.

3. Setting the front legs too close together (fig. G-1) or too far apart (fig. G-2). Properly, they should be straight down from the shoulder, parallel to each other and perpendicular to the ground (fig. G-3).

4. Setting the hind or rear legs too close to the front legs (fig. G-4) or too far back from them (fig. G-5). In either case, you will distort the dog's topline and be likely to put the dog off balance.

FIGURE G-2

FIGURE G-3

FIGURE G-4/G-8

FIGURE G-5/G-8

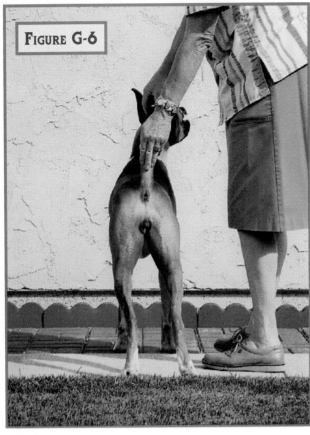

FIGURE G-6

FIGURE G-7A

5. Setting the hind legs too close together (fig. G-6) or too far apart (fig. G-7). Ideally, the hocks to the foot should be almost perpendicular to the ground, and, if you dropped a plumbline from the rearmost projection of the upper thigh below the tail to the ground, the plumbline should drop just in front of the rear foot. The rear feet should be set a footprint or so wider on each side than the front have been set (fig. G-7-A).

6. Do not permit your dog in the finished stack to "count the clouds" by holding the muzzle higher than the skull (fig. G-8). See fig. G-4 and G-5.

7. Bunching the dog's neck skin in front of the collar (fig. G-9).

FIGURE G-7

FIGURE G-9

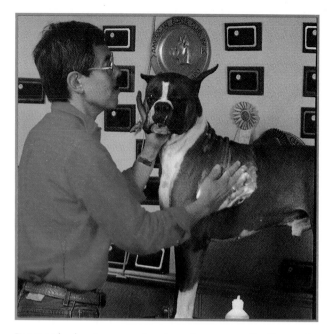

For speedy cleaning, a no rinse type shampoo application can be used to remove any surface dirt and to give the coat an added sheen. Photograph by Isabelle Francais.

On a positive note, here are some more suggestions: When gaiting your dog in the ring, move him at a steady trot unless directed otherwise by the judge. You and the dog should be only far enough apart so that you do not interfere with each other and are spaced at a safe distance from the dog ahead of yours. Do not permit the dog behind to crowd yours. Maintain control over your dog, as he may become excited around others. You are the master! The ring belongs to the judge, but your dog and his behavior are your responsibility. Take note of the diagrams of the commonly used movement patterns.

Grooming preparation should include cleanliness of body, coat, ears and teeth; also, trimming of toenails. Before bathing the Boxer, apply a small amount of petroleum jelly over the top of the dog's nose and over and around the rectal area. Gently rub this in to soften any crusty material. This will allow its removal without causing irritation during the bath. Use a *mild* shampoo. I

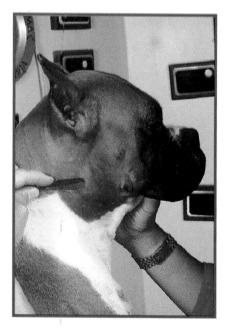

Use a flea comb on a daily basis during flea season so that you can avoid applying any preparations to the dog that contain toxic substances. Photograph by Isabelle Francais.

Never probe deeply into the Boxer's ear. Use a cotton swab to remove any dirt from the dog's ear. Photograph by Isabelle Francais.

like to dilute it so it will rinse out thoroughly. If my Boxers have unwanted guests, I flea comb on a daily basis so I do not have to use toxic substances that may accumulate in their systems and cause illness. Wet the dog thoroughly with warm water, except for the ears and face. You can clean this area with a wash cloth. After the dog is rinsed and wet, apply the diluted shampoo to the back of the neck, over the top of the body and down each leg and foot. Do not let the dog lick the shampoo because this can cause an upset stomach. It is a matter of training. Needless to say, during the bath, it is important that your dog is on a non-slip surface and restrained so he cannot leap out of the bathing container or off a grooming table.

Now back to the wet soapy dog. Massage the shampoo into the coat, under the body and tail area, legs and feet. Then rinse the dog very well all over except for the ears and face. If the arm pits and between the hind legs feel free of soapy residue, then you have probably done a good job. If the dog's legs or white markings do not look clean, you will have to rewash those areas. If you avoid getting water around or into the ears or in the nostrils, the tendency to shake is greatly reduced. I further reduce this by keeping some hand pressure on the dog's neck. After rinsing, I palm off the excess water and towel dry. If necessary, because of the temperature, I use a hand-held dryer. Keep the other hand on the dog so you can monitor the heat. Your Boxer will love all this attention. Keep this experience a good time. It adds to your bond with the dog.

Now, you are ready to clean the ears. Plastic cotton swabs are stronger and less apt to break than wooden ones. Have plenty on hand. With the dog restrained on a grooming table or sitting between your legs with his back to you, pull the ear gently up with one hand. With your other hand, take the swab down into the ear and, with a rotating lifting motion, lift out whatever wax or dirt you can. Continue doing this, working your way up to the upper ear, but be certain to use a clean swab with each effort. This will guard against knocking loose material down into the canal of the ear. Repeat this procedure with the other ear.

If you clean the teeth and gums of your dog on a regular basis, you will have nothing special to do for show preparation. Use of gauze as a pad or wrapped around your finger tip will suffice for a toothbrush. Use light firm pressure from the gumline to the end of the tooth. Work out any impacted hair. Use a tooth scaler to remove any hard scale. Hold the edge of the tool close to the gum against the tooth and press toward the end of the tooth. You can break away the hard scale without hurting the gums if you are firm, confident and careful. But, if you do draw blood or irritate the gums, apply some oral antiseptic to the sore area.

Trimming your dog's nails on a regular basis will maintain shortness in length. This makes the foot look more compact and may aid in the strength of the pastern, both desirable characteristics. The hard part of the top end of the nail is what I cut or file so I do not injure

Keep the Boxer's nails short and neat, using a guillotine-type clipper or an electirc grinder most efficient for nail grooming. Photograph by Isabelle Francais.

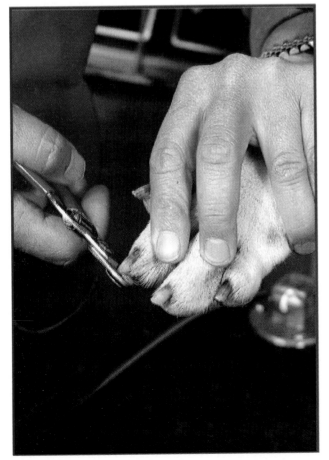

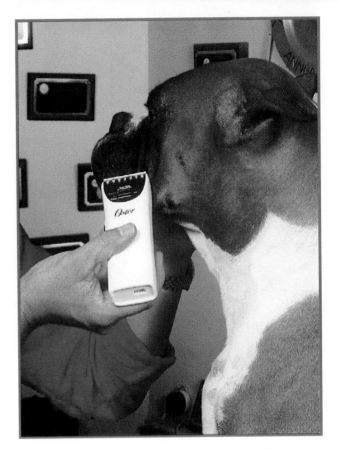

Although some breeders use a clipper on the Boxer's muzzle, a blunt-ended scissors to clip the whiskers is the more reliable approach. Photograph by Isabelle Francais.

the quick, which is the very sensitive soft vascular center part that is often present near the bottom end of the nail. When you are holding your dog's leg and foot to do this work, be careful not to pull the leg into an unnatural position. If the dog would then struggle, it could be painful and cause great difficulty in completing your task. Your grip in holding the foot or leg should be firm but not so forceful that it is painful. Again, training helps.

The hair cut should clean up and sharpen the outline of your Boxer. As you cut the whiskers on the muzzle, slip a finger under the lip and press the whisker out so you can trim it closer to the skin without shaving the adjoining hair. This is scissors work, as are the eyebrows, cheek and chin hairs. Keep the scissors held and pointed in a safe manner. Before you trim the hair along the cut edge of the ear, around the base and up the inside, put a small amount of cotton into the previously cleaned ear. This will keep any hair from dropping down into the ear where it could cause irritation. Trim off hair sticking out where the front dewclaws were removed, under the lower edge of the flank and on the underbelly, if it is excessive. Also, trim the rough hair from the underside and end of the tail and the cowlick at the backside of each rear leg. Groom the neck, back, shoulders and rear legs of loose hair with a rubber curry comb, or small damp Turkish towel. You can bring up the coat shine with very light application of mineral oil. Add a dab of petroleum jelly to the top of the nose to add the polished touch. You can dust some cornstarch into the white markings, but wipe off the excess. Your Boxer should look pretty sharp now. Good luck and have fun!

OBEDIENCE TRAINING AND THE SHOW DOG

When exhibitors think of obedience training, they automatically focus in on competition-level precision. No wonder most breed people refuse to even consider obedience training for their show prospects. However, among the many theories and methods, at least one program provides a sound foundation for obedience and show prospects alike. Breed people have always realized the importance of socialization and regularly take their three- to six-month-old puppies to matches for the experience. The obedience trainers have organized this process into a six-week program known as Kindergarten Puppy Training or KPT.

Understanding how the dam communicates with her puppies will simplify how you "talk" to your puppy. Puppies grow up responding to growls, barks, cooing, shakes and paws.

Bringing home a new Jacquet puppy to Patti and David Rutelege's family—here's Jacquet's Empress.

Kindergarten Puppy Training

There are hundreds of trainers throughout the country who will not start obedience work until the puppy is six to nine months old. KPT should start at about three months, but classes will accept puppies up to six months of age. While still young and amenable, the pups are introduced to the basic commands in a relaxed, non-compulsive environment.

On the first day, each owner arrives with a bouncing baby puppy adorned with a buckle collar attached to a six-foot lead. The atmosphere is charged with barely restrained enthusiasm as each pup tries to play with the one next in line. Enter the instructor, who will attempt to impose a little calm reason into the melee by introducing the dominant down.

The dominant down is a simple technique that will stand the owner and the dog in good stead for the rest of their lives together. For many, this is their first introduction to how to "talk dog." Basically, the owner is replacing the mother dog in the puppy's life. The puppy is laid on its side with the owner placing a hand on the neck and on the groin area. If the puppy struggles, the owner growls at him until he submits. With practice, the owner will be able to sit beside the puppy without placing the restraining hands. Ultimately, the owner will merely have to assume a dominant posture with the adult dog to have him submit. After the first few weeks, the dominant down is used only for correction of misbehavior. This exercise establishes the owner as the "leader of the pack" as well as reassures the young puppy that someone is in charge and will take care of him.

While the puppies are in the dominant down position, the instructor begins the first of many discussions concerning responsible dog ownership, canine anatomy, training philosophy, psychology, etc. In addition, there will be a weekly question-and-answer period as well as a problem-solving session, if needed. At the close of the talk, the pups are released and most will jump up and eagerly "kiss" their owners. Note that a puppy that does not "kiss" the owner, but walks away from the situation, has not truly submitted.

Now everyone is ready to begin working. Each week, the instructor reviews the exercises learned in the prior class and then introduces a few new ones or additional parts to those already learned.

Finally, about 10 to 15 minutes before the class ends, all the puppies are released and allowed to run and play with each other. The instructor will watch each of the puppy's behavior toward the other puppies and will point out distinctive actions and explain what they mean. Generally, precision is not expected, food is used liberally and praise is applied enthusiastically.

So what does this do for the conformation exhibitor? First of all, it provides an excellent foundation on which to build. The dog's attention has become focused on you and he has become immune to distractions. Food has been used to elicit the desired behavior, making the transition to conformation baiting a simple step. Secondly, taking the puppy to unfamiliar locations for training will help establish a "work time" as opposed to a "play time." It is then a simple task to get the puppy to connect the show ring with "work time." Finally, you and your puppy have begun to work as a team. Breed people tend to forget that the dog and the handler are a team. However, when you watch the flashier show dogs, you realize that there is a special relationship between the two that make them stand out in a crowd.

While KPT offers many advantages for the conformation exhibitor, it does not have the drawbacks commonly associated with obedience training. Since the commands are taught in a light and easy manner, they do not become firmly ingrained at this point, which is why the next class recommended is beginners, where

Puppy dreams for the future champion from Jacquet Boxers. Owner, Olive Beaudreau Lee.

The author Richard Tomita proudly showing off two Jacquet puppies. Intelligence, temperament and, of course, the physical attributes described in the Boxer standard guide every breeding at Jacquet.

you continue to work on the exercises learned in KPT. While the puppy knows the basics of the commands, the handler has the opportunity to concentrate on the commands needed, such as stand-stay. In addition, after only six weeks, the new handler is not firmly entrenched in the two-handed handling method. Using food helps since you hold food in one hand and the lead in the other.

With a KPT-trained puppy, you have many options. You can stop obedience training immediately and begin conformation handling classes; you can continue on in obedience; or you can do both, even though it takes more effort and specialized training than doing one activity at a time. Many conformation enthusiasts first show their dogs and then return to obedience training as a way to do something else with a dog after he has retired. In that case, the KPT training has laid a foundation upon which you can build at a later date.

BRACE OF BOXERS

BY LUCY LE COMTE

A brace of Boxers is a rare and exciting event presented only at a limited number of dog shows. If you ever have the chance to see one, enjoy the moment; it will probably be a once-in-a-lifetime experience for many reasons.

The AKC rule for the Brace class is only that both dogs forming the brace, or pair, must have identical ownership. In the ring, each brace is examined by the judge and the one presenting the most similarity to each other is the winner. Therefore, the ideal is to have two dogs who are so similar that they look alike. The likelihood of owning two show Boxers who seem identical is very slim, especially for the small- or medium-sized breeders, because most Boxers kept for showing or breeding purposes have markings that can be of infinite variety, as in the fawn or brindle shades of their coats. When it comes to the judging for the Best Brace in Working Group or Best Brace in Show, the Boxers must compete against other dogs that have limited to no markings or variations, like Samoyeds, Rottweilers, Maltese, etc. Consequently, the Boxers are clearly at a disadvantage.

The exuberance and willfulness of the Boxers may add to the spectacle but at the same time present a major difficulty: Finding a handler willing to take on the challenge offered by the handling of a Boxer brace and capable of keeping the brace under control at all times so that the dogs move in unison is extremely tough.

When you finally succeed to knock down all the barriers raised against the formation of a Boxer brace to create a successful one, you are more than happy and proud when they finally go around the ring like old pros.

Can. Ch. Kenon's Gold Ribbon and Kenon's Gold Drizzle O'Kanabec, littermates bred by Kenneth Lau and owned by Lucy Le Comte and N. Haineault, handled by Karen T. Speck to a Working Group Brace first.

Guest author Nancy Widmayer at age 14 with her beloved pet and partner Jacquet's Riefler, with whom she competed in Junior Showmanship for several years.

JUNIOR SHOWMANSHIP

BY NANCY WIDMAYER DOYLE

At most dog shows, there is a separate and unique kind of competition known as Junior Showmanship. Instead of individual breeds of dogs vying for points, young boys and girls compete with their own dogs and these can be of any recognized breed. Age and skill divide the Juniors' rings. Novice Junior represents the youngest exhibitors (10 to 13 years old) who have not yet won three first-place ribbons. Open Junior is for competitors from 10 to 13 years old who have won at least three first-place ribbons. Everyone hopes to win at least eight "firsts" in one competitive year to qualify for Junior Showmanship classes at "The Garden"—Westminster Kennel Club's annual national competition at Madison Square Garden in New York City each February. Novice Senior classes consist of those exhibitors between 14 and 18 years old who have not yet won three first-place ribbons. The largest of all Junior Showmanship rings is Open Senior, and it encompasses those between 14 and 18 years old who have won more than three first-place ribbons. They are in very keen competition for the minimum eight first-place ribbons necessary to grace the rings at Madison Square Garden.

Since there are a limited number of opportunities to compete for a specific number of wins, it is safe to say that some of the most avid and fiercest of all competition takes place in the Open Senior Junior Showmanship rings of dog shows. Whereas a canine competitor in the breed ring continuously accumulates winners' points toward an AKC championship, Junior Showmanship competitors are constantly watching the calendar, since every year the slate is wiped clean. The eight wins must be earned anew annually and before the competitor's 17th birthday. Many a tearful loser can be observed as the opportunity is lost.

Standing ringside, one will see many different vignettes...the backstage parent assessing his or her child's "performance," the overjoyed winners or disappointed losers, the camaraderie of most of the competitors who see each other at almost every dog show, but best of all is the magical relationship that exists between the junior and his or her dog. The competitions come and go, and the rules may change a bit from year to year, but the child and dog connection is and always should be the reason for this competition. Some judges recognize it and regard it, and some (alas!) only reward the competitor with the perfect dog. This ring does not exist solely for champions and their owners. It is not only possible but a frequent occurrence that non-champions win with their masters. One reason is that the love and caring of these particular dogs are part of the intangible ingredient of the showmanship apparent in this ring. A definite, recognizable bonding has taken place

Marianne Coviello competes at the Junior Showmanship Nationals at Westminster Kennel Club in 1993.

Nancy Widmayer at age 13, winning Junior Showmanship class with Jacquet's Riefler under Breeder Judge Hal Bierman.

in the careful training of a dog owned and adored by its junior exhibitor. And when that dog is a Boxer, there can be an even higher level of the ideal combination.

Many breeds are exhibited in large numbers in the juniors' ring. Toys and Sporting dogs abound. Far rarer is a dog from the Working Group and, in particular, the Boxer. They aren't accustomed by nature to standing still for long periods of time— sometimes up to 45 minutes in a crowded Junior Showmanship class. They're so "tuned in" to every noise and activity around the ring, it's difficult for them not to react as the watchdogs. However, a well-trained junior can transfer his knowl-

Junior Handler Kriste Kaemmlein handles Jacquet's Flaming Brandy (by Ch. Cachet's Mad Max of TuRo ex Jacquet's Diamond Lady).

Nancy Widmayer winning Best Junior Handler with Jacquet's Jolie Jeune Fille at the 1985 New Jersey Boxer Club.

edge and patience into a superb and stylish sight when he gaits his beautiful Boxer around the ring and goes through the different paces required by each judge. Of course, it's a bonus to handle a Boxer because their naturally animated faces draw a lot of attention in a ring of less-animated dogs. I know I was at an advantage with my Boxer when I was in Junior Showmanship competition. Frequently, when my dog and I would arrive ringside I'd hear, "Oh no, the Boxer girl is here today."

I began training my Boxer when he was a puppy. His ears were still taped when we brought him home. We went to weekly dog handling classes where I schooled him to gait and stop as necessary, to stand for examination by the instructor (or judge), as well as to stand for long periods of time while the other dogs in the class were being examined. I've got to interject right here how appreciative my family and I all were for the training opportunities I had. The White Plains School of Animal Training, headed by Barbara Dille, was a short drive from home and I really had excellent and very personalized training there. In addition, we often drove to the New Jersey classes offered by the Ramapo Kennel Club, one of the few clubs that offer handling classes. Their dedication and determination to provide the training opportunity even though the locations used to change frequently was commendable and, as with so many things in life, it was the faithfulness of a few, like Vic and Jane Schwarz and Rick Tomita, who saw to it that we all had continuing opportunities to practice our dogs. They also had the patience and a good sense of humor in enduring puppy training, which is totally different than working with a trained dog. At any rate, my little puppy finally learned to be "stacked" into the proper standing position, and as he matured he learned to be baited into enticing and outstanding expressions. We were a team. When we were ready, we traveled weekly to dog shows.

A very young Marylou Wilderson-Hatfield, competing in Junior Showmanship with Rolling Hill's Fancy Free, owned by Edgar and Florence Wilderson, circa 1968. Today Marylou is one of the fancy's favorite Boxer handlers. Judge, Ed Hoffman.

My Boxer always knew when I meant business in the ring. Sometimes, just to test me, he'd act up a little on the first leg of a triangular gaiting pattern, but just a stern look from me or the tone of my voice or a tiny jerk of his soft choke show collar put him back into the show dog mode and he'd complete the exercise perfectly. We won a lot over the years and he always knew when we had won. It was a "high" I'll never forget. I'll also never forget his sense of humor and his clownish way of trying to humble me in the ring from time to time. Boxers are incredibly intelligent and intuitive. They seem to know just when to get you. But they also respect your superiority (our friend Carol Benjamin would refer to me as the Alpha in that canine relationship) and my Boxer always did what I asked of him—ultimately.

Marianne Coviello handling Ch. Rajah III (by Galaxy's Milkyway v Chal Vic ex Margales Toshiba of Kellyman) to a specialty BOW at Westchester in 1991. Rajah was found through Boxer Rescue, and what an asset she turned out to be!

David C. Brown with Sakura's Magic Fantasy, winning Best Junior Handler at Beverly Hills KC in 1987. Owners, Bill and Sandy Brown.

Back to the training scene, I learned very well how to hide my dog's faults, accentuate his squareness, keep his tail up and flex his hocks. The latter brought me to the front of a class on the New England circuit one summer when Jane Forsyth was judging. She informed everyone in the class that I knew how to flex my dog's hocks and that they should all watch me and learn how. I was thrilled and embarrassed at the same time...and then amused for the rest of the circuit when, each day as I arrived ringside, various of my fellow competitors from that infamous day all told me *not* to flex my dog's hocks. It had been such a thrill to win under Jane Forsyth and the other times that week (I was really on my way toward eight wins that year) that I just smiled at them and laughed.

Winning is always fun, but it was even more fun with a Boxer because of my dog's joyous attitude—one of the Boxer's best traits——exuded with either a high leap or a special prance or just his marvelously twinkling eyes when we looked at each other "nose to nose." I so vividly remember the day I won my eighth first place and was assured of a place at the Garden. As we tore back to the van I felt that we practically flew. The funny thing is that my mother said we looked like we were floating together to the van and that our feet almost never hit the ground.

I guess this is as good a place as any to comment on the fact that none of the training, showing and all that goes

with it would be possible without one or two devoted parents. You just can't imagine how much their support and willingness to drive anywhere, anytime in this stage of my life meant to me. Frankly, unless you have the support of a parent or two, there's no way this can be done.

As I'm writing this for Rick's book, I'm 24 years old. I've graduated from college and am newly married. But I'd have to say that some of my best childhood memories are of my Boxers at home, the training classes and puppy training sessions at Jacquet Kennels and, most of all, my Junior Showmanship competitions. I learned a lot about myself and the world. I value the opportunity to have learned how to compete under intense pressure and maintain my cool, I thoroughly enjoyed the responsibility of caring for dogs in my life and, most of all, I remember how truly special my relationship was with my own dogs—both in the ring and out at all times. My friends were always envious of the beautiful Boxers my family had. Many of my friends were not allowed to have dogs at all, much less a purebred, so they always came to our house and wanted to play with our dogs.

I was born into a home with Boxers who were loved and prized, and I consider it a rare privilege to have grown up with them and to have learned, firsthand, what good friends and how truly marvelous Boxers are.

Ch. Bee-Mike's Grand Illusion (by Ch. Marquam Hill's Traper of TuRo ex Ch. Bee-Mike's Ebony 'N' Ivory), bred and owned by Bruce and Betty Mentzer, produced three champions, including Ch. Bee-Mike's Kaleidoscope.

Ch. Dieterich's Satin Lace (by Dieterich's Handsome Charles ex Diamond Lulu Belle), owned by Muriel Dieterich and bred by Violeta Rodriguez.

Ch. Ruhlend's Swiss Miss (by Ch. K-9's Swiss Yodeler ex Amber's Annah), handled by Carol Howell, bred by Kathryn Whiston, owned by William and Ruth Leek.

Ch. Dieterich Ebony Mist (by Dieterich's Major Diamond ex Belle's Geisha Doll), owned by Muriel Dieterich and Sandy Gauthier.

Am-Ber. Ch. Dieterich's Diamond Ace (by Dieterich's Major Diamond ex Belle's Geisha Doll), owned by Muriel Dieterich and Lucille Neil, bred by Vi Campo.

Am-Ber. Ch. Crescent Lane's Stilleto (by Int. Ch. Mephisto's Stakatto ex Ch. Cresent Lanes Sure Thing), bred by Arleen Freer and Pedro Rodriguez and owned by Arlene Freer.

Ch. Camgene's Likely Tummaykit (by Ch. Benjoman of Five T's ex Ch. Camgene's Canadian Souvenir), bred and owned by Eugene and Hedy Haas.

Ch. Mystery's Show Bis, SOM (by Ch. Ell Bee's Just Watch Out ex Ch. Mystery's Cherokee Maiden), bred by Richard and Denise Calbert and owned with Mr. and Mrs. Judson Streicher.

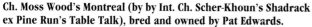

Ch. K-9's Swiss Yodeler, CD (by Ch. Von Schorer's Mountain Music ex Calypso Heidi), bred by R. Weingartner, owned by William and Ruth Leek.

Ch. Moss Wood's Montreal (by by Int. Ch. Scher-Khoun's Shadrack ex Pine Run's Table Talk), bred and owned by Pat Edwards.

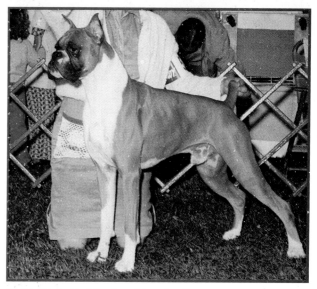

Ch. Mar-Ray's Dashing Lee, SOM, (by Ch. Yours True Lee ex Mar-Ray's Delilah), bred by George Freer and owned by Mary Freer and Rev. Robert Tuttle.

Ch Bullock's Isaiah (by Ch. Marquam Hill's Traper of TuRo ex Ch. Bullock's Corinthian Maid), bred by Greg Bullock.

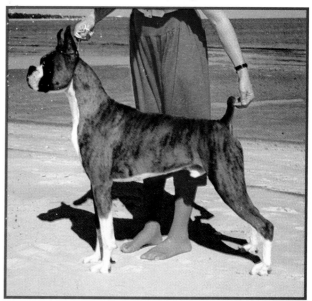

Ch. J. & R.'s Sir John (by Ch. Wilderson's Demos ex Ch. NuRo's Ruffles and Flourishes) bred and owned by John and Ruth Fry.

Ch. J. & R.'s Southern Belle (by Ch. Wilderson's Demos ex Ch. NuRo's Ruffles and Flourishes), owned by breeders John and Ruth Fry with Jack and Sandra Bazebeer.

Ch. Flying Apache Uprising, DOM (by Ch. Flying Apache Regal Rococo ex Ch. Brier Court's Independence), bred by Patricia Adams, owned by Russell K. Anderson.

Ch. Keil's High Society, DOM (by Ch. Salgray's Market Wise ex Ch. Weber's High Falutin), bred and owned by John Keil.

Ch. Foxwood's Nicholas, CD (by Me-Don's Special Revue ex Foxwood's Dasha), owned and bred by Irene Fox.

Ch. Scarborough Norman Knight, SOM (by Ch. Huffand's Nice Enough ex Ch. Gerhard's Calliope), bred by Audrey Gerhardy with owners Jason and Virginia Zurflieh.

Ch. Wakefield's Buckwheat (by Ch. J and R's Senators Choice ex Wakewood's Tamarack), owned by William and Nina Farthing.

Ch. Keil's Dynasty, SOM (by Ch. Salgray's Market Wise ex Ch. Keil's Hello Dolly), owned by John Keil, a SOM in the US and Canada.

Ch. Kojak von San Remo (by Ch. Happy Ours Fortune de Jacquet ex Galicia von San Remo), owned by Frank Scelfo and Liane Dimitroff.

Ch. Bee-Mike's Ebony 'N' Ivory (by Ch. Shieldmont's Dimension ex Ch. Bee-Mike's Carbon Copy), bred and owned by Bruce and Betty Mentzer.

Ch. Bropat's Red Alert of Asgard, SOM (by Ch. Araby's Short Stop, SOM ex Ch. Bropat's Fandancer, DOM), owned by breeder Pat Brown with Trudy O'Brien, proved an influential sire, especially in the southeast US and Florida.

Ch. Shieldmont's Lets Make a Deal, SOM (by Ch. Shieldmont's Judge N' Jury ex Ch. Shieldmont's Haunting Haze), bred by Richard and Nancy Shields and owned by Mr. and Mrs. Judson Streicher.

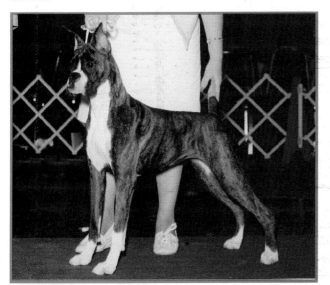

Ch. Aries Golden Tiffany, DOM (by Am-Can. Ch. Strawberry's Caballero ex Ch. Ramrod's Tara's Aries), bred and owned by Marilou Ruboyianes.

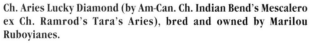

Ch. Shamrock's Mahogany Roxie (by Ch. Smokey's Magnum Force ex Ch. Jacquet's Susannha), owned by Robert and Peggy Otto, bred by B. and D. Spivey and R. Tomita.

Ch. Aries Lucky Diamond (by Am-Can. Ch. Indian Bend's Mescalero ex Ch. Ramrod's Tara's Aries), bred and owned by Marilou Ruboyianes.

Ch. Bar-Rows Enchantment (by Baldr's Sun Smoke ex Bar-Row's Gold Kameo), bred and owned by Allen and Helen Row.

Am-Can. Ch. Keil's Vision, SOM (by Ch. Keil's Dynasty ex Ch. Keil's High Society), bred and owned by John Keil.

Am-Jap-Int. Ch. Arrow's Sky High (by Ch. Happy Ours Fortune de Jacquet ex Jacquet's Nicole Arrow), bred by Richard Tomita with owners Theresa Langan and Sharon Klics. Owner in Japan Sadao Kikuchi.

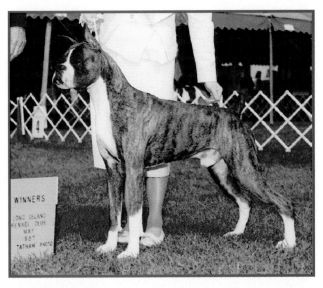

Ch. Lynnrod's Fiddler on the Roof (by Ch. TuRo's Accolade ex Lynnrod's Four Leaf Clover), bred and owned by Vivian Plummer and Mary Frantz.

Ch. Donley's Torrance of Omaha (by Ch. Baldr's Sun Smoke ex Donley's Bettina), owned by Bill Brown and Bob Donley.

Ch. Stamped Ellen's Alley (by Ch. TuRo's Dakota of Shar-Rea ex Ch. Ellen's Alley Lovely), owned by Larry and Janet Sinclair and bred by Sheila Fraser, sired five champions.

Ch. Smokey's Magnum Force (by Bauerhofs Hobbitt ex Philadel's Gypsy Wonder), a BIS winner for Shamrock Boxers, owned by Dale and Deborah Spivey.

Ch. Ewo's Tie Breaker, SOM (by Ch. Heldenbrand's Jet Breaker ex Ch. Ewo's Crystal), owned and bred by Earl W. Overstreet.

Ch. Breezewood's Ace of Spades (by Ch. Berena's Tribute to Fa-Fa ex Ch. Breezewood's One Mo' Time), owned by Janette A. Stitt, bred by Christine Baum.

Am-Can. Ch. Keil's Wimbledon, SOM (by Am-Can. Ch. Keil's Vision ex Am-Can. Ch. Keil's Renaissance), bred and owned by John Keil.

Ch. Hancock's Klondike Gold, TT (by Ch. Doggone Gold Ransom ex Ch. Moon Valley's Image), bred by Robert Hancock, Jr.

Ch. Jacquet's Black Watch (by Ch. Cachet's Mad Max of TuRo ex Jacquet's Diamond Lady), bred and owned by Richard Tomita.

Ch. Seasides Ewo Surf Breaker, SOM (by Ch. Heldenbrand's Jet Breaker ex Ch. Ewo's Crystal), bred by Earl Overstreet, owned by Jerry and Alison Miller.

Ch. Sam-Boz's My Sebastian of KM (by Ch . Kellymars Sebastian Jacquet ex Red's Samantha of The Hill), bred and owned by Richard and Erma Benjamin.

Ch. Moss Wood's Aspen Gold (by Am-Can. Ch. Wagner Wilverday Famous Amos ex Ch. Moss Woods Sadie Thompson), bred by P. Fields, P. Edwards and D. Piburn, owned by Gail Warner.

Ch. Luv-a-Lee's Cool Dude v. Mariday (by Ch. Luv-a-Lee's Red Baron ex Mariday's Glory Days), bred by Marylou Testa, owned by Yetta Meisel.

Am-Can. Ch. Kenon's Gold Ribbon (by Ch. Kenon's Black Gold ex Candy Kisses Keno of Kenon), bred by Ken Lou, owned by L. Lecomte and N. Haineault.

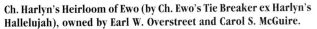

Ch. Harlyn's Clear Choice of Ewo (by Ch. Ewo's Tie Breaker ex Ch. Harlyn's Clearly a Classic), owned by Earl W. Overstreet and Carol S. McGuire.

Ch. Harlyn's Heirloom of Ewo (by Ch. Ewo's Tie Breaker ex Harlyn's Hallelujah), owned by Earl W. Overstreet and Carol S. McGuire.

Lyndell's Joel Flashin Star (by Ch. Lyndell's Music Man ex Ch. Lyndell's Musicle), bred by Ed Woodel and owned by Joseph Grasso.

Am-Can. Ch. Sig's Starfire (by Ch. Arriba's Footloose ex Sig's Totsie Pop), bred by C. and R. Washington and C. Idzik, owned by Paul and Cynthia Starr.

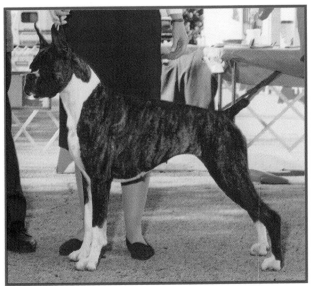

Ch. Silkwood's Coquette (by Ch. Bitwyn's Flying Apache Chief ex Ch. Bitwyns Uptown Girl), bred by Karen Ontell and Winifred Bitler and owned by Jeff and Karen Ontell.

Am-Can. Ch. Arriba's R.J. Spritz, CD (by Ch. Von Schorer's Canadian Caper ex Arriba's Happy Day), bred by Ted Fickes, owned by Mr. and Mrs. R. De Rosa.

Am-Can. Ch. Woods End Million Heir, SOM (by Ch. Keil's Dynasty ex Ch. Woods End Moon Whisper), bred and owned by Mrs. Jack Billhardt.

Am-Can. Ch. Scher-Khoun's Tarantella (by Int. Ch. Scher-Khoun's Shadrack ex Can. Ch. Donfarel's Fashions Fancy), bred by Shirley and Ben de Boer and owned by Jason and Virginia Zurflieh.

Ch. Scarborough's Living Proof, DOM (by Am-Can. Ch. Golden Haze Tuxedo ex Ch. Scarborough Barbara Allen), owned by breeders Jason and Virginia with C. Snelson and M. Holloman.

Ch. Jacquet's Firesong (by Ch. Jacquet's Prince of Fortune ex Jacquet's Cerissa), bred by R. and P. Shupak and Richard Tomita, owned by Dennis and Marie Snell and Richard Tomita.

Ch. Scarborough's City Lights (by Int. Ch. Gray Roy's Minstrel Boy ex Am-Can. Ch. Scher-Khoun's Tarantella), bred by Jason and Virginia Zurflieh, became the foundation bitch for owner Audrey Gerhardy.

Am-Can-Ber. Ch. Woods End Crown Sable, SOM (by Ch. Keil's Dynasty ex Ch. Woods End Moon Whisper), owned by breeder Mrs. Jack Billhardt.

Am-Can. Ch. Vimar's We Believe in Magic, SOM (by Am-Can. Ch. Vimar's EST ex Ebony Image of Ellen's Alley), bred by Vic Lanksbury, owned by Margaret Lanksbury.

Ch. Arriba's Occult (by Ch. Arriba's Crescendo ex Arriba's Luicretin), bred by Ted Fickes, owned by Dr. Theodore S. Fickes and Marylou Wilderson.

Ch. Wilderson's Demos, SOM (by Ch. Arriba's Crescendo ex Ch. Rococo's Tangerine), bred by F. and E. Wilderson, owned by Marylou Wilderson.

Am-Can. Ch. Fiero's Ceaser Apollo (by Am-Can. Ch. Fiero's Smash Fit ex Fiero's Iva-Natu), littermate to Tailo owned by Michael Bruning and Carol Nesbitt, bred by Ingrid Feder.

SELECTING AND TRAINING THE OBEDIENCE BOXER

BY MARILYN KREJCI AND CLAUDINE RAYMO

Training a Boxer is not much different than training most other dog breeds. As a rule, Boxers are smart and learn very quickly. Shy, aloof, boisterous and rebellious dogs are found in every breed. The greatest difference among dogs is the amount of time their owners have put into the training. The trainer who is firm, fair, pleasant, patient and ready with praise will quickly enjoy the rewards of a job well done—a happily obedient dog.

No matter what your reason for buying a puppy—show, obedience or a family pet—you should always know what to look for when viewing litters. If you do your homework before you begin your puppy search, you will be able to make the best choice. Call several breeders and ask about any litters they have or may know about. Be prepared to ask for any medical information on the parents, pups and older dogs of the same breeding. An obedience dog must be sound. Chances are unsound parents will produce unsound puppies. Reputable breeders will be happy to provide you the information you need.

At eight years of age, Marilyn's Summer Tan of Asgard, UDT (by Ch. Shieldmont's Dimension ex Ch. Asgards Southern Belle), retrieving over the high jump. Owners, Steve and Marilyn J. Krejci.

The first (and only) Boxer to earn an AKC Obedience Trial Championship: OTCh. Marilyn's Tinamarie of Bropat, UDT (by Ch. Bropat's Red Alert of Asgard ex Rumac's Everything Nice), doing her thing over the bar jump. Owners, Steve and Marilyn J. Krejci.

When looking at litters, resist the urge to buy the first puppy you see. Quietly observe how the puppies interact. Are they lively, curious, outgoing and playful? Or do they look around nervously and act cautiously about their surroundings? Puppies should adjust quickly to new surroundings, so don't be fooled into thinking that "they just aren't used to this room." Ask to see the mother and, if possible, the father—observe their temperaments. If either parent is vicious, or extremely nervous, it would be best to pass on that litter.

Once you have found a nice-looking litter, and you are pleased with the parents, start watching the individual pups. A happy, outgoing, curious puppy is your best bet. The shy, quiet puppy may need more socializing than you can give. Likewise, the quiet, laid-back puppy may make a good pet but will not be an easy obedience prospect. Watch how the pups react to sudden noises. If they recover quickly from the noise, do they go and investigate it, or do they run away? Look for the puppy who plays freely, gets into everything and is outgoing. In the future, these qualities will come into play in your training.

Once you have brought your puppy home, make sure you keep him socialized. Take him to various places like parks and your friends' homes and take him out on frequent walks. Get him adjusted to wearing a collar and walking on a lead. Taking your puppy to puppy kindergarten can be very helpful. He will learn how to interact with other puppies and people as well as learn some basic obedience commands. You can begin more serious training at four months of age. When your Boxer puppy is ready for basic classes, try to find an obedience club in your area if you haven't already done so. It is here that you can observe the various methods used by different trainers and choose one with whom you are comfortable. Once you begin training, stick to one method so as not to confuse your Boxer. Be open to suggestions, but don't be demanding of your dog. Find an instructor who uses upbeat, positive methods as Boxers are both intelligent and sensitive. Avoid the harsh, brow-beating types. A good instructor will make the dog feel like it is doing something good. If he gives a correction, does he quickly praise the dog afterward? Dogs cannot learn on a human's level of understanding, so a good instructor will work with the dog on the dog's level.

"Rowdie," doing a perfect sit front during the recall exercise.

Banta Sweet Brentwood D'Lite at age six weeks, getting an early start in the scent discrimination exercise. Breeder-owners, Mary Banta and Patricia Mullen.

THREE RULES OF TRAINING

The three most important rules in dog training are: consistency, praise and patience.

Consistency is crucial. Stick to one method, use only one command for each exercise and have only one family member work the dog. By being consistent in these areas, you are making it easier for the dog to learn. Continue with one method until your Boxer has learned that lesson. The only exception would be if the dog was not catching on at all. In that case, a different method should be tried. The point is to not continually change methods—this would only confuse the dog and frustrate the owner.

Use one-word commands. Keep it simple. The dog will understand easy-sounding words that aren't contradicting themselves. For instance, use "sit" instead of "sit down."

The second rule, praise is a vital part of every happy team. Your training should always be on a pleasant upbeat note. This not only helps keep the dog's attention but it also encourages proper behavior. Always use a pleasant voice and keep your actions calm but approving. If you get too excited, your Boxer may get out of hand, as all happy Boxers are prone to do. A simple pat on the chest will put him in seventh heaven.

Along with praise goes food training. Although it is not necessary, food gives an added incentive and is used by many top trainers today. Now when we say "food," we are talking about a *treat* that you give your dog for a successfully completed exercise. It may be small chunks of hotdog, dried liver or some other small tasty morsel. The proper use of food will give measurable results in your training. It can be used to teach your dog the proper heel position, and it can speed up recalls. More importantly, food training is probably the best way to teach your dog to stay attentive to you. If you do not have your dog's attention, you will quickly lose control of your training and, eventually, of your Boxer. Teaching the dog to "watch me" should be one of the first things you work on. Once the dog is consistently paying attention, the rest of your training will go much smoother.

The third vital key to successful dog training is patience. The quickest and surest way to lose all the ground you have gained is to lose your temper. Many dogs reach

Guest author Marilyn J. Krejci's Marilyn's TyBreaker of Asgard (Breaker), being taught to come to front on command, part of the recall exercise.

The dog sits straight in front of the handler after coming on command. He is now ready to finish, or go to heel.

The end result: a beautiful straight sit after finishing.

The dog is in the down-stay with his attention on the handler. Slight tension on the lead reinforces the stay.

Teaching the sit, the handler gently pushes down in the hip area while the right hand controls the dog.

Guest author Marilyn J. Krejci reinforces the "watch me" exercise with Breaker. Note the dog's eye contact with handler.

Breaker on a sit-stay while reinforcing the "watch-me." This is also the position used when working the recall exercise.

Breaker demonstrating the proper heel position. Note the dog's head is turned to watch the handler.

Front view of proper heel position.

a learning plateau in their training where they seem to forget everything. It is at this point where you may get very frustrated. If you keep yourself calm and work through the problems slowly and with lots of encouragement, you will make it through just fine. There will be many times when your patience will be tested. If you lose your temper you could damage the bond with your Boxer. If things aren't going well, stop what you are doing, take a short break, do something the dog knows and enjoys and end the session on a happy note. This way you won't sour the dog on his training.

CORRECTION

There are times when you will have to correct your dog. Knowing when to correct and when not to is a great tool in training. Don't correct him for not doing something he hasn't learned yet, but, on the other hand, do correct him for refusing to do something he has been taught. A correction can be anything from an angry voice to an ear pinch. Collar corrections are the most common and the most effective when done properly. Unfortunately, a bad collar correction can be disastrous. All corrections should be quick and firm. Follow them with

Stevenstar Summer Solstice, CDX, owned by Marcella Mushovic.

plentiful praise. Do not brow-beat the dog as this will only serve to lessen his trust in you. Remember to deliver your commands in a firm and no-nonsense voice. There is no room for squeaky and whining voices.

Another important point to remember in training is to never call your dog to punish him. He will only learn to run from you at the sound of his name. If the dog has done something wrong, such as messing in the house or chewing your shoes, you need to catch him in the act or else he will have little idea why you are upset. Dogs cannot comprehend your yelling about something he did four hours earlier. You will only confuse and worry him.

Ch. Somerset's Alpha Romeo (by Ch. Berena's Gemini Splashdown ex Ch. Somerset's Lady Liberty), demonstrating the heel on leash exercise in the Novice class. Breeders, Eugene Menendez and Gerald Connell, owned with Patricia Mullen.

A BOXER IN CONDITION

Obedience dogs of any breed should always be well conditioned. Boxers are working dogs and therefore should be in excellent shape. Your Boxer requires a couple good walks daily as well as an occasional romp to keep in good condition. If you are working in the advanced classes, make sure your dog is used to jumping before you attempt these exercises. An overweight or unhealthy dog may injure himself on the jumps. The importance of good breeding comes into play here. A competition dog must be physically sound to withstand daily training and practice. An unsound dog will break down very quickly. Along with proper physical conditioning goes good nutrition. Feed your dog a well-balanced diet to keep him at his top potential. An underweight or overweight dog makes a poor sight in the ring.

Brentwood's Sweet Sundie, UD, owned by Mary Banta and Patricia Mullen, performing in the scent discrimination in the Utility class.

Rowdie, retrieving on the flat exercise in the Open class.

Rowdie, over the high jump in the Open class.

OBEDIENCE COMPETITION

Once you have graduated from the basics, and you wish to continue training, you can then work in a Novice class. It is here that you will expand upon the basic exercises and begin to apply them to a trial-oriented training schedule. Once you are ready to move on to competition level training, you can work in a Novice competition class. Here you can polish your performance and prepare to enter the shows.

Once you have entered a show, make sure you and the dog are ready for the big day. Groom your dog to look his best. Make sure he is clean and healthy, and trim his whiskers if you desire. Make sure you have dressed neatly. A well-turned-out team looks sharper in the ring.

Once you have earned your Companion Dog title, which is the title that you can earn in Novice competition, you may want to move on to the advanced classes. Most training clubs offer advanced classes and will be able to assist you in your training needs.

Boxers are not a common sight in the obedience rings anymore. In 1991, only 97 obedience titles were earned by Boxers: 80 Companion Dog (CD) titles, 14 Companion Dog Excellent (CDX) titles and 3 Utility Dog (UD) titles. Very few people continue on to the advanced (CDX, UD) classes. Of those, a few continue to compete for the pure enjoyment of it. The present-day regulars include Ella Dupree, Shirley Bavilaqua, Mary Banta, Claudine Raymo and Marilyn and Steve Krejci, the latter of which have earned over 35 titles on Boxers since 1977. These great obedience-titled Boxers include: Marilyn's Little Bit, UDT, VB (UD-TD); Marilyn's Mandy, CD, TD; Marilyn's Tuff Decision, UDT, VB; Marilyn's Southern Sand, UDT; Marilyn's Summer Tan of Asgard, UDT; Ha-Mar Something Special, UDT; Scarborough Seeing Double, UDT; Marilyn's Lucky Niki of Asgard, UDT; and OTCh. Marilyn's Tinamarie of Bropat, UDT (the only Boxer to hold the coveted Obedience Trial Championship in the US).

Rowdie, Shawna, Duchess and Mario on the long sit exercise in the Novice class.

OTCh. Marilyn's Tinamarie of Bropat, UDT, owned by Steve and Marilyn J. Krejci.

The Tampa Bay Boxer Club's 1992 Dog Obedience Clubs of Florida Team included: Mike and Mary Ainsley with Doc, CD and Missy, CD; Wendy Mayhall with July, CD; Claudine Raymo with Wood, CD and Sarah, CDX; Debra Neufeld with Java, CDX; and Illeana Nadal with Laika, UD.

Owned by guest author Karla Spitzer, this is U-CD Harpo the Marker, CDX, CGC, Tracking Certified, retrieving dumbbell over the high jump.

Five pros: Marilyn's Summer Tan of Asgard, UDT, Marilyn's Suzi Q of Petrie, Marilyn's Lucky Niki of Asbard, UDT, Marilyn's TyBreaker of Asgard, and OTCh. Marilyn's Tinamarie of Bropat. Owners, Steve and Marilyn J. Krejci.

OBEDIENCE "TRIALS"

BY KARLA SPITZER

I think that everyone who gets bit by the "dog bug" and wants to compete in dog obedience gets it from the first dog or dogs they ever knew. Usually, of course, that first experience was a good one and, one way or another, it leads them to the Novice A ring.

I want to tell you about my trip to and notes from the Novice A ring, in hopes that it may inspire you to do the same. There are many nasty rumors out there that Boxers "don't do obedience" and are "nothing but couch potatoes." I disagree, as you'll see, and I hope that when you're done reading this, you'll do the same.

I grew up on a farm/ranch in North Dakota where "working" herding dogs were an important part of life. That first, most important dog in my life was an English Shepherd, now a rare breed. "Rover" was truly a prince among dogs, and he set a tone for dog-loving in my life that has continued on to today and beyond.

My parents' ranch bordered on a larger lake that is one of the major migratory stops for almost all ducks, geese and other upland game that fly from Canada, south and back each year with the change of the seasons. Because of the lake and the hunting, hunters from all over the region—Minneapolis, Chicago, Denver, Kansas City, etc.—come to hunt in the area.

The hunters had a tendency to leave dogs behind. We assumed that these beautiful sporting dogs (mostly pointers and retrievers, as I recall, but once a purebred Dachshund!) had somehow disappointed them. It seemed that the hunters expected the good-hearted farmers and ranchers in the area to give these dogs a

Ranison Prince Boy, CDX, showing off his great balance in a trial.

home. They were partly right. Most farmers and ranchers in that area are kind-hearted, but they also had limited pocketbooks. Often the dogs became injured or turned feral and had to be shot.

It was with the Dachshund that I was on my way to becoming a bona fide dog rescuer. Someone had left her in the little town of Streeter where I went to school. I refused to leave her after piano lessons one fine Thursday in sixth grade. I was sitting on the curb in an early November snow with my piano books and this poor little dog when my father found us. He tried to talk me out of keeping her...he knew something I didn't. She was really, really pregnant. But I wouldn't go home without her, and he also knew I could be really, really determined (I prefer that to "stubborn"), and so my career as a dog rescuer was launched.

"Penny" (that was her color—like a brand new penny) came home with us, and within 48 hours, she had six pups—a bunch of "Heinz-Fifty-Sevens" if ever there were any, and I had the challenging task of finding good homes for all of them. My father felt that with all the herding dogs (over the years, we had English Shepherds, Border Collies, Collies, German Shepherds and crosses of every conceivable kind), life on a ranch, even as an indoor dog, would be too dangerous for her. He felt that she didn't understand cattle, and probably couldn't learn.

We gave her to my aunt, who re-named her "Queenie." Queenie lived for another 12 years until she died of old age. One of her daughters, Holly, and one of her sons, Pepper, eventually came back to live with us. Like any good breeder, I had a lifetime return policy! All the rest of the pups stayed with their families, and lived to ripe old ages. At my 20-year high school class

Harpo, jumping the hurdle. Owner, Karla Spitzer.

reunion, people I hadn't seen for years came up to me to remind me of those pups and how much they had loved them!

Eventually, my father relaxed his policy on having other than herding dogs—that's how Holly and Pepper got in the door, so to speak. Dad's last dog, while he still had cattle, was a Labrador Retriever/Border Collie cross! Not only could Blackie herd, he could retrieve and hunt rabbits like nobody's business!

Holly and Pepper died while I was in high school, and I left my last dog, a Collie named Sandie, with my parents when I went off to college. That was in the days when people still let their dogs roam loose at times, and other than having dogs follow me back to campus frequently, I didn't have another dog for a long, long time.

And what I learned from all those poor abandoned hunting dogs was that nothing takes the place of good training. It will keep an owner happy with a dog in the long-term.

After college, I lived in Canada and England. It was while I was in England that I fell madly in love with—guess what? Boxers! Of the un-cropped variety.

U-CD Cleo, CDX, CGC, Tracking Certified, heading for the flyball box. Owner, Scott Friedman.

Aust. Ch. Phoenix Ginger Rogers, owned by Michele Roberts, through the tire jump.

For many years, after I returned to the U.S., I had a career and other things to think about, but I did what I had done all through high school and college, I dog-sat. When I lived in northern California, I helped a friend manage a kennel of German Shepherds for an out-of-country owner. It was purely a love of dogs on my part, and it was a breed I knew.

I also dog-sat for a friend that had a cross-breed bitch so vicious, no kennel would take her. My friend didn't tell me this. Another friend let this minor little detail slip a few days after I'd begun what seemed to be a perfectly amicable house-sitting situation with "Wallye." Oh well. Wallye and I had a perfectly good time, which has tended to be my experience with dogs in general, including the 100 or so rescue dogs I've worked with throughout my life.

Then I moved to southern California and finally got around to having another dog of my own, and guess what I found? Boxers!

Anyway, I found a litter—two, actually. The owners had two bitches who had whelped at the same time—one fawn and one brindle. I had made up my mind I wanted a brindle male.

What we came home with was Cleo. A white female with brown ears, a brown spot on her rear, black mascara-like smudges around her eyes and lungs like no other puppy I'd ever experienced. My husband, Scott, fell totally in love with her and vice versa. And so, when she cried all night, it was he who got to sleep on the floor with her. (Of course, had it been a brindle male, I would have been the one who slept on the floor with him...)

Known at our house as "the puppy from hell," Cleo made me re-evaluate everything I ever thought I knew about dogs. I read everything I could about training dogs. She hated being crated—she cried so loud, I was afraid the neighbors would call the ASPCA; she could have cared less about being house-trained; she was a finicky eater; and unlike any puppy we ever had growing up, she loved to run off to see the world!

Well, enter Waldo. I figured she must be lonely, so I called Boxer Rescue, and they had an older dog—a big, dark brindle. Scott, Cleo and I went to meet him. It was pretty much love at first sight. The people at the kennel said I was the first person he'd even looked at, and when he met Scott and Cleo (then four months old), he was definitely sold on coming home with us.

Not only was Waldo (no, I don't know what his "real" name was, but he looked like a Waldo to me...what's more, he answered to it!) a big hit with Cleo—especially his ears and his hamstrings, but he was a big hit with Scott and me. On one of the first nights he was with us, he bounced a screen door right out of its tracks going out to our backyard to investigate a sound he didn't like! Needless to say, we were impressed.

As Cleo approached the grand old age of one, our (now beloved) Waldo showed some really clear signs of slowing down. He was, after all, an "older" dog when we got him. So, that fall, we went in search of another puppy.

This time, though, I did the sensible, responsible thing...I contacted several breeders in the area, and I

Ranison Prince Boy, CDX, over the spread hurdle, moving at a speedy pace.

made appointments to see the litters. Harpo's was first, and against all my best-laid, common sense plans, I fell totally in love, and bought Harpo with my heart—not my head. He was the first and only puppy I saw. And, more important, he was the right puppy.

This time I got my wish. A male brindle—unlike Waldo, Harpo is flashier and red. His breeder, Mariola Clements, warned me that he was "pretty energetic," but after Cleo, I figured nothing could phase me.

As unlike Cleo as two puppies of the same breed could be, he still *never* wants to see the world unless it's with me; even the mildest "no" was cast in stone to him; he never put his teeth on us or played rough; and if he ever had any doubts about what to do, he'd sit down, right where he was, and think about it. This was a *very* good puppy. (Maybe the Dog Star was smiling on me after Cleo?)

After a little hesitation, Cleo seemed pretty happy to have a lively young playmate, and Waldo got a break.

Aust. Ch. Phoenix Ginger Rogers, over the A-frame.

Whatever it was that Waldo said to Harpo about not biting his hamstrings and ears, it was effective. Harpo *never* bit Waldo's ears or hamstrings, but Cleo's were another story.

Waldo seemed stern with young Harpo, but he had a good heart and a soft spot. This time, when the new puppy cried at night, it was Waldo who laid down next to him to comfort him. (Fortunately, I didn't have to be the one!)

Unfortunately, when Harpo was about seven months old, our wonderful Waldo was diagnosed with a fibro-sarcoma. He was diagnosed in February of 1992, and died on September 17 (amidst a flood of tears from Scott and me). Before he died, I was fascinated to watch him teach Harpo everything he knew about being a guard dog, I think...

They'd go outside to the yard. Waldo would "stack"—intent upon something, then Harpo would do the same thing. It seemed, at times, that there were so many minor adjustments to be made, but then what do I know about being a male Boxer guard dog?

Prince in action over the spread hurdles.

Ginger, making it look easy!! Aust. Ch. Phoenix Ginger Rogers (by Vimars Magic Goes On ex Phoenix the Dame), bred by M. and T. Carter and owned by Michele Roberts.

At any rate, because Cleo was the "puppy from hell," when Harpo hit three-and-a-half months and Cleo about a year-and-a-half, Cleo and Scott went to novice obedience and Harpo and I went to puppy class. The rest, as they say, is history.

We were hooked. Although I'd had a lot to do with dogs, I'd never done formal obedience as a sport. And since I was relatively new to Boxers, no one told me it was impossible! (To start with...) So, undeterred by any facts whatsoever, we went off to obedience classes optimistically. Our only thought was to have "good" dogs, or at least one good dog (Harpo), and one passable one (Cleo).

We were lucky enough to land in one of Shirley Indelicato's "Obedience Preferred" classes. I'll never forget teaching Harpo to do a "down." He'd go down all right, on his back with his paws waving. Shirley looked at him and said, "You know, he could be a good obedience dog."

I have no idea what it was that she saw in him at that point, but we were hooked.

We learned the Novice exercises. In an American Kennel Club trial, the exercises are as follows: heel on leash, figure eight, stand for examination, heel off leash, recall, one-minute group sits and three-minute group downs. This looks and sounds easy, but it's deceptive! If you've never put a title on a dog in AKC before, you enter in Novice A. Novice A is basically for the handlers. Everyone there is as new to the sport as you are. Experienced handlers take their novice dogs into the Novice B.

In a United Kennel Club trial, the exercises are slightly different. While you heel on leash, do your figure eight, stand for examination, heel off leash and sit, the recall is over a jump at a height equal to the dog's shoulders, not exceeding 24 inches, whichever is less.

The down is in the ring with the other dog working its first three exercises, and the dog "honors" (stays down) for however long that takes! As in the AKC, experienced handlers, or handlers who have novice titles on the dog in some other club (AKC, ASCA, etc.) take their novice dogs into Novice B.

In either category in AKC, if you successfully pass with a score of 170 or more on three different occasions with three different judges, you and your dog will have earned the title "Companion Dog" —"CD" to those of us in the know—which follows the dog's registered name. In UKC, you may earn your three "legs" under two different judges, and you earn the title "United Companion Dog"—"U-CD," which, like a championship title, is placed before the dog's registered name.

After Novice, we learned the Open exercises. In an AKC trial, the Open exercises are as follows: heel off-lead, drop on recall, retrieve a dumbbell on the flat, retrieve a dumbbell over a jump, jump over the broad jump (twice the length of the high jump—most Boxers will jump 28" and 56", 30" and 60", or 32" and 64"). The sit is three minutes with the handler out of sight of the dog. The down is five minutes with the handler out of sight of the dog. Open A is for dogs that have won the CD title, but have not yet won a CDX (Companion Dog Excellent, the Open title). Open B is for people who have either won an Obedience Trial Championship or who are working toward that title or a Utility Dog Excellent title.

In UKC trials, the exercises are heel off leash with a steward walking through the ring in the opposite direc-

Harpo, figuring out the scent discrimination articles. Owner, Karla Spitzer.

tion. The drop on recall also occurs with a steward walking in the opposite direction once the dog has dropped. There is a retrieve on the flat and over the jump. Again, the jumps are shoulder height to 24 inches, whichever is less. The broad jump is twice the height of the high jump. While the first dog is working, the honoring dog is in the ring with its owner out of sight. The sit is a three-minute group sit with the owners out of sight.

The title you receive from AKC is "Companion Dog Excellent"—CDX. It is placed after the dog's registered name. The title you receive from UKC is the "United Companion Dog Excellent"—U-CDX, and it goes before the dog's registered name.

Then there is Utility—the college degree of dog titles. In AKC Utility, the dog must heel off leash to do signal exercises, which include a stand, stay, drop, sit and come. Then the dog must select two articles scented by you, one at a time, from a pile of eleven at a time. (The other ten are scented by the judge). That's followed by a directed retrieve of gloves which are placed across the ring from you and your dog by a steward. Next comes the moving stand and examination. In this exercise, you must stand your dog and leave him or her while you're moving. The judge examines your dog, and you call your dog to heel. The final exercise of this Zen grueler is the directed jumping. This is the exercise where after all those years of teaching your dog a recall under any and all circumstances, you must teach your dog to go away from you for a minimum of 20 feet, turn and sit awaiting your next command! Then you direct the dog to either the high jump or the bar. (The judge gets to call that one.) Dogs who are eligible to show in Utility A are the dogs who have earned a CDX, but who have not won the UD title.

In UKC Utility, the exercises are much the same. The honoring dog is in the ring for the signal exercises with its owner in sight, but with their backs to the dog. The dog is only required to retrieve the metal articles, but it is required to do two directed retrieves with the gloves.

The title earned in AKC is the "Utility Dog"—UD. It is placed after the dog's registered name. In UKC, the title is "United Utility Dog"—U-UD, and it is placed before a dog's registered name.

In January of 1994, the AKC added an additional title to the list of titles that could be earned by a dog in obedience—the Utility Dog Excellent. To earn a UDX, the dog must qualify in both Open B and Utility B on the same day in ten different trials. As far as I know, the UKC does not have an equivalent title.

The last of the obedience titles that AKC grants is the great-grandfather or grandmother of them all. "OTCh," or Obedience Trial Champion, is placed in front of a dog's registered name. In order to do this, the dog needs to win 100 points, including a first place in Utility B, a first place in Open B, and one additional first place in either Utility or Open B, under three different judges. The number of points that you win is based upon how many dogs were entered in the trial and which place you were in, first or second. (I think the human side of this team probably needs an advanced degree in math in order to earn this title...)

So that's obedience...and how are Boxers doing? According to the book *The Intelligence of Dogs*, in a compilation of judges' opinions on Boxers' performances at obedience trials, not so good. Forty-fifth in fact. What that means in practical terms is that most judges think that Boxers aren't very smart in obedience.

According to the American Kennel Club, for the year 1993, 72 Boxers received their Companion Dog titles; eight received their Companion Dog Excellent titles; and three received their Utility Dog Excellent titles.

To get back to Boxers being smart, how many of you out there really think your Boxer is dumb? If I'm not mistaken, not many. My dogs can open sliding doors

Harpo at the flyball box. Owner, Karla Spitzer.

and doors with door knobs. Harpo and Kosmo can pretty much figure out days of the week. They know which days they train and which days they have lessons. (Maybe Cleo can too, but she's not letting on it she can...)

As one of my trainers (Boxer breeder Liz Farrell) once told me, Boxers were bred for herding, hunting and guarding. In the early days, before Frau Stockmann and friends took an interest, they were the indigenous dogs of Europe. They mostly herded and hunted and guarded whatever needed guarding. They were the "bull-baiters." Remember the story of Frau Stockmann's first dog, Pluto, who took down a stag in his old age? And all those old pictures from medieval Europe that had various sized mastiff-type dogs guarding the castles?

Well, in order to do any of that, you have to have a dog who can scan its horizons. So the dog we know as the modern-day Boxer evolved for centuries to be able to watch its horizons. The Boxer was an independent working dog.

When we take this dog into the obedience ring, its instincts are going to tell it to keep an eye on things for you. Also, I've yet to meet a Boxer who wasn't a quick-take. And most trainers are inclined to want to repeat exercises until it bores most Boxers almost to tears. And a bored Boxer is usually a stubborn Boxer.

It's a dog who's saying, "Did that, been there...And I'm not going to do it again. If you want to throw that dumbbell one more time, *you* get it."

Still this isn't all bad. The important thing I've learned in working with my Boxers is that if I can show them very clearly what I want them to do in the first place, it doesn't take that much to teach them. They don't train like the dogs who are generally considered the really "top" obedience competitors such as Border Collies,

Jacquet's Heliocentric, training for tracking with guest author Karla Spitzer.

Harpo flies back from the flyball box.

Golden Retrievers, German Shepherds, Poodles and Shelties. Except for Poodles, the rest are all sporting or herding dogs. These are dogs who were bred to work very closely with man.

Boxers, I feel, have a much wider range of interest. And often, I find that they will learn a great deal by watching (so make sure they're watching good dogs!). This is not always good news when it comes to training for obedience. But it is good to know about how your "off-breed obedience dog" learns.

Your Boxer will probably never retrieve a stick out of water as often as a Golden Retriever, or chase a ball as often as a Border Collie. However, if you'll respect the intelligence and nobility that your dog has, you can have a fine, competitive obedience dog nevertheless. You've got a dog who is smarter in more areas than most, you just need to be more creative in getting him or her to work with *you*. Once I learned that if Harpo did something well one time and let it go at that instead of repeating things, we really began accelerating in our ability and our trial scores.

What happens with most Boxers if you repeat things too much in one session is that they'll decide one of two things: (1) Since they've already done it, even if they've done it right, something must be wrong, so they'll do it differently. (2) Since they've already done it, it's *boring*, and they'll try to make it more interesting, therefore doing it differently.

So since what you wanted was more of the same, getting multiple repeats can be pretty self-defeating. My advice? Don't do it. If you like to do the same things over and over again, get a Border Collie or a Golden Retriever. If you want an efficient dog, get a Boxer.

A little tip on going into classes with your Boxer: If you live in an area where there aren't any other Boxers showing, you can assume that no one in the area really knows how to train them. There are always Boxers around, but a lot of trainers don't have a lot of experience with them or other members of the Working Group. If the trainer you consider taking lessons with says things like, "Boxers are stubborn, they'll never do it," etc., consider going elsewhere. If they have a sense of humor and seem good with dogs in general, you might want to stay. If they say you can only train a Boxer with a "pinch color and a cattle prod," run the other way. You can bet your Boxer will!

I was very lucky to have found some marvelous trainers—Shirley Indelicato, Linda Zapp and Liz Farrell. I found and left very quickly some others whose names will not be mentioned including one who said that Cleo was so stubborn, she should have been put down at birth! I admit she has a mind of her own, but she's still my best buddy as I sit writing in my office, and she's the world's best cuddler. She can take or leave formal obedience, but she loves agility, and basically, she loves doing anything with Scott and me.

She's a great dog, and although I joke about her being our "bad" dog, she's really a wonderful gem of a personality. She is, however, a "type" of Boxer, and since she was our very first puppy, we've learned a lot about how to deal with her. Unless your dog is totally vicious, people-aggressive, ill-bred, or so dominant that you're frightened of it, don't let anyone tell you that your dog is bad, stubborn or stupid. If it's not doing what you want, you just haven't built up the communication skills to let it know what to do to please you. Even though the general belief is that Boxers are stubborn, I think that it's more that they're watchful, careful and economical with their movements and decisions. And frankly, I think that's a good attribute of the breed. If you go on with obedience, you will find there are many areas where there are differences from the popular obedience breeds.

For instance, if you attempt to teach your Boxer moving and stationary attention, remember that you will probably not get the same "appearance" of attention as the so-called "hot" obedience breeds. Some of those Border Collies, Goldens and Aussies can wrap their heads right around in front of their handlers and look like they're glued to their handler's thighs! Boxers don't have that level of neck flexibility or interest, besides which, in their own little heart of hearts they *know* their real job is to watch out for *you*. Nevertheless, when they understand the concept of attention and that it is their job to watch you while staying in the heel position, they can give you the same precision that any other breed can. They just won't be as obvious about looking at you. And I feel it is their nature, if they aren't looking in self-confidence, to heel a little wider.

Since Boxers can jump, do agility and air-scene like nobody's business, there is no reason why you can't go as far as you like in any of the dog sports. You just need to respect your particular dog's abilities, and not lump him or her into too many "dog" categories (too stubborn, too slow, too stupid and so on). You might find out that he/she is just a little too smart and has you all figured out! And far be it from any Boxer to disappoint its owner if the owner thinks the Boxer can't do something! This is one of the almost scary aspects of Boxers. If you think your dog can't do something, it won't. If you think it can, it will. I've seen this time and time again when I'm working with friends to try to train their dogs. The dog will almost always do what I want with no force or fight and just a bit of encouragement, thus

Headed for the flyball box.

totally amazing their owners. It's because I *believe* they can do it. I think Boxers are *very* intuitive. This is one area where if you think your dog can do it, it can and will do it. But not without some reasonable and thoughtful training, of course!

Like me, you might have an incredibly ecstatic Gemini social butterfly—Harpo; or you might have an independent "attitude" Taurus—Cleo; or you might have a balanced thoughtful Libra smarts like my pup, Kosmo. Whatever type of Boxer you have, if all else fails, you can have heart to heart talks before you go into an obedience ring. If we're having a "flat" day, Harpo and I often do.

Our talks go something like this: "Okay, Harps, you can do this. You know it, and I know it."

No response.

"You're as good as any other dog here, any day."

Yawn.

"Come on, we've spent so much time training, you've got to show these other dogs Boxers can do it!"

Slight eyebrow raised as Harpo glances around, gauging the competition.

"Look, if you're really good, you can kiss the judge afterwards..."

This brings out some enthusiasm. Harpo loves people and I don't think he's shown in a ring yet where he hasn't wanted to kiss the judge—not that that's earned us any extra points or anything—he just likes it.

"Just please don't embarrass me, okay?"

Genuine look of surprise from Harpo, "Who, moi? Embarrass you?! Karla, I'm hurt you'd even think it!"

And bless his little heart, he generally comes through. Although I find obedience competition nerve-racking at times, I still try to make it fun. When our number is called, I turn proudly to my beautiful friend and say,

Can. Ch-OTCh.-U-CDX Foxwood's Crown Jewel, UD, AD, NAD, CGC, TDI (by Am-Can. Ch. Woods End Crown Sable ex Foxwood's Katybeth of Jaimax), owned by Ella M. DuPree and bred by Irene Fox and Janice Fournier, competing in advanced agility.

"It's show time!" That's our cue we're going into the ring. Almost every judge we've ever showed under has said how happy he looks in the ring. (And some have said how nervous I look!)

Does Harpo like applause? You bet your boots. And like everyone else, he has his days when he's really styling. So much so that a few people have burst into tears when we beat them out of a ribbon place. I was amazed that someone would cry about the "shame" of being beaten by a Boxer.

Harpo the bog-hearted just felt bad that they cried. Personally, I'm not sure his generous attitude helped. Possibly the only thing worse than being beaten by a Boxer might be said Boxer feeling sorry for you later?

Well, in addition to learning about the various dog classes, Scott and I learned how to "steward" at matches and trials, and we found a whole new circle of friends throughout the Southern California area. And we (almost) never looked back.

Not even the night Cleo quite cheerfully ran off at an Open class, nearly getting herself killed and scaring the rest of the class almost to death.

Not even when she ran out of the ring to run around the show grounds. Everybody smiled—they'd rarely seen a happier dog.

Not even when Harpo hid under the judge's raincoat in the rain during his first obedience match in Novice at eight months. He wouldn't come out. The judge and stewards howled with laughter. (Guess who didn't?)

Not even when Harpo refused to recall out of the shade when the thermometer rose quickly and unexpectedly from the mid-60s to over 100 degrees at his first AKC Novice trial. He refused to take his eyes off Judge Selma Ashley as if asking, "Please don't make her make me do this!"

Not even when Harpo went into his first Open ring at a match, off-lead, kissed the judge, kissed the stewards and generally anyone else available. Not even when he failed his first UKC Open trial attempt for the same...

Not even when he left the fly-ball ring to kiss all spectators on the sides.

Not even when an unsupervised toddler ran up to Harpo at a show, raising the ire of a nearby Doberman, and flopped down on Harpo (even though I don't have any, Harpo loves children). When the horrified father came to reclaim the toddler, Harpo growled...at the father *and* the irritated Doberman. When I handed the child over with apologies, Harpo looked at me indignantly as if to say, "Look, I won that kid fair and square. She came to *me*. How can you give her back?! We don't even know this guy!"

Ch. Jacquet's Cebele, CD (by Int. Ch. Jacquet's Novarese ex Ch. Jacquet's Geneve), finishing her first obedience title, bred and owned by Debbie Alport and Richard Tomita.

Jacquet's Big Guy, CD, owned and handled by Sam Rodman, bred by Richard Tomita.

In the summer of 1994, Cleo turned four on May 20, and Harpo turned three on June 16. They both finished their CDs and U-CDs. Harpo placed second once and third twice in AKC, and he placed first and third for his U-CD. Harpo finished his U-CD on June 19 and his AKC CD on July 2. Cleo finished her AKC CD on July 8, and her U-CD on September 3. She placed second place on two legs of her U-CD.

Cleo started obedience first, but basically, she's a party girl and won't do anything if it's not fun. Basically, Harpo is still his good, loving self, and he really wants to please. Both are trained for Open, and Harpo is in class, training for Utility.

Harpo, discerning his utility articles. Owner, Karla Spitzer.

Ch. Foxwood's Krystal Karosel, Am-Can. CD, CGC, TDI, DOM, owned by Ella M. DuPree and bred by Irene Fox and Janice Fournier, through the tire jump at an advanced agility trial. She is the littermate to Crown Jewel, proving that brains and looks run in the family.

And in the meantime, in January of 1993, another old Boxer rescue dog, Gretel, came to live with us. She lived through the Topanga-Malibu fire with us last fall, and the violence of the Northridge Earthquake on January 17, 1994. Both events were pretty traumatizing to all of us. In spite of everything, Gretel seemed very happy with us. Still, amid another flood of tears and three days of eerie, mournful howling by Harpo, who loved her, she left us on May 23, 1994.

In the "other" meantime, Harpo did sire a litter in 1993, and Kosmo came to our house in December of 1993. He looks like his dad, and they'll make a great brace. Bred for temperament and obedience, Kosmo and a brother and sister came in first, second and fourth in their first Novice class graduation in April.

And when Kosmo cried at night? Harpo the bighearted was right there, and Gretel was the best "Grandma" ever. Cleo seemed a little disgusted that another Harpo-looking puppy came through the front door.

"Top Dog"

Living in the Los Angeles area gives one a lot of access to dog sports in general. After our first Novice classes, Scott and I were asked to join the K-9 Obedience Club, Inc., where we went on to learn a great deal more about obedience and related events. (More importantly, we met some really great people).

One important annual event to the dog world in southern California is called "Top Dog." If you say "Top Dog" to any southern Californian dog obedience person, it will conjure up for them images of great obedience dogs putting on great performances, and one of the most intense competitions they're likely to see. There is a great deal of pride in having been on a Top Dog team, and a great deal of envy for those who would like to be able to "make the cut."

Top Dog is sponsored by the Southern California Dog Obedience Council. "SCDOC," as it's known, consists of 36 member obedience clubs and another half-dozen or so scent hurdle teams. SCDOC sponsors programs dedicated to the welfare of dogs and to educating the public about dogs and responsible dog ownership. In southern California, it produces a calendar of dog events and, of course, the annual Top Dog competition for all its member clubs.

Unlike regular obedience competition, which sets the abilities of dog against dog, Top Dog sets obedience club against obedience club. Of course, each obedience club wants its best dogs to represent them. Needless to say, competition for a place on the Top Dog team can be fierce. It is a great honor to be on a team.

1994 was a tough year for the K-9 Obedience Club, Inc. With a majority of its members living within ten miles of the epicenter of the January 17, 1994 Northridge Earthquake, everyone's minds were on things like how long it was going to take to get their houses fixed, their garden walls up and other little essentials like that.

The result was the 1994 Top Dog competition was not an issue. None of the regular "old-timers" even wanted to go. I was disappointed that we weren't going to have a Top Dog team. Here I was, with this really well-trained dog who could compete. My Boxer, Harpo, while not a 200 dog—high 180s, low 190s—had been very, very consistent. In seven trials, his score had only varied a point-and-a-half. Because one Top Dog team strategy is to have dogs who are consistent, I thought we could be an asset. After all, a bad day for a consistent dog who has respectable scores is less damaging to a team than one who scores high one day and bombs or fails to qualify the next.

I expressed my disappointment at the meeting while the discussion about not going to Top Dog was going on. To my surprise, several faces turned to me and said, "Okay, Karla, you do it. You be the captain."

To which I said, "You guys are kidding, right?"

After all, I'm still a Novice A person, and basically will be until I've taken Harpo all the way through Utility. I was sure they had to be kidding.

They weren't. And suddenly, there I was, a rank novice with an "off-breed" obedience dog—albeit a good one—and I was the captain.

Needless to say, I was still faced with the original problem. What good was it to be the captain of the Top Dog team if *no one* wanted to go?

And there were lots of reasons why no one wanted to go in addition to earthquake related ones...believe me, I heard them all!

No one wanted to make the long trip down to San Marcos (three plus hours on busy freeways), spend the night in a hotel lugging their dogs and the necessary paraphernalia. And especially, no one wanted to drive all that way and eat cold fried chicken and cole slaw!

An additional problem was that I didn't have a clue about how to captain a Top Dog team. Given these handicaps, how was I going to find nine dogs and handlers who would go?

Being the kind of person who likes to do a good job, I was a little bummed. However, never one to be deterred (for long, anyway), I began to formulate a plan. I'd offer a bribe. I'd prepare a gourmet lunch, champagne and hors d'ouerves in my room the night before to celebrate the event.

Well, it worked. Offering a gourmet lunch got me the commitment of a team, and, you know that line from an old Beatles tune, "I'll get by with a little help from my friends?" I actually learned to be a Top Dog captain.

Initially, I only had four dogs: Carol Pyles volunteered to go with her Belgian Malinois, Bandit. He'd be our Open dog. I figured that I'd take Harpo as a Novice dog, and my husband's dog, Cleo (our white/parti colored "dog of a different color" Boxer) as a Novice dog. Doreen Kropf volunteered her Border Collie, Mega, for Novice also.

Ideally, you should have three dogs in each category—Novice, Open and Utility. Then you have two competitors and a good, solid alternate should anything happen to one of the competitors before the big day. In any case, I was still short five dogs—the whole Utility category and two Open dogs.

After revealing the menu for lunch and with help from K-9 board member Carol Pyles, current president and nationally known obedience judge and trainer Shirley Indelicato, board members Dottie Ambrose and Florence Spring and a lot of moral support from training buddies Roz Vincent, Jocelyn Hartsy and Florence Blecher , the four dogs grew into a real team of nine. Not only that, but we had a really solid "fun" team! Nanette Cox, our club artist, even made us wonderful matching Top Dog earrings!

The path leading up to the "big day" wasn't without its burps and gurgles, though.

Cleo disqualified herself from the team by blithely and cheerfully running out of the ring in two differ-

The 1994 K-9 Obedience Club, Inc., **Top Dog Team** included guest author and team captain Karla Spitzer competing with the only Boxer, U-CD Harpo the Marker, CD, CGC.

ent trials during the time I had to make my decisions for the team.

Then my Utility handlers were in dispute about who got to be the alternate! Since people usually fight to be *on* the team as a *competitor*, this was a little unusual. I think it reflects the tone of the earthquake year...we made the final decision the day of Top Dog!

I had to figure out:

(1) How to transport my three dogs and all the gear they need to safely show on hot summer days (Stuff them in my biggest crate in my Jeep, and cram everything else around it.);

(2) How to pack and transport a gourmet picnic lunch for 16 to 20 people, keeping it refrigerated and fresh (Use big ice chests and lots of ice, seal them with electrical tape—this was so effective, I accidentally froze the red grape, red lettuce and chicken breast salad!);

(3) What to do with all my "captain's" paper work and related material (Take a briefcase and hope to find it in the Jeep once I got down there!);

(4) How to plan team practices (Shirley Indelicato graciously allowed us to set up next to her classes on Thursday nights.);

(5) How to get agreement on team T-shirts (Just call, quote a price and ask for a size...) and,

(6) What I was going to do if (heaven forbid!) one of my dogs and/or handlers were injured or didn't show up (I was just planning to panic on that one...).

I learned that wearing a captain's and hostess's hat, 170+ miles from home isn't nearly as easy as it sounds, either. (Not that, come to think of it, it ever

sounded easy...) It may have had something to do with a half-a-dozen people coming and going and those four or five extra dogs.

A rather minor mishap occurred. Sometime during the evening before Top Dog my (then) nine-month-old puppy, Kosmo, discovered that he liked champagne. A curious puppy, he unfortunately managed to knock over a glass or two of champagne, which he lapped up before anyone could get to him. After the first one, he was hooked, and kept his eager eye on all glasses that didn't have anyone's hand on them.

He probably didn't drink that much; after two attempts, we were wise to him. But, I can only assume poor Kosmo was hung over in a major way the next day. My normally sweet and loving pup turned into Cujo the Worst—growling and snarling at any dog who even looked at him. As this behavior never happened before or since, I can only guess he was one unhappy puppy with a walloping headache! (I feel that I should qualify the "champagne" part by saying that there were only two bottles and a non-alcoholic sparking cider for about a dozen people. Most people didn't want to be hung over to show their dogs the next day. The champagne was intended to make us think that this even was festive and fun, not just a lot of work!)

The day of the Top Dog finally dawned—very hot and humid. Harpo was one of only two Boxers represented out of somewhere between 200–300 dogs. In the end, mostly because we had enough Novice dogs, and no other available Open dogs besides Bandit (the Belgian Malinois) and Fiona (the Irish Water Spaniel), I made Harpo the Open alternate. He was doing very well in Open. I felt he could do a good job if he had to, which at that point, I was hoping he wouldn't. I certainly had my hands full with everything else! Not only had I been doing the cooking and entertaining, I had to find out where my team was showing and when, and all kinds of extra "captain's" duties that I had not anticipated.

However, the alternates are required to do sits and downs, just in case anything happens to the first two dogs between their sits and downs and when they go in the ring. I think Harpo felt the weight of this new responsibility greatly. I'm told he was like a statue on his sits and downs. (In Open, the handler is out of sight.)

How did my team do? Great—for a major earthquake year. (We were 16th out of the 36 teams listed.) Going down to San Diego County was a welcome relief from

Jacquet's Hazel, CD, CGC (by Ch. Goldfield's Dorian de Jacquet ex Jacquet's Diana), owned by Nancy Thacher.

the rubble of the earthquake clean-up in the San Fernando Valley. The gourmet picnic lunch, once it thawed out from my anti-food poisoning precautions, was a great hit. In fact, the whole event became so jolly, some of the senior members (who shall remain nameless) went so far as to have a water fight!

In the end, our wonderful Novice A team of Marcia Krause and Basset Hound Roxanne were the stars of the day. K-9's highest scoring dog and handler team, they were asked to represent SCDOC in the competition against the Northern California Dog Obedience Council team.

Everyone else just mostly had fun. In our wonderful new purple and gold T-shirts and earrings, we represented the K-9 Obedience Club with pride. We were a very eclectic team, and while I'm told by an SCDOC official that there have occasionally been Boxers in "Top Dog" over the years, there haven't been many.

DRILL TEAM

The Boxer Rebellion Obedience Drill Team of the Boxer Club of San Fernando Valley flushed with success on completing their premier performance on September 17, 1994.

Along about the fall of 1993, with all my K-9 Obedience Club, Inc. training buddies talking about getting "legs" toward their obedience titles at their breed specialties, I began to wonder why there was no obedience at Boxer specialties. After all, if Beagles, Basset Hounds, Cardigan Welsh Corgis, Irish Water Spaniels and other slightly "off" breeds for obedience could have obedience trials at their specialties, why not Boxers?

Well, I found that there are two clubs north of me, one in the San Francisco area and one in Seattle, that did. But I really wasn't quite ready for that kind of trip in 1993. Talking to friends in the Boxer Club of San Fernando Valley, everyone said the same things to me that I'd been told about training a Boxer for obedience in general. "They're too stubborn; they don't do obedience," and so on. Nevertheless, eventually they said "Okay, Karla, you do it. You be the obedience chairman."

It seemed fairly straightforward at the time. I knew of six Boxers who either had or were working toward their CDs: Lisa Handley with Bud; Marianne Legere with Bixby; Nancy Heckert with Molly; Susi McGrew with Toby; my husband, Scott Friedman with Cleo; and me with Harpo.

After reading all the AKC regulations for shows, I found that you only need six dogs entered in an obedience trial to get a leg toward a title in a specialty. Well, if I knew personally of six Boxers in the Los Angeles area who were training in obedience, it stood to reason that there were likely to be more that I didn't know about.

So, I set about to find out from AKC what was required. They wanted a questionnaire telling them how many members were interested, and then, how many people had actually put an obedience title on a dog. Ouch.

At the point of the questionnaire (spring of 1994), we only had three people who'd successfully done this. Confident that number would change shortly, I rallied on. The next steps were having an approved exhibition, then matches and sanctioned matches and then, *maybe*, we'd be permitted to put on a licensed obedience trial.

Well, by this time, I'd made it through being the K-9 "Top Dog" captain, and I figured I could do anything! All these hoops didn't phase me *until* I started thinking about putting on an obedience demonstration. By now my friend Nancy, with her Boxer, Molly, had moved to northern California and was no longer available for participation. The other five dogs had their CDs, but I'd be the first to admit that unless you're showing a dog yourself, or you simply love the sport, watching an obedience ring—especially Novice—can be pretty boring. Four of the CD dogs were practicing for their CDXs (Companion Dog Excellent), but none of them were necessarily going to be ready to do an Open demonstration by the day of our specialty.

In the meantime, we had started a little Boxer practice group. Susan Jackson of Reward's Boxers was excited to have someone else in the club who was interested in obedience, and so, on Tuesday nights throughout the summer, she, with several of her show dogs; Betty Aikenhead of Sandhill's Boxers with some of her show dogs; Diane Reyes and Kenny Pawlek with their puppy, Mugsy; and Scott and I with Cleo, Harpo and Kosmo, would get together to practice obedience.

As the summer wore on, and our specialty got closer, I became a little worried. I was really uncertain of what to do. I fantasized a little about doing something to music, but discarded it as too frivolous...unlikely to work.

Finally, I confided my concerns to Susan. I'd known Susan for many years through our mutual interest in dog rescue. She'd given me advice on more than one occasion about what to do with problematic dogs in problematic situations. Not only was she a kennel owner

was a Doberman drill team, and there were whole books of drills we could use if we couldn't figure out one of our own.

Thus, the Boxer Rebellion Obedience Drill Team was born!

At first, we had a hard time coming up with enough dogs. The dogs Susan was working with, Reward's Ropin' the Wind (Windy) and Reward's Esquire of Bix-L (Archie), weren't going to be available. Windy was going on a show circuit with Jimmie and Wendy Bettis, and Archie, at about six months, was too young.

Well, Frau Stockmann's Dog Star must have been giggling about us. Susan was keeping Jimmie and Wendy's American/Canadian Champion, Treceder's Jazzy Jet (J-J), to begin putting an obedience title on

The Boxer Rebellion Obedience Drill Team of the Boxer Club of the San Fernando Valley included: C. George Trist with Bud, Kathleen Merwin with Mister, Diane Reyes with Kosmo, Kenny Pawlek with Mugsy, Susi McGrew with Toby, Scott Friedman with Cleo, Lisa Handley with Bud, Susan Jackson with JJ, and Karla Spitzer with Harpo.

and breeder, but she'd been in and out of the sport of obedience for a lot longer than I had.

I told her frankly that I was stumped. She asked me what I was thinking of doing, and I jokingly said I thought watching basic obedience was so boring we'd be better off doing something choreographed to music.

To my amazement, she enthusiastically agreed! She said in the "old days," when she had Dobermans, there

The Drill Team in 1997 with Boxers handled by Susan Jackson, Kenny Pawlek, Scott Friedman, Karen Van Hoepen, Kathleen Merwin, Ellen Saul, Diane Reyes, Karla Spitzer, and Dolores Caprino.

him. Diane Reyes's and Kenny Pawlek's Mugsy had enough basic obedience, and Diane would handle our pup, Mugsy's brother, Kosmo. Initially, we had five dogs—Harpo, Cleo, J-J, Mugsy and Kosmo. Two CD dogs, one champion and two pups. Not an auspicious beginning.

I listened to a lot of music, then thought about the dog's abilities (varied, to say the least!), and came up with a piece that I thought we could handle. It was the "Love Theme" from the movie *St. Elmo's Fire*. It moved at a good pace, but had some natural stopping points. Also, it wasn't too long or too short—four minutes and thirty seconds.

So, one hot, muggy early August day, Scott and I and Harpo met Susan at Pierce College in Woodland Hills, California, the site of our forthcoming show. We marked off an area for a ring, and with poor, patient Harpo in tow, we tried out dozens of different drill movements to go with the music.

Jacquet's Otis Odyssey, CDX, sired by Ch. Jacquet's Greggson, owned by Pat V. Smith.

Then we decided that five dogs just weren't enough. We thought about all our "Boxer friends," wondering who might be silly or game enough to want to do this with us. Marianne Legere had already told me she couldn't be available because she was the show secretary and she would be too busy. Susi McGrew lives in Orange County, which was a long drive. Lisa Handley lives in Ventura County, which was a long way, too, but not nearly as long as coming from Orange County. Susan had a friend, Kathleen Merwin, in Sylmar that had a pup out of Susan's Ch. Cheroakee Bix-l's Leah on Me (Cory) who was about 18 months old.

So Susan and I went home to call our "Boxer friends," and to my amazement, they all wanted to come and be a part of the team!

When we got together the next week to practice, we had eight dogs and han-

dlers! Karla and Harpo; Susan and J-J; Lisa and Bud; Scott and Cleo; Diane and Kosmo; Kathleen and Mister; Susi and Toby; and Kenny and Mugsy.

What we did first was to walk out the pattern as a team—handlers only. Since we had two pinwheels (we got ambitious putting the drill together!), this was more challenging than it might sound.

The dogs were absolutely fascinated watching us! Talk about getting their attention! I'm sure it did the obedience dogs' hearts good to see us marching around in the hot sun for hours without them.

Finally, when we (the people) could put it together with the music, we added the dogs. To our surprise, it went even better. Remember, we weren't doing anything fancy. Just a series of starts, stops, sits, turns and about-turns—except for the killer pinwheels. And we were doing this with four dogs who had recently received their novice obedience titles (CDs), one champion who was just learning formal obedience, a young dog and two pups. We couldn't make it too hard...to say nothing of the fact that we were finding it *very* hard to keep our lines straight ourselves!

Well, the Dog Star was probably really laughing at this point, because we felt too good about things. On our next practice, Susi couldn't make it, and Diane had been rear-ended in an automobile accident. The remains of our team practiced anyway with strict instructions to me to slow down. I move fast in the ring to keep up Harpo's interest and attention!

I slowed down, but we didn't seem as in sync as we had been. Then, the batteries in my boom-box died, and we had no music at all. Still, we soldiered on...

When the premium list went out, I got a call from Lois Trist (Kami Ko N' Kini's Boxers) from San Diego County asking if she and George could be part of the demonstration. I said, "Sure." I sent the title of the song we were going to use, a diagram of the drill, and instructions that we were going to wear white tops with blue bottoms. So now we were up to ten dogs!

Skanes Pure Strength, CD, imported from England by owner Rick M. Daniel.

Then again, on the other hand, maybe not. Toby, Susi's dog, got a very fast growth on his foot that seemed to be giving him some serious trouble. Susi didn't think he'd be able to be in the drill. And Diane was having a lot of trouble with her back, so she didn't think she could take Kosmo. Susan fell and badly strained her left wrist and wasn't sure she could handle at all!! We seemed to be back at eight or fewer dogs, and no time for everyone to get together to practice.

Oh well...

I didn't have much time to worry about it. I had volunteered to do the same gourmet picnic (maybe a calling of mine?) for the Judges' Lunch that I'd done for K-9's Top Dog team, and I had a lot of food preparation to do. Plus dog baths, plus picking up the sweepstakes judge, Rick Tomita, at the airport and on the way to the specialty. At that point, I was just hoping they wouldn't drum any of us out of the Boxer Club of San Fernando Valley for gross embarrassment or something as a result of the drill team.

As I think about it later, I could get into this Dog Star thing because Toby recovered, so Susi brought him. Diane recovered enough so she could handle Kosmo. Lois didn't bring Peaches, her dog, but George had brought Bud (Ch. Kami-Ko N'Kini's Burgermeister), as he was entered in the Burbank Kennel Club Obedience Trial the next day. Susan was well enough to handle anything!

We had planned to do at least one walk-through before we went into the ring, but it wasn't meant to be. I stuck George and Bud in between Susi and Toby and Kenny and Mugsy. My instructions to George were. "Follow Susi, this is easy." My instructions to Susi and Kenny included a very brief introduction, "George, this is Kenny and Susi...Susi and Kenny, George...George is going in between you guys, help him out..."

And worse, I realized, as we lined up, (a) my team, including myself, were really nervous! and (b) the crowd was really watching!

Well, I had to turn on the music sometime, so I yelled to the team, "Are you ready?" And as required, they yelled back, "Ready!"

Fortunately, I love the music. I had gone over it in my mind so many times that I felt right at home with it...at first. We entered the ring—slowly—it was really hot, went all the way around, came up the middle and halted, just as we had practiced. I glanced back to see if all eight other team members and dogs were with me—they were—when the crowd burst into applause!

That totally threw me...only once have I had "performance applause" in the obedience ring—Harpo had done a really stunning job of off-leash heeling that earned him second place. I concluded that something else must be going on and tried to look around to see what it was.

Behind me, Susan figured out why I froze. She hissed at me, "These are breed people. They've never seen nine Boxers sit in the ring on command before at the same time. Keep moving!"

I did, but I was clearly a little thrown by the early applause. I called an about-turn when I should have called a left at one point. (Half of my team believed me—the other half knew better, including Susan, thank heavens!)

And poor Harpo was very nervous, too. I live in an area of rural Los Angeles County where a lot of people let their dogs free, and he's been jumped a few times on leash. I think that all the strange dogs close to the ring, the testosterone and the bitches in heat made him worry about the possible ramifications. I had a hard time keeping him focused on me. Then, we nearly lost our second pinwheel, I have no idea why, but every time we did a sit, or caught up with each other, there was that wonderful applause.

Our ending was a great hit. We had the dogs do a down, one at a time, in a domino effect, starting with me and Harpo, to the wail of the saxophone at the end of the song. And that turned out perfectly!

What a crowd. They thought we were great. And while we didn't do everything just exactly right, we did a lot of things right, and next time, we'd be even better.

So, in our own small way, we really were great. Nobody else I know is trying to do this. We have great dogs (they're Boxers!) and a great group of people who were awfully good sports about being in the drill team. What more could you ask for?

"Geronimooooo!" This is Tarzan of Twin Acres with owner-breeder at Auger's K-9 Kollege. Bred by Fred Procopio, Tarzan is by Ch. Happy Ours Fortune de Jacquet out of Katherine of Twin Acres.

Ch. Gabriela of Halakau, UD became Hawaii's first Utility Dog Boxer. She is owned by Paul and Janis Goto and bred by Robert and Madeline Gage.

Heldenbrand's Dream Lover, CD, owner-bred by Andy and Elvina Heldenbrand.

Will Michaels, CD, CGC, TT, TDI with owner Ann Lettis and judge Carol Brower. Will is a Delta Society Pet and Partner.

Hawaii 5-O (that's five Obedience dogs from Hawaii owned by Paul and Janis Goto): Ch. Seawest Chocklateee Supriz, CD, bred by Diane McGlauflin; Ch. Gabriela of Halakau, UD, bred by Robert and Madeline Gage; Ch. Halakau's Brown Bomber, bred by the Gotos; Halakau's Hawaiian Punch, bred by the Gotos; and Ch. Merrilane's Monument, CD, bred by Merrilane Kennels, Reta George and Dr. Harold Rumbel.

Blanca's Lady "J", CD with owner Sherril Webb, winning third leg of her Canadian CD.

Ch. Merrilane's Monument, CD (by Ch. Merrilane's Knockout, SOM ex Merrilane's Liberty Belle), bred by Merrilane Kennels, Reta George and Dr. Harold Rumbel, owned by Paul and Janis Goto and Lois Matthews.

Cheyenne on the seesaw at an agility trial, owned by Cheri Bush.

Can. Ch-OTCh.-U-CDX Foxwood's Crown Jewel, UD, AD, NAD, CGC, TDI, bred by Irene Fox and Janice Fournier, owned by Ella M. DuPree, competes at an advanced agility trial.

Here's Hawaii 5-O showing off their ribbons and brute strength: Ch. Seawest Chocklateee Supriz, CD; Ch. Gabriela of Halakau, UD; Ch. Halakau's Brown Bomber; Halakau's Hawaiian Punch; and Ch. Merrilane's Monument, CD. Owners, Paul and Janis Goto.

Cheyenne over the A-frame.

Cheyenne through the tire jump.

Tekoneva's Yippee Yi O (by Tekoneva's Firefox ex Tekoneva Eglantine), owned by Cheri Bush.

Cheyenne through the weave poles.

Keil's Strike Force going through the tunnel. Owner, Cheri Bush.

Weave, weave...

BOXER PUBLICATIONS

BOXER REVIEW

BY KRIS DAHL

I was tremendously honored and flattered that my dear friend Rick Tomita, of more years than I can count, asked for a write-up about the *Boxer Review* and its impact on the world-wide Boxer fancy. Since its inception in 1956—yes, that is more than four decades of continued publishing—it has grown in acceptance around the world. It is with no small amount of pride that we state that its international circulation grows with each issue as fanciers realize that to be a part of the "wonderful world of Boxers" is to share goals, aspirations and problems with the entire world. No club, no country is an "island unto itself." There is a common denominator that binds us all together: the desire to create the "perfect Boxer."

This point was vividly dramatized as the *Review* began the first of many international Boxer issues years ago. Over the years, the *Review* has traveled to Brazil, South Africa, Australia, England, Germany and Mexico, and always with the same result. As interviews were conducted with club members and individual fanciers, one recurring statement seemed to be prevalent. We, in the United States, often think we are unique in the Boxer world. We are not. We share the same problems about clubs, health problems, politics the world over—you name it—it is universal. That in itself binds us all together and, only together, through the sharing of new ideas in research, health, welfare, etc., can we all reach that common goal.

No club, breeder or fancier can lay claim that the problems he faces are his and his alone. Every issue of the *Review* attests to that, for our foreign subscribers devour each issue and learn from our educational ideas and share their thoughts and reactions in future issues. It would also be safe to say that American imports in Japan, Australia and Brazil (to name a few) were secured from displays in the *Review*. With these international issues, along with our regular issues and comments from individuals from other countries, we feel we are rendering a real service by opening up the lines of communication in the "wonderful world of Boxers." It is a service that we believe in and are happy to do as often as we can.

International issues, well supported with advertisements of Boxers in each country featured, have led people to correspond with other breeders around the world, people they didn't even know existed until they saw pedigrees, names and addresses in another part of the world. Dogs are exported and imported, ideas are exchanged, new friends are made...and the "wonderful world of Boxers" begins to become a little smaller.

This exchange of ideas and research into the many common goals and aspirations we all have for the Boxer is vital if we are all to achieve perfection or at least close to it. The *Review* is more than happy to be the liaison. If you are interested in your country becoming an international feature in the *Review*, remember—I have camera, tape recorder/will travel!

BOXER QUARTERLY

Boxer Quarterly was started in the United Kingdom in 1986 by Andrew Brace. After it changed hands it was kept going for its new owner, David Cavill, by Di Johnson, a Boxer enthusiast well known in the dog world for her Dicarol Great Danes.

Early in 1994 Eddie Banks, Keith Jump and Tim Hutchings, who are all involved with successful show kennels, namely Sunhawk Norwatch, Susancar and Winuwuk respectively, took over *Boxer Quarterly* and are now producing a very successful, informative and entertaining glossy magazine for all Boxer people worldwide with three issues annually available by direct subscription.

The March 1995 cover of *Boxer Review*.

SCRAPBOOKS OF BOXER CHAMPIONS

BY STURLENE ARNOLD

The *Scrapbooks of Boxer Champions* are different than any other books available on the Boxer breed. This 26-volume set is my contribution to the Boxer breed. It has taken 22 years of research and the compiling of the thousands of pages they contain.

What my scrapbooks contain are pictures, when available, and pedigrees of every Boxer champion, and the Producers of Merit. The first Boxer Champion was published in 1915. These books are updated monthly with the new champions as they are published. They are in a loose-leaf format so the pages can be added alphabetically.

These books are a valuable source for studying pedigrees. They will familiarize you with all the champions that there have been. A person can spend hours, days, weeks or even months studying the many lines. In this manner you are able to see how the different breeders got to where they are, not only in the past but also in the present.

These books also show what these Boxers produced—their champion kids as well as their obedience-titled get.

The *Scrapbooks* are easy to understand and the set now has been broken down so that all the ABC-CKC Sires and Dams of Merit are contained in a separate

Guest author Sturlene Arnold handles her first show bitch, Shalimar's Wah-Sha She Maiden (by Sweet Sinbad of Shalimar ex Peppermint Patti), bred by Lillian Yaeger. Sturlene's dedication to the *Boxer Scrapbooks* and keeping Boxer statistics for the US and Canada is awe-inspiring. Thanks to her tireless work, the author can trust that the thousands of pedigrees presented in this book are as accurate as humanly possible.

set. All the Boxers are represented in this two volume set. This set is special. I've done the Sires on blue paper and the Dams on pink paper. The dogs in this set can be found in most of the pedigrees of today's Boxers.

The *Scrapbooks* take up a vast majority of my time, keeping them current and making sure all the information is correct. You might say I'm obsessed with my work, but it's all for the purpose of making sure none of these champions will ever be forgotten and so people can see that a dog is not just a name on a pedigree. These books are the history of the breed. The books are privately published by this author.

Left: The March 1995 cover of Boxer Quarterly.

BOXERS IN COMMUNITY SERVICE

BOXER THERAPY DOGS

BY ANN LETTIS, CHAIRPERSON, CERTIFIED EVALUATORS, THERAPY DOGS INTERNATIONAL

The personality of the Boxer makes this dog an ideal canine to use in therapy work with humans. A self-assured, outgoing temperament coupled with an uncanny sense of knowing when to behave make the breed an ideal choice for working with institutional bound people.

In Nova Scotia, Canada, Donna and Wilfred Wheten of Dawnwolf Boxers "work" their championship Boxers at the regional psychiatric hospital with young people and adults suffering from a variety of mental disorders. Since 1989 the Whetens and their dogs (sometimes four

mans through their lead and Mae was living proof of this canine intuition. She would change and adapt with the needs of each patient. She could be seen one minute frolicking and playing with a boisterous, outgoing individual, and five minutes later passively pulling a wheelchair and timid occupant around the gymnasium. Mae was a wonder to watch, a treasure to own and an outstanding therapy dog. The Boxers who have followed in her footsteps have continued the tradition of excellence in the therapy visitation field.

The Whetens start their dogs at initial therapy work usually between the ages of nine to twelve months, depending on the self-confidence of the puppy. Youngsters are always accompanied by an older and more experienced dog and are under the ever watchful eye of their owners to monitor behavior, reactions and safety. Requests for Boxer visitations to other wards and to special education classes within the local school system as well as to senior citizen residences leave the demand for the Whetens' dogs greater than they can fill.

This working relationship between man and Boxer benefits all those involved in different ways. The Whetens gain a sense of satisfaction by contribut-

Delta Pet and Partner, Will Michaels, CD, TT, TDI, CGC with Ann Lettis, visiting a nursing-home patient.

at a time), make biweekly visits to residential wards. Unpredictable behavior and sudden outbursts on the part of the patients are all taken in stride by the dogs. It is the nature of the Boxer to be respectfully inquisitive and their affection is honestly and openly given in circumstances that would make many humans shy away.

The Whetens' first therapy Boxer, Canadian Champion C. & M.'s Mae West (out of Canadian Champion Jacquet's Maine Trooper) was a natural. Seeing Mae work and being a small part of making the magic materialize served as the impetus for the Whetens' future work with Boxers in the therapy field. Long after she was gone, the images of Mae working with patients still remains vivid. It is often said that intelligent dogs can sense hu-

ing to their community, and the Boxers gain a unique experience that benefits their personal development while allowing them to act as goodwill ambassadors of the breed. Most importantly, disadvantaged people who might otherwise not have had the opportunity have a chance to interact with another living creature, form a sometimes much needed unconditional friendship and benefit from this relationship in a way that broadens their experiences while living in a limited environment. Visits from our beloved Boxers give many of these patients hope of what tomorrow and the next visit will bring.

The reaction one encounters when announcing his/her dog is a registered therapy dog is extremely varied.

Some individuals feel this means your dog is undergoing psychotherapy, while others only know by the tone of your voice that your dog must be doing something very special, but they are not really sure what it is. Fortunately the "therapy dog" is gaining public recognition for this contribution to the community. This is a dog who visits every type of institution, bringing companionship to those who feel alone, words to the lips of those who have not found it necessary to communicate with humans, smiles to those who have been apathetic and movement to those who previously had no will to move, but now they reach out to pat the dog on the head.

A certain amount of training goes into a potential therapy dog. Therapy Dog International uses the AKC Canine Good Citizen test, with the addition of service equipment, to test dogs for registration with their organization. Dogs of good stable temperament who respond well to gently given commands succeed in this special area of the canine world. Once in a while there is that special dog, the one that truly knows what each resident is all about, the one that isn't just happy in his work, but who gives a part of himself to each individual according to their special needs. I have had the honor of working and living with just such a dog, my Boxer, Will Michaels, CD (Companion Dog), TT (Temperament Tested), TDI (Therapy Dog International), CGC (Canine Good Citizen) and Delta Society Pet & Partner.

Anyone even slightly familiar with the Boxer breed is well aware of their high energy. Leave the house for five minutes and they welcome you home with the same enthusiasm witnessed in the Rose Bowl Parade. Boxers don't discriminate, friends and family are treated equally and, to this breed, every living entity falls into this category. Therefore, it is especially amazing to watch the Boxer work as a therapy dog. There seems to be a special instinct that enables this breed to suddenly move as if in slow motion, with the added ability to convert their energy and strength into that of the smallest lap dog. To witness this is truly an experience.

My Will began his therapy career working in a nursing home where his daughter Hope has now taken his place. His career change came about when I received a phone call from Eden II, a day care program for autistic children.

Mary Jane Gill, Ph.D. was the psychologist who initiated the idea of bringing a dog into the program, since some of the children had a dog phobia. These particular children made it impossible for teachers to take the class for walks in the community and when a dog came to visit, their excessive reactions caused the other children to become afraid of animals. Using James as an example, he was a 13-year-old autistic boy who functioned at the severe level. He could communicate using a combination of verbal speech and sign language. He reacted to dogs with *extreme* fear. When a dog approached on the sidewalk, James would run away in fright with no awareness of potential dangers such as traffic. This was exactly the type of challenge Will loved. Although his lifestyle did not include children, being a Boxer, Will possessed the breed's natural love of them.

Jeswils First Hope Michaels, CD, daughter of Will Michaels, also a therapy dog. Owner, Ann Lettis.

In the beginning of the therapy, James's phobia was so severe that he showed fear reactions to stuffed dogs and pictures of them. I discussed the situation with my good friend, Dr. Mary Burch, who in turn helped us formulate specific sessions for James. Dr. Burch was extremely interested since to the best of her knowledge, while this area of therapy dog work may have been previously implemented, there was no documentation. Will was the first dog to be so documented.

The doctors and I did not care if James ever touched Will, we were only attempting to overcome his stress when a dog was present. Needless to say, the first time he reached out and touched Will, the room was silent. We shared that moment with tears, smiles and emotions that will never be forgotten. The Boxer's love of children is difficult for them to contain, still, Will gently interacts with all; however, he goes even further with those who are afraid. Without any commands he will lay on the floor, not a muscle moving, not an ear twitching, when they come into the room. Will knows that all the work he has accomplished could be ruined by one sudden movement, so his eyes promise these children they need not feel threatened and they have come to believe him.

I know the day will come when these special children will no longer have Will, he is ten-and-a-half now. It's difficult to think how they will handle the loss for they need him as much as I do. What is not difficult is knowing that they will never be without a Boxer, nor will I.

TRIBUTE TO BIXBY

BY KARLA SPITZER

What does Boxer Cheroakee's Trial by Fire, CD, a.k.a. Marianne Legere's Bixby, have in common with wonder dogs like Lassie, White Fang, Old Yeller and Rin Tin Tin? After recently completing his CD with Marianne, he's a bona fide life-saver and hero, and not just on TV or in stories.

Early on the morning of April 26, 1994, around 2:00 a.m., Bixby, with great determination and persistence, repeatedly poked Marianne until she woke up fully. Normally, we wouldn't appreciate this untimely persistence in a dog, but this poking may have saved her life. Due to a bout with polio in her youth, Marianne must sleep with a mini-respirator in order to ensure that she continues to breathe and that her lungs remain inflated.

Once fully awake and aware, Marianne realized from the sound the respirator was making that something was wrong, and Bixby was anxious for her to understand this! The tube leading from the respirator to Marianne had somehow disconnected and Bixby seemed to know, because of the unusual sound the machine was making, that Marianne needed to fix the situation ASAP.

Marianne Legere giving Bixby instructions

Once awake, Marianne did, of course, correct the problem with the respirator. But later, when she thought about the implications of the disconnected tube, she was amazed, overwhelmed and grateful that Bixby was able to sense the seriousness of the situation.

Unable to call her friends to tell them about Bixby's intelligent act (it's still around 2:00 in the morning!), Marianne turned to Bixby. But was he available for comment? No. It was 2:00 a.m. Marianne, his beloved person, was safe once again and Bixby?...Fast asleep.

Bixby also does useful things such as picking up dropped items and giving them to Marianne and bringing things to her from her mother, who may be in another room.

Cheroakee's Trial By Fire, CD, owned by Marianne Legere, winning his CD title. "Bixby" is a true working dog and helps his owner with her everyday chores.

Cherokee Oaks Panache is a therapy dog and working toward her CD title, learning how to fill Bixby's footsteps.

518

Bixby, picking up Marianne's keys.

Bixby, wearing his backpack carrying Marianne's purse and other possessions.

Bixby, steadying Marianne as she moves from her wheelchair to the armchair.

Bixby, guarding Marianne's wheelchair—a real deterrent for theft.

SEEING EYE® DOGS

German Shepherds were the first breed to be trained as guides for blind people, and they continue to serve admirably in that capacity. But Boxers, too, can function as loyal and trustworthy guides. They are friendly dogs with small frames yet strong pull. In fact, one graduate of The Seeing Eye®, who will use only Boxers, says, "They're very proud when they do their work. Their loyalty is just unexplainable."

This graduate adds, "They travel well and aren't afraid of anything. They are willing to please when they are in harness, but playful out of harness. They feel what a person feels and pick up the mood of the family. They're very observant and aware of everything."

The Seeing Eye®, the world's oldest dog guide school, used Boxers extensively in the 1940s and 1950s. Another Seeing Eye® graduate, Jack Hayes, played baseball for the Washington Senators in the 1930s. He is remembered as the first player to wear a helmet and as a Seeing Eye graduate who always had Boxers. Today, the organization tries to keep a few Boxers available each year for fanciers of the breed and for people with allergies to long-haired coats.

Seeing Eye® Boxers undergo the same rigorous training as the German Shepherds, Labrador Retrievers and Golden Retrievers for which the school is known.

Charlotte Gotz and her first guide dog Abby.

Charlotte Gotz and Casey at the entrance to J-B Pet Supply Wholesale, the author's mail-order business in Oakland, New Jersey.

Seeing Eye® pups are raised in the homes of volunteers in New Jersey and parts of Pennsylvania and Delaware. During the year or so the pups live in these volunteer homes, they are taught basic obedience, exposed to the types of social situations they will encounter as working dogs and given lots of love. A dog raised in a kennel doesn't have the firm foundation of love and trust or the experience in cars, stores and similar environments as does a dog raised amid a nurturing family.

When the pup is about 14 months old, he returns to The Seeing Eye® to begin his formal training in guide work. He is assigned to a sighted instructor who works with a "string" of ten dogs for a period of three months. The dog is taught to guide along progressively more difficult routes in downtown Morristown, and to navigate through heavy pedestrian and vehicular traffic.

At the successful completion of this training, the dog is matched with a blind person. Person and dog then train under the supervision of the instructor for an additional 20 to 27 days. The last portion of the training period is tailored to fit each individual's needs. City dwellers, for example, go to New York to learn to negotiate subways. People who live in rural areas learn to walk safely along curbless roadways.

Since its founding in 1929, The Seeing Eye has matched over 10,000 specially bred and trained dog guides with blind people from throughout the United States and Canada. The organization is a philanthropy and receives no government aid.

DEVOTION TO LOVE

BY CHARLOTTE GOTZ

Since that fateful day in January 1969, when I woke up to a world of blackness, my world had been steadily going down hill. My anger and resentment were vented on my children, my husband and anyone within five miles of me. I had to quit my job in advertising and sales and my travels were limited to anywhere anyone would take me. My independence was gone and I was now completely dependent on others. I studied cane travel and was deemed very proficient by my instructor. On my first solo trip I got lost in our driveway and was lucky to make it back to the house. Through all the heartaches my very best friend, Rosemary Goodrich, stood by me, constantly trying to convince me to go for a guide dog from "The Seeing Eye." Her constant persistence paid off. In April 1975, I went to The Seeing Eye. On Sunday at lunch we were informed what breed of dog we would get and its name. I was now in my room waiting patiently for a Boxer named Tanya. In a few short minutes I would embark on a whole new life—go to places I had never dared to travel to, conquer the unconquerable, make my mark in the world and once again become a real person.

Tanya had a stubborn streak a mile long. If she didn't wish to do something, she didn't do it. Part of her training was to fetch a glove from the floor, which she suddenly decided not to do. In the evening when the trainer would work with her, echoes of "fetch, damn it, fetch" would echo throughout the dorm. Tanya would sit, fold her ears back and stare just past the trainer as if to say, "Make me." In time he won out and she fetched.

Our training period went very well until the third week, when Tanya was distracted and walked me into a parking meter. It was a quick trip to the hospital to check for broken ribs.

To me Tanya was the most beautiful dog in the world. She had an overshot jaw, a cockeyed nose, a tongue that was too long to keep in her mouth and two front teeth that stuck out of her face like a bulldog's. Our arrival home was greeted by my 11-year-old-daughter with, "What an ugly dog!" My 10-year-old son seemed very indifferent to both of us.

Tanya was a real lady with a very sexy gait. Her rear end would swing from side to side as she traveled down the street in harness. When we went for an afternoon walk, we would pass a yard with two dogs fenced in. When they started to bark, Tanya would slow down as we passed them, hold her head up a little higher and look straight ahead. Once we were past she would pick up to her normal speed and continue on her way. Once while out shopping we were crossing a street when a pickup truck came from the side street and turned right in front of us. Tanya turned in front of my children and myself, stopping all of us while the truck sped by. She stopped me many times in this manner, even to the point of once being grazed by a car. The spot of her injury later became the beginning of a cancerous tumor.

Tanya and I had been together for about four years when my husband Wayne, our children and I took a trip to England with a group of students. I had to leave Tanya at home with my mother because of the quarantine laws pertaining to animals going into Great Britain. I gave Tanya my fuzzy bath robe to sleep on and from what I was told, she did. When I called home my mother put the phone by Tanya's ear so I could talk to her. When the phone call was done she would lay down on the robe and bury her nose in it. She was a family dog when not in harness, getting along very well with any member of the family. Definitely not a one person dog, but very devoted to me. We were more than just a team, we were one. I think our trip away from her was harder on me than it was on her. When we came home, she completely ignored me but walked over to one of the suitcases, laid

Charlotte Gotz and Casey visit with author Richard Tomita and his partner Bill Scolnik at the office of J-B Pet Supply Wholesale. Casey, bred by author Richard Tomita and supplied to The Seeing Eye in Morristown, New Jersey, finished at the top of her class.

down next to it and whined very softly. When I opened the suitcase, she put her nose into it and took out a small bag with the toy I had brought as a gift for her. I held her, cried a lot and vowed I would never leave her again.

Tanya was a very prim and proper lady. When we were on the street and people would stop and talk about how pretty she was or how well behaved, she would sit with her chest out, her ears pointed straight up and a look of "what do you expect, I'm from The Seeing Eye."

Tanya had two vices: she loved balloons and cigarettes. Friends of ours owned a pancake house a short distance from where we lived. When we went there to eat we would get an orange balloon for her and blow it up. If it wasn't an orange balloon she didn't want it. She would look so proud as we walked out of the restaurant with the balloon in her overshot jaw. When driving home in our station wagon she would sit in the back with the tied end of the blown-up balloon in her mouth looking out the window for everyone to see. She was so careful with the balloon it would last up to a week before it burst.

Her other habit, this one bad, was an addiction to cigarettes. At first it was to just the cigarette butt. We would walk down the street and she would lap up a butt without breaking stride until one day she threw up, then her addiction centered on exhaled smoke. She would sit lapping the smoke in the air with her tongue when any-one exhaled or left their cigarette burning in an ashtray. This was a habit I tried to but could not break until she finally succumbed to lung cancer.

Tanya was with me constantly, even when not in har-ness. Once while I was hanging clothes on the line out-side I noticed a tomato smell in the air and then Tanya walked by. She had been in the garden picking and eat-ing the little cherry tomatoes from the vines. She did get confused once when she ran from the house to the backyard and mistook a large tomato for a racquet ball. She was certainly surprised as she grabbed the "ball" on the run and it squooshed in her mouth.

Charlotte Gotz with Abby and a latch-hook tribute to her first dog, Tanya: "Love Leads the Way."

Tamoron's Brindy Bandit, sired by Ch. Jacquet's Jesse James, is a Seeing Eye dog and therapy dog, owned by Noel White and bred by Joy Iannaconi.

On Easter Sunday 1982, Tanya became very sick and we rushed her to an animal emergency clinic in the evening. Exploratory surgery found that a tumor on Tanya's spleen had burst and that she had cancer. The vet brought her dog from home for a blood transfusion to replace the blood that was lost and performed sur-gery. Tanya was up and around the next day as soon as the anesthetic wore off but she stayed under the vet's care for another day. I would try anything to help my baby. We managed to get the Illinois School of Veteri-nary Medicine to examine Tanya and help us make a decision. They concluded she was in no pain or discom-fort as yet and all the cancer had been removed. Che-motherapy was the only solution left. My veterinarian, Dr. Ken Martinsek, agreed to administer the treatments and for six months gave of his time and love, charging me only for the medication, coming in on weekends and holidays when she needed fluids. For a period of time she lived free of any cancer, but that was short lived. The cancer developed in her lungs and there was no hope left. Finally my daughter, who called this dog ugly, carried her out to do her duty for the last time. We then took that inevitable trip to the vet. Tanya is still with me today, in a brass urn on the headboard of our bed. With-out her to guide me both physically and mentally, I might not be alive today.

Tanya was put to sleep on a Friday morning and I left town with my girlfriend for the weekend. When I returned home I had my husband call all the Boxer ken-nels in the area to find a pet Boxer. My life already seemed very empty. We picked up Dixie, a 14-month-old Boxer who had been returned to the breeder. We found out much later she had been abused and branded as mean. She had to be caged at night and tried to rip the metal cage apart. Many times we had to use pliers and wrenches to get the door of the cage open. When I left for The Seeing Eye, my husband determined Dixie would never be left alone or caged. All through my 21-day stay at The Seeing Eye, the family alternated being with her, taking her for rides, letting her sleep with them and many other means of expressing love. When I came home with Abby, they greeted each other outside before I entered the house. There was never a problem and we were a family of six. Dixie's meanness was only in some person's imagination. Dixie was the most gentle dog I ever knew and she never hurt any living thing. Once she caught a fly in her mouth but she spit it out and it flew away.

If Tanya was headstrong and determined, Abby, my second Boxer, was stubborn and pigheaded. I received her on January 3, 1983 at The Seeing Eye. When she was brought to me on Sunday afternoon, she curled up in the corner and completely ignored me. Her guide work was good but her attitude towards me left something to be desired. Crossing the street was not a problem but when we were on the sidewalk, she would walk me into ruts, cracks, holes or anything else. It took quite a few heartaches, sprained ankles and many months before we became a team. I would have sent Abby back to The Seeing Eye except she would have had to be crated and I just could not do that to her. I found out much later that Abby had been a kennel dog before she was donated and had never lived in a house until she was 15 months old. She had never been given love and she did not know how to give it in return. In the period of adjustment that we went through, Abby never made a mess in the house or any place she should not have. Abby was a very clean dog and must have thought it beneath her to be dirty or messy.

As a team we became as one. Abby was a one person dog and I was that one. She had many health problems. She had two bouts of pancreatis and five ulcerated corneas through her life. Each time she bounced back with no lasting effects or lack of desire to work. While recovering, she never failed to do her work to near perfection nor at any time allowed me to be in an unsafe situation. After her first surgery when she came out of the anesthetic, she started to hyperventilate. I was called at home and told about her problem. Within an hour, I was at her side and she started to calm down. We were allowed to take her home that day. During the second surgery, I stayed in the waiting room, and at subsequent surgeries, Abby was brought to me and laid on a blanket in the waiting room so she would see me when she recovered. She would usually come out of the anesthetic between 12:00 and 2:00 while the clinic was closed. It was Abby's own private room. Normally Dr. Martinsek never lets the animals leave before 24 hours. Because of Abby's hyperventilating and knowing the good care she would receive from us, an exception was made and she slept that evening at home. I was at her side throughout the

Casey with her trainer Lee Bolling on graduation day from The Seeing Eye. Casey is the full litter sister to Jacquet's Holden, the author's present house dog.

night and in the morning she ate, did her duty and went back to sleep.

When Abby was six-and-a-half, we became grandparents and I became a babysitter. I normally pulled the stroller and Abby had to learn there were new sizes to contend with and others who came first when it was necessary.

The longer we were together, the more we communicated without words. We would walk a mile and a half to the bank and take care of our business. Abby would seem to know afterwards if I wanted to go home, and leave by the same door, or continue shopping and leave by the opposite door. In the mall, she would know which door to go to without a command. Abby would also fetch anything for me. If I were to drop a spoon putting it in the dishwasher, Abby would find it. If I dropped the back clip of my pierced earring, Abby would come and put her nose by it so I could find it. She took great pride in being able to assist me and in just being with me.

We became such a good team that we moved forward with my life. I was now going to try things that I never could do before. My husband and I joined the Order of the Eastern Star and I became an officer. The Eastern Star is a Masonic-affiliated organization for men and women. My first office just required a lecture to memorize, which I did. My second station required several lectures plus a lot of floor work: presenting guests, escorting the American flag and escorting candidates through initiation. There is a lot of intricate work and training in the marches. I would work through the floor work with a sighted person with Abby at heel. At a corner where we would turn I would stop, have Abby sit, tap the floor with my foot and tell her, "That's a good girl." At each turn I would repeat this procedure. I would not use her all the time and sometimes she would be on a long leash to my chair. Once while the American flag was being presented and I was 20 feet away from my chair, Abby found my glass of water beneath my chair and, being thirsty, decided to take a drink. We had to stop for several seconds while everyone watched Abby when they all heard the slurping. We continued to do the work and each year advanced until we were head of our chapter. Abby was a true Eastern Star dog. We visited many chapters and she became known through the state and even in several other states. There were always several special people to her as she was special to them, and she would always pick them out in a crowd. When we went to visit after a meeting, I could drop her harness and she would go to her special friends and sit, and they would talk to her and she would tilt her head to the side and listen. She was a beautiful dog. She was a brindle from the East Coast and her striping was blended and not pronounced.

Casey, working with trainer Lee Bolling.

Our two Boxers got along extremely well. There was never a harsh word or discord between them. Dixie would stay at home while Abby, Wayne and I went out, and she would greet us lovingly on our return. She seemed to know Abby's place was with me while her place was at home.

We did take the two of them out together many times, especially at Christmas time. Christmas was Abby's favorite time. We would drive through different areas that were decorated and lit. Her head would swivel from side to side when both sides of the street were lit.

After ten years with my Abby, I had to make a hard decision. Abby was starting to slow down and her hindquarters were starting to give her problems. We just had Dixie put to sleep because of a pinched nerve in the spine and loss of mobility in the rear legs along with a bad heart. Dr. Martinsek would constantly monitor our dogs until we felt they were in pain or discomfort. The January class at The Seeing Eye would be starting soon, and there was a Boxer named Casey waiting for me.

In January 1994, I left Abby at home with my husband and returned once again to The Seeing Eye. Wayne had to take off from work because of a knee injury so I knew Abby would be in good hands. My biggest concern was that she would pine away for me, not eat and starve to death. My worries were unfounded as when I came home, Abby was several pounds heavier and very attached to my husband. He was several pounds heavier too and very attached to Abby.

"The Changing of the Guide": Retired at 12 years of age, Abby and the new Jacquet Seeing Eye dog Casey, in the home of Charlotte Gotz.

When they brought Casey to me, I said, "Casey come!" She ran to me, covered me with kisses and gave me her heart. We knew instantly that we would be a team. The first day in town I said "Abby forward!" She took me up to the corner of Maple and Miller and stopped at the curb. My trainer tapped me on the shoulder and said, "Oh, you really work well together and you know what? I bet if you use her name, she will work even better." I never realized I used Abby's name. When I handed my husband Abby's leash when I left, part of me stayed at home with her.

Part of our training requires a traffic check. That is when a trainer, driving a car, will aim for the student and dog when they are crossing a street or driveway. Casey never hesitated but pulled me backwards six steps. This was the first time I was ever guided with both of us going in reverse. Several times we had traffic checks like this, once returning to the curb from the middle of the road.

Casey would love to play when we were in our room. I had brought a Nylabone® from home for my dog to play with. Casey would throw the bone around sometimes, having it land under the bed or dresser. Once it landed in the bathtub. Then she would just stand there and cry ever so slightly, just pleading with me to retrieve it for her.

Casey is a fawn colored Boxer with a black face and white toes. People have nicknamed her "Twinkle Toes" because when she travels down the street, her toes seem to sparkle as she trots on by. She is a beautiful Boxer with the disposition of a puppy. Her attitude on life is to see everything, do everything, go everywhere and get to know everyone she meets. This, however, has not interfered with her work. She is better in her work now, at three years old, than Tanya or Abby were in their entire lives. I could almost guess the way she was raised and the type of people her breeder and owner were by the loving disposition that just radiates from her. I now babysit for four grandchildren. Casey is my assistant sitter and worships the children with a passion.

After I returned home, Wayne, Casey and I had to do some shopping. It was a cold March day with about an inch of snow on the ground. We had just stepped off the curb and were crossing the parking lot to get to our car, when all of a sudden Casey turned in front of me and stretched her neck in front of my husband, stopping him. We never saw the car that decided to make a U-turn and come our way. Casey had stopped and saved both of us. My dogs have saved me many times. When Abby was 11 years old, we were out completing several errands. It was a windy day and I didn't hear the car as I was about to cross a driveway. Abby stopped and I didn't know why. I put my hand out to give Abby the forward sign and touched the moving car. These are the things my dogs do for me. I love my dogs and to me there is no dog like a Boxer.

It was November of 1994 and my Abby's legs were getting weaker and weaker. I so wanted to have her make it through Christmas. In December, Abby slowed down in her eating. On a Saturday morning we took Abby into the vet and we all came to a hard decision. She was not in pain yet, but was becoming disoriented and suffered from a loss of appetite. She had lost considerable weight and the cause was unknown. Blood work six months before had shown nothing and an electrocardiogram had shown only minor problems. Whatever the reason, the time had come. I let Casey give her a kiss, then asked my husband to leave the room and take Casey with him. Oh God, I died right along with her. But I was by her side at the end as she was by mine though her life. I held her as she fell into that eternal sleep and wondered if I could go on. The vet called my husband in so he could say good-bye, then carried her in the back. Casey sensed the sorrow in my life and laid on my lap on the way home.

Casey is now our only child at home. She loves our grandchildren and takes Cheerios from between the fingers of the one- and two-year-olds. She plays a little rougher with our five-year-old grandson but never ever to the point of hurting him. I don't believe Casey knows how to hurt or to be aggressive to children. My husband, Casey and I went to New Jersey for our vacation and saw a stage play off- Broadway. When we left the theater a mounted policeman dismounted and tied his horse to the parking meter. Casey came up the steps, staring at the horse, and walked slowly towards it. I pulled her back and the officer mentioned it was alright as his horse liked dogs. Well! Casey just had to see what this big dog really looked like. They got closer and closer. Casey stretched her neck and the horse put its head down. They were nose to nose checking each other out when all of a sudden Casey gave that big dog a great big slurpy kiss across the nose. The horse lifted its head up in surprise and Casey just stood there looking at it. The expression on her face said what she was thinking: "Hi buddy!" Casey has several wrinkles in her forehead and as her ears move, so do the wrinkles. These traits give her face expression and personality.

We attended a "Council of the Blind" Convention in Chicago which lasted for a week. Of the 600 ageists at the convention, she was the only Boxer. I truly feel sorry that there are so many people less fortunate than myself. The reason I usually get a Boxer is that my husband is allergic to dogs. I groom my dogs once a day, which gets the dander out, and I vacuum the house each afternoon. Casey and I also volunteer to give presentations and lectures on blindness and guide dogs. We have talked to school children from preschool to high school as well as fraternal organizations, woman's clubs, men's clubs, senior groups, church groups, youth organizations, professional woman's organizations and many others. Many people still do not know about guide dogs and how they are used. Nor do they know that a guide dog is permitted entry with the blind person to all facilities. Since my first Boxer I have learned much about them. With their loving disposition I feel secure about their behavior towards other people and children.

Seeing Eye dog Lucy with trainer Ed Oathouse, donated by Jacquet Boxers.

My first year as head of our Eastern Star chapter, I had the theme "Love Leads the Way" with Tanya's picture on the cover of our program. The second time through our theme was "Someone to Watch Over Me" with a picture of Abby and a big stuffed panda on the cover of our program. The last year there was a picture of Abby and Casey on the cover and my theme was "Devotion is Love."

I will close as I once closed one chapter of my life and opened a new one. It was 1994 and I had my Abby, age and experience, and my Casey, youth and vitality. It was a year that would bring forth both sorrowful and joyful memories. I had my Casey to guide me and it was the first year of Abby's retirement. It was Abby's love and devotion that helped me through the roughest times and gave me the courage to continue when I faltered along the way. My life had been placed in her hands and she had taken care of it very well. As time moves on, so must our lives. No matter how sad the inevitable may be, we must be thankful when we are able to prepare for it. Now, Casey is here, at my side, to assist and guide me on my journey through life. I am thankful each day for those two gentle miracles of God whose only purpose in life is to guide, serve and love; and must cram it all into those few short years they are here with us. Theirs is a life of devotion and love.

In April 1995 my husband, Casey and I went to New Jersey to visit the Seeing Eye in Morristown and to fulfill a dream I've always had. I wanted to thank personally the donors of one of my Boxers. Rick Tomita was the only donor I was able to meet. It was a lovely trip but the first time we drove through Morristown, Casey shook like a leaf in the wind. When we did go to visit, she was working and there was no problem. When we finally met with Rick in Oakland, there was no doubt in my mind that Casey recognized him at once. As soon as I put the harness down she was covering him with kisses from ear to ear and her tail was wagging fast. We visited the whole afternoon and got to see the Jacquet Kennels

Seeing Eye dog Lucy, bred by the author.

and all of the Boxers. It was such a thrill to hold a two-day-old Boxer and realize that my Casey was once such a tiny thing. When we visited the J-B Wholesale warehouse, Holden, the on-site watchdog, was put in his cage. Casey greeted him through the bars. Holden was released and he welcomed us to the warehouse. We have heard so much about Holden that it seemed as if we already knew him. Casey was taken out of harness and she played with Holden for over an hour. Out of harness she is a regular Boxer and she showed everyone that she still runs and plays with the best of them. Guide dogs out of harness are normal dogs, and Casey proved no exception.

Perhaps the reason I love Boxers so much is that they never seem to grow up. When the problems of life get me down and I become depressed and feel alone, my Casey will find a way to make me laugh and be happy once again. One time she even picked up and carried three shoes in her mouth and brought them to me.

We owe much to the state of New Jersey and the people in it. As battles for freedom and independence were once fought there, a different battle ensues there: the battle of blind persons training with guide dogs to gain their independence to be able to travel about freely and safely without a sighted person as a guide. Approximately 11,000 students have graduated from The Seeing Eye in Morristown with new freedom granted them by an assisting guide dog.

I would like to thank several people for allowing this chapter to take place. First and foremost I thank The Seeing Eye, Inc. of Morristown, New Jersey for allowing me to be one of their students and making it possible for me to receive three beautiful Boxers.

Mr. Ed Oathouse for training Tanya, the prim and proper lady, for working with me the 28 days of my first stay at The Seeing Eye and for teaching me the proper way to use a guide dog. To learn the commands and to follow my dog, above all to get myself out of any situation that may arise, for teaching me integrity, stability and determination.

Mr. Drew Gibben for training my second dog, Abby, the brindle Boxer. For convincing me during my 21-day stay that Abby could one day be a loving and devoted guide dog, someone who would be a part of my life and heart.

Mr. Lee Bolling for training Casey, my third Boxer, the black faced twinkled-toed puppy who I am afraid may someday grow up, and again, Mr. Gibben who continued the training until I arrived. The one who showed me all of my perseverance, all of my determination and all of my stamina paid off in my becoming a good guide dog user.

Betty Montgomery for donating one of her Boxers, J.R. Crackmonts Abigail, my Abby, to The Seeing Eye so that I could live a normal life.

To Richard Tomita for donating Casey, my little squirt, who is helping me to continue with my life and even to dream the impossible dream.

It is unfortunate that I do not know who to thank for my Tanya. My heartfelt thanks go out for my lady for she was number one and number one is always special.

She allowed me to screw up, then learn and conquer, always at my side.

Rosemary Goodrich, my adopted sister, who has listened to my problems and encouraged me to get up when I fell, move forward when I stepped back and to keep on trying when everything went wrong. She has shared my joys and my sorrows for we have walked in each other's shoes and have walked the same path of life.

Dr. Kenneth Martinsek, for without him I would not have had my Tanya for seven and one half years, my Abby for eleven years and now my Casey for eighteen months. His devotion and concern in the care of my babies has helped see them through many problems. His concern for me has been more than I could ever ask for or even imagine when I called him at odd hours of the night at home.

To all the people who have been a part of my life these last 13 years, I thank you for making life possible and livable and accepting my Seeing Eye Boxers.

My daughter Christina and son Wayne Paul II, for never feeling as if my Boxers were put before them but accepting them as a part of me, never becoming jealous and treating my girls as if we were all one family.

Most of all my husband, Wayne, who wrote this beautiful chapter with all my thoughts, my ideas, my dreams, all my hopes and our everyday life. For without you none of this would be possible. I thank you for standing by me after that fatal day of January 11, 1969 that changed our lives. After which our lives were enriched by Tanya, my lady; Abby, my love; and Casey, my little squirt.

Casey, relaxing at home.

Lucy is one cool guide dog.

A very special thank you to all the Boxer breeders and owners who have donated these wonderful animals for guide dogs and so enriched the lives of we who are so fortunate enough to receive them.

Dear Rick,

There is not a day that goes by that your Casey does not cease to amaze me. Today I went for a haircut. A girl about 12 houses away does this for me. It was across a street and through the snow banks. Casey slowed down as we came to icy spots on the sidewalk and found a clear path through the snow bank to the street. She walked down the block and stopped at the driveway to the house, then turned in when I gave her the command. We had walked to this girl's house only two times before. She is such a terrific dog and guide. I give her many more liberties than normal and much more than Seeing Eye would approve of. Since she is a Boxer, she is a different type of dog. Never once when I have had her harness in my hand has she done anything but work to perfection, nor act in any way she should not. I never intend to attempt to change her nature or her personality as long as her work is as perfect as it is. Out of harness or on leash, she is a Boxer. If it is no problem to you, we would like to see you this coming summer. My husband Wayne has a cousin in East Orange, NJ, where we would stay. When I had to have my Abby put to sleep there was a large hole in my heart and a vast emptiness. Casey was there to fill that vast void and she gave me the love I needed to look forward to another day. She is such a clown and goof that she brings much joy and laughter into our lives. I hope whoever received Lucy is as happy with her as I am with Casey. With all our love,

Charlotte and Casey

BOXERS IN CARDA

BY KARLA SPITZER

Dedicated to the Memory of Bannor

CARDA, Inc. (California Rescue Dog Association) is a nonprofit, tax-exempt organization that provides volunteer dog/handler teams to search for people lost in wilderness areas and other unusual circumstances, such as urban search and rescue for earthquake and fire victims. CARDA certifies the dog/handler teams "mission ready" as proof that they can undergo the rigors involved in a life and death search.

The volunteers who search for lost people must spend hundreds of hours training and conditioning not only their dogs but themselves as well for the challenging physical circumstances that they often face when undertaking a search. These volunteers are on call 24 hours a day. They live with a beeper or pager at all times. They are prepared to leave their jobs, taking vacation time if they must, occasionally facing very real danger in order to participate in the searches to save another person's life.

The following is about two very special people, Rhonda Dyer and Cindy Clark, and four very special Boxers—Juba, Tanis, Bannor and Trooper—who are,

The badge of Bannor.

have been, or are becoming certified members of the California Rescue Dog Association.

Should I ever need to be rescued (heaven forbid!), I can think of no one I would rather have rescue me than one of these two wonderful women and a cheerful, determined Boxer.

Juba, Tanis and Rhonda Dyer of San Jose, California

After watching a video of dog rescue teams searching for victims of the 1985 Mexico City Earthquake, Rhonda Dyer of San Jose, California, wondered what she would have to do to teach her Boxer puppy to do this kind of search and rescue work.

Rhonda found a local contact for CARDA. In December of 1985, when Jedapay's Jaunty Juba was 14 weeks old, she and Rhonda went to their first CARDA training session. (Juba's AKC titles include Companion Dog Excellent and Tracking Dog).

After learning to search and scent (actually, all dogs know how to search and scent—what they learn is how to do what they do naturally on command when we ask them), after many hours of socialization and after learning how to swim, Juba was approaching her "mission ready" test. To pass the test, Juba had to find a subject in a 40-acre area within two hours. And *then* she had to do longer, more difficult searches! (160 acres and two people!)

Juba passed both tests. By March 7, 1986, she had her final certification to become the first Boxer to be registered as a "mission ready" wilderness search dog with CARDA. Later, she was trained in water rescue to find drowning victims. Juba, like many other dogs, has a sense of smell so acute that she can smell victims even underwater.

In CARDA, Juba became what is known as an "area" dog, or one of the dogs that would sniff out *any* human scent within the designated area. Area dogs cover distances farther and faster than any other

Bannor, wading through the water.

part of the search team. In searches covering larger geographic areas, the "area" dogs "clear" the area quickly so that the search can be narrowed down and the victim found more quickly. Since dogs can go where humans can't, use of the area dogs has that added advantage. Area dogs are also most valuable in situations where no "scent" article is available. In disasters, they notify their handlers of the presence of any human scent.

Later, when they were more experienced with wilderness searches, Rhonda and Juba trained for evidence and urban disaster searches. Training Juba for disaster readiness consisted of many repetitions of slow and steady drills over agility equipment to give her confidence on different types of surfaces. This was crucial to Juba's safety, especially in California, where because of significant seismic or "earthquake" activity, the rescue dogs need to learn not to move even if the surface they are standing on does.

Juba's training paid off. On October 17, 1989, the Loma Prieta Earthquake rocked San Francisco and the surrounding area. The next day, Rhonda and Juba were assigned to search at the Cypress structure in Oakland. The Cypress structure is that memorable part of the Interstate 8-80 freeway that collapsed, trapping between 50 to 60 people and their cars for several days.

Following the search at the Cypress structure, Rhonda and Juba were transferred to the Pacific Garden Mall, a charming older section of downtown Santa Cruz, which had sustained considerable damage. Many persons were known to be missing in this area. Santa Cruz's close proximity to the epicenter of the earthquake, the time of day (early evening) and the charming old turn-of-the-century construction proved to be a deadly combination.

Juba, searching a collapsed building after an earthquake.

Tanis on agility ramp.

In Santa Cruz, Rhonda and Juba spent their time searching for survivors. Juba did her job very well, searching over the rubble of collapsed buildings with ease. All the hours of agility training showed as she slowly and carefully climbed over the remains of the many shattered buildings. Juba was one of the dogs who indicated a presence of a body in one collapsed building in the Pacific Garden Mall, and eventually, all the missing persons were accounted for.

Then in September of 1991, a fire storm—another California specialty—ravaged the Oakland Hills area across the bay from San Francisco. Helping in the search for bodies and survivors after the fire storm was the most dangerous situation that Juba and Rhonda had faced.

It took three days for the surface to cool enough to safely search. And even after three days, only the surface of the burn area had cooled. A mere three to four inches down from the surface were embers hot enough to cause severe burns. So in addition to facing the problem of loose and moving rubble, Juba and Rhonda also faced the possibility of being badly injured. Neverthe-

Tanis and Rhonda Dyer, searching on the swamp.

less, Juba and Rhonda worked tirelessly. They searched for people for four days.

Does Juba have an opinion of who she likes to find? Yes.

According to Rhonda, Juba prefers to find her victims alive, and has much less enthusiasm for cadavers. Still, as Rhonda points out, searches for (known) cadavers also provide a valuable service. These searches are performed in order to give the family a certain knowledge, a final outcome. And in some cases, cadaver searches produce vital evidence. So search and rescue dogs must be willing to search for remains.

Around the time of the Oakland Fire in 1991, Rhonda had begun testing Boxer puppies from litters in her area. She was looking for another likely prospect as a search and rescue dog. Juba was a pretty, petite, fine-boned bitch, and her many long, hard searches had taken a toll on her.

After the fire, Rhonda came home with Topaz Forgotten Realms (a.k.a. Tanis), one of the last of Merrilane's Knockout's daughters. Tanis went through the same training as Juba, and passed her final wilderness test searches in April of 1993. Tanis, like Juba, is an area dog. On December 1, 1993, Rhonda and Tanis were called to assist law enforcement officials in the Polly Klaas kidnapping in Petaluma, in northern California.

Juba is retired now from search and rescue work, though Rhonda says she'll continue her obedience work toward a Utility Dog title. For now, the search and rescue career for Tanis has just begun.

Bannor, Trooper and Cindy Clark of Oak View, California

Meanwhile, in Oak View, Ventura County, California, much closer to the Los Angeles area, we have another search and rescue team. Cindy and Bannor (Dolor's Bannor of Hearthrall—born November 19, 1985) participated in many missing person searches. Cindy and Bannor started search and rescue work when Bannor was two.

Cindy, Bannor and Trooper have a different role in search and rescue than Rhonda with Juba and Tanis. Bannor and Trooper became "trailing" dogs, or one of the search dogs who scents only for a specific scent. Trailing dogs go where the scent of the person has fallen or been blown by the wind. The role of trailing dogs differs from that of police trained dogs or area dogs. Police dogs follow the crushed vegetation caused by a fleeing person.

Trailing dogs are "scent discriminating" and have to have a correct scent guide. Usually this is something that only the missing person has worn or touched. Under the right weather conditions, a trailing dog with a correct scent guide could find one specific child in Disneyland.

After many hours of training, Bannor distinguished himself with extraordinary Boxer intelligence. He received the highest score for his "mission ready" test of any dogs in southern California, including Bloodhounds! Not only that, but Bannor trailed his "victim" on a ten-day-old trail that his victim/tester had inadvertently laid while he was hiking in the area with his wife ten days prior to the test!

The tests Bannor had to pass *before* the big "mission ready" test were: (1) trailing—24, 48 and 72-hour-old trails; (2) city search and wilderness search;

Juba, working after a fire in Oakland, California.

(3) socializing—traveling in a pick-up with four other dogs on a bumpy road; (4) swimming test; (5) helicopter entrance/exit with engine and rotors on; (6) car identification; (7) cadaver finds; (8) water finds from a boat.

Bannor's first real search was for a man named Scottie, who had a mental age of five. Scottie became lost on an outing in the Santa Barbara Mountains area.

After 36 hours of trailing, Bannor and Cindy were sent home. It was very, very hot, and Bannor's feet had developed blisters. Cindy wouldn't have known this if she hadn't seen them because Bannor hadn't limped, slowed down or made any kind of complaint. Bannor had his scent, and he was determined to find the person that belonged to it.

Seven days or so later, Cindy's CARDA supervisor called Cindy to tell her that Scottie had been found—dead. As Cindy relayed this painful information to her husband, Bruce, Bannor looked at her, jumped up, threw his head back and howled a long mournful howl. Somewhere in his big Boxer heart, Bannor knew what this message meant. He felt a great sadness for a person named Scottie whom he only met through scent, and to whom something awful and final had happened.

Although he did many searches, one of Bannor's most important and fun roles was the "Hug-A-Tree" program for children. This program, for kindergarten through sixth grade, is designed to teach children wilderness safety.

Bannor went with Cindy to schools to teach children what to do just in case they ever got lost in the wilderness. Cindy would explain to the children that to prepare to go into the wilderness, you need to take a whistle and a trash bag. If you get lost, you need to stop, hug a tree, blow your whistle—it will last a lot longer than your voice—and wear your trash bag for warmth and to stay dry.

As a reward for their attentiveness and willingness to learn the important points from the slide show program, Cindy would have Bannor "sing" for the children. He was a great hit, and he always loved to have the children pet him. Since Cindy and Bannor did about 25 assemblies over a period of five years, talking to 20 to 500 children at a time, many children met Bannor. Cindy says that frequently, children on the street recognize and remember her as "Bannor's mom!"

Bannor and Cindy's last search was a very difficult one. They were flown by airplane in crowded conditions to Blythe, California, in the Sonoran Desert. This was Bannor's first airplane flight, and he slept on the luggage on the way to Blythe. Along with other rescue dogs, volunteers and law enforcement officials, they were taken to a place near the Arizona/California border where a dove hunter had disappeared. High temperatures (even at midnight) and rugged terrain made this search so challenging that several of the desert-trained search teams had to be hospitalized.

Tanis, working for the first time on concrete rubble with Rhonda Dyer.

Trooper, guarding Cindy's gear.

A smiling Trooper trails a scent.

Bannor took Cindy to within 500 hundred feet of the victim two days before the victim was actually found. Bannor and Cindy could not get closer because of an apiary of 40 hives of bees. The bees were swarming to keep the hives cool...a dangerous situation all in itself. Because no other search dogs were indicating this area as a "find," Bannor's "find" was not taken seriously at first.

Two days later, when all other trails led to the same general area, Cindy managed to convince her supervisor to have another look. Once the bees could be settled down, the victim was found. Bannor had been right, after all.

Cindy and Bannor flew home with Bannor sleeping on top of the luggage. A month later, on November 1, 1993, Bannor died of a lympho-sarcoma, just days short of his eighth birthday. Cindy and her family were devastated. CARDA, the children of Ventura County and the Los Angeles County Sheriff's Department lost a great and valuable friend.

Cindy's Letter to Bannor

Dear Bannor,

Friend, companion, search and rescue dog par excellent! I miss you so! You took me on many adventures, but I knew that I was safe with you.

We had such exciting searches together. We would trail the lost person for hours on end. You keep your concentration and determination to find that lost person. I admire your ability not to give up so much!

Our career as a K-9 search and rescue team all started when you were two years old. In your early training, you showed so much promise that it gave me the "stick-to-it-ive-ness" to get myself in shape. You

Trooper gets the scent.

would take me to the training victim at a dead run the last 500 yards!

When we were on the boat in water rescue training, it took another handler and me to keep you from jumping overboard to help the diver.

The part of training that was hardest for you was walking up to the helicopter when the engine was on. Your first trip took two handlers and a hot dog to get you there.

It was only because of you that I kept up with the training that took us two years. You were so good at trailing that I

Tanis finds her lost person on a mission-ready test.

had to keep up my training to make the team as a mission ready handler.

As I sit here writing this, our pager is beeping. A search has been called for a four-year-old child. It brings tears to my eyes as I remember how you would sit by my pager waiting for a search to be called. You were always ready and willing to help with such enthusiasm.

At the Command Post, you were always so friendly to the family of the victim and other searchers. It helped everyone to calm down by being able to pet you and look into your smiling face.

It was wonderful living and working with you. You were my special partner, and I will never forget you, beloved Bannor.

Your partner,
Cindy Clark

In spite of the sadness of losing such a special friend, Cindy and her family, like most Boxer lovers, couldn't be without a Boxer for long.

Shortly after Bannor died, a new puppy of a similar breeding became available. Trooper's Golden Echo (a.k.a. "Trooper"), born September 2, 1993, came to the Clark home to be Cindy's son's dog. Although Trooper belongs to Ryan, yes, Cindy is training him for search and rescue work, and, yes, he's very, very good.

At four-and-one-half-months, Trooper successfully trailed his first person, Cindy's son, Ryan, from outside of the locked driver's door of a car into the woods to his location. Little Trooper "found" his first person. This surprised Cindy. She was certain that Ryan had gone in another direction. But Trooper was right. As Cindy says, "Always trust your dog." Or in this case, your puppy.

At ten months, Trooper followed a 16-hour-old trail for one mile perfectly. Trooper did this after three other dogs had already worked the trail. Two of the dogs were "mission ready."

Trooper lived up to his name—he was not distracted, nor was he influenced by where the other dogs had gone. He worked independently. He successfully avoided a scent pool that had derailed the other dogs. (A scent pool happens when the scene concentrates in one area because of wind, terrain, vegetation or other conditions. If large and intense enough, it can confuse even a well-trained dog into thinking the victim is in the area, when this is not the case.) Trooper was the only one who followed the "victim's" exact trail, although all four dogs eventually "found" the "victim."

At one year old, Trooper was being trained for cadaver work (buried bodies), water rescue and city and wilderness trailing. In December of 1994, Trooper and Cindy faced his "mission ready" test.

If there were ever any dogs who could prove that the old adage about Boxers not doing anything just isn't true, it is Juba and Bannor, now retired or gone, and Tanis and Trooper. These Boxers have proven repeatedly that they are talented, motivated, willing and able to learn. They have made valuable contributions to saving the lives of other people. Thanks to special people like Rhonda Dyer and Cindy Clark, who seem to be very skilled at bringing out the best in their Boxers, the rest of us have something to aspire to.

Cindy Clark and Trooper.

Ch. Benjoman of 5 T's with owner Josephine Thomson.

OUR LIVES WITH BOXERS

The many beautiful faces that fill our homes and hearts:
Top left: Ch. Arrow's Skys the Limit of R-J, bred by Zina
De Rosa and Theresa Langan, and owned by Edward F.
Hoffman and T. Langan. *Top right:* Am-Can-Ber. Ch.
Woods End Crown Sable, SOM, owned by Mrs. Jack L.
Billhardt. *Bottom right:* Ch. Vagabond's Son of a Gun,
owned by Ken and Beverly Larson.

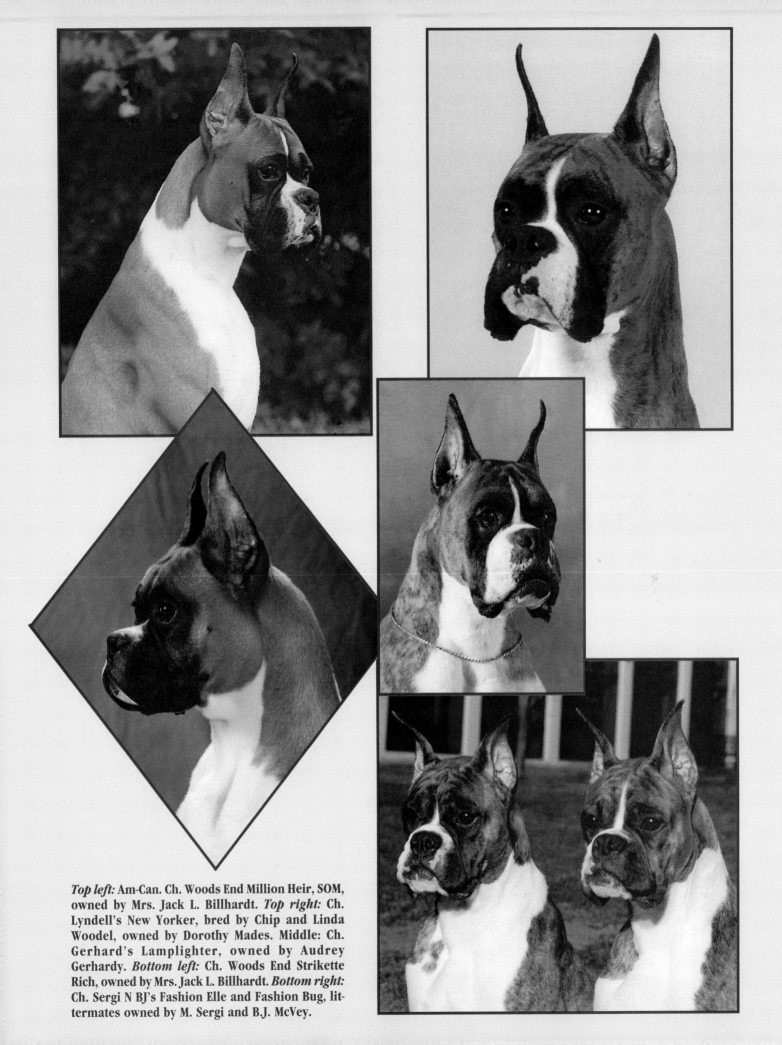

Top left: Am-Can. Ch. Woods End Million Heir, SOM, owned by Mrs. Jack L. Billhardt. *Top right:* Ch. Lyndell's New Yorker, bred by Chip and Linda Woodel, owned by Dorothy Mades. Middle: Ch. Gerhard's Lamplighter, owned by Audrey Gerhardy. *Bottom left:* Ch. Woods End Strikette Rich, owned by Mrs. Jack L. Billhardt. *Bottom right:* Ch. Sergi N BJ's Fashion Elle and Fashion Bug, littermates owned by M. Sergi and B.J. McVey.

On the beach at the Jersey shore, here's the irrepressibly photogenic Jacquet's Bosco, therapy dog, owned by Spiros Michals, digging up his copy of the author's first book *A New Owner's Guide to Boxers*.

Lower left: "The end is nigh....." Here's Jacquet's Bud, CD. *Lower right:* "We'll frolick and play the Norwegian way...."

Jacquet Boxers are nothing you can shake a stick at....and get it back. Here's Ch. Jacquet's Corbet, Ch. Jacquet's Jeunet, Ch. J and R's Urbin of Jacquet and Jacquet's Rajah, all cobred by author Richard Tomita and owned by Evelyn and Lorraine Mazzei and Elaine Votta.

Jacquet's Denfert with a thoroughbred friend. Owner, Ashley Scattergood.

THE CITY BOXER

BY DAVID WOLLOWICK

New York City, surely a city of cities, provides a great life for a Boxer. People may say suburban or country life is the best for a dog, but there are many advantages for a dog that lives in the city. I've met several people walking dogs in the city who were only visiting. All say that now that they have experienced dog life in New York, it's much better than in their suburban communities.

First, there is lots of great park space where your Boxer can run. In fact, on the Upper West Side, you really aren't more than three blocks from any park. The city thoughtfully provided several large fenced-in dog runs. Also, there are a few large fields where dogs congregate naturally. These spaces are larger than the average back yard. There's plenty of space in which our Boxer, Casey, and even some retired racing Greyhounds can achieve a long steady gallop.

The greatest advantage in the city is the other dogs. Casey has made many friends whom she is always excited to see and play with during morning and evening walks. Casey can play and run for hours with this steady stream of dogs that come to her favorite field in the park. I'm convinced that a dog who stays fenced in a suburban yard all day with no other dogs to play with can't have a better life than Casey. I'm also convinced that the socialization with other dogs makes for a happier, better adjusted Boxer. Casey also gets a lot of people's attention. Boxers in the city are a rarity. Retrievers of all kinds seem to be the most popular. People stop us all the time and admire how beautiful she is. I don't think many people have really seen a good Boxer and appreciate how magnificent this breed can be. Of course Casey loves all the attention, which is another advantage of the city.

We live in a large apartment building. The doorman makes a great mid-day dog walker. There are lots of people only an elevator ride away willing to take care of Casey when we go away.

Looking out over her Manhattan neighborhood is Jacquet's Princess Grace, owned by Rick and Ellen Lehrer.

As you can see, we feel Boxers are wonderful dogs and being in the city should not be a deterrent. In our case, the city has helped develop a Boxer who is a happy, healthy dog and a terrific addition to our family.

Boxers, as a breed, are one of the ideal dogs for city life. While their nature is people-friendly, their look can be a deterrent should trouble arise. In addition, the short coat sheds only a little and the docked tail does not present the potential for leg slapping during tail wagging in small spaces (i.e., elevators).

Bugsy Cruikshank spending time with owners in the park.

Above: The race through Central Park.... Casey and friend.

Lower left: Promenade on the streets of Nice, France. Photo courtesy of Siegi Lehmann.

Lower right: Crossing the street around Riverside Drive in New York City.

Water fun from around the world. *Above:* Can. Ch. Jaegerhouse Canine Canuck is captain. *Below:* Staying cool in the pool.

Above: The Hawaiian Boxers of Janis Goto, enjoying some water sports. *Below:* Jacquet water sports: Nicquee cooling off in New Jersey. Owned by Madeline and Tom Tomaszewsky.

Above: Sandra Wildman, splashing about in the pond at Wildax with Eng. Ch. Tonantron All Glory of Wildax. *Below:* Ch. Goldfield's Idol Maker and Jacquet's Darby with Kurt and Georgia Grammer, paddling through their lake in New York state.

Above: Jacquet's Maxine has been trained to hunt wild caribou, lawn ornaments and Wagnerian sopranos. Owner and trainer, Sieglinde Lehmann. *Below:* Two Jacquet Boxers sired by Int. Ch. Jacquet's Urko: Ch. Jacquet's Maja and Jacquet's Jazzbow, bred by Carole Shea and the author.

Left: Boxella's Rosanna, bred by Joseph Heine and C. Hughes and owned by J. O'Neil. *Below:* Proving his superior intelligence, here's Tanner, owned by Ella M. Du Pree, raising his editorial.

Above: Ven-PR-Dom-SoAm. Ch. Richaire's Solid Gold, bred by Claire Tolagian and owned by Doris, Oscar and Richardo Rivero. *Below:* Jacquet's Stella, at five months, owned by Jay Louie.

Above: Bullie, peeking through the tall grass, unmowed by owner and photographer Kelly Ferrandez. *Below:* Jacquet's Bronson of Dieterich, owned by Bill and Marge Dunn.

Above: Jessica Starr, sharing with Barney and Mandy. *Middle:* "How 'bout a drink?!" *Bottom:* Ryan Clark with canine heroes Ember and Bannor.

Boxers fill our lives and our children's lives as well. Thanks to our many contributors for sharing all their "kids" with us. *Above:* Joshua Abramson and Bruno. Below: Chelsea and Sarah Ames.

Above: Corey Dunn is well protected by Jacquet's Bronson of Dieterich, owned by William and Marge Dunn and Richard Tomita.. **Below left:** Flavia D'Urso and her two handsome companions, Alex and Gea, owned by Stallario and Katherine D'Urso, who kindly translated the Italian section of this book. **Below right:** Kevin Kenny at 8 years old and the four-month-old Davonna. His mother Debbie is a loyal assistant at Jacquet.

Next to children, Boxers prefer sleep! *Left:* Catherine and Daniella Devaney napping with Jacquet's Hobbes. Co-owned by Ann Rizzo. *Middle left:* "Zzzzz" by Ram, owned by Laszlo Cheffolway and Lilian Gustafsson. *Middle right:* Kerry, Brute and Trooper audition as couch potatoes.

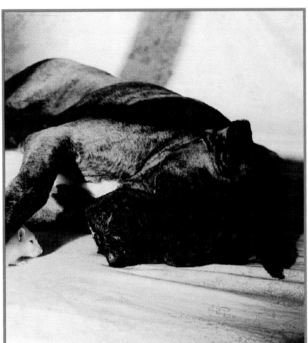

The Boxer family of Patti Rutledge, all handsome snoozers.

Top left: Kyle and the 14-year-old Ch. Goldfield's Idol Maker, snoozing in the sun. *Top right:* Ch. Jacquet's River Run, all run out. Owners, Gary and Mary Kalfin, who own an inn that welcomes dogs in Ammagansett, New York. *Middle left:* Germrotthaus Moka, cuddling with the family cat, owned by L. Lecomte and N. Haineault. *Middle right:* A basket of three Vikenje Boxers. *Bottom:* Jessica Starr, sleeping with Ch. Sig's Starfire.

Above: The "Fiddle" litter from Intrends of Melbourne, Australia, owned by Judy Horton. *Below:* Aust. Ch. Tobana Chattahoochee and Natalie Robbins.

Above: Jacquet's Kaiser owned by Shozo Kawakami of Japan. *Below:* Jacquet's Frances Abercrombie, known as "Abby" to owners Carole and John Hessels.

Above: Patti Rutledge and two Jacquet Boxer puppies sent to her as holiday gifts by her uncle and aunt, Dr. and Mrs. Herbert R. Axelrod. *Below:* Ch. Hollycrests Oodles of Noodles and daughter Two Faced, owned by Cheryl J. Colby.

Above: In good hands, Jason Ellis with Am-Can. Ch. Arriba's Zingara, owned by Carol Nesbitt and Dr. T. S. Fickes. *Below:* Champ and Frosty, making friends. Owner, Matt Plumser.

GERIATRICS

Through good care, proper diet, exercise and a lot of love, Boxers can live a good long life. It used to be that seven to nine years was good. Today, 11 to 14 years seems the average age. It is fortunate the Boxer is not in fashion, not in the "Top Ten" of the most popular dogs. Present-day breeders are very conscientious and breed very carefully, more concerned with learning from the research by the top veterinary colleges to find means of prolonging the life of the Boxer.

I feed my Boxers the highest grade food with natural ingredients. I try to stay away from foods with chemical preservatives. There are many excellent dry foods on the market to choose from. We use the lamb and rice formula at our kennel mixed with fresh cooked beef, lamb or chicken to soak the dry food and to make the food more appetizing. If you cannot cook for them, then choose canned foods with the least amount of preservatives.

For the senior citizen, there are excellent supplements to help the Boxer grow old gracefully. I found beta carotene is helpful to discourage tumors and cancer. There is a pelletized form just for dogs. If arthritis is beginning to creep into the joints and makes walking a chore or painful, instead of aspirin-based anti-inflammatories, I use a natural supplement made from the succulent yucca. These can be found in certain mail-order dog-supply catalogs or some of the specialty dog food and supply stores.

Some of the ailments such as urinary problems or constant vomiting can be remedied by changing to prescription diets, which can be provided by veterinarians. Always consult your veterinarian for these special diets.

Obesity is one of the major problems with old age and it is up to the owner to control excess weight, which

At eleven-and-a-half years of age, Ch. Merrilane's April Holiday, SOM, who goes by the call name "Pokey," with friend Bryan.

is always stressful to your dog's vital organs. Fortunately, there are many diets for overweight dogs available and you might put your dog on these diets. They are lower in calories and high in fiber content so that you can feed a full meal instead of cutting back on regular meals. I cook carrots, celery, turnips and green beans in beef or chicken broth, not bouillon, made from marrow bones, soup bones or chicken parts. The dogs will love it and love you for preparing this lowfat, low-calorie treat.

Boxers slow down in their golden years. This is Jacquet's Pandion at twelve years of age.

Above: Marylou Hatfield handles Ch. Jacquet's Amaryllis (by Ch. Happy Ours Fortune de Jacquet ex Ch. Jacquet's Canterbury Belle), still going strong in winning the Veterans class. Bred by Rick Tomita and Michele McArdle and owned by Marie De Finis. *Below:* A senior from Glencotta Kennels owned by Lillian Wainwright.

Above: Aust. Ch. Sjecoin Winter Forecast, at ten-and-a-half years old, spending time with some neighborhood kids. Owners, D. and R. Brace. *Below:* Sadie, at eleven years of age, using her K-9 cart after her hindquarters stopped functioning normally. Owned by Maurene Butterworth, Sadie still has much zest for living.

Above: "Oh, say, can you see!" Ch. Jacquet's Amaryllis. *Below:* Buster Douglas, owned by Dr. Jack and Debbie Crawford, is the fourth Boxer in Dr. Jack's life. Once a Boxer man, always a Boxer man, Dr. Jack intends one day to breed a great line of Boxers all his own.

Above: Boxers thrive around the world...from pole to pole. This is "Rex," owned by Hank and Candy Bartos of North Pole, Alaska. *Below:* Br. Ch. Warena's Amadeus is a real knockout!

Top left: Patti and David Rutledge and some of her beautiful Boxer clan. *Top right:* Leaping Lyndee Lu, Am-Can. CD, with a tall, dark and handsome friend. Owner, Ella M. Du Pree. *Bottom left:* Ch. Cherkei's High Cotton (by Ch. Golden Haze Tuxedo ex Ch. Cherkei's Arriba Wicked Calita), bred and owned by Keith and Cheryl Robbins, and co-owned by Jack and Kathy Fitzpatrick. Handled by Cheryl Robbins, today a well-respected AKC judge. *Bottom right:* Ch. Cherkei's Son-of-a-Gun (by Ch. Salgray's Good Grief ex Baron's Lady Come Lately), a Best in Show winner owned by Keith and Cheryl Robbins, and the sire of 12 American champions.

"Red ball in the pocket," spinning her magic is Jacquet's Little Miss Magic, owned by Jeff and Missy Mathis and bred by the author.

MGM's Rowdy Robert Redford, the much-loved house dog of Victor and Anita Clemente, enjoying the winter snow.

Boxer pups 3 1/2 weeks, bred by Hope and Barry Blazer.

Chief is being caressed by a foster-cared raccoon orphan, owned and photographed by Cindy S. White.

Ch. Sirrocco's Kiss by The Book (by Ch. Golden Haze Tuxedo ex Sirrocco's Kiss N Tell), bred by Kathleen Gould and handler Diane Mallet. Owners, R. Culberson, B. Weber, D. Mallet, J. and B. Korson. She is the number one Boxer for 1997 and is among the top ten Working dogs.

Maxine, owned by Siege Lehmann, with her new friend, a Korat (a rare cat breed from Thailand).

Above: Ch. Kreyon Image of Papillon (by Ch. Kreyon's Easy Money ex Ch. Kreyon's Delta Dawn II), bred by Margaret Krey and owned by Jeffrey and Nan Kramer. *Below:* Carlwen's Joie de Vivre, DOM (by Ch. My-R's Haybinder of Holly Lane ex Ch. Carlwens Free Spirit), bred by Wendy Ness and owned with Melva and Melvin Hatfield.

Above: Ch. Hi Hat's Moonshadow v Jacquet, handled to finish by co-owner Nancy Wainwright. Breeders, Leni Kaplan and Richard Tomita. *Below:* Ch. Caymans Dapper Dan (by Ch. Rusric's Vaga-bond Prince ex Ch. El Sirrah's Cayman Gold), bred by Sydney Brown and owned by Richard and Marsha Servetnick.

Above left: Ch. El Sirrah's Cayman Gold, DOM, bred by Lois Harris and Constance Hunter, and owned by Sydney L. Brown. *Above right:* Ch. TuRo's Cachet with Chic Ceccarini. *Below left:* At just ten months, Ch. Kellymar's The Beat Goes On (by Ch. Kellymar's Sebastian Jacquet ex Brookside's Motif de Jacquet), owned by Mary Leibensperger and bred by Patricia Fink. *Below right:* Ch. Beaufront's First Edition (by Ch. Moon Valley's Sun N' Shadow ex Miksan's Molly Maguire) was the much-beloved homebred champion of owner Billie and David McFadden, author of *The New Boxer*. Handler, John L. Horan.

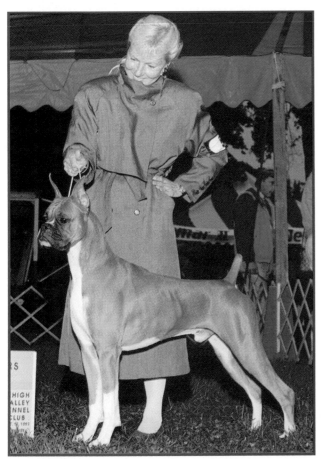

Above: Ch. Moon Valley's Main Attraction (by Ch. Tall Oaks Desert Dazzler ex Ch. Moon Valley's Image), a top show dog from the early 1990s, the grandson of Traper and Famous Amos, bred by Ida Baum, handled by Richard and Chris Baum and owned by Ray Culberson, Bill Weber and Olive B. Lee. *Below:* Siegi Lehmann with the lovely Maxine.

Above: The formative years... Mr. and Mrs. Warren Tillapaugh's Jacquet pup Betsy acquaints herself with granddaughter Sarah. *Below:* Rufus and Mary Frances Burleson with two of their lovely champions, Ch. Marburl's Chamissa and Ch. Marburl's Strawberry Soda.

The first lady of the ABC National: Ch. Kiebla's Tradition of TuRo, DOM, owned by Bruce and Jeannie Korson and handled by Christine Baum, bred by Kitty Barker and TuRo Boxers.

Named to commemorate another great winner, this is Ch. Laureate Kiss Me Kate, bred by Margaret Benshoff, owned by Clinton and Eileen Sherburne, and handled by Gary Steele.

Judge Mrs. Billie Mc Fadden, an active fundraising enthusiast for Boxer health research and a determined breed Rescue advocate, awards. Jacquet's Cellini (by Ch. Jacquet's Greggson ex Ch. Jacquet's Frederica), bred by Bill Lyle, Dorothy Fink and Rick Tomita, handled elegantly by Kriste Kaemline. Thanks to Mrs. Mc Fadden's tireless pioneer work, our Boxers are living healthier, longer lives with all of us.

Ch. Har-Vel's Gold Express, SOM (by Ch. Marburl's Joshua ex Har-Vel's Sweet 'N Sassy) is the famed sire of Ch. Rochil's Grande Marshall. Owners, Pat Niles and Perry Combest: breeders, Velda I. and Harold Rounsaville. Handler, Michael Shepherd.

Ch. Darkstar's Wings of Desire (by Ch. Jacquet's Lord of Thunder ex Jacquet's Amethyst Queen), from the first litter of breeders Robert and Pamela Bober, one of many upcoming breeders who have based their lines on the author's line.

Ch. Darkstar's Shadow of Thor (by Ch. Jacquet's Lord of Thunder ex Jacquet's Amethyst Queen) is the first homebred champion of breeders Robert and Pamela Bober, who owns him with Charles Kahora. Pamela proudly handles to this BOW win.

Ch. Har-Vel's Josh's Gold, CD, SOM (by Ch. Marburl's Joshua ex Har-Vel's Sweet 'N Sassy), bred by Velda I. and Harold Rounsaville, owned by Sandra Lynch.

Ch. Jacquet's Commander, bred and owned by Bill Lyle and Dorothy Fink, looking particularly smashing on his way to the title.

The breeder's commitment to produce better and better Boxers must never falter—here's inspiration in the making, at six-and-a-half weeks. Bred by Joe and Laura Manello.

Ch. Oliver's Solid Gold, DOM (by Ch. Har-Vel's Gold Chips ex Oliver's Mer-Lu-Ia), bred by Emmett and Mary Oliver and owned by Velda I. Rounsaville.

With her own kind of flash, Ch. Jacquet's Faline (by Ch. Merrilane's April Fashion ex Jacquet's Painted Lady), bred by Richard Tomita, and owned by Bernie and Georgine Schwerdtfeger. The first plain Boxer to finish in over two decades in early 1980's!

RESCUE

BY MICHELE MCARDLE

The mandate of any breed Rescue group is to respond quickly when one of the breed needs a new home. Calls for help come at all hours from animal shelters, dog wardens, the police, caring citizens who have found a Boxer, families who've fallen on hard times, and the occasional breeder who honors the commitment to "take back" a puppy "of any age."

It falls to only a few dedicated individuals who truly love the breed to pick up, transport, medically treat and shelter the often frightened and always confused sick adolescent or creaky geriatric.

Vicki Fox, a dedicated Rescue worker, with a Boxer she saved from going to the pound.

Michele McArdle, the backbone of Boxer Rescue in Connecticut and much of the Tri-State area, with fellow Rescuer Kevin Link and new Boxer adopter, Catherine Aspenson.

Fifteen years ago Rescue calls were not nearly as frequent as nowadays and were mostly about lost or abandoned dogs who had ended up in a pound. Over subsequent years, the Rescue message has been passed along and shelters, pounds, veterinarians, pet supply stores and the police all know Michele McArdle of Boxer Rescue Service, Inc., in Nowalk, Connecticut and Jean Loubriel of the Demarest, New Jersey group are the "Boxer Ladies" in the Northeast. Their network of helper contacts extend essentially from Bangor, Maine to Buffalo, New York to Philadelphia and every place in between.

Lost and abandoned Boxers represent only a small percentage of dogs placed by Rescue. Domestic and international job transfers, divorce, illness, apartments turning into "No Dog" condos are only some of the diverse reasons for Boxer Rescue. Many of these dogs would have been euthanized as their owners ran out of options. More than 150 Boxers are placed in the Northeast by BRS every year.

Some Boxers are easy to find new home for, like healthy youngsters, where older, sick, cranky dogs take a little longer, sometimes a lot longer—and the expenses mount. Nonetheless, we always find a home. Spaying neutering, heartworm treatment in addition to other medical emergencies and veterinary costs, boarding,

transportation and phone charges become increasingly burdensome and disheartening. We do it because they are worth it and bring untold joy to their new families.

The American Boxer Rescue Association (ABRA for short) has done nothing short of magic in the years since they've been established. Author Richard Tomita strongly supports the efforts of ABRA and the local Rescue groups that work daily to make a difference. All breeders are urged to become more involved and supportive of Rescue groups as the over-population and euthanasia problem reflects poorly on everyone who loves this great breed. Keep Boxers out of the shelters and out of the statistics. Breeders' expertise for evaluating temperament and health is vital for the better rehoming of Boxers in the community.

"Rocky," a four-year-old rescued Boxer, with his hew family Sean and Brandon Gunter, the nephews of new owners Todd and Rhonda Phillips.

A REAL-LIFE RESCUE STORY

BY JANE FOURNIER

All too often in Rescue, Boxers come into our homes in poor condition, but this one broke our hearts.

On June 1, 1997, a one-and-a-half-year-old male was turned over to an animal lover who knew about him (but had never seen him). When she arrived to adopt him, she laid her eyes upon the dog with his owner hosing him down with cold water "because he was dirty."

Still covered with the residue of feces and urine, he was rushed to an emergency vet clinic. He weighed in at 25 pounds, unable to walk or even hold his head up. He was stabilized and put on intravenous and small feedings several times a day. He spent four days under the vet's care. The adopter was unable to afford the cost of the emergency hospitalization and called to see if Boxer Rescue could help.

Indeed we could!

Upon his release, he weighed 36 pounds. He was given antibiotics to help heal the open sores and fed six small meals per day, then four, and finally, when his system could handle a large meal, two per day. He was not housebroken. Because he was still so weak that he could not hold up his head, climb stairs, or walk any distance, his adopters had to carry him in and out of doors for several days. His veterinary records from his previous owner indicated that he weighed 49 pounds on February 28, which is to say that he lost 24 pounds in the three months prior to his rescue.

Within just six weeks, after being fed a diet of lamb and rice all-natural puppy and adult kibble, boiled hamburger, baby beef and lamb, fat-free yogurt and cottage cheese, plus 500 units of vitamin C and pet tabs daily, he weighed a whopping 65 pounds! He is extremely gentle and loving and is now housebroken. Despite his traumatic experience, he is a typical Boxer who loves the world and is eager to please.

Although his former owner (who considers herself a "breeder") stated that he refused to eat because his mother was leashed and not in the house, he has never missed one meal since he was rescued.

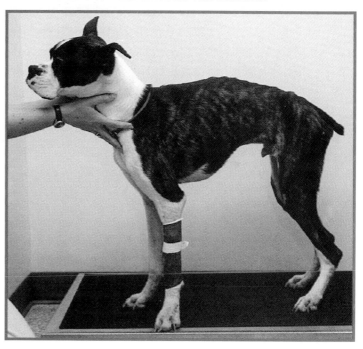

Above: **June 1, 1997, rescued at 25 pounds and dying....***Below:* **after six weeks of proper care, nutrition and TLC....July 15, 1997, 65 pounds and thriving!** *What does Boxer Rescue mean to you?*

APPENDIX
SIRES AND DAMS OF MERIT

This Appendix represents the research work of Sturlene Arnold. Our first two lists present the top ten Sires and Dams of Merit in the US and Canada and the number of champion progeny produced. Secondly, you will find the list of all the current American Boxer Club and Canadian Boxer Club Sires and Dams of Merit. On this roster, each Sire and Dam of Merit is presented by name with his/her parents.

The ABC Sire or Dam of Merit award is very prestigious and has been instituted for many years—the award is intended for the Boxer not its owners or breeders. A dog must have produced a total of seven or more champions to attain this award, and the bitch must have produced four or more champion offspring. Initially, the the Canadian Boxer Club Sires and Dams of Merit were bestowed upon club members only. Through the efforts of Larry Dosier and myself, the CKC now awards the SOM and DOM to all worthy Canadian Boxers (not only those owned by club members).

Of course, many future great dogs are producing offspring and soon will attain the coveted titles of Sires and Dams of Merit. Please keep in mind that the statistics change all the time. If I missed anyone's dog, I apologize, it is not intentional. *This appendix is current until October 1, 1997.*

TOP TEN SIRES OF MERIT IN THE US AND CANADA

All the Top Ten Sires have earned the distinction of Sire of Merit in the United States and Canada. Since some of these sires have progeny still competing in the show ring, these statistics are by no means final.

Name of Dog	Number of Champions Sired
1. Int. Ch. Scher-Khoun's Shadrack	111
2. Int. Ch. Millan's Fashion Hint	108
3. Ch. Bang Away of Sirrah Crest	86
4. Ch. Marquam Hill's Traper of TuRo	82
5. Ch. Salgray's Fashion Plate	68
6. Int. Ch. Mephisto's Soldier of Fortune	62
7. Am-Can. Ch. Fiero's Tally-Ho Tailo	59
8. Am-Can. Ch. Golden Haze Tuxedo	57
9. Ch. Jered's Spellbinder	56
10. Ch. Berena's Gemini Splashdown	50

TOP TEN DAMS OF MERIT IN THE US AND CANADA

Name of Bitch	Number of Champions Produced
1. Ger. Ch. Gretel v Hohenneuffen (ABC/DOM)	11
1. Ch. Holly Lane's Windstorm (ABC/DOM)	11
1. Savoye's Satin Shadow of Ajay (CKC/DOM)	11
1. Can. Ch. Verwood's Lollipop (CKC/DOM)	11
5. Can. Ch. Chat Away of Blossomlea (CKC/DOM)	10
5. Merrilane's Mad Passion, CD (ABC/DOM)	10
7. Can. Ch. Donessle's Foxfire (CKC/DOM)	9
7. Heigh Ho Bramble (ABC/DOM)	9
7. Jacquet's Kiri Te Kanawa (ABC/DOM)	9
7. Can. Ch. Karmel's Dante's Sassafras (CKC/DOM)	9
7. Miss Raheba of May-Will (ABC/DOM)	9
7. Can. Ch. Scher-Khoun's Autumn Concerto (CKC/DOM)	9

SIRES OF MERIT

Am-Can. Ch. Acadia's Conquistador (by Am-Can. Ch. Trimanor's Baccus ex Can. Ch. Blueline's California Gold) CKC/SOM.

Ch. Aimeebee's Apoppin' (by Int. Ch. Eldic's Darius ex Ch. Upnatem of Woodcrest) ABC/SOM.

Am-Can. Ch. Ajays Ralph Lauren (by Can. Ch. TuRo's Kristian Dior ex Can. Ch. Ajays Tammy Faye B) CKC/SOM.

Am-Can. Ch. Amerglo Bellringer, UD (by Ch. Ruda River Rings The Bell ex Amerglo Elegantstar) ABC/SOM.

Ch. Apollo of San Joaquin (by Whirlaway of Mazelaine, CD ex Gay Lady Inga of San Joaquin) ABC/SOM.

Ch. Araby's BlackWatch (by Ch. Marquam Hill's Traper of TuRo ex Ch. Lilliputs Black Magic) ABC/SOM.

Ch. Araby's Shortstop (by Am-Can. Ch. Von Schorer's Moon Shadow ex Moon Valley's Merry Weather) ABC/SOM.

Am-Can. Ch. Aracrest's Amnesty (by Int. Ch. Millan's Fashion Hint ex Am-Can. Ch. Aracrest's Trinkett) CKC/SOM.

Am-Can. Ch. Aracrest's Creed (by Ch. Mystery's Show Bis ex Ch. Belasco's Panache) CKC/SOM.

Am-Can. Ch. Aracrest's Jered (by Int. Ch. Scher-Khoun's Shadrack ex Can. Ch. Jocolu's Charming Fashion) ABC/SOM.

Am-Can. Ch. Aracrest's Kaylib (by Int. Ch. Scher-Khoun's Shadrack ex Can. Ch. Jocolu's Charming Fashion) ABC/SOM.

Ch. Aracrest's Talisman (by Ch. Omega's Rockfire ex Can. Ch. Aracrest's Velvet Sensation) ABC/CKC/SOM.

Ch. Archduke of Valcar (by Int. Ch. Dorian von Marienhof of Mazelaine ex Ch. Valwa von Dom) ABC/SOM.

Am-Can. Ch. Arriba's Associate of Karjean (by Ch. Arriba's Crescendo ex Ch. Arriba's Zingara) ABC/CKC/SOM.

Ch. Arriba's Cherkei OH Boy (by Am-Can. Ch. Moon Valley's Sun N' Shadow ex Ch. Arriba's Cherkei Fancy Free) ABC/SOM.

Ch. Arriba's Crescendo (by Ch. Arriba's Excelsior ex Arriba's Debutante) ABC/SOM.

Ch. Arriba's Footloose (by Ch. Marquam Hill's Traper of TuRo ex Ch. Arriba's Lady Revue) ABC/SOM.

Ch. Arriba's Knight Revue (by Ch. Salgray's Ambush ex Ch. Arriba's Castanet) ABC/SOM.

Ch. Baldr's Sun Smoke (by Ch. Moon Valley's Sunsation ex Baldr's Xstacy) ABC/SOM.

Ch. Bang Away of Sirrah Crest (by Int. Ch. Ursa Major of Sirrah Crest ex Verily Verily of Sirrah Crest) ABC/CKC/SOM.

Ch. Barisle's Dash of Magic (by Am-Can. Ch. Vimar's We Believe In Magic ex Ch. Marburls Scarlett Cord) ABC/SOM.

Ch. Barisle's Special Premium (by Ch. Mystery's Show Bis ex Ch. Marburl's Scarlet Cord) ABC/SOM.

Am-Can. Ch. Barrage of Quality Hill (by Ch. Bang Away of Sirrah Crest ex Valley Grove's Applause) ABC/SOM.

Ch. Becrelen's Import (by Int. Ch. Millan's Fashion Hint ex Salgray's Bonus Baby) ABC/SOM.

Am-Can. Ch. Bellcrest Just Watch Me (by Ch. Ell Bee's Just Watch Out ex Bellcrest's Encore) ABC/CKC/SOM.

Ch. Benjoman of Five T's (by Am-Can. Ch. Scher-Khoun's Abednego ex Tudosal's Ruffels) ABC/SOM.

Ch. Berena's Gemini Splashdown (by Am-Can. Ch. Wagner Wilverday Famous Amos ex Summerbird Leading Lady) ABC/CKC/SOM.

Ch. Berena's Tribute To Fa-Fa (by Am-Can. Ch. Wagner Wilverday Famous Amos ex Summerbird Leading Lady) ABC/SOM.

Ch. Bladan's U-Chetnik (by Ch. Sir Galahad of Bladan, CDX ex Blue Glow of Bladan) ABC/SOM.

Can. Ch. Blaze of Marcus (by Ch. Janacee's Marcus ex Bob-Ell's Golden Penny) CKC/SOM.

Ch. Box M Irving De Keefer (by Ch. Box M Tropic Storm ex Ms Kaleonakula) ABC/SOM.

Can. Ch. Bracara's Artistic Action (by Ch. Salgray's Ambush ex Can. Ch. Gaylord's Eminent Emblem) CKC/SOM.

Am-Can. Ch. Bracara's Haymaker (by Ch. Salgray's Market Wise ex Can. Ch. Bracara's Special Action) CKC/SOM.

Ch. Braemerwood Happy Tracks (by Int. Ch. Millan's Fashion Hint ex Braemerwood Comin' Thru) ABC/SOM.

Ch. Brayshaw's Masquerader (by Ch. Brayshaw's Mr. Morgan Roberts ex Wakefield's Bang Up Lassie) ABC/SOM.

Ch. Breezewood's Equal Time (by Int. Ch. Moon Valley's Sun N'Shadow ex Ch. Sarazak's Sizzle) ABC/SOM.

Ch. Brettendale's Stampede (by Am-Can. Ch. Donessle's Cassino ex Ch. Paragon's Nite Shade) ABC/SOM.

Ch. Bridgewood's B.K. Kahuna (by Ch. Telstar's Good Time Charlie ex Ginger's Gold 'N Glow) ABC/SOM.

Ch. Bropat's Red Alert of Asgard (by Ch. Araby's Shortstop ex Ch. Bropat's Fandancer) ABC/SOM.

Ch. Bubbling Over of Lilac Hedge (by Int. Ch. Lustig von Dom of Tulgey Wood ex Heigh Ho Bramble) ABC/SOM.

Ch. But Good of Lilac Hedge (by Int. Ch. Lustig von Dom of Tulgey Wood ex Heigh Ho Bramble) ABC/SOM.

Ch. Cachet's Mad Max of TuRo (by Ch. TuRo's Empire ex Ch. TuRo's Cachet) ABC/SOM.

Ch. Cajon's Calling Card (by Am-Can. Ch. Barrage of Quality Hill ex Ch. Treceder's Sequence) ABC/SOM.

Ch. Canyonair Hickory Dick, CD (by Ch. Mazelaine's Masterpiece ex Canyonair Diamond Lil, CD) ABC/CKC/SOM.

Ch. Canyonair's Man on Fire (by Ch. Canyonair Hickory Dick, CD ex Rie-Mac's Dorable Darlin) ABC/SOM.

Ch. Canzonet's Musical Matinee (by Ch. Canzonet's Music Man ex Canzonet's Miss Scarlet) ABC/SOM.

Ch. Capriana's Bragabout (by Ch. Flintwood's Rabble Rouser ex Capriana's Tara) ABC/SOM.

Am-Can. Ch. Capriana's Renegade (by Ch. Marquam Hill's Comanche ex M.G.M.'s Matched Pennies Echo) ABC/SOM.

Ch. Captain Lookout of Thorhall (by Am-Can. Ch. Keppy-L of May-Will ex Happy Talk of Thorhall) ABC/CKC/SOM.

Ch. Carlwen's Sean of Erin (by Ch. Salgray's Ovation ex Ch. Carlwen's Scotch Mischief) ABC/SOM.

Ch. Castro's Midnight Special (by Ch. Ell Bee's Just Watch Out ex Ch. Dasel's Spring Fantasy, CD) ABC/SOM.

Ch. Cava-Lane's Moving On (by Ch. Salgray's Good Grief ex Ch. Cava-Lane's Gorgeous Babe) ABC/SOM.

Ch. Cedar Hill's Capital Classic (by Ch. Aracrest's Talisman ex Cedarhyl's Crystal of Katandy) ABC/SOM.

Can. Ch. Cee-Jay's Mister Mike, CD (by Can. Ch. Donessle's Spring Fever ex Calmar's Chatterbox) CKC/SOM.

Ch. Cherkei's Desperado (by Ch. Cherkei's Legendary Lawman ex Ch. Milray's Mistique) ABC/SOM.

Ch. Cherkei's High Cotton (by Am-Can. Ch. Golden Haze Tuxedo ex Ch. Cherkei Arriba Wicked Calita) ABC/SOM.

Ch. Cherkei's Son-Of-A-Gun (by Ch. Salgray's Good Grief ex Baron's Lady Come Lately) ABC/SOM.

Can. Ch. Cinnrhee's Grand Slam (by Am-Can. Ch. Acadia's Conquistador ex Can. Ch. Cinnrhee's She's Trump) CKC/SOM.

Am-Can. Ch. Cinnrhee's Mug Shot (by Ch. Marquam Hill's Traper of TuRo ex Can. Ch. Dallenlee's Cinnamon Spice) CKC/SOM.

Ch. Cochise of Cherokee Oaks (by Ch. Helixview Galant Charger ex Copper Penny of Cherokee Oaks) ABC/SOM.

Am-Can. Ch. Conquistador's Adagio (by Int. Ch. Scher-Khoun's Meshack ex Can. Ch. Mephisto's Candy Princess) CKC/SOM.

Can. Ch. Conquistador's Impressario (by Can. Ch. Adagio's Andante Conquistador ex Can. Ch. Conquistador's Val Halla) CKC/SOM.

Ch. Dapper Dan III, CD (by Arriba's Repeat Performance ex Ch. Merrilane's Paper Doll) ABC/SOM.

Ch. Dauber of Tulgey Wood (by Int. Ch. Lustig von Dom ex Ginger of Mazelaine) ABC/SOM.

Ch. Dempsey's Copper Gentleman (by Ch. Jered's Spellbinder ex Fontana's Crimson Mist) ABC/SOM.

Am-Can. Ch. Diamondaire's Dealer's Choice (by Am-Can. Ch. Haviland's Count Royal ex Verwood's Nina Never Knew) CKC/SOM.

Am-Can. Ch. Doggone Ounce of Gold (by Int. Ch. Mephisto's Vendetta ex Ch. Orrkid's First Lady) ABC/SOM.

Am-Can. Ch. Donessle's Cassino (by Can. Ch. Donessle's Crusader ex Donessle's Solitaire) ABC/CKC/SOM.

Can. Ch. Donessle's Crusader (by Int. Ch. Scher-Khoun's Meshack ex Can. Ch. Donessle's Foxfire) CKC/SOM.

Am-Can. Ch. Donessle's Diplomat (by Int. Ch. Scher-Khoun's Meshack ex Can. Ch. Donessle's Foxfire) CKC/SOM.

Can. Ch. Donessle's Simon Sez (by Arg-Can. Ch. Donessle's Spring Torrent ex Can. Ch. Donessle's Twilight Magic) CKC/SOM.

Can. Ch. Donessle's Spring Fever (by Am-Can. Ch. Donessle's Diplomat ex Can. Ch. Scher-Khoun's Dark Rhapsody) CKC/SOM.

Int. Ch. Dorian von Marienhof of Mazelaine (by Int. Ch. Xerxes von Dom ex Saxonia's Andl) ABC/SOM.

Ch. Dormac's Gunslinger (by Ch. Salgray's Ambush ex Dormac's Risque) ABC/SOM.

Am-Can. Ch. Dornlea's Free Spirit (by Ch. Dornlea's Grand Slam ex Kamursart Aloha Licorice) ABC/SOM.

Ch. Duke Cronian (by Int. Ch. Dorian von Marienhof of Mazelaine ex Ch. Crona von Zwergeck) ABC/SOM.

Am-Can. Ch. Echo's Believe It or Not (by Ch. Araby's Black Watch ex Can. Ch. Echo's Desiree) ABC/SOM.

Ch. Edjer of Baldr (by Int. Ch. Aracrest's Jered ex Cherokee Rose of Baldr) ABC/SOM.

Am-Can. Ch. Eldic's Darius (by Am-Can. Ch. Barrage of Quality Hill ex Eldic's Beaux Brite) ABC/SOM.

Ch. Eldic's Landlord (by Int. Ch. Eldic's Darius ex Eldic's Dark Dream) ABC/SOM.

Can. Ch. Elharlen's Critics Choice (by Am-Can. Ch. Woods End Crown Sable ex Elharlen's Wavelore) CKC/SOM.

Ch. Elixir of Raineylane (by Mazelaine's Kapellmeister ex Amiable Mandy of Raineylane) ABC/CKC/SOM.

Ch. Ell Bee's Just Watch Out (by Ch. Moreleen's Al-le-lu-ia ex Ell Bee's Young Kipper) ABC/SOM.

Am-Can. Ch. Ell Bee's Sooner Bee Travlin (by Am-Can. Ch. Ell Bee's Son of Bis ex Am-Can. Ch. Bellcrest Just It From Ell Bee) ABC/SOM.

Ch. Endymion of Mazelaine (by Int. Ch. Dorian v Marienhof of Mazelaine ex Mazelaine Theodosia) ABC/SOM.

Ch. Evergreen's Bogart (by Ch. Salgray's KO Aracrest ex Ch. Salgray's Fame of Evergreen) ABC/SOM.

Ch. Evergreen's Class Act (by Ch. Salgray's KO Aracrest ex Evergreen's Image of Delight) ABC/SOM.

Ch. Evo-Wen's Impressario (by Ch. Evo-Wen's Big Story ex Evo-Wen's Mecque Mecque) ABC/SOM.

Ch. Ewo's Tie Breaker (by Ch. Heldenbrand's Jet Breaker ex Ch. Ewo's Crystal) ABC/SOM.

Ger. Ch. Fachinger von Neu-Drosedow (by Int. Ch. Sigurd von Dom ex Digalen von Neu-Drosedow) ABC/SOM.

Am-Can. Ch. Fiero's Tally-Ho Tailo (by Am-Can. Ch. Fiero's Smash Hit ex Fiero's Iva-Natu) ABC/CKC/SOM.

Can. Ch. Fisher's Nashewa Kelso, CD (by Can. Ch. Mellow Brew of Ellen's Alley ex Can. Ch. Fisher's Tuffina Roy-Al) CKC/SOM.

Ch. Flintwood's Bag N'Baggage (by Ch. Flintwood's Places Please ex Ch. Morgenshern of Kresthallo) ABC/SOM.

Ch. Flintwood's Linebacker (by Ch. Flintwood's Sundowner ex Ch. Flintwood's Fontessa) ABC/SOM.

Ch. Flintwood's Rabble Rouser (by Ch. Brayshaw's Masquerader ex Flintwood's Banned in Boston) ABC/SOM.

Ch. Flintwood's Sundowner (by Ch. Flintwood's Bag N'Bagagge ex Ch. Sans Souci of Kresthallo) ABC/SOM.

Ch. Frazer's Parade Meister (by Mazelaine's Kapellmeister ex Frazer's Miss Boots) ABC/SOM.

Can. Ch. Gaylord's Eminent Escort (by Gaylord's Coy Challenge ex Can. Ch. Gaylord's Black Ballet) CKC/SOM.

Can. Ch. Gaylord's Gallant Gentleman (by Ch. Treceder's Sequel ex Can. Ch. Gaymitz Jet Flight) CKC/SOM.

Am-Can. Ch. Gaymitz Jolly Roger (by Am-Can. Ch. Salgray's Flying High ex Can. Ch. Gaymitz Dash O' Fire) CKC/SOM.

Ch. Gerhard's Lamplighter (by Ch. Regail Bo-Jack ex Ch. Scarborough City Lights) ABC/SOM.

Can. Ch. Glencotta's Magnum (by Am-Can. Ch. Jodi's Jubilation ex Capital Hill's Musical Hit) CKC/SOM.

Ch. Glennroe Rum Runner (by Ch. Telstar's Front Runner ex Glennroe Elated Echo O'Dolor) ABC/SOM.

Can. Ch. Golden Haze Snow Drift, CDX (by Can. Ch. Cher-Lane's Bombardier ex Am-Can. Ch. Golden Haze Stole the Action) CKC/SOM.

Am-Can. Ch. Golden Haze Tuxedo (by Ch. Marquam Hill's Traper of TuRo ex Can. Ch. Golden Haze Stole The Ring) ABC/CKC/SOM.

Am-Ber-Can. Ch. Gray Roy's Minstrel Boy (by Gray Roy's Mr. Lightning ex Gray Roy's Lollipop) ABC/CKC/SOM.

Ch. Happy Ours Fortune De Jacquet (by Ch. Merrilane's April Holiday ex Jacquet's Painted Lady) ABC/SOM.

Ch. Har-Vel's Gold Express (by Int. Ch. Marburl's Joshua ex Har-Vel's Sweet-N'Sassy) ABC/SOM.

Ch. Har-Vel's Josh's Gold, CD (by Int. Ch. Marburl's Joshua ex Har-Vel's Sweet-N'Sassy) ABC/SOM.

Am-Can. Ch. Haviland's Count Royal (by Can. Ch. Haviland's Jacks or Better ex Can. Ch. Haviland's Renegade Lady) CKC/SOM.

Can. Ch. Haviland's Jacks or Better (by Int. Ch. Scher-Khoun's Shadrack ex Can. Ch. Haviland's Gamblin Lady) CKC/SOM.

Can. Ch. Haviland's Renegade Storm (by Am-Can. Ch. Capriana's Renegade ex Can. Ch. Calendar Girl of Haviland) CKC/SOM.

Am-Can. Ch. Haviland's Royal Sable (by Am-Can. Ch. Woods End Crown Sable ex Can. Ch. Tradonalee's Miss Classic) CKC/SOM.

Ch. Haviland's Storm-Away (by Ch. Bang Away of Sirrah Crest ex Haviland's El Wendie) CKC/SOM.

Ch. Heldenbrand's Heart Breaker (by Ch. Heldenbrand's Jedi Knight ex Ch. Wheatland's Gem v Heldenbrand) ABC/SOM.

Ch. Heldenbrand's Jet Breaker (by Ch. Heldenbrand's Heart Breaker ex Heldenbrand's Jetta Jovina) ABC/CKC/SOM.

Am-Can-Mex. Ch. Helixview Noble Knight (by Ch. Bang Away of Sirrah Crest ex Int. Ch. Wil-Elen's Fashion Plate) ABC/SOM.

Ch. Herndon's Peeless Panda (by Ch. Holly Lane's Winter Forecast ex Ch. Herndon's Desert Flyer) ABC/SOM.

Ch. Herndon's Pure Magic (by Ch. Herndon's Peerless Panda ex Herndon's Black Magic) ABC/SOM.

Ch. Hi-Tech's Arbitrage (by Am-Can. Ch. Fiero's Tally-Ho Tailo ex Ch. Boxerton Hollyhock) ABC/SOM.

Can. Ch. Holiday's Amerigo (by Ch. Marquam Hill's Traper of TuRo ex Can. Ch. Holiday's Front Page) CKC/SOM.

Ch. Hollycrest's Farm Hand (by Ch. Heldenbrand's Jedi Knight ex Peckham's Lady Phaedra) ABC/SOM.

Ch. Hollycrest's Stage Hand (by Ch. Brettendale's Stampede ex Ch. Hi-Hill's Rave Review) ABC/SOM.

Ch. Holly Lane's Diamond Replay (by Int. Ch. Scher-Khoun's Meshack ex Ch. Holly Lane's Windstorm) ABC/CKC/SOM.

Ch. Holly Lane's Disk Wheel (by Holly Lane's Wire Wheels ex Holly Lane's Cissy) ABC/SOM.

Ch. Holly Lane's Dream Peddler, CD (by Ch. Aracrest's Courier of Holly Lane ex Shane's Lady ABC/SOM.

Ch. Holly Lane's Flamboyant Carlon (by Ch. Salgray's KO Aracrest ex Ch. Carlon's Classy Chasis) ABC/SOM.

Ch. Holly Lane's Inherit The Wind (by Ch. My-R's Haybinder of Holly Lane ex Ch. Holly Lane's Winter Fantasy) ABC/SOM.

Ch. Holly Lane's Praire Chief (by Ch. Holly Lane's Inherit The Wind ex Holly Lane's Taskaloosa) ABC/SOM.

Ch. Holly Lane's Wildwind (by Ch. Brayshaw's Masquerader ex Ch. Holly Lane's Cookie) ABC/SOM.

Ch. Holly Lane's Winter Storm (by Int. Ch. Scher-Khoun's Meshack ex Ch. Holly Lane's Windstorm) ABC/SOM.

Can. Ch. Honeywood Copperplate (by Ch. Salgray's Fashion Plate ex Can. Ch. Honeywood Bittersweet) CKC/SOM.

Can. Ch. Hot Spell of Blossomlea (by Ch. Jered's Spellbinder ex Can. Ch. Painted Besom of Blossomlea) CKC/SOM.

Ch. Huck Hill's Rampage (by Alidan's Nautical White Cap ex Mill River's Bewildered) ABC/SOM.

Ch. Huffand's Irish Rebel (by Ch. Benjoman of Five T's ex Ch. Huffand's Charade) ABC/SOM.

Ch. Huffand's Nice Enough (by Ch. Merrilane's April Fashion ex Ch. Huffand's High Society) ABC/SOM.

Ch. Ingo von Heger Se Sumbula (by Ger. Ch. Fachinger von Neu-Drosedow ex Jojo von Dom) ABC/SOM.

Ch. Jacquet's Brass Idol (by Ch. Merrilane's April Fashion ex Jacquet's Perigal) ABC/SOM.

Ch. Jacquet's Greggson (by Int. Ch. Jacquet's Novarese ex Int. Ch. Jacquet's Aliage of Goldfield) ABC/SOM.

Int. Ch. Jacquet's Novarese (by Int. Ch. Jacquet's Agassiz ex Angel Angelli) ABC/SOM.

Am-Ber-Can-Jap. Ch. Jacquet's Urko (by Ch. Happy Ours Fortune De Jacquet ex Ch. Jacquet's Candy Dancer) ABC/SOM.

Ch. Jacquet's Zephan (by Ch. Rocky of Shawnee Trail ex Ronel's Jacquet Satie) ABC/SOM.

Can. Ch. Jaegerhouse's Victorara (by Ch. Aracrest's Talisman ex Can. Ch. Jaegerhouse's Golden Goddess) CKC/SOM.

Ch. Jered's Sovereign (by Ch. Bang Away of Sirrah Crest ex Ch. Jered's Sweet Stuff) ABC/SOM.

Ch. Jered's Spellbinder (by Ch. Elixir of Raineylane ex Hot Copy of Gay Oaks) ABC/SOM.

Ch. Jodi's Jeremiah (by Am-Can. Ch. Sherilyn's Sheridan ex Plymouth's Pride and Joy) ABC/SOM.

Am-Can. Ch. Jodi's Jubilation (by Am-Can. Ch. Sherilyn's Sheridan ex Hollycrest's Little Bit, CD) ABC/CKC/SOM.

Am-Can. Jodi's Riptide (by Am-Can. Ch. Jodi's Jeremiah ex Lady Star Heritage) ABC/SOM.

Ch. Jo-San's Future Time (by Ch. Har-Vel's Josh's Gold, CD ex Har-Vel's Gold Dust) ABC/SOM.

Am-Can. Ch. Josha's Linebacker, CD, CGC (by Am-Can. Golden Haze Tuxedo ex TuRo's Cameo of Campisi) ABC/CKC/SOM.

Am-Can. Ch. Keil's Circuit Breaker (by Am-Can. Ch. Keil's Vision ex Ch. Keil's Fatal Attraction) CKC/SOM.

Ch. Keil's Dynasty (by Ch. Salgray's Market Wise ex Ch. Keil's Hello Dolly) ABC/CKC/SOM.

Am-Can. Ch. Keil's Vision (by Ch. Keil's Dynasty ex Ch. Keil's High Society) ABC/SOM.

Am-Can. Ch. Keil's Wimbledon (by Am-Can. Ch. Keil's Vision ex Am-Can. Ch. Keil's Renaissance).

Ch. King's Mojave (by Ch. Tall Oaks Desert Dazzler ex Ch. Vandown's Laguna Rose) ABC/SOM.

Ch. Kobang of Sirrah Crest (by Ch. Duke Cronian ex Kantatrix of Mazelaine) ABC/SOM.

Ch. Kreyon's Easy Money (by Ch. Berena's Gemini Splashdown ex Kreyon's Borrowed Change) ABC/SOM.

Ch. Kricket's Jonathan (by Int. Ch. Marburl's Joshua ex Ch. Kricket's Dyn-O-Mite) ABC/SOM.

Ch. Leblanc's Back Door Johnny (by Ch. Janeda's Stage Door Johnny ex Am-Can. Ch. Leblanc's High Concerto) ABC/SOM.

Ch. Lewgin Lane's Whizz Bang (by Ch. Bang Away of Sirrah Crest ex Major Karla of Lewgin Lane) ABC/SOM.

Can. Ch. Lounsbury's Flashback To Rupik (by Am-Can. Ch. Bellcrest Just Watch Me ex Can. Ch. Lounsbury's Divinity) CKC/SOM.

Int. Ch. Lustig von Dom of Tulgey Wood (by Zorn von Dom ex Esta von der Wuerm) ABC/SOM.

Am-Can. Ch. Mahderf's El Chico (by Int. Ch. Dorian von Marienhof of Mazelaine ex Ch. Mahderf's Miss Eva) ABC/SOM.

Can. Ch. Malimi's Sailor of Allsorts (by Can. Ch. Malimi's Licorice Allsort ex Can. Ch. Malimi's Kissed by Magic) CKC/SOM.

Am-Can-Mex. Ch. Marburl's Joshua (by Ch. Moreleen's Al-le-lu-ia ex Marburl's Fireball) ABC/SOM.

Ch. Marjack's Golden Windjammer (by Ch. Captain Lookout of Thorhall ex Int. Ch. Marjack's Golden Mist) ABC/SOM.

Ch. Marquam Hill's Comanche (by Ch. Bang Away of Sirrah Crest ex Legacy of Clover Downs) ABC/SOM.

Ch. Marquam Hill's Traper of TuRo (by Int. Ch. Mephisto's Vendetta ex Ch. TuRo's Whisper of Five T's) ABC/CKC/SOM.

Am-Can. Ch. Marquam Hill's Trigger of TuRo (by Int. Ch. Mephisto's Vendetta ex Ch. TuRo's Whisper of Five T's) ABC/SOM.

Ch. Mar-Ray's Dashing Lee (by Ch. Yours True Lee ex Mar-Ray's Delilah) ABC/SOM.

Am-Can. Ch. Marshall's Fashion Magic (by Am-Can. Ch. Rodonna's Renegade Soldier ex Kamursart's Hannah) CKC/SOM.

Mazelaine's Kapellmeister (by Ch. Mazelaine's Legend ex Ch. Volante of Mazelaine) ABC/SOM.

Ch. Mazelaine's Masterpiece (by Ch. Bubbling Over of Lilac Hedge ex Omen of Mazelaine) ABC/SOM.

Ch. Mazelaine's Zazarac Brandy (by Am-Can. Ch. Merry Monarch ex Ch. Warbady of Mazelaine) ABC/SOM.

Me-Don's Special Revue (by Ch. Arriba's Knight Revue ex Me-Don's On The Road) ABC/SOM.

Am-Can. Ch. Memorylane's Avenger (by Can. Ch. Millan's Jet Fashion ex Memorylane's Desiree) ABC/SOM.

Can. Ch. Memorylane's Fascination (by Gaylord's Coy Challenge ex Can. Ch. Ringmaster's High Fashion) CKC/SOM.

Am-Can-Ber. Ch. Memorylane's Fashion Escort (by Int. Ch. Millan's Fashion Hint ex Beechnut of Blossomlea) CKC/SOM.

Am-Can. Ch. Mephisto's Citizen Kane (by Am-Mex. Ch. Dean-Erik's Razin Kane ex Am-Can. Ch. Mephisto's Black Sabbath) CKC/SOM.

Am-Can. Ch. Mephisto's Guns and Roses (by Am-Can. Ch. Mephisto's Rosenkavalier ex Mephisto's Queen of Spades) CKC/SOM.

Can-Nor. Ch. Mephisto's High Noon (by Int. Ch. Scher-Khoun's Shadrack ex Can. Ch. Verwood's Lollipop) CKC/SOM.

Am-Can. Ch. Mephisto's Rosenkavalier (by Ch. Berena's Gemini Splashdown ex Am-Can. Ch. Mephisto's Black Sabbath) CKC/SOM.

Am-Can. Ch. Mephisto's The Godfather (by Am-Mex. Ch. Dean-Erik's Razin Kane ex Am-Can. Ch. Mephisto's Black Sabbath) CKC/SOM.

Am-Ber-Can. Ch. Mephisto's Soldier of Fortune (by Int. Ch. Scher-Khoun's Shadrack ex Can. Ch. Verwood's Lollipop) ABC/CKC/SOM.

Am-Can-Ber. Ch. Mephisto's Vendetta (by Nor-Can. Ch. Mephisto's High Noon ex Can. Ch. Scher-Khoun's Autumn Concerto) ABC/CKC/SOM.

Can. Ch. Mephisto's Zorro of Leblanc (by Int. Ch. Mephisto's Vendetta ex Am-Can. Ch. Leblanc's High Concerto) CKC/SOM.

Ch. Merrilane's April Fashion (by Ch. Merrilane's Holiday Fashion ex Ch. Merrilane's April Love) ABC/SOM.

Ch. Merrilane's April Holiday (by Ch. Merrilane's Holiday Fashion ex Ch. Merrilane's April Love) ABC/SOM.

Ch. Merrilane's Holiday Fashion (by Int. Ch. Millan's Fashion Hint ex Merrilane's Mad Passion, CD) ABC/SOM.

Ch. Merrilane's Knockout (by Ch. Merrilane's April Holiday ex Ch. Jacquet's Mercer) ABC/SOM.

Ch. Merrilane's Mad Magic of Jofra (by Ch. Eldic's Landlord ex Merrilane's Mad Passion, CD) ABC/SOM.

Am-Can. Ch. Merry Monarch (by Am-Can. Ch. Mahderf's El Chico ex Jem of the Season) ABC/SOM.

Am-Ber-Can. Ch. Millan's Fashion Hint (by Ch. Salgray's Fashion Plate ex Int. Ch. Gaymitz Jet Action) ABC/CKC/SOM.

Ch. Milray's Winsome of Will-Ve's (by Ch. Salgray's Market Wise ex Ch. Milray's Mistique) ABC/SOM.

Am-Can-Mex. Ch. Monarch's Ego of Garakonti, CD (by Am-Can. Ch. Merry Monarch ex Ch. Pansy of Sierralair) ABC/SOM.

Ch. Moon Valley's Main Attraction (by Ch. Tall Oaks Desert Dazzler ex. Ch. Moon Valley's Image) ABC/SOM.

Am-Can. Ch. Moon Valley's Solar Flare (by Am-Can. Ch. Von Schorer's Moon Shadow ex Moon Valley's Merry Weather) ABC/CKC/SOM.

Am-Can. Ch. Moon Valley's Sun N'Shadow (by Am-Can. Ch. Von Schorer's Moon Shadow ex Moon Valley's Merry Weather) ABC/CKC/SOM.

Ch. Moon Valley's Sunsation (by Am-Can. Ch. Moon Valley's Solar Flare ex Moon Valley's Summer Shade) ABC/SOM.

Ch. Moreleen's Al-le-lu-ia (by Ch. Salgray's Ambush ex Merwin Hill's Flare Up) ABC/SOM.

Ch. Moreleen Meralota v Imladris (by Ch. Sir Lancelot of Box Run ex Moreleen's ESP) ABC/SOM.

Am-Can. Ch. Moss Wood's Zinger Zapper (by Int. Ch. Moon Valley's Solar Flare ex Moss Wood's Sweet Surrender) ABC/CKC/SOM.

Ch. My-R's Haybinder of Holly Lane (by Ch. Holly Lane's Wildwind ex Ch. My-R's Sensation) ABC/SOM.

Ch. Mystery's Show Bis (by Ch. Ell Bee's Just Watch Out ex Ch. Mystery's Cherokee Maiden) ABC/SOM.

Ch. Nemrac's Ali Bey (by Ch. Aimeebee's Ido Ido ex Pashee Baba) ABC/SOM.

Niklofs Columbo (by Ch. Moreleen's Al-le-lu-ia ex Di Liso's Melody) ABC/SOM.

Ch. Norhaven's Gladiator (by Ch. Treceder's Sequel ex Norhaven's Desire) ABC/SOM.

Ch. Notelrac's Major Beau (by Am-Can. Ch. Scher-Khoun's Abednego ex Tudosal's Ruffels) ABC/SOM.

Ch. Omega's Rockfire (by Int. Ch. Scher-Khoun's Shadrack ex Ch. Weber's Hustling Black Garter) ABC/SOM.

Ch. Omega's Tycoon (by Ch Aracrest's Talisman ex Ch. Omega's Maja) ABC/SOM.

Ch. Philanderer of Woodcrest (by Int. Ch. Eldic's Darius ex Katydid of Woodcrest) ABC/SOM.

Ch. Piccolo v.d. Stuttgarter (by Int. Ch. Utz von Dom of Mazelaine ex Glenda v.d. Stuttgarter) ABC/SOM.

Ch. Pinebrook's Innuendo (by Am-Can. Ch. Pinebrook's Well Tailored ex Fiero's Cassie) ABC/SOM.

Ch. Pinebrook's Radiation (by Candlewood's Straight Shot ex Oliver's HappyTalk) ABC/SOM.

Can. Ch. Pinepath's Gemini (by Int. Ch. Moon Valley's Sun N'Shadow ex Can. Ch. Pinepath's Sweet Gypsy Bee) CKC/SOM.

Am-Can. Ch. Pinepath's Night Watch (by Am-Can. Ch. Fiero's Tally-Ho ex Am-Can. Ch. Greenhaven's Ebony at Pinepath) ABC/CKC/SOM.

Am-Can. Ch. Playboy Candy Kisses (by Hi-Tone's Diamond Jim Brady ex Cleopatra's Candy Kisses) CKC/SOM.

Ch. Popham's Firebrand (by Ch. Helixview Galant Charger ex Amerglo Belle Star) ABC/SOM.

Ch. Quisto's Cornerstone (by Int. Ch. Aracrest's Jered ex Quisto's Queen Bee) ABC/SOM.

Ch. Raineylane's Paladin (by Del Mar's Double Dare ex Raineylane's Silky Sue) ABC/SOM.

Can. Ch. Rayshar's Magic Moment, TT, CD (by Ch. Marquam Hill's Traper of TuRo ex Can. Ch. Rayshar's Frosted Velvet) CKC/SOM.

Ch. Renno's Kountry Kid (by Ch. Bee-Jay's Come Fly With Me ex Renno's Tiger Stripe) ABC/SOM.

Rexob's Heritage of Trimanor (by Am-Can. Ch. Trimanor's Baccus ex Trimanor's Moonlighting Melody) CKC/SOM.

Can. Ch. Richmar's Rising Rocket (by Ch. Khorasan's Atomic ex Richmar's Hi Boots) CKC/SOM.

Ch. Rochil's Grande Marshall (by Ch. Har-Vel's Gold Express ex Ch. Rochil's Kallista of Marburl) ABC/SOM.

Ch. Rockalane's Country Sunset (by Ch. Vel-Kel's Big Ben ex Rocklane's Call Me Troubles) ABC/SOM.

Am-Can. Ch. Rodonna's El Segundo (by Wo-Kan-Da's Surveyor ex Can. Ch. Romar's Sheena) CKC/SOM.

Can. Ch. Rodonna's Renegade Crusader (by Am-Can. Ch. Rodonna's Renegade Soldier ex Can. Ch. King's Apache Sassoon) CKC/SOM.

Am-Can. Ch. Rodonna's Renegade Soldier (by Int. Ch. Mephisto's Soldier of Fortune ex Rodonna's Future Shock) CKC/SOM.

Ch. Sajac's Royal Savage (by Ch. Salgray's Ambush ex Carlwen's Candy Striper) ABC/SOM.

Ch. Salgray's Ambush (by Am-Can. Ch. Salgray's Flying High ex Ch. Salgray's Flaming Ember) ABC/SOM.

Ch. Salgray's Balladeer (by Am-Can. Ch. Salgray's Battle Chief ex Ch. Salgray's Dixie Gal) ABC/SOM.

Am-Can. Ch. Salgray's Battle Chief (by Am-Can. Ch. Barrage of Quality Hill ex Ch. Slipper of Grayarlin) ABC/SOM.

Ch. Salgray's Bojangles (by Ch. Salgray's Ovation ex Elharlen's Camero) ABC/SOM.

Ch. Salgray's Expresso (by Ch. Salgray's Minute Man ex Salgray's Autumn Years) ABC/SOM.

Ch. Salgray's Fashion Plate (by Am-Can. Ch. Salgray's Battle Chief ex Am-Can. Ch. Marquam Hill's Flamingo) ABC/CKC/SOM.

Am-Can. Ch. Salgray's Flying High (by Am-Can. Ch. Salgray's Battle Chief ex Am-Can. Ch. Marquam Hill's Flamingo) ABC/CKC/SOM.

Ch. Salgray's Good Grief (by Ch. Salgray's Ambush ex Ch. Salgray's Out of Bounds) ABC/SOM.

Am-Can. Ch. Salgray's Hijinx O'Thorn Crest (by Am-Can. Ch. Woods End Crown Sable ex Ch. Salgray's Call Me Madam) ABC/SOM.

Ch. Salgray's KO Aracrest (by Ch. Salgray's Market Wise ex Can. Ch. Aracrest Rhinegold) ABC/SOM.

Ch. Salgray's Market Wise (by Ch. Salgray's Ambush ex Ch. Salgray's Jitterbug) ABC/SOM.

Ch. Salgray's Ovation (by Am-Can. Ch. Salgray's Flying High ex Can. Ch. Salgray's Roulette) ABC/SOM.

Ch. Salgray's Royal Flush (by Ch. Salgray's Ambush ex Ch. Salgray's Zetta of Dormac) ABC/SOM.

Ch. Sam-El's Maker's Mark (by Ch. Omega's Rockfire ex Sam-El's O'Shannon) ABC/SOM.

Ch. Scarborough Norman Knight (by Ch. Huffand's Nice Enough ex Ch. Gerhard's Calliope) ABC/SOM.

Ch. Scarborough Silversmith (by Int. Ch. Gray Roy's Minstrel Boy ex Am-Can. Ch. Scher-Khoun's Tarantella) ABC/SOM.

Ch. Scarlet Oak Rocco (by Am-Can. Ch. Memorylane's Avenger ex Ch. Millan's Gay Bug) ABC/SOM.

Am-Can. Ch. Scher-Khoun's Abednego (by Int. Ch. Scher-Khoun's Shadrack ex Can. Ch. Scher-Khoun's Carousel) ABC/SOM.

Am-Ber-Can. Ch. Scher-Khoun's Meshack (by Int. Ch. Scher-Khoun's Shadrack ex Int. Ch. Scher-Khoun's Syncopation) ABC/CKC/SOM.

Am-Ber-Can. Ch. Scher-Khoun's Shadrack (by Int. Ch. Millan's Fashion Hint ex Can. Ch. Scher-Khoun's Carousel) ABC/CKC/SOM.

Ch. Schoolmaster of Mazelaine (by Ch. Endymion of Mazelaine ex Psyche of Mazelaine) ABC/SOM.

Am-Can. Ch. Scottlea's Billy Be Damned (by Int. Ch. Scher-Khoun's Shadrack ex Can. Ch. Fan-Ton's Fashion Flair) CKC/SOM.

Am-Can. Ch. Seaside's Ewo Surf Breaker (by Ch. Heldenbrand's Jet Breaker ex Ch. Ewo's Crystal) ABC/SOM.

Sergi's N BJ's Junior Strut (by Am-Can. Ch. Wincaster's Tyger of Huffand ex Ch. Niklofs Empress of TuRo) ABC/SOM.

Can. Ch. Shadowlane's Othello (by Can. Ch. Donessle's Spring Fever ex Can. Ch. Shadowdale's Love That Lady) CKC/SOM.

Am-Can. Ch. Sherilyn's Sheridan (by Ch. Karjean's Premonition ex Sherilyn's Sorti-Special) ABC/SOM.

Ch. Shieldmont's Dimension (by Int. Ch. Moon Valley's Sun N'Shadow ex Ch. Holly Lane's Beads) ABC/SOM.

Ch. Shieldmont's Game Plan (by Ch. Shieldmont's Dimension ex Ch. Donessle's Night Wind) ABC/SOM.

Ch. Shieldmont's Issues N Answers (by Am-Can. Ch. Wagner Wilverday Famous Amos ex Ch. Shieldmont's Focal Point) ABC/SOM.

Ch. Shieldmont's Judge N'Jury (by Ch. Shieldmont's Issues N Answers ex Ch. Donessle's Night Wind) ABC/SOM.

Ch. Shieldmont's Let's Make A Deal (by Ch. Shieldmont's Judge N'Jury ex Ch. Shieldmont's Haunting Haze) ABC/SOM.

Int. Ch. Sigurd von Dom of Barmere (by Iwein von Dom ex Belinde Hassia) ABC/SOM.

Ch. Sir Galahad of Bladan, CDX (by Ch. Brokas von Germanenstolz of Bladan ex Ch. Nemesis of Mazelaine) ABC/SOM.

Can. Ch. Soldier's Mark of Norbourne (by Int. Ch. Mephisto's Soldier of Fortune ex Ch. Sensuous Heidi, CD) CKC/SOM.

Am-Can. Ch. Soldier's Pride of Norbourne (by Int. Ch. Mephisto's Soldier of Fortune ex Ch. Sensuous Heidi, CD) CKC/SOM.

Ch. Sorrelane's Student Prince (by Ch. Evo-Wen's Dynamo ex Berge's Sky Angel) ABC/SOM.

Ch. Sortilair's Flaming Star (by Ch. Glenshire's Major Spark ex Sortilair's Dusty Star) ABC/SOM.

Am-Can. Ch. Spark Plug (by Ch. Zack von Dom ex Royal Lessa v Koenig) ABC/SOM.

Can. Ch. Standfast of Blossomlea (by Ruda River's Happy Go Lucky ex Ber-Can. Ch. Fireside Chat of Blossomlea) CKC/SOM.

Can. Ch. Starview's Black Gold (by Can. Ch. Soldier's Mark of Norbourne ex Can. Ch. Billie's Country Classic) CKC/SOM.

Can. Ch. Starview's Mystery Mark (by Can. Ch. Starview's Black Gold ex Can. Ch. Starview's Sugar and Spice, CD) CKC/SOM.

Am-Can. Ch. Strawberry's Caballero (by Can. Ch. Mephisto's Bandalero ex Ch. Indian Bend's Swiss Moca) ABC/SOM.

Ch. Summit View's Fuzz Buster (by Am-Can. Ch. Diamondaire's Dealer's Choice ex Am-Can. Ch. Summit View's Dutch Treat) ABC/SOM.

Ch. Summit View's Legal Tender (by Ch. Summit View's Fuzz Buster ex Am-Can. Ch. Summit View's Ambrosia) ABC/SOM.

Ch. Sundarby's Fleetwood Mac (by Ch TuRo's Empire ex Ch. Sundarby's Cover Girl) ABC/SOM.

Am-Can. Ch. Sunset Fonz of Five T's (by Am-Can. Ch. Memorylane's Sunset ex Terri of Tall Timbers) ABC/SOM.

Ch. Talisman's Vigilante (by Ch. Aracrest's Talisman ex Ch. Talisman's Chantilly Lace) ABC/SOM.

Ch. Tall Oaks Desert Dazzler (by Am-Can. Ch. Wagner Wilverday Famous Amos ex Tall Oaks Solar Flame) ABC/SOM.

Can. Ch. Tarabran's Electra Cadet, CDX (by Can. Ch. Gaylord's Eminent Escort ex Can. Ch. Scher-Khoun's Tara) CKC/SOM.

Ch. Telstar's Front Runner (by Ch. Telstar's Court Jester ex Ch. Telstar's Pride-N-Joy) ABC/SOM.

Ch. Telstar's Good Time Charlie (by Ch. Berena's Gemini Splashdown ex Telstar's High Fidelity) ABC/SOM.

Ch. Telstar's Highflyer (by Ch. Araby's Shortstop ex Ch. Glennroe Opensesame) ABC/SOM.

Ch. Telstar's Starmaker (by Int. Ch. Mephisto's Vendetta ex Telstar's Peppermint Pleaser) ABC/SOM.

Ch. Tolfan's Total Eclipse (by Ch. TuRo's Native Dancer ex Mephisto's Razzle Dazzle) ABC/SOM.

Am-Can. Ch. Tradonalee's Bismark (by Ch. Holly Lane's Diamond Replay ex Can. Ch. Cinderella of Tradonalee) ABC/SOM.

Can. Ch. Tradonalee's Classic Sensation (by Ch. Berena's Gemini Splashdown ex Am-Can. Ch. Carlon's Classy Catrina) CKC/SOM.

Ch. Treceder's Selection (by Ch. Jered's Spellbinder ex Ch. Treceder's High Falutin) ABC/SOM.

Ch. Treceder's Sequel (by Ch. Treceder's Selection ex Ch. Treceder's Shady Lady) ABC/CKC/SOM.

Ch. Treceder's Shine Boy (by Ch. Treceder's Selection ex Treceder's Show Piece) ABC/SOM.

Ch. Trefoil's Choir Boy (by Int. Ch. Gray Roy's Minstrel Boy ex Kaseba's Show Girl) ABC/SOM.

Am-Can. Ch. Trefoil's Dylan of Donessle (by Int. Ch. Gray Roy's Minstrel Boy ex Can. Ch. Donessle's Miss Fancy) ABC/SOM.

Am-Can. Ch. Trimanor's Baccus (by Can. Ch. Donessle's Crusader ex Am-Can. Ch. Trimanor's Fair Antoinette) CKC/SOM.

Can. Ch. Trimanor's I Don't Give A Damn (by Am-Can. Ch. Bellcrest Just Watch Me) CKC/SOM.

Am-Can. Ch. Trimanor Pinepath's Hudson Bay (by Can. Ch. Pinepath's Gemini ex Pinepath's Fair Cleopatra) CKC/SOM.

Can. Ch. Trimanor's Rolls Royce Bentley (by Can. Ch. Trimanor's Lincoln Continental ex Can. Ch. Trimanor's Fatal Attraction) CKC/SOM.

Ch. Tudosal's Whizzard of Laurel Hill (by TuRo's Escappade ex Tudosal's Onyx of Laurel Hill) ABC/SOM.

Ch. TuRo's Accolade (by Ch. Marquam Hill's Traper of TuRo ex TuRo's Katrina of Cross Bar) ABC/SOM.

Am-Can. Ch. TuRo's Dakota of Shar-Rea (by Ch. TuRo's Tidal Wave ex Ch. TuRo's Cherub of DJ) ABC/SOM.

Ch. TuRo's Empire (by Ch. Marquam Hill's Traper of TuRo ex Ch. TuRo's Touche) ABC/SOM.

TuRo's Escappade (by Ch. Marquam Hill's Traper of TuRo ex Ch. TuRo's Touche) ABC/SOM.

Can. Ch. TuRo's Kristian Dior (by Ch. Marquam Hill's Traper of TuRo ex TuRo's Snapshot) ABC/CKC/SOM.

Ch. TuRo's Native Dancer (by Int. Ch. Millan's Fashion Hint ex Am. Ch. Hansparke's Fashion Fair) ABC/SOM.

Am-Can. Ch. Ursa Major of Sirrah Crest (by Ch. Yobang of Sirrah Crest ex Umbra of Sirrah Crest, CD) ABC/SOM.

Int. Ch. Utz von Dom of Mazelaine (by Zorn von Dom ex Esta von der Wuerm) ABC/SOM.

Can. Ch. Vanan's Dreadnaught (by Int. Ch. Scher-Khoun's Shadrack ex Rochdale's Halo) CKC/SOM.

Ch. Vancroft's Primetime (by Ch. Misty Valley's Curtain Call ex Ch. Vancroft's Vogue) ABC/SOM.

Ch. Vandown-King's Fire Alert (by Ch. Bropat's Red Alert of Asgard ex Ch. Vandown's Laguna Rose) ABC/SOM.

Am-Can. Ch. Vannassau's Step-In-Time (by Can. Ch. Gramlich's Win-Fall ex Can. Ch. Beaucrest's Fashion Image) CKC/SOM.

Am-Can. Ch. V-E Admiral of Renrew (by Ch. Max v Hohenneuffen ex Ch. Overture of Mazelaine) ABC/SOM.

Ch. Vel-Kel's Big Ben (by Am-Can. Ch. Scher-Khoun's Abednego ex Interlude's Rain Drop) ABC/SOM.

Am-Can. Ch. Verwood's Thief in the Night (by Int. Ch. Moon Valley's Sun N'Shadow ex Verwood's Utter Nonsense) CKC/SOM.

Ch. Vick Wick of Sirrah Crest (by Ch. Xebony of Sirrah Crest ex Ch. Questa of Sirrah Crest) ABC/SOM.

Ch. Vihabra's Gold 'N Zephyr (by Ch. Merrilane's Vihabra Gold 'N Key ex Alumar's Pink Champagne) ABC/SOM.

Am-Can. Ch. Vimar's EST (by Ch. Holly Lane's Diamond Reply ex Vimar's Lil Bit A Breeze) ABC/SOM.

Am-Can. Ch. Vimar's We Believe In Magic (by Am-Can. Ch. Vimar's EST ex Ebony Image of Ellen's Alley) ABC/CKC/SOM.

Ch. Virgo's Market Boomer (by Ch. Shieldmont's Let's Make a Deal ex Ch. Virgo's Totally Awesome) ABC/SOM.

Am-Can. Ch. Von Schorer's Moon Shadow (by Int. Ch. Millan's Fashion Hint ex Ch. Nadora's Black Lace) ABC/SOM.

Am-Can. Ch. Waagmeester's Hari-Mac (by Waagmeester's Show Boy ex Waagmeester's Miss Priss) CKC/SOM.

Am-Can. Ch. Wagner Wilverday Famous Amos (by Ch. Marquam Hill's Traper of TuRo ex Ch. Wagner's Vision of Wilvirday) ABC/SOM.

Ch. Warlord of Mazelaine (by Int. Ch. Utz von Dom of Mazelaine ex Ch. Symphony of Mazelaine) ABC/SOM.

Ch. Wedge Hollow's Hasty Harry (by Ch. Canzonet's Musical Matinee ex Wedge Hollows Clever Colleen) ABC/SOM.

Ch. Wichita of Cherokee Oaks (by Int. Ch. Helixview Noble Knight ex Cherokee Oaks Flame Princess) ABC/SOM.

Ch. Wilderson's Demos (by Ch. Arriba's Crescendo ex Ch. Rococo's Tangerine) ABC/SOM.

Am-Can. Ch. Wincaster's Tyger of Huffand (by Ch. Huffand's Irish Rebel ex Can. Ch. Jocolu's Buttons and Bows) ABC/SOM.

Can. Ch. Wo-Kan-Da's Triumph (by Can. Ch. Wo-Kan-Da's Golden Warrior ex Can. Ch. Her Majesty of Blossomlea) CKC/SOM.

Am-Can. Ch. Woods End Crown Sable (by Ch. Keil's Dynasty ex Ch. Woods End Moon Whisper) ABC/CKC/SOM.

Am-Can. Ch. Woods End Million Heir (by Ch. Keils' Dynasty ex Ch. Woods End Moon Whisper) ABC/SOM.

Can. Ch. Wyncroft's Etcetera (by Can. Ch. Seefeld Post Laureate ex Seefeld Artiste Model of Carnbrae) CKC/SOM.

Ch. Yactor of Tulgey Wood (by Int. Ch. Lustig v Dom of Tulgey Wood ex Elda of Tulgey Wood) ABC/SOM.

Ch. Yobang of Sirrah Crest (by Ch. Duke Cronian ex Maderia of Sirrah Crest) ABC/SOM.

Ch. Yours True Lee (by Ch. Helixview Fine-N-Dandee ex Ch. True Lee Fair) ABC/SOM.

Ch. Zack von Dom (by Ger. Ch. Heiner v Zwergeck ex Petra von Dom) ABC/SOM.

Am-Can. Ch. Zephyr's Heaven Help Us (by Am-Can. Ch. Golden Haze Tuxedo ex Can. Ch. Kpark Shout It Out) CKC/SOM.

Zorn von Dom (by Int. Ch. Sigurd v Dom ex Dudel von Pfarrhaus) ABC/SOM.

DAMS OF MERIT

Can. Ch. Abbyroad's Dizzie Miss Lizzie (by Ch. Brettendale's Stampede ex Can. Ch. Abbyroad's Added Touch) CKC/DOM.

Ackland's Scheherazade (by Int. Ch. Ackland's Student Prince ex Mackaman's Merry Berry) ABC/DOM.

Ch. Ada v Trauntal of Barmere (by Tanko v Haidhausen ex Fricka v Berggeist) ABC/DOM.

Ch. Aeronay's Lady Boneva (by Ch. Brasun's Legionnaire ex Pleasant Valley's Cricket) ABC/DOM.

Can. Ch. Ainsdale April Misty Valley (by Am-Can. Ch. Bellcrest Just Watch Me ex Can. Ch. Ainsdale August Delite) CKC/DOM.

Can. Ch. Ainsdale August Delite (by Am-Can. Ch. Donessle's Cassino ex Can. Ch. Ainsdale Double Delite) CKC/DOM.

Can. Ch. Ainsdale Double Delite (by Am-Can. Ch. Trimanor Pinepaths Hudson Bay ex Can. Ch. Trimanor's Fair Delilah) CKC/DOM.

Can. Ch. Ajays Chanel (by Can. Ch. TuRo's Kristian Dior ex Can. Ch. Ajays Tammy Faye B) CKC/DOM.

Am-Can. Ch. Ajays Ruby Teusday (by Can. Ch. Tradonalees Classic Sensation ex Savoye's Satin Shadow of Ajay) CKC/DOM.

Can. Ch. Ajays Tammy Faye B (by Ch. Berena's Gemini Splashdown ex Can. Ch. Zephyr's Time Is Money) CKC/DOM.

Aljo's Beauty Spot of Armac (by Armac's Deka Demon ex Misty's Princess Lou) ABC/DOM.

Can. Ch. Allison X-Mas Carrol (by Can. Ch. Mazelaine's Aces High ex Can. Ch. Allison Carrol) CKC/DOM.

Amber Lady III, CDX (by Cerberus of Glen-Sed ex Bingo Kid of Mars) ABC/DOM.

Ch. Anchic's Passion of TuRo (by Ch. TuRo's Accolade ex Tiffany XVIII) ABC/DOM.

Anitra of Mazelaine (by Int. Ch. Check v Hunnenstein ex Ch. Landa of Mazelaine) ABC/DOM.

Can. Ch. Aperion Bevenuta of Elharlen (by Can. Ch. Elharlen's Comanchero ex Traveller of Haviland) CKC/DOM.

Aracrest's Fashion Krickett (by Int. Ch. Millan's Fashion Hint ex Am-Can. Ch. Aracrest's Trinkett) CKC/DOM.

Aracrest's Victorian Revival (by Am-Can. Ch. Aracrest's Creed ex Can. Ch. Hershey's In Vogue) CKC/DOM.

Can. Ch. Ariel of Karavan (by Ch. Brass Bound of Briarnole ex Beau Belle of Showline) CKC/DOM.

Ch. Aries Golden Tiffany (by Am-Can. Ch. Strawberry's Caballero ex Ch. Ramrod's Tara Aries) ABC/DOM.

Ch. Arriba's Cherkei Fancy Free (by Ch. Marquam Hill's Traper of TuRo ex Ch. Arriba's Lady Revue) ABC/DOM.

Ch. Arriba's Lady Revue (by Ch. Arriba's Knight Revue ex Betlow's Foxy Lady of Arriba) ABC/DOM.

Arriba's Ultimate (by Ch. Arriba's Crescendo ex Ch. Arriba's Jubilee) ABC/DOM.

Ch. Arriba's Zechin (by Int. Ch. Scher-Khoun's Shadrack ex Ch. Arriba's Jubilee) ABC/DOM.

Ch. Asgard's Southern Belle (by Ch. Bropat's Commotion ex Asgard's Hi-Performance) ABC/DOM.

Can. Ch. Backchat of Blossomlea 2nd (by Am-Can. Ch. Salgray's Flying High ex Ber-Can. Ch. Fireside Chat of Blossomlea) CKC/DOM.

Ch. Bainridge O'Suzana of Karlyna (by Ch. Hala's Apache Rising Son ex Wesan's Sassy Sorceress) ABC/DOM.

Baldr's Angela Shoreline (by Ch. Sara-Sien Adonis of Shoreline ex Baldr's Xtravaganza) ABC/DOM.

Ch. Baldr's Superchic (by Ch. Laureate X-Cel-A-Rator ex Ch. Black Toad Penelope) ABC/DOM.

Can. Ch. Beaucrest's Fashion Flair (by Am-Can. Ch. Style Setter of Kargotor ex Can. Ch. Beaucrest's Cherokee Princess) CKC/DOM.

Can. Ch. Beaucrest's Fashion Image (by Can. Ch. Barnaby Jones of Terid-Don ex Can. Ch. Beaucrest's Moonlight Shadow) CKC/DOM.

Beaupix's Shennanigan's (by Ch. Araby's Shortstop ex Ch. Jacquet's Fanfare of Beaupix) ABC/DOM.

Bellcrest's Encore (by Am-Can. Ch. Wincaster's Stargazer ex Can. Ch. Bellcrest's Critique, CD) CKC/DOM.

Am-Can. Ch. Bellcrest Sooner Be Me (by Am-Can. Ch. Ell Bee's Son of Bis ex Am-Can. Ch. Bellcrest Just It From Ell Bee) CKC/DOM.

Can. Ch. Bellgary's Mahogany Velvet (by Can. Ch. Bellegary's Denver Dividend ex Can. Ch. Verwood's Countess Kali) CKC/DOM.

Can. Ch. Billie's Country Classic (by Int. Ch. Mephisto's Vendetta ex Can. Ch. Billie's Country Gold) CKC/DOM.

Ch. Bitwyn's Star of Kings Pt. (by Ch. Vel-Kel's Big Ben ex Bitwyn's New England Summer) ABC/DOM.

Blanka v Fohlnhof Se Sumbula (by Alf v Uracher Wasserfall ex Eukutol v Neu- Drosedow) ABC/DOM.

Can. Ch. Bobby Pin of Blossomlea (by Am-Can. Ch. Salgray's Flying High ex Ber-Can. Ch. Fireside Chat of Blossomlea) CKC/DOM.

Ch. Bonita of Cross Acres (by Eagle of Tulgey Wood ex Bravenhartz Ionic Irene) ABC/DOM.

Bourbonhill's Summer Mist (by Ch. Bourbonhill's Noble Knight ex Scojem's Gingerbread Lady) ABC/DOM.

Ch. Boxerton Hollyhock (by Ch. Tall Oaks Desert Dazzler ex Boxerton Empress Tree) ABC/DOM.

Box M Cover Girl of Seawest (by Ch. Box M Irving De Keefer ex Ch. Caesar's Reno Showgirl) ABC/DOM.

Can. Ch. Bracara's Artistic of Gaylord (by Ch. Salgray's Ambush ex Can. Ch. Gaylord's Eminent Emblem) CKC/DOM.

Can. Ch. Bracara's Special Action (by Can. Ch. Bracara's Artistic Action ex Can. Ch. Gaylord's Special Selection) CKC/DOM.

Braemerwood Comin' Thru (by Ed-Ru's Golden Boy ex Salgray's Ambasara of Hargayle) ABC/DOM.

Ch. Braemerwood Joy of Heritage (by Ch. Braemerwood Happy Tracks ex Spring Sonnet of Heritage) ABC/DOM.

Ch. Breezewood's One Mo' Time (by Int. Ch. Moon Valley's Sun N'Shadow ex Ch. Sarazak's Sizzle) ABC/DOM.

Ch. Brettendale's Sidekik Karalot (by Ch. Brettendale's Stampede ex Brettendale's Susannah) ABC/DOM.

Ch. Brier Court's Independence (by Ch. Flying Apache Walking Tall ex Ch. Blythe Spirit of Brier Court) ABC/DOM.

Can. Ch. Brintan Sugar Plum (by Int. Ch. Mephisto's Soldier of Fortune ex Can. Ch. Marbelton Plum Silly, CD) CKC/DOM.

Ch. Bropat's Fandancer (by Ch. TuRo's Native Dancer ex Siboney's Fantastica Bropat) ABC/DOM.

Ch. Bruhnwall's Venus (by Am-Can. Ch. Baron of Brightwood ex Red Feather) ABC/DOM.

Ch. Buemar's Flashdance (by Ch. Kricket's Jonathan ex Ch. Braemerwood Star of Buemar) ABC/DOM.

Can. Ch. Bullock's Influence Elharlen (by Ch. Marquam Hill's Traper of TuRo ex Ch. Bullock's Corinthian Maid) CKC/DOM.

Buma's Champagne Lady (by Ch. Mtn Aire's Top of The Rockies ex Buma's Pina Kolada) ABC/DOM.

Can. Ch. Canyonair's Autumn Breeze (by Ch. Bang Away of Sirrah Crest ex Canyonair's Nicklette, CD) CKC/DOM.

Canyonair Diamond Lil, CD (by Ch. Endymion of Mazelaine ex Ornadoon of Sirrah Crest) ABC/DOM.

Ch. Canyonair Honey Chile (by Ch. Mazelaine's Masterpiece ex Canyonair Diamond Lil, CD) ABC/DOM.

Am-Can-Ber. Ch. Carlon's Classy Catrina (by Ch. My-R's Haybinder of Holly Lane ex Ch. Carlon's Sassy N'Classy) CKC/DOM.

Ch. Carlon's Classy Chasis (by Ch. My-R's Haybinder of Holly Lane ex Ch. Carlon's Sassy N'Classy) ABC/DOM.

Ch. Carlon's Sassy N'Classy (by Ch. Moreleen Meralota v Imladris ex Ch. TuRo's Truffian) ABC/DOM.

Carlwen's Joie De Vivre (by Ch. My-R's Haybinder of Holly Lane ex Ch. Carlwen's Free Spirit) ABC/DOM.

Carlwen's Juliet von Barrage (by Am-Can. Ch. Barrage of Quality Hill ex Carlwen's Duchess von Veto) ABC/DOM.

Am-Can. Ch. Cascade's Winter Kiss (by Ch. Berena's Tribute To Fa-Fa ex Ch. Cascade's Sweet Sixteen) CKC/DOM.

Cava-Lane's Velvet Touch (by Cava-Lane's Top Secret ex Sorrelane's Tar Baby) ABC/DOM.

Can. Ch. Cayman's Gold Legacy (by Am-Can. Ch. Mephisto's Apollo ex Ch. El Sirrah's Cayman Gold) CKC/DOM.

Ch. Cayman's Sweet Nandi (by Ch. Rusric's Vagabond Prince ex Ch. El Sirrah's Cayman Gold) ABC/DOM.

Can. Ch. Cedarlodge's Miss Chanel, CDX (by Am-Can. Ch. Malabar's Cracker ex Can. Ch. Seefield Wisnowski Mona Lisa) CKC/DOM.

Can. Ch. Chardepado's Golden Girl (by Ch. Keil's Dynasty ex Can. Ch. Sweet Rhapsody) CKC/DOM.

Can. Ch. Chardepado's Good Golly Ms Molly (by Am-Can. Ch. Acadia's Conquistador ex Can. Ch. Sweet Rhapsody) CKC/DOM.

Can. Ch. Chat Away of Blossomlea (by Ch. Bang Away of Sirrah Crest ex Can. Ch. Painted Besom of Blossomlea) CKC/DOM.

Ch. Cherkei Arriba Wicked Calita (by Ch. Cherkei's Desperado ex Ch. Me-Don's Annie Oakley of Cherkei) ABC/DOM.

Cherkei's Hot Issue (by Ch. Cherkei's Oak Ridge Boy ex Shoals Misty Lady) ABC/DOM.

Ch. Chocolatina De Miro (by Ch. Chocolate De Miro ex Belle's Geisha Doll) ABC/DOM.

Can. Ch. Cinderella of Tradonalee (by Int. Ch. Memorylane's Fashion Escort ex Helixview Miss B-Haven) CKC/DOM.

Claremont's Hickory (by Ch. Berena's Gemini Splashdown ex Bentbrook's Belle Sinclair) ABC/DOM.

Clinaude's Ginger Snap (by Clinaude's Ace ex Abigail of Galewood) ABC/DOM.

Colonel's Black Velvet (by Int. Ch. Millan's Fashion Hint ex Ginger and Spice) CKC/DOM.

Conquistador's E of Snuffbox (by Int. Ch. Gray Roy's Minstrel Boy ex Ch. Ja-Ka-Ri's Chechonya, CD) CKC/DOM.

Cora v d Blutenau (by Ger. Ch. Edler v Isarstrand ex Alma) ABC/DOM.

Ch. Creekwood's New Beginning (by Ch. Torin of Creekwood ex La-Lyn Creekwood Nut-N-Honey) ABC/DOM.

Ch. Crona v Zwergeck (by Int. Ch. Lustig v Dom of Tulgey ex Britta v Konigssee) ABC/DOM.

Ch. Cynra's Chanel (by Ch. Berena's Gemini Splashdown ex Cynra's Tango) ABC/DOM.

Ch. Cynra's Confetti (by Ch. Talisman's Candyman of Cynra ex Cynra's Trilogy) ABC/DOM.

Cynthia v Tal (by Ch. Hermes v Uracher Wasserfall se Sumbula ex Ch. Cynthia of Mazelaine) ABC/DOM.

Ch. Dagmar of Mazelaine (by Ch. Argue v Konigssee of Mazelaine ex Anitra of Mazelaine) ABC/DOM.

Can. Ch. Dallenlee's Cinnamon Spice (by Am-Can. Ch. Cedarlodge's Mr. St. Laurent ex Can. Ch. Dallenlee's Royal Sable, CD) CKC/DOM.

Can. Ch. Dallenlee's Royal Sable, CD (by Am-Can. Ch. Haviland's Count Royal ex Can. Ch. Cedarlodge's Miss Chanel, CDX) CKC/DOM.

Can. Ch. Dark Maiden of Hampton 2nd (by Duke of Wye Valley ex Haviland's Dark Mist) CKC/DOM.

Dasel's Cristel Star (by Int. Ch. Brumble Carolina Star ex Scampan's Cristel Windjammer) ABC/DOM.

Ch. Dasel's Spring Fantasy, CD (by Am-Can. Ch. Moss Wood's Zinger Zapper ex Dasel's Cristel Star) ABC/DOM.

Ch. Debut's Private Dancer (by Ch. Mival's Coming Fashion ex Ch. Debut's Private Audition) ABC/DOM.

Ch. De-Miro's Rosa De Lejos (by Ch. Barman's Golden Nugget ex Ch. Kalua De Miro) ABC/DOM.

Can. Ch. Diamondaire's New Sensation (by Can. Ch. Dreamboat's Future Hope ex Diamondaire's Royal Reflection) CKC/DOM.

Diamondaire's Step-In-Out, CD (by Can. Ch. Diamondaire's Dynamo ex Can. Ch. Sancurt's Rhapsodi O'Diamondaire) CKC/DOM.

Di Liso's Omega (by Ch. Moreleen's Apachie Ambush ex Di Liso's Ouija) ABC/DOM.

Am-Can. Ch. DJ's Jezzabell (by Ch. DJ's Memory Maker ex DJ's Brycrest Tiara) CKC/DOM.

Can. Ch. Donessle's Enchantress (by Int. Ch. Scher-Khoun's Meshack ex Can. Ch. Donessle's Foxfire) CKC/DOM.

Can. Ch. Donessle's Foxfire (by Int. Ch. Gray Roy's Minstrel Boy ex Can. Ch. Donessle's Miss Fancy) CKC/DOM.

Can. Ch. Donessle's Miss Fancy (by Int. Ch. Scher-Khoun's Shadrack ex Hansparke's Dynamite Dot) ABC/CKC/DOM.

Can. Ch. Donessle's On The Double (by Donessle's Going Places ex Donessle's Sadie) CKC/DOM.

Can. Ch. Donessle's That Girl (by Am-Can. Ch. Arriba's Associate of Karjean ex Can. Ch. Donessle's Twilight Magic) CKC/DOM.

Can. Ch. Donessle's Twilight Magic (by Int. Ch. Moon Valley's Sun N'Shadow ex Can. Ch. Donessle's Enchantress) CKC/DOM.

Can. Ch. Dorado's Crystal Walker (by Am-Can. Ch. Mephisto's Rosenkavalier ex Tokyo Rose) CKC/DOM.

Dormac's Risque (by Ch. Salgray's Ovation ex Ch. Dormac's Delightful Rhapsody) ABC/DOM.

Ebony Image of Ellen's Alley (by Ch. My-R's Haybinder of Holly Lane ex Molly Plum of Ellen's Alley) ABC/DOM.

Edelweiss (by Ch. Talisman of Pine Run ex Int. Ch. Gaymitz Jet Action) CKC/DOM.

Ch. El Encanto's Chantaje Jacquet (by Int. Ch. Jacquet's Novarese ex Ch. Jacquet's Maja) ABC/DOM.

Can. Ch. Elharlen's Great Expectations (by Elharlen's Xanthous ex Can. Ch. Elharlen's Quintessence) CKC/DOM.

Elharlen's Odessa (by Can. Ch. Elharlen's Critics Choice ex Can. Ch. Elharlen's Great Expectations) CKC/DOM.

Can. Ch. Elharlen's Optimum Choice (by Can. Ch. Donessle's Mile-Hi ex Can. Ch. Elharlen's Fair Warning) CKC/DOM.

Elharlen's Wavelore (by Ch. Salgray's Expresso ex Elharlen's Quasar) CKC/DOM.

Ch. El Sirrah's Cayman Gold (by Am-Can. Ch. Doggone Ounce of Gold ex El Sirrah's Critic's Choice) ABC/DOM.

Ch. El Wendie of Rockland (by Ch. Konzert of Mazelaine ex Tilda of Rockland) ABC/DOM.

Esta V D Wuerm (by Int. Ch. Sigurd v Dom ex Ger. Ch. Uni v d Wuerm) ABC/DOM.

Ch. Ewo's Crystal (by Ch. Cedar Hill's Capital Classic ex Ewo's Jasmine) ABC/DOM.

Ch. Exuberant of Woodcrest (by Ch. Philanderer of Woodcrest ex Eldic's Onederful) ABC/DOM.

Can. Ch. Falconhurst's Front Paige News (by Can. Ch. Rayshar's Magic Moment, CD ex Can. Ch. Falconhurst's Fashion Blaze) CKC/DOM.

Flintwood's Banned In Boston (by Ch. Flintwood's Places Please ex Ch. Morgenshern of Kresthallo) ABC/DOM.

Ch. Flying Apache Uprising (by Ch. Flying Apache Regal Rococo ex Ch. Brier Court's Independence) ABC/DOM.

Foresthill's The Magic Touch (by Am-Can. Ch. Donessle's Cassino ex Jocolu's Trivia) CKC/DOM.

Ch. Fowler's Good Golly Ms Molly (by Lake Bay's Last Hurrah ex Von Witzel's Glanz Brun Augen) ABC/DOM.

Foxwood's Katybeth of Jaimax (by Ch. Foxwood's Nicholas, CD ex Kawa's Mocha Midge) ABC/DOM.

Ch. Foxwood's Krystal Karosel, CDX (by Am-Can. Ch. Woods End Crown Sable ex Foxwood's Katybeth of Jaimax) ABC/DOM.

Can. Ch. Gaylord's Black Ballet (by Am-Can. Ch. Jered's Stacked Deck ex Can. Ch. Gaylord's Shady Lady) CKC/DOM.

Can. Ch. Gaylord's Candy Lady of Gaymitz (by Ch. Treceder's Sequel ex Can. Ch. Gaymitz Jet Flight) CKC/DOM.

Can. Ch. Gaylord's Echo of The Past (by Can. Ch. Donessle's Crusader ex Can. Ch. Gaylord's Vaguely Modest) CKC/DOM.

Can. Ch. Gaylord's Eminent Encore (by Gaylord's Coy Challenge ex Can. Ch. Gaylord's Black Ballet) CKC/DOM.

Can. Ch. Gaylord's Loyal Legacy (by Can. Ch. Gaylord's Immaculate Imp ex Can. Ch. Gaylord's Black Ballet) CKC/DOM.

Can. Ch. Gaylord's Midnite Madness (by Am-Can. Ch. Donessle's Cassino ex Can. Ch. Gaylord's Northern Dancer) CKC/DOM.

Can. Ch. Gaylord's Special Selection (by Can. Ch. Gaylord's Eminent Escort ex Can. Ch. Bracara's Artistic of Gaylord) CKC/DOM.

Can. Ch. Gaylord's Vaguely Modest (by Can. Ch. Gaylord's Kopper Kane ex Can. Ch. Gaylord's Popular Paige) CKC/DOM.

Can. Ch. Gaymitz Dash O'Fire (by Can. Ch. Standfast of Blossomlea ex Ber/Can. Ch. Gaymitz Spelling Bee) ABC/CKC/DOM.

Can. Ch. Gaymitz Jet Flight (by Am-Can. Ch. Salgray's Flying High ex Can. Ch. Gaymitz Dash O'Fire) CKC/DOM.

Ch. Gerhard's R'NR Encore (by Ch. Gerhard's Lamplighter ex Brettendale's Firecracker) ABC/DOM.

Ch. Gerhard's String of Pearls (by Ch. Scarborough Norman Knight ex Ch. Gerhard's Harbor Lights) ABC/DOM.

Can. Ch. Gerlils Flashy First (by Am-Can. Ch. Siegel's Royal Coachman ex Can. Ch. Boxwood's First Choice, CD) CKC/DOM.

Can. Ch. Glencotta's Baroness (by Can. Ch. Glencotta's Riot Act ex Can. Ch. Pandora's Barbara of B'Kara) CKC/DOM.

Glencotta's Loose Change (by Verre-Way's Showcase ex Willarea's Backtalk) CKC/DOM.

Can. Ch. Glencotta's Sultana (by Am-Can. Ch. Glencotta's Magnum ex Houndhaven's Dark Delight) CKC/DOM.

Ch. Glennroe Alexandria (by Ch. Glennroe Eldorado ex Glennroe Our Golden Gadabout, CD) ABC/DOM.

Ch. Glennroe Ingenue (by Ch. Glennroe Eldorado ex Glennroe Dulzura) ABC/DOM.

Ch. Glennroe Opensesame (by Ch. Clinel's Lil Abner ex Ch. Glennroe Ingenue) ABC/DOM.

Ch. Glennroe Tequila Sunrise (by Ch. Glennroe Rum Runner ex Lyn-El's Daisy Mae) ABC/DOM.

Can. Ch. Golden Haze April Showers (by Can. Ch. Golden Haze Snow Drift, CDX ex Can. Ch. Moss Wood's Zippity Do Da) ABC/CKC/DOM.

Am-Can. Ch. Golden Haze Just One Look (by Am-Can. Ch. Bellcrest Just Watch Me ex Can. Ch. Golden Haze April Showers) CKC/DOM.

Goldenshine Dana (by Can. Ch. Trimanor's I Don't Give A Damm ex Lilli) CKC/DOM.

Ch. Gorgeous of Jofra (by Deneb of Jofra ex Crescendo of Jofra) ABC/DOM.

Ger. Ch. Gretel v Hohenneuffen (by Ger. Ch. Hansl v Biederstein ex Cilly v Hohenneuffen) ABC/DOM.

Ch. Ha-Mar Hint of Shady Lady (by Int. Ch. Millan's Fashion Hint ex Ha-Mar Ringside Gossip) ABC/DOM.

Hancocks Sabatha of Kameo (by Can. Ch. Mephisto's Bandalero ex Ch. Creme De La Creme De Kameo) ABC/DOM.

Am-Can. Ch. Hansparke's Fashion Fair (by Int. Ch. Millan's Fashion Hint ex Ch. Hansparke Pride of Step Aside) ABC/DOM.

Can. Ch. Hansparke's Sweet Charlotte (by Can. Ch. Malabar's Anthony Earp ex Can. Ch. Kerra- Laine's Step-Aside) CKC/DOM.

Haviland's Clarissa (by Can. Ch. Haviland's Zipper ex Woolacott's December Bride) CKC/DOM.

Can. Ch. Haviland's Gai-Beau (by Can. Ch. Haviland's Gai-Time ex Haviland's Storm Lark) CKC/DOM.

Can. Ch. Haviland's Gai-Bow (by Can. Ch. Haviland's Renegade Storm ex Can. Ch. Haviland's Gai-Beau) CKC/DOM. **Haviland's Royal Carnival** (by Am-Can. Ch. Haviland's Royal Sable ex Haviland's Eye Catcher) CKC/DOM.

Ch. Hazlyn's Zippity Do-Dah (by Mazelaine's Galway ex Vel-Hi's Kapella) ABC/DOM.

Heigh Ho Bramble (by Int. Ch. Dorian v Marienhof of Mazelaine ex Mazelaine Quagga) ABC/DOM.

Heldenbrand's Jetta Jovina (by Ch. Heldenbrand's Kansas Twister ex Misty Mountain Rhodes) ABC/DOM.

Ch. Heldenbrand's Raven Holly Lane (by Ch. Holly Lane's Prairie Chief ex Heldenbrand's Jetta Jovina) ABC/DOM.

Ch. Heleva Heart Stealer, CD, TT (by Ch. Notelrac's Notorious ex Beth-El's Heleva One) ABC/DOM.

Ch. Herndon's Desert Flyer (by Am-Can. Ch. Salgray's Flying High ex Ch. Bilger's Lady of Leisure) ABC/DOM.

High Spot Letti (by Armin v Hanseatenhof Stoeckersburg ex Delma v d Stoeckersburg) ABC/DOM.

Ch. Hi-Hill's Rave Review (by Ch. Heldenbrand's Ks Kid by Peddler ex Hi-Hill's Summer Shadows) ABC/DOM.

Ch. Hi-Winds Grand Illusion (by Ch. Echo's California Cruiser ex Claremonts Jenny of Hi-Winds) ABC/DOM.

Can. Ch. Holiday's Front Page (by Am-Can. Ch. Arriba's Associate of Karjean ex Root's High Magic, CD) CKC/DOM.

Hollycrest's Little Bit, CD (by Am-Can. Ch. Scher-Khoun's Abednego ex Grr-Aces Valkyrie) ABC/DOM.

Ch. Holly Lane's Cookie (by Ch. Flintwood's Sundowner ex Sarazan's Love Story) ABC/DOM.

Can. Ch. Hollylane's Irish Gold (by Ch. Huffand's Irish Rebel ex Golden Haviland's Edition) CKC/DOM.

Hollylane's Irish Mist (by Ch. Huffand's Irish Rebel v. Golden Haviland's Edition) CKC/DOM.

Holly Lane's Spring Breeze (by Ch. Holly Lane's Wind and Fire ex Ch. Holly Lane's Winter Wind) ABC/DOM.

Holly Lane's Taskaloosa (by Ch. My-R's Haybinder of Holly Lane ex Ch. Holly Lane's Baubles) ABC/DOM.

Ch. Holly Lane's Windstorm (by Ch. Brayshaw's Masquerader ex Ch. Holly Lane's Cookie) ABC/DOM.

Ch. Holly Lane's Winter Fantasy (by Int. Ch. Scher-Khoun's Meshack ex Ch. Holly Lane's Windstorm) ABC/DOM.

Howcurt's Autumn Jubilee (by Ch. Berena's Gemini Splashdown ex Telstar's Spellbound) ABC/DOM.

Ch. Huffand's Charade (by Ch. Arriba's High Hopes ex Arriba's Ultimate) ABC/DOM.

Ch. Huffand's Obsession of Arriba (by Am-Can. Ch. Golden Haze Tuxedo ex Ch. Americana's Megan By Huffand) ABC/DOM.

Can. Ch. Hyde Park Hi Hopes of K-Park (by Am-Can. Ch. Bellcrest Just Watch Me ex Hyde Park Folly) CKC/DOM.

Ch. Hy Hopes Sweet Stuff (by Ch. Evo-Wen's Impressario ex Ch. Helixview Golden Promise) ABC/DOM.

Indian Bend's Cissy (by Pomelo Park's Midnight Prancer ex Indian Bend's Wind Song) ABC/DOM.

Indian Bend's Maria (by Int. Ch. Scher-Khoun's Shadrack ex Indian Bend's Wind Song) ABC/DOM.

Can. Ch. Indy De Kiritowi (by Ch. Salgray's Valentino ex Can. Ch. Gaylord's Echo of The Past) CKC/DOM.

Ch. Jacaway's Satin Doll (by Jacaway's Life of the Party ex Ch. Jacaway's Lovely Lisa) ABC/DOM.

Ch. Jacquet's Canterbury Belie (by Ch. Jacquet's Zephan ex Ch. Jacquet's Chelsea) ABC/DOM.

Ch. Jacquet's Goldfield Rubi Doux (by Ch. Merrilane's April Fashion ex Jacquet's Hot Summer) ABC/DOM.

Ch. Jacquet's Jolie (by Ch. Jacquet's Zephan ex Ms Libschon of Rochelle) ABC/DOM.

Jacquet's Kiri Te Kanawa (by Ch. Jacquet's Gaspard ex Nutwood's Renata De Jacquet) ABC/DOM.

Jacquet's Perigal (by Ch. Tamberlaine's Polished Brass ex Jacquet's Rekah) ABC/DOM.

Can. Ch. Jaegerhouse's Scotia Bluenose (by Can. Ch. Donessle's Spring Fever ex Diamondaire's Step-N-Out, CD) CKC/DOM.

Can. Ch. Jandaire's Burnt Sienna (by Can. Ch. Standfast of Blossomlea ex Chataway's Chico of Blossomlea) CKC/DOM.

J and Ps Kisses Galore (by Can. Ch. Trimanor's Lincoln Continental ex Suzie "Q") CKC/DOM.

Ch. Janeda's Nokomis (by Am-Can. Ch. Von Schorer's Moon Shadow ex Hallmark Hill's King's Ransom) ABC/DOM.

Ch. Ja-Ru's Swamp Fire (by Ch. Los Aroble's King Kong ex Rancho Chiquito's Comet) ABC/DOM.

Jered's Sky Siren (by Ch. Bang Away of Sirrah Crest ex Ch. Jered's Sweet Stuff) ABC/DOM.

Can. Ch. Jocolu's Charming Fashion (by Int. Ch. Millan's Fashion Hint ex Jocolu's Miss Win-Sum) ABC/CKC/DOM.

Can. Ch. Jocolu's Susanna (by Int. Ch. Millan's Fashion Hint ex Ev-Lyn's Sabre Gal, CD) CKC/DOM.

Jocolu's Trivia (by Can. Ch. Donessle's Spring Fever ex Tigre of Jocolu) CKC/DOM.

Ch. Jojac's Magic Moment (by Int. Ch. Millan's Fashion Hint ex Arriba's Gavotte) ABC/DOM.

Ch. Jopa's Twilight Romance (by Ch. Wagner Wilverday Famous Amos ex Camnic's Great Pride of Jopa) ABC/DOM.

Ch. Jopa's Weekend Fantasy (by Ch. Zat's So of Woodcrest ex Camnic's Great Pride of Jopa) ABC/DOM.

Jordannas Chantilly Lace (by Can. Ch. Ainsdale Stonwall Jackson, CD ex Can. Ch. Donaby's Fancy Touch) CKC/DOM.

Ch. Joy's Joyous Lady (by Ch. Tuff E'Nuff of Bigaboda ex Ginger Peachie of Galaday) ABC/DOM.

K-9's Twister (by Ch. Treceder's Sequel ex Lazy Lawn's Tantalizin' Twist) ABC/DOM.

Can. Ch. Kadenza's Ain't I Somethin (by Can. Ch. Toniks Cruz Control at Kadenza ex Can. Ch. Dreamboat's Fawn Baroness) CKC/DOM.

Ch. Kalua De Miro (by Ch. Milray's Winsome of Will-Ve's ex Ch. De Nada De Miro) ABC/DOM.

Kamursart's Hannah (by Am-Can. Ch. Vimar's We Believe in Magic ex Ch. Warjoy's Kit 'N Kaboodle) CKC/DOM.

Can. Ch. Karmel's Dante Sassafras (by Ch. Berena's Gemini Splashdown ex Jacquet's Kiri Te Kanawa) CKC/DOM.

Kar-Neil's Karma Kelly (by Candlewood's Lite My Fire ex Kar-Neil's Straight Laced) ABC/DOM.

Kaseba's Show Girl (by Am-Can. Ch. Peablo's Black Bishop ex Ch. Treceder's Show Boat) ABC/DOM.

Ch. Keil's High Society (by Ch. Salgray's Market Wise ex Ch. Weber's High Falutin') ABC/DOM.

Keil's Katrina (by Ch. Salgray's Market Wise ex Ch. Weber's High Falutin') ABC/DOM.

Am-Can. Ch. Keil's Renaissance (by Ch. Marquam Hill's Traper of TuRo ex Ch. Keil's High Society) ABC/DOM.

Ch. Kiebla's Tradition of TuRo (by TuRo's Escappade ex Ch. Kiebla's Mercy) ABC/DOM.

Konchita of Cross Acres (by Ch. Serius of Cross Acres ex Fancy of Cross Acres) ABC/DOM.

Ch. Kreyon's Delta Dawn II (by Ch. Rochils Grande Marshall ex Kreyon's Added Attraction) ABC/DOM.

Lady Charlotte of Box Run (by Ch. Oliver's Custom Cut ex Oliver's Moonbeam) ABC/DOM.

Lady Margaret IV (by Ch. Camnic's Fiddle ex Duchess of Sleepy Hollow) ABC/DOM.

Leblanc's Just Allas (by Ch. Mystery's Show Bis ex Leblanc's Just Stitches) ABC/DOM.

Am-Can. Ch. Leblanc's Just Nicole (by Ch. Leblanc's Back Door Johnny ex Leblanc's Just Allas) ABC/DOM.

Legacy of Clover Downs (by Ch. Jered's Sovereign ex Zizzle Zee of Sirrah Crest) ABC/DOM.

Can. Ch. Leopold's Knockout Kelly (by Int. Ch. Mephisto's Soldier of Fortune ex Can. Ch. Veralyn's Lucious Lady Leopold) CKC/DOM.

Lin Mar's Love Always O'Philadel (by Ch. Heldenbrand's Jet Breaker ex Philadel's Winter Solstice) ABC/DOM.

Can. Ch. Lounsbury's Sweet Miss Conduct (by Am-Can. Ch. Wincaster's Stargazer ex Can. Ch. Donessle's Spring Serenade) CKC/DOM.

Ch. Lucy's Gold Thread (by Ch. Har-Vel's Gold Express ex Von Rohr's Lady Lucy) ABC/DOM.

Malabar's Belinda Earp (by Can. Ch. Boxella's Wyatt Earp ex Malabar's Bewitching) CKC/DOM.

Malabar's Stand Pat 2nd (by Can. Ch. Standfast of Blossomlea ex Can. Ch. Malabar's Fait Accompli) CKC/DOM.

Can. Ch. Manor Hill's Lady Ann, CD (by Ch. Merrilane's April Fashion ex Ch. Jacquet's First Lady) ABC/CKC/DOM.

Ch. Marburl's Scarlet Cord (by Ch. Holly Oaks Lord Rochambeau ex Ch. Marburl's Rehab of Wesan) ABC/DOM.

Am-Can. Ch. Marjack's Golden Mist (by Ch. Salal's Sure Conceit ex Marjack's Golden Girl) ABC/DOM.

Can. Ch. Marko's Medousa Gorgons (by Can. Ch. Gaylord's Duneden's Pride ex Marko's Aegis Aramis) CKC/SOM.

Marlene v Burcham (by Ch. Gayborne of Briarnole ex Gretchen v Burcham) ABC/DOM.

Am-Can. Ch. Marquam Hill's Flamingo (by Am-Can. Ch. Barrage of Quality Hill ex Legacy of Clover Downs) ABC/DOM.

Ch. Marwal's Satisfactual (by Ch. Bang Away of Sirrah Crest ex Am-Can. Ch. Hazlyn's Zippity Do-Dah) ABC/DOM.

Can. Ch. McAdam's Rodonna Pride In Mind (by Am-Can. Ch. Soldier's Pride of Norbourne ex Tokyo Rose) CKC/DOM.

McKarge's Irish Jade (by Am-Can. Ch. Jodi's Jeremiah ex McKarge's Tara) ABC/DOM.

Memorylane's Desiree (by Int. Ch. Memorylane's Fashion Escort ex Can. Ch. Ringmaster's High Fashion) CKC/DOM.

Am-Can. Ch. Mephisto's Black Sabbath (by Ch. Marquam Hill's Traper of TuRo ex Can. Ch. Mephisto's Autumns Romance) ABC/CKC/DOM.

Can. Ch. Mephisto's Calypso of Leblanc (by Int. Ch. Mephisto's Vendetta ex Am-Can. Ch. Leblanc's High Concerto) CKC/DOM.

Mephisto's Queen of Spades (by Am-Mex. Ch. Dean-Erik's Razin Kane ex Am-Can. Ch. Mephisto's Black Sabbath) CKC/DOM.

Can. Ch. Mephisto's Scarlet Lady (by Int. Ch. Mephisto's Soldier of Fortune ex Can. Ch. Scher-Khoun's Autumn Concerto) CKC/DOM.

Ch. Merrilane's Hot Pants (by Int. Ch. Memorylane's Fashion Escort ex Merrilane's Mad Passion, CD) ABC/DOM.

Merrilane's Mad Passion, CD (by Ch. Merrilane's Silver Dollar ex Bar Nymph's Medallion) ABC/DOM.

Merwin Hill's Gibson Girl (by Ch. Bilger's Parade Away ex Bilger's Golden Debbie) ABC/DOM.

Millan's Miss Palmyra (by Int. Ch. Millan's Fashion Hint ex Can. Ch. Tagwood's Spring Fashion) ABC/DOM.

Miss Raheba of May-Will (by Ch. Sir Commando of Virwill ex Vixen of Betsallane) ABC/DOM.

Ch. Missy's Debutante (by Ch. Salgray's Market Wise ex Hyde Park Missy) ABC/DOM.

Ch. Misty Maid of Thorhall (by Ch. Captain Lookout of Thorhall ex Robinson's Gret-Haven Pandora) ABC/DOM.

Moon Valley's Summer Shade (by Am-Can. Ch. Moss Wood's Zinger Zapper ex Araby's Made In Moon Valley) ABC/DOM.

Moreleen's ESP (by Ch. Moreleen's Al-le-lu-ia ex Ch. Moreleen's Abracadabra) ABC/DOM.

Ch. Morgenshern of Kresthallo (by Ch. Steeplechase Up and Away ex Malmhus Girl About Town) ABC/DOM.

Moss Wood's Frosty Morn (by Am-Can. Ch. Wagner Wilverday Famous Amos ex Ch. Moss Wood's Sadie Thompson) ABC/DOM.

Ch. Moss Wood's Sadie Thompson (by Ch. Moss Wood's Wynnin Waze ex Am-Can. Ch. Moss Wood's Zing-A-Ling) ABC/DOM.

Am-Can. Ch. Moss Wood's Zing-A-Ling (by Int. Ch. Moon Valley's Solar Flare ex Moss Wood's Sweet Surrender) ABC/DOM.

Am-Can. Ch. Moss Wood's Zippity Do-Da (by Int. Ch. Moon Valley's Solar Flare ex Moss Wood's Sweet Surrender) CKC/DOM.

Myshadow's Sparkle (by Can. Ch. Arrow of Fortune Rodonna ex Myshadow's Designer's Dream) CKC/DOM.

Nagerroc's Boom Boom (by Am-Can. Ch. Barrage of Quality Hill ex Malmhus Girl About Town) ABC/DOM.

Ch. Nemesis of Mazelaine (by Int. Ch. Dorian v Marienhof of Mazelaine ex Ch. Dagmar of Mazelaine) ABC/DOM.

Ch. Nocturne of Mazelaine (by Int. Ch. Dorian v Marienhof of Mazelaine ex Ch. Dagmar of Mazelaine) ABC/DOM.

Can. Ch. Notgnillew's Unity (by Can. Ch. Rayshar's Velvet Bask ex Raisin'Cain) CKC/DOM.

Ch. Nu-Ro's Ruffles and Flourishes (by Ch. Hanky Panky of Woodcrest ex Ch. NuRo's MacNamara Lace) ABC/DOM.

Ch. Oliver's Solid Gold (by Ch. Har-Vel's Gold Chips ex Oliver's Meri-lu-ia) ABC/DOM.

Omega's Windfire (by Ch. Aracrest's Talisman ex Omega's Lovefire) ABC/DOM.

Ch. Orrkid's April Love (by Baldr's Gathering Storm ex Thornhilda Baldr) ABC/DOM.

Ch. Paddy v Hohenneuffen of Barmere (by Ger. Ch. Hansl v Biederstein ex Ida v Hohenneuffen) ABC/DOM.

Can. Ch. Painted Besom of Blossomlea (by Can. Ch. Zack's Zebedee of Ringtru ex Leibling of Blossomlea) CKC/DOM.

Can. Ch. Pandora's Barbara of B'Kara (by Can. Ch. Honeywood Bellringer ex Park-Et Pandora, CD) CKC/DOM.

Pandora's Sweet Lady (by Can. Ch. Honeywood Bellringer ex Park-Et Pandora, CD) CKC/DOM.

Patcha's Brocade (by Int. Ch. Helixview Noble Knight ex Ch. Patcha's Velvet Touch) ABC/DOM.

Can. Ch. Piccadillys Amber Magic (by Can. Ch. Telstar's Lourd of Piccadillys ex Can. Ch. Starview's Tamara, CD) CKC/DOM.

Pinebrook's Forever Amber (by Ch. Pinebrook's Apricot Brandy ex Pinebrook's Amy) ABC/DOM.

Can. Ch. Pinepath's On The Road Again (by Am-Can. Ch. Acadia's Conquistador ex Am-Can. Ch. Country Times Candy Apple) CKC/DOM.

Can. Ch. Pinepath's Raisen Kane (by Can. Ch. Pinepath's Union Jack ex Pinepath's Nobel Prize) CKC/DOM.

Can. Ch. Pinepath's Sweet Gypsy Bee (by Int. Ch. Scher-Khoun's Shadrack ex Pinepath's Mini-Bee) CKC/DOM.

Pine Run's Table Talk (by Am-Can. Ch. Jered's Stacked Deck ex Ch. Pine Run's Torchlite) ABC/DOM.

Prina Pro Patria Chelsie (by Can. Ch. Pinepath's Union Jack ex Terid-Don's Pinepaths Sun Ray) CKC/DOM.

Can. Ch. Rayshar's Frosted Velvet (by Am-Can. Ch. Verwood's Thief In The Night ex Can. Ch. Verwood's Sun Mist, CD) CKC/DOM.

Renno's Tiger Stripe (by Ch. Renno's Front Page ex Renno's Impish Image) ABC/DOM.

Ch. R-J's Twice As Nice (by Ch. Arriba's R-J Spritz, CD ex Miss Brandy Dee) ABC/DOM.

Rochdale's Halo (by Can. Ch. Haviland's Renegade Storm ex Dark Halo) CKC/DOM.

Ch. Rochil's Kallista of Marburl (by Int. Ch. Marburl's Joshua ex Ch. Marburl's Nugget) ABC/DOM.

Ch. Rococo's Bright Magic (by Ch. Evo-Wen's Impressario ex Ch. Halo of Twin Willows) ABC/DOM.

Can. Ch. Rodonna's Lady For Pengalli (by Am-Can. Ch. Marshall's Fashion Magic ex Can. Ch. Candy K Blackjax Wild Romance) CKC/DOM.

Can. Ch. Rodonna's Legacy To Pengalli (by Can. Ch. Rodonna's Renegade Crusader ex Can. Ch. McAdam's Rodonna Pride In Mind) CKC/DOM.

Ch. Rummer Run's Mary Jane (by Ch. Bropat's Red Alert of Asgard ex Ch. Dante's Class Act) ABC/DOM.

Can. Ch. Rupik Play Back (by Can. Ch. Lounsbury's Flashback To Rupik ex Bella Dora of Rupik) CKC/DOM.

Ry-Neal's Vision of Perfection (by Ch. Noble Thor Buckingham ex Talisman's Beckwin Vanna) ABC/DOM.

Ch. Salgray's Auntie Mame (by Am-Can. Ch. Salgray's Flying High ex Ch. Salgray's Flaming Ember) ABC/DOM.

Salgray's Autumn Years (by Ch. Salgray's Ovation ex Salgray's Visa Versa) ABC/DOM.

Ch. Salgray's Call Me Madam (by Ch. Salgray's Valentino ex Salgray's Tall Tales) ABC/DOM.

Ch. Salgray's Jitterbug (by Int. Ch. Millan's Fashion Hint ex Ch. Salgray's Memory Book) ABC/DOM.

Can. Ch. Salgray's Roulette (by Am-Can. Ch. Barrage of Quality Hill ex Salgray's Soda Pop) ABC/DOM.

Can. Ch. Sancurt's Rhapsodi O'Diamondaire (by Am-Can. Ch. Aracrest's Amnesty ex Scher-Khoun's High Sierra) CKC/DOM.

Sandhill's Meet The Press (by Ch. Shieldmont's Issues N Answers ex Ch. Bee-Mike's Foxfire) ABC/DOM.

Ch. Sans Souci of Kresthallo (by Ch. Steeplechase Up and Away ex Malmhus Girl About Town) ABC/DOM.

Sarazak's Sister Smudge (by Ch. Cardona's Vanzetti ex Sarazak's Captivator) ABC/DOM.

Ch. Sarazak's Sizzle (by Ch. TuRo's Trumpet ex Sarazak's Captivator) ABC/DOM.

Ch. Sarkel's Promise of Cross Bars, CD, CGC (by Cross Bar's Gabber Dean Hays, CD ex Sarkel's Misty Morning) ABC/DOM.

Savoye's Satin Shadow of Ajay (by Ch. Marquam Hill's Traper of TuRo ex TuRo's Tiffany of Savoye) CKC/DOM.

Ch. Scarborough Living Proof (by Am-Can. Ch. Golden Haze Tuxedo ex Ch. Scarborough Barbara Allen) ABC/DOM.

Scarborough Soliloquy (by Int. Ch. Gray Boy's Minstrel Boy ex Am-Can. Ch. Scher-Khoun's Tarantella) ABC/DOM.

Can. Ch. Scher-Khoun's Autumn Concerto (by Int. Ch. Scher-Khoun's Shadrack ex Can. Ch. Scher-Khoun's Apricot Brandy) CKC/DOM.

Scher-Khoun's Carbon Copy (by Int. Ch. Scher-Khoun's Meshack ex Can. Ch. Scher-Khoun's Dark Rhapsody) CKC/DOM.

Am-Can. Ch. Scher-Khoun's Coquette (by Int. Ch. Millan's Fashion Hint ex Can. Ch. Backchat of Blossomlea 2nd) CKC/DOM.

Can. Ch. Scher-Khoun's Dark Rhapsody (by Int. Ch. Scher-Khoun's Shadrack ex Can. Ch. Donfaral's Fashion's Fancy) CKC/DOM.

School's Simple Addition (by Ch. Jo-San's Future Time ex CJ's Memory Lil O'Schoolmaster) ABC/DOM.

Seawest Athenas Box M Madness (by Ch. Seawest Yuri Nuff of Box M ex Keka) ABC/DOM.

Can. Ch. Seefeld Wisnowski Mona Lisa (by Eng. Ch. Seefeld Picasso ex Parakay Miss Lexington) CKC/DOM.

Can. Ch. Sensuous Heidi, CD (by Can. Ch. Beaucrest's Hite of Fashion ex Can. Ch. Norbourne's Sensuous Annie) CKC/DOM.

Can. Ch. Serenade of Mark Hill (by Can. Ch. Haviland's Renegade Storm ex Sugar N'Spice of Blossomlea) CKC/DOM.

Ch. Sergi's Classic Design (by Ch. Huffand's Nice Enough ex BJ's Sergi's Honey Acres) ABC/DOM.

Sergi's N BJ's Original Design (by Ch. Huffand's Nice Enough ex BJ's Sergi's Honey Acres) ABC/DOM.

Shadowdale Dance To The Music (by Am-Can. Ch. Donessle's Cassino ex Can. Ch. Shadowdale's Sheer Delight) CKC/DOM.

Ch. Sheer Magic of Jeamar, CD (by Ch. Camgene's Likely Tummaykit ex C Magic Maker's One and Only) ABC/DOM.

Ch. Sher 'Ed N V Me Too (by Ch. Renno's Sertain Solution ex Ch. Shar-IV's Sunsational Kandy) ABC/DOM.

Siegel's Honey Babe (by Ch. Valatham's Pow-Wow ex Sadoff's Daisy Mae) ABC/CKC/DOM.

Skidoo's No Frills (by Ch. Summit Views Legal Tender ex Ch. Skidoo's Instant Replay, TT) ABC/DOM.

Spring Willow's My Tammy Too (by Lindenfeld's Short Stop ex Spring Willow's Tamara) ABC/DOM.

Stapleton's Beau Allure (by Ch. Xavier's Beau Geste ex Sirrah Crest Acclaim) ABC/DOM.

Can. Ch. Starview's Black Magic (by Can. Ch. Governor William of Starview ex Can. Ch. Sweet Cinnamon at Starview) CKC/DOM.

Can. Ch. Starview's Sugar and Spice, CD (by Can. Ch. Soldier's Mark of Norbourne ex Can. Ch. Billie's Country Classic) CKC/DOM.

Sultan's Diamond Belle (by Ch. Shieldmont's Dimension ex Ch. Asgard's Southern Belle) ABC/DOM.

Summerbird Leading Lady (by Am-Can. Ch. Arriba's Associate of Karjean ex Summerbird Important Date) ABC/DOM.

Summit View's Blaze of Glory (by Summit View's Bell Ringer ex Summit View's Ravishing Ruby) ABC/DOM.

Am-Can. Ch. Summit View's Mya of Ruffian (by Ch. Summit View's Fuzz Buster ex Bellcrest Just Jezebel) ABC/DOM.

Swagger of Mazelaine (by Int. Ch. Utz von Dom of Mazelaine ex Lorelei of Mazelaine) ABC/DOM.

Ch. Symphony of Mazelaine (by Int. Ch. Dorian von Marienhof of Mazelaine ex Ch. Crona von Zwergeck) ABC/DOM.

Tallassee's Enough's Enough (by Ch. Huffand's Nice Enough ex Tallassee's Nightwood) ABC/DOM.

Can. Ch. Tasha, CD (by Am-Can. Ch. Bonel's Rusty Jones ex Jaegerhouse's Providence) CKC/DOM.

Ch. Telstar's Moon Pebbles (by Ch. Berena's Gemini Splashdown ex Ch. Telstar's Bambi) ABC/DOM.

Ch. Tenebo's Sable Doll (by Am-Can. Ch. Woods End Crown Sable ex Tenebo's Copper Doll) ABC/DOM.

Terra Oak's Gal Sal (by Ch. Pinebrook's Radiation ex Emwal's Maggie O) ABC/DOM.

Thanque Poko (by Ch. Merrilane's Holiday Fashion ex Treceder's Medianoche) ABC/DOM.

Thanque Yankee Doodle Joy (by Am-Can. Ch. Vimar's EST ex Ch. Thanque Taos) ABC/DOM.

Ch. Thorwood's Rubicon (by Ch. Arriba's Knight Review ex Ch. Gray Roy's Party Girl) ABC/DOM.

Can. Ch. TKO's Black Onyx (by Can. Ch. Holiday's Amerigo ex Can. Ch. Fashion Brittany Limousine) CKC/DOM.

TNT's Gracie Allen (by Duke The Rowdy Rascal ex Bambi Boe) ABC/DOM.

Tokyo Rose (by Ajay's Bo Victor ex Brite Light) CKC/DOM.

Ch. Touchstone's Shaia (by Ch. TuRo's Accolade ex Kennebecs Show-N-Tell) ABC/DOM.

Can. Ch. Tradonalee's Miss Classic (by Ch. Holly Lane's Prairie Chief ex Am-Can. Ch. Carlon's Classy Catrina) CKC/DOM.

Trimanor's Fair Ambrosia (by Am-Can. Ch. Cinnrhee's Mugshot ex Trimanor's Poetry In Motion) CKC/DOM.

Can. Ch. Trimanor's Fair Delilah (by Am-Can. Ch. Moss Wood's Zinger Zapper ex Am-Can. Ch. Trimanor Fair Antoinette) CKC/DOM.

Trimanor's Lady In Command (by Can. Ch. Trimanor's Command Performance ex Can. Ch. Trimanor's Leading Lady) CKC/DOM.

Trimanor's Poetry In Motion (by Am-Can. Ch. Moon Valley's Solar Flare ex Can. Ch. Trimanor's Scarlet O'Hara) CKC/DOM.

Can. Ch. Trimanor's Scarlet O'Hara (by Can. Ch. Donessle's Crusader ex Am-Can. Ch. Trimanor's Fair Antoinette) CKC/DOM.

Can. Ch. Trimanor's Taste of Honey (by Am-Can. Ch. Trimanor's Baccus ex Trimanor's Poetry In Motion) CKC/DOM.

Tudosal's Ruffels (by Tudosal's Ramrod ex Tudosal's Miss Minx) ABC/DOM.

Ch. TuRo's Angel Fire of DJ (by Ch. TuRo's Native Dancer ex TuRo's Cross Fire) ABC/DOM.

Can. Ch. TuRo's Ebony of Anchic (by Ch. TuRo's Accolade ex Tiffany XVIII) ABC/DOM.

TuRo's Katrina of Cross Bar (by Ch. TuRo's Native Dancer ex Cross Bar's Noel) ABC/DOM.

TuRo's Locket of Harelhaus (by Ch. TuRo's Applause ex Vimar's Hocus-Pocus) ABC/DOM.

Ch. TuRo's Magic Spell (by Ch. Braemerwood's Happy Tracks ex Hansparke's Dominique) ABC/DOM.

Ch. TuRo's Tigger of Five T's (by Ch. Benjoman of Five T's ex Ch. TuRo's Vanity Fair) ABC/DOM.

Ch. TuRo's Touche (by Ch. Benjoman of Five T's ex Ch. Holly Lane's Baubles) ABC/DOM.

Ch. TuRo's Truffian (by Ch. TuRo's Native Dancer ex Hansparke's Dominique) ABC/DOM.

Ch. TuRo's Vanity Fair (by Int. Ch. Aracrest's Kaylib ex Ch. Hansparke's Fashion Fair) ABC/DOM.

Ch. TuRo's Whisper of Five T's (by Ch. Benjoman of Five T's ex Ch. TuRo's Vanity Fair) ABC/DOM.

Ch. Valkyrie's Hera (by Am-Can. Ch. Moss Wood's Zinger Zapper ex Valkyrie's Freya) ABC/DOM.

Ch. Valley Hi's Rainmaker of Sunar (by Ch. Kamursart's Hi Ho Warjoy ex Valley Highs Classic Design) ABC/DOM.

Can. Ch. Valmax Aurora (by Am-Can. Ch. Beaulaine's Boambo ex Joriemoeur Katie) CKC/DOM.

Ch. Vandowns Black Velvet (by Ch. Vandown-Kings Fire Alert ex Ch. Vagabond's Brown Sugar) ABC/DOM.

Ch. Vandown's Laguna Rose (by Ch. Merrilane's Knockout ex Sonic Song of Mystic Hills) ABC/DOM.

Can. Ch. Veralyn's Luscious Lady Leopold (by Can. Ch. Gaylord's Gallant Gentleman ex Tudosal's Gracious Me) CKC/DOM.

Verand's Cloudy Dawn (by Ch. My-R's Wizard ex Peter's Pamuramic, CD) ABC/DOM.

Can. Ch. Verwood's Countess Kali (by Am-Can. Ch. Haviland's Count Royal ex Can. Ch. Verwood's Quinella) CKC/DOM.

Verwood's Ivory Tower (by Verwood's Himself ex Can. Ch. Verwood's Bewitched) CKC/DOM.

Can. Ch. Verwood's Lollipop (by Int. Ch. Millan's Fashion Hint ex Can. Ch. Verwood's Keepsake) CKC/DOM.

Verwood's Nina Never Knew (by Am-Can. Ch. Verwood's King of Spades ex Can. Ch. Verwood's Miss Boots) CKC/DOM.

Can. Ch. Verwood's Quinella (by Ch. Salgray's Ovation ex Can. Ch. Verwood's Miss Muffet) CKC/DOM.

Can. Ch. Verwood's Sun Mist, CD (by Int. Ch. Moon Valley's Sun N'Shadow ex Can. Ch. Diamondaire's Apache Lace) CKC/DOM.

Ch. Vihabra's Magin's Irish Gold (by Ch. Marquam Hill's Trigger of TuRo ex Ch. Vihabra's Stardust) ABC/DOM.

Ch. Vihabra's Stardust (by Ch. Merrilane's Fashion Star ex Merrilane's Touchdown Benroe) ABC/DOM.

Ch. Virgo's Destiny (by Ch. Keil's Dynasty ex Ch. Merrilane's Look-out) ABC/DOM.

Ch. Virgo's Moon Zapper (by Am-Can. Ch. Moss Wood's Zinger Zapper ex Virgo's Moon Lilly) ABC/DOM.

Ch. Von Schaum's Panhandle Rose (by Niklofs Columbo ex Von Schaum's Missy) ABC/DOM.

Ch. Von Schorer's Miss Knock About (by Evo-Wen's Knock Out ex Von Schorer's Noble Lisa) ABC/DOM.

Ch. Warjoy's Kismet (by Am-Can. Ch. Vimar's EST ex Warjoy's Box-R Reflection) ABC/DOM.

Can. Ch. Washakie of Warchief (by Am-Can. Ch. Style Setter of Kargotor ex Duchess Anne of Romar) CKC/DOM.

Ch. Weber's High Falutin' (by Ch. Vel-Kel's Big Ben ex Ch. Ringmaster's Standing Ovation) ABC/DOM.

Can. Ch. Wedge Hollows Busy Bee (by Am-Can. Ch. Rodonna's Renegade Soldier ex Am-Can. Ch. Wedge Hollows Wallis Winsor) CKC/DOM.

Wesan's Faith Alone (by Ch. Benjoman of Five T's ex Ch. K-Nine's Monique) ABC/DOM.

Ch. Wesan's Sun Daze (by Ch. Baldr's Sun Smoke ex Wesan's Rainy Daze) ABC/DOM.

Can. Ch. Wild Rock's Mam'Selle (by Wild Rock's Incentive ex Wild Rock's Gingerbread) CKC/DOM.

Wild Rock's Toot 'N'Annie (by Can. Ch. Pinepaths Fifth Dimension ex Can. Ch. Wild Rock's Medley) CKC/DOM.

Am-Can-Mex. Ch. Wil-Elen's Fashion Plate (by Monarch's Eager Lad of Tarzana ex Wil-Elen's Cindy) ABC/DOM.

Wo-Kan-Da's Honey-B (by Bob-Ell's Raz Ma Taz ex Wo-Kan-Da's Tang) CKC/DOM.

Ch. Woods End Moon Whisper (by Ch. Marquam Hill's Traper of TuRo ex Ch. Woods End Moon Mist) ABC/DOM.

Ch. Yller of Mazelaine (by Int. Ch. Utz v Dom of Mazelaine ex Cilla v d Marenore) ABC/DOM.

Can. Ch. Zephyr's Money Talks, CD (by Am-Can. Ch. Golden Haze Tuxedo ex Can. Ch. Golden Haze April Showers) CKC/DOM.

Can. Ch. Zephyr's Time Is Money (by Am-Can. Ch. Golden Haze Tuxedo ex Can. Ch. Golden Haze April Showers) CKC/DOM.

INDEX

Page numbers in **boldface** refer to illustrations.
For the reader's convenience, titles have been omitted from all names.